D1081982

 **2017 Edition**

Compendium of Professional Responsibility

RULES *and* STANDARDS

Cover design by ABA Design.

Nothing contained in this book is to be considered as the rendering of legal advice for specific cases, and readers are responsible for obtaining such advice from their own legal counsel. This book and any forms and agreements herein are intended for educational and informational purposes only.

No part of this publication may be reproduced, stored in a retrieval system, or transmitted in any form or by any means, electronic, mechanical, photocopying, recording, or otherwise, without the prior written permission of the publisher. For permission contact the ABA Copyrights & Contracts Department, copyright@americanbar.org or via fax at (312)988-6030.

21 20 19 18 17   5 4 3 2 1

©2017 by the American Bar Association. All rights reserved.

Printed in the United States of America.

ISBN: 978-1-63425-947-7

The ABA Model Rules of Professional Conduct (©2013), including Preamble, Scope, Terminology, and Comment, were adopted by the ABA House of Delegates on August 2, 1983, and amended in 1987, 1989, 1990, 1991, 1992, 1993, 1994, 1995, 1997, 1998, 2000, 2002, 2003, 2007, 2008, 2009, 2012, 2013, 2016, and 2017.

The ABA Model Code of Professional Responsibility (©1981) was adopted by the ABA House of Delegates on August 12, 1969 and amended in 1970, 1974, 1975, 1976, 1977, 1978, 1979, and 1980.

The ABA Model Code of Judicial Conduct (©2010) was adopted by the ABA House of Delegates on August 7, 1990 and amended in 1997, 1999, 2003, 2007 and 2010.

The ABA Canons of Professional Ethics (©1957) were adopted by the ABA House of Delegates on August 27, 1908 and amended in 1928, 1933, 1937, 1940, 1942, 1943, 1951, and 1956.

The ABA Standards for Imposing Lawyer Sanctions (©1992) were adopted by the ABA House of Delegates on February 10, 1986 and amended on February 4, 1992.

ABA Guidelines for Litigation Conduct ©1998. Reprinted by permission.

ABA Formal Ethics Opinion 93-379 © 1993; ABA Formal Ethics Opinion 95-390 © 1995; ABA Formal Ethics Opinion 96-402 © 1996; ABA Formal Ethics Opinion 99-414 © 1999; ABA Formal Ethics Opinion 09-455 © 2009; ABA Formal Ethics Opinion 10-457 © 2010; ABA Formal Ethics Opinion 466 © 2014; ABA Formal Ethics Opinion 471 © 2015; ABA Formal Ethics Opinion 472 © 2015.

ABA Model Rules for Client Protection (©2007)
Adding formal ethics opinions from the 2017 MRPC

Discounts are available for books ordered in bulk. Special consideration is given to state bars, CLE programs and other bar-related organizations. Inquire at Publications, Planning and Marketing, American Bar Association, 321 N. Clark Street, Chicago, Illinois 60654.

www.ShopABA.org

CENTER FOR PROFESSIONAL RESPONSIBILITY
PUBLICATIONS BOARD
2017–2018

John P. Sahl, *Chair*
Akron, Ohio

Susan Saab Fortney
Fort Worth, Texas

Natasha T. Martin
Seattle, Washington

Arthur F. Greenbaum
Columbus, Ohio

Maritza I. Reyes
Orlando, Florida

Mark L. Tuft
San Francisco, California

AMERICAN BAR ASSOCIATION
CENTER FOR PROFESSIONAL RESPONSIBILITY

Director
Tracy L. Kepler

Dedicated to the memory of
Jeanne P. Gray
Director, ABA Center for Professional Responsibility,
1982–2013

Contents

ABA Model Rules, Codes and Guidelines

Preface

The 2017 edition of the American Bar Association Center for Professional Responsibility *Compendium of Professional Responsibility Rules and Standards* gathers together for immediate reference the essential legal ethics materials needed by lawyers and judges in their daily practice, law students in their exploration of the standards of their new profession, and legal scholars in their analysis of the changing currents that influence professional regulation.

The first section of the *Compendium* presents models for ethical and professional conduct and standards for enforcing that conduct that have been developed by the American Bar Association. These models have been used as the foundation for most state regulations and as interpretive guidance for the courts in their resolution of professional responsibility issues. Despite the local variations in the way they have been adopted (occasionally significant), they serve to familiarize the reader with the philosophy of lawyer regulation and can be used to initiate review of substantive issues unfamiliar to the lawyer, student or scholar.

In addition, the *Compendium* contains a selection of federal Rules and Standards that are commonly needed in the general practice of law, and in practice before the SEC and IRS, and that impact upon a number of ethical rules of conduct, such as the rules regarding competence and meritorious claims and contentions.

Information on the composition, jurisdiction and procedures of the ABA Standing Committee on Ethics and Professional Responsibility is included to explain how ABA ethics rules are formulated and interpreted. In addition, seven of the Committee's Formal Ethics Opinions that address important areas of lawyer conduct have been included.

The Center thanks the West Group for its generous gift of the West Professional Responsibility Law Library, the resource for much of the work performed by the Center.

Other Center for Professional Responsibility books of interest to Compendium users may include:

- Annotated Model Rules of Professional Conduct (Eighth Edition)
- Annotated Model Code of Judicial Conduct (Second Edition)
- Annotated Standards for Imposing Lawyer Sanctions
- Lawyer Law: Comparing the ABA Model Rules of Professional Conduct with the ALI Restatement (Third) of the Law Governing Lawyers

- ABA/BNA Lawyers' Manual on Professional Conduct (available through Bloomberg BNA)
- Legal Ethics: The Lawyer's Deskbook on Professional Responsibility (available through Thomson Reuters)
- The Paralegal's Guide to Professional Responsibility (Fourth Edition)
- A Legislative History of the Model Rules: The Development of the ABA Model Rules of Professional Conduct, 1982-2013
- Formal Ethics Opinions, 1999-2013
- Model Rules of Professional Conduct and Model Code of Judicial Conduct mobile apps (available through the iStore)

For more information, visit the Center's Web site at
http://www.americanbar.org/groups/professional_responsibility.html

ABA Model Rules of Professional Conduct

The ABA Model Rules of Professional Conduct,
including Preamble, Scope, Terminology and Comment,
were adopted by the ABA House of Delegates on August 2, 1983,
and amended in 1987, 1989, 1990, 1991, 1992, 1993, 1994, 1995,
1997, 1998, 2000, 2002, 2003, 2007, 2008, 2009, 2012, 2013 and 2016.

ABA STANDING COMMITTEE ON ETHICS AND PROFESSIONAL RESPONSIBILITY
2017–2018

BARBARA S. GILLERS, *Chair*
New York, NY

DOUGLAS RICHMOND,
Chicago, IL

JOHN M. BARKETT
Miami, FL

MICHAEL H. RUBIN
Baton Rouge, LA

WENDY WEN YU CHANG
Los Angeles, CA

LYNDA C. SHELY
Scottsdale, AZ

DANIEL J. CROTHERS
Bismark, ND

ELIZABETH C. TARBERT
Tallahassee, FL

KEITH ROBERT FISHER
Arlington, VA

ALLISON L. WOOD
Chicago, IL

Board of Governors Liaison
PENINA KESSLER LIEBER
Pittsburgh, PA

AMERICAN BAR ASSOCIATION
CENTER FOR PROFESSIONAL RESPONSIBILITY

Director
TRACY L. KEPLER

Ethics Counsel
DENNIS A. RENDLEMAN

Contents

ABA Model
Rules of
Professional
Conduct

COUNSELOR

ADVOCATE

TRANSACTIONS WITH PERSONS OTHER THAN CLIENTS

LAW FIRMS AND ASSOCIATIONS

PUBLIC SERVICE

INFORMATION ABOUT LEGAL SERVICES

MAINTAINING THE INTEGRITY
OF THE PROFESSION

APPENDICES

ABA Model
Rules of
Professional
Conduct

Preface

For more than one hundred years, the American Bar Association has provided leadership in legal ethics and professional responsibility through the adoption of professional standards that serve as models of the regulatory law governing the legal profession.

On August 27, 1908, the Association adopted the original Canons of Professional Ethics. These were based principally on the Code of Ethics adopted by the Alabama Bar Association in 1887, which in turn had been borrowed largely from the lectures of Judge George Sharswood, published in 1854 as Professional Ethics, and from the fifty resolutions included in David Hoffman's A Course of Legal Study (2d ed. 1836). Piecemeal amendments to the Canons occasionally followed.

In 1913, the Standing Committee on Professional Ethics of the American Bar Association was established to keep the Association informed about state and local bar activities concerning professional ethics. In 1919 the name of the Committee was changed to the Committee on Professional Ethics and Grievances; its role was expanded in 1922 to include issuing opinions "concerning professional conduct, and particularly concerning the application of the tenets of ethics thereto." In 1958 the Committee on Professional Ethics and Grievances was separated into two committees: a Committee on Professional Grievances, with authority to review issues of professional misconduct, and a Committee on Professional Ethics with responsibility to express its opinion concerning proper professional and judicial conduct. The Committee on Professional Grievances was discontinued in 1971. The name of the Committee on Professional Ethics was changed to the Committee on Ethics and Professional Responsibility in 1971 and remains so.

In 1964, at the request of President Lewis F. Powell Jr., the House of Delegates of the American Bar Association created a Special Committee on Evaluation of Ethical Standards (the "Wright Committee") to assess whether changes should be made in the then-current Canons of Professional Ethics. In response, the Committee produced the Model Code of Professional Responsibility. The Model Code was adopted by the House of Delegates on August 12, 1969, and subsequently by the vast majority of state and federal jurisdictions.

In 1977, the American Bar Association created the Commission on Evaluation of Professional Standards to undertake a comprehensive rethinking of the ethical premises and problems of the legal profession. Upon evaluating the Model Code and determining that amendment of the Code would not achieve a comprehensive statement of the law governing the legal profession, the Commission commenced a six-year study and drafting process that produced the Model Rules of Professional Conduct. The Model Rules were adopted by the House of Delegates of the American Bar Association on August 2, 1983.

Between 1983 and 2002, the House amended the Rules and Comments on fourteen different occasions. In 1997, the American Bar Association created the Commission on Evaluation of the Rules of Professional Conduct ("Ethics 2000 Commission") to comprehensively review the Model Rules and propose amendments as deemed appropriate. On February 5, 2002 the House of Delegates adopted a series of amendments that arose from this process.

In 2000, the American Bar Association created the Commission on Multijurisdictional Practice to research, study and report on the application of current ethics and bar admission rules to the multijurisdictional practice of law. On August 12, 2002 the House of Delegates adopted amendments to Rules 5.5 and 8.5 as a result of the Commission's work and recommendations.

In 2002, the American Bar Association created the Task Force on Corporate Responsibility to examine systemic issues relating to corporate responsibility arising out of the unexpected and traumatic bankruptcy of Enron and other Enron-like situations that had shaken confidence in the effectiveness of the governance and disclosure systems applicable to public companies in the United States. In August 11-12, 2003, the House of Delegates adopted amendments to Rules 1.6 and 1.13 as a result of the Task Force's work and recommendations.

In 2009, the American Bar Association created the Commission on Ethics 20/20 to perform a thorough review of the ABA Model Rules of Professional Conduct and the U.S. system of lawyer regulation in the context of advances in technology and global legal practice developments. On August 6, 2012 and February 11, 2013 the House of Delegates adopted a series of amendments to the Rules and Comments as a result of the Commission's work and recommendations.

The American Bar Association continues to pursue its goal of assuring the highest standards of professional competence and ethical conduct. The Standing Committee on Ethics and Professional Responsibility, charged with interpreting the professional standards of the Association and recommending appropriate amendments and clarifications, issues opinions interpreting the Model Rules of Professional Conduct and the Model Code of Judicial Conduct. The opinions of the Committee are published by the American Bar Association in a series of bound volumes containing opinions from 1924 through 2013 and as individual PDFs starting with the 1984 opinions.

Requests that the Committee issue opinions on particular questions of professional and judicial conduct should be directed to the American Bar Association, Center for Professional Responsibility, 321 N. Clark Street, Chicago, Illinois 60654.

ABA Model Rules of Professional Conduct

ABA COMMISSION ON EVALUATION OF PROFESSIONAL STANDARDS (1977–1983)

ROBERT W. MESERVE, *Chair*
Boston, Massachusetts

MARVIN E. FRANKEL
New York, New York

RICHARD H. SINKFIELD
Atlanta, Georgia

ALAN BARTH
Washington, D.C.

LOIS C. HARRISON
Lakeland, Florida

WILLIAM B. SPANN, JR.
Atlanta, Georgia

ARNO H. DENECKE
Salem, Oregon

ROBERT O. HETLAGE
St. Louis, Missouri

SAMUEL D. THURMAN
Salt Lake City, Utah

THOMAS EHRLICH
Washington, D.C.

ROBERT B. McKAY
New York, New York

ROBERT J. KUTAK
Omaha, Nebraska
Former Chair

JANE FRANK-HARMAN
Washington, D.C.

L. CLAIR NELSON
Washington, D.C.

LIAISONS

MICHAEL FRANCK
Lansing, Michigan
*Standing Committee on
Professional Discipline*

JOHN C. DEACON
Jonesboro, Arkansas
Board of Governors

H. WILLIAM ALLEN
Little Rock, Arkansas
*Standing Committee on
Ethics and Professional
Responsibility*

THOMAS Z. HAYWARD, JR.
Chicago, Illinois

CONSULTANTS

BETTY B. FLETCHER
Seattle, Washington

L. RAY PATTERSON
Atlanta, Georgia

JOHN F. SUTTON, JR.
Austin, Texas

REPORTER

GEOFFREY C. HAZARD, JR.
New Haven, Connecticut

ASSISTANT REPORTERS

THOMAS J. McCORMICK
Washington, D.C.

DANIEL S. REYNOLDS
DeKalb, Illinois

COMMISSION ON EVALUATION OF PROFESSIONAL STANDARDS
Chair's Introduction

The Commission on Evaluation of Professional Standards was appointed in the summer of 1977 by former ABA President William B. Spann, Jr. Chaired by Robert J. Kutak until his death in early 1983, the Commission was charged with evaluating whether existing standards of professional conduct provided comprehensive and consistent guidance for resolving the increasingly complex ethical problems in the practice of law. For the most part, the Commission looked to the former ABA Model Code of Professional Responsibility, which served as a model for the majority of state ethics codes. The Commission also referred to opinions of the ABA Standing Committee on Ethics and Professional Responsibility, as well as to decisions of the United States Supreme Court and of state supreme courts. After thoughtful study, the Commission concluded that piecemeal amendment of the Model Code would not sufficiently clarify the profession's ethical responsibilities in light of changed conditions. The Commission therefore commenced a drafting process that produced numerous drafts, elicited voluminous comment, and launched an unprecedented debate on the ethics of the legal profession.

On January 30, 1980, the Commission presented its initial suggestions to the bar in the form of a Discussion Draft of the proposed Model Rules of Professional Conduct. The Discussion Draft was subject to the widest possible dissemination and interested parties were urged to offer comments and suggestions. Public hearings were held around the country to provide forums for expression of views on the draft.

In the year following the last of these public hearings, the Commission conducted a painstaking analysis of the submitted comments and attempted to integrate into the draft those which seemed consistent with its underlying philosophy. The product of this analysis and integration was presented on May 31, 1981, as the proposed Final Draft of the Model Rules of Professional Conduct. This proposed Final Draft was submitted in two formats. The first format, consisting of blackletter Rules and accompanying Comments in the so-called restatement format, was submitted with the Commission's recommendation that it be adopted. The alternative format was patterned after the Model Code and consisted of Canons, Ethical Considerations, and Disciplinary Rules. In February 1982, the House of Delegates by substantial majority approved the restatement format of the Model Rules.

The proposed Final Draft was submitted to the House of Delegates for debate and approval at the 1982 Annual Meeting of the Association in San Francisco. Many organizations and interested parties offered their comments in the form of proposed amendments to the Final Draft. In the time allotted on its agenda, however, the House debated only proposed amendments to Rule 1.5. Consideration of the remainder of the document was deferred until the 1983 Midyear Meeting in New Orleans. The proposed Final Draft, as amended by the House in San Francisco, was reprinted in the November 1982 issue of the *ABA Journal*.

At the 1983 Midyear Meeting the House resumed consideration of the Final Draft. After two days of often vigorous debate, the House completed its review of the proposed amendments to the blackletter Rules. Many amendments, particularly in the area of confidentiality, were adopted. Debate on a Preamble, Scope, Terminology, and Comments, rewritten to reflect the New Orleans amendments, was deferred until the 1983 Annual Meeting in Atlanta, Georgia.

On March 11, 1983, the text of the blackletter Rules as approved by the House in February, together with the proposed Preamble, Scope, Terminology, and Comments, was circulated to members of the House, Section and Committee chairs, and all other interested parties. The text of the Rules reflected the joint efforts of the Commission and the House Drafting Committee to incorporate the changes approved by the House and to ensure stylistic continuity and uniformity. Recipients of the draft were again urged to submit comments in the form of proposed amendments. The House Committees on Drafting and Rules and Calendar met on May 23, 1983, to consider all of the proposed amendments that had been submitted in response to this draft. In addition, discussions were held among concerned parties in an effort to reach accommodation of the various positions. On July 11, 1983, the final version of the Model Rules was again circulated.

The House of Delegates commenced debate on the proposed Preamble, Scope, Terminology, and Comments on August 2, 1983. After four hours of debate, the House completed its consideration of all the proposed amendments and, upon motion of the Commission, the House voted to adopt the Model Rules of Professional Conduct, together with the ancillary material as amended. The task of the Commission had ended and it was discharged with thanks.

Throughout the drafting process, active participants included not only the members of the Commission but also the Sections and Committees of the American Bar Association and national, state, and local bar organizations. The work of the Commission was subject to virtually continuous scrutiny by academicians, practicing lawyers, members of the press, and the judiciary. Consequently, every provision of the Model Rules reflects the thoughtful consideration and hard work of many dedicated professionals. Because of their input, the Model Rules are truly national in derivation. The Association can take immense pride in its continued demonstration of leadership in the area of professional responsibility.

The Model Rules of Professional Conduct are intended to serve as a national framework for implementation of standards of professional conduct. Although the Commission endeavored to harmonize and accommodate the views of all the participants, no set of national standards that speaks to such a diverse constituency as the legal profession can resolve each issue to the complete satisfaction of every affected party. Undoubtedly there will be those who take issue with one or another of the Rules' provisions. Indeed, such dissent from individual provisions is expected. And the Model Rules, like all model legislation, will be subject to modification at the level of local implementation. Viewed as a whole, however, the Model Rules represent a responsible approach to the ethical practice of law and are consistent with professional obligations imposed by other law, such as constitutional, corporate, tort, fiduciary, and agency law.

I should not end this report without speaking of the Commission's debt to many people who have aided us in our deliberations, and have devoted time, energy, and goodwill to the advancement of our work over the last six years. It would probably be impossible to name each of the particular persons whose help was significant to us, and it surely would be unfortunate if the name of anyone were omitted from the list. We are, and shall remain, deeply grateful to the literally hundreds of people who aided us with welcome and productive suggestions. We think the bar should be grateful to each of them, and to our deceased members, Alan Barth of the District of Columbia, who we hardly had time to know, Bill Spann, who became a member after the conclusion of his presidential term, and our original chair, Bob Kutak.

The long work of the Commission and its resulting new codification of the ethical rules of practice demonstrate, it is submitted, the commitment of the American lawyer to his or her profession and to achievement of the highest standards.

Robert W. Meserve
September 1983

ABA COMMISSION ON EVALUATION OF THE RULES OF PROFESSIONAL CONDUCT (1997–2002)

HON. E. NORMAN VEASEY, *Chair*
Wilmington, Delaware

MARGARET C. LOVE
Washington, D.C.

LAWRENCE J. FOX
Philadelphia, Pennsylvania

SUSAN R. MARTYN
Toledo, Ohio

ALBERT C. HARVEY
Memphis, Tennessee

DAVID T. MCLAUGHLIN
New London, New Hampshire

GEOFFREY C. HAZARD, JR.
Swarthmore, Pennsylvania

RICHARD E. MULROY
Ridgewood, New Jersey

HON. PATRICK E. HIGGINBOTHAM
Dallas, Texas

LUCIAN T. PERA
Memphis, Tennessee

W. LOEBER LANDAU
New York, New York

HON. HENRY RAMSEY, JR. (Ret.)
Berkeley, California

HON. LAURIE D. ZELON
Los Angeles, California

LIAISONS

JAMES B. LEE
Salt Lake City, Utah
Board of Governors

SETH ROSNER
Greenfield Center, New York
Board of Governors

REPORTERS

NANCY J. MOORE
Boston, Massachusetts
Chief Reporter

THOMAS D. MORGAN (1998–1999)
Washington, D.C.

CARL A. PIERCE
Knoxville, Tennessee

CENTER FOR PROFESSIONAL RESPONSIBILITY

JEANNE P. GRAY
Chicago, Illinois
Director

CHARLOTTE K. STRETCH, *Counsel*
Chicago, Illinois

SUSAN M. CAMPBELL, *Paralegal*
Chicago, Illinois

COMMISSION ON EVALUATION OF THE
RULES OF PROFESSIONAL CONDUCT ("ETHICS 2000")

Chair's Introduction

In mid-1997, ABA President Jerome J. Shestack, his immediate predecessor, N. Lee Cooper, and his successor, Philip S. Anderson had the vision to establish the "Ethics 2000" Commission. These three leaders persuaded the ABA Board of Governors that the Model Rules adopted by the ABA House of Delegates in 1983 needed comprehensive review and some revision, and this project was launched. Though some might have thought it premature to reopen the Model Rules to such a rigorous general reassessment after only fourteen years, the evaluation process has proven that the ABA leadership was correct.

One of the primary reasons behind the decision to revisit the Model Rules was the growing disparity in state ethics codes. While a large majority of states and the District of Columbia had adopted some version of the Model Rules (then thirty-nine, now forty-two), there were many significant differences among the state versions that resulted in an undesirable lack of uniformity—a problem that had been exacerbated by the approximately thirty amendments to the Model Rules between 1983 and 1997. A few states had elected to retain some version of the 1969 Model Code of Professional Responsibility, and California remained committed to an entirely separate system of lawyer regulation.

But it was not only the patchwork pattern of state regulation that motivated the ABA leaders of 1997 to take this action. There were also new issues and questions raised by the influence that technological developments were having on the delivery of legal services. The explosive dynamics of modern law practice and the anticipated developments in the future of the legal profession lent a sense of urgency as well as a substantive dimension to the project. These developments were underscored by the work then underway on the American Law Institute's *Restatement of the Law Governing Lawyers*.

There was also a strong countervailing sense that there was much to be valued in the existing concepts and articulation of the Model Rules. The Commission concluded early on that these valuable aspects of the Rules should not be lost or put at risk in our revision effort. As a result, the Commission set about to be comprehensive, but at the same time conservative, and to recommend change only where necessary. In balancing the need to preserve the good with the need for improvement, we were mindful of Thomas Jefferson's words of nearly 185 years ago, in a letter concerning the

ABA Model
Rules of
Professional
Conduct

Virginia Constitution, that "moderate imperfections had better be borne with; because, when once known, we accommodate ourselves to them, and find practical means of correcting their ill effects."

Thus, we retained the basic architecture of the Model Rules. We also retained the primary disciplinary function of the Rules, resisting the temptation to preach aspirationally about "best practices" or professionalism concepts. Valuable as the profession might find such guidance, it would not have—and should not be misperceived as having—a regulatory dimension. We were, however, always conscious of the educational role of the Model Rules. Finally, we tried to keep our changes to a minimum: when a particular provision was found not to be "broken" we did not try to "fix" it. Even so, as the reader will note, the Commission ended up making a large number of changes: some are relatively innocuous and nonsubstantive, in the nature of editorial or stylistic changes; others are substantive but not particularly controversial; and a few are both substantive and controversial.

The deliberations of the Commission did not take place in a vacuum and our determinations are not being pronounced *ex cathedra*. Rather, they are products of thorough research, scholarly analysis, and thoughtful consideration. Of equal importance, they have been influenced by the views of practitioners, scholars, other members of the legal profession, and the public. All these constituencies have had continual access to and considerable—and proper—influence upon the deliberations of the Commission throughout this process.

I must pause to underscore the openness of our process. We held over fifty days of meetings, all of which were open, and ten public hearings at regular intervals over a four-and-a-half-year period. There were a large number of interested observers at our meetings, many of whom were members of our Advisory Council of 250-plus persons, to offer comments and suggestions. Those observations were very helpful and influential in shaping the Report. Our public discussion drafts, minutes, and Report were available on our website for the world to see and comment upon. As a consequence, we received an enormous number of excellent comments and suggestions, many of which were adopted in the formulation of our Report.

Moreover, we encouraged state and local bar associations, ABA sections and divisions, other professional organizations, and the judiciary to appoint specially designated committees to work with and counsel the Commission. This effort was successful, and the Commission benefitted significantly from the considered views of these groups.

In heeding the counsel of these advisors, we were constantly mindful of substantial and high-velocity changes in the legal profession, particularly over the past decade. These changes have been highlighted by increased public scrutiny of lawyers and an awareness of their influential role in the formation and implementation of public policy; persistent concerns about lawyer honesty, candor, and civility; external competitive and technological pressures on the legal profession; internal pressures on law firm organization and management raised by sheer size, as well as specialization and lawyer mobility; jurisdictional and governance issues, such as multidisciplinary and multijurisdictional practice; special concerns of lawyers in nontraditional practice settings, such as government lawyers and in-house counsel; and the need to enhance public trust and confidence in the legal profession.

At the end of the day, our goal was to develop Rules that are comprehensible to the public and provide clear guidance to the practitioner. Our desire was to preserve all that is valuable and enduring about the existing Model Rules, while at the same time adapting them to the realities of modern law practice and the limits of professional discipline. We believe our product is a balanced blend of traditional precepts and forward-looking provisions that are responsive to modern developments. Our process has been thorough, painstaking, open, scholarly, objective, and collegial.

It is impossible here to go into detail about the changes proposed by the Commission. The changes recommended by the Commission clarified and strengthened a lawyer's duty to communicate with the client; clarified and strengthened a lawyer's duty to clients in certain specific problem areas; responded to the changing organization and structure of modern law practice; responded to new issues and questions raised by the influence that technological developments are having on the delivery of legal services; clarified existing Rules to provide better guidance and explanation to lawyers; clarified and strengthened a lawyer's obligations to the tribunal and to the justice system; responded to the need for changes in the delivery of legal services to low- and middle-income persons; and increased protection of third parties.

The ABA House of Delegates began consideration of the Commission's Report at the August 2001 Annual Meeting in Chicago and completed its review at the February 2002 Midyear Meeting in Philadelphia. At the August 2002 Annual Meeting in Washington, D.C., the ABA House of Delegates considered and adopted additional amendments to the Model Rules sponsored by the ABA Commission on Multijurisdictional Practice and the ABA Standing Committee on Ethics and Professional Responsibility. As state supreme courts consider implementation of these newly revised Rules, it is our fervent hope that the goal of uniformity will be the guiding beacon.

In closing, the Commission expresses its gratitude to the law firm of Drinker Biddle & Reath, whose generous contribution helped make possible the continued, invaluable support of the Commission's Chief Reporter. I also want to express personally my gratitude to and admiration for my colleagues. The chemistry, goodwill, good humor, serious purpose, collegiality, and hard work of the Commission members, Reporters, and ABA staff have been extraordinary. The profession and the public have been enriched beyond measure by their efforts. It has been a pleasure and a privilege for me to work with all of them.

Hon. E. Norman Veasey
August 2002

PREAMBLE AND SCOPE

PREAMBLE:
A LAWYER'S RESPONSIBILITIES

[1] A lawyer, as a member of the legal profession, is a representative of clients, an officer of the legal system and a public citizen having special responsibility for the quality of justice.

[2] As a representative of clients, a lawyer performs various functions. As advisor, a lawyer provides a client with an informed understanding of the client's legal rights and obligations and explains their practical implications. As advocate, a lawyer zealously asserts the client's position under the rules of the adversary system. As negotiator, a lawyer seeks a result advantageous to the client but consistent with requirements of honest dealings with others. As an evaluator, a lawyer acts by examining a client's legal affairs and reporting about them to the client or to others.

[3] In addition to these representational functions, a lawyer may serve as a third-party neutral, a nonrepresentational role helping the parties to resolve a dispute or other matter. Some of these Rules apply directly to lawyers who are or have served as third-party neutrals. See, e.g., Rules 1.12 and 2.4. In addition, there are Rules that apply to lawyers who are not active in the practice of law or to practicing lawyers even when they are acting in a nonprofessional capacity. For example, a lawyer who commits fraud in the conduct of a business is subject to discipline for engaging in conduct involving dishonesty, fraud, deceit or misrepresentation. See Rule 8.4.

[4] In all professional functions a lawyer should be competent, prompt and diligent. A lawyer should maintain communication with a client concerning the representation. A lawyer should keep in confidence information relating to representation of a client except so far as disclosure is required or permitted by the Rules of Professional Conduct or other law.

[5] A lawyer's conduct should conform to the requirements of the law, both in professional service to clients and in the lawyer's business and personal affairs. A lawyer should use the law's procedures only for legitimate purposes and not to harass or intimidate others. A lawyer should demonstrate respect for the legal system and for those who serve it, including judges, other lawyers and public officials. While it is a lawyer's duty, when necessary, to challenge the rectitude of official action, it is also a lawyer's duty to uphold legal process.

[6] As a public citizen, a lawyer should seek improvement of the law, access to the legal system, the administration of justice and the quality of

service rendered by the legal profession. As a member of a learned profession, a lawyer should cultivate knowledge of the law beyond its use for clients, employ that knowledge in reform of the law and work to strengthen legal education. In addition, a lawyer should further the public's understanding of and confidence in the rule of law and the justice system because legal institutions in a constitutional democracy depend on popular participation and support to maintain their authority. A lawyer should be mindful of deficiencies in the administration of justice and of the fact that the poor, and sometimes persons who are not poor, cannot afford adequate legal assistance. Therefore, all lawyers should devote professional time and resources and use civic influence to ensure equal access to our system of justice for all those who because of economic or social barriers cannot afford or secure adequate legal counsel. A lawyer should aid the legal profession in pursuing these objectives and should help the bar regulate itself in the public interest.

[7] Many of a lawyer's professional responsibilities are prescribed in the Rules of Professional Conduct, as well as substantive and procedural law. However, a lawyer is also guided by personal conscience and the approbation of professional peers. A lawyer should strive to attain the highest level of skill, to improve the law and the legal profession and to exemplify the legal profession's ideals of public service.

[8] A lawyer's responsibilities as a representative of clients, an officer of the legal system and a public citizen are usually harmonious. Thus, when an opposing party is well represented, a lawyer can be a zealous advocate on behalf of a client and at the same time assume that justice is being done. So also, a lawyer can be sure that preserving client confidences ordinarily serves the public interest because people are more likely to seek legal advice, and thereby heed their legal obligations, when they know their communications will be private.

[9] In the nature of law practice, however, conflicting responsibilities are encountered. Virtually all difficult ethical problems arise from conflict between a lawyer's responsibilities to clients, to the legal system and to the lawyer's own interest in remaining an ethical person while earning a satisfactory living. The Rules of Professional Conduct often prescribe terms for resolving such conflicts. Within the framework of these Rules, however, many difficult issues of professional discretion can arise. Such issues must be resolved through the exercise of sensitive professional and moral judgment guided by the basic principles underlying the Rules. These principles include the lawyer's obligation zealously to protect and pursue a client's legitimate interests, within the bounds of the law, while maintaining a pro-

fessional, courteous and civil attitude toward all persons involved in the legal system.

[10] The legal profession is largely self-governing. Although other professions also have been granted powers of self-government, the legal profession is unique in this respect because of the close relationship between the profession and the processes of government and law enforcement. This connection is manifested in the fact that ultimate authority over the legal profession is vested largely in the courts.

[11] To the extent that lawyers meet the obligations of their professional calling, the occasion for government regulation is obviated. Self-regulation also helps maintain the legal profession's independence from government domination. An independent legal profession is an important force in preserving government under law, for abuse of legal authority is more readily challenged by a profession whose members are not dependent on government for the right to practice.

[12] The legal profession's relative autonomy carries with it special responsibilities of self-government. The profession has a responsibility to assure that its regulations are conceived in the public interest and not in furtherance of parochial or self-interested concerns of the bar. Every lawyer is responsible for observance of the Rules of Professional Conduct. A lawyer should also aid in securing their observance by other lawyers. Neglect of these responsibilities compromises the independence of the profession and the public interest which it serves.

[13] Lawyers play a vital role in the preservation of society. The fulfillment of this role requires an understanding by lawyers of their relationship to our legal system. The Rules of Professional Conduct, when properly applied, serve to define that relationship.

SCOPE

[14] The Rules of Professional Conduct are rules of reason. They should be interpreted with reference to the purposes of legal representation and of the law itself. Some of the Rules are imperatives, cast in the terms "shall" or "shall not." These define proper conduct for purposes of professional discipline. Others, generally cast in the term "may," are permissive and define areas under the Rules in which the lawyer has discretion to exercise professional judgment. No disciplinary action should be taken when the lawyer chooses not to act or acts within the bounds of such discretion. Other Rules define the nature of relationships between the lawyer and others. The Rules are thus partly obligatory and disciplinary and partly constitutive and descriptive in that they define a lawyer's professional role. Many of the Com-

ments use the term "should." Comments do not add obligations to the Rules but provide guidance for practicing in compliance with the Rules.

[15] The Rules presuppose a larger legal context shaping the lawyer's role. That context includes court rules and statutes relating to matters of licensure, laws defining specific obligations of lawyers and substantive and procedural law in general. The Comments are sometimes used to alert lawyers to their responsibilities under such other law.

[16] Compliance with the Rules, as with all law in an open society, depends primarily upon understanding and voluntary compliance, secondarily upon reinforcement by peer and public opinion and finally, when necessary, upon enforcement through disciplinary proceedings. The Rules do not, however, exhaust the moral and ethical considerations that should inform a lawyer, for no worthwhile human activity can be completely defined by legal rules. The Rules simply provide a framework for the ethical practice of law.

[17] Furthermore, for purposes of determining the lawyer's authority and responsibility, principles of substantive law external to these Rules determine whether a client-lawyer relationship exists. Most of the duties flowing from the client-lawyer relationship attach only after the client has requested the lawyer to render legal services and the lawyer has agreed to do so. But there are some duties, such as that of confidentiality under Rule 1.6, that attach when the lawyer agrees to consider whether a client-lawyer relationship shall be established. See Rule 1.18. Whether a client-lawyer relationship exists for any specific purpose can depend on the circumstances and may be a question of fact.

[18] Under various legal provisions, including constitutional, statutory and common law, the responsibilities of government lawyers may include authority concerning legal matters that ordinarily reposes in the client in private client-lawyer relationships. For example, a lawyer for a government agency may have authority on behalf of the government to decide upon settlement or whether to appeal from an adverse judgment. Such authority in various respects is generally vested in the attorney general and the state's attorney in state government, and their federal counterparts, and the same may be true of other government law officers. Also, lawyers under the supervision of these officers may be authorized to represent several government agencies in intragovernmental legal controversies in circumstances where a private lawyer could not represent multiple private clients. These Rules do not abrogate any such authority.

[19] Failure to comply with an obligation or prohibition imposed by a Rule is a basis for invoking the disciplinary process. The Rules presup-

pose that disciplinary assessment of a lawyer's conduct will be made on the basis of the facts and circumstances as they existed at the time of the conduct in question and in recognition of the fact that a lawyer often has to act upon uncertain or incomplete evidence of the situation. Moreover, the Rules presuppose that whether or not discipline should be imposed for a violation, and the severity of a sanction, depend on all the circumstances, such as the willfulness and seriousness of the violation, extenuating factors and whether there have been previous violations.

[20] Violation of a Rule should not itself give rise to a cause of action against a lawyer nor should it create any presumption in such a case that a legal duty has been breached. In addition, violation of a Rule does not necessarily warrant any other nondisciplinary remedy, such as disqualification of a lawyer in pending litigation. The Rules are designed to provide guidance to lawyers and to provide a structure for regulating conduct through disciplinary agencies. They are not designed to be a basis for civil liability. Furthermore, the purpose of the Rules can be subverted when they are invoked by opposing parties as procedural weapons. The fact that a Rule is a just basis for a lawyer's self-assessment, or for sanctioning a lawyer under the administration of a disciplinary authority, does not imply that an antagonist in a collateral proceeding or transaction has standing to seek enforcement of the Rule. Nevertheless, since the Rules do establish standards of conduct by lawyers, a lawyer's violation of a Rule may be evidence of breach of the applicable standard of conduct.

[21] The Comment accompanying each Rule explains and illustrates the meaning and purpose of the Rule. The Preamble and this note on Scope provide general orientation. The Comments are intended as guides to interpretation, but the text of each Rule is authoritative.

ABA Model
Rules of
Professional
Conduct

RULE 1.0: TERMINOLOGY

(a) "Belief" or "believes" denotes that the person involved actually supposed the fact in question to be true. A person's belief may be inferred from circumstances.

(b) "Confirmed in writing," when used in reference to the informed consent of a person, denotes informed consent that is given in writing by the person or a writing that a lawyer promptly transmits to the person confirming an oral informed consent. See paragraph (e) for the definition of "informed consent." If it is not feasible to obtain or transmit the writing at the time the person gives informed consent, then the lawyer must obtain or transmit it within a reasonable time thereafter.

(c) "Firm" or "law firm" denotes a lawyer or lawyers in a law partnership, professional corporation, sole proprietorship or other association authorized to practice law; or lawyers employed in a legal services organization or the legal department of a corporation or other organization.

(d) "Fraud" or "fraudulent" denotes conduct that is fraudulent under the substantive or procedural law of the applicable jurisdiction and has a purpose to deceive.

(e) "Informed consent" denotes the agreement by a person to a proposed course of conduct after the lawyer has communicated adequate information and explanation about the material risks of and reasonably available alternatives to the proposed course of conduct.

(f) "Knowingly," "known," or "knows" denotes actual knowledge of the fact in question. A person's knowledge may be inferred from circumstances.

(g) "Partner" denotes a member of a partnership, a shareholder in a law firm organized as a professional corporation, or a member of an association authorized to practice law.

(h) "Reasonable" or "reasonably" when used in relation to conduct by a lawyer denotes the conduct of a reasonably prudent and competent lawyer.

(i) "Reasonable belief" or "reasonably believes" when used in reference to a lawyer denotes that the lawyer believes the matter in question and that the circumstances are such that the belief is reasonable.

(j) "Reasonably should know" when used in reference to a lawyer denotes that a lawyer of reasonable prudence and competence would ascertain the matter in question.

(k) "Screened" denotes the isolation of a lawyer from any participation in a matter through the timely imposition of procedures within a firm that are reasonably adequate under the circumstances to protect information that the isolated lawyer is obligated to protect under these Rules or other law.

(l) "Substantial" when used in reference to degree or extent denotes a material matter of clear and weighty importance.

(m) "Tribunal" denotes a court, an arbitrator in a binding arbitration proceeding or a legislative body, administrative agency or other body acting in an adjudicative capacity. A legislative body, administrative agency or other body acts in an adjudicative capacity when a neutral official, after the presentation of evidence or legal argument by a party or parties, will render a binding legal judgment directly affecting a party's interests in a particular matter.

(n) "Writing" or "written" denotes a tangible or electronic record of a communication or representation, including handwriting, typewriting, printing, photostating, photography, audio or videorecording, and electronic communications. A "signed" writing includes an electronic sound, symbol or process attached to or logically associated with a writing and executed or adopted by a person with the intent to sign the writing.

Comment

Confirmed in Writing

[1] If it is not feasible to obtain or transmit a written confirmation at the time the client gives informed consent, then the lawyer must obtain or transmit it within a reasonable time thereafter. If a lawyer has obtained a client's informed consent, the lawyer may act in reliance on that consent so long as it is confirmed in writing within a reasonable time thereafter.

Firm

[2] Whether two or more lawyers constitute a firm within paragraph (c) can depend on the specific facts. For example, two practitioners who share office space and occasionally consult or assist each other ordinarily would not be regarded as constituting a firm. However, if they present themselves to the public in a way that suggests that they are a firm or conduct themselves as a firm, they should be regarded as a firm for purposes of the Rules. The terms of any formal agreement between associated lawyers are relevant in determining whether they are a firm, as is the fact that they have mutual access to information concerning the clients they serve. Furthermore, it is relevant in doubtful cases to consider the underlying purpose of the Rule

that is involved. A group of lawyers could be regarded as a firm for purposes of the Rule that the same lawyer should not represent opposing parties in litigation, while it might not be so regarded for purposes of the Rule that information acquired by one lawyer is attributed to another.

[3] With respect to the law department of an organization, including the government, there is ordinarily no question that the members of the department constitute a firm within the meaning of the Rules of Professional Conduct. There can be uncertainty, however, as to the identity of the client. For example, it may not be clear whether the law department of a corporation represents a subsidiary or an affiliated corporation, as well as the corporation by which the members of the department are directly employed. A similar question can arise concerning an unincorporated association and its local affiliates.

[4] Similar questions can also arise with respect to lawyers in legal aid and legal services organizations. Depending upon the structure of the organization, the entire organization or different components of it may constitute a firm or firms for purposes of these Rules.

Fraud

[5] When used in these Rules, the terms "fraud" or "fraudulent" refer to conduct that is characterized as such under the substantive or procedural law of the applicable jurisdiction and has a purpose to deceive. This does not include merely negligent misrepresentation or negligent failure to apprise another of relevant information. For purposes of these Rules, it is not necessary that anyone has suffered damages or relied on the misrepresentation or failure to inform.

Informed Consent

[6] Many of the Rules of Professional Conduct require the lawyer to obtain the informed consent of a client or other person (e.g., a former client or, under certain circumstances, a prospective client) before accepting or continuing representation or pursuing a course of conduct. See, e.g., Rules 1.2(c), 1.6(a) and 1.7(b). The communication necessary to obtain such consent will vary according to the Rule involved and the circumstances giving rise to the need to obtain informed consent. The lawyer must make reasonable efforts to ensure that the client or other person possesses information reasonably adequate to make an informed decision. Ordinarily, this will require communication that includes a disclosure of the facts and circumstances giving rise to the situation, any explanation reasonably necessary to inform the client or other person of the material advantages and disadvantages of the proposed course of conduct and a discussion of the client's or

other person's options and alternatives. In some circumstances it may be appropriate for a lawyer to advise a client or other person to seek the advice of other counsel. A lawyer need not inform a client or other person of facts or implications already known to the client or other person; nevertheless, a lawyer who does not personally inform the client or other person assumes the risk that the client or other person is inadequately informed and the consent is invalid. In determining whether the information and explanation provided are reasonably adequate, relevant factors include whether the client or other person is experienced in legal matters generally and in making decisions of the type involved, and whether the client or other person is independently represented by other counsel in giving the consent. Normally, such persons need less information and explanation than others, and generally a client or other person who is independently represented by other counsel in giving the consent should be assumed to have given informed consent.

[7] Obtaining informed consent will usually require an affirmative response by the client or other person. In general, a lawyer may not assume consent from a client's or other person's silence. Consent may be inferred, however, from the conduct of a client or other person who has reasonably adequate information about the matter. A number of Rules require that a person's consent be confirmed in writing. See Rules 1.7(b) and 1.9(a). For a definition of "writing" and "confirmed in writing," see paragraphs (n) and (b). Other Rules require that a client's consent be obtained in a writing signed by the client. See, e.g., Rules 1.8(a) and (g). For a definition of "signed," see paragraph (n).

Screened

[8] This definition applies to situations where screening of a personally disqualified lawyer is permitted to remove imputation of a conflict of interest under Rules 1.10, 1.11, 1.12 or 1.18.

[9] The purpose of screening is to assure the affected parties that confidential information known by the personally disqualified lawyer remains protected. The personally disqualified lawyer should acknowledge the obligation not to communicate with any of the other lawyers in the firm with respect to the matter. Similarly, other lawyers in the firm who are working on the matter should be informed that the screening is in place and that they may not communicate with the personally disqualified lawyer with respect to the matter. Additional screening measures that are appropriate for the particular matter will depend on the circumstances. To implement, reinforce and remind all affected lawyers of the presence of the screening, it may be appropriate for the firm to undertake such procedures as a written under-

taking by the screened lawyer to avoid any communication with other firm personnel and any contact with any firm files or other information, including information in electronic form, relating to the matter, written notice and instructions to all other firm personnel forbidding any communication with the screened lawyer relating to the matter, denial of access by the screened lawyer to firm files or other information, including information in electronic form, relating to the matter and periodic reminders of the screen to the screened lawyer and all other firm personnel.

[10] In order to be effective, screening measures must be implemented as soon as practical after a lawyer or law firm knows or reasonably should know that there is a need for screening.

CLIENT-LAWYER RELATIONSHIP

RULE 1.1: COMPETENCE

A lawyer shall provide competent representation to a client. Competent representation requires the legal knowledge, skill, thoroughness and preparation reasonably necessary for the representation.

Comment

Legal Knowledge and Skill

[1] In determining whether a lawyer employs the requisite knowledge and skill in a particular matter, relevant factors include the relative complexity and specialized nature of the matter, the lawyer's general experience, the lawyer's training and experience in the field in question, the preparation and study the lawyer is able to give the matter and whether it is feasible to refer the matter to, or associate or consult with, a lawyer of established competence in the field in question. In many instances, the required proficiency is that of a general practitioner. Expertise in a particular field of law may be required in some circumstances.

[2] A lawyer need not necessarily have special training or prior experience to handle legal problems of a type with which the lawyer is unfamiliar. A newly admitted lawyer can be as competent as a practitioner with long experience. Some important legal skills, such as the analysis of precedent, the evaluation of evidence and legal drafting, are required in all legal problems. Perhaps the most fundamental legal skill consists of determining what kind of legal problems a situation may involve, a skill that necessarily transcends any particular specialized knowledge. A lawyer can provide adequate representation in a wholly novel field through necessary study.

Competent representation can also be provided through the association of a lawyer of established competence in the field in question.

[3] In an emergency a lawyer may give advice or assistance in a matter in which the lawyer does not have the skill ordinarily required where referral to or consultation or association with another lawyer would be impractical. Even in an emergency, however, assistance should be limited to that reasonably necessary in the circumstances, for ill-considered action under emergency conditions can jeopardize the client's interest.

[4] A lawyer may accept representation where the requisite level of competence can be achieved by reasonable preparation. This applies as well to a lawyer who is appointed as counsel for an unrepresented person. See also Rule 6.2.

Thoroughness and Preparation

[5] Competent handling of a particular matter includes inquiry into and analysis of the factual and legal elements of the problem, and use of methods and procedures meeting the standards of competent practitioners. It also includes adequate preparation. The required attention and preparation are determined in part by what is at stake; major litigation and complex transactions ordinarily require more extensive treatment than matters of lesser complexity and consequence. An agreement between the lawyer and the client regarding the scope of the representation may limit the matters for which the lawyer is responsible. See Rule 1.2(c).

Retaining or Contracting With Other Lawyers

[6] Before a lawyer retains or contracts with other lawyers outside the lawyer's own firm to provide or assist in the provision of legal services to a client, the lawyer should ordinarily obtain informed consent from the client and must reasonably believe that the other lawyers' services will contribute to the competent and ethical representation of the client. See also Rules 1.2 (allocation of authority), 1.4 (communication with client), 1.5(e) (fee sharing), 1.6 (confidentiality), and 5.5(a) (unauthorized practice of law). The reasonableness of the decision to retain or contract with other lawyers outside the lawyer's own firm will depend upon the circumstances, including the education, experience and reputation of the nonfirm lawyers; the nature of the services assigned to the nonfirm lawyers; and the legal protections, professional conduct rules, and ethical environments of the jurisdictions in which the services will be performed, particularly relating to confidential information.

[7] When lawyers from more than one law firm are providing legal services to the client on a particular matter, the lawyers ordinarily should consult with each other and the client about the scope of their respective

representations and the allocation of responsibility among them. See Rule 1.2. When making allocations of responsibility in a matter pending before a tribunal, lawyers and parties may have additional obligations that are a matter of law beyond the scope of these Rules.

Maintaining Competence

[8] To maintain the requisite knowledge and skill, a lawyer should keep abreast of changes in the law and its practice, including the benefits and risks associated with relevant technology, engage in continuing study and education and comply with all continuing legal education requirements to which the lawyer is subject.

Definitional Cross-References

"Reasonably" *See* Rule 1.0(h)

RULE 1.2: SCOPE OF REPRESENTATION AND ALLOCATION OF AUTHORITY BETWEEN CLIENT AND LAWYER

(a) Subject to paragraphs (c) and (d), a lawyer shall abide by a client's decisions concerning the objectives of representation and, as required by Rule 1.4, shall consult with the client as to the means by which they are to be pursued. A lawyer may take such action on behalf of the client as is impliedly authorized to carry out the representation. A lawyer shall abide by a client's decision whether to settle a matter. In a criminal case, the lawyer shall abide by the client's decision, after consultation with the lawyer, as to a plea to be entered, whether to waive jury trial and whether the client will testify.

(b) A lawyer's representation of a client, including representation by appointment, does not constitute an endorsement of the client's political, economic, social or moral views or activities.

(c) A lawyer may limit the scope of the representation if the limitation is reasonable under the circumstances and the client gives informed consent.

(d) A lawyer shall not counsel a client to engage, or assist a client, in conduct that the lawyer knows is criminal or fraudulent, but a lawyer may discuss the legal consequences of any proposed course of conduct with a client and may counsel or assist a client to make a good faith effort to determine the validity, scope, meaning or application of the law.

Comment

Allocation of Authority between Client and Lawyer

[1] Paragraph (a) confers upon the client the ultimate authority to determine the purposes to be served by legal representation, within the limits imposed by law and the lawyer's professional obligations. The decisions specified in paragraph (a), such as whether to settle a civil matter, must also be made by the client. See Rule 1.4(a)(1) for the lawyer's duty to communicate with the client about such decisions. With respect to the means by which the client's objectives are to be pursued, the lawyer shall consult with the client as required by Rule 1.4(a)(2) and may take such action as is impliedly authorized to carry out the representation.

[2] On occasion, however, a lawyer and a client may disagree about the means to be used to accomplish the client's objectives. Clients normally defer to the special knowledge and skill of their lawyer with respect to the means to be used to accomplish their objectives, particularly with respect to technical, legal and tactical matters. Conversely, lawyers usually defer to the client regarding such questions as the expense to be incurred and concern for third persons who might be adversely affected. Because of the varied nature of the matters about which a lawyer and client might disagree and because the actions in question may implicate the interests of a tribunal or other persons, this Rule does not prescribe how such disagreements are to be resolved. Other law, however, may be applicable and should be consulted by the lawyer. The lawyer should also consult with the client and seek a mutually acceptable resolution of the disagreement. If such efforts are unavailing and the lawyer has a fundamental disagreement with the client, the lawyer may withdraw from the representation. See Rule 1.16(b)(4). Conversely, the client may resolve the disagreement by discharging the lawyer. See Rule 1.16(a)(3).

[3] At the outset of a representation, the client may authorize the lawyer to take specific action on the client's behalf without further consultation. Absent a material change in circumstances and subject to Rule 1.4, a lawyer may rely on such an advance authorization. The client may, however, revoke such authority at any time.

[4] In a case in which the client appears to be suffering diminished capacity, the lawyer's duty to abide by the client's decisions is to be guided by reference to Rule 1.14.

Independence from Client's Views or Activities

[5] Legal representation should not be denied to people who are unable to afford legal services, or whose cause is controversial or the subject of popular disapproval. By the same token, representing a client does not constitute approval of the client's views or activities.

Agreements Limiting Scope of Representation

[6] The scope of services to be provided by a lawyer may be limited by agreement with the client or by the terms under which the lawyer's services are made available to the client. When a lawyer has been retained by an insurer to represent an insured, for example, the representation may be limited to matters related to the insurance coverage. A limited representation may be appropriate because the client has limited objectives for the representation. In addition, the terms upon which representation is undertaken may exclude specific means that might otherwise be used to accomplish the client's objectives. Such limitations may exclude actions that the client thinks are too costly or that the lawyer regards as repugnant or imprudent.

[7] Although this Rule affords the lawyer and client substantial latitude to limit the representation, the limitation must be reasonable under the circumstances. If, for example, a client's objective is limited to securing general information about the law the client needs in order to handle a common and typically uncomplicated legal problem, the lawyer and client may agree that the lawyer's services will be limited to a brief telephone consultation. Such a limitation, however, would not be reasonable if the time allotted was not sufficient to yield advice upon which the client could rely. Although an agreement for a limited representation does not exempt a lawyer from the duty to provide competent representation, the limitation is a factor to be considered when determining the legal knowledge, skill, thoroughness and preparation reasonably necessary for the representation. See Rule 1.1.

[8] All agreements concerning a lawyer's representation of a client must accord with the Rules of Professional Conduct and other law. See, e.g., Rules 1.1, 1.8 and 5.6.

Criminal, Fraudulent and Prohibited Transactions

[9] Paragraph (d) prohibits a lawyer from knowingly counseling or assisting a client to commit a crime or fraud. This prohibition, however, does not preclude the lawyer from giving an honest opinion about the actual consequences that appear likely to result from a client's conduct. Nor does the fact that a client uses advice in a course of action that is criminal or fraudulent of itself make a lawyer a party to the course of action. There is a critical distinction between presenting an analysis of legal aspects of questionable conduct and recommending the means by which a crime or fraud might be committed with impunity.

[10] When the client's course of action has already begun and is continuing, the lawyer's responsibility is especially delicate. The lawyer is required to avoid assisting the client, for example, by drafting or delivering documents that the lawyer knows are fraudulent or by suggesting how the

wrongdoing might be concealed. A lawyer may not continue assisting a client in conduct that the lawyer originally supposed was legally proper but then discovers is criminal or fraudulent. The lawyer must, therefore, withdraw from the representation of the client in the matter. See Rule 1.16(a). In some cases, withdrawal alone might be insufficient. It may be necessary for the lawyer to give notice of the fact of withdrawal and to disaffirm any opinion, document, affirmation or the like. See Rule 4.1.

[11] Where the client is a fiduciary, the lawyer may be charged with special obligations in dealings with a beneficiary.

[12] Paragraph (d) applies whether or not the defrauded party is a party to the transaction. Hence, a lawyer must not participate in a transaction to effectuate criminal or fraudulent avoidance of tax liability. Paragraph (d) does not preclude undertaking a criminal defense incident to a general retainer for legal services to a lawful enterprise. The last clause of paragraph (d) recognizes that determining the validity or interpretation of a statute or regulation may require a course of action involving disobedience of the statute or regulation or of the interpretation placed upon it by governmental authorities.

[13] If a lawyer comes to know or reasonably should know that a client expects assistance not permitted by the Rules of Professional Conduct or other law or if the lawyer intends to act contrary to the client's instructions, the lawyer must consult with the client regarding the limitations on the lawyer's conduct. See Rule 1.4(a)(5).

Definitional Cross-References
"Fraudulent" *See* Rule 1.0(d)
"Informed consent" *See* Rule 1.0(e)
"Knows" *See* Rule 1.0(f)
"Reasonable" *See* Rule 1.0(h)

RULE 1.3: DILIGENCE

A lawyer shall act with reasonable diligence and promptness in representing a client.

Comment
[1] A lawyer should pursue a matter on behalf of a client despite opposition, obstruction or personal inconvenience to the lawyer, and take whatever lawful and ethical measures are required to vindicate a client's cause or endeavor. A lawyer must also act with commitment and dedication to the interests of the client and with zeal in advocacy upon the client's behalf. A

lawyer is not bound, however, to press for every advantage that might be realized for a client. For example, a lawyer may have authority to exercise professional discretion in determining the means by which a matter should be pursued. See Rule 1.2. The lawyer's duty to act with reasonable diligence does not require the use of offensive tactics or preclude the treating of all persons involved in the legal process with courtesy and respect.

[2] A lawyer's work load must be controlled so that each matter can be handled competently.

[3] Perhaps no professional shortcoming is more widely resented than procrastination. A client's interests often can be adversely affected by the passage of time or the change of conditions; in extreme instances, as when a lawyer overlooks a statute of limitations, the client's legal position may be destroyed. Even when the client's interests are not affected in substance, however, unreasonable delay can cause a client needless anxiety and undermine confidence in the lawyer's trustworthiness. A lawyer's duty to act with reasonable promptness, however, does not preclude the lawyer from agreeing to a reasonable request for a postponement that will not prejudice the lawyer's client.

[4] Unless the relationship is terminated as provided in Rule 1.16, a lawyer should carry through to conclusion all matters undertaken for a client. If a lawyer's employment is limited to a specific matter, the relationship terminates when the matter has been resolved. If a lawyer has served a client over a substantial period in a variety of matters, the client sometimes may assume that the lawyer will continue to serve on a continuing basis unless the lawyer gives notice of withdrawal. Doubt about whether a client-lawyer relationship still exists should be clarified by the lawyer, preferably in writing, so that the client will not mistakenly suppose the lawyer is looking after the client's affairs when the lawyer has ceased to do so. For example, if a lawyer has handled a judicial or administrative proceeding that produced a result adverse to the client and the lawyer and the client have not agreed that the lawyer will handle the matter on appeal, the lawyer must consult with the client about the possibility of appeal before relinquishing responsibility for the matter. See Rule 1.4(a)(2). Whether the lawyer is obligated to prosecute the appeal for the client depends on the scope of the representation the lawyer has agreed to provide to the client. See Rule 1.2.

[5] To prevent neglect of client matters in the event of a sole practitioner's death or disability, the duty of diligence may require that each sole practitioner prepare a plan, in conformity with applicable rules, that designates another competent lawyer to review client files, notify each client of the lawyer's death or disability, and determine whether there is a need for immediate protective action. Cf. Rule 28 of the American Bar Association

Model Rules for Lawyer Disciplinary Enforcement (providing for court appointment of a lawyer to inventory files and take other protective action in absence of a plan providing for another lawyer to protect the interests of the clients of a deceased or disabled lawyer).

Definitional Cross-References

"Reasonable" *See* Rule 1.0(h)

RULE 1.4: COMMUNICATION

(a) A lawyer shall:

(1) promptly inform the client of any decision or circumstance with respect to which the client's informed consent, as defined in Rule 1.0(e), is required by these Rules;

(2) reasonably consult with the client about the means by which the client's objectives are to be accomplished;

(3) keep the client reasonably informed about the status of the matter;

(4) promptly comply with reasonable requests for information; and

(5) consult with the client about any relevant limitation on the lawyer's conduct when the lawyer knows that the client expects assistance not permitted by the Rules of Professional Conduct or other law.

(b) A lawyer shall explain a matter to the extent reasonably necessary to permit the client to make informed decisions regarding the representation.

Comment

[1] Reasonable communication between the lawyer and the client is necessary for the client effectively to participate in the representation.

Communicating with Client

[2] If these Rules require that a particular decision about the representation be made by the client, paragraph (a)(1) requires that the lawyer promptly consult with and secure the client's consent prior to taking action unless prior discussions with the client have resolved what action the client wants the lawyer to take. For example, a lawyer who receives from opposing counsel an offer of settlement in a civil controversy or a proffered plea bargain in a criminal case must promptly inform the client of its substance unless the client has previously indicated that the proposal will be accept-

able or unacceptable or has authorized the lawyer to accept or to reject the offer. See Rule 1.2(a).

[3] Paragraph (a)(2) requires the lawyer to reasonably consult with the client about the means to be used to accomplish the client's objectives. In some situations—depending on both the importance of the action under consideration and the feasibility of consulting with the client —this duty will require consultation prior to taking action. In other circumstances, such as during a trial when an immediate decision must be made, the exigency of the situation may require the lawyer to act without prior consultation. In such cases the lawyer must nonetheless act reasonably to inform the client of actions the lawyer has taken on the client's behalf. Additionally, paragraph (a)(3) requires that the lawyer keep the client reasonably informed about the status of the matter, such as significant developments affecting the timing or the substance of the representation.

[4] A lawyer's regular communication with clients will minimize the occasions on which a client will need to request information concerning the representation. When a client makes a reasonable request for information, however, paragraph (a)(4) requires prompt compliance with the request, or if a prompt response is not feasible, that the lawyer, or a member of the lawyer's staff, acknowledge receipt of the request and advise the client when a response may be expected. A lawyer should promptly respond to or acknowledge client communications.

Explaining Matters

[5] The client should have sufficient information to participate intelligently in decisions concerning the objectives of the representation and the means by which they are to be pursued, to the extent the client is willing and able to do so. Adequacy of communication depends in part on the kind of advice or assistance that is involved. For example, when there is time to explain a proposal made in a negotiation, the lawyer should review all important provisions with the client before proceeding to an agreement. In litigation a lawyer should explain the general strategy and prospects of success and ordinarily should consult the client on tactics that are likely to result in significant expense or to injure or coerce others. On the other hand, a lawyer ordinarily will not be expected to describe trial or negotiation strategy in detail. The guiding principle is that the lawyer should fulfill reasonable client expectations for information consistent with the duty to act in the client's best interests, and the client's overall requirements as to the character of representation. In certain circumstances, such as when a lawyer asks a client to consent to a representation affected by a conflict of interest, the client must give informed consent, as defined in Rule 1.0(e).

[6] Ordinarily, the information to be provided is that appropriate for a client who is a comprehending and responsible adult. However, fully informing the client according to this standard may be impracticable, for example, where the client is a child or suffers from diminished capacity. See Rule 1.14. When the client is an organization or group, it is often impossible or inappropriate to inform every one of its members about its legal affairs; ordinarily, the lawyer should address communications to the appropriate officials of the organization. See Rule 1.13. Where many routine matters are involved, a system of limited or occasional reporting may be arranged with the client.

Withholding Information

[7] In some circumstances, a lawyer may be justified in delaying transmission of information when the client would be likely to react imprudently to an immediate communication. Thus, a lawyer might withhold a psychiatric diagnosis of a client when the examining psychiatrist indicates that disclosure would harm the client. A lawyer may not withhold information to serve the lawyer's own interest or convenience or the interests or convenience of another person. Rules or court orders governing litigation may provide that information supplied to a lawyer may not be disclosed to the client. Rule 3.4(c) directs compliance with such rules or orders.

Definitional Cross-References

"Informed consent" *See* Rule 1.0(e)
"Knows" *See* Rule 1.0(f)
"Reasonably" *See* Rule 1.0(h)

RULE 1.5: FEES

(a) A lawyer shall not make an agreement for, charge, or collect an unreasonable fee or an unreasonable amount for expenses. The factors to be considered in determining the reasonableness of a fee include the following:

(1) the time and labor required, the novelty and difficulty of the questions involved, and the skill requisite to perform the legal service properly;

(2) the likelihood, if apparent to the client, that the acceptance of the particular employment will preclude other employment by the lawyer;

(3) the fee customarily charged in the locality for similar legal services;

(4) the amount involved and the results obtained;

(5) the time limitations imposed by the client or by the circumstances;

(6) the nature and length of the professional relationship with the client;

(7) the experience, reputation, and ability of the lawyer or lawyers performing the services; and

(8) whether the fee is fixed or contingent.

(b) The scope of the representation and the basis or rate of the fee and expenses for which the client will be responsible shall be communicated to the client, preferably in writing, before or within a reasonable time after commencing the representation, except when the lawyer will charge a regularly represented client on the same basis or rate. Any changes in the basis or rate of the fee or expenses shall also be communicated to the client.

(c) A fee may be contingent on the outcome of the matter for which the service is rendered, except in a matter in which a contingent fee is prohibited by paragraph (d) or other law. A contingent fee agreement shall be in a writing signed by the client and shall state the method by which the fee is to be determined, including the percentage or percentages that shall accrue to the lawyer in the event of settlement, trial or appeal; litigation and other expenses to be deducted from the recovery; and whether such expenses are to be deducted before or after the contingent fee is calculated. The agreement must clearly notify the client of any expenses for which the client will be liable whether or not the client is the prevailing party. Upon conclusion of a contingent fee matter, the lawyer shall provide the client with a written statement stating the outcome of the matter and, if there is a recovery, showing the remittance to the client and the method of its determination.

(d) A lawyer shall not enter into an arrangement for, charge, or collect:

(1) any fee in a domestic relations matter, the payment or amount of which is contingent upon the securing of a divorce or upon the amount of alimony or support, or property settlement in lieu thereof; or

(2) a contingent fee for representing a defendant in a criminal case.

(e) A division of a fee between lawyers who are not in the same firm may be made only if:

(1) the division is in proportion to the services performed by each lawyer or each lawyer assumes joint responsibility for the representation;

(2) the client agrees to the arrangement, including the share each lawyer will receive, and the agreement is confirmed in writing; and

(3) the total fee is reasonable.

Comment

Reasonableness of Fee and Expenses

[1] Paragraph (a) requires that lawyers charge fees that are reasonable under the circumstances. The factors specified in (1) through (8) are not exclusive. Nor will each factor be relevant in each instance. Paragraph (a) also requires that expenses for which the client will be charged must be reasonable. A lawyer may seek reimbursement for the cost of services performed in-house, such as copying, or for other expenses incurred in-house, such as telephone charges, either by charging a reasonable amount to which the client has agreed in advance or by charging an amount that reasonably reflects the cost incurred by the lawyer.

Basis or Rate of Fee

[2] When the lawyer has regularly represented a client, they ordinarily will have evolved an understanding concerning the basis or rate of the fee and the expenses for which the client will be responsible. In a new client-lawyer relationship, however, an understanding as to fees and expenses must be promptly established. Generally, it is desirable to furnish the client with at least a simple memorandum or copy of the lawyer's customary fee arrangements that states the general nature of the legal services to be provided, the basis, rate or total amount of the fee and whether and to what extent the client will be responsible for any costs, expenses or disbursements in the course of the representation. A written statement concerning the terms of the engagement reduces the possibility of misunderstanding.

[3] Contingent fees, like any other fees, are subject to the reasonableness standard of paragraph (a) of this Rule. In determining whether a particular contingent fee is reasonable, or whether it is reasonable to charge any form of contingent fee, a lawyer must consider the factors that are relevant under the circumstances. Applicable law may impose limitations on contingent fees, such as a ceiling on the percentage allowable, or may require a lawyer to offer clients an alternative basis for the fee. Applicable law also may apply to situations other than a contingent fee, for example, government regulations regarding fees in certain tax matters.

Terms of Payment

[4] A lawyer may require advance payment of a fee, but is obliged to return any unearned portion. See Rule 1.16(d). A lawyer may accept property in payment for services, such as an ownership interest in an enterprise, providing this does not involve acquisition of a proprietary interest in the cause of action or subject matter of the litigation contrary to Rule 1.8 (i). However, a fee paid in property instead of money may be subject to the requirements of Rule 1.8(a) because such fees often have the essential qualities of a business transaction with the client.

[5] An agreement may not be made whose terms might induce the lawyer improperly to curtail services for the client or perform them in a way contrary to the client's interest. For example, a lawyer should not enter into an agreement whereby services are to be provided only up to a stated amount when it is foreseeable that more extensive services probably will be required, unless the situation is adequately explained to the client. Otherwise, the client might have to bargain for further assistance in the midst of a proceeding or transaction. However, it is proper to define the extent of services in light of the client's ability to pay. A lawyer should not exploit a fee arrangement based primarily on hourly charges by using wasteful procedures.

Prohibited Contingent Fees

[6] Paragraph (d) prohibits a lawyer from charging a contingent fee in a domestic relations matter when payment is contingent upon the securing of a divorce or upon the amount of alimony or support or property settlement to be obtained. This provision does not preclude a contract for a contingent fee for legal representation in connection with the recovery of post-judgment balances due under support, alimony or other financial orders because such contracts do not implicate the same policy concerns.

Division of Fee

[7] A division of fee is a single billing to a client covering the fee of two or more lawyers who are not in the same firm. A division of fee facilitates association of more than one lawyer in a matter in which neither alone could serve the client as well, and most often is used when the fee is contingent and the division is between a referring lawyer and a trial specialist. Paragraph (e) permits the lawyers to divide a fee either on the basis of the proportion of services they render or if each lawyer assumes responsibility for the representation as a whole. In addition, the client must agree to the arrangement, including the share that each lawyer is to receive, and the agreement must be confirmed in writing. Contingent fee agreements must be in a

writing signed by the client and must otherwise comply with paragraph (c) of this Rule. Joint responsibility for the representation entails financial and ethical responsibility for the representation as if the lawyers were associated in a partnership. A lawyer should only refer a matter to a lawyer whom the referring lawyer reasonably believes is competent to handle the matter. See Rule 1.1.

[8] Paragraph (e) does not prohibit or regulate division of fees to be received in the future for work done when lawyers were previously associated in a law firm.

Disputes over Fees

[9] If a procedure has been established for resolution of fee disputes, such as an arbitration or mediation procedure established by the bar, the lawyer must comply with the procedure when it is mandatory, and, even when it is voluntary, the lawyer should conscientiously consider submitting to it. Law may prescribe a procedure for determining a lawyer's fee, for example, in representation of an executor or administrator, a class or a person entitled to a reasonable fee as part of the measure of damages. The lawyer entitled to such a fee and a lawyer representing another party concerned with the fee should comply with the prescribed procedure.

Definitional Cross-References

"Confirmed in writing" *See* Rule 1.0(b)
"Firm" *See* Rule 1.0(c)
"Writing" and "Written" and "Signed" *See* Rule 1.0(n)

RULE 1.6: CONFIDENTIALITY OF INFORMATION

(a) A lawyer shall not reveal information relating to the representation of a client unless the client gives informed consent, the disclosure is impliedly authorized in order to carry out the representation or the disclosure is permitted by paragraph (b).

(b) A lawyer may reveal information relating to the representation of a client to the extent the lawyer reasonably believes necessary:

(1) to prevent reasonably certain death or substantial bodily harm;

(2) to prevent the client from committing a crime or fraud that is reasonably certain to result in substantial injury to the financial interests or property of another and in furtherance of which the client has used or is using the lawyer's services;

(3) to prevent, mitigate or rectify substantial injury to the financial interests or property of another that is reasonably certain to result or has resulted from the client's commission of a crime or fraud in furtherance of which the client has used the lawyer's services;

(4) to secure legal advice about the lawyer's compliance with these Rules;

(5) to establish a claim or defense on behalf of the lawyer in a controversy between the lawyer and the client, to establish a defense to a criminal charge or civil claim against the lawyer based upon conduct in which the client was involved, or to respond to allegations in any proceeding concerning the lawyer's representation of the client;

(6) to comply with other law or a court order; or

(7) to detect and resolve conflicts of interest arising from the lawyer's change of employment or from changes in the composition or ownership of a firm, but only if the revealed information would not compromise the attorney-client privilege or otherwise prejudice the client.

(c) A lawyer shall make reasonable efforts to prevent the inadvertent or unauthorized disclosure of, or unauthorized access to, information relating to the representation of a client.

Comment

[1] This Rule governs the disclosure by a lawyer of information relating to the representation of a client during the lawyer's representation of the client. See Rule 1.18 for the lawyer's duties with respect to information provided to the lawyer by a prospective client, Rule 1.9(c)(2) for the lawyer's duty not to reveal information relating to the lawyer's prior representation of a former client and Rules 1.8(b) and 1.9(c)(1) for the lawyer's duties with respect to the use of such information to the disadvantage of clients and former clients.

[2] A fundamental principle in the client-lawyer relationship is that, in the absence of the client's informed consent, the lawyer must not reveal information relating to the representation. See Rule 1.0(e) for the definition of informed consent. This contributes to the trust that is the hallmark of the client-lawyer relationship. The client is thereby encouraged to seek legal assistance and to communicate fully and frankly with the lawyer even as to embarrassing or legally damaging subject matter. The lawyer needs this information to represent the client effectively and, if necessary, to advise the client to refrain from wrongful conduct. Almost without exception, clients

come to lawyers in order to determine their rights and what is, in the complex of laws and regulations, deemed to be legal and correct. Based upon experience, lawyers know that almost all clients follow the advice given, and the law is upheld.

[3] The principle of client-lawyer confidentiality is given effect by related bodies of law: the attorney-client privilege, the work product doctrine and the rule of confidentiality established in professional ethics. The attorney-client privilege and work product doctrine apply in judicial and other proceedings in which a lawyer may be called as a witness or otherwise required to produce evidence concerning a client. The rule of client-lawyer confidentiality applies in situations other than those where evidence is sought from the lawyer through compulsion of law. The confidentiality rule, for example, applies not only to matters communicated in confidence by the client but also to all information relating to the representation, whatever its source. A lawyer may not disclose such information except as authorized or required by the Rules of Professional Conduct or other law. See also Scope.

[4] Paragraph (a) prohibits a lawyer from revealing information relating to the representation of a client. This prohibition also applies to disclosures by a lawyer that do not in themselves reveal protected information but could reasonably lead to the discovery of such information by a third person. A lawyer's use of a hypothetical to discuss issues relating to the representation is permissible so long as there is no reasonable likelihood that the listener will be able to ascertain the identity of the client or the situation involved.

Authorized Disclosure

[5] Except to the extent that the client's instructions or special circumstances limit that authority, a lawyer is impliedly authorized to make disclosures about a client when appropriate in carrying out the representation. In some situations, for example, a lawyer may be impliedly authorized to admit a fact that cannot properly be disputed or to make a disclosure that facilitates a satisfactory conclusion to a matter. Lawyers in a firm may, in the course of the firm's practice, disclose to each other information relating to a client of the firm, unless the client has instructed that particular information be confined to specified lawyers.

Disclosure Adverse to Client

[6] Although the public interest is usually best served by a strict rule requiring lawyers to preserve the confidentiality of information relating to the representation of their clients, the confidentiality rule is subject to limited exceptions. Paragraph (b)(1) recognizes the overriding value of life and

physical integrity and permits disclosure reasonably necessary to prevent reasonably certain death or substantial bodily harm. Such harm is reasonably certain to occur if it will be suffered imminently or if there is a present and substantial threat that a person will suffer such harm at a later date if the lawyer fails to take action necessary to eliminate the threat. Thus, a lawyer who knows that a client has accidentally discharged toxic waste into a town's water supply may reveal this information to the authorities if there is a present and substantial risk that a person who drinks the water will contract a life-threatening or debilitating disease and the lawyer's disclosure is necessary to eliminate the threat or reduce the number of victims.

[7] Paragraph (b)(2) is a limited exception to the rule of confidentiality that permits the lawyer to reveal information to the extent necessary to enable affected persons or appropriate authorities to prevent the client from committing a crime or fraud, as defined in Rule 1.0(d), that is reasonably certain to result in substantial injury to the financial or property interests of another and in furtherance of which the client has used or is using the lawyer's services. Such a serious abuse of the client-lawyer relationship by the client forfeits the protection of this Rule. The client can, of course, prevent such disclosure by refraining from the wrongful conduct. Although paragraph (b)(2) does not require the lawyer to reveal the client's misconduct, the lawyer may not counsel or assist the client in conduct the lawyer knows is criminal or fraudulent. See Rule 1.2(d). See also Rule 1.16 with respect to the lawyer's obligation or right to withdraw from the representation of the client in such circumstances, and Rule 1.13(c), which permits the lawyer, where the client is an organization, to reveal information relating to the representation in limited circumstances.

[8] Paragraph (b)(3) addresses the situation in which the lawyer does not learn of the client's crime or fraud until after it has been consummated. Although the client no longer has the option of preventing disclosure by refraining from the wrongful conduct, there will be situations in which the loss suffered by the affected person can be prevented, rectified or mitigated. In such situations, the lawyer may disclose information relating to the representation to the extent necessary to enable the affected persons to prevent or mitigate reasonably certain losses or to attempt to recoup their losses. Paragraph (b)(3) does not apply when a person who has committed a crime or fraud thereafter employs a lawyer for representation concerning that offense.

[9] A lawyer's confidentiality obligations do not preclude a lawyer from securing confidential legal advice about the lawyer's personal responsibility to comply with these Rules. In most situations, disclosing information to secure such advice will be impliedly authorized for the lawyer to carry out the

representation. Even when the disclosure is not impliedly authorized, paragraph (b)(4) permits such disclosure because of the importance of a lawyer's compliance with the Rules of Professional Conduct.

[10] Where a legal claim or disciplinary charge alleges complicity of the lawyer in a client's conduct or other misconduct of the lawyer involving representation of the client, the lawyer may respond to the extent the lawyer reasonably believes necessary to establish a defense. The same is true with respect to a claim involving the conduct or representation of a former client. Such a charge can arise in a civil, criminal, disciplinary or other proceeding and can be based on a wrong allegedly committed by the lawyer against the client or on a wrong alleged by a third person, for example, a person claiming to have been defrauded by the lawyer and client acting together. The lawyer's right to respond arises when an assertion of such complicity has been made. Paragraph (b)(5) does not require the lawyer to await the commencement of an action or proceeding that charges such complicity, so that the defense may be established by responding directly to a third party who has made such an assertion. The right to defend also applies, of course, where a proceeding has been commenced.

[11] A lawyer entitled to a fee is permitted by paragraph (b)(5) to prove the services rendered in an action to collect it. This aspect of the rule expresses the principle that the beneficiary of a fiduciary relationship may not exploit it to the detriment of the fiduciary.

[12] Other law may require that a lawyer disclose information about a client. Whether such a law supersedes Rule 1.6 is a question of law beyond the scope of these Rules. When disclosure of information relating to the representation appears to be required by other law, the lawyer must discuss the matter with the client to the extent required by Rule 1.4. If, however, the other law supersedes this Rule and requires disclosure, paragraph (b)(6) permits the lawyer to make such disclosures as are necessary to comply with the law.

Detection of Conflicts of Interest

[13] Paragraph (b)(7) recognizes that lawyers in different firms may need to disclose limited information to each other to detect and resolve conflicts of interest, such as when a lawyer is considering an association with another firm, two or more firms are considering a merger, or a lawyer is considering the purchase of a law practice. See Rule 1.17, Comment [7]. Under these circumstances, lawyers and law firms are permitted to disclose limited information, but only once substantive discussions regarding the new relationship have occurred. Any such disclosure should ordinarily include no more than the identity of the persons and entities involved in

a matter, a brief summary of the general issues involved, and information about whether the matter has terminated. Even this limited information, however, should be disclosed only to the extent reasonably necessary to detect and resolve conflicts of interest that might arise from the possible new relationship. Moreover, the disclosure of any information is prohibited if it would compromise the attorney-client privilege or otherwise prejudice the client (e.g., the fact that a corporate client is seeking advice on a corporate takeover that has not been publicly announced; that a person has consulted a lawyer about the possibility of divorce before the person's intentions are known to the person's spouse; or that a person has consulted a lawyer about a criminal investigation that has not led to a public charge). Under those circumstances, paragraph (a) prohibits disclosure unless the client or former client gives informed consent. A lawyer's fiduciary duty to the lawyer's firm may also govern a lawyer's conduct when exploring an association with another firm and is beyond the scope of these Rules.

[14] Any information disclosed pursuant to paragraph (b)(7) may be used or further disclosed only to the extent necessary to detect and resolve conflicts of interest. Paragraph (b)(7) does not restrict the use of information acquired by means independent of any disclosure pursuant to paragraph (b)(7). Paragraph (b)(7) also does not affect the disclosure of information within a law firm when the disclosure is otherwise authorized, see Comment [5], such as when a lawyer in a firm discloses information to another lawyer in the same firm to detect and resolve conflicts of interest that could arise in connection with undertaking a new representation.

[15] A lawyer may be ordered to reveal information relating to the representation of a client by a court or by another tribunal or governmental entity claiming authority pursuant to other law to compel the disclosure. Absent informed consent of the client to do otherwise, the lawyer should assert on behalf of the client all nonfrivolous claims that the order is not authorized by other law or that the information sought is protected against disclosure by the attorney-client privilege or other applicable law. In the event of an adverse ruling, the lawyer must consult with the client about the possibility of appeal to the extent required by Rule 1.4. Unless review is sought, however, paragraph (b)(6) permits the lawyer to comply with the court's order.

[16] Paragraph (b) permits disclosure only to the extent the lawyer reasonably believes the disclosure is necessary to accomplish one of the purposes specified. Where practicable, the lawyer should first seek to persuade the client to take suitable action to obviate the need for disclosure. In any case, a disclosure adverse to the client's interest should be no greater than the lawyer reasonably believes necessary to accomplish the purpose. If the

disclosure will be made in connection with a judicial proceeding, the disclosure should be made in a manner that limits access to the information to the tribunal or other persons having a need to know it and appropriate protective orders or other arrangements should be sought by the lawyer to the fullest extent practicable.

[17] Paragraph (b) permits but does not require the disclosure of information relating to a client's representation to accomplish the purposes specified in paragraphs (b)(1) through (b)(6). In exercising the discretion conferred by this Rule, the lawyer may consider such factors as the nature of the lawyer's relationship with the client and with those who might be injured by the client, the lawyer's own involvement in the transaction and factors that may extenuate the conduct in question. A lawyer's decision not to disclose as permitted by paragraph (b) does not violate this Rule. Disclosure may be required, however, by other Rules. Some Rules require disclosure only if such disclosure would be permitted by paragraph (b). See Rules 1.2(d), 4.1(b), 8.1 and 8.3. Rule 3.3, on the other hand, requires disclosure in some circumstances regardless of whether such disclosure is permitted by this Rule. See Rule 3.3(c).

Acting Competently to Preserve Confidentiality

[18] Paragraph (c) requires a lawyer to act competently to safeguard information relating to the representation of a client against unauthorized access by third parties and against inadvertent or unauthorized disclosure by the lawyer or other persons who are participating in the representation of the client or who are subject to the lawyer's supervision. See Rules 1.1, 5.1 and 5.3. The unauthorized access to, or the inadvertent or unauthorized disclosure of, information relating to the representation of a client does not constitute a violation of paragraph (c) if the lawyer has made reasonable efforts to prevent the access or disclosure. Factors to be considered in determining the reasonableness of the lawyer's efforts include, but are not limited to, the sensitivity of the information, the likelihood of disclosure if additional safeguards are not employed, the cost of employing additional safeguards, the difficulty of implementing the safeguards, and the extent to which the safeguards adversely affect the lawyer's ability to represent clients (e.g., by making a device or important piece of software excessively difficult to use). A client may require the lawyer to implement special security measures not required by this Rule or may give informed consent to forgo security measures that would otherwise be required by this Rule. Whether a lawyer may be required to take additional steps to safeguard a client's information in order to comply with other law, such as state and federal laws that govern data privacy or that impose notification require-

ments upon the loss of, or unauthorized access to, electronic information, is beyond the scope of these Rules. For a lawyer's duties when sharing information with nonlawyers outside the lawyer's own firm, see Rule 5.3, Comments [3]-[4].

[19] When transmitting a communication that includes information relating to the representation of a client, the lawyer must take reasonable precautions to prevent the information from coming into the hands of unintended recipients. This duty, however, does not require that the lawyer use special security measures if the method of communication affords a reasonable expectation of privacy. Special circumstances, however, may warrant special precautions. Factors to be considered in determining the reasonableness of the lawyer's expectation of confidentiality include the sensitivity of the information and the extent to which the privacy of the communication is protected by law or by a confidentiality agreement. A client may require the lawyer to implement special security measures not required by this Rule or may give informed consent to the use of a means of communication that would otherwise be prohibited by this Rule. Whether a lawyer may be required to take additional steps in order to comply with other law, such as state and federal laws that govern data privacy, is beyond the scope of these Rules.

Former Client

[20] The duty of confidentiality continues after the client-lawyer relationship has terminated. See Rule 1.9(c)(2). See Rule 1.9(c)(1) for the prohibition against using such information to the disadvantage of the former client.

Definitional Cross-References
"Firm" *See* Rule 1.0(c)
"Fraud" *See* Rule 1.0(d)
"Informed consent" *See* Rule 1.0(e)
"Reasonable" and "Reasonably" *See* Rule 1.0(h)
"Reasonably believes" *See* Rule 1.0(i)
"Substantial" *See* Rule 1.0(l)

RULE 1.7: CONFLICT OF INTEREST: CURRENT CLIENTS

(a) Except as provided in paragraph (b), a lawyer shall not represent a client if the representation involves a concurrent conflict of interest. A concurrent conflict of interest exists if:

(1) the representation of one client will be directly adverse to another client; or

(2) there is a significant risk that the representation of one or more clients will be materially limited by the lawyer's responsibilities to another client, a former client or a third person or by a personal interest of the lawyer.

(b) Notwithstanding the existence of a concurrent conflict of interest under paragraph (a), a lawyer may represent a client if:

(1) the lawyer reasonably believes that the lawyer will be able to provide competent and diligent representation to each affected client;

(2) the representation is not prohibited by law;

(3) the representation does not involve the assertion of a claim by one client against another client represented by the lawyer in the same litigation or other proceeding before a tribunal; and

(4) each affected client gives informed consent, confirmed in writing.

Comment

General Principles

[1] Loyalty and independent judgment are essential elements in the lawyer's relationship to a client. Concurrent conflicts of interest can arise from the lawyer's responsibilities to another client, a former client or a third person or from the lawyer's own interests. For specific Rules regarding certain concurrent conflicts of interest, see Rule 1.8. For former client conflicts of interest, see Rule 1.9. For conflicts of interest involving prospective clients, see Rule 1.18. For definitions of "informed consent" and "confirmed in writing," see Rule 1.0(e) and (b).

[2] Resolution of a conflict of interest problem under this Rule requires the lawyer to: 1) clearly identify the client or clients; 2) determine whether a conflict of interest exists; 3) decide whether the representation may be undertaken despite the existence of a conflict, i.e., whether the conflict is consentable; and 4) if so, consult with the clients affected under paragraph (a) and obtain their informed consent, confirmed in writing. The clients affected under paragraph (a) include both of the clients referred to in paragraph (a)(1) and the one or more clients whose representation might be materially limited under paragraph (a)(2).

[3] A conflict of interest may exist before representation is undertaken, in which event the representation must be declined, unless the lawyer obtains the informed consent of each client under the conditions of paragraph (b). To determine whether a conflict of interest exists, a lawyer should adopt reasonable procedures, appropriate for the size and type of firm and practice, to determine in both litigation and non-litigation matters the persons

and issues involved. See also Comment to Rule 5.1. Ignorance caused by a failure to institute such procedures will not excuse a lawyer's violation of this Rule. As to whether a client-lawyer relationship exists or, having once been established, is continuing, see Comment to Rule 1.3 and Scope.

[4] If a conflict arises after representation has been undertaken, the lawyer ordinarily must withdraw from the representation, unless the lawyer has obtained the informed consent of the client under the conditions of paragraph (b). See Rule 1.16. Where more than one client is involved, whether the lawyer may continue to represent any of the clients is determined both by the lawyer's ability to comply with duties owed to the former client and by the lawyer's ability to represent adequately the remaining client or clients, given the lawyer's duties to the former client. See Rule 1.9. See also Comments [5] and [29].

[5] Unforeseeable developments, such as changes in corporate and other organizational affiliations or the addition or realignment of parties in litigation, might create conflicts in the midst of a representation, as when a company sued by the lawyer on behalf of one client is bought by another client represented by the lawyer in an unrelated matter. Depending on the circumstances, the lawyer may have the option to withdraw from one of the representations in order to avoid the conflict. The lawyer must seek court approval where necessary and take steps to minimize harm to the clients. See Rule 1.16. The lawyer must continue to protect the confidences of the client from whose representation the lawyer has withdrawn. See Rule 1.9(c).

Identifying Conflicts of Interest: Directly Adverse

[6] Loyalty to a current client prohibits undertaking representation directly adverse to that client without that client's informed consent. Thus, absent consent, a lawyer may not act as an advocate in one matter against a person the lawyer represents in some other matter, even when the matters are wholly unrelated. The client as to whom the representation is directly adverse is likely to feel betrayed, and the resulting damage to the client-lawyer relationship is likely to impair the lawyer's ability to represent the client effectively. In addition, the client on whose behalf the adverse representation is undertaken reasonably may fear that the lawyer will pursue that client's case less effectively out of deference to the other client, i.e., that the representation may be materially limited by the lawyer's interest in retaining the current client. Similarly, a directly adverse conflict may arise when a lawyer is required to cross-examine a client who appears as a witness in a lawsuit involving another client, as when the testimony will be damaging to the client who is represented in the lawsuit. On the other hand, simultane-

ABA Model Rules of Professional Conduct

ous representation in unrelated matters of clients whose interests are only economically adverse, such as representation of competing economic enterprises in unrelated litigation, does not ordinarily constitute a conflict of interest and thus may not require consent of the respective clients.

[7] Directly adverse conflicts can also arise in transactional matters. For example, if a lawyer is asked to represent the seller of a business in negotiations with a buyer represented by the lawyer, not in the same transaction but in another, unrelated matter, the lawyer could not undertake the representation without the informed consent of each client.

Identifying Conflicts of Interest: Material Limitation

[8] Even where there is no direct adverseness, a conflict of interest exists if there is a significant risk that a lawyer's ability to consider, recommend or carry out an appropriate course of action for the client will be materially limited as a result of the lawyer's other responsibilities or interests. For example, a lawyer asked to represent several individuals seeking to form a joint venture is likely to be materially limited in the lawyer's ability to recommend or advocate all possible positions that each might take because of the lawyer's duty of loyalty to the others. The conflict in effect forecloses alternatives that would otherwise be available to the client. The mere possibility of subsequent harm does not itself require disclosure and consent. The critical questions are the likelihood that a difference in interests will eventuate and, if it does, whether it will materially interfere with the lawyer's independent professional judgment in considering alternatives or foreclose courses of action that reasonably should be pursued on behalf of the client.

Lawyer's Responsibilities to Former Clients and Other Third Persons

[9] In addition to conflicts with other current clients, a lawyer's duties of loyalty and independence may be materially limited by responsibilities to former clients under Rule 1.9 or by the lawyer's responsibilities to other persons, such as fiduciary duties arising from a lawyer's service as a trustee, executor or corporate director.

Personal Interest Conflicts

[10] The lawyer's own interests should not be permitted to have an adverse effect on representation of a client. For example, if the probity of a lawyer's own conduct in a transaction is in serious question, it may be difficult or impossible for the lawyer to give a client detached advice. Similarly, when a lawyer has discussions concerning possible employment with

an opponent of the lawyer's client, or with a law firm representing the opponent, such discussions could materially limit the lawyer's representation of the client. In addition, a lawyer may not allow related business interests to affect representation, for example, by referring clients to an enterprise in which the lawyer has an undisclosed financial interest. See Rule 1.8 for specific Rules pertaining to a number of personal interest conflicts, including business transactions with clients. See also Rule 1.10 (personal interest conflicts under Rule 1.7 ordinarily are not imputed to other lawyers in a law firm).

[11] When lawyers representing different clients in the same matter or in substantially related matters are closely related by blood or marriage, there may be a significant risk that client confidences will be revealed and that the lawyer's family relationship will interfere with both loyalty and independent professional judgment. As a result, each client is entitled to know of the existence and implications of the relationship between the lawyers before the lawyer agrees to undertake the representation. Thus, a lawyer related to another lawyer, e.g., as parent, child, sibling or spouse, ordinarily may not represent a client in a matter where that lawyer is representing another party, unless each client gives informed consent. The disqualification arising from a close family relationship is personal and ordinarily is not imputed to members of firms with whom the lawyers are associated. See Rule 1.10.

[12] A lawyer is prohibited from engaging in sexual relationships with a client unless the sexual relationship predates the formation of the client-lawyer relationship. See Rule 1.8(j).

Interest of Person Paying
for a Lawyer's Service

[13] A lawyer may be paid from a source other than the client, including a co-client, if the client is informed of that fact and consents and the arrangement does not compromise the lawyer's duty of loyalty or independent judgment to the client. See Rule 1.8(f). If acceptance of the payment from any other source presents a significant risk that the lawyer's representation of the client will be materially limited by the lawyer's own interest in accommodating the person paying the lawyer's fee or by the lawyer's responsibilities to a payer who is also a co-client, then the lawyer must comply with the requirements of paragraph (b) before accepting the representation, including determining whether the conflict is consentable and, if so, that the client has adequate information about the material risks of the representation.

ABA Model Rules of Professional Conduct

ABA Model
Rules of
Professional
Conduct

Prohibited Representations

[14] Ordinarily, clients may consent to representation notwithstanding a conflict. However, as indicated in paragraph (b), some conflicts are nonconsentable, meaning that the lawyer involved cannot properly ask for such agreement or provide representation on the basis of the client's consent. When the lawyer is representing more than one client, the question of consentability must be resolved as to each client.

[15] Consentability is typically determined by considering whether the interests of the clients will be adequately protected if the clients are permitted to give their informed consent to representation burdened by a conflict of interest. Thus, under paragraph (b)(1), representation is prohibited if in the circumstances the lawyer cannot reasonably conclude that the lawyer will be able to provide competent and diligent representation. See Rule 1.1 (competence) and Rule 1.3 (diligence).

[16] Paragraph (b)(2) describes conflicts that are nonconsentable because the representation is prohibited by applicable law. For example, in some states substantive law provides that the same lawyer may not represent more than one defendant in a capital case, even with the consent of the clients, and under federal criminal statutes certain representations by a former government lawyer are prohibited, despite the informed consent of the former client. In addition, decisional law in some states limits the ability of a governmental client, such as a municipality, to consent to a conflict of interest.

[17] Paragraph (b)(3) describes conflicts that are nonconsentable because of the institutional interest in vigorous development of each client's position when the clients are aligned directly against each other in the same litigation or other proceeding before a tribunal. Whether clients are aligned directly against each other within the meaning of this paragraph requires examination of the context of the proceeding. Although this paragraph does not preclude a lawyer's multiple representation of adverse parties to a mediation (because mediation is not a proceeding before a "tribunal" under Rule 1.0(m)), such representation may be precluded by paragraph (b)(1).

Informed Consent

[18] Informed consent requires that each affected client be aware of the relevant circumstances and of the material and reasonably foreseeable ways that the conflict could have adverse effects on the interests of that client. See Rule 1.0(e) (informed consent). The information required depends on the nature of the conflict and the nature of the risks involved. When representation of multiple clients in a single matter is undertaken, the information must include the implications of the common representation, including pos-

sible effects on loyalty, confidentiality and the attorney-client privilege and the advantages and risks involved. See Comments [30] and [31] (effect of common representation on confidentiality).

[19] Under some circumstances it may be impossible to make the disclosure necessary to obtain consent. For example, when the lawyer represents different clients in related matters and one of the clients refuses to consent to the disclosure necessary to permit the other client to make an informed decision, the lawyer cannot properly ask the latter to consent. In some cases the alternative to common representation can be that each party may have to obtain separate representation with the possibility of incurring additional costs. These costs, along with the benefits of securing separate representation, are factors that may be considered by the affected client in determining whether common representation is in the client's interests.

Consent Confirmed in Writing

[20] Paragraph (b) requires the lawyer to obtain the informed consent of the client, confirmed in writing. Such a writing may consist of a document executed by the client or one that the lawyer promptly records and transmits to the client following an oral consent. See Rule 1.0(b). See also Rule 1.0(n) (writing includes electronic transmission). If it is not feasible to obtain or transmit the writing at the time the client gives informed consent, then the lawyer must obtain or transmit it within a reasonable time thereafter. See Rule 1.0(b). The requirement of a writing does not supplant the need in most cases for the lawyer to talk with the client, to explain the risks and advantages, if any, of representation burdened with a conflict of interest, as well as reasonably available alternatives, and to afford the client a reasonable opportunity to consider the risks and alternatives and to raise questions and concerns. Rather, the writing is required in order to impress upon clients the seriousness of the decision the client is being asked to make and to avoid disputes or ambiguities that might later occur in the absence of a writing.

Revoking Consent

[21] A client who has given consent to a conflict may revoke the consent and, like any other client, may terminate the lawyer's representation at any time. Whether revoking consent to the client's own representation precludes the lawyer from continuing to represent other clients depends on the circumstances, including the nature of the conflict, whether the client revoked consent because of a material change in circumstances, the reasonable expectations of the other clients and whether material detriment to the other clients or the lawyer would result.

Consent to Future Conflict

[22] Whether a lawyer may properly request a client to waive conflicts that might arise in the future is subject to the test of paragraph (b). The effectiveness of such waivers is generally determined by the extent to which the client reasonably understands the material risks that the waiver entails. The more comprehensive the explanation of the types of future representations that might arise and the actual and reasonably foreseeable adverse consequences of those representations, the greater the likelihood that the client will have the requisite understanding. Thus, if the client agrees to consent to a particular type of conflict with which the client is already familiar, then the consent ordinarily will be effective with regard to that type of conflict. If the consent is general and open-ended, then the consent ordinarily will be ineffective, because it is not reasonably likely that the client will have understood the material risks involved. On the other hand, if the client is an experienced user of the legal services involved and is reasonably informed regarding the risk that a conflict may arise, such consent is more likely to be effective, particularly if, e.g., the client is independently represented by other counsel in giving consent and the consent is limited to future conflicts unrelated to the subject of the representation. In any case, advance consent cannot be effective if the circumstances that materialize in the future are such as would make the conflict nonconsentable under paragraph (b).

Conflicts in Litigation

[23] Paragraph (b)(3) prohibits representation of opposing parties in the same litigation, regardless of the clients' consent. On the other hand, simultaneous representation of parties whose interests in litigation may conflict, such as coplaintiffs or codefendants, is governed by paragraph (a)(2). A conflict may exist by reason of substantial discrepancy in the parties' testimony, incompatibility in positions in relation to an opposing party or the fact that there are substantially different possibilities of settlement of the claims or liabilities in question. Such conflicts can arise in criminal cases as well as civil. The potential for conflict of interest in representing multiple defendants in a criminal case is so grave that ordinarily a lawyer should decline to represent more than one codefendant. On the other hand, common representation of persons having similar interests in civil litigation is proper if the requirements of paragraph (b) are met.

[24] Ordinarily a lawyer may take inconsistent legal positions in different tribunals at different times on behalf of different clients. The mere fact that advocating a legal position on behalf of one client might create precedent adverse to the interests of a client represented by the lawyer in an unrelated matter does not create a conflict of interest. A conflict of interest

ABA Model Rules of Professional Conduct

exists, however, if there is a significant risk that a lawyer's action on behalf of one client will materially limit the lawyer's effectiveness in representing another client in a different case; for example, when a decision favoring one client will create a precedent likely to seriously weaken the position taken on behalf of the other client. Factors relevant in determining whether the clients need to be advised of the risk include: where the cases are pending, whether the issue is substantive or procedural, the temporal relationship between the matters, the significance of the issue to the immediate and long-term interests of the clients involved and the clients' reasonable expectations in retaining the lawyer. If there is significant risk of material limitation, then absent informed consent of the affected clients, the lawyer must refuse one of the representations or withdraw from one or both matters.

[25] When a lawyer represents or seeks to represent a class of plaintiffs or defendants in a class-action lawsuit, unnamed members of the class are ordinarily not considered to be clients of the lawyer for purposes of applying paragraph (a)(1) of this Rule. Thus, the lawyer does not typically need to get the consent of such a person before representing a client suing the person in an unrelated matter. Similarly, a lawyer seeking to represent an opponent in a class action does not typically need the consent of an unnamed member of the class whom the lawyer represents in an unrelated matter.

Nonlitigation Conflicts

[26] Conflicts of interest under paragraphs (a)(1) and (a)(2) arise in contexts other than litigation. For a discussion of directly adverse conflicts in transactional matters, see Comment [7]. Relevant factors in determining whether there is significant potential for material limitation include the duration and intimacy of the lawyer's relationship with the client or clients involved, the functions being performed by the lawyer, the likelihood that disagreements will arise and the likely prejudice to the client from the conflict. The question is often one of proximity and degree. See Comment [8].

[27] For example, conflict questions may arise in estate planning and estate administration. A lawyer may be called upon to prepare wills for several family members, such as husband and wife, and, depending upon the circumstances, a conflict of interest may be present. In estate administration the identity of the client may be unclear under the law of a particular jurisdiction. Under one view, the client is the fiduciary; under another view the client is the estate or trust, including its beneficiaries. In order to comply with conflict of interest rules, the lawyer should make clear the lawyer's relationship to the parties involved.

[28] Whether a conflict is consentable depends on the circumstances. For example, a lawyer may not represent multiple parties to a negotiation

whose interests are fundamentally antagonistic to each other, but common representation is permissible where the clients are generally aligned in interest even though there is some difference in interest among them. Thus, a lawyer may seek to establish or adjust a relationship between clients on an amicable and mutually advantageous basis; for example, in helping to organize a business in which two or more clients are entrepreneurs, working out the financial reorganization of an enterprise in which two or more clients have an interest or arranging a property distribution in settlement of an estate. The lawyer seeks to resolve potentially adverse interests by developing the parties' mutual interests. Otherwise, each party might have to obtain separate representation, with the possibility of incurring additional cost, complication or even litigation. Given these and other relevant factors, the clients may prefer that the lawyer act for all of them.

Special Considerations in Common Representation

[29] In considering whether to represent multiple clients in the same matter, a lawyer should be mindful that if the common representation fails because the potentially adverse interests cannot be reconciled, the result can be additional cost, embarrassment and recrimination. Ordinarily, the lawyer will be forced to withdraw from representing all of the clients if the common representation fails. In some situations, the risk of failure is so great that multiple representation is plainly impossible. For example, a lawyer cannot undertake common representation of clients where contentious litigation or negotiations between them are imminent or contemplated. Moreover, because the lawyer is required to be impartial between commonly represented clients, representation of multiple clients is improper when it is unlikely that impartiality can be maintained. Generally, if the relationship between the parties has already assumed antagonism, the possibility that the clients' interests can be adequately served by common representation is not very good. Other relevant factors are whether the lawyer subsequently will represent both parties on a continuing basis and whether the situation involves creating or terminating a relationship between the parties.

[30] A particularly important factor in determining the appropriateness of common representation is the effect on client-lawyer confidentiality and the attorney-client privilege. With regard to the attorney-client privilege, the prevailing rule is that, as between commonly represented clients, the privilege does not attach. Hence, it must be assumed that if litigation eventuates between the clients, the privilege will not protect any such communications, and the clients should be so advised.

[31] As to the duty of confidentiality, continued common representation will almost certainly be inadequate if one client asks the lawyer not to dis-

close to the other client information relevant to the common representation. This is so because the lawyer has an equal duty of loyalty to each client, and each client has the right to be informed of anything bearing on the representation that might affect that client's interests and the right to expect that the lawyer will use that information to that client's benefit. See Rule 1.4. The lawyer should, at the outset of the common representation and as part of the process of obtaining each client's informed consent, advise each client that information will be shared and that the lawyer will have to withdraw if one client decides that some matter material to the representation should be kept from the other. In limited circumstances, it may be appropriate for the lawyer to proceed with the representation when the clients have agreed, after being properly informed, that the lawyer will keep certain information confidential. For example, the lawyer may reasonably conclude that failure to disclose one client's trade secrets to another client will not adversely affect representation involving a joint venture between the clients and agree to keep that information confidential with the informed consent of both clients.

[32] When seeking to establish or adjust a relationship between clients, the lawyer should make clear that the lawyer's role is not that of partisanship normally expected in other circumstances and, thus, that the clients may be required to assume greater responsibility for decisions than when each client is separately represented. Any limitations on the scope of the representation made necessary as a result of the common representation should be fully explained to the clients at the outset of the representation. See Rule 1.2(c).

[33] Subject to the above limitations, each client in the common representation has the right to loyal and diligent representation and the protection of Rule 1.9 concerning the obligations to a former client. The client also has the right to discharge the lawyer as stated in Rule 1.16.

Organizational Clients

[34] A lawyer who represents a corporation or other organization does not, by virtue of that representation, necessarily represent any constituent or affiliated organization, such as a parent or subsidiary. See Rule 1.13(a). Thus, the lawyer for an organization is not barred from accepting representation adverse to an affiliate in an unrelated matter, unless the circumstances are such that the affiliate should also be considered a client of the lawyer, there is an understanding between the lawyer and the organizational client that the lawyer will avoid representation adverse to the client's affiliates, or the lawyer's obligations to either the organizational client or the new client are likely to limit materially the lawyer's representation of the other client.

ABA Model Rules of Professional Conduct

[35] A lawyer for a corporation or other organization who is also a member of its board of directors should determine whether the responsibilities of the two roles may conflict. The lawyer may be called on to advise the corporation in matters involving actions of the directors. Consideration should be given to the frequency with which such situations may arise, the potential intensity of the conflict, the effect of the lawyer's resignation from the board and the possibility of the corporation's obtaining legal advice from another lawyer in such situations. If there is material risk that the dual role will compromise the lawyer's independence of professional judgment, the lawyer should not serve as a director or should cease to act as the corporation's lawyer when conflicts of interest arise. The lawyer should advise the other members of the board that in some circumstances matters discussed at board meetings while the lawyer is present in the capacity of director might not be protected by the attorney-client privilege and that conflict of interest considerations might require the lawyer's recusal as a director or might require the lawyer and the lawyer's firm to decline representation of the corporation in a matter.

Definitional Cross-References

"Confirmed in writing" *See* Rule 1.0(b)
"Informed consent" *See* Rule 1.0(e)
"Reasonably believes" *See* Rule 1.0(i)
"Tribunal" *See* Rule 1.0(m)

RULE 1.8: CONFLICT OF INTEREST: CURRENT CLIENTS: SPECIFIC RULES

(a) A lawyer shall not enter into a business transaction with a client or knowingly acquire an ownership, possessory, security or other pecuniary interest adverse to a client unless:

(1) the transaction and terms on which the lawyer acquires the interest are fair and reasonable to the client and are fully disclosed and transmitted in writing in a manner that can be reasonably understood by the client;

(2) the client is advised in writing of the desirability of seeking and is given a reasonable opportunity to seek the advice of independent legal counsel on the transaction; and

(3) the client gives informed consent, in a writing signed by the client, to the essential terms of the transaction and the lawyer's role in the transaction, including whether the lawyer is representing the client in the transaction.

(b) A lawyer shall not use information relating to representation of a client to the disadvantage of the client unless the client gives informed consent, except as permitted or required by these Rules.

(c) A lawyer shall not solicit any substantial gift from a client, including a testamentary gift, or prepare on behalf of a client an instrument giving the lawyer or a person related to the lawyer any substantial gift unless the lawyer or other recipient of the gift is related to the client. For purposes of this paragraph, related persons include a spouse, child, grandchild, parent, grandparent or other relative or individual with whom the lawyer or the client maintains a close, familial relationship.

(d) Prior to the conclusion of representation of a client, a lawyer shall not make or negotiate an agreement giving the lawyer literary or media rights to a portrayal or account based in substantial part on information relating to the representation.

(e) A lawyer shall not provide financial assistance to a client in connection with pending or contemplated litigation, except that:

(1) a lawyer may advance court costs and expenses of litigation, the repayment of which may be contingent on the outcome of the matter; and

(2) a lawyer representing an indigent client may pay court costs and expenses of litigation on behalf of the client.

(f) A lawyer shall not accept compensation for representing a client from one other than the client unless:

(1) the client gives informed consent;

(2) there is no interference with the lawyer's independence of professional judgment or with the client-lawyer relationship; and

(3) information relating to representation of a client is protected as required by Rule 1.6.

(g) A lawyer who represents two or more clients shall not participate in making an aggregate settlement of the claims of or against the clients, or in a criminal case an aggregated agreement as to guilty or nolo contendere pleas, unless each client gives informed consent, in a writing signed by the client. The lawyer's disclosure shall include the existence and nature of all the claims or pleas involved and of the participation of each person in the settlement.

(h) A lawyer shall not:

(1) make an agreement prospectively limiting the lawyer's liability to a client for malpractice unless the client is independently represented in making the agreement; or

(2) settle a claim or potential claim for such liability with an unrepresented client or former client unless that person is advised in writing of the desirability of seeking and is given a reasonable opportunity to seek the advice of independent legal counsel in connection therewith.

(i) A lawyer shall not acquire a proprietary interest in the cause of action or subject matter of litigation the lawyer is conducting for a client, except that the lawyer may:

(1) acquire a lien authorized by law to secure the lawyer's fee or expenses; and

(2) contract with a client for a reasonable contingent fee in a civil case.

(j) A lawyer shall not have sexual relations with a client unless a consensual sexual relationship existed between them when the client-lawyer relationship commenced.

(k) While lawyers are associated in a firm, a prohibition in the foregoing paragraphs (a) through (i) that applies to any one of them shall apply to all of them.

Comment

Business Transactions between Client and Lawyer

[1] A lawyer's legal skill and training, together with the relationship of trust and confidence between lawyer and client, create the possibility of overreaching when the lawyer participates in a business, property or financial transaction with a client, for example, a loan or sales transaction or a lawyer investment on behalf of a client. The requirements of paragraph (a) must be met even when the transaction is not closely related to the subject matter of the representation, as when a lawyer drafting a will for a client learns that the client needs money for unrelated expenses and offers to make a loan to the client. The Rule applies to lawyers engaged in the sale of goods or services related to the practice of law, for example, the sale of title insurance or investment services to existing clients of the lawyer's legal practice. See Rule 5.7. It also applies to lawyers purchasing property from estates they represent. It does not apply to ordinary fee arrangements between client and lawyer, which are governed by Rule 1.5, although its requirements must be met when the lawyer accepts an interest in the client's business or other nonmonetary property as payment of all or part of a fee. In addition, the Rule does not apply to standard commercial transactions between the lawyer and the client for products or services that the client generally markets to others, for example, banking or brokerage services, medical services, products manufactured or distributed by the client, and utilities' services.

In such transactions, the lawyer has no advantage in dealing with the client, and the restrictions in paragraph (a) are unnecessary and impracticable.

[2] Paragraph (a)(1) requires that the transaction itself be fair to the client and that its essential terms be communicated to the client, in writing, in a manner that can be reasonably understood. Paragraph (a)(2) requires that the client also be advised, in writing, of the desirability of seeking the advice of independent legal counsel. It also requires that the client be given a reasonable opportunity to obtain such advice. Paragraph (a)(3) requires that the lawyer obtain the client's informed consent, in a writing signed by the client, both to the essential terms of the transaction and to the lawyer's role. When necessary, the lawyer should discuss both the material risks of the proposed transaction, including any risk presented by the lawyer's involvement, and the existence of reasonably available alternatives and should explain why the advice of independent legal counsel is desirable. See Rule 1.0(e) (definition of informed consent).

[3] The risk to a client is greatest when the client expects the lawyer to represent the client in the transaction itself or when the lawyer's financial interest otherwise poses a significant risk that the lawyer's representation of the client will be materially limited by the lawyer's financial interest in the transaction. Here the lawyer's role requires that the lawyer must comply, not only with the requirements of paragraph (a), but also with the requirements of Rule 1.7. Under that Rule, the lawyer must disclose the risks associated with the lawyer's dual role as both legal adviser and participant in the transaction, such as the risk that the lawyer will structure the transaction or give legal advice in a way that favors the lawyer's interests at the expense of the client. Moreover, the lawyer must obtain the client's informed consent. In some cases, the lawyer's interest may be such that Rule 1.7 will preclude the lawyer from seeking the client's consent to the transaction.

[4] If the client is independently represented in the transaction, paragraph (a)(2) of this Rule is inapplicable, and the paragraph (a)(1) requirement for full disclosure is satisfied either by a written disclosure by the lawyer involved in the transaction or by the client's independent counsel. The fact that the client was independently represented in the transaction is relevant in determining whether the agreement was fair and reasonable to the client as paragraph (a)(1) further requires.

Use of Information Related to Representation

[5] Use of information relating to the representation to the disadvantage of the client violates the lawyer's duty of loyalty. Paragraph (b) applies when the information is used to benefit either the lawyer or a third person, such as another client or business associate of the lawyer. For example, if

ABA Model
Rules of
Professional
Conduct

a lawyer learns that a client intends to purchase and develop several parcels of land, the lawyer may not use that information to purchase one of the parcels in competition with the client or to recommend that another client make such a purchase. The Rule does not prohibit uses that do not disadvantage the client. For example, a lawyer who learns a government agency's interpretation of trade legislation during the representation of one client may properly use that information to benefit other clients. Paragraph (b) prohibits disadvantageous use of client information unless the client gives informed consent, except as permitted or required by these Rules. See Rules 1.2(d), 1.6, 1.9(c), 3.3, 4.1(b), 8.1 and 8.3.

Gifts to Lawyers

[6] A lawyer may accept a gift from a client, if the transaction meets general standards of fairness. For example, a simple gift such as a present given at a holiday or as a token of appreciation is permitted. If a client offers the lawyer a more substantial gift, paragraph (c) does not prohibit the lawyer from accepting it, although such a gift may be voidable by the client under the doctrine of undue influence, which treats client gifts as presumptively fraudulent. In any event, due to concerns about overreaching and imposition on clients, a lawyer may not suggest that a substantial gift be made to the lawyer or for the lawyer's benefit, except where the lawyer is related to the client as set forth in paragraph (c).

[7] If effectuation of a substantial gift requires preparing a legal instrument such as a will or conveyance, the client should have the detached advice that another lawyer can provide. The sole exception to this Rule is where the client is a relative of the donee.

[8] This Rule does not prohibit a lawyer from seeking to have the lawyer or a partner or associate of the lawyer named as executor of the client's estate or to another potentially lucrative fiduciary position. Nevertheless, such appointments will be subject to the general conflict of interest provision in Rule 1.7 when there is a significant risk that the lawyer's interest in obtaining the appointment will materially limit the lawyer's independent professional judgment in advising the client concerning the choice of an executor or other fiduciary. In obtaining the client's informed consent to the conflict, the lawyer should advise the client concerning the nature and extent of the lawyer's financial interest in the appointment, as well as the availability of alternative candidates for the position.

Literary Rights

[9] An agreement by which a lawyer acquires literary or media rights concerning the conduct of the representation creates a conflict between the

interests of the client and the personal interests of the lawyer. Measures suitable in the representation of the client may detract from the publication value of an account of the representation. Paragraph (d) does not prohibit a lawyer representing a client in a transaction concerning literary property from agreeing that the lawyer's fee shall consist of a share in ownership in the property, if the arrangement conforms to Rule 1.5 and paragraphs (a) and (i).

Financial Assistance

[10] Lawyers may not subsidize lawsuits or administrative proceedings brought on behalf of their clients, including making or guaranteeing loans to their clients for living expenses, because to do so would encourage clients to pursue lawsuits that might not otherwise be brought and because such assistance gives lawyers too great a financial stake in the litigation. These dangers do not warrant a prohibition on a lawyer lending a client court costs and litigation expenses, including the expenses of medical examination and the costs of obtaining and presenting evidence, because these advances are virtually indistinguishable from contingent fees and help ensure access to the courts. Similarly, an exception allowing lawyers representing indigent clients to pay court costs and litigation expenses regardless of whether these funds will be repaid is warranted.

Person Paying for a Lawyer's Services

[11] Lawyers are frequently asked to represent a client under circumstances in which a third person will compensate the lawyer, in whole or in part. The third person might be a relative or friend, an indemnitor (such as a liability insurance company) or a co-client (such as a corporation sued along with one or more of its employees). Because third-party payers frequently have interests that differ from those of the client, including interests in minimizing the amount spent on the representation and in learning how the representation is progressing, lawyers are prohibited from accepting or continuing such representations unless the lawyer determines that there will be no interference with the lawyer's independent professional judgment and there is informed consent from the client. See also Rule 5.4(c) (prohibiting interference with a lawyer's professional judgment by one who recommends, employs or pays the lawyer to render legal services for another).

[12] Sometimes, it will be sufficient for the lawyer to obtain the client's informed consent regarding the fact of the payment and the identity of the third-party payer. If, however, the fee arrangement creates a conflict of interest for the lawyer, then the lawyer must comply with Rule 1.7. The lawyer must also conform to the requirements of Rule 1.6 concerning confidential-

ABA Model
Rules of
Professional
Conduct

ity. Under Rule 1.7(a), a conflict of interest exists if there is significant risk that the lawyer's representation of the client will be materially limited by the lawyer's own interest in the fee arrangement or by the lawyer's responsibilities to the third-party payer (for example, when the third-party payer is a co-client). Under Rule 1.7(b), the lawyer may accept or continue the representation with the informed consent of each affected client, unless the conflict is nonconsentable under that paragraph. Under Rule 1.7(b), the informed consent must be confirmed in writing.

Aggregate Settlements

[13] Differences in willingness to make or accept an offer of settlement are among the risks of common representation of multiple clients by a single lawyer. Under Rule 1.7, this is one of the risks that should be discussed before undertaking the representation, as part of the process of obtaining the clients' informed consent. In addition, Rule 1.2(a) protects each client's right to have the final say in deciding whether to accept or reject an offer of settlement and in deciding whether to enter a guilty or nolo contendere plea in a criminal case. The rule stated in this paragraph is a corollary of both these Rules and provides that, before any settlement offer or plea bargain is made or accepted on behalf of multiple clients, the lawyer must inform each of them about all the material terms of the settlement, including what the other clients will receive or pay if the settlement or plea offer is accepted. See also Rule 1.0(e) (definition of informed consent). Lawyers representing a class of plaintiffs or defendants, or those proceeding derivatively, may not have a full client-lawyer relationship with each member of the class; nevertheless, such lawyers must comply with applicable rules regulating notification of class members and other procedural requirements designed to ensure adequate protection of the entire class.

Limiting Liability and Settling Malpractice Claims

[14] Agreements prospectively limiting a lawyer's liability for malpractice are prohibited unless the client is independently represented in making the agreement because they are likely to undermine competent and diligent representation. Also, many clients are unable to evaluate the desirability of making such an agreement before a dispute has arisen, particularly if they are then represented by the lawyer seeking the agreement. This paragraph does not, however, prohibit a lawyer from entering into an agreement with the client to arbitrate legal malpractice claims, provided such agreements are enforceable and the client is fully informed of the scope and effect of the agreement. Nor does this paragraph limit the ability of lawyers to practice in the form of a limited-liability entity, where permitted by law, provided

that each lawyer remains personally liable to the client for his or her own conduct and the firm complies with any conditions required by law, such as provisions requiring client notification or maintenance of adequate liability insurance. Nor does it prohibit an agreement in accordance with Rule 1.2 that defines the scope of the representation, although a definition of scope that makes the obligations of representation illusory will amount to an attempt to limit liability.

[15] Agreements settling a claim or a potential claim for malpractice are not prohibited by this Rule. Nevertheless, in view of the danger that a lawyer will take unfair advantage of an unrepresented client or former client, the lawyer must first advise such a person in writing of the appropriateness of independent representation in connection with such a settlement. In addition, the lawyer must give the client or former client a reasonable opportunity to find and consult independent counsel.

Acquiring Proprietary Interest in Litigation

[16] Paragraph (i) states the traditional general rule that lawyers are prohibited from acquiring a proprietary interest in litigation. Like paragraph (e), the general rule has its basis in common law champerty and maintenance and is designed to avoid giving the lawyer too great an interest in the representation. In addition, when the lawyer acquires an ownership interest in the subject of the representation, it will be more difficult for a client to discharge the lawyer if the client so desires. The Rule is subject to specific exceptions developed in decisional law and continued in these Rules. The exception for certain advances of the costs of litigation is set forth in paragraph (e). In addition, paragraph (i) sets forth exceptions for liens authorized by law to secure the lawyer's fees or expenses and contracts for reasonable contingent fees. The law of each jurisdiction determines which liens are authorized by law. These may include liens granted by statute, liens originating in common law and liens acquired by contract with the client. When a lawyer acquires by contract a security interest in property other than that recovered through the lawyer's efforts in the litigation, such an acquisition is a business or financial transaction with a client and is governed by the requirements of paragraph (a). Contracts for contingent fees in civil cases are governed by Rule 1.5.

Client-Lawyer Sexual Relationships

[17] The relationship between lawyer and client is a fiduciary one in which the lawyer occupies the highest position of trust and confidence. The relationship is almost always unequal; thus, a sexual relationship between lawyer and client can involve unfair exploitation of the lawyer's fiduciary

role, in violation of the lawyer's basic ethical obligation not to use the trust of the client to the client's disadvantage. In addition, such a relationship presents a significant danger that, because of the lawyer's emotional involvement, the lawyer will be unable to represent the client without impairment of the exercise of independent professional judgment. Moreover, a blurred line between the professional and personal relationships may make it difficult to predict to what extent client confidences will be protected by the attorney-client evidentiary privilege, since client confidences are protected by privilege only when they are imparted in the context of the client-lawyer relationship. Because of the significant danger of harm to client interests and because the client's own emotional involvement renders it unlikely that the client could give adequate informed consent, this Rule prohibits the lawyer from having sexual relations with a client regardless of whether the relationship is consensual and regardless of the absence of prejudice to the client.

[18] Sexual relationships that predate the client-lawyer relationship are not prohibited. Issues relating to the exploitation of the fiduciary relationship and client dependency are diminished when the sexual relationship existed prior to the commencement of the client-lawyer relationship. However, before proceeding with the representation in these circumstances, the lawyer should consider whether the lawyer's ability to represent the client will be materially limited by the relationship. See Rule 1.7(a)(2).

[19] When the client is an organization, paragraph (j) of this Rule prohibits a lawyer for the organization (whether inside counsel or outside counsel) from having a sexual relationship with a constituent of the organization who supervises, directs or regularly consults with that lawyer concerning the organization's legal matters.

Imputation of Prohibitions

[20] Under paragraph (k), a prohibition on conduct by an individual lawyer in paragraphs (a) through (i) also applies to all lawyers associated in a firm with the personally prohibited lawyer. For example, one lawyer in a firm may not enter into a business transaction with a client of another member of the firm without complying with paragraph (a), even if the first lawyer is not personally involved in the representation of the client. The prohibition set forth in paragraph (j) is personal and is not applied to associated lawyers.

Definitional Cross-References

"Firm" *See* Rule 1.0(c)

"Informed consent" *See* Rule 1.0(e)

"Knowingly" *See* Rule 1.0(f)

"Substantial" *See* Rule 1.0(l)

"Writing" and "Signed" *See* Rule 1.0(n)

RULE 1.9: DUTIES TO FORMER CLIENTS

(a) A lawyer who has formerly represented a client in a matter shall not thereafter represent another person in the same or a substantially related matter in which that person's interests are materially adverse to the interests of the former client unless the former client gives informed consent, confirmed in writing.

(b) A lawyer shall not knowingly represent a person in the same or a substantially related matter in which a firm with which the lawyer formerly was associated had previously represented a client

   (1) whose interests are materially adverse to that person; and

   (2) about whom the lawyer had acquired information

protected by Rules 1.6 and 1.9(c) that is material to the matter; unless the former client gives informed consent, confirmed in writing.

(c) A lawyer who has formerly represented a client in a matter or whose present or former firm has formerly represented a client in a matter shall not thereafter:

   (1) use information relating to the representation to the disadvantage of the former client except as these Rules would permit or require with respect to a client, or when the information has become generally known; or

   (2) reveal information relating to the representation except as these Rules would permit or require with respect to a client.

Comment

[1] After termination of a client-lawyer relationship, a lawyer has certain continuing duties with respect to confidentiality and conflicts of interest and thus may not represent another client except in conformity with this Rule. Under this Rule, for example, a lawyer could not properly seek to rescind on behalf of a new client a contract drafted on behalf of the former client. So also a lawyer who has prosecuted an accused person could not properly represent the accused in a subsequent civil action against the government concerning the same transaction. Nor could a lawyer who has represented multiple clients in a matter represent one of the clients against the others in the same or a substantially related matter after a dispute arose among the clients in that matter, unless all affected clients give informed consent. See Comment [9]. Current and former government lawyers must comply with this Rule to the extent required by Rule 1.11.

[2] The scope of a "matter" for purposes of this Rule depends on the facts of a particular situation or transaction. The lawyer's involvement in

a matter can also be a question of degree. When a lawyer has been directly involved in a specific transaction, subsequent representation of other clients with materially adverse interests in that transaction clearly is prohibited. On the other hand, a lawyer who recurrently handled a type of problem for a former client is not precluded from later representing another client in a factually distinct problem of that type even though the subsequent representation involves a position adverse to the prior client. Similar considerations can apply to the reassignment of military lawyers between defense and prosecution functions within the same military jurisdictions. The underlying question is whether the lawyer was so involved in the matter that the subsequent representation can be justly regarded as a changing of sides in the matter in question.

[3] Matters are "substantially related" for purposes of this Rule if they involve the same transaction or legal dispute or if there otherwise is a substantial risk that confidential factual information as would normally have been obtained in the prior representation would materially advance the client's position in the subsequent matter. For example, a lawyer who has represented a businessperson and learned extensive private financial information about that person may not then represent that person's spouse in seeking a divorce. Similarly, a lawyer who has previously represented a client in securing environmental permits to build a shopping center would be precluded from representing neighbors seeking to oppose rezoning of the property on the basis of environmental considerations; however, the lawyer would not be precluded, on the grounds of substantial relationship, from defending a tenant of the completed shopping center in resisting eviction for nonpayment of rent. Information that has been disclosed to the public or to other parties adverse to the former client ordinarily will not be disqualifying. Information acquired in a prior representation may have been rendered obsolete by the passage of time, a circumstance that may be relevant in determining whether two representations are substantially related. In the case of an organizational client, general knowledge of the client's policies and practices ordinarily will not preclude a subsequent representation; on the other hand, knowledge of specific facts gained in a prior representation that are relevant to the matter in question ordinarily will preclude such a representation. A former client is not required to reveal the confidential information learned by the lawyer in order to establish a substantial risk that the lawyer has confidential information to use in the subsequent matter. A conclusion about the possession of such information may be based on the nature of the services the lawyer provided the former client and information that would in ordinary practice be learned by a lawyer providing such services.

Lawyers Moving Between Firms

[4] When lawyers have been associated within a firm but then end their association, the question of whether a lawyer should undertake representation is more complicated. There are several competing considerations. First, the client previously represented by the former firm must be reasonably assured that the principle of loyalty to the client is not compromised. Second, the rule should not be so broadly cast as to preclude other persons from having reasonable choice of legal counsel. Third, the rule should not unreasonably hamper lawyers from forming new associations and taking on new clients after having left a previous association. In this connection, it should be recognized that today many lawyers practice in firms, that many lawyers to some degree limit their practice to one field or another, and that many move from one association to another several times in their careers. If the concept of imputation were applied with unqualified rigor, the result would be radical curtailment of the opportunity of lawyers to move from one practice setting to another and of the opportunity of clients to change counsel.

[5] Paragraph (b) operates to disqualify the lawyer only when the lawyer involved has actual knowledge of information protected by Rules 1.6 and 1.9(c). Thus, if a lawyer while with one firm acquired no knowledge or information relating to a particular client of the firm, and that lawyer later joined another firm, neither the lawyer individually nor the second firm is disqualified from representing another client in the same or a related matter even though the interests of the two clients conflict. See Rule 1.10(b) for the restrictions on a firm once a lawyer has terminated association with the firm.

[6] Application of paragraph (b) depends on a situation's particular facts, aided by inferences, deductions or working presumptions that reasonably may be made about the way in which lawyers work together. A lawyer may have general access to files of all clients of a law firm and may regularly participate in discussions of their affairs; it should be inferred that such a lawyer in fact is privy to all information about all the firm's clients. In contrast, another lawyer may have access to the files of only a limited number of clients and participate in discussions of the affairs of no other clients; in the absence of information to the contrary, it should be inferred that such a lawyer in fact is privy to information about the clients actually served but not those of other clients. In such an inquiry, the burden of proof should rest upon the firm whose disqualification is sought.

[7] Independent of the question of disqualification of a firm, a lawyer changing professional association has a continuing duty to preserve confidentiality of information about a client formerly represented. See Rules 1.6 and 1.9(c).

ABA Model Rules of Professional Conduct

[8] Paragraph (c) provides that information acquired by the lawyer in the course of representing a client may not subsequently be used or revealed by the lawyer to the disadvantage of the client. However, the fact that a lawyer has once served a client does not preclude the lawyer from using generally known information about that client when later representing another client.

[9] The provisions of this Rule are for the protection of former clients and can be waived if the client gives informed consent, which consent must be confirmed in writing under paragraphs (a) and (b). See Rule 1.0(e). With regard to the effectiveness of an advance waiver, see Comment [22] to Rule 1.7. With regard to disqualification of a firm with which a lawyer is or was formerly associated, see Rule 1.10.

Definitional Cross-References

"Confirmed in writing" *See* Rule 1.0(b)
"Firm" *See* Rule 1.0(c)
"Informed consent" *See* Rule 1.0(e)
"Knowingly" and "Known" *See* Rule 1.0(f)
"Writing" *See* Rule 1.0(n)

RULE 1.10: IMPUTATION OF CONFLICTS OF INTEREST: GENERAL RULE

(a) While lawyers are associated in a firm, none of them shall knowingly represent a client when any one of them practicing alone would be prohibited from doing so by Rules 1.7 or 1.9, unless

(1) the prohibition is based on a personal interest of the disqualified lawyer and does not present a significant risk of materially limiting the representation of the client by the remaining lawyers in the firm; or

(2) the prohibition is based upon Rule 1.9(a) or (b), and arises out of the disqualified lawyer's association with a prior firm, and

(i) the disqualified lawyer is timely screened from any participation in the matter and is apportioned no part of the fee therefrom;

(ii) written notice is promptly given to any affected former client to enable the former client to ascertain compliance with the provisions of this Rule, which shall include a description of the screening procedures employed; a statement of the firm's and of the screened lawyer's compliance with these Rules; a statement that review may be available before a tribunal; and an agreement by the firm to respond promptly to any written inquiries or objections by the former client about the screening procedures; and

(iii) certifications of compliance with these Rules and with the screening procedures are provided to the former client by the screened lawyer and by a partner of the firm, at reasonable intervals upon the former client's written request and upon termination of the screening procedures.

(b) When a lawyer has terminated an association with a firm, the firm is not prohibited from thereafter representing a person with interests materially adverse to those of a client represented by the formerly associated lawyer and not currently represented by the firm, unless:

(1) the matter is the same or substantially related to that in which the formerly associated lawyer represented the client; and

(2) any lawyer remaining in the firm has information protected by Rules 1.6 and 1.9(c) that is material to the matter.

(c) A disqualification prescribed by this Rule may be waived by the affected client under the conditions stated in Rule 1.7.

(d) The disqualification of lawyers associated in a firm with former or current government lawyers is governed by Rule 1.11.

Comment

Definition of "Firm"

[1] For purposes of the Rules of Professional Conduct, the term "firm" denotes lawyers in a law partnership, professional corporation, sole proprietorship or other association authorized to practice law; or lawyers employed in a legal services organization or the legal department of a corporation or other organization. See Rule 1.0(c). Whether two or more lawyers constitute a firm within this definition can depend on the specific facts. See Rule 1.0, Comments [2]–[4].

Principles of Imputed Disqualification

[2] The rule of imputed disqualification stated in paragraph (a) gives effect to the principle of loyalty to the client as it applies to lawyers who practice in a law firm. Such situations can be considered from the premise that a firm of lawyers is essentially one lawyer for purposes of the rules governing loyalty to the client, or from the premise that each lawyer is vicariously bound by the obligation of loyalty owed by each lawyer with whom the lawyer is associated. Paragraph (a)(1) operates only among the lawyers currently associated in a firm. When a lawyer moves from one firm to another, the situation is governed by Rules 1.9(b) and 1.10(a)(2) and 1.10(b).

ABA Model
Rules of
Professional
Conduct

[3] The rule in paragraph (a) does not prohibit representation where neither questions of client loyalty nor protection of confidential information are presented. Where one lawyer in a firm could not effectively represent a given client because of strong political beliefs, for example, but that lawyer will do no work on the case and the personal beliefs of the lawyer will not materially limit the representation by others in the firm, the firm should not be disqualified. On the other hand, if an opposing party in a case were owned by a lawyer in the law firm, and others in the firm would be materially limited in pursuing the matter because of loyalty to that lawyer, the personal disqualification of the lawyer would be imputed to all others in the firm.

[4] The rule in paragraph (a) also does not prohibit representation by others in the law firm where the person prohibited from involvement in a matter is a nonlawyer, such as a paralegal or legal secretary. Nor does paragraph (a) prohibit representation if the lawyer is prohibited from acting because of events before the person became a lawyer, for example, work that the person did while a law student. Such persons, however, ordinarily must be screened from any personal participation in the matter to avoid communication to others in the firm of confidential information that both the nonlawyers and the firm have a legal duty to protect. See Rules 1.0(k) and 5.3.

[5] Rule 1.10(b) operates to permit a law firm, under certain circumstances, to represent a person with interests directly adverse to those of a client represented by a lawyer who formerly was associated with the firm. The Rule applies regardless of when the formerly associated lawyer represented the client. However, the law firm may not represent a person with interests adverse to those of a present client of the firm, which would violate Rule 1.7. Moreover, the firm may not represent the person where the matter is the same or substantially related to that in which the formerly associated lawyer represented the client and any other lawyer currently in the firm has material information protected by Rules 1.6 and 1.9(c).

[6] Rule 1.10(c) removes imputation with the informed consent of the affected client or former client under the conditions stated in Rule 1.7. The conditions stated in Rule 1.7 require the lawyer to determine that the representation is not prohibited by Rule 1.7(b) and that each affected client or former client has given informed consent to the representation, confirmed in writing. In some cases, the risk may be so severe that the conflict may not be cured by client consent. For a discussion of the effectiveness of client waivers of conflicts that might arise in the future, see Rule 1.7, Comment [22]. For a definition of informed consent, see Rule 1.0(e).

[7] Rule 1.10(a)(2) similarly removes the imputation otherwise required by Rule 1.10(a), but unlike section (c), it does so without requiring that there

be informed consent by the former client. Instead, it requires that the procedures laid out in sections (a)(2)(i)-(iii) be followed. A description of effective screening mechanisms appears in Rule 1.0(k). Lawyers should be aware, however, that, even where screening mechanisms have been adopted, tribunals may consider additional factors in ruling upon motions to disqualify a lawyer from pending litigation.

[8] Paragraph (a)(2)(i) does not prohibit the screened lawyer from receiving a salary or partnership share established by prior independent agreement, but that lawyer may not receive compensation directly related to the matter in which the lawyer is disqualified.

[9] The notice required by paragraph (a)(2)(ii) generally should include a description of the screened lawyer's prior representation and be given as soon as practicable after the need for screening becomes apparent. It also should include a statement by the screened lawyer and the firm that the client's material confidential information has not been disclosed or used in violation of the Rules. The notice is intended to enable the former client to evaluate and comment upon the effectiveness of the screening procedures.

[10] The certifications required by paragraph (a)(2)(iii) give the former client assurance that the client's material confidential information has not been disclosed or used inappropriately, either prior to timely implementation of a screen or thereafter. If compliance cannot be certified, the certificate must describe the failure to comply.

[11] Where a lawyer has joined a private firm after having represented the government, imputation is governed by Rule 1.11(b) and (c), not this Rule. Under Rule 1.11(d), where a lawyer represents the government after having served clients in private practice, nongovernmental employment or in another government agency, former-client conflicts are not imputed to government lawyers associated with the individually disqualified lawyer.

[12] Where a lawyer is prohibited from engaging in certain transactions under Rule 1.8, paragraph (k) of that Rule, and not this Rule, determines whether that prohibition also applies to other lawyers associated in a firm with the personally prohibited lawyer.

Definitional Cross-References

"Firm" *See* Rule 1.0(c)
"Knowingly" *See* Rule 1.0(f)
"Partner" *See* Rule 1.0(g)
"Screened" *See* Rule 1.0(k)
"Tribunal" *See* Rule 1.0(m)
"Written" *See* Rule 1.0(n)

RULE 1.11: SPECIAL CONFLICTS OF INTEREST FOR FORMER AND CURRENT GOVERNMENT OFFICERS AND EMPLOYEES

(a) Except as law may otherwise expressly permit, a lawyer who has formerly served as a public officer or employee of the government:

(1) is subject to Rule 1.9(c); and

(2) shall not otherwise represent a client in connection with a matter in which the lawyer participated personally and substantially as a public officer or employee, unless the appropriate government agency gives its informed consent, confirmed in writing, to the representation.

(b) When a lawyer is disqualified from representation under paragraph (a), no lawyer in a firm with which that lawyer is associated may knowingly undertake or continue representation in such a matter unless:

(1) the disqualified lawyer is timely screened from any participation in the matter and is apportioned no part of the fee therefrom; and

(2) written notice is promptly given to the appropriate government agency to enable it to ascertain compliance with the provisions of this Rule.

(c) Except as law may otherwise expressly permit, a lawyer having information that the lawyer knows is confidential government information about a person acquired when the lawyer was a public officer or employee, may not represent a private client whose interests are adverse to that person in a matter in which the information could be used to the material disadvantage of that person. As used in this Rule, the term "confidential government information" means information that has been obtained under governmental authority and which, at the time this Rule is applied, the government is prohibited by law from disclosing to the public or has a legal privilege not to disclose and which is not otherwise available to the public. A firm with which that lawyer is associated may undertake or continue representation in the matter only if the disqualified lawyer is timely screened from any participation in the matter and is apportioned no part of the fee therefrom.

(d) Except as law may otherwise expressly permit, a lawyer currently serving as a public officer or employee:

(1) is subject to Rules 1.7 and 1.9; and

(2) shall not:

(i) participate in a matter in which the lawyer participated personally and substantially while in private practice or nongovernmental employment, unless the appropriate government agency gives its informed consent, confirmed in writing; or

(ii) negotiate for private employment with any person who is involved as a party or as lawyer for a party in a matter in which the lawyer is participating personally and substantially, except that a lawyer serving as a law clerk to a judge, other adjudicative officer or arbitrator may negotiate for private employment as permitted by Rule 1.12(b) and subject to the conditions stated in Rule 1.12(b).

(e) As used in this Rule, the term "matter" includes:

(1) any judicial or other proceeding, application, request for a ruling or other determination, contract, claim, controversy, investigation, charge, accusation, arrest or other particular matter involving a specific party or parties, and

(2) any other matter covered by the conflict of interest rules of the appropriate government agency.

Comment

[1] A lawyer who has served or is currently serving as a public officer or employee is personally subject to the Rules of Professional Conduct, including the prohibition against concurrent conflicts of interest stated in Rule 1.7. In addition, such a lawyer may be subject to statutes and government regulations regarding conflict of interest. Such statutes and regulations may circumscribe the extent to which the government agency may give consent under this Rule. See Rule 1.0(e) for the definition of informed consent.

[2] Paragraphs (a)(1), (a)(2) and (d)(1) restate the obligations of an individual lawyer who has served or is currently serving as an officer or employee of the government toward a former government or private client. Rule 1.10 is not applicable to the conflicts of interest addressed by this Rule. Rather, paragraph (b) sets forth a special imputation rule for former government lawyers that provides for screening and notice. Because of the special problems raised by imputation within a government agency, paragraph (d) does not impute the conflicts of a lawyer currently serving as an officer or employee of the government to other associated government officers or employees, although ordinarily it will be prudent to screen such lawyers.

[3] Paragraphs (a)(2) and (d)(2) apply regardless of whether a lawyer is adverse to a former client and are thus designed not only to protect the

ABA Model
Rules of
Professional
Conduct

former client, but also to prevent a lawyer from exploiting public office for the advantage of another client. For example, a lawyer who has pursued a claim on behalf of the government may not pursue the same claim on behalf of a later private client after the lawyer has left government service, except when authorized to do so by the government agency under paragraph (a). Similarly, a lawyer who has pursued a claim on behalf of a private client may not pursue the claim on behalf of the government, except when authorized to do so by paragraph (d). As with paragraphs (a)(1) and (d)(1), Rule 1.10 is not applicable to the conflicts of interest addressed by these paragraphs.

[4] This Rule represents a balancing of interests. On the one hand, where the successive clients are a government agency and another client, public or private, the risk exists that power or discretion vested in that agency might be used for the special benefit of the other client. A lawyer should not be in a position where benefit to the other client might affect performance of the lawyer's professional functions on behalf of the government. Also, unfair advantage could accrue to the other client by reason of access to confidential government information about the client's adversary obtainable only through the lawyer's government service. On the other hand, the rules governing lawyers presently or formerly employed by a government agency should not be so restrictive as to inhibit transfer of employment to and from the government. The government has a legitimate need to attract qualified lawyers as well as to maintain high ethical standards. Thus a former government lawyer is disqualified only from particular matters in which the lawyer participated personally and substantially. The provisions for screening and waiver in paragraph (b) are necessary to prevent the disqualification rule from imposing too severe a deterrent against entering public service. The limitation of disqualification in paragraphs (a)(2) and (d)(2) to matters involving a specific party or parties, rather than extending disqualification to all substantive issues on which the lawyer worked, serves a similar function.

[5] When a lawyer has been employed by one government agency and then moves to a second government agency, it may be appropriate to treat that second agency as another client for purposes of this Rule, as when a lawyer is employed by a city and subsequently is employed by a federal agency. However, because the conflict of interest is governed by paragraph (d), the latter agency is not required to screen the lawyer as paragraph (b) requires a law firm to do. The question of whether two government agencies should be regarded as the same or different clients for conflict of interest purposes is beyond the scope of these Rules. See Rule 1.13 Comment [9].

[6] Paragraphs (b) and (c) contemplate a screening arrangement. See

Rule 1.0(k) (requirements for screening procedures). These paragraphs do not prohibit a lawyer from receiving a salary or partnership share established by prior independent agreement, but that lawyer may not receive compensation directly relating the lawyer's compensation to the fee in the matter in which the lawyer is disqualified.

[7] Notice, including a description of the screened lawyer's prior representation and of the screening procedures employed, generally should be given as soon as practicable after the need for screening becomes apparent.

[8] Paragraph (c) operates only when the lawyer in question has knowledge of the information, which means actual knowledge; it does not operate with respect to information that merely could be imputed to the lawyer.

[9] Paragraphs (a) and (d) do not prohibit a lawyer from jointly representing a private party and a government agency when doing so is permitted by Rule 1.7 and is not otherwise prohibited by law.

[10] For purposes of paragraph (e) of this Rule, a "matter" may continue in another form. In determining whether two particular matters are the same, the lawyer should consider the extent to which the matters involve the same basic facts, the same or related parties, and the time elapsed.

Definitional Cross-References
"Confirmed in writing" *See* Rule 1.0(b)
"Firm" *See* Rule 1.0(c)
"Informed consent" *See* Rule 1.0(e)
"Knowingly" and "Knows" *See* Rule 1.0(f)
"Screened" *See* Rule 1.0(k)
"Written" *See* Rule 1.0(n)

RULE 1.12: FORMER JUDGE, ARBITRATOR, MEDIATOR OR OTHER THIRD-PARTY NEUTRAL

(a) Except as stated in paragraph (d), a lawyer shall not represent anyone in connection with a matter in which the lawyer participated personally and substantially as a judge or other adjudicative officer or law clerk to such a person or as an arbitrator, mediator or other third-party neutral, unless all parties to the proceeding give informed consent, confirmed in writing.

(b) A lawyer shall not negotiate for employment with any person who is involved as a party or as lawyer for a party in a matter in which the lawyer is participating personally and substantially as a judge or other adjudicative officer or as an arbitrator, mediator

ABA Model
Rules of
Professional
Conduct

or other third-party neutral. A lawyer serving as a law clerk to a judge or other adjudicative officer may negotiate for employment with a party or lawyer involved in a matter in which the clerk is participating personally and substantially, but only after the lawyer has notified the judge or other adjudicative officer.

(c) If a lawyer is disqualified by paragraph (a), no lawyer in a firm with which that lawyer is associated may knowingly undertake or continue representation in the matter unless:

(1) the disqualified lawyer is timely screened from any participation in the matter and is apportioned no part of the fee therefrom; and

(2) written notice is promptly given to the parties and any appropriate tribunal to enable them to ascertain compliance with the provisions of this rule.

(d) An arbitrator selected as a partisan of a party in a multimember arbitration panel is not prohibited from subsequently representing that party.

Comment

[1] This Rule generally parallels Rule 1.11. The term "personally and substantially" signifies that a judge who was a member of a multimember court, and thereafter left judicial office to practice law, is not prohibited from representing a client in a matter pending in the court, but in which the former judge did not participate. So also the fact that a former judge exercised administrative responsibility in a court does not prevent the former judge from acting as a lawyer in a matter where the judge had previously exercised remote or incidental administrative responsibility that did not affect the merits. Compare the Comment to Rule 1.11. The term "adjudicative officer" includes such officials as judges pro tempore, referees, special masters, hearing officers and other parajudicial officers, and also lawyers who serve as part-time judges. Paragraphs C(2), D(2) and E(2) of the Application Section of the Model Code of Judicial Conduct provide that a part-time judge, judge pro tempore or retired judge recalled to active service, shall not "act as a lawyer in a proceeding in which the judge has served as a judge or in any other proceeding related thereto." Although phrased differently from this Rule, those Rules correspond in meaning.

[2] Like former judges, lawyers who have served as arbitrators, mediators or other third-party neutrals may be asked to represent a client in a matter in which the lawyer participated personally and substantially. This Rule forbids such representation unless all of the parties to the proceedings give their informed consent, confirmed in writing. See Rule 1.0(e)

and (b). Other law or codes of ethics governing third-party neutrals may impose more stringent standards of personal or imputed disqualification. See Rule 2.4.

[3] Although lawyers who serve as third-party neutrals do not have information concerning the parties that is protected under Rule 1.6, they typically owe the parties an obligation of confidentiality under law or codes of ethics governing third-party neutrals. Thus, paragraph (c) provides that conflicts of the personally disqualified lawyer will be imputed to other lawyers in a law firm unless the conditions of this paragraph are met.

[4] Requirements for screening procedures are stated in Rule 1.0(k). Paragraph (c)(1) does not prohibit the screened lawyer from receiving a salary or partnership share established by prior independent agreement, but that lawyer may not receive compensation directly related to the matter in which the lawyer is disqualified.

[5] Notice, including a description of the screened lawyer's prior representation and of the screening procedures employed, generally should be given as soon as practicable after the need for screening becomes apparent.

Definitional Cross-References

"Confirmed in writing" *See* Rule 1.0(b)

"Firm" *See* Rule 1.0(c)

"Informed consent" *See* Rule 1.0(e)

"Knowingly" *See* Rule 1.0(f)

"Screened" *See* Rule 1.0(k)

"Tribunal" *See* Rule 1.0(m)

"Writing" and "Written" *See* Rule 1.0(n)

RULE 1.13: ORGANIZATION AS CLIENT

(a) A lawyer employed or retained by an organization represents the organization acting through its duly authorized constituents.

(b) If a lawyer for an organization knows that an officer, employee or other person associated with the organization is engaged in action, intends to act or refuses to act in a matter related to the representation that is a violation of a legal obligation to the organization, or a violation of law that reasonably might be imputed to the organization, and that is likely to result in substantial injury to the organization, then the lawyer shall proceed as is reasonably necessary in the best interest of the organization. Unless the lawyer reasonably believes that it is not necessary in the best interest of the organization to do so, the lawyer shall refer the matter to higher authority in the organization, including, if warranted by the circumstances, to the highest authority that can act on behalf of the organization as determined by applicable law.

(c) Except as provided in paragraph (d), if

(1) despite the lawyer's efforts in accordance with paragraph (b) the highest authority that can act on behalf of the organization insists upon or fails to address in a timely and appropriate manner an action or a refusal to act, that is clearly a violation of law; and

(2) the lawyer reasonably believes that the violation is reasonably certain to result in substantial injury to the organization,

then the lawyer may reveal information relating to the representation whether or not Rule 1.6 permits such disclosure, but only if and to the extent the lawyer reasonably believes necessary to prevent substantial injury to the organization.

(d) Paragraph (c) shall not apply with respect to information relating to a lawyer's representation of an organization to investigate an alleged violation of law, or to defend the organization or an officer, employee or other constituent associated with the organization against a claim arising out of an alleged violation of law.

(e) A lawyer who reasonably believes that he or she has been discharged because of the lawyer's actions taken pursuant to paragraphs (b) or (c), or who withdraws under circumstances that require or permit the lawyer to take action under either of those paragraphs, shall proceed as the lawyer reasonably believes necessary to assure that the organization's highest authority is informed of the lawyer's discharge or withdrawal.

(f) In dealing with an organization's directors, officers, employees, members, shareholders or other constituents, a lawyer shall explain the identity of the client when the lawyer knows or reasonably should know that the organization's interests are adverse to those of the constituents with whom the lawyer is dealing.

(g) A lawyer representing an organization may also represent any of its directors, officers, employees, members, shareholders or other constituents, subject to the provisions of Rule 1.7. If the organization's consent to the dual representation is required by Rule 1.7, the consent shall be given by an appropriate official of the organization other than the individual who is to be represented, or by the shareholders.

Comment

The Entity as the Client

[1] An organizational client is a legal entity, but it cannot act except through its officers, directors, employees, shareholders and other constituents. Officers, directors, employees and shareholders are the constituents of the corporate organizational client. The duties defined in this Comment apply equally to unincorporated associations. "Other constituents" as used in this Comment means the positions equivalent to officers, directors, employees and shareholders held by persons acting for organizational clients that are not corporations.

[2] When one of the constituents of an organizational client communicates with the organization's lawyer in that person's organizational capacity, the communication is protected by Rule 1.6. Thus, by way of example, if an organizational client requests its lawyer to investigate allegations of wrongdoing, interviews made in the course of that investigation between the lawyer and the client's employees or other constituents are covered by Rule 1.6. This does not mean, however, that constituents of an organizational client are the clients of the lawyer. The lawyer may not disclose to such constituents information relating to the representation except for disclosures explicitly or impliedly authorized by the organizational client in order to carry out the representation or as otherwise permitted by Rule 1.6.

[3] When constituents of the organization make decisions for it, the decisions ordinarily must be accepted by the lawyer even if their utility or prudence is doubtful. Decisions concerning policy and operations, including ones entailing serious risk, are not as such in the lawyer's province. Paragraph (b) makes clear, however, that when the lawyer knows that the organization is likely to be substantially injured by action of an officer or other constituent that violates a legal obligation to the organization or is in violation of law that might be imputed to the organization, the lawyer must proceed as is reasonably necessary in the best interest of the organization. As defined in Rule 1.0(f), knowledge can be inferred from circumstances, and a lawyer cannot ignore the obvious.

[4] In determining how to proceed under paragraph (b), the lawyer should give due consideration to the seriousness of the violation and its consequences, the responsibility in the organization and the apparent motivation of the person involved, the policies of the organization concerning such matters, and any other relevant considerations. Ordinarily, referral to a higher authority would be necessary. In some circumstances, however, it may be appropriate for the lawyer to ask the constituent to reconsider the matter; for example, if the circumstances involve a constituent's innocent misunderstanding of law and subsequent acceptance of the lawyer's advice,

ABA Model
Rules of
Professional
Conduct

the lawyer may reasonably conclude that the best interest of the organization does not require that the matter be referred to higher authority. If a constituent persists in conduct contrary to the lawyer's advice, it will be necessary for the lawyer to take steps to have the matter reviewed by a higher authority in the organization. If the matter is of sufficient seriousness and importance or urgency to the organization, referral to higher authority in the organization may be necessary even if the lawyer has not communicated with the constituent. Any measures taken should, to the extent practicable, minimize the risk of revealing information relating to the representation to persons outside the organization. Even in circumstances where a lawyer is not obligated by Rule 1.13 to proceed, a lawyer may bring to the attention of an organizational client, including its highest authority, matters that the lawyer reasonably believes to be of sufficient importance to warrant doing so in the best interest of the organization.

[5] Paragraph (b) also makes clear that when it is reasonably necessary to enable the organization to address the matter in a timely and appropriate manner, the lawyer must refer the matter to higher authority, including, if warranted by the circumstances, the highest authority that can act on behalf of the organization under applicable law. The organization's highest authority to whom a matter may be referred ordinarily will be the board of directors or similar governing body. However, applicable law may prescribe that under certain conditions the highest authority reposes elsewhere, for example, in the independent directors of a corporation.

Relation to Other Rules

[6] The authority and responsibility provided in this Rule are concurrent with the authority and responsibility provided in other Rules. In particular, this Rule does not limit or expand the lawyer's responsibility under Rules 1.8, 1.16, 3.3 or 4.1. Paragraph (c) of this Rule supplements Rule 1.6(b) by providing an additional basis upon which the lawyer may reveal information relating to the representation, but does not modify, restrict, or limit the provisions of Rule 1.6(b)(1) – (6). Under paragraph (c) the lawyer may reveal such information only when the organization's highest authority insists upon or fails to address threatened or ongoing action that is clearly a violation of law, and then only to the extent the lawyer reasonably believes necessary to prevent reasonably certain substantial injury to the organization. It is not necessary that the lawyer's services be used in furtherance of the violation, but it is required that the matter be related to the lawyer's representation of the organization. If the lawyer's services are being used by an organization to further a crime or fraud by the organization, Rules 1.6(b)(2) and 1.6(b)(3) may permit the lawyer to disclose confidential information.

In such circumstances Rule 1.2(d) may also be applicable, in which event, withdrawal from the representation under Rule 1.16(a)(1) may be required.

[7] Paragraph (d) makes clear that the authority of a lawyer to disclose information relating to a representation in circumstances described in paragraph (c) does not apply with respect to information relating to a lawyer's engagement by an organization to investigate an alleged violation of law or to defend the organization or an officer, employee or other person associated with the organization against a claim arising out of an alleged violation of law. This is necessary in order to enable organizational clients to enjoy the full benefits of legal counsel in conducting an investigation or defending against a claim.

[8] A lawyer who reasonably believes that he or she has been discharged because of the lawyer's actions taken pursuant to paragraph (b) or (c), or who withdraws in circumstances that require or permit the lawyer to take action under either of these paragraphs, must proceed as the lawyer reasonably believes necessary to assure that the organization's highest authority is informed of the lawyer's discharge or withdrawal.

Government Agency

[9] The duty defined in this Rule applies to governmental organizations. Defining precisely the identity of the client and prescribing the resulting obligations of such lawyers may be more difficult in the government context and is a matter beyond the scope of these Rules. See Scope [18]. Although in some circumstances the client may be a specific agency, it may also be a branch of government, such as the executive branch, or the government as a whole. For example, if the action or failure to act involves the head of a bureau, either the department of which the bureau is a part or the relevant branch of government may be the client for purposes of this Rule. Moreover, in a matter involving the conduct of government officials, a government lawyer may have authority under applicable law to question such conduct more extensively than that of a lawyer for a private organization in similar circumstances. Thus, when the client is a governmental organization, a different balance may be appropriate between maintaining confidentiality and assuring that the wrongful act is prevented or rectified, for public business is involved. In addition, duties of lawyers employed by the government or lawyers in military service may be defined by statutes and regulation. This Rule does not limit that authority. See Scope.

Clarifying the Lawyer's Role

[10] There are times when the organization's interest may be or become adverse to those of one or more of its constituents. In such circumstances

the lawyer should advise any constituent, whose interest the lawyer finds adverse to that of the organization of the conflict or potential conflict of interest, that the lawyer cannot represent such constituent, and that such person may wish to obtain independent representation. Care must be taken to assure that the individual understands that, when there is such adversity of interest, the lawyer for the organization cannot provide legal representation for that constituent individual, and that discussions between the lawyer for the organization and the individual may not be privileged.

[11] Whether such a warning should be given by the lawyer for the organization to any constituent individual may turn on the facts of each case.

Dual Representation

[12] Paragraph (g) recognizes that a lawyer for an organization may also represent a principal officer or major shareholder.

Derivative Actions

[13] Under generally prevailing law, the shareholders or members of a corporation may bring suit to compel the directors to perform their legal obligations in the supervision of the organization. Members of unincorporated associations have essentially the same right. Such an action may be brought nominally by the organization, but usually is, in fact, a legal controversy over management of the organization.

[14] The question can arise whether counsel for the organization may defend such an action. The proposition that the organization is the lawyer's client does not alone resolve the issue. Most derivative actions are a normal incident of an organization's affairs, to be defended by the organization's lawyer like any other suit. However, if the claim involves serious charges of wrongdoing by those in control of the organization, a conflict may arise between the lawyer's duty to the organization and the lawyer's relationship with the board. In those circumstances, Rule 1.7 governs who should represent the directors and the organization.

Definitional Cross-References

"Knows" *See* Rule 1.0(f)

"Reasonably" *See* Rule 1.0(h)

"Reasonably believes" *See* Rule 1.0(i)

"Reasonably should know" *See* Rule 1.0(j)

"Substantial" *See* Rule 1.0(l)

RULE 1.14: CLIENT WITH DIMINISHED CAPACITY

(a) When a client's capacity to make adequately considered decisions in connection with a representation is diminished, whether because of minority, mental impairment or for some other reason, the lawyer shall, as far as reasonably possible, maintain a normal client-lawyer relationship with the client.

(b) When the lawyer reasonably believes that the client has diminished capacity, is at risk of substantial physical, financial or other harm unless action is taken and cannot adequately act in the client's own interest, the lawyer may take reasonably necessary protective action, including consulting with individuals or entities that have the ability to take action to protect the client and, in appropriate cases, seeking the appointment of a guardian ad litem, conservator or guardian.

(c) Information relating to the representation of a client with diminished capacity is protected by Rule 1.6. When taking protective action pursuant to paragraph (b), the lawyer is impliedly authorized under Rule 1.6(a) to reveal information about the client, but only to the extent reasonably necessary to protect the client's interests.

Comment

[1] The normal client-lawyer relationship is based on the assumption that the client, when properly advised and assisted, is capable of making decisions about important matters. When the client is a minor or suffers from a diminished mental capacity, however, maintaining the ordinary client-lawyer relationship may not be possible in all respects. In particular, a severely incapacitated person may have no power to make legally binding decisions. Nevertheless, a client with diminished capacity often has the ability to understand, deliberate upon, and reach conclusions about matters affecting the client's own well-being. For example, children as young as five or six years of age, and certainly those of ten or twelve, are regarded as having opinions that are entitled to weight in legal proceedings concerning their custody. So also, it is recognized that some persons of advanced age can be quite capable of handling routine financial matters while needing special legal protection concerning major transactions.

[2] The fact that a client suffers a disability does not diminish the lawyer's obligation to treat the client with attention and respect. Even if the person has a legal representative, the lawyer should as far as possible

accord the represented person the status of client, particularly in maintaining communication.

[3] The client may wish to have family members or other persons participate in discussions with the lawyer. When necessary to assist in the representation, the presence of such persons generally does not affect the applicability of the attorney-client evidentiary privilege. Nevertheless, the lawyer must keep the client's interests foremost and, except for protective action authorized under paragraph (b), must look to the client, and not family members, to make decisions on the client's behalf.

[4] If a legal representative has already been appointed for the client, the lawyer should ordinarily look to the representative for decisions on behalf of the client. In matters involving a minor, whether the lawyer should look to the parents as natural guardians may depend on the type of proceeding or matter in which the lawyer is representing the minor. If the lawyer represents the guardian as distinct from the ward, and is aware that the guardian is acting adversely to the ward's interest, the lawyer may have an obligation to prevent or rectify the guardian's misconduct. See Rule 1.2(d).

Taking Protective Action

[5] If a lawyer reasonably believes that a client is at risk of substantial physical, financial or other harm unless action is taken, and that a normal client-lawyer relationship cannot be maintained as provided in paragraph (a) because the client lacks sufficient capacity to communicate or to make adequately considered decisions in connection with the representation, then paragraph (b) permits the lawyer to take protective measures deemed necessary. Such measures could include: consulting with family members, using a reconsideration period to permit clarification or improvement of circumstances, using voluntary surrogate decisionmaking tools such as durable powers of attorney or consulting with support groups, professional services, adult-protective agencies or other individuals or entities that have the ability to protect the client. In taking any protective action, the lawyer should be guided by such factors as the wishes and values of the client to the extent known, the client's best interests and the goals of intruding into the client's decisionmaking autonomy to the least extent feasible, maximizing client capacities and respecting the client's family and social connections.

[6] In determining the extent of the client's diminished capacity, the lawyer should consider and balance such factors as: the client's ability to articulate reasoning leading to a decision, variability of state of mind and ability to appreciate consequences of a decision; the substantive fairness of a decision; and the consistency of a decision with the known long-term com-

mitments and values of the client. In appropriate circumstances, the lawyer may seek guidance from an appropriate diagnostician.

[7] If a legal representative has not been appointed, the lawyer should consider whether appointment of a guardian ad litem, conservator or guardian is necessary to protect the client's interests. Thus, if a client with diminished capacity has substantial property that should be sold for the client's benefit, effective completion of the transaction may require appointment of a legal representative. In addition, rules of procedure in litigation sometimes provide that minors or persons with diminished capacity must be represented by a guardian or next friend if they do not have a general guardian. In many circumstances, however, appointment of a legal representative may be more expensive or traumatic for the client than circumstances in fact require. Evaluation of such circumstances is a matter entrusted to the professional judgment of the lawyer. In considering alternatives, however, the lawyer should be aware of any law that requires the lawyer to advocate the least restrictive action on behalf of the client.

Disclosure of the Client's Condition

[8] Disclosure of the client's diminished capacity could adversely affect the client's interests. For example, raising the question of diminished capacity could, in some circumstances, lead to proceedings for involuntary commitment. Information relating to the representation is protected by Rule 1.6. Therefore, unless authorized to do so, the lawyer may not disclose such information. When taking protective action pursuant to paragraph (b), the lawyer is impliedly authorized to make the necessary disclosures, even when the client directs the lawyer to the contrary. Nevertheless, given the risks of disclosure, paragraph (c) limits what the lawyer may disclose in consulting with other individuals or entities or seeking the appointment of a legal representative. At the very least, the lawyer should determine whether it is likely that the person or entity consulted with will act adversely to the client's interests before discussing matters related to the client. The lawyer's position in such cases is an unavoidably difficult one.

Emergency Legal Assistance

[9] In an emergency where the health, safety or a financial interest of a person with seriously diminished capacity is threatened with imminent and irreparable harm, a lawyer may take legal action on behalf of such a person even though the person is unable to establish a client-lawyer relationship or to make or express considered judgments about the matter, when the person or another acting in good faith on that person's behalf has consulted with the lawyer. Even in such an emergency, however, the lawyer should not act

unless the lawyer reasonably believes that the person has no other lawyer, agent or other representative available. The lawyer should take legal action on behalf of the person only to the extent reasonably necessary to maintain the status quo or otherwise avoid imminent and irreparable harm. A lawyer who undertakes to represent a person in such an exigent situation has the same duties under these Rules as the lawyer would with respect to a client.

[10] A lawyer who acts on behalf of a person with seriously diminished capacity in an emergency should keep the confidences of the person as if dealing with a client, disclosing them only to the extent necessary to accomplish the intended protective action. The lawyer should disclose to any tribunal involved and to any other counsel involved the nature of his or her relationship with the person. The lawyer should take steps to regularize the relationship or implement other protective solutions as soon as possible. Normally, a lawyer would not seek compensation for such emergency actions taken.

Definitional Cross-References

"Reasonably" *See* Rule 1.0(h)
"Reasonably believes" *See* Rule 1.0(i)
"Substantial" *See* Rule 1.0(l)

RULE 1.15: SAFEKEEPING PROPERTY

(a) A lawyer shall hold property of clients or third persons that is in a lawyer's possession in connection with a representation separate from the lawyer's own property. Funds shall be kept in a separate account maintained in the state where the lawyer's office is situated, or elsewhere with the consent of the client or third person. Other property shall be identified as such and appropriately safeguarded. Complete records of such account funds and other property shall be kept by the lawyer and shall be preserved for a period of [five years] after termination of the representation.

(b) A lawyer may deposit the lawyer's own funds in a client trust account for the sole purpose of paying bank service charges on that account, but only in an amount necessary for that purpose.

(c) A lawyer shall deposit into a client trust account legal fees and expenses that have been paid in advance, to be withdrawn by the lawyer only as fees are earned or expenses incurred.

(d) Upon receiving funds or other property in which a client or third person has an interest, a lawyer shall promptly notify the client or third person. Except as stated in this Rule or otherwise permitted by law or by agreement with the client, a lawyer shall promptly deliver to the client or third person any funds or other property that the client or third person is entitled to receive and, upon request by the client or third person, shall promptly render a full accounting regarding such property.

(e) When in the course of representation a lawyer is in possession of property in which two or more persons (one of whom may be the lawyer) claim interests, the property shall be kept separate by the lawyer until the dispute is resolved. The lawyer shall promptly distribute all portions of the property as to which the interests are not in dispute.

Comment

[1] A lawyer should hold property of others with the care required of a professional fiduciary. Securities should be kept in a safe deposit box, except when some other form of safekeeping is warranted by special circumstances. All property that is the property of clients or third persons, including prospective clients, must be kept separate from the lawyer's business and personal property and, if monies, in one or more trust accounts. Separate trust accounts may be warranted when administering estate monies or acting in similar fiduciary capacities. A lawyer should maintain on a current basis books and records in accordance with generally accepted accounting practice and comply with any recordkeeping rules established by law or court order. See, e.g., ABA Model Rules for Client Trust Account Records.

[2] While normally it is impermissible to commingle the lawyer's own funds with client funds, paragraph (b) provides that it is permissible when necessary to pay bank service charges on that account. Accurate records must be kept regarding which part of the funds are the lawyer's.

[3] Lawyers often receive funds from which the lawyer's fee will be paid. The lawyer is not required to remit to the client funds that the lawyer reasonably believes represent fees owed. However, a lawyer may not hold funds to coerce a client into accepting the lawyer's contention. The disputed portion of the funds must be kept in a trust account and the lawyer should suggest means for prompt resolution of the dispute, such as arbitration. The undisputed portion of the funds shall be promptly distributed.

[4] Paragraph (e) also recognizes that third parties may have lawful claims against specific funds or other property in a lawyer's custody, such as a client's creditor who has a lien on funds recovered in a personal injury action. A lawyer may have a duty under applicable law to protect such third-party claims against wrongful interference by the client. In such cases, when the third-party claim is not frivolous under applicable law, the law-

yer must refuse to surrender the property to the client until the claims are resolved. A lawyer should not unilaterally assume to arbitrate a dispute between the client and the third party, but, when there are substantial grounds for dispute as to the person entitled to the funds, the lawyer may file an action to have a court resolve the dispute.

[5] The obligations of a lawyer under this Rule are independent of those arising from activity other than rendering legal services. For example, a lawyer who serves only as an escrow agent is governed by the applicable law relating to fiduciaries even though the lawyer does not render legal services in the transaction and is not governed by this Rule.

[6] A lawyers' fund for client protection provides a means through the collective efforts of the bar to reimburse persons who have lost money or property as a result of dishonest conduct of a lawyer. Where such a fund has been established, a lawyer must participate where it is mandatory, and, even when it is voluntary, the lawyer should participate.

RULE 1.16: DECLINING OR TERMINATING REPRESENTATION

(a) Except as stated in paragraph (c), a lawyer shall not represent a client or, where representation has commenced, shall withdraw from the representation of a client if:

(1) the representation will result in violation of the Rules of Professional Conduct or other law;

(2) the lawyer's physical or mental condition materially impairs the lawyer's ability to represent the client; or

(3) the lawyer is discharged.

(b) Except as stated in paragraph (c), a lawyer may withdraw from representing a client if:

(1) withdrawal can be accomplished without material adverse effect on the interests of the client;

(2) the client persists in a course of action involving the lawyer's services that the lawyer reasonably believes is criminal or fraudulent;

(3) the client has used the lawyer's services to perpetrate a crime or fraud;

(4) the client insists upon taking action that the lawyer considers repugnant or with which the lawyer has a fundamental disagreement;

(5) the client fails substantially to fulfill an obligation to the lawyer regarding the lawyer's services and has been given

reasonable warning that the lawyer will withdraw unless the obligation is fulfilled;

(6) the representation will result in an unreasonable financial burden on the lawyer or has been rendered unreasonably difficult by the client; or

(7) other good cause for withdrawal exists.

(c) A lawyer must comply with applicable law requiring notice to or permission of a tribunal when terminating a representation. When ordered to do so by a tribunal, a lawyer shall continue representation notwithstanding good cause for terminating the representation.

(d) Upon termination of representation, a lawyer shall take steps to the extent reasonably practicable to protect a client's interests, such as giving reasonable notice to the client, allowing time for employment of other counsel, surrendering papers and property to which the client is entitled and refunding any advance payment of fee or expense that has not been earned or incurred. The lawyer may retain papers relating to the client to the extent permitted by other law.

Comment

[1] A lawyer should not accept representation in a matter unless it can be performed competently, promptly, without improper conflict of interest and to completion. Ordinarily, a representation in a matter is completed when the agreed-upon assistance has been concluded. See Rules 1.2(c) and 6.5. See also Rule 1.3, Comment [4].

Mandatory Withdrawal

[2] A lawyer ordinarily must decline or withdraw from representation if the client demands that the lawyer engage in conduct that is illegal or violates the Rules of Professional Conduct or other law. The lawyer is not obliged to decline or withdraw simply because the client suggests such a course of conduct; a client may make such a suggestion in the hope that a lawyer will not be constrained by a professional obligation.

[3] When a lawyer has been appointed to represent a client, withdrawal ordinarily requires approval of the appointing authority. See also Rule 6.2. Similarly, court approval or notice to the court is often required by applicable law before a lawyer withdraws from pending litigation. Difficulty may be encountered if withdrawal is based on the client's demand that the lawyer engage in unprofessional conduct. The court may request an explanation for the withdrawal, while the lawyer may be bound to keep confidential the facts that would constitute such an explanation. The lawyer's statement that

ABA Model
Rules of
Professional
Conduct

professional considerations require termination of the representation ordinarily should be accepted as sufficient. Lawyers should be mindful of their obligations to both clients and the court under Rules 1.6 and 3.3.

Discharge

[4] A client has a right to discharge a lawyer at any time, with or without cause, subject to liability for payment for the lawyer's services. Where future dispute about the withdrawal may be anticipated, it may be advisable to prepare a written statement reciting the circumstances.

[5] Whether a client can discharge appointed counsel may depend on applicable law. A client seeking to do so should be given a full explanation of the consequences. These consequences may include a decision by the appointing authority that appointment of successor counsel is unjustified, thus requiring self-representation by the client.

[6] If the client has severely diminished capacity, the client may lack the legal capacity to discharge the lawyer, and in any event the discharge may be seriously adverse to the client's interests. The lawyer should make special effort to help the client consider the consequences and may take reasonably necessary protective action as provided in Rule 1.14.

Optional Withdrawal

[7] A lawyer may withdraw from representation in some circumstances. The lawyer has the option to withdraw if it can be accomplished without material adverse effect on the client's interests. Withdrawal is also justified if the client persists in a course of action that the lawyer reasonably believes is criminal or fraudulent, for a lawyer is not required to be associated with such conduct even if the lawyer does not further it. Withdrawal is also permitted if the lawyer's services were misused in the past even if that would materially prejudice the client. The lawyer may also withdraw where the client insists on taking action that the lawyer considers repugnant or with which the lawyer has a fundamental disagreement.

[8] A lawyer may withdraw if the client refuses to abide by the terms of an agreement relating to the representation, such as an agreement concerning fees or court costs or an agreement limiting the objectives of the representation.

Assisting the Client upon Withdrawal

[9] Even if the lawyer has been unfairly discharged by the client, a lawyer must take all reasonable steps to mitigate the consequences to the client. The lawyer may retain papers as security for a fee only to the extent permitted by law. See Rule 1.15.

Definitional Cross-References

"Fraud" and "Fraudulent" *See* Rule 1.0(d)

"Reasonable" *See* Rule 1.0(h)

"Reasonably believes" *See* Rule 1.0(i)

"Tribunal" *See* Rule 1.0(m)

RULE 1.17: SALE OF LAW PRACTICE

A lawyer or a law firm may sell or purchase a law practice, or an area of law practice, including good will, if the following conditions are satisfied:

(a) The seller ceases to engage in the private practice of law, or in the area of practice that has been sold, [in the geographic area] [in the jurisdiction] (a jurisdiction may elect either version) in which the practice has been conducted;

(b) The entire practice, or the entire area of practice, is sold to one or more lawyers or law firms;

(c) The seller gives written notice to each of the seller's clients regarding:

(1) the proposed sale;

(2) the client's right to retain other counsel or to take possession of the file; and

(3) the fact that the client's consent to the transfer of the client's files will be presumed if the client does not take any action or does not otherwise object within ninety (90) days of receipt of the notice.

If a client cannot be given notice, the representation of that client may be transferred to the purchaser only upon entry of an order so authorizing by a court having jurisdiction. The seller may disclose to the court in camera information relating to the representation only to the extent necessary to obtain an order authorizing the transfer of a file.

(d) The fees charged clients shall not be increased by reason of the sale.

Comment

[1] The practice of law is a profession, not merely a business. Clients are not commodities that can be purchased and sold at will. Pursuant to this Rule, when a lawyer or an entire firm ceases to practice, or ceases to practice in an area of law, and other lawyers or firms take over the representation, the selling lawyer or firm may obtain compensation for the reasonable value of the practice as may withdrawing partners of law firms. See Rules 5.4 and 5.6.

Termination of Practice by the Seller

[2] The requirement that all of the private practice, or all of an area of practice, be sold is satisfied if the seller in good faith makes the entire practice, or the area of practice, available for sale to the purchasers. The fact that a number of the seller's clients decide not to be represented by the purchasers but take their matters elsewhere, therefore, does not result in a violation. Return to private practice as a result of an unanticipated change in circumstances does not necessarily result in a violation. For example, a lawyer who has sold the practice to accept an appointment to judicial office does not violate the requirement that the sale be attendant to cessation of practice if the lawyer later resumes private practice upon being defeated in a contested or a retention election for the office or resigns from a judiciary position.

[3] The requirement that the seller cease to engage in the private practice of law does not prohibit employment as a lawyer on the staff of a public agency or a legal services entity that provides legal services to the poor, or as in-house counsel to a business.

[4] The Rule permits a sale of an entire practice attendant upon retirement from the private practice of law within the jurisdiction. Its provisions, therefore, accommodate the lawyer who sells the practice on the occasion of moving to another state. Some states are so large that a move from one locale therein to another is tantamount to leaving the jurisdiction in which the lawyer has engaged in the practice of law. To also accommodate lawyers so situated, states may permit the sale of the practice when the lawyer leaves the geographical area rather than the jurisdiction. The alternative desired should be indicated by selecting one of the two provided for in Rule 1.17(a).

[5] This Rule also permits a lawyer or law firm to sell an area of practice. If an area of practice is sold and the lawyer remains in the active practice of law, the lawyer must cease accepting any matters in the area of practice that has been sold, either as counsel or co-counsel or by assuming joint responsibility for a matter in connection with the division of a fee with another lawyer as would otherwise be permitted by Rule 1.5(e). For example, a lawyer with a substantial number of estate planning matters and a substantial number of probate administration cases may sell the estate planning portion of the practice but remain in the practice of law by concentrating on probate administration; however, that practitioner may not thereafter accept any estate planning matters. Although a lawyer who leaves a jurisdiction or geographical area typically would sell the entire practice, this Rule permits the lawyer to limit the sale to one or more areas of the practice, thereby preserving the lawyer's right to continue practice in the areas of the practice that were not sold.

Sale of Entire Practice or Entire Area of Practice

[6] The Rule requires that the seller's entire practice, or an entire area of practice, be sold. The prohibition against sale of less than an entire practice area protects those clients whose matters are less lucrative and who might find it difficult to secure other counsel if a sale could be limited to substantial fee-generating matters. The purchasers are required to undertake all client matters in the practice or practice area, subject to client consent. This requirement is satisfied, however, even if a purchaser is unable to undertake a particular client matter because of a conflict of interest.

Client Confidences, Consent and Notice

[7] Negotiations between seller and prospective purchaser prior to disclosure of information relating to a specific representation of an identifiable client no more violate the confidentiality provisions of Model Rule 1.6 than do preliminary discussions concerning the possible association of another lawyer or mergers between firms, with respect to which client consent is not required. See Rule 1.6(b)(7). Providing the purchaser access to detailed information relating to the representation, such as the client's file, however, requires client consent. The Rule provides that before such information can be disclosed by the seller to the purchaser the client must be given actual written notice of the contemplated sale, including the identity of the purchaser, and must be told that the decision to consent or make other arrangements must be made within 90 days. If nothing is heard from the client within that time, consent to the sale is presumed.

[8] A lawyer or law firm ceasing to practice cannot be required to remain in practice because some clients cannot be given actual notice of the proposed purchase. Since these clients cannot themselves consent to the purchase or direct any other disposition of their files, the Rule requires an order from a court having jurisdiction authorizing their transfer or other disposition. The court can be expected to determine whether reasonable efforts to locate the client have been exhausted, and whether the absent client's legitimate interests will be served by authorizing the transfer of the file so that the purchaser may continue the representation. Preservation of client confidences requires that the petition for a court order be considered in camera. (A procedure by which such an order can be obtained needs to be established in jurisdictions in which it presently does not exist).

[9] All elements of client autonomy, including the client's absolute right to discharge a lawyer and transfer the representation to another, survive the sale of the practice or area of practice.

Fee Arrangements Between Client and Purchaser

[10] The sale may not be financed by increases in fees charged the clients of the practice. Existing arrangements between the seller and the client as to fees and the scope of the work must be honored by the purchaser.

Other Applicable Ethical Standards

[11] Lawyers participating in the sale of a law practice or a practice area are subject to the ethical standards applicable to involving another lawyer in the representation of a client. These include, for example, the seller's obligation to exercise competence in identifying a purchaser qualified to assume the practice and the purchaser's obligation to undertake the representation competently (see Rule 1.1); the obligation to avoid disqualifying conflicts, and to secure the client's informed consent for those conflicts that can be agreed to (see Rule 1.7 regarding conflicts and Rule 1.0(e) for the definition of informed consent); and the obligation to protect information relating to the representation (see Rules 1.6 and 1.9).

[12] If approval of the substitution of the purchasing lawyer for the selling lawyer is required by the rules of any tribunal in which a matter is pending, such approval must be obtained before the matter can be included in the sale (see Rule 1.16).

Applicability of the Rule

[13] This Rule applies to the sale of a law practice of a deceased, disabled or disappeared lawyer. Thus, the seller may be represented by a non-lawyer representative not subject to these Rules. Since, however, no lawyer may participate in a sale of a law practice which does not conform to the requirements of this Rule, the representatives of the seller as well as the purchasing lawyer can be expected to see to it that they are met.

[14] Admission to or retirement from a law partnership or professional association, retirement plans and similar arrangements, and a sale of tangible assets of a law practice, do not constitute a sale or purchase governed by this Rule.

[15] This Rule does not apply to the transfers of legal representation between lawyers when such transfers are unrelated to the sale of a practice or an area of practice.

Definitional Cross-References

"Law firm" See Rule 1.0(c)
"Written" See Rule 1.0(n)

RULE 1.18: DUTIES TO PROSPECTIVE CLIENT

(a) A person who consults with a lawyer about the possibility of forming a client-lawyer relationship with respect to a matter is a prospective client.

(b) Even when no client-lawyer relationship ensues, a lawyer who has learned information from a prospective client shall not use or reveal that information, except as Rule 1.9 would permit with respect to information of a former client.

(c) A lawyer subject to paragraph (b) shall not represent a client with interests materially adverse to those of a prospective client in the same or a substantially related matter if the lawyer received information from the prospective client that could be significantly harmful to that person in the matter, except as provided in paragraph (d). If a lawyer is disqualified from representation under this paragraph, no lawyer in a firm with which that lawyer is associated may knowingly undertake or continue representation in such a matter, except as provided in paragraph (d).

(d) When the lawyer has received disqualifying information as defined in paragraph (c), representation is permissible if:

(1) both the affected client and the prospective client have given informed consent, confirmed in writing; or:

(2) the lawyer who received the information took reasonable measures to avoid exposure to more disqualifying information than was reasonably necessary to determine whether to represent the prospective client; and

(i) the disqualified lawyer is timely screened from any participation in the matter and is apportioned no part of the fee therefrom; and

(ii) written notice is promptly given to the prospective client.

Comment

[1] Prospective clients, like clients, may disclose information to a lawyer, place documents or other property in the lawyer's custody, or rely on the lawyer's advice. A lawyer's consultations with a prospective client usually are limited in time and depth and leave both the prospective client and the lawyer free (and sometimes required) to proceed no further. Hence, prospective clients should receive some but not all of the protection afforded clients.

[2] A person becomes a prospective client by consulting with a lawyer about the possibility of forming a client-lawyer relationship with respect to a matter. Whether communications, including written, oral, or electronic

communications, constitute a consultation depends on the circumstances. For example, a consultation is likely to have occurred if a lawyer, either in person or through the lawyer's advertising in any medium, specifically requests or invites the submission of information about a potential representation without clear and reasonably understandable warnings and cautionary statements that limit the lawyer's obligations, and a person provides information in response. See also Comment [4]. In contrast, a consultation does not occur if a person provides information to a lawyer in response to advertising that merely describes the lawyer's education, experience, areas of practice, and contact information, or provides legal information of general interest. Such a person communicates information unilaterally to a lawyer, without any reasonable expectation that the lawyer is willing to discuss the possibility of forming a client-lawyer relationship, and is thus not a "prospective client." Moreover, a person who communicates with a lawyer for the purpose of disqualifying the lawyer is not a "prospective client."

[3] It is often necessary for a prospective client to reveal information to the lawyer during an initial consultation prior to the decision about formation of a client-lawyer relationship. The lawyer often must learn such information to determine whether there is a conflict of interest with an existing client and whether the matter is one that the lawyer is willing to undertake. Paragraph (b) prohibits the lawyer from using or revealing that information, except as permitted by Rule 1.9, even if the client or lawyer decides not to proceed with the representation. The duty exists regardless of how brief the initial conference may be.

[4] In order to avoid acquiring disqualifying information from a prospective client, a lawyer considering whether or not to undertake a new matter should limit the initial consultation to only such information as reasonably appears necessary for that purpose. Where the information indicates that a conflict of interest or other reason for non-representation exists, the lawyer should so inform the prospective client or decline the representation. If the prospective client wishes to retain the lawyer, and if consent is possible under Rule 1.7, then consent from all affected present or former clients must be obtained before accepting the representation.

[5] A lawyer may condition a consultation with a prospective client on the person's informed consent that no information disclosed during the consultation will prohibit the lawyer from representing a different client in the matter. See Rule 1.0(e) for the definition of informed consent. If the agreement expressly so provides, the prospective client may also consent to the lawyer's subsequent use of information received from the prospective client.

[6] Even in the absence of an agreement, under paragraph (c), the lawyer is not prohibited from representing a client with interests adverse to

those of the prospective client in the same or a substantially related matter unless the lawyer has received from the prospective client information that could be significantly harmful if used in the matter.

[7] Under paragraph (c), the prohibition in this Rule is imputed to other lawyers as provided in Rule 1.10, but, under paragraph (d)(1), imputation may be avoided if the lawyer obtains the informed consent, confirmed in writing, of both the prospective and affected clients. In the alternative, imputation may be avoided if the conditions of paragraph (d)(2) are met and all disqualified lawyers are timely screened and written notice is promptly given to the prospective client. See Rule 1.0(k) (requirements for screening procedures). Paragraph (d)(2)(i) does not prohibit the screened lawyer from receiving a salary or partnership share established by prior independent agreement, but that lawyer may not receive compensation directly related to the matter in which the lawyer is disqualified.

[8] Notice, including a general description of the subject matter about which the lawyer was consulted, and of the screening procedures employed, generally should be given as soon as practicable after the need for screening becomes apparent.

[9] For the duty of competence of a lawyer who gives assistance on the merits of a matter to a prospective client, see Rule 1.1. For a lawyer's duties when a prospective client entrusts valuables or papers to the lawyer's care, see Rule 1.15.

Definitional Cross-References

"Confirmed in writing" *See* Rule 1.0(b)
"Firm" *See* Rule 1.0(c)
"Informed consent" *See* Rule 1.0(e)
"Knowingly" *See* Rule 1.0(f)
"Reasonable" and "Reasonably" *See* Rule 1.0(h)
"Screened" *See* Rule 1.0(k)
"Written" *See* Rule 1.0(n)

COUNSELOR

RULE 2.1: ADVISOR

In representing a client, a lawyer shall exercise independent professional judgment and render candid advice. In rendering advice, a lawyer may refer not only to law but to other considerations such as moral, economic, social and political factors, that may be relevant to the client's situation.

Comment

Scope of Advice

[1] A client is entitled to straightforward advice expressing the lawyer's honest assessment. Legal advice often involves unpleasant facts and alternatives that a client may be disinclined to confront. In presenting advice, a lawyer endeavors to sustain the client's morale and may put advice in as acceptable a form as honesty permits. However, a lawyer should not be deterred from giving candid advice by the prospect that the advice will be unpalatable to the client.

[2] Advice couched in narrow legal terms may be of little value to a client, especially where practical considerations, such as cost or effects on other people, are predominant. Purely technical legal advice, therefore, can sometimes be inadequate. It is proper for a lawyer to refer to relevant moral and ethical considerations in giving advice. Although a lawyer is not a moral advisor as such, moral and ethical considerations impinge upon most legal questions and may decisively influence how the law will be applied.

[3] A client may expressly or impliedly ask the lawyer for purely technical advice. When such a request is made by a client experienced in legal matters, the lawyer may accept it at face value. When such a request is made by a client inexperienced in legal matters, however, the lawyer's responsibility as advisor may include indicating that more may be involved than strictly legal considerations.

[4] Matters that go beyond strictly legal questions may also be in the domain of another profession. Family matters can involve problems within the professional competence of psychiatry, clinical psychology or social work; business matters can involve problems within the competence of the accounting profession or of financial specialists. Where consultation with a professional in another field is itself something a competent lawyer would recommend, the lawyer should make such a recommendation. At the same time, a lawyer's advice at its best often consists of recommending a course of action in the face of conflicting recommendations of experts.

Offering Advice

[5] In general, a lawyer is not expected to give advice until asked by the client. However, when a lawyer knows that a client proposes a course of action that is likely to result in substantial adverse legal consequences to the client, the lawyer's duty to the client under Rule 1.4 may require that the lawyer offer advice if the client's course of action is related to the representation. Similarly, when a matter is likely to involve litigation, it may be necessary under Rule 1.4 to inform the client of forms of dispute resolution that might constitute reasonable alternatives to litigation. A lawyer ordinar-

ily has no duty to initiate investigation of a client's affairs or to give advice that the client has indicated is unwanted, but a lawyer may initiate advice to a client when doing so appears to be in the client's interest.

RULE 2.2 (DELETED 2002)

RULE 2.3: EVALUATION FOR
USE BY THIRD PERSONS

(a) A lawyer may provide an evaluation of a matter affecting a client for the use of someone other than the client if the lawyer reasonably believes that making the evaluation is compatible with other aspects of the lawyer's relationship with the client.

(b) When the lawyer knows or reasonably should know that the evaluation is likely to affect the client's interests materially and adversely, the lawyer shall not provide the evaluation unless the client gives informed consent.

(c) Except as disclosure is authorized in connection with a report of an evaluation, information relating to the evaluation is otherwise protected by Rule 1.6.

Comment
Definition

[1] An evaluation may be performed at the client's direction or when impliedly authorized in order to carry out the representation. See Rule 1.2. Such an evaluation may be for the primary purpose of establishing information for the benefit of third parties; for example, an opinion concerning the title of property rendered at the behest of a vendor for the information of a prospective purchaser, or at the behest of a borrower for the information of a prospective lender. In some situations, the evaluation may be required by a government agency; for example, an opinion concerning the legality of the securities registered for sale under the securities laws. In other instances, the evaluation may be required by a third person, such as a purchaser of a business.

[2] A legal evaluation should be distinguished from an investigation of a person with whom the lawyer does not have a client-lawyer relationship. For example, a lawyer retained by a purchaser to analyze a vendor's title to property does not have a client-lawyer relationship with the vendor. So also, an investigation into a person's affairs by a government lawyer or by special counsel employed by the government, is not an evaluation as that

ABA Model Rules of Professional Conduct

term is used in this Rule. The question is whether the lawyer is retained by the person whose affairs are being examined. When the lawyer is retained by that person, the general rules concerning loyalty to client and preservation of confidences apply, which is not the case if the lawyer is retained by someone else. For this reason, it is essential to identify the person by whom the lawyer is retained. This should be made clear not only to the person under examination, but also to others to whom the results are to be made available.

Duties Owed to Third Person and Client

[3] When the evaluation is intended for the information or use of a third person, a legal duty to that person may or may not arise. That legal question is beyond the scope of this Rule. However, since such an evaluation involves a departure from the normal client-lawyer relationship, careful analysis of the situation is required. The lawyer must be satisfied as a matter of professional judgment that making the evaluation is compatible with other functions undertaken in behalf of the client. For example, if the lawyer is acting as advocate in defending the client against charges of fraud, it would normally be incompatible with that responsibility for the lawyer to perform an evaluation for others concerning the same or a related transaction. Assuming no such impediment is apparent, however, the lawyer should advise the client of the implications of the evaluation, particularly the lawyer's responsibilities to third persons and the duty to disseminate the findings.

Access to and Disclosure of Information

[4] The quality of an evaluation depends on the freedom and extent of the investigation upon which it is based. Ordinarily a lawyer should have whatever latitude of investigation seems necessary as a matter of professional judgment. Under some circumstances, however, the terms of the evaluation may be limited. For example, certain issues or sources may be categorically excluded, or the scope of search may be limited by time constraints or the noncooperation of persons having relevant information. Any such limitations that are material to the evaluation should be described in the report. If after a lawyer has commenced an evaluation, the client refuses to comply with the terms upon which it was understood the evaluation was to have been made, the lawyer's obligations are determined by law, having reference to the terms of the client's agreement and the surrounding circumstances. In no circumstances is the lawyer permitted to knowingly make a false statement of material fact or law in providing an evaluation under this Rule. See Rule 4.1.

Obtaining Client's Informed Consent

[5] Information relating to an evaluation is protected by Rule 1.6. In many situations, providing an evaluation to a third party poses no significant risk to the client; thus, the lawyer may be impliedly authorized to disclose information to carry out the representation. See Rule 1.6(a). Where, however, it is reasonably likely that providing the evaluation will affect the client's interests materially and adversely, the lawyer must first obtain the client's consent after the client has been adequately informed concerning the important possible effects on the client's interests. See Rules 1.6(a) and 1.0(e).

Financial Auditors' Requests for Information

[6] When a question concerning the legal situation of a client arises at the instance of the client's financial auditor and the question is referred to the lawyer, the lawyer's response may be made in accordance with procedures recognized in the legal profession. Such a procedure is set forth in the American Bar Association Statement of Policy Regarding Lawyers' Responses to Auditors' Requests for Information, adopted in 1975.

Definitional Cross-References

"Informed consent" See Rule 1.0(e)
"Knows" See Rule 1.0(f)
"Reasonably believes" See Rule 1.0(i)
"Reasonably should know" See Rule 1.0(j)

RULE 2.4: LAWYER SERVING
AS THIRD-PARTY NEUTRAL

(a) A lawyer serves as a third-party neutral when the lawyer assists two or more persons who are not clients of the lawyer to reach a resolution of a dispute or other matter that has arisen between them. Service as a third-party neutral may include service as an arbitrator, a mediator or in such other capacity as will enable the lawyer to assist the parties to resolve the matter.

(b) A lawyer serving as a third-party neutral shall inform unrepresented parties that the lawyer is not representing them. When the lawyer knows or reasonably should know that a party does not understand the lawyer's role in the matter, the lawyer shall explain the difference between the lawyer's role as a third-party neutral and a lawyer's role as one who represents a client.

ABA Model
Rules of
Professional
Conduct

Comment

[1] Alternative dispute resolution has become a substantial part of the civil justice system. Aside from representing clients in dispute-resolution processes, lawyers often serve as third-party neutrals. A third-party neutral is a person, such as a mediator, arbitrator, conciliator or evaluator, who assists the parties, represented or unrepresented, in the resolution of a dispute or in the arrangement of a transaction. Whether a third-party neutral serves primarily as a facilitator, evaluator or decisionmaker depends on the particular process that is either selected by the parties or mandated by a court.

[2] The role of a third-party neutral is not unique to lawyers, although, in some court-connected contexts, only lawyers are allowed to serve in this role or to handle certain types of cases. In performing this role, the lawyer may be subject to court rules or other law that apply either to third-party neutrals generally or to lawyers serving as third-party neutrals. Lawyer-neutrals may also be subject to various codes of ethics, such as the Code of Ethics for Arbitrators in Commercial Disputes prepared by a joint committee of the American Bar Association and the American Arbitration Association or the Model Standards of Conduct for Mediators jointly prepared by the American Bar Association, the American Arbitration Association and the Society of Professionals in Dispute Resolution.

[3] Unlike nonlawyers who serve as third-party neutrals, lawyers serving in this role may experience unique problems as a result of differences between the role of a third-party neutral and a lawyer's service as a client representative. The potential for confusion is significant when the parties are unrepresented in the process. Thus, paragraph (b) requires a lawyer-neutral to inform unrepresented parties that the lawyer is not representing them. For some parties, particularly parties who frequently use dispute-resolution processes, this information will be sufficient. For others, particularly those who are using the process for the first time, more information will be required. Where appropriate, the lawyer should inform unrepresented parties of the important differences between the lawyer's role as third-party neutral and a lawyer's role as a client representative, including the inapplicability of the attorney-client evidentiary privilege. The extent of disclosure required under this paragraph will depend on the particular parties involved and the subject matter of the proceeding, as well as the particular features of the dispute-resolution process selected.

[4] A lawyer who serves as a third-party neutral subsequently may be asked to serve as a lawyer representing a client in the same matter. The conflicts of interest that arise for both the individual lawyer and the lawyer's law firm are addressed in Rule 1.12.

[5] Lawyers who represent clients in alternative dispute-resolution processes are governed by the Rules of Professional Conduct. When the dispute-resolution process takes place before a tribunal, as in binding arbitration (see Rule 1.0(m)), the lawyer's duty of candor is governed by Rule 3.3. Otherwise, the lawyer's duty of candor toward both the third-party neutral and other parties is governed by Rule 4.1.

Definitional Cross-References

"Knows" *See* Rule 1.0(f)

"Reasonably should know" *See* Rule 1.0(j)

ADVOCATE

RULE 3.1: MERITORIOUS CLAIMS AND CONTENTIONS

A lawyer shall not bring or defend a proceeding, or assert or controvert an issue therein, unless there is a basis in law and fact for doing so that is not frivolous, which includes a good faith argument for an extension, modification or reversal of existing law. A lawyer for the defendant in a criminal proceeding, or the respondent in a proceeding that could result in incarceration, may nevertheless so defend the proceeding as to require that every element of the case be established.

Comment

[1] The advocate has a duty to use legal procedure for the fullest benefit of the client's cause, but also a duty not to abuse legal procedure. The law, both procedural and substantive, establishes the limits within which an advocate may proceed. However, the law is not always clear and never is static. Accordingly, in determining the proper scope of advocacy, account must be taken of the law's ambiguities and potential for change.

[2] The filing of an action or defense or similar action taken for a client is not frivolous merely because the facts have not first been fully substantiated or because the lawyer expects to develop vital evidence only by discovery. What is required of lawyers, however, is that they inform themselves about the facts of their clients' cases and the applicable law and determine that they can make good faith arguments in support of their clients' positions. Such action is not frivolous even though the lawyer believes that the client's position ultimately will not prevail. The action is frivolous, however, if the lawyer is unable either to make a good faith argument on the merits of

the action taken or to support the action taken by a good faith argument for an extension, modification or reversal of existing law.

[3] The lawyer's obligations under this Rule are subordinate to federal or state constitutional law that entitles a defendant in a criminal matter to the assistance of counsel in presenting a claim or contention that otherwise would be prohibited by this Rule.

RULE 3.2: EXPEDITING LITIGATION

A lawyer shall make reasonable efforts to expedite litigation consistent with the interests of the client.

Comment

[1] Dilatory practices bring the administration of justice into disrepute. Although there will be occasions when a lawyer may properly seek a postponement for personal reasons, it is not proper for a lawyer to routinely fail to expedite litigation solely for the convenience of the advocates. Nor will a failure to expedite be reasonable if done for the purpose of frustrating an opposing party's attempt to obtain rightful redress or repose. It is not a justification that similar conduct is often tolerated by the bench and bar. The question is whether a competent lawyer acting in good faith would regard the course of action as having some substantial purpose other than delay. Realizing financial or other benefit from otherwise improper delay in litigation is not a legitimate interest of the client.

Definitional Cross-References

"Reasonable" *See* Rule 1.0(h)

RULE 3.3: CANDOR TOWARD THE TRIBUNAL

(a) A lawyer shall not knowingly:

(1) make a false statement of fact or law to a tribunal or fail to correct a false statement of material fact or law previously made to the tribunal by the lawyer;

(2) fail to disclose to the tribunal legal authority in the controlling jurisdiction known to the lawyer to be directly adverse to the position of the client and not disclosed by opposing counsel; or

(3) offer evidence that the lawyer knows to be false. If a lawyer, the lawyer's client, or a witness called by the lawyer, has offered material evidence and the lawyer comes to know

of its falsity, the lawyer shall take reasonable remedial measures, including, if necessary, disclosure to the tribunal. A lawyer may refuse to offer evidence, other than the testimony of a defendant in a criminal matter, that the lawyer reasonably believes is false.

(b) A lawyer who represents a client in an adjudicative proceeding and who knows that a person intends to engage, is engaging or has engaged in criminal or fraudulent conduct related to the proceeding shall take reasonable remedial measures, including, if necessary, disclosure to the tribunal.

(c) The duties stated in paragraphs (a) and (b) continue to the conclusion of the proceeding, and apply even if compliance requires disclosure of information otherwise protected by Rule 1.6.

(d) In an ex parte proceeding, a lawyer shall inform the tribunal of all material facts known to the lawyer that will enable the tribunal to make an informed decision, whether or not the facts are adverse.

Comment

[1] This Rule governs the conduct of a lawyer who is representing a client in the proceedings of a tribunal. See Rule 1.0(m) for the definition of "tribunal." It also applies when the lawyer is representing a client in an ancillary proceeding conducted pursuant to the tribunal's adjudicative authority, such as a deposition. Thus, for example, paragraph (a)(3) requires a lawyer to take reasonable remedial measures if the lawyer comes to know that a client who is testifying in a deposition has offered evidence that is false.

[2] This Rule sets forth the special duties of lawyers as officers of the court to avoid conduct that undermines the integrity of the adjudicative process. A lawyer acting as an advocate in an adjudicative proceeding has an obligation to present the client's case with persuasive force. Performance of that duty while maintaining confidences of the client, however, is qualified by the advocate's duty of candor to the tribunal. Consequently, although a lawyer in an adversary proceeding is not required to present an impartial exposition of the law or to vouch for the evidence submitted in a cause, the lawyer must not allow the tribunal to be misled by false statements of law or fact or evidence that the lawyer knows to be false.

Representations by a Lawyer

[3] An advocate is responsible for pleadings and other documents prepared for litigation, but is usually not required to have personal knowledge of matters asserted therein, for litigation documents ordinarily present assertions by the client, or by someone on the client's behalf, and not assertions by the lawyer. Compare Rule 3.1. However, an assertion purporting

to be on the lawyer's own knowledge, as in an affidavit by the lawyer or in a statement in open court, may properly be made only when the lawyer knows the assertion is true or believes it to be true on the basis of a reasonably diligent inquiry. There are circumstances where failure to make a disclosure is the equivalent of an affirmative misrepresentation. The obligation prescribed in Rule 1.2(d) not to counsel a client to commit or assist the client in committing a fraud applies in litigation. Regarding compliance with Rule 1.2(d), see the Comment to that Rule. See also the Comment to Rule 8.4(b).

Legal Argument

[4] Legal argument based on a knowingly false representation of law constitutes dishonesty toward the tribunal. A lawyer is not required to make a disinterested exposition of the law, but must recognize the existence of pertinent legal authorities. Furthermore, as stated in paragraph (a)(2), an advocate has a duty to disclose directly adverse authority in the controlling jurisdiction that has not been disclosed by the opposing party. The underlying concept is that legal argument is a discussion seeking to determine the legal premises properly applicable to the case.

Offering Evidence

[5] Paragraph (a)(3) requires that the lawyer refuse to offer evidence that the lawyer knows to be false, regardless of the client's wishes. This duty is premised on the lawyer's obligation as an officer of the court to prevent the trier of fact from being misled by false evidence. A lawyer does not violate this Rule if the lawyer offers the evidence for the purpose of establishing its falsity.

[6] If a lawyer knows that the client intends to testify falsely or wants the lawyer to introduce false evidence, the lawyer should seek to persuade the client that the evidence should not be offered. If the persuasion is ineffective and the lawyer continues to represent the client, the lawyer must refuse to offer the false evidence. If only a portion of a witness's testimony will be false, the lawyer may call the witness to testify but may not elicit or otherwise permit the witness to present the testimony that the lawyer knows is false.

[7] The duties stated in paragraphs (a) and (b) apply to all lawyers, including defense counsel in criminal cases. In some jurisdictions, however, courts have required counsel to present the accused as a witness or to give a narrative statement if the accused so desires, even if counsel knows that the testimony or statement will be false. The obligation of the advocate under the Rules of Professional Conduct is subordinate to such requirements. See also Comment [9].

[8] The prohibition against offering false evidence only applies if the lawyer knows that the evidence is false. A lawyer's reasonable belief that evidence is false does not preclude its presentation to the trier of fact. A lawyer's knowledge that evidence is false, however, can be inferred from the circumstances. See Rule 1.0(f). Thus, although a lawyer should resolve doubts about the veracity of testimony or other evidence in favor of the client, the lawyer cannot ignore an obvious falsehood.

[9] Although paragraph (a)(3) only prohibits a lawyer from offering evidence the lawyer knows to be false, it permits the lawyer to refuse to offer testimony or other proof that the lawyer reasonably believes is false. Offering such proof may reflect adversely on the lawyer's ability to discriminate in the quality of evidence and thus impair the lawyer's effectiveness as an advocate. Because of the special protections historically provided criminal defendants, however, this Rule does not permit a lawyer to refuse to offer the testimony of such a client where the lawyer reasonably believes but does not know that the testimony will be false. Unless the lawyer knows the testimony will be false, the lawyer must honor the client's decision to testify. See also Comment [7].

Remedial Measures

[10] Having offered material evidence in the belief that it was true, a lawyer may subsequently come to know that the evidence is false. Or, a lawyer may be surprised when the lawyer's client, or another witness called by the lawyer, offers testimony the lawyer knows to be false, either during the lawyer's direct examination or in response to cross-examination by the opposing lawyer. In such situations or if the lawyer knows of the falsity of testimony elicited from the client during a deposition, the lawyer must take reasonable remedial measures. In such situations, the advocate's proper course is to remonstrate with the client confidentially, advise the client of the lawyer's duty of candor to the tribunal and seek the client's cooperation with respect to the withdrawal or correction of the false statements or evidence. If that fails, the advocate must take further remedial action. If withdrawal from the representation is not permitted or will not undo the effect of the false evidence, the advocate must make such disclosure to the tribunal as is reasonably necessary to remedy the situation, even if doing so requires the lawyer to reveal information that otherwise would be protected by Rule 1.6. It is for the tribunal then to determine what should be done—making a statement about the matter to the trier of fact, ordering a mistrial or perhaps nothing.

[11] The disclosure of a client's false testimony can result in grave consequences to the client, including not only a sense of betrayal but also loss

of the case and perhaps a prosecution for perjury. But the alternative is that the lawyer cooperate in deceiving the court, thereby subverting the truth-finding process which the adversary system is designed to implement. See Rule 1.2(d). Furthermore, unless it is clearly understood that the lawyer will act upon the duty to disclose the existence of false evidence, the client can simply reject the lawyer's advice to reveal the false evidence and insist that the lawyer keep silent. Thus the client could in effect coerce the lawyer into being a party to fraud on the court.

Preserving Integrity of Adjudicative Process

[12] Lawyers have a special obligation to protect a tribunal against criminal or fraudulent conduct that undermines the integrity of the adjudicative process, such as bribing, intimidating or otherwise unlawfully communicating with a witness, juror, court official or other participant in the proceeding, unlawfully destroying or concealing documents or other evidence or failing to disclose information to the tribunal when required by law to do so. Thus, paragraph (b) requires a lawyer to take reasonable remedial measures, including disclosure if necessary, whenever the lawyer knows that a person, including the lawyer's client, intends to engage, is engaging or has engaged in criminal or fraudulent conduct related to the proceeding.

Duration of Obligation

[13] A practical time limit on the obligation to rectify false evidence or false statements of law and fact has to be established. The conclusion of the proceeding is a reasonably definite point for the termination of the obligation. A proceeding has concluded within the meaning of this Rule when a final judgment in the proceeding has been affirmed on appeal or the time for review has passed.

Ex Parte Proceedings

[14] Ordinarily, an advocate has the limited responsibility of presenting one side of the matters that a tribunal should consider in reaching a decision; the conflicting position is expected to be presented by the opposing party. However, in any ex parte proceeding, such as an application for a temporary restraining order, there is no balance of presentation by opposing advocates. The object of an ex parte proceeding is nevertheless to yield a substantially just result. The judge has an affirmative responsibility to accord the absent party just consideration. The lawyer for the represented party has the correlative duty to make disclosures of material facts known to the lawyer and that the lawyer reasonably believes are necessary to an informed decision.

Withdrawal

[15] Normally, a lawyer's compliance with the duty of candor imposed by this Rule does not require that the lawyer withdraw from the representation of a client whose interests will be or have been adversely affected by the lawyer's disclosure. The lawyer may, however, be required by Rule 1.16(a) to seek permission of the tribunal to withdraw if the lawyer's compliance with this Rule's duty of candor results in such an extreme deterioration of the client-lawyer relationship that the lawyer can no longer competently represent the client. Also see Rule 1.16(b) for the circumstances in which a lawyer will be permitted to seek a tribunal's permission to withdraw. In connection with a request for permission to withdraw that is premised on a client's misconduct, a lawyer may reveal information relating to the representation only to the extent reasonably necessary to comply with this Rule or as otherwise permitted by Rule 1.6.

Definitional Cross-References

"Fraudulent" *See* Rule 1.0(d)
"Knowingly" and "Known" and "Knows" *See* Rule 1.0(f)
"Reasonable" *See* Rule 1.0(h)
"Reasonably believes" *See* Rule 1.0(i)
"Tribunal" *See* Rule 1.0(m)

RULE 3.4: FAIRNESS TO OPPOSING PARTY AND COUNSEL

A lawyer shall not:

(a) unlawfully obstruct another party's access to evidence or unlawfully alter, destroy or conceal a document or other material having potential evidentiary value. A lawyer shall not counsel or assist another person to do any such act;

(b) falsify evidence, counsel or assist a witness to testify falsely, or offer an inducement to a witness that is prohibited by law;

(c) knowingly disobey an obligation under the rules of a tribunal, except for an open refusal based on an assertion that no valid obligation exists;

(d) in pretrial procedure, make a frivolous discovery request or fail to make reasonably diligent effort to comply with a legally proper discovery request by an opposing party;

(e) in trial, allude to any matter that the lawyer does not reasonably believe is relevant or that will not be supported by admissible evidence, assert personal knowledge of facts in issue

ABA Model
Rules of
Professional
Conduct

except when testifying as a witness, or state a personal opinion as to the justness of a cause, the credibility of a witness, the culpability of a civil litigant or the guilt or innocence of an accused; or

(f) request a person other than a client to refrain from voluntarily giving relevant information to another party unless:

(1) the person is a relative or an employee or other agent of a client; and

(2) the lawyer reasonably believes that the person's interests will not be adversely affected by refraining from giving such information.

Comment

[1] The procedure of the adversary system contemplates that the evidence in a case is to be marshalled competitively by the contending parties. Fair competition in the adversary system is secured by prohibitions against destruction or concealment of evidence, improperly influencing witnesses, obstructive tactics in discovery procedure, and the like.

[2] Documents and other items of evidence are often essential to establish a claim or defense. Subject to evidentiary privileges, the right of an opposing party, including the government, to obtain evidence through discovery or subpoena is an important procedural right. The exercise of that right can be frustrated if relevant material is altered, concealed or destroyed. Applicable law in many jurisdictions makes it an offense to destroy material for purpose of impairing its availability in a pending proceeding or one whose commencement can be foreseen. Falsifying evidence is also generally a criminal offense. Paragraph (a) applies to evidentiary material generally, including computerized information. Applicable law may permit a lawyer to take temporary possession of physical evidence of client crimes for the purpose of conducting a limited examination that will not alter or destroy material characteristics of the evidence. In such a case, applicable law may require the lawyer to turn the evidence over to the police or other prosecuting authority, depending on the circumstances.

[3] With regard to paragraph (b), it is not improper to pay a witness's expenses or to compensate an expert witness on terms permitted by law. The common law rule in most jurisdictions is that it is improper to pay an occurrence witness any fee for testifying and that it is improper to pay an expert witness a contingent fee.

[4] Paragraph (f) permits a lawyer to advise employees of a client to refrain from giving information to another party, for the employees may identify their interests with those of the client. See also Rule 4.2.

Definitional Cross-References

"Knowingly" *See* Rule 1.0(f)
"Reasonably" *See* Rule 1.0(h)
"Reasonably believes" *See* Rule 1.0(i)
"Tribunal" *See* Rule 1.0(m)

RULE 3.5: IMPARTIALITY AND DECORUM OF THE TRIBUNAL

A lawyer shall not:

(a) seek to influence a judge, juror, prospective juror or other official by means prohibited by law;

(b) communicate ex parte with such a person during the proceeding unless authorized to do so by law or court order;

(c) communicate with a juror or prospective juror after discharge of the jury if:

(1) the communication is prohibited by law or court order;

(2) the juror has made known to the lawyer a desire not to communicate; or

(3) the communication involves misrepresentation, coercion, duress or harassment; or

(d) engage in conduct intended to disrupt a tribunal.

Comment

[1] Many forms of improper influence upon a tribunal are proscribed by criminal law. Others are specified in the ABA Model Code of Judicial Conduct, with which an advocate should be familiar. A lawyer is required to avoid contributing to a violation of such provisions.

[2] During a proceeding a lawyer may not communicate ex parte with persons serving in an official capacity in the proceeding, such as judges, masters or jurors, unless authorized to do so by law or court order.

[3] A lawyer may on occasion want to communicate with a juror or prospective juror after the jury has been discharged. The lawyer may do so unless the communication is prohibited by law or a court order but must respect the desire of the juror not to talk with the lawyer. The lawyer may not engage in improper conduct during the communication.

[4] The advocate's function is to present evidence and argument so that the cause may be decided according to law. Refraining from abusive or obstreperous conduct is a corollary of the advocate's right to speak on behalf of litigants. A lawyer may stand firm against abuse by a judge but should avoid reciprocation; the judge's default is no justification for similar derelic-

tion by an advocate. An advocate can present the cause, protect the record for subsequent review and preserve professional integrity by patient firmness no less effectively than by belligerence or theatrics.

[5] The duty to refrain from disruptive conduct applies to any proceeding of a tribunal, including a deposition. See Rule 1.0(m).

Definitional Cross-References

"Known" *See* Rule 1.0(f)

"Tribunal" *See* Rule 1.0(m)

RULE 3.6: TRIAL PUBLICITY

(a) A lawyer who is participating or has participated in the investigation or litigation of a matter shall not make an extrajudicial statement that the lawyer knows or reasonably should know will be disseminated by means of public communication and will have a substantial likelihood of materially prejudicing an adjudicative proceeding in the matter.

(b) Notwithstanding paragraph (a), a lawyer may state:

(1) the claim, offense or defense involved and, except when prohibited by law, the identity of the persons involved;

(2) information contained in a public record;

(3) that an investigation of a matter is in progress;

(4) the scheduling or result of any step in litigation;

(5) a request for assistance in obtaining evidence and information necessary thereto;

(6) a warning of danger concerning the behavior of a person involved, when there is reason to believe that there exists the likelihood of substantial harm to an individual or to the public interest; and

(7) in a criminal case, in addition to subparagraphs (1) through (6):

(i) the identity, residence, occupation and family status of the accused;

(ii) if the accused has not been apprehended, information necessary to aid in apprehension of that person;

(iii) the fact, time and place of arrest; and

(iv) the identity of investigating and arresting officers or agencies and the length of the investigation.

(c) Notwithstanding paragraph (a), a lawyer may make a statement that a reasonable lawyer would believe is required to protect a client from the substantial undue prejudicial effect of recent publicity not initiated by the lawyer or the lawyer's client. A statement made pursuant to this paragraph shall be limited to such information as is necessary to mitigate the recent adverse publicity.

(d) No lawyer associated in a firm or government agency with a lawyer subject to paragraph (a) shall make a statement prohibited by paragraph (a).

Comment

[1] It is difficult to strike a balance between protecting the right to a fair trial and safeguarding the right of free expression. Preserving the right to a fair trial necessarily entails some curtailment of the information that may be disseminated about a party prior to trial, particularly where trial by jury is involved. If there were no such limits, the result would be the practical nullification of the protective effect of the rules of forensic decorum and the exclusionary rules of evidence. On the other hand, there are vital social interests served by the free dissemination of information about events having legal consequences and about legal proceedings themselves. The public has a right to know about threats to its safety and measures aimed at assuring its security. It also has a legitimate interest in the conduct of judicial proceedings, particularly in matters of general public concern. Furthermore, the subject matter of legal proceedings is often of direct significance in debate and deliberation over questions of public policy.

[2] Special rules of confidentiality may validly govern proceedings in juvenile, domestic relations and mental disability proceedings, and perhaps other types of litigation. Rule 3.4(c) requires compliance with such rules.

[3] The Rule sets forth a basic general prohibition against a lawyer's making statements that the lawyer knows or should know will have a substantial likelihood of materially prejudicing an adjudicative proceeding. Recognizing that the public value of informed commentary is great and the likelihood of prejudice to a proceeding by the commentary of a lawyer who is not involved in the proceeding is small, the Rule applies only to lawyers who are, or who have been involved in the investigation or litigation of a case, and their associates.

[4] Paragraph (b) identifies specific matters about which a lawyer's statements would not ordinarily be considered to present a substantial likelihood of material prejudice, and should not in any event be considered prohibited by the general prohibition of paragraph (a). Paragraph (b) is not intended to be an exhaustive listing of the subjects upon which a lawyer may make a statement, but statements on other matters may be subject to paragraph (a).

[5] There are, on the other hand, certain subjects that are more likely than not to have a material prejudicial effect on a proceeding, particularly when they refer to a civil matter triable to a jury, a criminal matter, or any other proceeding that could result in incarceration. These subjects relate to:

(1) the character, credibility, reputation or criminal record of a party, suspect in a criminal investigation or witness, or the identity of a witness, or the expected testimony of a party or witness;

(2) in a criminal case or proceeding that could result in incarceration, the possibility of a plea of guilty to the offense or the existence or contents of any confession, admission, or statement given by a defendant or suspect or that person's refusal or failure to make a statement;

(3) the performance or results of any examination or test or the refusal or failure of a person to submit to an examination or test, or the identity or nature of physical evidence expected to be presented;

(4) any opinion as to the guilt or innocence of a defendant or suspect in a criminal case or proceeding that could result in incarceration;

(5) information that the lawyer knows or reasonably should know is likely to be inadmissible as evidence in a trial and that would, if disclosed, create a substantial risk of prejudicing an impartial trial; or

(6) the fact that a defendant has been charged with a crime, unless there is included therein a statement explaining that the charge is merely an accusation and that the defendant is presumed innocent until and unless proven guilty.

[6] Another relevant factor in determining prejudice is the nature of the proceeding involved. Criminal jury trials will be most sensitive to extrajudicial speech. Civil trials may be less sensitive. Non-jury hearings and arbitration proceedings may be even less affected. The Rule will still place limitations on prejudicial comments in these cases, but the likelihood of prejudice may be different depending on the type of proceeding.

[7] Finally, extrajudicial statements that might otherwise raise a question under this Rule may be permissible when they are made in response to statements made publicly by another party, another party's lawyer, or third persons, where a reasonable lawyer would believe a public response is required in order to avoid prejudice to the lawyer's client. When prejudicial statements have been publicly made by others, responsive statements may have the salutary effect of lessening any resulting adverse impact on the adjudicative proceeding. Such responsive statements should be limited to contain only such information as is necessary to mitigate undue prejudice created by the statements made by others.

[8] See Rule 3.8(f) for additional duties of prosecutors in connection with extrajudicial statements about criminal proceedings.

Definitional Cross-References

"Firm" *See* Rule 1.0(c)
"Knows" *See* Rule 1.0(f)
"Reasonable" *See* Rule 1.0(h)
"Reasonably should know" *See* Rule 1.0(j)
"Substantial" *See* Rule 1.0(l)

RULE 3.7: LAWYER AS WITNESS

(a) A lawyer shall not act as advocate at a trial in which the lawyer is likely to be a necessary witness unless:

(1) the testimony relates to an uncontested issue;

(2) the testimony relates to the nature and value of legal services rendered in the case; or

(3) disqualification of the lawyer would work substantial hardship on the client.

(b) A lawyer may act as advocate in a trial in which another lawyer in the lawyer's firm is likely to be called as a witness unless precluded from doing so by Rule 1.7 or Rule 1.9.

Comment

[1] Combining the roles of advocate and witness can prejudice the tribunal and the opposing party and can also involve a conflict of interest between the lawyer and client.

Advocate-Witness Rule

[2] The tribunal has proper objection when the trier of fact may be confused or misled by a lawyer serving as both advocate and witness. The opposing party has proper objection where the combination of roles may prejudice that party's rights in the litigation. A witness is required to testify on the basis of personal knowledge, while an advocate is expected to explain and comment on evidence given by others. It may not be clear whether a statement by an advocate-witness should be taken as proof or as an analysis of the proof.

[3] To protect the tribunal, paragraph (a) prohibits a lawyer from simultaneously serving as advocate and necessary witness except in those circumstances specified in paragraphs (a)(1) through (a)(3). Paragraph (a)(1) recognizes that if the testimony will be uncontested, the ambiguities in the dual role are purely theoretical. Paragraph (a)(2) recognizes that where the testimony concerns the extent and value of legal services rendered in the action in which the testimony is offered, permitting the lawyers to testify

avoids the need for a second trial with new counsel to resolve that issue. Moreover, in such a situation the judge has firsthand knowledge of the matter in issue; hence, there is less dependence on the adversary process to test the credibility of the testimony.

[4] Apart from these two exceptions, paragraph (a)(3) recognizes that a balancing is required between the interests of the client and those of the tribunal and the opposing party. Whether the tribunal is likely to be misled or the opposing party is likely to suffer prejudice depends on the nature of the case, the importance and probable tenor of the lawyer's testimony, and the probability that the lawyer's testimony will conflict with that of other witnesses. Even if there is risk of such prejudice, in determining whether the lawyer should be disqualified, due regard must be given to the effect of disqualification on the lawyer's client. It is relevant that one or both parties could reasonably foresee that the lawyer would probably be a witness. The conflict of interest principles stated in Rules 1.7, 1.9 and 1.10 have no application to this aspect of the problem.

[5] Because the tribunal is not likely to be misled when a lawyer acts as advocate in a trial in which another lawyer in the lawyer's firm will testify as a necessary witness, paragraph (b) permits the lawyer to do so except in situations involving a conflict of interest.

Conflict of Interest

[6] In determining if it is permissible to act as advocate in a trial in which the lawyer will be a necessary witness, the lawyer must also consider that the dual role may give rise to a conflict of interest that will require compliance with Rules 1.7 or 1.9. For example, if there is likely to be substantial conflict between the testimony of the client and that of the lawyer the representation involves a conflict of interest that requires compliance with Rule 1.7. This would be true even though the lawyer might not be prohibited by paragraph (a) from simultaneously serving as advocate and witness because the lawyer's disqualification would work a substantial hardship on the client. Similarly, a lawyer who might be permitted to simultaneously serve as an advocate and a witness by paragraph (a)(3) might be precluded from doing so by Rule 1.9. The problem can arise whether the lawyer is called as a witness on behalf of the client or is called by the opposing party. Determining whether or not such a conflict exists is primarily the responsibility of the lawyer involved. If there is a conflict of interest, the lawyer must secure the client's informed consent, confirmed in writing. In some cases, the lawyer will be precluded from seeking the client's consent. See Rule 1.7. See Rule 1.0(b) for the definition of "confirmed in writing" and Rule 1.0(e) for the definition of "informed consent."

[7] Paragraph (b) provides that a lawyer is not disqualified from serving as an advocate because a lawyer with whom the lawyer is associated in a firm is precluded from doing so by paragraph (a). If, however, the testifying lawyer would also be disqualified by Rule 1.7 or Rule 1.9 from representing the client in the matter, other lawyers in the firm will be precluded from representing the client by Rule 1.10 unless the client gives informed consent under the conditions stated in Rule 1.7.

Definitional Cross-References

"Firm" *See* Rule 1.0(c)

"Substantial" *See* Rule 1.0(l)

RULE 3.8: SPECIAL RESPONSIBILITIES OF A PROSECUTOR

The prosecutor in a criminal case shall:

(a) refrain from prosecuting a charge that the prosecutor knows is not supported by probable cause;

(b) make reasonable efforts to assure that the accused has been advised of the right to, and the procedure for obtaining, counsel and has been given reasonable opportunity to obtain counsel;

(c) not seek to obtain from an unrepresented accused a waiver of important pretrial rights, such as the right to a preliminary hearing;

(d) make timely disclosure to the defense of all evidence or information known to the prosecutor that tends to negate the guilt of the accused or mitigates the offense, and, in connection with sentencing, disclose to the defense and to the tribunal all unprivileged mitigating information known to the prosecutor, except when the prosecutor is relieved of this responsibility by a protective order of the tribunal;

(e) not subpoena a lawyer in a grand jury or other criminal proceeding to present evidence about a past or present client unless the prosecutor reasonably believes:

(1) the information sought is not protected from disclosure by any applicable privilege;

(2) the evidence sought is essential to the successful completion of an ongoing investigation or prosecution; and

(3) there is no other feasible alternative to obtain the information;

(f) except for statements that are necessary to inform the public of the nature and extent of the prosecutor's action and

ABA Model Rules of Professional Conduct

that serve a legitimate law enforcement purpose, refrain from making extrajudicial comments that have a substantial likelihood of heightening public condemnation of the accused and exercise reasonable care to prevent investigators, law enforcement personnel, employees or other persons assisting or associated with the prosecutor in a criminal case from making an extrajudicial statement that the prosecutor would be prohibited from making under Rule 3.6 or this Rule.

(g) When a prosecutor knows of new, credible and material evidence creating a reasonable likelihood that a convicted defendant did not commit an offense of which the defendant was convicted, the prosecutor shall:

(1) promptly disclose that evidence to an appropriate court or authority, and

(2) if the conviction was obtained in the prosecutor's jurisdiction,

(i) promptly disclose that evidence to the defendant unless a court authorizes delay, and

(ii) undertake further investigation, or make reasonable efforts to cause an investigation, to determine whether the defendant was convicted of an offense that the defendant did not commit.

(h) When a prosecutor knows of clear and convincing evidence establishing that a defendant in the prosecutor's jurisdiction was convicted of an offense that the defendant did not commit, the prosecutor shall seek to remedy the conviction.

Comment

[1] A prosecutor has the responsibility of a minister of justice and not simply that of an advocate. This responsibility carries with it specific obligations to see that the defendant is accorded procedural justice, that guilt is decided upon the basis of sufficient evidence, and that special precautions are taken to prevent and to rectify the conviction of innocent persons. The extent of mandated remedial action is a matter of debate and varies in different jurisdictions. Many jurisdictions have adopted the ABA Standards for Criminal Justice Relating to the Prosecution Function, which are the product of prolonged and careful deliberation by lawyers experienced in both criminal prosecution and defense. Competent representation of the sovereignty may require a prosecutor to undertake some procedural and remedial measures as a matter of obligation. Applicable law may require other measures by the prosecutor and knowing disregard of those obligations or a systematic abuse of prosecutorial discretion could constitute a violation of Rule 8.4.

[2] In some jurisdictions, a defendant may waive a preliminary hearing and thereby lose a valuable opportunity to challenge probable cause. Accordingly, prosecutors should not seek to obtain waivers of preliminary hearings or other important pretrial rights from unrepresented accused persons. Paragraph (c) does not apply, however, to an accused appearing *pro se* with the approval of the tribunal. Nor does it forbid the lawful questioning of an uncharged suspect who has knowingly waived the rights to counsel and silence.

[3] The exception in paragraph (d) recognizes that a prosecutor may seek an appropriate protective order from the tribunal if disclosure of information to the defense could result in substantial harm to an individual or to the public interest.

[4] Paragraph (e) is intended to limit the issuance of lawyer subpoenas in grand jury and other criminal proceedings to those situations in which there is a genuine need to intrude into the client-lawyer relationship.

[5] Paragraph (f) supplements Rule 3.6, which prohibits extrajudicial statements that have a substantial likelihood of prejudicing an adjudicatory proceeding. In the context of a criminal prosecution, a prosecutor's extrajudicial statement can create the additional problem of increasing public condemnation of the accused. Although the announcement of an indictment, for example, will necessarily have severe consequences for the accused, a prosecutor can, and should, avoid comments which have no legitimate law enforcement purpose and have a substantial likelihood of increasing public opprobrium of the accused. Nothing in this Comment is intended to restrict the statements which a prosecutor may make which comply with Rule 3.6(b) or 3.6(c).

[6] Like other lawyers, prosecutors are subject to Rules 5.1 and 5.3, which relate to responsibilities regarding lawyers and nonlawyers who work for or are associated with the lawyer's office. Paragraph (f) reminds the prosecutor of the importance of these obligations in connection with the unique dangers of improper extrajudicial statements in a criminal case. In addition, paragraph (f) requires a prosecutor to exercise reasonable care to prevent persons assisting or associated with the prosecutor from making improper extrajudicial statements, even when such persons are not under the direct supervision of the prosecutor. Ordinarily, the reasonable care standard will be satisfied if the prosecutor issues the appropriate cautions to law enforcement personnel and other relevant individuals.

[7] When a prosecutor knows of new, credible and material evidence creating a reasonable likelihood that a person outside the prosecutor's jurisdiction was convicted of a crime that the person did not commit, paragraph (g) requires prompt disclosure to the court or other appropriate authority,

such as the chief prosecutor of the jurisdiction where the conviction occurred. If the conviction was obtained in the prosecutor's jurisdiction, paragraph (g) requires the prosecutor to examine the evidence and undertake further investigation to determine whether the defendant is in fact innocent or make reasonable efforts to cause another appropriate authority to undertake the necessary investigation, and to promptly disclose the evidence to the court and, absent court-authorized delay, to the defendant. Consistent with the objectives of Rules 4.2 and 4.3, disclosure to a represented defendant must be made through the defendant's counsel, and, in the case of an unrepresented defendant, would ordinarily be accompanied by a request to a court for the appointment of counsel to assist the defendant in taking such legal measures as may be appropriate.

[8] Under paragraph (h), once the prosecutor knows of clear and convincing evidence that the defendant was convicted of an offense that the defendant did not commit, the prosecutor must seek to remedy the conviction. Necessary steps may include disclosure of the evidence to the defendant, requesting that the court appoint counsel for an unrepresented indigent defendant and, where appropriate, notifying the court that the prosecutor has knowledge that the defendant did not commit the offense of which the defendant was convicted.

[9] A prosecutor's independent judgment, made in good faith, that the new evidence is not of such nature as to trigger the obligations of sections (g) and (h), though subsequently determined to have been erroneous, does not constitute a violation of this Rule.

Definitional Cross-References

"Known" and "Knows" *See* Rule 1.0(f)
"Reasonable" *See* Rule 1.0(h)
"Reasonably believes" *See* Rule 1.0(i)
"Substantial" *See* Rule 1.0(l)
"Tribunal" *See* Rule 1.0(m)

RULE 3.9: ADVOCATE IN NONADJUDICATIVE PROCEEDINGS

A lawyer representing a client before a legislative body or administrative agency in a nonadjudicative proceeding shall disclose that the appearance is in a representative capacity and shall conform to the provisions of Rules 3.3(a) through (c), 3.4(a) through (c), and 3.5.

Comment

[1] In representation before bodies such as legislatures, municipal councils, and executive and administrative agencies acting in a rule-making or policy-making capacity, lawyers present facts, formulate issues and advance argument in the matters under consideration. The decision-making body, like a court, should be able to rely on the integrity of the submissions made to it. A lawyer appearing before such a body must deal with it honestly and in conformity with applicable rules of procedure. See Rules 3.3(a) through (c), 3.4(a) through (c) and 3.5.

[2] Lawyers have no exclusive right to appear before nonadjudicative bodies, as they do before a court. The requirements of this Rule therefore may subject lawyers to regulations inapplicable to advocates who are not lawyers. However, legislatures and administrative agencies have a right to expect lawyers to deal with them as they deal with courts.

[3] This Rule only applies when a lawyer represents a client in connection with an official hearing or meeting of a governmental agency or a legislative body to which the lawyer or the lawyer's client is presenting evidence or argument. It does not apply to representation of a client in a negotiation or other bilateral transaction with a governmental agency or in connection with an application for a license or other privilege or the client's compliance with generally applicable reporting requirements, such as the filing of income-tax returns. Nor does it apply to the representation of a client in connection with an investigation or examination of the client's affairs conducted by government investigators or examiners. Representation in such matters is governed by Rules 4.1 through 4.4.

TRANSACTIONS WITH PERSONS OTHER THAN CLIENTS

RULE 4.1: TRUTHFULNESS IN STATEMENTS TO OTHERS

In the course of representing a client a lawyer shall not knowingly:

(a) make a false statement of material fact or law to a third person; or

(b) fail to disclose a material fact when disclosure is necessary to avoid assisting a criminal or fraudulent act by a client, unless disclosure is prohibited by Rule 1.6.

Comment

Misrepresentation

[1] A lawyer is required to be truthful when dealing with others on a client's behalf, but generally has no affirmative duty to inform an opposing party of relevant facts. A misrepresentation can occur if the lawyer incorporates or affirms a statement of another person that the lawyer knows is false. Misrepresentations can also occur by partially true but misleading statements or omissions that are the equivalent of affirmative false statements. For dishonest conduct that does not amount to a false statement or for misrepresentations by a lawyer other than in the course of representing a client, see Rule 8.4.

Statements of Fact

[2] This Rule refers to statements of fact. Whether a particular statement should be regarded as one of fact can depend on the circumstances. Under generally accepted conventions in negotiation, certain types of statements ordinarily are not taken as statements of material fact. Estimates of price or value placed on the subject of a transaction and a party's intentions as to an acceptable settlement of a claim are ordinarily in this category, and so is the existence of an undisclosed principal except where nondisclosure of the principal would constitute fraud. Lawyers should be mindful of their obligations under applicable law to avoid criminal and tortious misrepresentation.

Crime or Fraud by Client

[3] Under Rule 1.2(d), a lawyer is prohibited from counseling or assisting a client in conduct that the lawyer knows is criminal or fraudulent. Paragraph (b) states a specific application of the principle set forth in Rule 1.2(d) and addresses the situation where a client's crime or fraud takes the form of a lie or misrepresentation. Ordinarily, a lawyer can avoid assisting a client's crime or fraud by withdrawing from the representation. Sometimes it may be necessary for the lawyer to give notice of the fact of withdrawal and to disaffirm an opinion, document, affirmation or the like. In extreme cases, substantive law may require a lawyer to disclose information relating to the representation to avoid being deemed to have assisted the client's crime or fraud. If the lawyer can avoid assisting a client's crime or fraud only by disclosing this information, then under paragraph (b) the lawyer is required to do so, unless the disclosure is prohibited by Rule 1.6.

Definitional Cross-References

"Fraudulent" *See* Rule 1.0(d)
"Knowingly" *See* Rule 1.0(f)

RULE 4.2: COMMUNICATION WITH PERSON REPRESENTED BY COUNSEL

In representing a client, a lawyer shall not communicate about the subject of the representation with a person the lawyer knows to be represented by another lawyer in the matter, unless the lawyer has the consent of the other lawyer or is authorized to do so by law or a court order.

Comment

[1] This Rule contributes to the proper functioning of the legal system by protecting a person who has chosen to be represented by a lawyer in a matter against possible overreaching by other lawyers who are participating in the matter, interference by those lawyers with the client-lawyer relationship and the uncounselled disclosure of information relating to the representation.

[2] This Rule applies to communications with any person who is represented by counsel concerning the matter to which the communication relates.

[3] The Rule applies even though the represented person initiates or consents to the communication. A lawyer must immediately terminate communication with a person if, after commencing communication, the lawyer learns that the person is one with whom communication is not permitted by this Rule.

[4] This Rule does not prohibit communication with a represented person, or an employee or agent of such a person, concerning matters outside the representation. For example, the existence of a controversy between a government agency and a private party, or between two organizations, does not prohibit a lawyer for either from communicating with nonlawyer representatives of the other regarding a separate matter. Nor does this Rule preclude communication with a represented person who is seeking advice from a lawyer who is not otherwise representing a client in the matter. A lawyer may not make a communication prohibited by this Rule through the acts of another. See Rule 8.4(a). Parties to a matter may communicate directly with each other, and a lawyer is not prohibited from advising a client concerning a communication that the client is legally entitled to make. Also, a lawyer having independent justification or legal authorization for communicating with a represented person is permitted to do so.

[5] Communications authorized by law may include communications by a lawyer on behalf of a client who is exercising a constitutional or other legal right to communicate with the government. Communications autho-

rized by law may also include investigative activities of lawyers representing governmental entities, directly or through investigative agents, prior to the commencement of criminal or civil enforcement proceedings. When communicating with the accused in a criminal matter, a government lawyer must comply with this Rule in addition to honoring the constitutional rights of the accused. The fact that a communication does not violate a state or federal constitutional right is insufficient to establish that the communication is permissible under this Rule.

[6] A lawyer who is uncertain whether a communication with a represented person is permissible may seek a court order. A lawyer may also seek a court order in exceptional circumstances to authorize a communication that would otherwise be prohibited by this Rule, for example, where communication with a person represented by counsel is necessary to avoid reasonably certain injury.

[7] In the case of a represented organization, this Rule prohibits communications with a constituent of the organization who supervises, directs or regularly consults with the organization's lawyer concerning the matter or has authority to obligate the organization with respect to the matter or whose act or omission in connection with the matter may be imputed to the organization for purposes of civil or criminal liability. Consent of the organization's lawyer is not required for communication with a former constituent. If a constituent of the organization is represented in the matter by his or her own counsel, the consent by that counsel to a communication will be sufficient for purposes of this Rule. Compare Rule 3.4(f). In communicating with a current or former constituent of an organization, a lawyer must not use methods of obtaining evidence that violate the legal rights of the organization. See Rule 4.4.

[8] The prohibition on communications with a represented person only applies in circumstances where the lawyer knows that the person is in fact represented in the matter to be discussed. This means that the lawyer has actual knowledge of the fact of the representation; but such actual knowledge may be inferred from the circumstances. See Rule 1.0(f). Thus, the lawyer cannot evade the requirement of obtaining the consent of counsel by closing eyes to the obvious.

[9] In the event the person with whom the lawyer communicates is not known to be represented by counsel in the matter, the lawyer's communications are subject to Rule 4.3.

Definitional Cross-References

"Knows" *See* Rule 1.0(f)

RULE 4.3: DEALING WITH UNREPRESENTED PERSON

In dealing on behalf of a client with a person who is not represented by counsel, a lawyer shall not state or imply that the lawyer is disinterested. When the lawyer knows or reasonably should know that the unrepresented person misunderstands the lawyer's role in the matter, the lawyer shall make reasonable efforts to correct the misunderstanding. The lawyer shall not give legal advice to an unrepresented person, other than the advice to secure counsel, if the lawyer knows or reasonably should know that the interests of such a person are or have a reasonable possibility of being in conflict with the interests of the client.

Comment

[1] An unrepresented person, particularly one not experienced in dealing with legal matters, might assume that a lawyer is disinterested in loyalties or is a disinterested authority on the law even when the lawyer represents a client. In order to avoid a misunderstanding, a lawyer will typically need to identify the lawyer's client and, where necessary, explain that the client has interests opposed to those of the unrepresented person. For misunderstandings that sometimes arise when a lawyer for an organization deals with an unrepresented constituent, see Rule 1.13(f).

[2] The Rule distinguishes between situations involving unrepresented persons whose interests may be adverse to those of the lawyer's client and those in which the person's interests are not in conflict with the client's. In the former situation, the possibility that the lawyer will compromise the unrepresented person's interests is so great that the Rule prohibits the giving of any advice, apart from the advice to obtain counsel. Whether a lawyer is giving impermissible advice may depend on the experience and sophistication of the unrepresented person, as well as the setting in which the behavior and comments occur. This Rule does not prohibit a lawyer from negotiating the terms of a transaction or settling a dispute with an unrepresented person. So long as the lawyer has explained that the lawyer represents an adverse party and is not representing the person, the lawyer may inform the person of the terms on which the lawyer's client will enter into an agreement or settle a matter, prepare documents that require the person's signature and explain the lawyer's own view of the meaning of the document or the lawyer's view of the underlying legal obligations.

Definitional Cross-References

"Knows" *See* Rule 1.0(f)

"Reasonable" *See* Rule 1.0(h)

"Reasonably should know" *See* Rule 1.0(j)

RULE 4.4: RESPECT FOR RIGHTS OF THIRD PERSONS

(a) In representing a client, a lawyer shall not use means that have no substantial purpose other than to embarrass, delay, or burden a third person, or use methods of obtaining evidence that violate the legal rights of such a person.

(b) A lawyer who receives a document or electronically stored information relating to the representation of the lawyer's client and knows or reasonably should know that the document or electronically stored information was inadvertently sent shall promptly notify the sender.

Comment

[1] Responsibility to a client requires a lawyer to subordinate the interests of others to those of the client, but that responsibility does not imply that a lawyer may disregard the rights of third persons. It is impractical to catalogue all such rights, but they include legal restrictions on methods of obtaining evidence from third persons and unwarranted intrusions into privileged relationships, such as the client-lawyer relationship.

[2] Paragraph (b) recognizes that lawyers sometimes receive a document or electronically stored information that was mistakenly sent or produced by opposing parties or their lawyers. A document or electronically stored information is inadvertently sent when it is accidentally transmitted, such as when an email or letter is misaddressed or a document or electronically stored information is accidentally included with information that was intentionally transmitted. If a lawyer knows or reasonably should know that such a document or electronically stored information was sent inadvertently, then this Rule requires the lawyer to promptly notify the sender in order to permit that person to take protective measures. Whether the lawyer is required to take additional steps, such as returning the document or deleting electronically stored information, is a matter of law beyond the scope of these Rules, as is the question of whether the privileged status of a document or electronically stored information has been waived. Similarly, this Rule does not address the legal duties of a lawyer who receives a document or electronically stored information that the lawyer knows or reason-

ably should know may have been inappropriately obtained by the sending person. For purposes of this Rule, "document or electronically stored information" includes, in addition to paper documents, email and other forms of electronically stored information, including embedded data (commonly referred to as "metadata"), that is subject to being read or put into readable form. Metadata in electronic documents creates an obligation under this Rule only if the receiving lawyer knows or reasonably should know that the metadata was inadvertently sent to the receiving lawyer.

[3] Some lawyers may choose to return a document or delete electronically stored information unread, for example, when the lawyer learns before receiving it that it was inadvertently sent. Where a lawyer is not required by applicable law to do so, the decision to voluntarily return such a document or delete electronically stored information is a matter of professional judgment ordinarily reserved to the lawyer. See Rules 1.2 and 1.4.

Definitional Cross-References
"Knows" *See* Rule 1.0(f)
"Reasonably should know" *See* Rule 1.0(j)
"Substantial" *See* Rule 1.0(l)

LAW FIRMS AND ASSOCIATIONS

RULE 5.1: RESPONSIBILITIES OF PARTNERS, MANAGERS, AND SUPERVISORY LAWYERS

(a) A partner in a law firm, and a lawyer who individually or together with other lawyers possesses comparable managerial authority in a law firm, shall make reasonable efforts to ensure that the firm has in effect measures giving reasonable assurance that all lawyers in the firm conform to the Rules of Professional Conduct.

(b) A lawyer having direct supervisory authority over another lawyer shall make reasonable efforts to ensure that the other lawyer conforms to the Rules of Professional Conduct.

(c) A lawyer shall be responsible for another lawyer's violation of the Rules of Professional Conduct if:

(1) the lawyer orders or, with knowledge of the specific conduct, ratifies the conduct involved; or

(2) the lawyer is a partner or has comparable managerial authority in the law firm in which the other lawyer practices, or has direct supervisory authority over the other lawyer, and knows of the conduct at a time when its consequences can be avoided or mitigated but fails to take reasonable remedial action.

ABA Model Rules of Professional Conduct

Comment

[1] Paragraph (a) applies to lawyers who have managerial authority over the professional work of a firm. See Rule 1.0(c). This includes members of a partnership, the shareholders in a law firm organized as a professional corporation, and members of other associations authorized to practice law; lawyers having comparable managerial authority in a legal services organization or a law department of an enterprise or government agency; and lawyers who have intermediate managerial responsibilities in a firm. Paragraph (b) applies to lawyers who have supervisory authority over the work of other lawyers in a firm.

[2] Paragraph (a) requires lawyers with managerial authority within a firm to make reasonable efforts to establish internal policies and procedures designed to provide reasonable assurance that all lawyers in the firm will conform to the Rules of Professional Conduct. Such policies and procedures include those designed to detect and resolve conflicts of interest, identify dates by which actions must be taken in pending matters, account for client funds and property and ensure that inexperienced lawyers are properly supervised.

[3] Other measures that may be required to fulfill the responsibility prescribed in paragraph (a) can depend on the firm's structure and the nature of its practice. In a small firm of experienced lawyers, informal supervision and periodic review of compliance with the required systems ordinarily will suffice. In a large firm, or in practice situations in which difficult ethical problems frequently arise, more elaborate measures may be necessary. Some firms, for example, have a procedure whereby junior lawyers can make confidential referral of ethical problems directly to a designated senior partner or special committee. See Rule 5.2. Firms, whether large or small, may also rely on continuing legal education in professional ethics. In any event, the ethical atmosphere of a firm can influence the conduct of all its members, and the partners may not assume that all lawyers associated with the firm will inevitably conform to the Rules.

[4] Paragraph (c) expresses a general principle of personal responsibility for acts of another. See also Rule 8.4(a).

[5] Paragraph (c)(2) defines the duty of a partner or other lawyer having comparable managerial authority in a law firm, as well as a lawyer who has direct supervisory authority over performance of specific legal work by another lawyer. Whether a lawyer has supervisory authority in particular circumstances is a question of fact. Partners and lawyers with comparable authority have at least indirect responsibility for all work being done by the firm, while a partner or manager in charge of a particular matter ordinarily also has supervisory responsibility for the work of other firm lawyers

engaged in the matter. Appropriate remedial action by a partner or manag-ing lawyer would depend on the immediacy of that lawyer's involvement and the seriousness of the misconduct. A supervisor is required to intervene to prevent avoidable consequences of misconduct if the supervisor knows that the misconduct occurred. Thus, if a supervising lawyer knows that a subordinate misrepresented a matter to an opposing party in negotiation, the supervisor as well as the subordinate has a duty to correct the resulting misapprehension.

[6] Professional misconduct by a lawyer under supervision could re-veal a violation of paragraph (b) on the part of the supervisory lawyer even though it does not entail a violation of paragraph (c) because there was no direction, ratification or knowledge of the violation.

[7] Apart from this Rule and Rule 8.4(a), a lawyer does not have dis-ciplinary liability for the conduct of a partner, associate or subordinate. Whether a lawyer may be liable civilly or criminally for another lawyer's conduct is a question of law beyond the scope of these Rules.

[8] The duties imposed by this Rule on managing and supervising law-yers do not alter the personal duty of each lawyer in a firm to abide by the Rules of Professional Conduct. See Rule 5.2(a).

Definitional Cross-References
"Firm" and "Law firm" *See* Rule 1.0(c)
"Knows" *See* Rule 1.0(f)
"Partner" *See* Rule 1.0(g)
"Reasonable" *See* Rule 1.0(h)

RULE 5.2: RESPONSIBILITIES OF A SUBORDINATE LAWYER

(a) A lawyer is bound by the Rules of Professional Conduct notwithstanding that the lawyer acted at the direction of another person.

(b) A subordinate lawyer does not violate the Rules of Professional Conduct if that lawyer acts in accordance with a supervisory lawyer's reasonable resolution of an arguable question of professional duty.

Comment
[1] Although a lawyer is not relieved of responsibility for a violation by the fact that the lawyer acted at the direction of a supervisor, that fact may be relevant in determining whether a lawyer had the knowledge required to

render conduct a violation of the Rules. For example, if a subordinate filed a frivolous pleading at the direction of a supervisor, the subordinate would not be guilty of a professional violation unless the subordinate knew of the document's frivolous character.

[2] When lawyers in a supervisor-subordinate relationship encounter a matter involving professional judgment as to ethical duty, the supervisor may assume responsibility for making the judgment. Otherwise a consistent course of action or position could not be taken. If the question can reasonably be answered only one way, the duty of both lawyers is clear and they are equally responsible for fulfilling it. However, if the question is reasonably arguable, someone has to decide upon the course of action. That authority ordinarily reposes in the supervisor, and a subordinate may be guided accordingly. For example, if a question arises whether the interests of two clients conflict under Rule 1.7, the supervisor's reasonable resolution of the question should protect the subordinate professionally if the resolution is subsequently challenged.

Definitional Cross-References

"Reasonable" *See* Rule 1.0(h)

RULE 5.3: RESPONSIBILITIES REGARDING NONLAWYER ASSISTANCE

With respect to a nonlawyer employed or retained by or associated with a lawyer:

(a) a partner, and a lawyer who individually or together with other lawyers possesses comparable managerial authority in a law firm shall make reasonable efforts to ensure that the firm has in effect measures giving reasonable assurance that the person's conduct is compatible with the professional obligations of the lawyer;

(b) a lawyer having direct supervisory authority over the nonlawyer shall make reasonable efforts to ensure that the person's conduct is compatible with the professional obligations of the lawyer; and

(c) a lawyer shall be responsible for conduct of such a person that would be a violation of the Rules of Professional Conduct if engaged in by a lawyer if:

(1) the lawyer orders or, with the knowledge of the specific conduct, ratifies the conduct involved; or

(2) the lawyer is a partner or has comparable managerial

authority in the law firm in which the person is employed, or has direct supervisory authority over the person, and knows of the conduct at a time when its consequences can be avoided or mitigated but fails to take reasonable remedial action.

Comment

[1] Paragraph (a) requires lawyers with managerial authority within a law firm to make reasonable efforts to ensure that the firm has in effect measures giving reasonable assurance that nonlawyers in the firm and nonlawyers outside the firm who work on firm matters act in a way compatible with the professional obligations of the lawyer. See Comment [6] to Rule 1.1 (retaining lawyers outside the firm) and Comment [1] to Rule 5.1 (responsibilities with respect to lawyers within a firm). Paragraph (b) applies to lawyers who have supervisory authority over such nonlawyers within or outside the firm. Paragraph (c) specifies the circumstances in which a lawyer is responsible for the conduct of such nonlawyers within or outside the firm that would be a violation of the Rules of Professional Conduct if engaged in by a lawyer.

Nonlawyers Within the Firm

[2] Lawyers generally employ assistants in their practice, including secretaries, investigators, law student interns, and paraprofessionals. Such assistants, whether employees or independent contractors, act for the lawyer in rendition of the lawyer's professional services. A lawyer must give such assistants appropriate instruction and supervision concerning the ethical aspects of their employment, particularly regarding the obligation not to disclose information relating to representation of the client, and should be responsible for their work product. The measures employed in supervising nonlawyers should take account of the fact that they do not have legal training and are not subject to professional discipline.

Nonlawyers Outside the Firm

[3] A lawyer may use nonlawyers outside the firm to assist the lawyer in rendering legal services to the client. Examples include the retention of an investigative or paraprofessional service, hiring a document management company to create and maintain a database for complex litigation, sending client documents to a third party for printing or scanning, and using an Internet-based service to store client information. When using such services outside the firm, a lawyer must make reasonable efforts to ensure that the services are provided in a manner that is compatible with the lawyer's pro-

fessional obligations. The extent of this obligation will depend upon the circumstances, including the education, experience and reputation of the nonlawyer; the nature of the services involved; the terms of any arrangements concerning the protection of client information; and the legal and ethical environments of the jurisdictions in which the services will be performed, particularly with regard to confidentiality. See also Rules 1.1 (competence), 1.2 (allocation of authority), 1.4 (communication with client), 1.6 (confidentiality), 5.4(a) (professional independence of the lawyer), and 5.5(a) (unauthorized practice of law). When retaining or directing a nonlawyer outside the firm, a lawyer should communicate directions appropriate under the circumstances to give reasonable assurance that the nonlawyer's conduct is compatible with the professional obligations of the lawyer.

[4] Where the client directs the selection of a particular nonlawyer service provider outside the firm, the lawyer ordinarily should agree with the client concerning the allocation of responsibility for monitoring as between the client and the lawyer. See Rule 1.2. When making such an allocation in a matter pending before a tribunal, lawyers and parties may have additional obligations that are a matter of law beyond the scope of these Rules.

Definitional Cross-References

"Firm" and "Law firm" *See* Rule 1.0(c)

"Knows" *See* Rule 1.0(f)

"Partner" *See* Rule 1.0(g)

"Reasonable" *See* Rule 1.0(h)

RULE 5.4: PROFESSIONAL INDEPENDENCE OF A LAWYER

(a) A lawyer or law firm shall not share legal fees with a nonlawyer, except that:

(1) an agreement by a lawyer with the lawyer's firm, partner, or associate may provide for the payment of money, over a reasonable period of time after the lawyer's death, to the lawyer's estate or to one or more specified persons;

(2) a lawyer who purchases the practice of a deceased, disabled, or disappeared lawyer may, pursuant to the provisions of Rule 1.17, pay to the estate or other representative of that lawyer the agreed-upon purchase price;

(3) a lawyer or law firm may include nonlawyer employees in a compensation or retirement plan, even though the plan is based in whole or in part on a profit-sharing arrangement; and

(4) a lawyer may share court-awarded legal fees with a nonprofit organization that employed, retained or recommended employment of the lawyer in the matter.

(b) A lawyer shall not form a partnership with a nonlawyer if any of the activities of the partnership consist of the practice of law.

(c) A lawyer shall not permit a person who recommends, employs, or pays the lawyer to render legal services for another to direct or regulate the lawyer's professional judgment in rendering such legal services.

(d) A lawyer shall not practice with or in the form of a professional corporation or association authorized to practice law for a profit, if:

(1) a nonlawyer owns any interest therein, except that a fiduciary representative of the estate of a lawyer may hold the stock or interest of the lawyer for a reasonable time during administration;

(2) a nonlawyer is a corporate director or officer thereof or occupies the position of similar responsibility in any form of association other than a corporation; or

(3) a nonlawyer has the right to direct or control the professional judgment of a lawyer.

Comment

[1] The provisions of this Rule express traditional limitations on sharing fees. These limitations are to protect the lawyer's professional independence of judgment. Where someone other than the client pays the lawyer's fee or salary, or recommends employment of the lawyer, that arrangement does not modify the lawyer's obligation to the client. As stated in paragraph (c), such arrangements should not interfere with the lawyer's professional judgment.

[2] This Rule also expresses traditional limitations on permitting a third party to direct or regulate the lawyer's professional judgment in rendering legal services to another. See also Rule 1.8(f) (lawyer may accept compensation from a third party as long as there is no interference with the lawyer's independent professional judgment and the client gives informed consent).

Definitional Cross-References

"Firm" and "Law firm" *See* Rule 1.0(c)
"Partner" *See* Rule 1.0(g)

RULE 5.5: UNAUTHORIZED PRACTICE OF LAW; MULTIJURISDICTIONAL PRACTICE OF LAW

(a) A lawyer shall not practice law in a jurisdiction in violation of the regulation of the legal profession in that jurisdiction, or assist another in doing so.

(b) A lawyer who is not admitted to practice in this jurisdiction shall not:

(1) except as authorized by these Rules or other law, establish an office or other systematic and continuous presence in this jurisdiction for the practice of law; or

(2) hold out to the public or otherwise represent that the lawyer is admitted to practice law in this jurisdiction.

(c) A lawyer admitted in another United States jurisdiction, and not disbarred or suspended from practice in any jurisdiction, may provide legal services on a temporary basis in this jurisdiction that:

(1) are undertaken in association with a lawyer who is admitted to practice in this jurisdiction and who actively participates in the matter;

(2) are in or reasonably related to a pending or potential proceeding before a tribunal in this or another jurisdiction, if the lawyer, or a person the lawyer is assisting, is authorized by law or order to appear in such proceeding or reasonably expects to be so authorized;

(3) are in or reasonably related to a pending or potential arbitration, mediation, or other alternative dispute resolution proceeding in this or another jurisdiction, if the services arise out of or are reasonably related to the lawyer's practice in a jurisdiction in which the lawyer is admitted to practice and are not services for which the forum requires pro hac vice admission; or

(4) are not within paragraphs (c)(2) or (c)(3) and arise out of or are reasonably related to the lawyer's practice in a jurisdiction in which the lawyer is admitted to practice.

(d) A lawyer admitted in another United States jurisdiction or in a foreign jurisdiction, and not disbarred or suspended from practice in any jurisdiction or the equivalent thereof, or a person otherwise lawfully practicing as an in-house counsel under the laws of a foreign jurisdiction, may provide legal services through an office or other systematic and continuous presence in this jurisdiction that:

(1) are provided to the lawyer's employer or its organizational affiliates; are not services for which the forum requires pro hac

vice admission; and, when performed by a foreign lawyer and requires advice on the law of this or another jurisdiction or of the United States, such advice shall be based upon the advice of a lawyer who is duly licensed and authorized by the jurisdiction to provide such advice; or

(2) are services that the lawyer is authorized by federal law or other law or rule to provide in this jurisdiction.

(e) For purposes of paragraph (d):

(1) the foreign lawyer must be a member in good standing of a recognized legal profession in a foreign jurisdiction, the members of which are admitted to practice as lawyers or counselors at law or the equivalent, and subject to effective regulation and discipline by a duly constituted professional body or a public authority; or

(2) the person otherwise lawfully practicing as an in-house counsel under the laws of a foreign jurisdiction must be authorized to practice under this rule by, in the exercise of its discretion, [the highest court of this jurisdiction].

Comment

[1] A lawyer may practice law only in a jurisdiction in which the lawyer is authorized to practice. A lawyer may be admitted to practice law in a jurisdiction on a regular basis or may be authorized by court rule or order or by law to practice for a limited purpose or on a restricted basis. Paragraph (a) applies to unauthorized practice of law by a lawyer, whether through the lawyer's direct action or by the lawyer assisting another person. For example, a lawyer may not assist a person in practicing law in violation of the rules governing professional conduct in that person's jurisdiction.

[2] The definition of the practice of law is established by law and varies from one jurisdiction to another. Whatever the definition, limiting the practice of law to members of the bar protects the public against rendition of legal services by unqualified persons. This Rule does not prohibit a lawyer from employing the services of paraprofessionals and delegating functions to them, so long as the lawyer supervises the delegated work and retains responsibility for their work. See Rule 5.3.

[3] A lawyer may provide professional advice and instruction to nonlawyers whose employment requires knowledge of the law; for example, claims adjusters, employees of financial or commercial institutions, social workers, accountants and persons employed in government agencies. Lawyers also may assist independent nonlawyers, such as paraprofessionals, who are authorized by the law of a jurisdiction to provide particular law-related services. In addition, a lawyer may counsel nonlawyers who wish to proceed pro se.

ABA Model
Rules of
Professional
Conduct

[4] Other than as authorized by law or this Rule, a lawyer who is not admitted to practice generally in this jurisdiction violates paragraph (b)(1) if the lawyer establishes an office or other systematic and continuous presence in this jurisdiction for the practice of law. Presence may be systematic and continuous even if the lawyer is not physically present here. Such a lawyer must not hold out to the public or otherwise represent that the lawyer is admitted to practice law in this jurisdiction. See also Rules 7.1(a) and 7.5(b).

[5] There are occasions in which a lawyer admitted to practice in another United States jurisdiction, and not disbarred or suspended from practice in any jurisdiction, may provide legal services on a temporary basis in this jurisdiction under circumstances that do not create an unreasonable risk to the interests of their clients, the public or the courts. Paragraph (c) identifies four such circumstances. The fact that conduct is not so identified does not imply that the conduct is or is not authorized. With the exception of paragraphs (d)(1) and (d)(2), this Rule does not authorize a U.S. or foreign lawyer to establish an office or other systematic and continuous presence in this jurisdiction without being admitted to practice generally here.

[6] There is no single test to determine whether a lawyer's services are provided on a "temporary basis" in this jurisdiction, and may therefore be permissible under paragraph (c). Services may be "temporary" even though the lawyer provides services in this jurisdiction on a recurring basis, or for an extended period of time, as when the lawyer is representing a client in a single lengthy negotiation or litigation.

[7] Paragraphs (c) and (d) apply to lawyers who are admitted to practice law in any United States jurisdiction, which includes the District of Columbia and any state, territory or commonwealth of the United States. Paragraph (d) also applies to lawyers admitted in a foreign jurisdiction. The word "admitted" in paragraphs (c), (d) and (e) contemplates that the lawyer is authorized to practice in the jurisdiction in which the lawyer is admitted and excludes a lawyer who while technically admitted is not authorized to practice, because, for example, the lawyer is on inactive status.

[8] Paragraph (c)(1) recognizes that the interests of clients and the public are protected if a lawyer admitted only in another jurisdiction associates with a lawyer licensed to practice in this jurisdiction. For this paragraph to apply, however, the lawyer admitted to practice in this jurisdiction must actively participate in and share responsibility for the representation of the client.

[9] Lawyers not admitted to practice generally in a jurisdiction may be authorized by law or order of a tribunal or an administrative agency to appear before the tribunal or agency. This authority may be granted pursuant to formal rules governing admission pro hac vice or pursuant to informal practice of the tribunal or agency. Under paragraph (c)(2), a lawyer does not violate this Rule when the lawyer appears before a tribunal or agency pur-

suant to such authority. To the extent that a court rule or other law of this jurisdiction requires a lawyer who is not admitted to practice in this jurisdiction to obtain admission pro hac vice before appearing before a tribunal or administrative agency, this Rule requires the lawyer to obtain that authority.

[10] Paragraph (c)(2) also provides that a lawyer rendering services in this jurisdiction on a temporary basis does not violate this Rule when the lawyer engages in conduct in anticipation of a proceeding or hearing in a jurisdiction in which the lawyer is authorized to practice law or in which the lawyer reasonably expects to be admitted pro hac vice. Examples of such conduct include meetings with the client, interviews of potential witnesses, and the review of documents. Similarly, a lawyer admitted only in another jurisdiction may engage in conduct temporarily in this jurisdiction in connection with pending litigation in another jurisdiction in which the lawyer is or reasonably expects to be authorized to appear, including taking depositions in this jurisdiction.

[11] When a lawyer has been or reasonably expects to be admitted to appear before a court or administrative agency, paragraph (c)(2) also permits conduct by lawyers who are associated with that lawyer in the matter, but who do not expect to appear before the court or administrative agency. For example, subordinate lawyers may conduct research, review documents, and attend meetings with witnesses in support of the lawyer responsible for the litigation.

[12] Paragraph (c)(3) permits a lawyer admitted to practice law in another jurisdiction to perform services on a temporary basis in this jurisdiction if those services are in or reasonably related to a pending or potential arbitration, mediation, or other alternative dispute resolution proceeding in this or another jurisdiction, if the services arise out of or are reasonably related to the lawyer's practice in a jurisdiction in which the lawyer is admitted to practice. The lawyer, however, must obtain admission pro hac vice in the case of a court-annexed arbitration or mediation or otherwise if court rules or law so require.

[13] Paragraph (c)(4) permits a lawyer admitted in another jurisdiction to provide certain legal services on a temporary basis in this jurisdiction that arise out of or are reasonably related to the lawyer's practice in a jurisdiction in which the lawyer is admitted but are not within paragraphs (c)(2) or (c)(3). These services include both legal services and services that non-lawyers may perform but that are considered the practice of law when performed by lawyers.

[14] Paragraphs (c)(3) and (c)(4) require that the services arise out of or be reasonably related to the lawyer's practice in a jurisdiction in which the lawyer is admitted. A variety of factors evidence such a relationship. The lawyer's client may have been previously represented by the lawyer, or may

be resident in or have substantial contacts with the jurisdiction in which the lawyer is admitted. The matter, although involving other jurisdictions, may have a significant connection with that jurisdiction. In other cases, significant aspects of the lawyer's work might be conducted in that jurisdiction or a significant aspect of the matter may involve the law of that jurisdiction. The necessary relationship might arise when the client's activities or the legal issues involve multiple jurisdictions, such as when the officers of a multinational corporation survey potential business sites and seek the services of their lawyer in assessing the relative merits of each. In addition, the services may draw on the lawyer's recognized expertise developed through the regular practice of law on behalf of clients in matters involving a particular body of federal, nationally-uniform, foreign, or international law. Lawyers desiring to provide pro bono legal services on a temporary basis in a jurisdiction that has been affected by a major disaster, but in which they are not otherwise authorized to practice law, as well as lawyers from the affected jurisdiction who seek to practice law temporarily in another jurisdiction, but in which they are not otherwise authorized to practice law, should consult the [*Model Court Rule on Provision of Legal Services Following Determination of Major Disaster*].

[15] Paragraph (d) identifies two circumstances in which a lawyer who is admitted to practice in another United States or a foreign jurisdiction, and is not disbarred or suspended from practice in any jurisdiction, or the equivalent thereof, may establish an office or other systematic and continuous presence in this jurisdiction for the practice of law. Pursuant to paragraph (c) of this Rule, a lawyer admitted in any U.S. jurisdiction may also provide legal services in this jurisdiction on a temporary basis. See also *Model Rule on Temporary Practice by Foreign Lawyers*. Except as provided in paragraphs (d)(1) and (d)(2), a lawyer who is admitted to practice law in another United States or foreign jurisdiction and who establishes an office or other systematic or continuous presence in this jurisdiction must become admitted to practice law generally in this jurisdiction.

[16] Paragraph (d)(1) applies to a U.S. or foreign lawyer who is employed by a client to provide legal services to the client or its organizational affiliates, i.e., entities that control, are controlled by, or are under common control with the employer. This paragraph does not authorize the provision of personal legal services to the employer's officers or employees. The paragraph applies to in-house corporate lawyers, government lawyers and others who are employed to render legal services to the employer. The lawyer's ability to represent the employer outside the jurisdiction in which the lawyer is licensed generally serves the interests of the employer and does not create an unreasonable risk to the client and others because the employer

is well situated to assess the lawyer's qualifications and the quality of the lawyer's work. To further decrease any risk to the client, when advising on the domestic law of a United States jurisdiction or on the law of the United States, the foreign lawyer authorized to practice under paragraph (d)(1) of this Rule needs to base that advice on the advice of a lawyer licensed and authorized by the jurisdiction to provide it.

[17] If an employed lawyer establishes an office or other systematic presence in this jurisdiction for the purpose of rendering legal services to the employer, the lawyer may be subject to registration or other requirements, including assessments for client protection funds and mandatory continuing legal education. See *Model Rule for Registration of In-House Counsel.*

[18] Paragraph (d)(2) recognizes that a U.S. or foreign lawyer may provide legal services in a jurisdiction in which the lawyer is not licensed when authorized to do so by federal or other law, which includes statute, court rule, executive regulation or judicial precedent. See, e.g., *Model Rule on Practice Pending Admission.*

[19] A lawyer who practices law in this jurisdiction pursuant to paragraphs (c) or (d) or otherwise is subject to the disciplinary authority of this jurisdiction. See Rule 8.5(a).

[20] In some circumstances, a lawyer who practices law in this jurisdiction pursuant to paragraphs (c) or (d) may have to inform the client that the lawyer is not licensed to practice law in this jurisdiction. For example, that may be required when the representation occurs primarily in this jurisdiction and requires knowledge of the law of this jurisdiction. See Rule 1.4(b).

[21] Paragraphs (c) and (d) do not authorize communications advertising legal services in this jurisdiction by lawyers who are admitted to practice in other jurisdictions. Whether and how lawyers may communicate the availability of their services in this jurisdiction is governed by Rules 7.1 to 7.5.

Definitional Cross-References

"Reasonably" *See* Rule 1.0(h)
"Tribunal" *See* Rule 1.0(m)

RULE 5.6: RESTRICTIONS ON RIGHT TO PRACTICE

A lawyer shall not participate in offering or making:
(a) a partnership, shareholders, operating, employment, or other similar type of agreement that restricts the right of a lawyer to practice after termination of the relationship, except an agreement concerning benefits upon retirement; or

ABA Model Rules of Professional Conduct

(b) an agreement in which a restriction on the lawyer's right to practice is part of the settlement of a client controversy.

Comment

[1] An agreement restricting the right of lawyers to practice after leaving a firm not only limits their professional autonomy but also limits the freedom of clients to choose a lawyer. Paragraph (a) prohibits such agreements except for restrictions incident to provisions concerning retirement benefits for service with the firm.

[2] Paragraph (b) prohibits a lawyer from agreeing not to represent other persons in connection with settling a claim on behalf of a client.

[3] This Rule does not apply to prohibit restrictions that may be included in the terms of the sale of a law practice pursuant to Rule 1.17.

RULE 5.7: RESPONSIBILITIES REGARDING LAW-RELATED SERVICES

(a) A lawyer shall be subject to the Rules of Professional Conduct with respect to the provision of law-related services, as defined in paragraph (b), if the law-related services are provided:

(1) by the lawyer in circumstances that are not distinct from the lawyer's provision of legal services to clients; or

(2) in other circumstances by an entity controlled by the lawyer individually or with others if the lawyer fails to take reasonable measures to assure that a person obtaining the law-related services knows that the services are not legal services and that the protections of the client-lawyer relationship do not exist.

(b) The term "law-related services" denotes services that might reasonably be performed in conjunction with and in substance are related to the provision of legal services, and that are not prohibited as unauthorized practice of law when provided by a nonlawyer.

Comment

[1] When a lawyer performs law-related services or controls an organization that does so, there exists the potential for ethical problems. Principal among these is the possibility that the person for whom the law-related services are performed fails to understand that the services may not carry with them the protections normally afforded as part of the client-lawyer relationship. The recipient of the law-related services may expect, for example, that the protection of client confidences, prohibitions against representation of

persons with conflicting interests, and obligations of a lawyer to maintain professional independence apply to the provision of law-related services when that may not be the case.

[2] Rule 5.7 applies to the provision of law-related services by a lawyer even when the lawyer does not provide any legal services to the person for whom the law-related services are performed and whether the law-related services are performed through a law firm or a separate entity. The Rule identifies the circumstances in which all of the Rules of Professional Conduct apply to the provision of law-related services. Even when those circumstances do not exist, however, the conduct of a lawyer involved in the provision of law-related services is subject to those Rules that apply generally to lawyer conduct, regardless of whether the conduct involves the provision of legal services. See, e.g., Rule 8.4.

[3] When law-related services are provided by a lawyer under circumstances that are not distinct from the lawyer's provision of legal services to clients, the lawyer in providing the law-related services must adhere to the requirements of the Rules of Professional Conduct as provided in paragraph (a)(1). Even when the law-related and legal services are provided in circumstances that are distinct from each other, for example through separate entities or different support staff within the law firm, the Rules of Professional Conduct apply to the lawyer as provided in paragraph (a)(2) unless the lawyer takes reasonable measures to assure that the recipient of the law-related services knows that the services are not legal services and that the protections of the client-lawyer relationship do not apply.

[4] Law-related services also may be provided through an entity that is distinct from that through which the lawyer provides legal services. If the lawyer individually or with others has control of such an entity's operations, the Rule requires the lawyer to take reasonable measures to assure that each person using the services of the entity knows that the services provided by the entity are not legal services and that the Rules of Professional Conduct that relate to the client-lawyer relationship do not apply. A lawyer's control of an entity extends to the ability to direct its operation. Whether a lawyer has such control will depend upon the circumstances of the particular case.

[5] When a client-lawyer relationship exists with a person who is referred by a lawyer to a separate law-related service entity controlled by the lawyer, individually or with others, the lawyer must comply with Rule 1.8(a).

[6] In taking the reasonable measures referred to in paragraph (a)(2) to assure that a person using law-related services understands the practical effect or significance of the inapplicability of the Rules of Professional Conduct, the lawyer should communicate to the person receiving the law-

related services, in a manner sufficient to assure that the person understands the significance of the fact, that the relationship of the person to the
business entity will not be a client-lawyer relationship. The communication
should be made before entering into an agreement for provision of or providing law-related services, and preferably should be in writing.

[7] The burden is upon the lawyer to show that the lawyer has taken
reasonable measures under the circumstances to communicate the desired
understanding. For instance, a sophisticated user of law-related services,
such as a publicly held corporation, may require a lesser explanation than
someone unaccustomed to making distinctions between legal services and
law-related services, such as an individual seeking tax advice from a law-
yer-accountant or investigative services in connection with a lawsuit.

[8] Regardless of the sophistication of potential recipients of law-related
services, a lawyer should take special care to keep separate the provision of
law-related and legal services in order to minimize the risk that the recipient
will assume that the law-related services are legal services. The risk of such
confusion is especially acute when the lawyer renders both types of services
with respect to the same matter. Under some circumstances the legal and
law-related services may be so closely entwined that they cannot be distinguished from each other, and the requirement of disclosure and consultation imposed by paragraph (a)(2) of the Rule cannot be met. In such a case a
lawyer will be responsible for assuring that both the lawyer's conduct and,
to the extent required by Rule 5.3, that of nonlawyer employees in the distinct entity that the lawyer controls complies in all respects with the Rules of
Professional Conduct.

[9] A broad range of economic and other interests of clients may be
served by lawyers' engaging in the delivery of law-related services. Examples of law-related services include providing title insurance, financial planning, accounting, trust services, real estate counseling, legislative lobbying,
economic analysis, social work, psychological counseling, tax preparation,
and patent, medical or environmental consulting.

[10] When a lawyer is obliged to accord the recipients of such services
the protections of those Rules that apply to the client-lawyer relationship,
the lawyer must take special care to heed the proscriptions of the Rules addressing conflict of interest (Rules 1.7 through 1.11, especially Rules 1.7(a)
(2) and 1.8(a), (b) and (f)), and to scrupulously adhere to the requirements
of Rule 1.6 relating to disclosure of confidential information. The promotion
of the law-related services must also in all respects comply with Rules 7.1
through 7.3, dealing with advertising and solicitation. In that regard, lawyers should take special care to identify the obligations that may be imposed
as a result of a jurisdiction's decisional law.

[11] When the full protections of all of the Rules of Professional Conduct do not apply to the provision of law-related services, principles of law external to the Rules, for example, the law of principal and agent, govern the legal duties owed to those receiving the services. Those other legal principles may establish a different degree of protection for the recipient with respect to confidentiality of information, conflicts of interest and permissible business relationships with clients. See also Rule 8.4 (Misconduct).

Definitional Cross-References
"Knows" *See* Rule 1.0(f)
"Reasonable" *See* Rule 1.0(h)

PUBLIC SERVICE

RULE 6.1: VOLUNTARY PRO BONO PUBLICO SERVICE

Every lawyer has a professional responsibility to provide legal services to those unable to pay. A lawyer should aspire to render at least (50) hours of pro bono publico legal services per year. In fulfilling this responsibility, the lawyer should:

(a) provide a substantial majority of the (50) hours of legal services without fee or expectation of fee to:

(1) persons of limited means; or

(2) charitable, religious, civic, community, governmental and educational organizations in matters that are designed primarily to address the needs of persons of limited means; and

(b) provide any additional services through:

(1) delivery of legal services at no fee or substantially reduced fee to individuals, groups or organizations seeking to secure or protect civil rights, civil liberties or public rights, or charitable, religious, civic, community, governmental and educational organizations in matters in furtherance of their organizational purposes, where the payment of standard legal fees would significantly deplete the organization's economic resources or would be otherwise inappropriate;

(2) delivery of legal services at a substantially reduced fee to persons of limited means; or

(3) participation in activities for improving the law, the legal system or the legal profession.

In addition, a lawyer should voluntarily contribute financial support to organizations that provide legal services to persons of limited means.

ABA Model Rules of Professional Conduct

Comment

[1] Every lawyer, regardless of professional prominence or professional work load, has a responsibility to provide legal services to those unable to pay, and personal involvement in the problems of the disadvantaged can be one of the most rewarding experiences in the life of a lawyer. The American Bar Association urges all lawyers to provide a minimum of 50 hours of pro bono services annually. States, however, may decide to choose a higher or lower number of hours of annual service (which may be expressed as a percentage of a lawyer's professional time) depending upon local needs and local conditions. It is recognized that in some years a lawyer may render greater or fewer hours than the annual standard specified, but during the course of his or her legal career, each lawyer should render on average per year, the number of hours set forth in this Rule. Services can be performed in civil matters or in criminal or quasi-criminal matters for which there is no government obligation to provide funds for legal representation, such as post-conviction death penalty appeal cases.

[2] Paragraphs (a)(1) and (2) recognize the critical need for legal services that exists among persons of limited means by providing that a substantial majority of the legal services rendered annually to the disadvantaged be furnished without fee or expectation of fee. Legal services under these paragraphs consist of a full range of activities, including individual and class representation, the provision of legal advice, legislative lobbying, administrative rule making and the provision of free training or mentoring to those who represent persons of limited means. The variety of these activities should facilitate participation by government lawyers, even when restrictions exist on their engaging in the outside practice of law.

[3] Persons eligible for legal services under paragraphs (a)(1) and (2) are those who qualify for participation in programs funded by the Legal Services Corporation and those whose incomes and financial resources are slightly above the guidelines utilized by such programs but nevertheless, cannot afford counsel. Legal services can be rendered to individuals or to organizations such as homeless shelters, battered women's centers and food pantries that serve those of limited means. The term "governmental organizations" includes, but is not limited to, public protection programs and sections of governmental or public sector agencies.

[4] Because service must be provided without fee or expectation of fee, the intent of the lawyer to render free legal services is essential for the work performed to fall within the meaning of paragraphs (a)(1) and (2). Accordingly, services rendered cannot be considered pro bono if an anticipated fee is uncollected, but the award of statutory attorneys' fees in a case originally accepted as pro bono would not disqualify such services from inclusion

under this section. Lawyers who do receive fees in such cases are encouraged to contribute an appropriate portion of such fees to organizations or projects that benefit persons of limited means.

[5] While it is possible for a lawyer to fulfill the annual responsibility to perform pro bono services exclusively through activities described in paragraphs (a)(1) and (2), to the extent that any hours of service remained unfulfilled, the remaining commitment can be met in a variety of ways as set forth in paragraph (b). Constitutional, statutory or regulatory restrictions may prohibit or impede government and public sector lawyers and judges from performing the pro bono services outlined in paragraphs (a)(1) and (2). Accordingly, where those restrictions apply, government and public sector lawyers and judges may fulfill their pro bono responsibility by performing services outlined in paragraph (b).

[6] Paragraph (b)(1) includes the provision of certain types of legal services to those whose incomes and financial resources place them above limited means. It also permits the pro bono lawyer to accept a substantially reduced fee for services. Examples of the types of issues that may be addressed under this paragraph include First Amendment claims, Title VII claims and environmental protection claims. Additionally, a wide range of organizations may be represented, including social service, medical research, cultural and religious groups.

[7] Paragraph (b)(2) covers instances in which lawyers agree to and receive a modest fee for furnishing legal services to persons of limited means. Participation in judicare programs and acceptance of court appointments in which the fee is substantially below a lawyer's usual rate are encouraged under this section.

[8] Paragraph (b)(3) recognizes the value of lawyers engaging in activities that improve the law, the legal system or the legal profession. Serving on bar association committees, serving on boards of pro bono or legal services programs, taking part in Law Day activities, acting as a continuing legal education instructor, a mediator or an arbitrator and engaging in legislative lobbying to improve the law, the legal system or the profession are a few examples of the many activities that fall within this paragraph.

[9] Because the provision of pro bono services is a professional responsibility, it is the individual ethical commitment of each lawyer. Nevertheless, there may be times when it is not feasible for a lawyer to engage in pro bono services. At such times a lawyer may discharge the pro bono responsibility by providing financial support to organizations providing free legal services to persons of limited means. Such financial support should be reasonably equivalent to the value of the hours of service that would have otherwise been provided. In addition, at times it may be more feasible to

satisfy the pro bono responsibility collectively, as by a firm's aggregate pro bono activities.

[10] Because the efforts of individual lawyers are not enough to meet the need for free legal services that exists among persons of limited means, the government and the profession have instituted additional programs to provide those services. Every lawyer should financially support such programs, in addition to either providing direct pro bono services or making financial contributions when pro bono service is not feasible.

[11] Law firms should act reasonably to enable and encourage all lawyers in the firm to provide the pro bono legal services called for by this Rule.

[12] The responsibility set forth in this Rule is not intended to be enforced through disciplinary process.

Definitional Cross-References

"Substantial" *See* Rule 1.0(l)

RULE 6.2: ACCEPTING APPOINTMENTS

A lawyer shall not seek to avoid appointment by a tribunal to represent a person except for good cause, such as:

(a) representing the client is likely to result in violation of the Rules of Professional Conduct or other law;

(b) representing the client is likely to result in an unreasonable financial burden on the lawyer; or

(c) the client or the cause is so repugnant to the lawyer as to be likely to impair the client-lawyer relationship or the lawyer's ability to represent the client.

Comment

[1] A lawyer ordinarily is not obliged to accept a client whose character or cause the lawyer regards as repugnant. The lawyer's freedom to select clients is, however, qualified. All lawyers have a responsibility to assist in providing pro bono publico service. See Rule 6.1. An individual lawyer fulfills this responsibility by accepting a fair share of unpopular matters or indigent or unpopular clients. A lawyer may also be subject to appointment by a court to serve unpopular clients or persons unable to afford legal services.

Appointed Counsel

[2] For good cause a lawyer may seek to decline an appointment to represent a person who cannot afford to retain counsel or whose cause is un-

popular. Good cause exists if the lawyer could not handle the matter competently, see Rule 1.1, or if undertaking the representation would result in an improper conflict of interest, for example, when the client or the cause is so repugnant to the lawyer as to be likely to impair the client-lawyer relationship or the lawyer's ability to represent the client. A lawyer may also seek to decline an appointment if acceptance would be unreasonably burdensome, for example, when it would impose a financial sacrifice so great as to be unjust.

[3] An appointed lawyer has the same obligations to the client as retained counsel, including the obligations of loyalty and confidentiality, and is subject to the same limitations on the client-lawyer relationship, such as the obligation to refrain from assisting the client in violation of the Rules.

Definitional Cross-References

"Tribunal" *See* Rule 1.0(m)

RULE 6.3: MEMBERSHIP IN LEGAL SERVICES ORGANIZATION

A lawyer may serve as a director, officer or member of a legal services organization, apart from the law firm in which the lawyer practices, notwithstanding that the organization serves persons having interests adverse to a client of the lawyer. The lawyer shall not knowingly participate in a decision or action of the organization:

(a) if participating in the decision or action would be incompatible with the lawyer's obligations to a client under Rule 1.7; or

(b) where the decision or action could have a material adverse effect on the representation of a client of the organization whose interests are adverse to a client of the lawyer.

Comment

[1] Lawyers should be encouraged to support and participate in legal service organizations. A lawyer who is an officer or a member of such an organization does not thereby have a client-lawyer relationship with persons served by the organization. However, there is potential conflict between the interests of such persons and the interests of the lawyer's clients. If the possibility of such conflict disqualified a lawyer from serving on the board of a legal services organization, the profession's involvement in such organizations would be severely curtailed.

ABA Model
Rules of
Professional
Conduct

[2] It may be necessary in appropriate cases to reassure a client of the organization that the representation will not be affected by conflicting loyalties of a member of the board. Established, written policies in this respect can enhance the credibility of such assurances.

Definitional Cross-References

"Law firm" *See* Rule 1.0(c)

"Knowingly" *See* Rule 1.0(f)

RULE 6.4: LAW REFORM ACTIVITIES AFFECTING CLIENT INTERESTS

A lawyer may serve as a director, officer or member of an organization involved in reform of the law or its administration notwithstanding that the reform may affect the interests of a client of the lawyer. When the lawyer knows that the interests of a client may be materially benefitted by a decision in which the lawyer participates, the lawyer shall disclose that fact but need not identify the client.

Comment

[1] Lawyers involved in organizations seeking law reform generally do not have a client-lawyer relationship with the organization. Otherwise, it might follow that a lawyer could not be involved in a bar association law reform program that might indirectly affect a client. See also Rule 1.2(b). For example, a lawyer specializing in antitrust litigation might be regarded as disqualified from participating in drafting revisions of rules governing that subject. In determining the nature and scope of participation in such activities, a lawyer should be mindful of obligations to clients under other Rules, particularly Rule 1.7. A lawyer is professionally obligated to protect the integrity of the program by making an appropriate disclosure within the organization when the lawyer knows a private client might be materially benefitted.

Definitional Cross-References

"Knows" *See* Rule 1.0(f)

RULE 6.5: NONPROFIT AND COURT-ANNEXED LIMITED LEGAL SERVICES PROGRAMS

(a) A lawyer who, under the auspices of a program sponsored by a nonprofit organization or court, provides short-term limited legal

services to a client without expectation by either the lawyer or the client that the lawyer will provide continuing representation in the matter:

> (1) is subject to Rules 1.7 and 1.9(a) only if the lawyer knows that the representation of the client involves a conflict of interest; and

> (2) is subject to Rule 1.10 only if the lawyer knows that another lawyer associated with the lawyer in a law firm is disqualified by Rule 1.7 or 1.9(a) with respect to the matter.

> (b) Except as provided in paragraph (a)(2), Rule 1.10 is inapplicable to a representation governed by this Rule.

Comment

[1] Legal services organizations, courts and various nonprofit organizations have established programs through which lawyers provide short-term limited legal services—such as advice or the completion of legal forms—that will assist persons to address their legal problems without further representation by a lawyer. In these programs, such as legal-advice hotlines, advice-only clinics or pro se counseling programs, a client-lawyer relationship is established, but there is no expectation that the lawyer's representation of the client will continue beyond the limited consultation. Such programs are normally operated under circumstances in which it is not feasible for a lawyer to systematically screen for conflicts of interest as is generally required before undertaking a representation. See, e.g., Rules 1.7, 1.9 and 1.10.

[2] A lawyer who provides short-term limited legal services pursuant to this Rule must secure the client's informed consent to the limited scope of the representation. See Rule 1.2(c). If a short-term limited representation would not be reasonable under the circumstances, the lawyer may offer advice to the client but must also advise the client of the need for further assistance of counsel. Except as provided in this Rule, the Rules of Professional Conduct, including Rules 1.6 and 1.9(c), are applicable to the limited representation.

[3] Because a lawyer who is representing a client in the circumstances addressed by this Rule ordinarily is not able to check systematically for conflicts of interest, paragraph (a) requires compliance with Rules 1.7 or 1.9(a) only if the lawyer knows that the representation presents a conflict of interest for the lawyer, and with Rule 1.10 only if the lawyer knows that another lawyer in the lawyer's firm is disqualified by Rules 1.7 or 1.9(a) in the matter.

[4] Because the limited nature of the services significantly reduces the risk of conflicts of interest with other matters being handled by the law-

ABA Model
Rules of
Professional
Conduct

yer's firm, paragraph (b) provides that Rule 1.10 is inapplicable to a representation governed by this Rule except as provided by paragraph (a)(2). Paragraph (a)(2) requires the participating lawyer to comply with Rule 1.10 when the lawyer knows that the lawyer's firm is disqualified by Rules 1.7 or 1.9(a). By virtue of paragraph (b), however, a lawyer's participation in a short-term limited legal services program will not preclude the lawyer's firm from undertaking or continuing the representation of a client with interests adverse to a client being represented under the program's auspices. Nor will the personal disqualification of a lawyer participating in the program be imputed to other lawyers participating in the program.

[5] If, after commencing a short-term limited representation in accordance with this Rule, a lawyer undertakes to represent the client in the matter on an ongoing basis, Rules 1.7, 1.9(a) and 1.10 become applicable.

Definitional Cross-References

"Law firm" *See* Rule 1.0(c)
"Knows" *See* Rule 1.0(f)

INFORMATION
ABOUT LEGAL SERVICES

RULE 7.1: COMMUNICATIONS
CONCERNING A LAWYER'S SERVICES

A lawyer shall not make a false or misleading communication about the lawyer or the lawyer's services. A communication is false or misleading if it contains a material misrepresentation of fact or law, or omits a fact necessary to make the statement considered as a whole not materially misleading.

Comment

[1] This Rule governs all communications about a lawyer's services, including advertising permitted by Rule 7.2. Whatever means are used to make known a lawyer's services, statements about them must be truthful.

[2] Truthful statements that are misleading are also prohibited by this Rule. A truthful statement is misleading if it omits a fact necessary to make the lawyer's communication considered as a whole not materially misleading. A truthful statement is also misleading if there is a substantial likelihood that it will lead a reasonable person to formulate a specific conclusion about the lawyer or the lawyer's services for which there is no reasonable factual foundation.

[3] An advertisement that truthfully reports a lawyer's achievements on behalf of clients or former clients may be misleading if presented so as to lead a reasonable person to form an unjustified expectation that the same results could be obtained for other clients in similar matters without reference to the specific factual and legal circumstances of each client's case. Similarly, an unsubstantiated comparison of the lawyer's services or fees with the services or fees of other lawyers may be misleading if presented with such specificity as would lead a reasonable person to conclude that the comparison can be substantiated. The inclusion of an appropriate disclaimer or qualifying language may preclude a finding that a statement is likely to create unjustified expectations or otherwise mislead the public.

[4] See also Rule 8.4(e) for the prohibition against stating or implying an ability to influence improperly a government agency or official or to achieve results by means that violate the Rules of Professional Conduct or other law.

RULE 7.2: ADVERTISING

(a) Subject to the requirements of Rules 7.1 and 7.3, a lawyer may advertise services through written, recorded or electronic communication, including public media.

(b) A lawyer shall not give anything of value to a person for recommending the lawyer's services except that a lawyer may

(1) pay the reasonable costs of advertisements or communications permitted by this Rule;

(2) pay the usual charges of a legal service plan or a not-for-profit or qualified lawyer referral service. A qualified lawyer referral service is a lawyer referral service that has been approved by an appropriate regulatory authority;

(3) pay for a law practice in accordance with Rule 1.17; and

(4) refer clients to another lawyer or a nonlawyer professional pursuant to an agreement not otherwise prohibited under these Rules that provides for the other person to refer clients or customers to the lawyer, if:

(i) the reciprocal referral agreement is not exclusive; and

(ii) the client is informed of the existence and nature of the agreement.

(c) Any communication made pursuant to this Rule shall include the name and office address of at least one lawyer or law firm responsible for its content.

ABA Model Rules of Professional Conduct

Comment

[1] To assist the public in learning about and obtaining legal services, lawyers should be allowed to make known their services not only through reputation but also through organized information campaigns in the form of advertising. Advertising involves an active quest for clients, contrary to the tradition that a lawyer should not seek clientele. However, the public's need to know about legal services can be fulfilled in part through advertising. This need is particularly acute in the case of persons of moderate means who have not made extensive use of legal services. The interest in expanding public information about legal services ought to prevail over considerations of tradition. Nevertheless, advertising by lawyers entails the risk of practices that are misleading or overreaching.

[2] This Rule permits public dissemination of information concerning a lawyer's name or firm name, address, email address, website, and telephone number; the kinds of services the lawyer will undertake; the basis on which the lawyer's fees are determined, including prices for specific services and payment and credit arrangements; a lawyer's foreign language ability; names of references and, with their consent, names of clients regularly represented; and other information that might invite the attention of those seeking legal assistance.

[3] Questions of effectiveness and taste in advertising are matters of speculation and subjective judgment. Some jurisdictions have had extensive prohibitions against television and other forms of advertising, against advertising going beyond specified facts about a lawyer, or against "undignified" advertising. Television, the Internet, and other forms of electronic communication are now among the most powerful media for getting information to the public, particularly persons of low and moderate income; prohibiting television, Internet, and other forms of electronic advertising, therefore, would impede the flow of information about legal services to many sectors of the public. Limiting the information that may be advertised has a similar effect and assumes that the bar can accurately forecast the kind of information that the public would regard as relevant. But see Rule 7.3(a) for the prohibition against a solicitation through a real-time electronic exchange initiated by the lawyer.

[4] Neither this Rule nor Rule 7.3 prohibits communications authorized by law, such as notice to members of a class in class action litigation.

Paying Others to Recommend a Lawyer

[5] Except as permitted under paragraphs (b)(1)-(b)(4), lawyers are not permitted to pay others for recommending the lawyer's services or for channeling professional work in a manner that violates Rule 7.3. A commu-

nication contains a recommendation if it endorses or vouches for a lawyer's credentials, abilities, competence, character, or other professional qualities. Paragraph (b)(1), however, allows a lawyer to pay for advertising and communications permitted by this Rule, including the costs of print directory listings, on-line directory listings, newspaper ads, television and radio airtime, domain-name registrations, sponsorship fees, Internet-based advertisements, and group advertising. A lawyer may compensate employees, agents and vendors who are engaged to provide marketing or client development services, such as publicists, public-relations personnel, business-development staff and website designers. Moreover, a lawyer may pay others for generating client leads, such as Internet-based client leads, as long as the lead generator does not recommend the lawyer, any payment to the lead generator is consistent with Rules 1.5(e) (division of fees) and 5.4 (professional independence of the lawyer), and the lead generator's communications are consistent with Rule 7.1 (communications concerning a lawyer's services). To comply with Rule 7.1, a lawyer must not pay a lead generator that states, implies, or creates a reasonable impression that it is recommending the lawyer, is making the referral without payment from the lawyer, or has analyzed a person's legal problems when determining which lawyer should receive the referral. See also Rule 5.3 (duties of lawyers and law firms with respect to the conduct of nonlawyers); Rule 8.4(a) (duty to avoid violating the Rules through the acts of another).

[6] A lawyer may pay the usual charges of a legal service plan or a not-for-profit or qualified lawyer referral service. A legal service plan is a prepaid or group legal service plan or a similar delivery system that assists people who seek to secure legal representation. A lawyer referral service, on the other hand, is any organization that holds itself out to the public as a lawyer referral service. Such referral services are understood by the public to be consumer-oriented organizations that provide unbiased referrals to lawyers with appropriate experience in the subject matter of the representation and afford other client protections, such as complaint procedures or malpractice insurance requirements. Consequently, this Rule only permits a lawyer to pay the usual charges of a not-for-profit or qualified lawyer referral service. A qualified lawyer referral service is one that is approved by an appropriate regulatory authority as affording adequate protections for the public. See, e.g., the American Bar Association's Model Supreme Court Rules Governing Lawyer Referral Services and Model Lawyer Referral and Information Service Quality Assurance Act (requiring that organizations that are identified as lawyer referral services (i) permit the participation of all lawyers who are licensed and eligible to practice in the jurisdiction and who meet reasonable objective eligibility requirements as may be established by the referral service

ABA Model Rules of Professional Conduct

for the protection of the public; (ii) require each participating lawyer to carry reasonably adequate malpractice insurance; (iii) act reasonably to assess client satisfaction and address client complaints; and (iv) do not make referrals to lawyers who own, operate or are employed by the referral service.)

[7] A lawyer who accepts assignments or referrals from a legal service plan or referrals from a lawyer referral service must act reasonably to assure that the activities of the plan or service are compatible with the lawyer's professional obligations. See Rule 5.3. Legal service plans and lawyer referral services may communicate with the public, but such communication must be in conformity with these Rules. Thus, advertising must not be false or misleading, as would be the case if the communications of a group advertising program or a group legal services plan would mislead the public to think that it was a lawyer referral service sponsored by a state agency or bar association. Nor could the lawyer allow in-person, telephonic, or real-time contacts that would violate Rule 7.3.

[8] A lawyer also may agree to refer clients to another lawyer or a non-lawyer professional, in return for the undertaking of that person to refer clients or customers to the lawyer. Such reciprocal referral arrangements must not interfere with the lawyer's professional judgment as to making referrals or as to providing substantive legal services. See Rules 2.1 and 5.4(c). Except as provided in Rule 1.5(e), a lawyer who receives referrals from a lawyer or nonlawyer professional must not pay anything solely for the referral, but the lawyer does not violate paragraph (b) of this Rule by agreeing to refer clients to the other lawyer or nonlawyer professional, so long as the reciprocal referral agreement is not exclusive and the client is informed of the referral agreement. Conflicts of interest created by such arrangements are governed by Rule 1.7. Reciprocal referral agreements should not be of indefinite duration and should be reviewed periodically to determine whether they comply with these Rules. This Rule does not restrict referrals or divisions of revenues or net income among lawyers within firms comprised of multiple entities.

Definitional Cross-References
"Law firm" *See* Rule 1.0(c)
"Written" *See* Rule 1.0(n)

RULE 7.3: SOLICITATION OF CLIENTS

(a) A lawyer shall not by in-person, live telephone or real-time electronic contact solicit professional employment when a significant motive for the lawyer's doing so is the lawyer's pecuniary gain, unless the person contacted:

(1) is a lawyer; or

(2) has a family, close personal, or prior professional relationship with the lawyer.

(b) A lawyer shall not solicit professional employment by written, recorded or electronic communication or by in-person, telephone or real-time electronic contact even when not otherwise prohibited by paragraph (a), if:

(1) the target of the solicitation has made known to the lawyer a desire not to be solicited by the lawyer; or

(2) the solicitation involves coercion, duress or harassment.

(c) Every written, recorded or electronic communication from a lawyer soliciting professional employment from anyone known to be in need of legal services in a particular matter shall include the words "Advertising Material" on the outside envelope, if any, and at the beginning and ending of any recorded or electronic communication, unless the recipient of the communication is a person specified in paragraphs (a)(1) or (a)(2).

(d) Notwithstanding the prohibitions in paragraph (a), a lawyer may participate with a prepaid or group legal service plan operated by an organization not owned or directed by the lawyer that uses in-person or telephone contact to solicit memberships or subscriptions for the plan from persons who are not known to need legal services in a particular matter covered by the plan.

Comment

[1] A solicitation is a targeted communication initiated by the lawyer that is directed to a specific person and that offers to provide, or can reasonably be understood as offering to provide, legal services. In contrast, a lawyer's communication typically does not constitute a solicitation if it is directed to the general public, such as through a billboard, an Internet banner advertisement, a website or a television commercial, or if it is in response to a request for information or is automatically generated in response to Internet searches.

[2] There is a potential for abuse when a solicitation involves direct in-person, live telephone or real-time electronic contact by a lawyer with someone known to need legal services. These forms of contact subject a person to the private importuning of the trained advocate in a direct interpersonal encounter. The person, who may already feel overwhelmed by the circumstances giving rise to the need for legal services, may find it difficult fully to evaluate all available alternatives with reasoned judgment and appropriate self-interest in the face of the lawyer's presence and insistence

upon being retained immediately. The situation is fraught with the possibility of undue influence, intimidation, and overreaching.

[3] This potential for abuse inherent in direct in-person, live telephone or real-time electronic solicitation justifies its prohibition, particularly since lawyers have alternative means of conveying necessary information to those who may be in need of legal services. In particular, communications can be mailed or transmitted by email or other electronic means that do not involve real-time contact and do not violate other laws governing solicitations. These forms of communications and solicitations make it possible for the public to be informed about the need for legal services, and about the qualifications of available lawyers and law firms, without subjecting the public to direct in-person, telephone or real-time electronic persuasion that may overwhelm a person's judgment.

[4] The use of general advertising and written, recorded or electronic communications to transmit information from lawyer to the public, rather than direct in-person, live telephone or real-time electronic contact, will help to assure that the information flows cleanly as well as freely. The contents of advertisements and communications permitted under Rule 7.2 can be permanently recorded so that they cannot be disputed and may be shared with others who know the lawyer. This potential for informal review is itself likely to help guard against statements and claims that might constitute false and misleading communications, in violation of Rule 7.1. The contents of direct in-person, live telephone or real-time electronic contact can be disputed and may not be subject to third-party scrutiny. Consequently, they are much more likely to approach (and occasionally cross) the dividing line between accurate representations and those that are false and misleading.

[5] There is far less likelihood that a lawyer would engage in abusive practices against a former client, or a person with whom the lawyer has a close personal or family relationship, or in situations in which the lawyer is motivated by considerations other than the lawyer's pecuniary gain. Nor is there a serious potential for abuse when the person contacted is a lawyer. Consequently, the general prohibition in Rule 7.3(a) and the requirements of Rule 7.3(c) are not applicable in those situations. Also, paragraph (a) is not intended to prohibit a lawyer from participating in constitutionally protected activities of public or charitable legal-service organizations or bona fide political, social, civic, fraternal, employee or trade organizations whose purposes include providing or recommending legal services to their members or beneficiaries.

[6] But even permitted forms of solicitation can be abused. Thus, any solicitation which contains information which is false or misleading within the meaning of Rule 7.1, which involves coercion, duress or harassment

within the meaning of Rule 7.3(b)(2), or which involves contact with someone who has made known to the lawyer a desire not to be solicited by the lawyer within the meaning of Rule 7.3(b)(1) is prohibited. Moreover, if after sending a letter or other communication as permitted by Rule 7.2 the lawyer receives no response, any further effort to communicate with the recipient of the communication may violate the provisions of Rule 7.3(b).

[7] This Rule is not intended to prohibit a lawyer from contacting representatives of organizations or groups that may be interested in establishing a group or prepaid legal plan for their members, insureds, beneficiaries or other third parties for the purpose of informing such entities of the availability of and details concerning the plan or arrangement which the lawyer or lawyer's firm is willing to offer. This form of communication is not directed to people who are seeking legal services for themselves. Rather, it is usually addressed to an individual acting in a fiduciary capacity seeking a supplier of legal services for others who may, if they choose, become prospective clients of the lawyer. Under these circumstances, the activity which the lawyer undertakes in communicating with such representatives and the type of information transmitted to the individual are functionally similar to and serve the same purpose as advertising permitted under Rule 7.2.

[8] The requirement in Rule 7.3(c) that certain communications be marked "Advertising Material" does not apply to communications sent in response to requests of potential clients or their spokespersons or sponsors. General announcements by lawyers, including changes in personnel or office location, do not constitute communications soliciting professional employment from a client known to be in need of legal services within the meaning of this Rule.

[9] Paragraph (d) of this Rule permits a lawyer to participate with an organization which uses personal contact to solicit members for its group or prepaid legal service plan, provided that the personal contact is not undertaken by any lawyer who would be a provider of legal services through the plan. The organization must not be owned by or directed (whether as manager or otherwise) by any lawyer or law firm that participates in the plan. For example, paragraph (d) would not permit a lawyer to create an organization controlled directly or indirectly by the lawyer and use the organization for the in-person or telephone solicitation of legal employment of the lawyer through memberships in the plan or otherwise. The communication permitted by these organizations also must not be directed to a person known to need legal services in a particular matter, but is to be designed to inform potential plan members generally of another means of affordable legal services. Lawyers who participate in a legal service plan must reasonably assure that the plan sponsors are in compliance with Rules 7.1, 7.2 and 7.3(b). See 8.4(a).

Definitional Cross-References

"Known" *See* Rule 1.0(f)

"Written" *See* Rule 1.0(n)

RULE 7.4: COMMUNICATION OF FIELDS OF PRACTICE AND SPECIALIZATION

(a) A lawyer may communicate the fact that the lawyer does or does not practice in particular fields of law.

(b) A lawyer admitted to engage in patent practice before the United States Patent and Trademark Office may use the designation "Patent Attorney" or a substantially similar designation.

(c) A lawyer engaged in Admiralty practice may use the designation "Admiralty," "Proctor in Admiralty" or a substantially similar designation.

(d) A lawyer shall not state or imply that a lawyer is certified as a specialist in a particular field of law, unless:

(1) the lawyer has been certified as a specialist by an organization that has been approved by an appropriate state authority or that has been accredited by the American Bar Association; and

(2) the name of the certifying organization is clearly identified in the communication.

Comment

[1] Paragraph (a) of this Rule permits a lawyer to indicate areas of practice in communications about the lawyer's services. If a lawyer practices only in certain fields, or will not accept matters except in a specified field or fields, the lawyer is permitted to so indicate. A lawyer is generally permitted to state that the lawyer is a "specialist," practices a "specialty," or "specializes in" particular fields, but such communications are subject to the "false and misleading" standard applied in Rule 7.1 to communications concerning a lawyer's services.

[2] Paragraph (b) recognizes the long-established policy of the Patent and Trademark Office for the designation of lawyers practicing before the Office. Paragraph (c) recognizes that designation of Admiralty practice has a long historical tradition associated with maritime commerce and the federal courts.

[3] Paragraph (d) permits a lawyer to state that the lawyer is certified as a specialist in a field of law if such certification is granted by an organiza-

tion approved by an appropriate state authority or accredited by the American Bar Association or another organization, such as a state bar association, that has been approved by the state authority to accredit organizations that certify lawyers as specialists. Certification signifies that an objective entity has recognized an advanced degree of knowledge and experience in the specialty area greater than is suggested by general licensure to practice law. Certifying organizations may be expected to apply standards of experience, knowledge and proficiency to insure that a lawyer's recognition as a specialist is meaningful and reliable. In order to insure that consumers can obtain access to useful information about an organization granting certification, the name of the certifying organization must be included in any communication regarding the certification.

RULE 7.5: FIRM NAMES
AND LETTERHEADS

(a) A lawyer shall not use a firm name, letterhead or other professional designation that violates Rule 7.1. A trade name may be used by a lawyer in private practice if it does not imply a connection with a government agency or with a public or charitable legal services organization and is not otherwise in violation of Rule 7.1.

(b) A law firm with offices in more than one jurisdiction may use the same name or other professional designation in each jurisdiction, but identification of the lawyers in an office of the firm shall indicate the jurisdictional limitations on those not licensed to practice in the jurisdiction where the office is located.

(c) The name of a lawyer holding a public office shall not be used in the name of a law firm, or in communications on its behalf, during any substantial period in which the lawyer is not actively and regularly practicing with the firm.

(d) Lawyers may state or imply that they practice in a partnership or other organization only when that is the fact.

Comment

[1] A firm may be designated by the names of all or some of its members, by the names of deceased members where there has been a continuing succession in the firm's identity or by a trade name such as the "ABC Legal Clinic." A lawyer or law firm may also be designated by a distinctive website address or comparable professional designation. Although the United States Supreme Court has held that legislation may prohibit the use of trade names in professional practice, use of such names in law practice is accept-

ABA Model
Rules of
Professional
Conduct

able so long as it is not misleading. If a private firm uses a trade name that includes a geographical name such as "Springfield Legal Clinic," an express disclaimer that it is a public legal aid agency may be required to avoid a misleading implication. It may be observed that any firm name including the name of a deceased partner is, strictly speaking, a trade name. The use of such names to designate law firms has proven a useful means of identification. However, it is misleading to use the name of a lawyer not associated with the firm or a predecessor of the firm, or the name of a nonlawyer.

[2] With regard to paragraph (d), lawyers sharing office facilities, but who are not in fact associated with each other in a law firm, may not denominate themselves as, for example, "Smith and Jones," for that title suggests that they are practicing law together in a firm.

Definitional Cross-References

"Firm" and "Law firm" *See* Rule 1.0(c)
"Substantial" *See* Rule 1.0(l)

RULE 7.6: POLITICAL CONTRIBUTIONS TO OBTAIN GOVERNMENT LEGAL ENGAGEMENTS OR APPOINTMENTS BY JUDGES

A lawyer or law firm shall not accept a government legal engagement or an appointment by a judge if the lawyer or law firm makes a political contribution or solicits political contributions for the purpose of obtaining or being considered for that type of legal engagement or appointment.

Comment

[1] Lawyers have a right to participate fully in the political process, which includes making and soliciting political contributions to candidates for judicial and other public office. Nevertheless, when lawyers make or solicit political contributions in order to obtain an engagement for legal work awarded by a government agency, or to obtain appointment by a judge, the public may legitimately question whether the lawyers engaged to perform the work are selected on the basis of competence and merit. In such a circumstance, the integrity of the profession is undermined.

[2] The term "political contribution" denotes any gift, subscription, loan, advance or deposit of anything of value made directly or indirectly to a candidate, incumbent, political party or campaign committee to influence or provide financial support for election to or retention in judicial or other government office. Political contributions in initiative and referendum elec-

tions are not included. For purposes of this Rule, the term "political contribution" does not include uncompensated services.

[3] Subject to the exceptions below, (i) the term "government legal engagement" denotes any engagement to provide legal services that a public official has the direct or indirect power to award; and (ii) the term "appointment by a judge" denotes an appointment to a position such as referee, commissioner, special master, receiver, guardian or other similar position that is made by a judge. Those terms do not, however, include (a) substantially uncompensated services; (b) engagements or appointments made on the basis of experience, expertise, professional qualifications and cost following a request for proposal or other process that is free from influence based upon political contributions; and (c) engagements or appointments made on a rotational basis from a list compiled without regard to political contributions.

[4] The term "lawyer or law firm" includes a political action committee or other entity owned or controlled by a lawyer or law firm.

[5] Political contributions are for the purpose of obtaining or being considered for a government legal engagement or appointment by a judge if, but for the desire to be considered for the legal engagement or appointment, the lawyer or law firm would not have made or solicited the contributions. The purpose may be determined by an examination of the circumstances in which the contributions occur. For example, one or more contributions that in the aggregate are substantial in relation to other contributions by lawyers or law firms, made for the benefit of an official in a position to influence award of a government legal engagement, and followed by an award of the legal engagement to the contributing or soliciting lawyer or the lawyer's firm would support an inference that the purpose of the contributions was to obtain the engagement, absent other factors that weigh against existence of the proscribed purpose. Those factors may include among others that the contribution or solicitation was made to further a political, social, or economic interest or because of an existing personal, family, or professional relationship with a candidate.

[6] If a lawyer makes or solicits a political contribution under circumstances that constitute bribery or another crime, Rule 8.4(b) is implicated.

Definitional Cross-References

"Law firm" *See* Rule 1.0(c)

MAINTAINING THE INTEGRITY OF THE PROFESSION

Rule 8.1: Bar Admission and Disciplinary Matters

An applicant for admission to the bar, or a lawyer in connection with a bar admission application or in connection with a disciplinary matter, shall not:

(a) knowingly make a false statement of material fact; or

(b) fail to disclose a fact necessary to correct a misapprehension known by the person to have arisen in the matter, or knowingly fail to respond to a lawful demand for information from an admissions or disciplinary authority, except that this Rule does not require disclosure of information otherwise protected by Rule 1.6.

Comment

[1] The duty imposed by this Rule extends to persons seeking admission to the bar as well as to lawyers. Hence, if a person makes a material false statement in connection with an application for admission, it may be the basis for subsequent disciplinary action if the person is admitted, and in any event may be relevant in a subsequent admission application. The duty imposed by this Rule applies to a lawyer's own admission or discipline as well as that of others. Thus, it is a separate professional offense for a lawyer to knowingly make a misrepresentation or omission in connection with a disciplinary investigation of the lawyer's own conduct. Paragraph (b) of this Rule also requires correction of any prior misstatement in the matter that the applicant or lawyer may have made and affirmative clarification of any misunderstanding on the part of the admissions or disciplinary authority of which the person involved becomes aware.

[2] This Rule is subject to the provisions of the Fifth Amendment of the United States Constitution and corresponding provisions of state constitutions. A person relying on such a provision in response to a question, however, should do so openly and not use the right of nondisclosure as a justification for failure to comply with this Rule.

[3] A lawyer representing an applicant for admission to the bar, or representing a lawyer who is the subject of a disciplinary inquiry or proceeding, is governed by the Rules applicable to the client-lawyer relationship, including Rule 1.6 and, in some cases, Rule 3.3.

Definitional Cross-References

"Knowingly" and "Known" *See* Rule 1.0(f)

RULE 8.2: JUDICIAL AND LEGAL OFFICIALS

(a) A lawyer shall not make a statement that the lawyer knows to be false or with reckless disregard as to its truth or falsity concerning the qualifications or integrity of a judge, adjudicatory officer or public legal officer, or of a candidate for election or appointment to judicial or legal office.

(b) A lawyer who is a candidate for judicial office shall comply with the applicable provisions of the Code of Judicial Conduct.

Comment

[1] Assessments by lawyers are relied on in evaluating the professional or personal fitness of persons being considered for election or appointment to judicial office and to public legal offices, such as attorney general, prosecuting attorney and public defender. Expressing honest and candid opinions on such matters contributes to improving the administration of justice. Conversely, false statements by a lawyer can unfairly undermine public confidence in the administration of justice.

[2] When a lawyer seeks judicial office, the lawyer should be bound by applicable limitations on political activity.

[3] To maintain the fair and independent administration of justice, lawyers are encouraged to continue traditional efforts to defend judges and courts unjustly criticized.

Definitional Cross-References

"Knows" *See* Rule 1.0(f)

RULE 8.3: REPORTING PROFESSIONAL MISCONDUCT

(a) A lawyer who knows that another lawyer has committed a violation of the Rules of Professional Conduct that raises a substantial question as to that lawyer's honesty, trustworthiness or fitness as a lawyer in other respects, shall inform the appropriate professional authority.

(b) A lawyer who knows that a judge has committed a violation of applicable rules of judicial conduct that raises a substantial question as to the judge's fitness for office shall inform the appropriate authority.

(c) This Rule does not require disclosure of information otherwise protected by Rule 1.6 or information gained by a lawyer or judge while participating in an approved lawyers assistance program.

Comment

[1] Self-regulation of the legal profession requires that members of the profession initiate disciplinary investigation when they know of a violation of the Rules of Professional Conduct. Lawyers have a similar obligation with respect to judicial misconduct. An apparently isolated violation may indicate a pattern of misconduct that only a disciplinary investigation can uncover. Reporting a violation is especially important where the victim is unlikely to discover the offense.

[2] A report about misconduct is not required where it would involve violation of Rule 1.6. However, a lawyer should encourage a client to consent to disclosure where prosecution would not substantially prejudice the client's interests.

[3] If a lawyer were obliged to report every violation of the Rules, the failure to report any violation would itself be a professional offense. Such a requirement existed in many jurisdictions but proved to be unenforceable. This Rule limits the reporting obligation to those offenses that a self-regulating profession must vigorously endeavor to prevent. A measure of judgment is, therefore, required in complying with the provisions of this Rule. The term "substantial" refers to the seriousness of the possible offense and not the quantum of evidence of which the lawyer is aware. A report should be made to the bar disciplinary agency unless some other agency, such as a peer review agency, is more appropriate in the circumstances. Similar considerations apply to the reporting of judicial misconduct.

[4] The duty to report professional misconduct does not apply to a lawyer retained to represent a lawyer whose professional conduct is in question. Such a situation is governed by the Rules applicable to the client-lawyer relationship.

[5] Information about a lawyer's or judge's misconduct or fitness may be received by a lawyer in the course of that lawyer's participation in an approved lawyers or judges assistance program. In that circumstance, providing for an exception to the reporting requirements of paragraphs (a) and (b) of this Rule encourages lawyers and judges to seek treatment through such a program. Conversely, without such an exception, lawyers and judges may hesitate to seek assistance from these programs, which may then result in additional harm to their professional careers and additional injury to the welfare of clients and the public. These Rules do not otherwise address the confidentiality of information received by a lawyer or judge participating in an approved lawyers assistance program; such an obligation, however, may be imposed by the rules of the program or other law.

Definitional Cross-References

"Knows" *See* Rule 1.0(f)

"Substantial" *See* Rule 1.0(l)

RULE 8.4: MISCONDUCT

It is professional misconduct for a lawyer to:

(a) violate or attempt to violate the Rules of Professional Conduct, knowingly assist or induce another to do so, or do so through the acts of another;

(b) commit a criminal act that reflects adversely on the lawyer's honesty, trustworthiness or fitness as a lawyer in other respects;

(c) engage in conduct involving dishonesty, fraud, deceit or misrepresentation;

(d) engage in conduct that is prejudicial to the administration of justice;

(e) state or imply an ability to influence improperly a government agency or official or to achieve results by means that violate the Rules of Professional Conduct or other law; or

(f) knowingly assist a judge or judicial officer in conduct that is a violation of applicable rules of judicial conduct or other law.

(g) engage in conduct that the lawyer knows or reasonably should know is harassment or discrimination on the basis of race, sex, religion, national origin, ethnicity, disability, age, sexual orientation, gender identity, marital status or socioeconomic status in conduct related to the practice of law. This paragraph does not limit the ability of a lawyer to accept, decline or withdraw from a representation in accordance with Rule 1.16. This paragraph does not preclude legitimate advice or advocacy consistent with these Rules.

Comment

[1] Lawyers are subject to discipline when they violate or attempt to violate the Rules of Professional Conduct, knowingly assist or induce another to do so or do so through the acts of another, as when they request or instruct an agent to do so on the lawyer's behalf. Paragraph (a), however, does not prohibit a lawyer from advising a client concerning action the client is legally entitled to take.

[2] Many kinds of illegal conduct reflect adversely on fitness to practice law, such as offenses involving fraud and the offense of willful failure to file an income tax return. However, some kinds of offenses carry no such impli-

ABA Model
Rules of
Professional
Conduct

cation. Traditionally, the distinction was drawn in terms of offenses involving "moral turpitude." That concept can be construed to include offenses concerning some matters of personal morality, such as adultery and comparable offenses, that have no specific connection to fitness for the practice of law. Although a lawyer is personally answerable to the entire criminal law, a lawyer should be professionally answerable only for offenses that indicate lack of those characteristics relevant to law practice. Offenses involving violence, dishonesty, breach of trust, or serious interference with the administration of justice are in that category. A pattern of repeated offenses, even ones of minor significance when considered separately, can indicate indifference to legal obligation.

[3] A lawyer who, in the course of representing a client, knowingly manifests by words or conduct, bias or prejudice based upon race, sex, religion, national origin, disability, age, sexual orientation or socioeconomic status, violates paragraph (d) when such actions are prejudicial to the administration of justice. Legitimate advocacy respecting the foregoing factors does not violate paragraph (d). A trial judge's finding that peremptory challenges were exercised on a discriminatory basis does not alone establish a violation of this rule.

[4] A lawyer may refuse to comply with an obligation imposed by law upon a good faith belief that no valid obligation exists. The provisions of Rule 1.2(d) concerning a good faith challenge to the validity, scope, meaning or application of the law apply to challenges of legal regulation of the practice of law.

[5] Lawyers holding public office assume legal responsibilities going beyond those of other citizens. A lawyer's abuse of public office can suggest an inability to fulfill the professional role of lawyers. The same is true of abuse of positions of private trust such as trustee, executor, administrator, guardian, agent and officer, director or manager of a corporation or other organization.

[6] A lawyer may refuse to comply with an obligation imposed by law upon a good faith belief that no valid obligation exists. The provisions of Rule 1.2(d) concerning a good faith challenge to the validity, scope, meaning or application of the law apply to challenges of legal regulation of the practice of law.

[7] Lawyers holding public office assume legal responsibilities going beyond those of other citizens. A lawyer's abuse of public office can suggest an inability to fulfill the professional role of lawyers. The same is true of abuse of positions of private trust such as trustee, executor, administrator, guardian, agent and officer, director or manager of a corporation or other organization.

Definitional Cross-References

"Fraud" *See* Rule 1.0(d)

"Knowingly and knows" *See* Rule 1.0(f)

"Reasonably should know" *See* Rule 1.0(j)

RULE 8.5: DISCIPLINARY AUTHORITY; CHOICE OF LAW

(a) **Disciplinary Authority.** A lawyer admitted to practice in this jurisdiction is subject to the disciplinary authority of this jurisdiction, regardless of where the lawyer's conduct occurs. A lawyer not admitted in this jurisdiction is also subject to the disciplinary authority of this jurisdiction if the lawyer provides or offers to provide any legal services in this jurisdiction. A lawyer may be subject to the disciplinary authority of both this jurisdiction and another jurisdiction for the same conduct.

(b) **Choice of Law.** In any exercise of the disciplinary authority of this jurisdiction, the rules of professional conduct to be applied shall be as follows:

(1) for conduct in connection with a matter pending before a tribunal, the rules of the jurisdiction in which the tribunal sits, unless the rules of the tribunal provide otherwise; and

(2) for any other conduct, the rules of the jurisdiction in which the lawyer's conduct occurred, or, if the predominant effect of the conduct is in a different jurisdiction, the rules of that jurisdiction shall be applied to the conduct. A lawyer shall not be subject to discipline if the lawyer's conduct conforms to the rules of a jurisdiction in which the lawyer reasonably believes the predominant effect of the lawyer's conduct will occur.

Comment

Disciplinary Authority

[1] It is longstanding law that the conduct of a lawyer admitted to practice in this jurisdiction is subject to the disciplinary authority of this jurisdiction. Extension of the disciplinary authority of this jurisdiction to other lawyers who provide or offer to provide legal services in this jurisdiction is for the protection of the citizens of this jurisdiction. Reciprocal enforcement of a jurisdiction's disciplinary findings and sanctions will further advance the purposes of this Rule. See, Rules 6 and 22, ABA *Model Rules for Lawyer Disciplinary Enforcement*. A lawyer who is subject to the disciplinary authority of this jurisdiction under Rule 8.5(a) appoints an official to be designated

171

ABA Model
Rules of
Professional
Conduct

by this court to receive service of process in this jurisdiction. The fact that the lawyer is subject to the disciplinary authority of this jurisdiction may be a factor in determining whether personal jurisdiction may be asserted over the lawyer for civil matters.

Choice of Law

[2] A lawyer may be potentially subject to more than one set of rules of professional conduct which impose different obligations. The lawyer may be licensed to practice in more than one jurisdiction with differing rules, or may be admitted to practice before a particular court with rules that differ from those of the jurisdiction or jurisdictions in which the lawyer is licensed to practice. Additionally, the lawyer's conduct may involve significant contacts with more than one jurisdiction.

[3] Paragraph (b) seeks to resolve such potential conflicts. Its premise is that minimizing conflicts between rules, as well as uncertainty about which rules are applicable, is in the best interest of both clients and the profession (as well as the bodies having authority to regulate the profession). Accordingly, it takes the approach of (i) providing that any particular conduct of a lawyer shall be subject to only one set of rules of professional conduct, (ii) making the determination of which set of rules applies to particular conduct as straightforward as possible, consistent with recognition of appropriate regulatory interests of relevant jurisdictions, and (iii) providing protection from discipline for lawyers who act reasonably in the face of uncertainty.

[4] Paragraph (b)(1) provides that as to a lawyer's conduct relating to a proceeding pending before a tribunal, the lawyer shall be subject only to the rules of professional conduct of that tribunal. As to all other conduct, including conduct in anticipation of a proceeding not yet pending before a tribunal, paragraph (b)(2) provides that a lawyer shall be subject to the rules of the jurisdiction in which the lawyer's conduct occurred, or, if the predominant effect of the conduct is in another jurisdiction, the rules of that jurisdiction shall be applied to the conduct. In the case of conduct in anticipation of a proceeding that is likely to be before a tribunal, the predominant effect of such conduct could be where the conduct occurred, where the tribunal sits or in another jurisdiction.

[5] When a lawyer's conduct involves significant contacts with more than one jurisdiction, it may not be clear whether the predominant effect of the lawyer's conduct will occur in a jurisdiction other than the one in which the conduct occurred. So long as the lawyer's conduct conforms to the rules of a jurisdiction in which the lawyer reasonably believes the predominant effect will occur, the lawyer shall not be subject to discipline under this Rule. With respect to conflicts of interest, in determining a lawyer's reasonable

belief under paragraph (b)(2), a written agreement between the lawyer and client that reasonably specifies a particular jurisdiction as within the scope of that paragraph may be considered if the agreement was obtained with the client's informed consent confirmed in the agreement.

[6] If two admitting jurisdictions were to proceed against a lawyer for the same conduct, they should, applying this rule, identify the same governing ethics rules. They should take all appropriate steps to see that they do apply the same rule to the same conduct, and in all events should avoid proceeding against a lawyer on the basis of two inconsistent rules.

[7] The choice of law provision applies to lawyers engaged in transnational practice, unless international law, treaties or other agreements between competent regulatory authorities in the affected jurisdictions provide otherwise.

Definitional Cross-References

"Reasonably believes" *See* Rule 1.0(i)
"Tribunal" *See* Rule 1.0(m)

ABA Model
Rules of
Professional
Conduct

APPENDIX A

Subject Guide

ABA Model Rules of Professional Conduct

ABA Model
Rules of
Professional
Conduct

APPENDIX B
Correlation Tables
TABLES A AND B: RELATED SECTIONS IN THE
ABA MODEL CODE OF PROFESSIONAL RESPONSIBILITY

TABLE A*

ABA MODEL RULES	ABA MODEL CODE
Competence	
Rule 1.1	EC 1-1, EC 1-2, EC 6-1, EC 6-2, EC 6-3, EC 6-4, EC 6-5, DR 6-101(A)
Scope of Representation and Allocation of Authority between Client and Lawyer	
Rule 1.2(a)	EC 5-12, EC 7-7, EC 7-8, DR 7-101(A)(1)
Rule 1.2(b)	EC 7-17
Rule 1.2(c)	EC 7-8, EC 7-9, DR 7-101(B)(1)
Rule 1.2(d)	EC 7-1, EC 7-2, EC 7-5, EC 7-22, DR 7-102(A)(6), (7), & (8), DR 7-106
Diligence	
Rule 1.3	EC 2-31, EC 6-4, EC 7-1, EC 7-38, DR 6-101(A)(3), DR 7-101(A)(1) & (3)
Communication	
Rule 1.4(a)	EC 7-8, EC 9-2, DR 2-110(C)(1)(c), DR 6-101(A)(3), DR 9-102(B)(1)
Rule 1.4(b)	EC 7-8
Fees	
Rule 1.5(a)	EC 2-16, EC 2-17, EC 2-18, DR 2-106(A) & (B)
Rule 1.5(b)	EC 2-19
Rule 1.5(c)	EC 2-20, EC 5-7
Rule 1.5(d)	EC 2-20, DR 2-106(C)
Rule 1.5(e)	EC 2-22, DR 2-107(A)

---

* Table A provides cross-references to related provisions, but only in the sense that the provisions consider substantially similar subject matter or reflect similar concerns. A cross-reference does not indicate that a provision of the ABA Model Code of Professional Responsibility has been incorporated by the provision of a Model Rule. The Canons of the Code are not cross-referenced.

ABA Model Rules of Professional Conduct

TABLE A *(continued)*

ABA MODEL RULES	ABA MODEL CODE
Confidentiality of Information	
Rule 1.6(a)	EC 4-1, EC 4-2, EC 4-3, EC 4-4, DR 4-101(A), (B), & (C)
Rule 1.6(b)(1)	EC 4-2, DR 4-101(C)(3), DR 7-102(B)
Rule 1.6(b)(2)	DR 4-101(C)(3)
Rule 1.6(b)(3)	None
Rule 1.6(b)(4)	None
Rule 1.6(b)(5)	DR 4-101(C)(4)
Rule 1.6(b)(6)	DR 4-101(C)(2)
Rule 1.6(b)(7)	None
Rule 1.6(c)	None
Conflict of Interest: Current Clients	
Rule 1.7(a)	EC 2-21, EC 5-1, EC 5-2, EC 5-3, EC 5-9, EC 5-11, EC 5-13, EC 5-14, EC 5-15, EC 5-17, EC 5-21, EC 5-22, EC 5-23, DR 5-101(A) & (B), DR 5-102, DR 5-104(A), DR 5-105(A) & (B), DR 5-107(A) & (B)
Rule 1.7(b)	EC 2-21, EC 5-15, EC 5-16, EC 5-17, EC 5-19, EC 5-23, DR 5-101(A) & (B), DR 5-102, DR 5-104(A), DR 5-105(C), DR 5-107(A)
Conflict of Interest: Current Clients: Specific Rules	
Rule 1.8(a)	EC 5-3, EC 5-5, DR 5-104(A)
Rule 1.8(b)	EC 4-5, DR 4-101(B)
Rule 1.8(c)	EC 5-1, EC 5-2, EC 5-5, EC 5-6
Rule 1.8(d)	EC 5-1, EC 5-3, EC 5-4, DR 5-104(B)
Rule 1.8(e)	EC 5-1, EC 5-3, EC 5-7, EC 5-8, DR 5-103(B)
Rule 1.8(f)	EC 2-21, EC 5-1, EC 5-22, EC 5-23, DR 5-107(A) & (B)
Rule 1.8(g)	EC 5-1, DR 5-106(A)
Rule 1.8(h)	EC 6-6, DR 6-102(A)
Rule 1.8(i)	EC 5-1, EC 5-7, DR 5-101(A), DR 5-103(A)
Rule 1.8(j)	None
Rule 1.8(k)	None
Duties to Former Clients	
Rule 1.9(a)	DR 5-105(C)
Rule 1.9(b)	EC 4-5, EC 4-6
Rule 1.9(c)	None
Imputation of Conflicts of Interest: General Rule	
Rule 1.10(a)	EC 4-5, DR 5-105(D)
Rule 1.10(b)	EC 4-5, DR 5-105(D)

TABLE A (continued)

ABA MODEL RULES	ABA MODEL CODE
Rule 1.10(c)	DR 5-105(A)
Rule 1.10(d)	None

Special Conflicts of Interest for Former and Current Government Officers and Employees

Rule 1.11(a)	EC 9-3, DR 9-101(B)
Rule 1.11(b)	None
Rule 1.11(c)	None
Rule 1.11(d)	EC 8-8
Rule 1.11(e)	None

Former Judge, Arbitrator, Mediator or Other Third-Party Neutral

Rule 1.12(a)&(b)	EC 5-20, EC 9-3, DR 9-101(A) & (B)
Rule 1.12(c)	DR 5-105(D)
Rule 1.12(d)	None

Organization as Client

Rule 1.13(a)	EC 5-18, EC 5-24
Rule 1.13(b)	EC 5-18, EC 5-24, DR 5-107(B)
Rule 1.13(c)	EC 5-18, EC 5-24, DR 5-105(D), DR 5-107(B)
Rule 1.13(d)	None
Rule 1.13(e)	None
Rule 1.13(f)	EC 5-16
Rule 1.13(g)	EC 4-4, EC 5-16, DR 5-105(B) & (C)

Client with Diminished Capacity

Rule 1.14(a)	EC 7-11, EC 7-12
Rule 1.14(b)	EC 7-12
Rule 1.14(c)	None

Safekeeping Property

Rule 1.15	EC 5-7, EC 9-5, EC 9-7, DR 5-103(A)(1), DR 9-102

Declining or Terminating Representation

Rule 1.16(a)(1)	EC 2-30, EC 2-31, EC 2-32, DR 2-103(E), DR 2-104(A), DR 2-109(A), DR 2-110(B)(1) & (2)
Rule 1.16(a)(2)	EC 1-6, EC 2-30, EC 2-31, EC 2-32, DR 2-110(B)(3), DR 2-110(C)(4)
Rule 1.16(a)(3)	EC 2-31, EC 2-32, DR 2-110(B)(4)
Rule 1.16(b)(1)	EC 2-32, DR 2-110(A)(2), DR 2-110(C)(5)
Rule 1.16(b)(2)	EC 2-31, EC 2-32, DR 2-110(C)(1)(b) & (c), DR 2-110(C)(2)

ABA Model
Rules of
Professional
Conduct

TABLE A *(continued)*

ABA MODEL RULES	ABA MODEL CODE
Rule 1.16(b)(3)	EC 2-31, EC 2-32, DR 2-110(C)(2)
Rule 1.16(b)(4)	EC 2-30, EC 2-31, EC 2-32, DR 2-110(C)(1)(d)
Rule 1.16(b)(5)	EC 2-31, EC 2-32, DR 2-110(C)(1)(f)(i)(j)
Rule 1.16(b)(6)	EC 2-32, DR 2-110(C)(1)(d) & (e)
Rule 1.16(b)(7)	EC 2-32, DR 2-110(C)(6)
Rule 1.16(c)	EC 2-32, DR 2-110(A)(1)
Rule 1.16(d)	EC 2-32, DR 2-110(A)(2) & (3)

Sale of Law Practice

Rule 1.17	None

Duties to Prospective Client

Rule 1.18	EC 4-1

Advisor

Rule 2.1	EC 5-11, EC 7-3, EC 7-8, DR 5-107(B)

Evaluation for Use by Third Persons

Rule 2.3	None

Lawyer Serving as Third-Party Neutral

Rule 2.4	EC 5-20

Meritorious Claims and Contentions

Rule 3.1	EC 7-1, EC 7-4, EC 7-5, EC 7-14, EC 7-25, DR 5-102(A)(5), DR 2-109(A)(B)(1), DR 7-102(A)(1) & (2)

Expediting Litigation

Rule 3.2	EC 7-20, DR 1-102(A)(5), DR 7-101(A)(1) & (2)

Candor toward the Tribunal

Rule 3.3(a)(1)	EC 7-4, EC 7-26, EC 7-32, EC 8-5, DR 1-102(A)(4) & (5), DR 7-102(A)(4) & (5)
Rule 3.3(a)(2)	EC 7-23, DR 1-102(A)(5), DR 7-106(B)(1)
Rule 3.3(a)(3)	EC 7-5, EC 7-6, EC 7-26, EC 8-5, DR 1-102(A)(4) & (5), DR 7-102(A)(4), (6), & (7), DR 7-102(B)(1) & (2)
Rule 3.3(b)	EC 7-5, EC 7-26, EC 7-27, EC 7-32, EC 8-5, DR 1-102(A)(4) & (5), DR 7-102(A)(4), (6), & (7), DR 7-102(B)(1) & (2), DR 7-108(G), DR 7-109(A) & (B)
Rule 3.3(c)	EC 8-5, DR 7-102(B)
Rule 3.3(d)	EC 7-24, EC 7-27

ABA Model Rules of Professional Conduct

TABLE A *(continued)*

ABA MODEL RULES	ABA MODEL CODE

Fairness to Opposing Party and Counsel

Rule 3.4(a)	EC 7-6, EC 7-27, DR 1-102(A)(4) & (5), DR 7-106(C)(7), DR 7-109(A) & (B)
Rule 3.4(b)	EC 7-6, EC 7-28, DR 1-102(A)(4), (5), & (6), DR 7-102(A)(6), DR 7-109(C)
Rule 3.4(c)	EC 7-22, EC 7-25, EC 7-38, DR 1-102(A)(5), DR 7-106(A), DR 7-106(C)(5) & (7)
Rule 3.4(d)	DR 1-102(A)(5), DR 7-106(A), DR 7-106(C)(7)
Rule 3.4(e)	EC 7-24, EC 7-25, DR 1-102(A)(5), DR 7-106(C)(1), (2), (3), & (4)
Rule 3.4(f)	EC 7-27, DR 1-102(A)(5), DR 7-104(A)(2), DR 7-109(B)

Impartiality and Decorum of the Tribunal

Rule 3.5(a)	EC 7-20, EC 7-29, EC 7-31, EC 7-32, EC 7-34, DR 7-106, DR 7-108, DR 7-109, DR 7-110, DR 8-101(A)
Rule 3.5(b)	EC 7-35, DR 7-108, DR 7-110(A) & (B)
Rule 3.5(c)	EC 7-29, EC 7-30, EC 7-31, EC 7-32, DR 7-108
Rule 3.5(d)	EC 7-20, EC 7-25, EC 7-36, EC 7-37, DR 7-101(A)(1), DR 7-106(C)(6)

Trial Publicity

| Rule 3.6 | EC 7-25, EC 7-33, DR 7-107 |

Lawyer as Witness

| Rule 3.7(a) | EC 5-9, EC 5-10, DR 5-101(B)(1) & (2), DR 5-102 |
| Rule 3.7(b) | EC 5-9, DR 5-101(B), DR 5-102 |

Special Responsibilities of a Prosecutor

Rule 3.8(a)	EC 7-11, EC 7-13, EC 7-14, DR 7-103(A)
Rule 3.8(b)	EC 7-11, EC 7-13
Rule 3.8(c)	EC 7-11, EC 7-13, EC 7-18
Rule 3.8(d)	EC 7-11, EC 7-13, DR 7-103(B)
Rule 3.8(e)	None
Rule 3.8(f)	EC 7-14

Advocate in Nonadjudicative Proceedings

| Rule 3.9 | EC 7-11, EC 7-15, EC 7-16, EC 8-4, EC 8-5, DR 7-106(B)(2), DR 9-101(C) |

Truthfulness in Statements to Others

| Rule 4.1 | EC 7-5, DR 7-102(A)(3), (4), (5), & (7), DR 7-102(B) |

TABLE A *(continued)*

ABA MODEL RULES	ABA MODEL CODE

Communication with Person Represented by Counsel

| Rule 4.2 | EC 2-30, EC 7-18, DR 7-104(A)(1) |

Dealing with Unrepresented Person

| Rule 4.3 | EC 2-3, EC 7-18, DR 7-104(A)(2) |

Respect for Rights of Third Persons

| Rule 4.4(a) | EC 7-10, EC 7-14, EC 7-21, EC 7-25, EC 7-29, EC 7-30, EC 7-37, DR 2-110(B)(1), DR 7-101(A)(1), DR 7-102(A)(1), DR 7-106(C)(2), DR 7-107(D), (E), & (F), DR 7-108(D), (E), & (F) |
| Rule 4.4(b) | None |

Responsibilities of Partners, Managers, and Supervisory Lawyers

| Rule 5.1(a)&(b) | EC 4-5, DR 4-101(D), DR 7-107(J) |
| Rule 5.1(c) | DR 1-102(A)(2), DR 1-103(A), DR 7-108(E) |

Responsibilities of a Subordinate Lawyer

| Rule 5.2 | None |

Responsibilities regarding Nonlawyer Assistance

Rule 5.3(a)	EC 3-6, EC 4-2, EC 4-5, EC 7-28, DR 4-101(D), DR 7-107(J)
Rule 5.3(b)	DR 1-102(A)(2), DR 7-107(J), DR 7-108(B), DR 7-108(E)
Rule 5.3(c)	None

Professional Independence of a Lawyer

Rule 5.4(a)	EC 2-33, EC 3-8, EC 5-24, DR 2-103(D)(1), DR 2-103(D)(2), DR 2-103(D)(4)(a), (d), (e), & (f), DR 3-102(A), DR 5-107(C)(3)
Rule 5.4(b)	EC 2-33, EC 3-8, DR 3-103(A)
Rule 5.4(c)	EC 2-33, EC 5-22, EC 5-23, DR 2-103(C), DR 5-107(B)
Rule 5.4(d)	EC 2-33, EC 3-8, DR 5-107(C)

Unauthorized Practice of Law; Multijurisdictional Practice of Law

Rule 5.5(a)	DR 3-101(A) & (B)
Rule 5.5(b)	None
Rule 5.5(c)	None
Rule 5.5(d)	None
Rule 5.5(e)	None

TABLE A *(continued)*

ABA MODEL RULES	ABA MODEL CODE

Restrictions on Right to Practice

Rule 5.6   DR 2-108

Responsibilities regarding Law-Related Services

Rule 5.7   None

Voluntary Pro Bono Publico Service

Rule 6.1   EC 1-2, EC 1-4, EC 2-1, EC 2-2, EC 2-16, EC 2-24,
                   EC 2-25, EC 6-2, EC 8-1, EC 8-2, EC 8-3, EC 8-7,
                   EC 8-9

Accepting Appointments

Rule 6.2 (a)   EC 2-1, EC 2-25, EC 2-27, EC 2-28, EC 2-29, EC 8-3
Rule 6.2(b)   EC 2-16, EC 2-25, EC 2-29, EC 2-30
Rule 6.2(c)   EC 2-25, EC 2-27, EC 2-29, EC 2-30

Membership in Legal Services Organization

Rule 6.3   EC 2-33, DR 5-101(A)

Law Reform Activities Affecting Client Interests

Rule 6.4   EC 2-33, DR 5-101(A), DR 8-101

Nonprofit and Court-Annexed Limited Legal Services Programs

Rule 6.5   None

Communications Concerning a Lawyer's Services

Rule 7.1   EC 2-8, EC 2-9, EC 2-10, DR 2-101(A), (B), (C),
                   (E), (F), & (G), DR 2-102(E)

Advertising

Rule 7.2(a)   EC 2-1, EC 2-2, EC 2-6, EC 2-7, EC 2-8, EC 2-15,
                   DR 2-101(B) & (H), DR 2-102(A) & (B), DR 2-103(B),
                   DR 2-104(A)(4) & (5)
Rule 7.2(b)   EC 2-8, EC 2-15, DR 2-101(I), DR 2-103(B), (C), & (D)
Rule 7.2(c)   None

Solicitation of Clients

Rule 7.3   EC 2-3, EC 2-4, EC 5-6, DR 2-103(A),
                   DR 2-103(C)(1), DR 2-103(D)(4)(b) & (c),
                   DR 2-104(A)(1), (2), (3), & (5)

ABA Model Rules of Professional Conduct

TABLE A *(continued)*

**ABA
MODEL RULES**

**ABA
MODEL CODE**

Communication of Fields of Practice and Specialization

Rule 7.4(a)	EC 2-1, EC 2-7, EC 2-8, EC 2-14, DR 2-101(B)(2), DR 2-102(A)(3), DR 2-102(E), DR 2-105(A)
Rule 7.4(b)	DR 2-105(A)(1)
Rule 7.4(c)	EC 2-14
Rule 7.4(d)	EC 2-8, EC 2-14, DR 2-105(A)(2) & (3)

Firm Names and Letterheads

Rule 7.5(a)	EC 2-11, EC 2-13, DR 2-102(A)(4), DR 2-102(B), (D), & (E), DR 2-105
Rule 7.5(b)	EC 2-11, DR 2-102(D)
Rule 7.5(c)	EC 2-11, EC 2-12, DR 2-102(B)
Rule 7.5(d)	EC 2-11, EC 2-13, DR 2-102(C)

*Political Contributions to Obtain Government
Legal Engagements or Appointments by Judges*

Rule 7.6	None

Bar Admission and Disciplinary Matters

Rule 8.1(a)	EC 1-1, EC 1-2, EC 1-3, DR 1-101(A) & (B)
Rule 8.1(b)	DR 1-102(A)(5), DR 1-103(B)

Judicial and Legal Officials

Rule 8.2(a)	EC 8-6, DR 8-102
Rule 8.2(b)	DR 8-103

Reporting Professional Misconduct

Rule 8.3	EC 1-3, DR 1-103(A)

Misconduct

Rule 8.4(a)	EC 1-5, EC 1-6, EC 9-6, DR 1-102(A)(1) & (2), DR 2-103(E), DR 7-102(A) & (B)
Rule 8.4(b)	EC 1-5, DR 1-102(A)(3) & (6), DR 7-102(A)(8), DR 8-101(A)(3)
Rule 8.4(c)	EC 1-5, EC 9-4, DR 1-102(A)(4), DR 8-101(A)(3)
Rule 8.4(d)	EC 3-9, EC 8-3, DR 1-102(A)(5), DR 3-101(B)
Rule 8.4(e)	EC 1-5, EC 9-2, EC 9-4, EC 9-6, DR 9-101(C)
Rule 8.4(f)	EC 1-5, EC 7-34, EC 9-1, DR 1-102(A)(3), (4), (5), & (6), DR 7-110(A), DR 8-101(A)(2)
Rule 8.4(g)	None

Disciplinary Authority; Choice of Law

Rule 8.5	None

TABLE B*

ABA MODEL CODE	ABA MODEL RULES
Canon 1: Integrity of Profession	
EC 1-1	Rules 1.1, 8.1(a)
EC 1-2	Rules 1.1, 6.1, 8.1(a)
EC 1-3	Rules 8.1(a), 8.3
EC 1-4	Rule 6.1
EC 1-5	Rule 8.4(a), (b), (c), (e), & (f)
EC 1-6	Rules 1.16(a)(2), 8.4(a)
DR 1-101	Rule 8.1(a)
DR 1-102(A)(1)	Rule 8.4(a)
DR 1-102(A)(2)	Rules 5.1(c), 5.3(b), 8.4(a)
DR 1-102(A)(3)	Rule 8.4(b) & (f)
DR 1-102(A)(4)	Rules 3.3(a)(1), (3), & (b), 3.4(a) & (b), 8.4(c) & (f)
DR 1-102(A)(5)	Rules 3.1, 3.2, 3.3(a) & (b), 3.4, 8.4(d) & (f)
DR 1-102(A)(6)	Rules 3.4(b), 8.4(b) & (f)
DR 1-103(A)	Rules 5.1(c), 8.3
DR 1-103(B)	Rule 8.1(b)
Canon 2: Making Counsel Available	
EC 2-1	Rules 6.1, 6.2(a), 7.2(a), 7.4
EC 2-2	Rules 6.1, 7.2(a)
EC 2-3	Rules 4.3, 7.3
EC 2-4	Rule 7.3
EC 2-5	None
EC 2-6	Rule 7.2(a)
EC 2-7	Rules 7.2(a), 7.4
EC 2-8	Rules 7.1, 7.2(a) & (b), 7.4
EC 2-9	Rule 7.1
EC 2-10	Rule 7.1
EC 2-11	Rule 7.5
EC 2-12	Rule 7.5(c)
EC 2-13	Rule 7.5(a) & (d)
EC 2-14	Rule 7.4
EC 2-15	Rule 7.2(a) & (b)
EC 2-16	Rules 1.5(a), 6.1, 6.2(b)

** Table B provides cross-references to related provisions, but only in the sense that the provisions consider substantially similar subject matter or reflect similar concerns. A cross-reference does not indicate that a provision of the ABA Model Code of Professional Responsibility has been incorporated by the provision of a Model Rule. The Canons of the Code are not cross-referenced.

ABA Model
Rules of
Professional
Conduct

TABLE B (*continued*)

ABA MODEL CODE	ABA MODEL RULES
EC 2-17	Rule 1.5(a)
EC 2-18	Rule 1.5(a)
EC 2-19	Rule 1.5(b)
EC 2-20	Rule 1.5(c) & (d)
EC 2-21	Rules 1.7(a), 1.8(f)
EC 2-22	Rule 1.5(e)
EC 2-23	None
EC 2-24	Rule 6.1
EC 2-25	Rules 6.1, 6.2
EC 2-26	None
EC 2-27	Rule 6.2(a) & (c)
EC 2-28	Rule 6.2(a)
EC 2-29	Rule 6.2
EC 2-30	Rules 1.16(a)(1) & (2), 1.16(b)(4), 4.2, 6.2(b) & (c)
EC 2-31	Rules 1.3, 1.16(a) & (b)
EC 2-32	Rule 1.16
EC 2-33	Rules 5.4, 6.3, 6.4
DR 2-101(A)	Rule 7.1
DR 2-101(B)	Rules 7.1, 7.2(a)
DR 2-101(C)	Rule 7.1
DR 2-101(D)	None
DR 2-101(E)	Rule 7.1
DR 2-101(F)	Rule 7.1
DR 2-101(G)	Rule 7.1
DR 2-101(H)	Rule 7.2
DR 2-101(I)	Rule 7.2(b)
DR 2-102(A)	Rules 7.2(a), 7.4
DR 2-102(B)	Rules 7.2(a), 7.5(a) & (c)
DR 2-102(C)	Rule 7.5(d)
DR 2-102(D)	Rule 7.5(a) & (b)
DR 2-102(E)	Rules 7.1, 7.4, 7.5(a)
DR 2-103(A)	Rule 7.3
DR 2-103(B)	Rule 7.2(a) & (b)
DR 2-103(C)	Rules 5.4(a), 7.2(b), 7.3
DR 2-103(D)	Rules 1.16(a)(1), 5.4(a), 7.2(b), 7.3
DR 2-103(E)	Rules 1.16(a), 7.2(a), 7.3
DR 2-104	Rules 1.16(a), 7.3
DR 2-105	Rule 7.4
DR 2-106(A)	Rule 1.5(a)

TABLE B *(continued)*

ABA MODEL CODE	ABA MODEL RULES
DR 2-106(B)	Rule 1.5(a)
DR 2-106(C)	Rule 1.5(d)
DR 2-107(A)	Rule 1.5(e)
DR 2-107(B)	Rule 5.4(a)(1)
DR 2-108(A)	Rule 5.6
DR 2-108(B)	Rule 5.6
DR 2-109(A)	Rules 1.16(a)(1), 3.1
DR 2-110(A)	Rule 1.16(b)(1), (c), & (d)
DR 2-110(B)	Rules 1.16(a), 3.1, 4.4(a)
DR 2-110(C)	Rules 1.4(a)(5), 1.16(a) & (b)

Canon 3: Unauthorized Practice

EC 3-1	None
EC 3-2	None
EC 3-3	Rule 8.4(e)
EC 3-4	None
EC 3-5	None
EC 3-6	Rule 5.3(a)
EC 3-7	None
EC 3-8	Rule 5.4(a), (b), & (d)
EC 3-9	Rule 8.4(d)
DR 3-101(A)	Rule 5.5(a)
DR 3-101(B)	Rules 5.5(a), 8.4(d)
DR 3-102	Rule 5.4(a)
DR 3-103	Rule 5.4(b)

Canon 4: Confidences and Secrets

EC 4-1	Rules 1.6(a), 1.18
EC 4-2	Rules 1.6(a) & (b)(1), 5.3(a)
EC 4-3	Rule 1.6(a)
EC 4-4	Rules 1.6(a), 1.13(g)
EC 4-5	Rules 1.8(b), 1.9(b), 1.10(a) & (b), 5.1(a) & (c), 5.3(a)
EC 4-6	Rule 1.9(b)
DR 4-101(A)	Rule 1.6(a)
DR 4-101(B)	Rules 1.6(a), 1.8(b), 1.9(b)
DR 4-101(C)	Rule 1.6(a) & (b)
DR 4-101(D)	Rules 5.1(a) & (b), 5.3(a) & (b)

ABA Model Rules of Professional Conduct

TABLE B *(continued)*

ABA MODEL CODE	ABA MODEL RULES
Canon 5: Independent Judgment	
EC 5-1	Rules 1.7(a), 1.8(c), (d), (e), (f), (g), & (i)
EC 5-2	Rules 1.7(a), 1.8(c)
EC 5-3	Rules 1.7, 1.8(a), (d), & (e)
EC 5-4	Rule 1.8(d)
EC 5-5	Rule 1.8(a) & (c)
EC 5-6	Rules 1.8(c), 7.3
EC 5-7	Rules 1.5(c), 1.8(e) & (i), 1.15
EC 5-8	Rule 1.8(e)
EC 5-9	Rules 1.7(a), 3.7
EC 5-10	Rule 3.7(a)
EC 5-11	Rules 1.7(a), 2.1
EC 5-12	Rule 1.2(a)
EC 5-13	Rule 1.7(a)
EC 5-14	Rule 1.7(a)
EC 5-15	Rule 1.7
EC 5-16	Rules 1.7(b), 1.13(f) & (g)
EC 5-17	Rule 1.7
EC 5-18	Rule 1.13(a), (b), & (c)
EC 5-19	Rule 1.7(b)
EC 5-20	Rules 1.12(a) & (b), 2.4
EC 5-21	Rule 1.7
EC 5-22	Rule 1.7
EC 5-23	Rules 1.7(a), 1.8(f), 5.4(c)
EC 5-24	Rules 1.13(a), (b), & (c), 5.4(a)
DR 5-101(A)	Rules 1.7, 1.8(i), 6.3, 6.4
DR 5-101(B)	Rules 1.7, 3.7
DR 5-102(A)	Rules 1.7, 3.7
DR 5-102(B)	Rules 1.7(b), 3.7
DR 5-103(A)	Rules 1.8(i), 1.15
DR 5-103(B)	Rule 1.8(e)
DR 5-104(A)	Rules 1.7, 1.8(a)
DR 5-104(B)	Rule 1.8(d)
DR 5-105(A)	Rules 1.7, 1.10(c)
DR 5-105(B)	Rules 1.7, 1.13(g)
DR 5-105(C)	Rules 1.7(b), 1.13(g), 1.9(a)
DR 5-105(D)	Rules 1.10(a), 1.12(c), 1.13(c)
DR 5-106	Rule 1.8(g)
DR 5-107(A)	Rules 1.7(b), 1.8(f)

TABLE B *(continued)*

ABA MODEL CODE	ABA MODEL RULES
DR 5-107(B)	Rules 1.7(a), 1.8(f), 1.13(b) & (c), 2.1, 5.4(c)
DR 5-107(C)	Rule 5.4(a) & (d)

Canon 6: Competence

EC 6-1	Rule 1.1
EC 6-2	Rules 1.1, 5.1(a) & (b), 6.1
EC 6-3	Rule 1.1
EC 6-4	Rules 1.1, 1.3
EC 6-5	Rule 1.1
EC 6-6	Rule 1.8(h)
DR 6-101	Rules 1.1, 1.3, 1.4(a)
DR 6-102	Rule 1.8(h)

Canon 7: Zeal Within the Law

EC 7-1	Rules 1.2(d), 1.3, 3.1
EC 7-2	Rule 1.2(d)
EC 7-3	Rule 2.1
EC 7-4	Rules 3.1, 3.3(a)(1)
EC 7-5	Rules 1.2(d), 3.1, 3.3(a)(3) & (b), 4.1
EC 7-6	Rule 3.4(a) & (b)
EC 7-7	Rule 1.2(a)
EC 7-8	Rules 1.2(a) & (c), 1.4, 2.1
EC 7-9	Rule 1.2(c)
EC 7-10	Rule 4.4(a)
EC 7-11	Rules 1.14(a), 3.8(a), (b), (c), & (d), 3.9
EC 7-12	Rule 1.14
EC 7-13	Rule 3.8
EC 7-14	Rules 3.1, 3.8(a) & (f), 4.4(a)
EC 7-15	Rule 3.9
EC 7-16	Rule 3.9
EC 7-17	Rule 1.2(b)
EC 7-18	Rules 3.8(c), 4.2, 4.3
EC 7-19	None
EC 7-20	Rules 3.2, 3.5(a) & (d)
EC 7-21	Rule 4.4(a)
EC 7-22	Rules 1.2(d), 3.4(c)
EC 7-23	Rule 3.3(a)(2)
EC 7-24	Rules 3.3(d), 3.4(e)
EC 7-25	Rules 3.1, 3.4(c) & (e), 3.5(d), 3.6, 4.4(a)
EC 7-26	Rule 3.3(a)(3) & (b)

TABLE B *(continued)*

ABA MODEL CODE	ABA MODEL RULES
EC 7-27	Rules 3.3(b) & (d), 3.4(a) & (f)
EC 7-28	Rules 3.4(b), 5.3(a)
EC 7-29	Rules 3.5(a) & (c), 4.4(a)
EC 7-30	Rules 3.5(c), 4.4(a)
EC 7-31	Rule 3.5(a) & (c)
EC 7-32	Rules 3.3(a)(1) & (b), 3.5(a) & (c)
EC 7-33	Rule 3.6
EC 7-34	Rules 3.5(a), 8.4(f)
EC 7-35	Rule 3.5(b)
EC 7-36	Rule 3.5(d)
EC 7-37	Rules 3.5(d), 4.4(a)
EC 7-38	Rules 1.3, 3.4(c)
EC 7-39	None
DR 7-101(A)	Rules 1.2(a), 1.3, 3.2, 3.5(d), 4.4(a)
DR 7-101(B)	Rules 1.2(b), 1.16(b)
DR 7-102(A)(1)	Rules 3.1, 4.4(a)
DR 7-102(A)(2)	Rule 3.1
DR 7-102(A)(3)	Rules 3.3(a)(1), (a)(3), & (b), 4.1
DR 7-102(A)(4)	Rules 3.3(a) & (b), 4.1
DR 7-102(A)(5)	Rules 3.3(a)(1), 4.1
DR 7-102(A)(6)	Rules 1.2(d), 3.3(b), 3.4(b)
DR 7-102(A)(7)	Rules 1.2(d), 3.3(a)(3) & (b), 4.1
DR 7-102(A)(8)	Rules 1.2(d), 8.4(a) & (b)
DR 7-102(B)	Rules 1.6(b)(1), 3.3(b) & (c), 4.1
DR 7-103(A)	Rule 3.8(a)
DR 7-103(B)	Rule 3.8(d)
DR 7-104	Rules 3.4(f), 4.2, 4.3
DR 7-105	None
DR 7-106(A)	Rules 1.2(d), 3.4(c) & (d), 3.5(a)
DR 7-106(B)	Rules 3.3(a)(2), 3.9
DR 7-106(C)	Rules 3.4(a), (c), (d), & (e), 3.5(d), 4.4(a)
DR 7-107(A)–(I)	Rule 3.6
DR 7-107(D)–(F)	Rule 4.4(a)
DR 7-107(J)	Rules 5.1(a) & (b), 5.3(a) & (b)
DR 7-108(A)	Rule 3.5(a), (b), & (c)
DR 7-108(B)	Rules 3.5(a), (b), & (c), 5.3(b)
DR 7-108(C)	Rule 3.5(a), (b), & (c)
DR 7-108(D)	Rules 3.5(c)(3), 4.4(a)
DR 7-108(E)	Rules 3.5(a), (b), & (c), 4.4(a), 5.1(c), 5.3(b)

TABLE B *(continued)*

ABA MODEL CODE	ABA MODEL RULES
DR 7-108(F)	Rules 3.5(a), (b), & (c), 4.4(a)
DR 7-108(G)	Rules 3.3(b), 3.5(c)
DR 7-109(A)	Rules 3.3(a)(1), (a)(3), & (b), 3.4(a)
DR 7-109(B)	Rules 3.3(b), 3.4(a) & (f)
DR 7-109(C)	Rule 3.4(b)
DR 7-110(A)	Rules 3.5(a), 8.4(f)
DR 7-110(B)	Rule 3.5(a) & (b)

Canon 8: Improving Legal System

EC 8-1	Rule 6.1
EC 8-2	Rule 6.1
EC 8-3	Rules 6.1, 6.2(a), 8.4(d)
EC 8-4	Rule 3.9
EC 8-5	Rules 3.3(a)(1), (a)(3), & (b), 3.9
EC 8-6	Rule 8.2(a)
EC 8-7	Rule 6.1
EC 8-8	Rule 1.11(d)
EC 8-9	Rule 6.1
DR 8-101	Rules 3.5, 8.4(b), (c), & (f)
DR 8-102	Rule 8.2(a)
DR 8-103	Rule 8.2(b)

Canon 9: Appearance of Impropriety

EC 9-1	Rule 8.4(f)
EC 9-2	Rules 1.4(a), 8.4(e)
EC 9-3	Rules 1.11(a), 1.12(a) & (b)
EC 9-4	Rule 8.4(c) & (e)
EC 9-5	Rule 1.15
EC 9-6	Preamble, Rule 8.4(e)
EC 9-7	Rule 1.15
DR 9-101(A)	Rule 1.12(a) & (b)
DR 9-101(B)	Rules 1.11(a), 1.12(a) & (b)
DR 9-101(C)	Rules 1.4(a)(5), 3.9, 8.4(e)
DR 9-102	Rules 1.4(a), 1.15

APPENDIX C

ABA Standing Committee On Ethics and Professional Responsibility

COMPOSITION AND JURISDICTION

The Standing Committee on Ethics and Professional Responsibility, which consists of ten members, may:

(1) by the concurrence of a majority of its members, express its opinion on proper professional or judicial conduct, either on its own initiative or when requested to do so by a member of the bar or the judiciary;

(2) periodically publish its issued opinions to the profession in summary or complete form and, on request, provide copies of opinions to members of the bar, the judiciary and the public;

(3) provide under its supervision informal responses to ethics inquiries the answers to which are substantially governed by applicable ethical codes and existing written opinions;

(4) on request, advise or otherwise assist professional organizations and courts in their activities relating to the development, modification and interpretation of statements of the ethical standards of the profession such as the Model Rules of Professional Conduct, the predecessor Model Code of Professional Responsibility and the Model Code of Judicial Conduct;

(5) recommend amendments to or clarifications of the Model Rules of Professional Conduct or the Model Code of Judicial Conduct; and

(6) adopt rules relating to the procedures to be used in issuing opinions, effective when approved by the Board of Governors.

[The above Composition and Jurisdiction statement is found at §31.7 of the Bylaws of the Association. The Rules of Procedure are not incorporated into the Bylaws.]

RULES OF PROCEDURE

1. The Committee may express its opinion on questions of proper professional and judicial conduct. The Model Rules of Professional Conduct and the Model Code of Judicial Conduct, as they may be amended or superseded, contain the standards to be applied. For as long as a significant number of jurisdictions continue to base their professional standards on the predecessor Model Code of Professional Responsibility, the Committee will continue to refer also to the Model Code in its opinions.

2. The Committee may issue an opinion on its own initiative or upon a request from a member of the bar or the judiciary or from a professional organization or a court.

3. The Committee may issue opinions of two kinds: Formal Opinions and Informal Opinions. Formal Opinions are those upon subjects the Committee determines to be of widespread interest or unusual importance. Other opinions are Informal Opinions. The Committee will assign to each opinion a non-duplicative identifying number, with distinction between Formal Opinions and Informal Opinions.

4. The Committee will not usually issue an opinion on a question that is known to be pending before a court in a proceeding in which the requestor is involved. The Committee's published opinions will not identify the person who was the requestor or whose conduct is the subject of the opinion. The Committee will not issue an opinion on a question of law.

5. The Committee may invite or accept written information relevant to a particular opinion from a person or persons interested in such an opinion before the Committee begins its work on an opinion. Ordinarily, the Committee will not invite anyone to make an oral presentation or argument in support of that position.

6. When a Committee or staff member receives an inquiry about the status of a draft opinion from anyone outside the Committee, the member may inform the inquirer that the Committee is considering the question. Draft opinions may, in appropriate circumstances, be shown to other interested ABA Committees and entities. Committee and staff members shall not, absent unusual circumstances, discuss the substance of pending opinions with the public, but may mention topics related to pending opinions in a general fashion.

7. Before issuing an opinion with respect to judicial conduct the Committee will submit the proposed opinion to the Judges' Advisory Committee and consider any objection or comment from the Judges' Advisory Committee and any member of it. The Committee may assume that the Judges' Advisory Committee and its members have no objection or comment if none is received by the Committee within 30 days after the submission.

8. If the Committee decides not to issue a requested opinion the requestor will be promptly notified.

9. The Committee will issue an opinion only with the concurrence of six members in a vote taken at a meeting or in a telephone conference call. When a Committee member votes against a position declaring a Committee policy, that vote may be recorded in the minutes, which may include the name of the dissenting Committee member. The minutes shall not reflect the names of Committee members voting for or against any non-Committee policy question except that a member's vote shall be recorded and identified

at the member's request. When drafting an opinion, policy statement or other document to be publicly disseminated, the Committee shall make every effort to reach a consensus. When, after a full examination of the issue and an exchange of views, the Committee cannot reach a consensus, a dissenting opinion may be appropriate to express the views of a Committee member or members. A member may place a statement of dissent in the Committee file or request that the dissent be published with the opinion.

10. The Chair may assign to one or more members the responsibility of preparing a proposed opinion for consideration by the Committee. The Committee will issue a requested opinion as promptly as feasible.

11. A Formal Opinion overrules an earlier Formal Opinion or Informal Opinion to the extent of conflict. An Informal Opinion overrules an earlier Informal Opinion to the extent of conflict but does not overrule an earlier Formal Opinion.

12. Opinions of the Committee issued before the effective dates of the Model Rules of Professional Conduct, the predecessor Model Code of Professional Responsibility and the Model Code of Judicial Conduct continue in effect to the extent not inconsistent with those standards and not overruled or limited by later opinions.

13. The Committee will make opinions and/or summaries of opinions available for publication in the American Bar Association journal. The Committee will cause Formal Opinions and Informal Opinions to be published in looseleaf form.

14. The Committee may through its staff arrange to provide informal responses to ethics inquiries the answers to which are substantially governed by applicable ethical codes and opinions of this Committee or other ethics committees. The staff will maintain a log of such inquiries that will periodically be reviewed by the Committee.

15. Information contained in Committee files relating to requests for opinions that would disclose the identity of the inquirer or the person whose conduct is the subject of the opinion will not voluntarily be disclosed by the Association without the consent of the affected persons.

JUDGES ADVISORY COMMITTEE

An adjunct committee of the Standing Committee on Ethics and Professional Responsibility, the Judges' Advisory Committee plays a vital role in the development of judicial ethics opinions by reviewing each of the Ethics Committee's draft opinions interpreting the provisions of the Model Code of Judicial Conduct. The Advisory Committee lends its experience and expertise to the Standing Committee to insure that those opinions are properly responsive to the administrative and substantive concerns of the bench.

APPENDIX D

ABA SPECIAL COMMITTEE ON IMPLEMENTATION OF THE MODEL RULES OF PROFESSIONAL CONDUCT (1983–1987)

MICHAEL FRANCK, *Chair*
Lansing, Michigan

EDWARD L. BENOIT
Twin Falls, Idaho

W. STELL HUIE
Atlanta, Georgia

ROGER BROSNAHAN
Minneapolis, Minnesota

JAMES T. JENNINGS
Roswell, New Mexico

WAYNE A. BUDD
Boston, Massachusetts

CAROLYN B. LAMM
Washington, D.C.

RICHARD M. COLEMAN
Los Angeles, California

LLOYD LOCHRIDGE
Austin, Texas

JOHN C. ELAM
Columbus, Ohio

LEON SILVERMAN
New York, New York

JOSEPH E. GALLAGHER
Scranton, Pennsylvania

E.C. WARD
Natchez, Mississippi

ROBERT O. HETLAGE
St. Louis, Missouri

BEN J. WEAVER
Indianapolis, Indiana

CENTER FOR PROFESSIONAL RESPONSIBILITY

GEORGE KUHLMAN
Special Counsel

APPENDIX E

AMENDMENTS TO THE MODEL RULES OF PROFESSIONAL CONDUCT (BY RULE)

Preamble
Amended 2002 per Midyear Meeting Report 401.

Scope
Amended 2002 per Midyear Meeting Report 401.

Rule 1.0
Amended 2002 per Midyear Meeting Report 401.

Amended 2009 per Midyear Meeting Report 109.

Amended 2012 per Annual Meeting Report 105A.

Rule 1.1
Amended 2002 per Midyear Meeting Report 401.

Amended 2012 per Annual Meeting Reports 105A and C.

Rule 1.2
Amended 2002 per Midyear Meeting Report 401.

Rule 1.3
Amended 2002 per Midyear Meeting Report 401.

Rule 1.4
Amended 2002 per Midyear Meeting Report 401.

Amended 2012 per Annual Meeting Report 105A.

Rule 1.5
Amended 2002 per Midyear Meeting Report 401.

Rule 1.6
Amended 2002 per Midyear Meeting Report 401.

Amended 2003 per Annual Meeting Report 119A.

Amended 2012 per Annual Meeting Reports 105A and F.

Rule 1.7
Amended 1987 per Midyear Meeting Report 121.

Amended 2002 per Midyear Meeting Report 401.

Rule 1.8
Amended 1987 per Midyear Meeting Report 121.

Amended 2002 per Midyear Meeting Report 401.

Rule 1.9
Amended 1987 per Midyear Meeting Report 121.

Amended 1989 per Midyear Meeting Report 120A.

Amended 2002 per Midyear Meeting Report 401.

Rule 1.10
Amended 1989 per Midyear Meeting Report 120A.

Amended 2002 per Midyear Meeting Report 401.

Amended 2009 per Midyear Meeting Report 109.

Amended 2009 per Annual Meeting Report 109.

Rule 1.11

Amended 1987 per Midyear
Meeting Report 121.

Amended 2002 per Midyear
Meeting Report 401.

Rule 1.12

Amended 1987 per Midyear
Meeting Report 121.

Amended 2002 per Midyear
Meeting Report 401.

Rule 1.13

Amended 2002 per Midyear
Meeting Report 401.

Amended 2003 per Annual
Meeting Report 119B.

Rule 1.14

Amended 1997 per Midyear
Meeting Report 113.

Amended 2002 per Midyear
Meeting Report 401.

Rule 1.15

Amended 2002 per Midyear
Meeting Report 401.

Rule 1.16

Amended 2002 per Midyear
Meeting Report 401.

Rule 1.17

Added 1990 per Midyear
Meeting Report 8A.

Amended 2002 per Midyear
Meeting Report 401.

Amended 2012 per Annual
Meeting Report 105F.

Rule 1.18

Added 2002 per Midyear
Meeting Report 401.

Amended 2012 per Annual
Meeting Report 105B.

Rule 2.1

Amended 2002 per Midyear
Meeting Report 401.

Rule 2.2

Deleted 2002 per Midyear
Meeting Report 401.

Rule 2.3

Amended 2002 per Midyear
Meeting Report 401.

Rule 2.4

Added 2002 per Midyear
Meeting Report 401.

Rule 3.1

Amended 2002 per Midyear
Meeting Report 401.

Rule 3.2

Amended 2002 per Midyear
Meeting Report 401.

Rule 3.3

Amended 2002 per Midyear
Meeting Report 401.

Rule 3.4

Amended 2002 per Midyear
Meeting Report 401.

Rule 3.5

Amended 2002 per Midyear
Meeting Report 401.

Rule 3.6

Amended 1994 per Annual
Meeting Report 100.

Amended 2002 per Midyear
Meeting Report 401.

Rule 3.7

Amended 2002 per Midyear
Meeting Report 401.

Rule 3.8

Amended 1990 per Midyear Meeting Report 118.

Amended 1994 per Annual Meeting Report 100.

Amended 1995 per Annual Meeting Report 101.

Amended 2002 per Midyear Meeting Report 401.

Amended 2008 per Midyear Meeting Report 105B.

Rule 3.9

Amended 2002 per Midyear Meeting Report 401.

Rule 4.1

Amended 2002 per Midyear Meeting Report 401.

Rule 4.2

Amended 1995 per Annual Meeting Report 100.

Amended 2002 per Midyear Meeting Report 401.

Rule 4.3

Amended 2002 per Midyear Meeting Report 401.

Rule 4.4

Amended 2002 per Midyear Meeting Report 401.

Amended 2012 per Annual Meeting Report 105A.

Rule 5.1

Amended 2002 per Midyear Meeting Report 401.

Rule 5.3

Amended 2002 per Midyear Meeting Report 401.

Amended 2012 per Annual Meeting Report 105C.

Rule 5.4

Amended 1990 per Midyear Meeting Report 8A.

Amended 2002 per Midyear Meeting Report 401.

Rule 5.5

Amended 2002 per Annual Meeting Report 201B.

Amended 2007 per Midyear Meeting Report 104.

Amended 2012 per Annual Meeting Reports 105 B and C.

Amended 2013 per Midyear Meeting Report 107A.

Amended 2016 per Midyear Meeting Report 103.

Rule 5.6

Amended 1990 per Midyear Meeting Report 8A.

Amended 2002 per Midyear Meeting Report 401.

Rule 5.7

Added 1994 per Midyear Meeting Report 113.

Amended 2002 per Midyear Meeting Report 401.

Rule 6.1

Amended 1993 per Midyear Meeting Report 8A.

Amended 2002 per Midyear Meeting Report 401.

Rule 6.3

Amended 1987 per Midyear Meeting Report 121.

Rule 6.5

Added 2002 per Midyear Meeting Report 401.

Rule 7.1

Amended 2002 per Midyear Meeting Report 401.

Amended 2012 per Annual Meeting Report 105B.

Rule 7.2

Amended 1989 per Midyear Meeting Report 120B.

Amended 1990 per Midyear Meeting Report 8A.

Amended 2002 per Midyear Meeting Report 401.

Amended 2002 per Annual Meeting Report 114.

Amended 2012 per Annual Meeting Report 105B

Rule 7.3

Amended 1989 per Midyear Meeting Reports 115 and 120B.

Amended 2002 per Midyear Meeting Report 401.

Amended 2012 per Annual Meeting Report 105B.

Rule 7.4

Amended 1989 per Midyear Meeting Report 121.

Amended 1992 per Annual Meeting Revised Report 128.

Amended 1994 per Annual Meeting Report 121.

Amended 2002 per Midyear Meeting Report 401.

Rule 7.5

Amended 2002 per Midyear Meeting Report 401.

Amended 2002 per Annual Meeting Report 114.

Rule 7.6

Added 2000 per Midyear Meeting Report 110.

Rule 8.1

Amended 2002 per Midyear Meeting Report 401.

Rule 8.3

Amended 1991 per Midyear Meeting Report 108C.

Amended 2002 per Midyear Meeting Report 401.

Rule 8.4

Amended 1998 per Annual Meeting Report 117.

Amended 2002 per Midyear Meeting Report 401.

Amended 2016 per Annual Meeting Report 109.

Rule 8.5

Amended 1993 per Annual Meeting Report 114.

Amended 2002 per Annual Meeting Report 201C.

Amended 2013 per Midyear Meeting Report 107D.

AMENDMENTS TO THE MODEL RULES OF PROFESSIONAL CONDUCT (BY DATE)

1987 Midyear Meeting
Rules 1.7, 1.8, 1.9, 1.11, 1.12 and 6.3

1989 Midyear Meeting
Rules 1.9, 1.10, 7.2, 7.3 and 7.4

1990 Midyear Meeting
Rules 1.17, 3.8, 5.4, 5.6 and 7.2

1991 Midyear Meeting
Rule 8.3

1992 Annual Meeting
Rule 7.4

1993 Midyear Meeting
Rule 6.1

1993 Annual Meeting
Rule 8.5

1994 Midyear Meeting
Rule 5.7

1994 Annual Meeting
Rules 3.6, 3.8 and 7.4

1995 Annual Meeting
Rules 3.8 and 4.2

1997 Midyear Meeting
Rule 1.14

1998 Annual Meeting
Rule 8.4

2000 Midyear Meeting
Rule 7.6

2002 Midyear Meeting
Preamble, Scope, Rules 1.0, 1.1, 1.2, 1.3, 1.4, 1.5, 1.6, 1.7, 1.8, 1.9, 1.10, 1.11, 1.12, 1.13, 1.14, 1.15, 1.16, 1.17, 1.18, 2.1, 2.2, 2.3, 2.4, 3.1, 3.2, 3.3, 3.4, 3.5, 3.6, 3.7, 3.8, 3.9, 4.1, 4.2, 4.3, 4.4, 5.1, 5.3. 5.4, 5.6, 5.7, 6.1, 6.5, 7.1, 7.2, 7.3, 7.4, 7.5, 8.1, 8.3 and 8.4

2002 Annual Meeting
Rules 5.5, 7.2, 7.5 and 8.5

2003 Annual Meeting
Rules 1.6 and 1.13

2007 Midyear Meeting
Rule 5.5

2008 Midyear Meeting
Rule 3.8

2009 Midyear Meeting
Rules 1.0 and 1.10

2009 Annual Meeting
Rule 1.10

2012 Annual Meeting
Rules 1.0, 1.1, 1.4, 1.6, 1.17, 1.18, 4.4, 5.3, 5.5, 7.1, 7.2 and 7.3

2013 Midyear Meeting
Rules 5.5 and 8.5

2016 Midyear Meeting
Rule 5.5

2016 Annual Meeting
Rule 8.4

ABA Model Code of Professional Responsibility

The Model Code of Professional Responsibility was adopted by the House of Delegates of the American Bar Association on August 12, 1969, and was amended by the House of Delegates in February 1970, February 1974, February 1975, August 1976, August 1977, August 1978, February 1979, February 1980, and August 1980.

Contents

Preface

On August 14, 1964, at the request of President Lewis F. Powell, Jr., the House of Delegates of the American Bar Association created a Special Committee on Evaluation of Ethical Standards to examine the then current Canons of Professional Ethics and to make recommendations for changes. That committee produced the Model Code of Professional Responsibility, which was adopted by the House of Delegates in 1969 and became effective January 1, 1970. The new Model Code revised the previous Canons in four principal particulars: (1) there were important areas involving the conduct of lawyers that were either only partially covered in or totally omitted from the Canons; (2) many Canons that were sound in substance were in need of editorial revision; (3) most of the Canons did not lend themselves to practical sanctions for violations; and (4) changed and changing conditions in our legal system and urbanized society required new statements of professional principles.

The original 32 Canons of Professional Ethics were adopted by the American Bar Association in 1908. They were based principally on the Code of Ethics adopted by the Alabama State Bar Association in 1887, which in turn has been borrowed largely from the lectures of Judge George Sharswood, published in 1854 under the title of *Professional Ethics*, and from the fifty resolutions included in David Hoffman's *A Course of Legal Study* (2d ed. 1836). Since then a limited number of amendments have been adopted on a piecemeal basis.

As far back as 1934 Mr. Justice (later Chief Justice) Harlan Fiske Stone, in his memorable address entitled The *Public Influence of the Bar*, made this observation:

> Before the Bar can function at all as a guardian of the public interests committed to its care, there must be appraisal and comprehension of the new conditions, and the chained relationship of the lawyer to his clients, to his professional brethren and to the public. That appraisal must pass beyond the petty details of form and manners which have been so largely the subject of our Codes of Ethics, to more fundamental consideration of the way in which our professional activities affect the welfare of society as a whole. Our canons of ethics for the most part are generalizations designed for an earlier era.

Largely in that spirit, the committee appointed by President Powell in 1964 reached unanimous conclusion that further piecemeal amendment of the original Canons would not suffice. It proceeded to compose the Model Code of Professional Responsibility in response to the perceived need for change in the statement of professional principles for lawyers.

While the opinions of the Committee on Professional Ethics of the American Bar Association had been published and given fairly wide distribution with resulting value to the bench and bar, they certainly were not conclusive as to the adequacy of the previous Canons. Because the opinions were nec-

ABA Model
Code of
Professional
Responsibility

essarily interpretations of the existing Canons, they tended to support the Canons and were critical of them only in the most unusual case. Since a large number of requests for opinions from the Committee on Professional Ethics dealt with the etiquette of law practice, advertising, partnership names, announcements and the like, there had been a tendency for many lawyers to assume that this was the exclusive field of interest of the Committee and that it was not concerned with the more serious questions of professional standards and obligations.

The previous Canons were not an effective teaching instrument and failed to give guidance to young lawyers beyond the language of the Canons themselves. There was no organized interrelationship between the Canons and they often overlapped. They were not cast in language designed for disciplinary enforcement and many abounded with quaint expressions of the past. Those Canons contained, nevertheless, many provisions that were sound in substance, and all of these were retained in the Model Code adopted in 1969. In the studies and meetings conducted by the committee which developed the present Model Code, the committee relied heavily upon the monumental Legal Ethics (1953) of Henry S. Drinker, who served with great distinction for nine years as Chairman of the Committee on Professional Ethics (known in his day as the Committee on Professional Ethics and Grievances) of the American Bar Association.

The Formal Opinions of the Committee on Ethics and Professional Responsibility were collected and published in a single volume in 1967, and since that time have been published continuously in loose-leaf form. (The name was changed in 1971 to the Standing Committee on Ethics and Professional Responsibility.) The Informal Opinions of the Committee on Ethics and Professional Responsibility were collected and published in a two-volume set in 1975, and since that time new opinions have been published continuously in loose-leaf form.

Since the adoption of the Model Code of Professional Responsibility in 1969 a number of amendments have been required due to decisions of the Supreme Court of the United States and lower courts relating to the provision of group legal services and the provision of additional legal services on a wide scale not only to indigents but also to persons of moderate means. Furthermore, recent decisions of the Supreme Court of the United States on the subject of the constitutionality of restrictive provisions in the Code relating to lawyer advertising have required a substantial revision of Canon 2 and of other portions of the present Model Code. These modifications in the Code are included in the present printing, up to and including the action taken by the House of Delegates in August of 1978. The Committee on Ethics and Professional Responsibility is mandated under the By-Laws of the American Bar Association (Article 30.7) to recommend appropriate amendments to or clarification of the Model Code. Additional changes are under consideration by the Committee with particular cognizance of recent Court decisions.

Preamble[1]

The continued existence of a free and democratic society depends upon recognition of the concept that justice is based upon the rule of law grounded in respect for the dignity of the individual and his capacity through reason for enlightened self-government.[2] Law so grounded makes justice possible, for only through such law does the dignity of the individual attain respect and protection. Without it, individual rights become subject to unrestrained power, respect for law is destroyed, and rational self-government is impossible.

Lawyers, as guardians of the law, play a vital role in the preservation of society. The fulfillment of this role requires an understanding by lawyers of their relationship with and function in our legal system.[3] A consequent obligation of lawyers is to maintain the highest standards of ethical conduct.

In fulfilling his professional responsibilities, a lawyer necessarily assumes various roles that require the performance of many difficult tasks. Not every situation which he may encounter can be foreseen,[4] but fundamental ethical principles are always present to guide him. Within the framework of these principles, a lawyer must with courage and foresight be able and ready to shape the body of the law to the ever-changing relationships of society.[5]

The Model Code of Professional Responsibility points the way to the aspiring and provides standards by which to judge the transgressor. Each lawyer must find within his own conscience the touchstone against which to test the extent to which his actions should rise above minimum standards. But in the last analysis it is the desire for the respect and confidence of the members of his profession and of the society which he serves that should provide to a lawyer the incentive for the highest possible degree of ethical conduct. The possible loss of that respect and confidence is the ultimate sanction. So long as its practitioners are guided by these principles, the law will continue to be a noble profession. This is its greatness and its strength, which permit of no compromise.

Preliminary Statement

In furtherance of the principles stated in the Preamble, the American Bar Association has promulgated this Model Code of Professional Responsibility, consisting of three separate but interrelated parts: Canons, Ethical Considerations, and Disciplinary Rules.[6] The Code is designed to be adopted by appropriate agencies both as an inspirational guide to the members of the profession and as a basis for disciplinary action when the conduct of a lawyer falls below the required minimum standards stated in the Disciplinary Rules.

Obviously the Canons, Ethical Considerations, and Disciplinary Rules cannot apply to non-lawyers; however, they do define the type of ethical conduct that the public has a right to expect not only of lawyers but also of their non-professional employees and associates in all matters pertaining to professional employment. A lawyer should ultimately be responsible for the conduct of his employees and associates in the course of the professional representation of the client.

The Canons are statements of axiomatic norms, expressing in general terms the standards of professional conduct expected of lawyers in their relationships with the public, with the legal system, and with the legal profession. They embody the general concepts from which the Ethical Consideration and the Disciplinary Rules are derived.

The Ethical Considerations are aspirational in character and represent the objectives toward which every member of the profession should strive. They constitute a body of principles upon which the lawyer can rely for guidance in many specific situations.[7]

The Disciplinary Rules, unlike the Ethical Considerations, are mandatory in character. The Disciplinary Rules state the minimum level of conduct below which no lawyer can fall without being subject to disciplinary action. Within the framework of fair trial,[8] the Disciplinary Rules should be uniformly applied to all lawyers,[9] regardless of the nature of their professional activities.[10] The Model Code makes no attempt to prescribe either disciplinary procedures or penalties[11] for violation of a Disciplinary Rule,[12] nor does it undertake to define standards for civil liability of lawyers for professional conduct. The severity of judgment against one found guilty of violating a Disciplinary Rule should be determined by the character of the offense and the attendant circumstances.[13] An enforcing agency, in applying the Disciplinary Rules, may find interpretive guidance in the basic principles embodied in the Canons and in the objectives reflected in the Ethical Considerations.

NOTES

1. The footnotes are intended merely to enable the reader to relate the provisions of this Model Code to the ABA Canons of Professional Ethics adopted in 1908, as amended, the Opinions of the ABA Committee on Professional Ethics, and a limited number of other sources; they are not intended to be an annotation of the views taken by the ABA Special Committee on Evaluation of Ethical Standards. Footnotes citing ABA Canons refer to the ABA Canons of Professional Ethics, adopted in 1908, as amended.

2. *Cf.* ABA CANONS OF PROFESSIONAL ETHICS, Preamble (1908).

3. "[T]he lawyer stands today in special need of a clear understanding of his obligations and of the vital connection between these obligations and the role his profession plays in society." *Professional Responsibility: Report of the Joint Conference,* 44 A.B.A. J. 1159, 1160 (1958).

4. "No general statement of the responsibilities of the legal profession can encompass all the situations in which the lawyer may be placed. Each position held by him makes its own peculiar demands. These demands the lawyer must clarify for himself in the light of the particular role in which he serves." *Professional Responsibility: Report of the Joint Conference,* 44 A.B.A. J. 1159, 1218 (1958).

5. "The law and its institutions change as social conditions change. They must change if they are to preserve, much less advance, the political and social values from which they derive their purpose and their life. This is true of the most important of legal institutions,

the profession of law. The profession, too, must change when conditions change in order to preserve and advance the social values that are its reasons for being." Cheatham, Availability of Legal Services: *The Responsibility of the Individual Lawyer and the Organized Bar*. 12 U.C.L.A. L. REV. 438, 440 (1965).

6. The Supreme Court of Wisconsin adopted a Code of Judicial Ethics in 1967. "The code is divided into standards and rules, the standards being statements of what the general desirable level of conduct should be, the rules being particular canons, the violation of which shall subject an individual judge to sanctions." In re Promulgation of a Code of Judicial Ethics, 36 Wis. 2d 252,255, 153 N.W.2d 873, 874 (1967). The portion of the Wisconsin Code of Judicial Ethics entitled "Standards" states that "[t]he following standards set forth the significant qualities of the ideal judge . . . ."*Id.*, 36 Wis. 2d at 256, 153 N.W. 2d at 875.

The portion entitled "Rules" states that [t]he court promulgates the following rules because the requirements of judicial conduct embodied therein are of sufficient gravity to warrant sanctions if they are not obeyed . . . ."*Id.*, 36 Wis. 2d at 259, 153 N.W.2d at 876.

7. "Under the conditions of modern practice it is peculiarly necessary that the lawyer should understand, not merely the established standards of professional conduct, but the reasons underlying these standards. Today the lawyer plays a changing and increasingly varied role. In many developing fields the precise contribution of the legal profession is as yet undefined." *Professional Responsibility: Report of the Joint Conference*, 44 A.B.A. J. 1159 (1958).

"A true sense of professional responsibility must derive from an understanding of the reasons that lie back of specific restraints, such as those embodied in the Canons. The grounds for the lawyer's peculiar obligations are to be found in the nature of his calling. The lawyer who seeks a clear understanding of his duties will be led to reflect on the special services his profession renders to society and the services it might render if its full capacities were realized. When the lawyer fully understands the nature of his office, he will then discern what restraints are necessary to keep that office wholesome and effective." *Id.*

8. "Disbarment, designed to protect the public, is a punishment or penalty imposed on the lawyer . . . . He is accordingly entitled to procedural due process, which includes fair notice of charge." *In re* Ruffalo, 390 U.S. 544, 550, 20 L. Ed.2d 117, 122, 88 S. Ct. 1222, 1226 (1968), *rehearing denied*, 391 U.S. 961, 20 L. Ed. 2d 874, 88 S. Ct. 1933(1968).

"A State cannot exclude a person from the practice of law or from any other occupation in a manner or for reasons that contravene the Due Process or Equal Protection Clause of the Fourteenth Amendment . . . . A State can require high standards of qualification . . . but any qualification must have a rational connection with the applicant's fitness or capacity to practice law." Schware v. Bd. of Bar Examiners, 353 U.S. 232, 239, 1 L. Ed. 2d 796, 801-02, 77 S. Ct. 752, 756 (1957).

"[A]n accused lawyer may expect that he will not be condemned out of a capricious self-righteousness or denied the essentials of a fair hearing." Kingsland v. Dorsey, 338 U.S. 318, 320, 94 L.Ed. 123, 126, 70 S. Ct. 123, 124-25 (1949).

"The attorney and counselor being, by the solemn judicial act of the court, clothed with his office, does not hold it as a matter of grace and favor. The right which it confers upon him to appear for suitors, and to argue causes, is something more than a mere indulgence, revocable at the pleasure of the court or at the command of the legislature. It is a right of which he can only be deprived by the judgment of the court for moral or professional delinquency." Ex parte Garland, 71 U.S. (4 Wall.) 333, 378-79,18 L. Ed. 366, 370 (1866).

See generally Comment, *Procedural Due Process and Character Hearings for Bar Applicants*, 15 STAN. L. REV. 500 (1963)

9. "The canons of professional ethics must be enforced by the Courts and must be respected by members of the Bar if we are to maintain public confidence in the integrity and impartiality of the administration of justice." In re Meeker, 76 N. M. 354, 357, 414 P.2d 862, 864 (1966), appeal dismissed 385 U.S. 449 (1967).

10. *See* ABA CANONS OF PROFESSIONAL ETHICS, CANON 45 (1908).

11. "Other than serving as a model or derivative source, the American Bar Association Model Code of Professional Responsibility plays no part in the disciplinary proceeding, except as a guide for consideration in adoption of local applicable rules for the regulation of conduct on the part of legal practitioners." ABA COMM. ON PROFESSIONAL ETHICS, INFORMAL OPINION No. 1420(1978) [hereinafter each Formal Opinion is cited as "*ABA Opinion*"]. For the purposes and intended effect of the American Bar Association Model Code of Professional Responsibility and of the opinions of the Standing Committee on Ethics and Professional Responsibility, see Informal Opinion No. 1420. "There is generally no prescribed discipline for any particular type of improper conduct. The disciplinary measures taken are discretionary with the courts, which may disbar, suspend, or merely censure the attorney as the nature of the offense and past indicia of character may warrant." Note, 43 CORNELL L.Q. 489, 495 (1958).

12. The Model Code seeks only to specify conduct for which a lawyer should be disciplined by courts and governmental agencies which have adopted it. Recommendations as to the procedures to be used in disciplinary actions are within the jurisdiction of the American Bar Association Standing Committee on Professional Discipline.

13. "The severity of the judgment of this court should be in proportion to the gravity of the offenses, the moral turpitude involved, and the extent that the defendant's acts and conduct affect his professional qualifications to practice law." Louisiana State Bar Ass'n v. Steiner, 204 La. 1073, 1092-93, 16 So. 2d 843, 850 (1944) (Higgins, J., concurring in decree).

"Certainly an erring lawyer who has been disciplined and who having paid the penalty has given satisfactory evidence of repentance and has been rehabilitated and restored to his place at the bar by the court which knows him best ought not to have what amounts to an order of permanent disbarment entered against him by a federal court solely on the basis of an earlier criminal record and without regard to his subsequent rehabilitation and present good character . . . . We think, therefore, that the district court should reconsider the appellant's application for admission and grant it unless the court finds it to be a fact that the appellant is not presently of good moral or professional character." In re Dreier, 258 F.2d 68, 69-70 (3d Cir. 1958).

CANON 1
A Lawyer Should Assist in Maintaining the Integrity and Competence of the Legal Profession

ETHICAL CONSIDERATIONS

EC 1-1   A basic tenet of the professional responsibility of lawyers is that every person in our society should have ready access to the independent professional services of a lawyer of integrity and competence. Maintaining the integrity and improving the competence of the bar to meet the highest standards is the ethical responsibility of every lawyer.

EC 1-2   The public should be protected from those who are not qualified to be lawyers by reason of a deficiency in education[1] or moral standards[2] or of other relevant factors[3] but who nevertheless seek to practice law. To assure the maintenance of high moral and educational standards of the legal profession, lawyers should affirmatively assist courts and other appropriate bodies in promulgating, enforcing, and improving requirements for admission to the bar.[4] In like manner, the bar has a positive obligation to aid in the continued improvement of all phases of pre-admission and post-admission legal education.

EC 1-3   Before recommending an applicant for admission, a lawyer should satisfy himself that the applicant is of good moral character. Although a lawyer should not become a self-appointed investigator or judge of applicants for admission, he should report to proper officials all unfavorable information he possesses relating to the character or other qualifications of an applicant.[5]

EC 1-4   The integrity of the profession can be maintained only if conduct of lawyers in violation of the Disciplinary Rules is brought to the attention of the proper officials. A lawyer should reveal voluntarily to those officials all unprivileged knowledge of conduct of lawyers which he believes clearly to be in violation of the Disciplinary Rules.[6] A lawyer should, upon request serve on and assist committees and boards having responsibility for the administration of the Disciplinary Rules.[7]

EC 1-5   A lawyer should maintain high standards of professional conduct and should encourage fellow lawyers to do likewise. He should be temperate and dignified, and he should refrain from all illegal and morally reprehensible conduct.[8] Because of his position in society, even minor violations of law by a lawyer may tend to lessen public confidence in the legal profession. Obedience to law exemplifies respect for law. To lawyers especially, respect for the law should be more than a platitude.

EC 1-6   An applicant for admission to the bar or a lawyer may be unqualified, temporarily or permanently, for other than moral and educational reasons, such as mental or emotional instability. Lawyers should be diligent in taking steps to see that during a period of disqualification such person is not granted a license or, if licensed, is not permitted to practice.9 In like manner, when the disqualification has terminated, members of the bar should assist such person in being licensed, or, if licensed, in being restored to his full right to practice.

DISCIPLINARY RULES

DR 1-101   Maintaining Integrity and Competence of the Legal Profession.

(A) A lawyer is subject to discipline if he has made a materially false statement in, or if he has deliberately failed to disclose a material fact requested in connection with, his application for admission to the bar.[10]

(B) A lawyer shall not further the application for admission to the bar of another person known by him to be unqualified in respect to character, education, or other relevant attribute.[11]

DR 1-102   Misconduct.

(A) A lawyer shall not:
    (1) Violate a Disciplinary Rule.
    (2) Circumvent a Disciplinary Rule through actions of another.[12]
    (3) Engage in illegal conduct involving moral turpitude.[13]
    (4) Engage in conduct involving dishonesty, fraud, deceit, or misrepresentation.
    (5) Engage in conduct that is prejudicial to the administration of justice.
    (6) Engage in any other conduct that adversely reflects on his fitness to practice law.[14]

DR 1-103   Disclosure of information to Authorities.

(A) A lawyer possessing unprivileged knowledge of a violation of DR 1-102 shall report such knowledge to a tribunal or other authority empowered to investigate or act upon such violation.[15]

(B) A lawyer possessing unprivileged knowledge or evidence concerning another lawyer or a judge shall reveal fully such knowledge or evidence upon proper request of a tribunal or other authority empowered to investigate or act upon the conduct of lawyers or judges.[16]

NOTES

1. "[W]e cannot conclude that all educational restrictions [on bar admission] are unlawful. We assume that few would deny that a grammar school education requirement

ABA Model Code of Professional Responsibility

before taking the bar examination was reasonable. Or that an applicant had to be able to read or write. Once we conclude that some restriction is proper, then it becomes a matter of degree—the problem of drawing the line.

. . . .

"We conclude the fundamental question here is whether Rule IV, Section 6 of the Rules pertaining to Admission of Applicants to the State Bar of Arizona is 'arbitrary, capricious and unreasonable.' We conclude an educational requirement of graduation from an accredited law school is not." Hackin v. Lockwood, 361 F.2d 499, 503-4 (9th Cir. 1966), *cert. denied*, 385 U.S. 960, 17 L. Ed. 2d 305, 87 S. Ct. 396 (1966).

2. "Every state in the United States, as a prerequisite for admission to the practice of law, requires that applicants possess 'good moral character.' Although the requirement is of judicial origin, it is now embodied in legislation in most states." Comment, *Procedural Due Process and Character Hearings for Bar Applicant*, 15 Stan. L. Rev. 500 (1963).

"Good character in the member of the bar is essential to the preservation of the courts. The duty and power of the court to guard its portals against intrusion by men and women who are mentally and morally dishonest, unfit because of bad character, evidenced by their course of conduct, to participate in the administrative law, would seem to be unquestioned in the matter of preservation of judicial dignity and integrity." In re Monaghan, 126 Vt. 53, 222 A.2d 665, 670 (1966).

"Fundamentally, the question involved in both situations [i.e. admission and disciplinary proceedings] is the same—is the applicant for admission or the attorney sought to be disciplined a fit and proper person to be permitted to practice law, and that usually turns upon whether he has committed or is likely to continue to commit acts of moral turpitude. At the time of oral argument the attorney for respondent frankly conceded that the test for admission and for discipline is and should be the same. We agree with this concession." Hallinan v. Comm. of Bar Examiners, 65 Cal. 2d 447, 453, 421, P.2d 76, 81, 55 Cal. Rptr. 228, 233(1966).

3. "Proceedings to gain admission to the bar are for the purpose of protecting the public and the courts from the ministrations of persons unfit to practice the profession. Attorneys are officers of the court appointed to assist the court in the administration of justice. Into their hands are committed the property, the liberty and sometimes the lives of their clients. This commitment demands a high degree of intelligence, knowledge of the law, respect for its function in society, sound and faithful judgment and, above all else, integrity of character in private and professional conduct." In re Monaghan, 126 Vt. 53, 222 A.2d 665, 676 (1966) (Holden, C.J., dissenting).

4. "A bar composed of lawyers of good moral character is objective but it is unnecessary to sacrifice vital freedoms in order to obtain that goal. It is also important both to society and the bar itself that lawyers be unintimidated—free to think, speak, and act as members of an Independent Bar." Konigsberg v. State Bar, 353 U.S. 252, 273, 1 L. Ed. 2d 810, 825, 77 S. Ct. 722, 733 (1957).

5. *See* ABA Canons of Professional Ethics, Canon 29 (1908).

6. ABA Canons of Professional Ethics, Canon 28 (1908) designates certain conduct as unprofessional and then states that: "A duty to the public and to the profession devolves upon every member of the Bar having knowledge of such practices upon the part of any practitioner immediately to inform thereof, to the end that the offender may be disbarred." ABA Canon 29 states a broader admonition: "Lawyers should expose without fear or favor before the proper tribunals corrupt or dishonest conduct in the profession."

7. "It is the obligation of the organized Bar and the individual lawyer to give unstinted cooperation and assistance to the highest court of the state in discharging its function and duty with respect to discipline and in purging the profession of the unworthy." *Report of the Special Committee on Disciplinary Procedures*, 80 A.B.A. Rep. 463, 470 (1955).

8. *Cf.* ABA Canons of Professional Ethics, Canon 32 (1908).

ABA Model
Code of
Professional
Responsibility

9. "We decline, on the present record, to disbar Mr. Sherman or to reprimand him—not because we condone his actions, but because, as heretofore indicated, we are concerned with whether he is mentally responsible for what he has done.

"The logic of the situation would seem to dictate the conclusion that, if he was mentally responsible for the conduct we have outlined, he should be disbarred; and, if he was not mentally responsible, he should not be permitted to practice law.

"However, the flaw in the logic is that he may have been mentally irresponsible [at the time of his offensive conduct] . . . , and, yet, have sufficiently improved in the almost two and one-half years intervening to be able to capably and competently represent his clients.
. . . .

"We would make clear that we are satisfied that a case has been made against Mr. Sherman, warranting a refusal to permit him to further practice law in this state unless he can establish his mental irresponsibility at the time of the offenses charged. The burden of proof is upon him.

"If he establish such mental irresponsibility, the burden is then upon him to establish his present capability to practice law." In re Sherman, 58 Wash. 2d 1, 6-7, 354 P.2d 888, 890 (1960), *cert. denied*, 371 U.S. 951, 9 L. Ed. 2d 499, 83 S. Ct. 506 (1963).

10. "This Court has the inherent power to revoke a license to practice law in this State, where such license was issued by this Court, and its issuance was procured by the fraudulent concealment, or by the false and fraudulent representation by the applicant of a fact which was manifestly material to the issuance of the license." North Carolina ex rel. Attorney General v. Gorson, 209 N.C. 320, 326, 183 S.E. 392, 395 (1936), *cert. denied*, 298 U.S. 662, 80 L. Ed. 1387, 56 S. Ct. 752 (1936).

11. *See* ABA CANONS OF PROFESSIONAL ETHICS, CANON 29 (1908).

12. In *ABA Opinion* 95 (1933), which held that a municipal attorney could not permit police officers to interview persons with claims against the municipality when the attorney knew the claimants to be represented by counsel, the Committee on Professional Ethics said:

"The law officer is, of course, responsible for the acts of those in his department who are under his supervision and control. Opinion 85. In re Robinson, 136 N.Y.S. 548 (affirmed 209 N.Y. 354-1912) held that it was a matter of disbarment for an attorney to adopt a general course of approving the unethical conduct of employees of his client, even though he did not actively participate therein.

"'. . . The attorney should not advise or sanction acts by his client which he himself should not do.' Opinion 75."

13. "The most obvious non-professional ground for disbarment is conviction for a felony. Most states make conviction for a felony grounds for automatic disbarment. Some of these states, including New York, make disbarment mandatory upon conviction for any felony, while others require disbarment only for those felonies which involve moral turpitude. There are strong arguments that some felonies, such as involuntary manslaughter, reflect neither on an attorney's fitness, trustworthiness, nor competence and, therefore, should not be grounds for disbarment but most states tend to disregard these arguments and, following the common law rule, make disbarment mandatory on conviction for any felony." Note, 43 CORNELL L.Q. 489, 490 (1958).

"Some states treat conviction for misdemeanors as grounds for automatic disbarment . . . . However, the vast majority, accepting the common law rule, require that the misdemeanor involve moral turpitude. While the definition of moral turpitude may prove difficult, it seems only proper that those minor offenses which do not affect the attorney's fitness to continue in the profession should not be grounds for disbarment. A good example is an assault and battery conviction which would not involve moral turpitude unless done with malice and deliberation." *Id.* at 491.

"The term 'moral turpitude' has been used in the law for centuries. It has been the subject of many decisions by the courts but has never been clearly defined because of the nature of the term. Perhaps the best general definition of the term 'moral turpitude' is that it imparts an act of baseness, vileness or depravity in the duties which one person owes to another or to society in general, which is contrary to the usual, accepted and customary rule of right and duty which a person should follow. 58 C.J.S. at page 1201. Although offenses against revenue laws have been held to be crimes of moral turpitude, it has also been held that the attempt to evade the payment of taxes due to the government or any subdivision thereof, while wrong and unlawful, does not involve moral turpitude. 58 C.J.S. at page 1205." Comm. on Legal Ethics v. Scheer, 149 W. Va. 721, 726-27, 143 S.E.2d 141, 145 (1965).

"The right and power to discipline an attorney, as one of its officers, is inherent in the court . . . . This power is not limited to those instances of misconduct wherein he has been employed, or has acted, in a professional capacity; but, on the contrary, this power may be exercised where his misconduct outside the scope of his professional relations shows him to be an unfit person to practice law." In re Wilson, 391 S.W.2d 914, 179-18 (Mo. 1965).

14. "It is a fair characterization of the lawyer's responsibility in our society that he stands 'as a shield,' to quote Devlin, J., in defense of right and to ward off wrong. From a profession charged with these responsibilities there must be exacted those qualities of truth-speaking, of a high sense of honor, of granite discretion, of the strictest observance of fiduciary responsibility, that have, throughout the centuries, been compendiously described as 'moral character.'" Schware v. Bd. of Bar Examiners, 353 U.S. 232, 247, 1 L. Ed. 2d 796, 806, 77 S. Ct. 752, 761 (1957) (Frankfurter, J., *concurring*).

"Particularly applicable here is Rule 4.47 providing that 'A lawyer should always maintain his integrity; and shall not willfully commit any act against the interest of the public; *nor shall he violate his duty to the courts or his clients; nor shall he, by any misconduct, commit any offense against the laws of Missouri or the United States of America, which amounts to a crime involving acts done by him contrary to justice, honesty, modesty or good morals;* nor shall he be guilty of any other misconduct whereby, for the protection of the public and those charged with the administration of justice, he should no longer be entrusted with the duties and responsibilities belonging to the office of an attorney.' "In re Wilson, 391 S.W.2d 914, 917 (Mo. 1965).

15. *See* ABA CANONS OF PROFESSIONAL ETHICS, CANON 29 (1908); *cf.* ABA CANONS OF PROFESSIONAL ETHICS, CANON 28 (1908).

16. *Cf.* ABA CANONS OF PROFESSIONAL ETHICS, CANONS 28 and 29 (1908).

CANON 2
A Lawyer Should Assist the Legal Profession in Fulfilling Its Duty to Make Legal Counsel Available

ETHICAL CONSIDERATIONS

EC 2-1   The need of members of the public for legal services[1] is met only if they recognize their legal problems, appreciate the importance of seeking assistance,[2] and are able to obtain the services of acceptable legal counsel.[3] Hence, important functions of the legal profession are to educate laymen to recognize their problems, to facilitate the process of intelligent selection of lawyers, and to assist in making legal services fully available.[4]

Recognition of Legal Problems

ABA Model Code of Professional Responsibility

EC 2-2   The legal profession should assist laypersons to recognize legal problems because such problems may not be self-revealing and often are not timely noticed. Therefore, lawyers should encourage and participate in educational and public relations programs concerning our legal system with particular reference to legal problems that frequently arise. Preparation of advertisements and professional articles for lay publications[5] and participation in seminars, lectures, and civic programs should be motivated by a desire to educate the public to an awareness of legal needs and to provide information relevant to the selection of the most appropriate counsel rather than to obtain publicity for particular lawyers. The problems of advertising on television require special consideration, due to the style, cost, and transitory nature of such media. If the interests of laypersons in receiving relevant lawyer advertising are not adequately served by print media and radio advertising, and if adequate safeguards to protect the public can reasonably be formulated, television advertising may serve a public interest.

EC 2-3   Whether a lawyer acts properly in volunteering in-person advice to a layperson to seek legal services depends upon the circumstances.[6] The giving of advice that one should take legal action could well be in fulfillment of the duty of the legal profession to assist laypersons in recognizing legal problems.[7] The advice is proper only if motivated by a desire to protect one who does not recognize that he may have legal problems or who is ignorant of his legal rights or obligations. It is improper if motivated by a desire to obtain personal benefit, secure personal publicity, or cause legal action to be taken merely to harass or injure another. A lawyer should not initiate an in-person contact with a non-client, personally or through a representative, for the purpose of being retained to represent him for compensation.

EC 2-4   Since motivation is subjective and often difficult to judge, the motives of a lawyer who volunteers in-person advice likely to produce legal controversy may well be suspect if he receives professional employment or other benefits as a result.[8] A lawyer who volunteers in-person advice that one should obtain the services of a lawyer generally should not himself accept employment, compensation, or other benefit in connection with that matter. However, it is not improper for a lawyer to volunteer such advice and render resulting legal services to close friends, relatives, former clients (in regard to matters germane to former employment), and regular clients.[9]

EC 2-5   A lawyer who writes or speaks for the purpose of educating members of the public to recognize their legal problems should carefully refrain from giving or appearing to give a general solution applicable to all apparently similar individual problems,[10] since slight changes in fact situations may require a material variance in the applicable advice; otherwise, the public may be misled and misadvised. Talks and writings by lawyers for laymen should caution them not to attempt to solve individual problems upon the basis of the information contained therein.[11]

Selection of a Lawyer: Generally

EC 2-6 Formerly a potential client usually knew the reputations of local lawyers for competency and integrity and therefore could select a practitioner in whom he had confidence. This traditional selection process worked well because it was initiated by the client and the choice was an informed one.

EC 2-7 Changed conditions, however, have seriously restricted the effectiveness of the traditional selection process. Often the reputations of lawyers are not sufficiently known to enable laymen to make intelligent choices.[12] The law has become increasingly complex and specialized. Few lawyers are willing and competent to deal with every kind of legal matter, and many laymen have difficulty in determining the competence of lawyers to render different types of legal services. The selection of legal counsel is particularly difficult for transients, persons moving into new areas, persons of limited education or means, and others who have little or no contact with lawyers.[13] Lack of information about the availability of lawyers, the qualifications of particular lawyers, and the expense of legal representation leads laypersons to avoid seeking legal advice.

EC 2-8 Selection of a lawyer by a layperson should be made on an informed basis. Advice and recommendation of third parties—relatives, friends, acquaintances, business associates, or other lawyers—and disclosure of relevant information about the lawyer and his practice may be helpful. A layperson is best served if the recommendation is disinterested and informed. In order that the recommendation be disinterested, a lawyer should not seek to influence another to recommend his employment. A lawyer should not compensate another person for recommending him, for influencing a prospective client to employ him, or to encourage future recommendations.[14] Advertisements and public communications, whether in law lists, telephone directories, newspapers, other forms of print media, television or radio, should be formulated to convey only information that is necessary to make an appropriate selection. Such information includes: (1) office information, such as name, including name of law firm and names of professional associates; addresses; telephone numbers; credit card acceptability; fluency in foreign languages; and office hours; (2) relevant biographical information; (3) description of the practice, but only by using designations and definitions authorized by [the agency having jurisdiction of the subject under state law], for example, one or more fields of law in which the lawyer or law firm practices; a statement that practice is limited to one or more fields of law; and/ or a statement that the lawyer or law firm specializes in a particular field of law practice, but only by using designations, definitions and standards authorized by [the agency having jurisdiction of the subject under state law]; and (4) permitted fee information. Self-laudation should be avoided.[15]

Selection of a Lawyer: Professional Notices and Listings

EC 2-9   The lack of sophistication on the part of many members of the public concerning legal services, the importance of the interests affected by the choice of a lawyer and prior experience with unrestricted lawyer advertising, require that special care be taken by lawyers to avoid misleading the public and to assure that the information set forth in any advertising is relevant to the selection of a lawyer. The lawyer must be mindful that the benefits of lawyer advertising depend upon its reliability and accuracy. Examples of information in lawyer advertising that would be deceptive include misstatements of fact, suggestions that the ingenuity or prior record of a lawyer rather than the justice of the claim are the principal factors likely to determine the result, inclusion of information irrelevant to selecting a lawyer, and representations concerning the quality of service, which cannot be measured or verified. Since lawyer advertising is calculated and not spontaneous, reasonable regulation of lawyer advertising designed to foster compliance with appropriate standards serves the public interest without impeding the flow of useful, meaningful, and relevant information to the public.

EC 2-10   A lawyer should ensure that the information contained in any advertising which the lawyer publishes, broadcasts or causes to be published or broadcast is relevant, is disseminated in an objective and understandable fashion, and would facilitate the prospective client's ability to compare the qualifications of the lawyers available to represent him. A lawyer should strive to communicate such information without undue emphasis upon style and advertising stratagems which serve to hinder rather than to facilitate intelligent selection of counsel. Because technological change is a recurrent feature of communications forms, and because perceptions of what is relevant in lawyer selection may change, lawyer advertising regulations should not be cast in rigid, unchangeable terms. Machinery is therefore available to advertisers and consumers for prompt consideration of proposals to change the rules governing lawyer advertising. The determination of any request for such change should depend upon whether the proposal is necessary in light of existing Code provisions, whether the proposal accords with standards of accuracy, reliability and truthfulness, and whether the proposal would facilitate informed selection of lawyers by potential consumers of legal services. Representatives of lawyers and consumers should be heard in addition to the applicant concerning any proposed change. Any change which is approved should be promulgated in the form of an amendment to the Code so that all lawyers practicing in the jurisdiction may avail themselves of its provisions.

EC 2-11   The name under which a lawyer conducts his practice may be a factor in the selection process.[16] The use of a trade name or an assumed name could mislead laymen concerning the identity, responsibility, and status of those practicing thereunder.[17] Accordingly, a lawyer in private practice should practice only under his own name, the name of a lawyer employing him, a designation containing the name of one or more of the lawyers practicing in a partnership, or, if permitted by law, the name of a professional legal corporation, which should be clearly designated as such. For many years some law firms have used a firm name retaining one or more names of deceased or retired partners and such practice is not improper if the firm is a bona fide successor of a firm in which the deceased or retired person was a member, if the use of the name is authorized by law or by contract, and if the public is not misled thereby.[18] However, the name of a partner who withdraws from a firm but continues to practice law should be omitted from the firm name in order to avoid misleading the public.

EC 2-12   A lawyer occupying a judicial, legislative, or public executive or administrative position who has the right to practice law concurrently may allow his name to remain in the name of the firm if he actively continues to practice law as a member thereof. Otherwise, his name should be removed from the firm name,[19] and he should not be identified as a past or present member of the firm; and he should not hold himself out as being a practicing lawyer.

EC 2-13   In order to avoid the possibility of misleading persons with whom he deals, a lawyer should be scrupulous in the representation of his professional status.[20] He should not hold himself out as being a partner or associate of a law firm if he is not one in fact,[21] and thus should not hold himself out as a partner or associate if he only shares offices with another lawyer.[22]

EC 2-14   In some instances a lawyer confines his practice to a particular field of law.[23] In the absence of state controls to insure the existence of special competence, a lawyer should not be permitted to hold himself out as a specialist or as having official recognition as a specialist, other than in the fields of admiralty, trademark, and patent law where a holding out as a specialist historically has been permitted. A lawyer may, however, indicate in permitted advertising, if it is factual, a limitation of his practice or one or more particular areas or fields of law in which he practices using designations and definitions authorized for that purpose by [the state agency having jurisdiction]. A lawyer practicing in a jurisdiction which certifies specialists must also be careful not to confuse laypersons as to his status. If a lawyer discloses areas of law in which he practices or to which he limits his practice, but is not certified in [the jurisdiction], he, and the designation authorized in [the jurisdiction], should avoid any implication that he is in fact certified.

EC 2-15   The legal profession has developed lawyer referral systems designed to aid individuals who are able to pay fees but need assistance in locating lawyers competent to handle their particular problems. Use of a lawyer referral system enables a layman to avoid an uninformed selection of a lawyer because such a system makes possible the employment of competent lawyers who have indicated an interest in the subject matter involved. Lawyers should support the principle of lawyer referral systems and should encourage the evolution of other ethical plans which aid in the selection of qualified counsel.

Financial Ability to Employ Counsel: Generally

EC 2-16   The legal profession cannot remain a viable force in fulfilling its role in our society unless its members receive adequate compensation for services rendered, and reasonable fees[24] should be charged in appropriate cases to clients able to pay them. Nevertheless, persons unable to pay all or a portion of a reasonable fee should be able to obtain necessary legal services,[25] and lawyers should support and participate in ethical activities designed to achieve that objective.[26]

Financial Ability to Employ Counsel:
Persons Able to Pay Reasonable Fees

EC 2-17   The determination of a proper fee requires consideration of the interests of both client and lawyer.[27] A lawyer should not charge more than a reasonable fee,[28] for excessive cost of legal service would deter laymen from utilizing the legal system in protection of their rights. Furthermore, an excessive charge abuses the professional relationship between lawyer and client. On the other hand, adequate compensation is necessary in order to enable the lawyer to serve his client effectively and to preserve the integrity and independence of the profession.[29]

EC 2-18   The determination of the reasonableness of a fee requires consideration of all relevant circumstances,[30] including those stated in the Disciplinary Rules. The fees of a lawyer will vary according to many factors, including the time required, his experience, ability, and reputation, the nature of the employment, the responsibility involved, and the results obtained. It is a commendable and long-standing tradition of the bar that special consideration is given in the fixing of any fee for services rendered a brother lawyer or a member of his immediate family.

EC 2-19   As soon as feasible after a lawyer has been employed, it is desirable that he reach a clear agreement with his client as to the basis of the fee charges to be made. Such a course will not only prevent later misunderstanding but will also work for good relations between the lawyer and the client. It is usually beneficial to reduce to writing the understanding of the parties regarding the fee, particularly when it is contingent. A lawyer should be mindful that many persons who desire to employ him may have had little or no experience with fee charges of lawyers, and for this reason he should explain fully to such persons the reasons for the particular fee arrangement he proposes.

EC 2-20 Contingent fee arrangements[31] in civil cases have long been commonly accepted in the United States in proceedings to enforce claims. The historical bases of their acceptance are that (1) they often, and in a variety of circumstances, provide the only practical means by which one having a claim against another can economically afford, finance, and obtain the services of a competent lawyer to prosecute his claim, and (2) a successful prosecution of the claim produces a res out of which the fee can be paid.[32] Although a lawyer generally should decline to accept employment on a contingent fee basis by one who is able to pay a reasonable fixed fee, it is not necessarily improper for a lawyer, where justified by the particular circumstances of a case, to enter into a contingent fee contract in a civil case with any client who, after being fully informed of all relevant factors, desires that arrangement. Because of the human relationships involved and the unique character of the proceedings, contingent fee arrangements in domestic relation cases are rarely justified. In administrative agency proceedings contingent fee contracts should be governed by the same consideration as in other civil cases. Public policy properly condemns contingent fee arrangements in criminal cases, largely on the ground that legal services in criminal cases do not produce a res with which to pay the fee.

EC 2-21 A lawyer should not accept compensation or any thing of value incident to his employment or services from one other than his client without the knowledge and consent of his client after full disclosure.[33]

EC 2-22 Without the consent of his client, a lawyer should not associate in a particular matter another lawyer outside his firm. A fee may properly be divided between lawyers[34] properly associated if the division is in proportion to the services performed and the responsibility assumed by each lawyer[35] and if the total fee is reasonable.

EC 2-23 A lawyer should be zealous in his efforts to avoid controversies over fees with clients[36] and should attempt to resolve amicably any differences on the subject.[37] He should not sue a client for a fee unless necessary to prevent fraud or gross imposition by the client.[38]

Financial Ability to Employ Counsel:
Persons Unable to Pay Reasonable Fees

EC 2-24 A layman whose financial ability is not sufficient to permit payment of any fee cannot obtain legal services, other than in cases where a contingent fee is appropriate, unless the services are provided for him. Even a person of moderate means may be unable to pay a reasonable fee which is large because of the complexity, novelty, or difficulty of the problem or similar factors.[39]

EC 2-25   Historically, the need for legal services of those unable to pay reasonable fees has been met in part by lawyers who donated their services or accepted court appointments on behalf of such individuals. The basic responsibility for providing legal services for those unable to pay ultimately rests upon the individual lawyer, and personal involvement in the problems of the disadvantaged can be one of the most rewarding experiences in the life of a lawyer. Every lawyer, regardless of professional prominence or professional workload, should find time to participate in serving the disadvantaged. The rendition of free legal services to those unable to pay reasonable fees continues to be an obligation of each lawyer, but the efforts of individual lawyers are often not enough to meet the need.[40] Thus it has been necessary for the profession to institute additional programs to provide legal services.[41] Accordingly, legal aid offices,[42] lawyer referral services, and other related programs have been developed, and others will be developed, by the profession.[43] Every lawyer should support all proper efforts to meet this need for legal services.[44]

Acceptance and Retention of Employment

EC 2-26   A lawyer is under no obligation to act as adviser or advocate for every person who may wish to become his client; but in furtherance of the objective of the bar to make legal services fully available, a lawyer should not lightly decline proffered employment. The fulfillment of this objective requires acceptance by a lawyer of his share of tendered employment which may be unattractive both to him and the bar generally.[45]

EC 2-27   History is replete with instances of distinguished and sacrificial services by lawyers who have represented unpopular clients and causes. Regardless of his personal feelings, a lawyer should not decline representation because a client or a cause is unpopular or community reaction is adverse.[46]

EC 2-28   The personal preference of a lawyer to avoid adversary alignment against judges, other lawyers,[47] public officials, or influential members of the community does not justify his rejection of tendered employment.

EC 2-29   When a lawyer is appointed by a court or requested by a bar association to undertake representation of a person unable to obtain counsel, whether for financial or other reasons, he should not seek to be excused from undertaking the representation except for compelling reasons.[48] Compelling reasons do not include such factors as the repugnance of the subject matter of the proceeding, the identity[49] or position of a person involved in the case, the belief of the lawyer that the defendant in a criminal proceeding is guilty,[50] or the belief of the lawyer regarding the merits of the civil case.[5s1]

EC 2-30 Employment should not be accepted by a lawyer when he is unable to render competent service[52] or when he knows or it is obvious that the person seeking to employ him desires to institute or maintain an action merely for the purpose of harassing or maliciously injuring another.[53] Likewise, a lawyer should decline employment if the intensity of his personal feeling, as distinguished from a community attitude, may impair his effective representation of a prospective client. If a lawyer knows a client has previously obtained counsel, he should not accept employment in the matter unless the other counsel approves[54] or withdraws, or the client terminates the prior employment.[55]

EC 2-31 Full availability of legal counsel requires both that persons be able to obtain counsel and that lawyers who undertake representation complete the work involved. Trial counsel for a convicted defendant should continue to represent his client by advising whether to take an appeal and, if the appeal is prosecuted, by representing him through the appeal unless new counsel is substituted or withdrawal is permitted by the appropriate court.

EC 2-32 A decision by a lawyer to withdraw should be made only on the basis of compelling circumstances,[56] and in a matter pending before a tribunal he must comply with the rules of the tribunal regarding withdrawal. A lawyer should not withdraw without considering carefully and endeavoring to minimize the possible adverse effect on the rights of his client and the possibility of prejudice to his client[57] as a result of his withdrawal. Even when he justifiably withdraws, a lawyer should protect the welfare of his client by giving due notice of his withdrawal,[58] suggesting employment of other counsel, delivering to the client all papers and property to which the client is entitled, cooperating with counsel, subsequently employed, and otherwise endeavoring to minimize the possibility of harm. Further, he should refund to the client any compensation not earned during the employment.[59]

EC 2-33 As a part of the legal profession's commitment to the principle that high quality legal services should be available to all, attorneys are encouraged to cooperate with qualified legal assistance organizations providing prepaid legal services, Such participation should at all times be in accordance with the basic tenets of the profession: independence, integrity, competence and devotion to the interests of individual clients. An attorney so participating should make certain that his relationship with a qualified legal assistance organization in no way interferes with his independent, professional representation of the interests of the individual client. An attorney should avoid situations in which officials of the organization who are not lawyers attempt to direct attorneys concerning the manner in which legal services are performed for individual members, and should also avoid situations in which considerations of economy are given undue weight in determining the attorneys employed by an organization or the legal services to be performed for the member or beneficiary rather than competence and quality of service. An attorney interested in maintaining the historic traditions of the profession and preserving the function of a lawyer as a trusted and independent advisor to individual members of society should carefully assess such factors when accepting employment by, or otherwise participating in, a particular qualified legal assistance organization, and while so participating should adhere to the highest professional standards of effort and competence.[60]

DISCIPLINARY RULES

DR 2-101   Publicity in General.

(A) A lawyer shall not, on behalf of himself, his partner, associate or any other lawyer affiliated with him or his firm, use or participate in the use of any form of public communication containing a false, fraudulent, misleading, deceptive, self-laudatory or unfair statement or claim.

(B) In order to facilitate the process of informed selection of a lawyer by potential consumers of legal services, a lawyer may publish or broadcast, subject to DR 2-103, the following information in print media distributed or over television or radio broadcast in the geographic area or areas in which the lawyer resides or maintains offices of in which a significant part of the lawyer's clientele resides, provided that the information disclosed by the lawyer in such publication or broadcast complies with DR 2-101(A), and is presented in a dignified manner.[61]

(1) Name, including name of law firm and names of professional associates; addresses and telephone numbers;

(2) One or more fields of law in which the lawyer or law firm practices, a statement that practice is limited to one or more fields of law, or a statement that the lawyer or law firm specializes in a particular field of law practice, to the extent authorized under DR 2-105;

(3) Date and place of birth;

(4) Date and place of admission to the bar of state and federal courts;

(5) Schools attended, with dates of graduation, degrees and other scholastic distinctions;

(6) Public or quasi-public offices;

(7) Military service;

(8) Legal authorships;

(9) Legal teaching positions;

(10) Memberships, offices, and committee assignments, in bar associations;

(11) Membership and offices in legal fraternities and legal societies;

(12) Technical and professional licenses;

(13) Memberships in scientific, technical and professional associations and societies;

(14) Foreign language ability;

(15) Names and addresses of bank references;

(16) With their written consent, names of clients regularly represented;

(17) Prepaid or group legal services programs in which the lawyer participates;

(18) Whether credit cards or other credit arrangements are accepted;

(19) Office and telephone answering service hours;

(20) Fee for an initial consultation;

(21) Availability upon request of a written schedule of fees and/or estimate of the fee to be charged for specific services;

(22) Contingent fee rates subject to DR 2-106(C), provided that the statement discloses whether percentages are computed before or after deduction of costs;

(23) Range of fees for services, provided that the statement discloses that the specific fee within the range which will be charged will vary depending upon the particular matter to be handled for each client and the client is entitled without obligation to an estimate of the fee within the range likely to be charged, in print size equivalent to the largest print used in setting forth the fee information;

(24) Hourly rate, provided that the statement discloses that the total fee charged will depend upon the number of hours which must be devoted to the particular matter to be handled for each client and the client is entitled to without obligation an estimate of the fee likely to be charged, in print size at least equivalent to the largest print used in setting forth the fee information;

(25) Fixed fees for specific legal services,* the description of which would not be misunderstood or be deceptive, provided that the statement discloses that the quoted fee will be available only to clients whose matters fall into the services described and that the client is entitled without obligation to a specific estimate of the fee likely to be charged in print size at least equivalent to the largest print used in setting forth the fee information.

(C) Any person desiring to expand the information authorized for disclosure in DR 2-101(B), or to provide for its dissemination through other forums may apply to [the agency having jurisdiction under state law]. Any such application shall be served upon [the agencies having jurisdiction under state law over the regulation of the legal profession and consumer matters] who shall be heard, together with the applicant, on the issue of whether the proposal is necessary in light of the existing provisions of the Code, accords with standards of accuracy, reliability and truthfulness, and would facilitate the process of informed selection of lawyers by potential consumers of legal services. The relief granted in response to any such application shall be promulgated as an amendment to DR 2-101(B), universally applicable to all lawyers.**

(D) If the advertisement is communicated to the public over television or radio, it shall be pre-recorded, approved for broadcast by the lawyer, and a recording of the actual transmission shall be retained by the lawyer.[62]

(E) If a lawyer advertises a fee for a service, the lawyer must render that service for no more than the fee advertised.

(F) Unless otherwise specified in the advertisement if a lawyer publishes any fee information authorized under DR 2-101(B) in a publication that is published more frequently than one time per month, the lawyer shall be bound by any representation made therein for a period of not less than 30 days after such publication. If a lawyer publishes any fee information authorized under DR 2-101(B) in a publication that is published once a month or less frequently, he shall be bound by any representation made therein until the publication of the succeeding issue. If a lawyer publishes any fee information authorized under DR 2-101(B) in a publication which has no fixed date for publication of a succeeding issue, the lawyer shall be bound by any representation made therein for a reasonable period of time after publication but in no event less than one year.

(G) Unless otherwise specified, if a lawyer broadcasts any fee information authorized under DR 2-101(B), the lawyer shall be bound by any representation made therein for a period of not less than 30 days after such broadcast.

(H) This rule does not prohibit limited and dignified identification of a lawyer as a lawyer as well as by name:

(1) In political advertisements when his professional status is germane to the political campaign or to a political issue.

(2) In public notices when the name and profession of a lawyer are required or authorized by law or are reasonably pertinent for a purpose other than the attraction of potential clients.

(3) In routine reports and announcements of a bona fide business, civic, professional, or political organization in which he serves as a director or officer.

(4) In and on legal documents prepared by him.

---

* The agency having jurisdiction under state law may desire to issue appropriate guidelines defining "specific legal services."

** The agency having jurisdiction under state law should establish orderly and expeditious procedures for ruling on such applications.

(5) In and on legal textbooks, treatises, and other legal publications, and in dignified advertisements thereof.

(I) A lawyer shall not compensate or give any thing of value to representatives of the press, radio, television, or other communication medium in anticipation of or in return for professional publicity in a news item.

DR 2-102   Professional Notices, Letterheads, and Offices.

(A) A lawyer or law firm shall not use or participate in the use of[63] professional cards, professional announcement cards, office signs, letterheads, telephone directory listings, law lists, legal directory listings, or similar professional notices or devices, except that the following may be used if they are in dignified form:

(1) A professional card of a lawyer identifying him by name and as a lawyer, and giving his addresses, telephone numbers, the name of his law firm, and any information permitted under DR 2-105. A professional card of a law firm may also give the names of members and associates. Such cards may be used for identification.

(2) A brief professional announcement card stating new or changed associations or addresses, change of firm name, or similar matters pertaining to the professional office of a lawyer or law firm, which may be mailed to lawyers, clients, former clients, personal friends, and relatives.[64] It shall not state biographical data except to the extent reasonably necessary to identify the lawyer or to explain the change in his association, but it may state the immediate past position of the lawyer.[65] It may give the names and dates of predecessor firms in a continuing line of succession. It shall not state the nature of the practice except as permitted under DR 2-105.[66]

(3) A sign on or near the door of the office and in the building directory identifying the law office. The sign shall not state the nature of the practice, except as permitted under DR 2-105.

(4) A letterhead of a lawyer identifying him by name and as a lawyer, and giving his addresses, telephone numbers, the name of his law firm, associates and any information permitted under DR 2-105. A letterhead of a law firm may also give the names of members and associates,[67] and names and dates relating to deceased and retired members.[68] A lawyer may be designated "Of Counsel" on a letterhead if he has a continuing relationship with a lawyer or law firm, other than as a partner or associate. A lawyer or law firm may be designated as "General Counsel" or by similar professional reference on stationery of a client if he or the firm devotes a substantial amount of professional time in the representation of that client.[69] The letterhead of a law firm may give the names and dates of predecessor firms in a continuing line of succession.

ABA Model
Code of
Professional
Responsibility

(B) A lawyer in private practice shall not practice under a trade name, a name that is misleading as to the identity of the lawyer or lawyers practicing under such name, or a firm name containing names other than those of one or more of the lawyers in the firm, except that the name of a professional corporation or professional association may contain "P.C." or "P.A." or similar symbols indicating the nature of the organization, and if otherwise lawful a firm may use as, or continue to include in, its name the name or names of one or more deceased or retired members of the firm or of a predecessor firm in a continuing line of succession.[70] A lawyer who assumes a judicial, legislative, or public executive or administrative post or office shall not permit his name to remain in the name of a law firm or to be used in professional notices of the firm during any significant period in which he is not actively and regularly practicing law as a member of the firm,[71] and during such period other members of the firm shall not use his name in the firm name or in professional notices of the firm.[72]

(C) A lawyer shall not hold himself out as having a partnership with one or more other lawyers or professional corporations[73] unless they are in fact partners.[74]

(D) A partnership shall not be formed or continued between or among lawyers licensed in different jurisdictions unless all enumerations of the members and associates of the firm on its letterhead and in other permissible listings make clear the jurisdictional limitations on those members and associates of the firm not licensed to practice in all listed jurisdictions;[75] however, the same firm name may be used in each jurisdiction.

(E) Nothing contained herein shall prohibit a lawyer from using or permitting the use of, in connection with his name, an earned degree or title derived therefrom indicating his training in the law.[76]

DR 2-103 Recommendation of Professional Employment.[77]

(A) A lawyer shall not, except as authorized in DR 2-101(B), recommend employment, as a private practitioner,[78] of himself, his partner, or associate to a layperson who has not sought his advice regarding employment of a lawyer.[79]

(B) A lawyer shall not compensate or give anything of value to a person or organization to recommend or secure his employment[80] by a client, or as a reward for having made a recommendation resulting in his employment[81] by a client, except that he may pay the usual and reasonable fees or dues charged by any of the organizations listed in DR 2-103(D).[82]

(C) A lawyer shall not request a person or organization to recommend or promote the use of his services or those of his partner or associate, or any other lawyer affiliated with him or his firm, as a private practitioner,[83] except as authorized in DR 2-101, and except that

(1) He may request referrals from a lawyer referral service operated, sponsored, or approved by a bar association and may pay its fees incident thereto.[84]

(2) He may cooperate with the legal service activities of any of the offices or organizations enumerated in DR 2-103(D) (1) through (4) and may perform legal services for those to whom he was recommended by it to do such work if:

    (a) The person to whom the recommendation is made is a member or beneficiary of such office or organizations; and

    (b) The lawyer remains free to exercise his independent professional judgment on behalf of his client.[85]

(D) A lawyer or his partner or associate or any other lawyer affiliated with him or his firm may be recommended, employed or paid by, or may cooperate with, one of the following offices or organizations that promote the use of his services or those of his partner or associate or any other lawyer affiliated with him or his firm if there is no interference with the exercise of independent professional judgment in behalf of his client:

(1) A legal aid office or public defender office:

    (a) Operated or sponsored by a duly accredited law school.

    (b) Operated or sponsored by a bona fide nonprofit community organization.

    (c) Operated or sponsored by a governmental agency.

    (d) Operated, sponsored, or approved by a bar association.[86]

(2) A military legal assistance office.

(3) A lawyer referral service operated, sponsored, or approved by a bar association.

(4) Any bona fide organization that recommends, furnishes or pays for legal services to its members or beneficiaries[87] provided the following conditions are satisfied:

    (a) Such organization, including any affiliate, is so organized and operated that no profit is derived by it from the rendition of legal services by lawyers, and that, if the organization is organized for profit, the legal services are not rendered by lawyers employed, directed, supervised or selected by it except in connection with matters where such organization bears ultimate liability of its member or beneficiary.

    (b) Neither the lawyer, nor his partner, nor associate, nor any other lawyer affiliated with him or his firm, nor any nonlawyer, shall have initiated or promoted such organization

ABA Model
Code of
Professional
Responsibility

for the primary purpose of providing financial or other benefit to such lawyer, partner, associate or affiliated lawyer.

(c) Such organization is not operated for the purpose of procuring legal work or financial benefit for any lawyer as a private practitioner outside of the legal services program of the organization.

(d) The member or beneficiary to whom the legal services are furnished, and not such organization, is recognized as the client of the lawyer in the matter.

(e) Any member or beneficiary who is entitled to have legal services furnished or paid for by the organization may, if such member or beneficiary so desires, select counsel other than that furnished, selected or approved by the organization for the particular matter involved; and the legal service plan of such organization provides appropriate relief for any member or beneficiary who asserts a claim that representation by counsel furnished, selected or approved would be unethical, improper or inadequate under the circumstances of the matter involved and the plan provides an appropriate procedure for seeking such relief.

(f) The lawyer does not know or have cause to know that such organization is in violation of applicable laws, rules of court and other legal requirements that govern its legal service operations.

(g) Such organization has filed with the appropriate disciplinary authority at least annually a report with respect to its legal service plan, if any, showing its terms, its schedule of benefits, its subscription charges, agreements with counsel, and financial results of its legal service activities or, if it has failed to do so, the lawyer does not know or have case to know of such failure.[88]

(E) A lawyer shall not accept employment when he knows or it is obvious that the person who seeks his services does so as a result of conduct prohibited under this Disciplinary Rule.

DR 2-104 Suggestion of Need of Legal Services.[89, 90]

(A) A lawyer who has given unsolicited advice to a layman that he should obtain counsel or take legal action shall not accept employment resulting from that advice,[91] except that:

(1) A lawyer may accept employment by a close friend, relative, former client (if the advice is germane to the former employment), or one whom the lawyer reasonably believes to be a client.[92]

(2) A lawyer may accept employment that results from his participa-

tion in activities designed to educate laymen to recognize legal problems, to make intelligent selection of counsel, or to utilize available legal services if such activities are conducted or sponsored by a qualified legal assistance organization.[93]

(3) A lawyer who is recommended, furnished or paid by any of the offices or organizations enumerated in DR 2-103(D)(1) through (4)[94] may represent a member or beneficiary thereof, to the extent and under the conditions prescribed therein.

(4) Without affecting his right to accept employment, a lawyer may speak publicly or write for publication on legal topics[95] so long as he does not emphasize his own professional experience or reputation and does not undertake to give individual advice.

(5) If success in asserting rights or defenses of his client in litigation in the nature of a class action is dependent upon the joinder of others, a lawyer may accept, but shall not seek, employment from those contacted for the purpose of obtaining their joinder.[96]

DR 2-105 Limitation of Practice.[97]

(A) A lawyer shall not hold himself out publicly as a specialist, as practicing in certain areas of law or as limiting his practice permitted under DR 2101(B), except as follows:

(1) A lawyer admitted to practice before the United States Patent and Trademark Office may use the designation "Patents," "Patent Attorney," or "Patent Lawyer," or "Registered Patent Attorney" or any combination of those terms, on his letterhead and office sign.

(2) A lawyer who publicly discloses fields of law in which the lawyer or the law firm practices or states that his practice is limited to one or more fields of law shall do so by using designations and definitions authorized and approved by [the agency having jurisdiction of the subject under state law].

(3) A lawyer who is certified as a specialist in a particular field of law or law practice by [the authority having jurisdiction under state law over the subject of specialization by lawyers] may hold himself out as such, but only in accordance with the rules prescribed by that authority.[98]

DR 2-106 Fees for Legal Services.[99]

(A) A lawyer shall not enter into an agreement for, charge, or collect an illegal or clearly excessive fee.[100]

(B) A fee is clearly excessive when, after a review of the facts, a lawyer of ordinary prudence would be left with a definite and firm conviction that the fee is in excess of a reasonable fee. Factors to be considered as guides in determining the reasonableness of a fee include the following:

(1) The time and labor required, the novelty and difficulty of the questions involved, and the skill requisite to perform the legal service properly.

(2) The likelihood, if apparent to the client, that the acceptance of the particular employment will preclude other employment by the lawyer.

(3) The fee customarily charged in the locality for similar legal services.

(4) The amount involved and the results obtained.

(5) The time limitations imposed by the client or by the circumstances.

(6) The nature and length of the professional relationship with the client.

(7) The experience, reputation, and ability of the lawyer or lawyers performing the services.

(8) Whether the fee is fixed or contingent.[101]

(C) A lawyer shall not enter into an arrangement for, charge, or collect a contingent fee for representing a defendant in a criminal case.[102]

DR 2-107 Division of Fees Among Lawyers.

(A) A lawyer shall not divide a fee for legal services with another lawyer who is not a partner in or associate of his law firm or law office, unless:

(1) The client consents to employment of the other lawyer after a full disclosure that a division of fees will be made.

(2) The division is made in proportion to the services performed and responsibility assumed by each.[103]

(3) The total fee of the lawyers does not clearly exceed reasonable compensation for all legal services they rendered the client.[104]

(B) This Disciplinary Rule does not prohibit payment to a former partner or associate pursuant to a separation or retirement agreement.

DR 2-108 Agreements Restricting the Practice of a Lawyer.

(A) A lawyer shall not be a party to or participate in a partnership or employment agreement with another lawyer that restricts the right of a lawyer to practice law after the termination of a relationship created by the agreement, except as a condition to payment of retirement benefits.[105]

(B) In connection with the settlement of a controversy or suit, a lawyer shall not enter into an agreement that restricts his right to practice law.

DR 2-109 Acceptance of Employment.

(A) A lawyer shall not accept employment on behalf of a person if he knows or it is obvious that such person wishes to:

(1) Bring a legal action, conduct a defense, or assert a position in litigation, or otherwise have steps taken for him, merely for the purpose of harassing or maliciously injuring any person.[106]

(2) Present a claim or defense in litigation that is not warranted under existing law, unless it can be supported by good faith argument for an extension, modification, or reversal of existing law.

DR 2-110   Withdrawal from Employment.[107]

(A) In general.

(1) If permission for withdrawal from employment is required by the rules of a tribunal, a lawyer shall not withdraw from employment in a proceeding before that tribunal without its permission.

(2) In any event, a lawyer shall not withdraw from employment until he has taken reasonable steps to avoid foreseeable prejudice to the rights of his client, including giving due notice to his client, allowing time for employment of other counsel, delivering to the client all papers and property to which the client is entitled, and complying with applicable laws and rules.

(3) A lawyer who withdraws from employment shall refund promptly any part of a fee paid in advance that has not been earned.

(B) Mandatory withdrawal. A lawyer representing a client before a tribunal, with its permission if required by its rules, shall withdraw from employment, and a lawyer representing a client in other matters shall withdraw from employment, if:

(1) He knows or it is obvious that his client is bringing the legal action, conducting the defense, or asserting a position in the litigation, or is otherwise having steps taken for him, merely for the purpose of harassing or maliciously injuring any person.

(2) He knows or it is obvious that his continued employment will result in violation of a Disciplinary Rule.[108]

(3) His mental or physical condition renders it unreasonably difficult for him to carry out the employment effectively.

(4) He is discharged by his client.

(C) Permissive withdrawal.[109] If DR 2-110(B) is not applicable, a lawyer may not request permission to withdraw in matters pending before a tribunal, and may not withdraw in other matters, unless such request or such withdrawal is because:

(1) His client:

(a) Insists upon presenting a claim or defense that is not warranted under existing law and cannot be supported by good faith argument for an extension, modification, or reversal of existing law.[110]

(b) Personally seeks to pursue an illegal course of conduct.

ABA Model
Code of
Professional
Responsibility

    (c) Insists that the lawyer pursue a course of conduct that is illegal or that is prohibited under the Disciplinary Rules.

    (d) By other conduct renders it unreasonably difficult for the lawyer to carry out his employment effectively.

    (e) Insists, in a matter not pending before a tribunal, that the lawyer engage in conduct that is contrary to the judgment and advice of the lawyer but not prohibited under the Disciplinary Rules.

    (f) Deliberately disregards an agreement or obligation to the lawyer as to expenses or fees.

(2) His continued employment is likely to result in a violation of a Disciplinary Rule.

(3) His inability to work with co-counsel indicates that the best interests of the client likely will be served by withdrawal.

(4) His mental or physical condition renders it difficult for him to carry out the employment effectively.

(5) His client knowingly and freely assents to termination of his employment.

(6) He believes in good faith, in a proceeding pending before a tribunal, that the tribunal will find the existence of other good cause for withdrawal.

NOTES

1. "Men have need for more than a system of law; they have need for a system of law which functions, and that means they have need for lawyers." Cheatham, *The Lawyer's Role and Surroundings*, 25 ROCKY MT. L. REV. 405 (1953).

2. "Law is not self-applying; men must apply and utilize it in concrete cases. But the ordinary man is incapable. He cannot know the principles of law or the rules guiding the machinery of law administration; he does not know how to formulate his desires with precision and to put them into writing he is ineffective in the presentation of his claims." *Id.*

3. "This need [to provide legal services] was recognized by . . . Mr. [Lewis F.] Powell [Jr., President, American Bar Association, 1963-64], who said: 'Looking at contemporary America realistically, we must admit that despite all our efforts to date (and these have not been insignificant), far too many persons are not able to obtain equal justice under law. This usually results because their poverty or their ignorance has prevented them from obtaining legal counsel.'" Address by E. Clinton Bamberger, Association of American Law Schools 1965 Annual Meeting, Dec. 28, 1965, in PROCEEDINGS, PART II, 1965, 61, 63-64 (1965).

"A wide gap separates the need for legal services and its satisfaction, as numerous studies reveal. Looked at from the side of the layman, one reason for the gap is poverty and the consequent inability to pay legal fees. Another set of reasons is ignorance of the need for and the value of legal services, and ignorance of where to find a dependable lawyer. There is fear of the mysterious processes and delays of the law, and there is fear of overreaching and overcharging by lawyers, a fear stimulated by the occasional exposure of shysters." Cheatham, *Availability of Legal Services: The Responsibility of the Individual Lawyer and of the Organized Bar*, 12 U.C.L.A. L. REV. 438 (1965).

4. "It is not only the right but the duty of the profession as a whole to utilize such

methods as may be developed to bring the services of its members to those who need them, so long as this can be done ethically and with dignity." *ABA Opinion* 320 (1968).

"[T]here is a responsibility on the bar to make legal services available to those who need them. The maxim, 'privilege brings responsibilities,' can be expanded to read, exclusive privilege to render public service brings responsibility to assure that the service is available to those in need of it." Cheatham, *Availability of Legal Services: The Responsibility of the Individual Lawyer and of the Organized Bar*, 12 U.C.L.A. L. Rev. 438, 443 (1965).

"The obligation to provide legal services for those actually caught up in litigation carries with it the obligation to make preventive legal advice accessible to all. It is among those unaccustomed to business affairs and fearful of the ways of the law that such advice is often most needed. If it is not received in time, the most valiant and skillful representation in court may come too late." *Professional Responsibility: Report of the Joint Conference*, 44 A.B.A. J. 1159, 1216 (1958).

5. "A lawyer may with propriety write articles for publications in which he gives information upon the law . . . ." ABA Canons of Professional Ethics, Canon 40 (1908).

6. *See* ABA Canons of Professional Ethics, Canon 28 (1908).

7. This question can assume constitutional dimensions: "We meet at the outset the contention that 'solicitation' is wholly outside the area of freedoms protected by the First Amendment. To this contention there are two answers. The first is that a State cannot foreclose the exercise of constitutional rights b mere labels. The second is that abstract discussion is not the only species of communication which the Constitution protects; the First Amendment also protects vigorous advocacy, certainly of lawful ends, against governmental intrusion . . . .

. . . .

"However valid may be Virginia's interest in regulating the traditionally illegal practice of barratry, maintenance and champerty, that interest does not justify the prohibition of the NAACP activities disclosed by this record. Malicious intent was of the essence of the common-law offenses of fomenting or stirring up litigation. And whatever may be or may have been true of suits against governments in other countries, the exercise in our own, as in this case of First Amendment rights to enforce Constitutional rights through litigation, as a matter of law, cannot be deemed malicious." NAACP v. Button, 371 U.S. 415, 429, 439-40, 9 L. Ed. 2d 405, 415-16, 422, 83 S. Ct. 328, 336, 341 (1963).

8. It is disreputable for an attorney to breed litigation by seeking out those who have claims for personal injuries or other grounds of action in order to secure them as clients. or to employ agents or runners, or to reward those who bring or influence the bringing of business to his office . . . . Moreover, it tends quite easily to the institution of baseless litigation and the manufacture of perjured testimony. From early times, this danger has been recognized in the law by the condemnation of the crime of common barratry, or the stirring up of suits or quarrels between individuals at law or otherwise." In re Ades, 6 F. Supp. 467, 474-75 (D. Mary. 1934).

9. "*Rule 2*.

"§ a . . . .

"[A] member of the State Bar shall not solicit professional employment by

"(1) Volunteering counsel or advice except where ties of blood relationship or trust make it appropriate." Cal. Business and Professions Code § 6076 (West 1962).

10. "*Rule 18* . . . A member of the State Bar shall not advise inquirers or render opinions to them through or in connection with a newspaper, radio or other publicity medium of any kind in respect to their specific legal problems, whether or not such attorney shall be compensated for his service." Cal. Business and Prof. Code § 6076 (West 1962).

11. "In any case where a member might well apply the advice given in the opinion to his individual affairs, the lawyer rendering the opinion [concerning problems common to members of an association and distributed to the members through a periodic bulletin]

ABA Model Code of Professional Responsibility

should specifically state that this opinion should not be relied on by any member as a basis for handling his individual affairs, but that in every case he should consult his counsel. In the publication of the opinion the association should make a similar statement." *ABA Opinion* 273 (1946).

12. "A group of recent interrelated changes bears directly on the availability of legal services. . . . [One] change is the constantly accelerating urbanization of the country and the decline of personal and neighborhood knowledge of whom to retain as a professional man." Cheatham, *Availability of Legal Services: The Responsibility of the Individual Lawyer and of the Organized Bar*, 12 U.C.L A. L. REV. 438, 440 (1965).

13. *Cf.* Cheatham, *A Lawyer When Needed: Legal Services for the Middle Classes*, 63 COLUM. L. REV. 973, 974 (1963).

14. *See* ABA CANONS OF PROFESSIONAL ETHICS, CANON 28 (1908).

15. Amended, August 1978, House Informational Report No. 118.

16. *Cf. ABA Opinion* 303 (1961).

17. *See* ABA CANONS OF PROFESSIONAL ETHICS, CANON 33 (1908).

18. *Id.*

"The continued use of a firm name by one or more surviving partners after the death of a member of the firm whose name is in the firm title is expressly permitted by the Canons of Ethics. The reason for this is that all of the partners have by their joint and several efforts over a period of years contributed to the good will attached to the firm name. In the case of a firm having widespread connections, this good will is disturbed by a change in firm name every time a name partner dies, and that reflects a loss in some degree of the good will to the building up of which the surviving partners have contributed their time, skill and labor through a period of years. To avoid this loss the firm name is continued, and to meet the requirements of the Canon the individuals constituting the firm from time to time are listed." *ABA Opinion* 267 (1945).

"Accepted local custom in New York recognizes that the name of a law firm does not necessarily identify the individual member of the firm, and hence the continued use of a firm name after the death of one or more partners is not a deception and is permissible.... The continued use of a deceased partner's name in the firm title is not affected by the fact that another partner withdraws from the firm and his name is dropped, or the name of the new partner is added to the firm name." Opinion No. 45, Committee on Professional Ethics, New York State Bar Ass'n, 39 N.Y. St. B.J. 455 (1967).

Cf. ABA Opinion 258 (1943).

19. *Cf.* ABA CANONS OF PROFESSIONAL ETHICS, CANON 33 (1908) and *ABA Opinion* 315 (1965).

20. *Cf. ABA Opinions* 283 (1950) and 81 (1932).

21. *See ABA Opinion* 316 (1967).

22. "The word 'associates' has a variety of meanings. Principally through custom the word when used on the letterheads of law firms has come to be regarded as describing those who are employees of the firm. Because the word has acquired this special significance in connection with the practice of the law the use of the word to describe lawyer relationships other than employer-employee is likely to be misleading." In re Sussman and Tanner, 241 Ore. 246, 248, 405 P.2d 355, 356 (1965).

According to *ABA Opinion* 310 (1963), use of the term "associates" would be misleading in two situations: (1) where two lawyers are partners and they share both responsibility and liability for the partnership; and (2) where two lawyers practice separately, sharing no responsibility or liability, and only share a suite of offices and some costs.

23. "For a long time, many lawyers have, of necessity, limited their practice to certain branches of law. The increasing complexity of the law and the demand of the public for more expertness on the part of the lawyer has, in the past few years—particularly in the last ten years—brought about specialization on an increasing scale." *Report of the Special Committee on Specialization and Specialized Legal Services*, 79 A.B.A. REP. 582, 584 (1954).

24. *See* ABA CANONS OF PROFESSIONAL ETHICS, CANON 12 (1908).

25. *Cf.* ABA CANONS OF PROFESSIONAL ETHICS, CANON 12 (1908).

26. "If there is any fundamental proposition of government on which all would agree, it is that one of the highest goals of society must be to achieve and maintain equality before the law. Yet this ideal remains an empty form of words unless the legal profession is ready to provide adequate representation for those unable to pay the usual fees." *Professional Representation: Report of the Joint Conference*, 44 A.B.A. J. 1159, 1216 (1958).

27. *See* ABA CANONS OF PROFESSIONAL ETHICS, CANON 12 (1908).

28. *Cf.* ABA CANONS OF PROFESSIONAL ETHICS, CANON 12 (1908).

29. "When members of the Bar are induced to render legal services for inadequate compensation, as a consequence the quality of the service rendered may be lowered, the welfare of the profession injured and the administration of justice made less efficient." *ABA Opinion* 302 (1961).

Cf. ABA Opinion 307 (1962).

30. *See* ABA CANONS OF PROFESSIONAL ETHICS, CANON 12 (1908).

31. *See* ABA CANONS OF PROFESSIONAL ETHICS, CANON 13; *see also* MACKINNON, CONTINGENT FEES FOR LEGAL SERVICES (1964) (a report of the American Bar Foundation).

"A contract for a reasonable contingent fee where sanctioned by law is permitted by Canon 13, but the client must remain responsible to the lawyer for expenses advanced by the latter. 'There is to be no barter of the privilege of prosecuting a cause for gain in exchange for the promise of the attorney to prosecute at his own expense.' (Cardozo, C. J. in Matter of Gilman, 251 N.Y. 265, 270-271.)" *ABA Opinion* 246 (1942).

32. *See* Comment, *Providing Legal Services for the Middle Class in Civil Matters: The Problem, the Duty and a Solution*, 26 U. PITT. L. REV. 811, 829 (1965).

33. *See* ABA CANONS OF PROFESSIONAL ETHICS, CANON 38 (1908).

"Of course, as . . . [Informal Opinion 679] points out, there must be full disclosure of the arrangement [that an entity other than the client pays the attorney's fee] by the attorney to the client . . . ." *ABA Opinion* 320 (1968).

34. "Only lawyers may share in . . . a division of fees, but . . . it is not necessary that both lawyers be admitted to practice in the same state, so long as the division was based on the division of services or responsibility." *ABA Opinion* 316 (1967)

35. *See* ABA CANONS OF PROFESSIONAL ETHICS, CANON 34 (1908).

"We adhere to our previous rulings that where a lawyer merely brings about the employment of another lawyer but renders no service and assumes no responsibility in the matter, a division of the latter's fee is improper. (Opinions 18 and 153).

"It is assumed that the bar, generally, understands what acts or conduct of a lawyer may constitute 'services' to a client within the intendment of Canon 12. Such acts or conduct invariably, if not always, involve 'responsibility' on the part of the lawyer, whether the word 'responsibility' be construed to denote the possible resultant legal or moral liability on the part of the lawyer to the client or to others, or the onus of deciding what should or should not be done in behalf of the client. The word 'service' in Canon 12 must be construed in this broad sense and may apply to the selection and retainer of associate counsel as well as to other acts or conduct in the client's behalf." *ABA Opinion* 204 (1940).

36. *See* ABA CANONS OF PROFESSIONAL ETHICS, CANON 14 (1908).

37. *Cf. ABA Opinion* 320 (1968).

38. *See* ABA CANONS OF PROFESSIONAL ETHICS, CANON 14 (1908).

"Ours is a learned profession, not a mere money-getting trade . . . . Suits to collect fees should be avoided. Only where the circumstances imperatively require, should resort be had to a suit to compel payment. And where a lawyer does resort to a suit to enforce payment of fees which involves a disclosure, he should carefully avoid any disclosure not clearly necessary to obtaining or defending his rights." *ABA Opinion* 250 (1943).

But cf. ABA Opinion 320 (1968).

ABA Model
Code of
Professional
Responsibility

39. "As a society increases in size, sophistication and technology, the body of laws which is required to control that society also increases in size, scope and complexity. With this growth, the law directly affects more and more facets of individual behavior, creating an expanding need for legal services on the part of the individual members of the society . . . . As legal guidance in social and commercial behavior increasingly becomes necessary, there will come a concurrent demand from the layman that such guidance be made available to him. This demand will not come from those who are able to employ the best legal talent, nor from those who can obtain legal assistance at little or no cost. It will come from the large 'forgotten middle income class,' who can neither afford to pay proportionately large fees nor qualify for ultra-low-cost services. The legal profession must recognize this inevitable demand and consider methods whereby it can be satisfied. If the profession fails to provide such methods, the laity will." Comment, *Providing Legal Services for the Middle Class in Civil Matters: The Problem, the Duty and a Solution*, 26 U. PITT. L REV. 811, 811-12 (1965).

"The issue is not whether we shall do something or do nothing. The demand for ordinary everyday legal justice is so great and the moral nature of the demand is so strong that the issue has become whether we devise, maintain, and support suitable agencies able to satisfy the demand or, by our own default, force the government to take over the job, supplant us, and ultimately dominate us." Smith, *Legal Service Offices for Persons of Moderate Means*, 1949 WIS. L REV. 416, 418 (1949).

40. "Lawyers have peculiar responsibilities for the just administration of the law and these responsibilities include providing advice and representation for needy persons. To a degree not always appreciated by the public at large, the bar has performed these obligations with zeal and devotion. The Committee is persuaded, however, that a system of justice that attempts, in mid-twentieth century America, to meet the needs of the financially incapacitated accused through primary or exclusive reliance on the uncompensated services of counsel will prove unsuccessful and inadequate . . . . A system of adequate representation, therefore, should be structured and financed in a manner reflecting its public importance . . . . We believe that fees for private appointed counsel should be set by the court within maximum limits established by the statute." REPORT OF THE ATTY GEN.'S COMM. ON POVERTY AND THE ADMINISTRATION OF CRIMINAL JUSTICE 41-43 (1963).

41. "At present this representation [of those unable to pay usual fees] is being supplied in some measure through the spontaneous generosity of individual lawyers, through legal aid societies, and—increasingly—through the organized efforts of the Bar. If those who stand in need of this service know of its availability and their need is in fact adequately met, the precise mechanism by which this service is provided becomes of secondary importance. It is of great importance, however, that both the impulse to render this service, and the plan for making that impulse effective, should arise within the legal profession itself." *Professional Responsibility: Report of the Joint Conference*, 44 A.B.A. J. 1159, 1216 (1958).

42. "Free legal clinics carried on by the organized bar are not ethically objectionable. On the contrary, they serve a very worthwhile purpose and should be encouraged." *ABA Opinion* 191 (1939).

43. "Whereas the American Bar Association believes that it is a fundamental duty of the bar to see to it that all persons requiring legal advice be able to attain it, irrespective of their economic status . . . .

"Resolved, that the Association approves and sponsors the setting up by state and local bar associations of lawyer referral plans and low-cost legal service methods for the purpose of dealing with cases of persons who might not otherwise have the benefit of legal advice . . . ." *Proceedings of the House of Delegates of the American Bar Association*, Oct. 30, 1946, 71 A.B.A. REP. 103,109-10(1946).

44. "The defense of indigent citizens, without compensation, is carried on throughout the country by lawyers representing legal aid societies, not only with the approval, but

with the commendation of those acquainted with the work. Not infrequently services are rendered out of sympathy or for other philanthropic reasons, by individual lawyers who do not represent legal aid societies. There is nothing whatever in the Canons to prevent a lawyer from performing such an act, nor should there be." *ABA Opinion* 148 (1935).

45. *But cf.* ABA CANONS OF PROFESSIONAL ETHICS, CANON 31 (1908).

46. "One of the highest services the lawyer can render to society is to appear in court on behalf of clients whose causes are in disfavor with the general public." *Professional Responsibility: Report of the Joint Conference*, 44 A.B.A. J. 1159, 1216 (1958).

One author proposes the following proposition to be included in "A Proper Oath for Advocates": "I recognize that it is sometimes difficult for clients with unpopular causes to obtain proper legal representation. I will do all that I can to assure that the client with the unpopular cause is properly represented, and that the lawyer representing such a client receives credit from and support of the bar for handling such a matter." Thode, *The Ethical Standard for the Advocate*, 39 TEXAS L. REV. 575, 592 (1961).

"§6068 . . . . It is the duty of an attorney:

. . . .

"(h) Never to reject, for any consideration personal to himself, the cause of the defenseless or the oppressed." CAL. BUSINESS AND PROFESSIONS CODE § 6068 (West 1962). Virtually the same language is found in the Oregon statutes at ORE. REV. STATS. Ch. 9 § 9.460(8). *See* Rostow, *The Lawyer and His Client*, 48 A.B.A. J. 25 and 146 (1962).

47. *See* ABA CANONS OF PROFESSIONAL ETHICS, CANONS 7 and 29 (1908).

"We are of the opinion that it is not professionally improper for a lawyer to accept employment to compel another lawyer to honor the just claim of a layman. On the contrary, it is highly proper that he do so. Unfortunately, there appears to be a widespread feeling among laymen that it is difficult, if not impossible, to obtain justice when they have claims against members of the Bar because other lawyers will not accept employment to proceed against them. The honor of the profession, whose members proudly style themselves officers of the court, must surely be sullied if its members bind themselves by custom to refrain from enforcing just claims of laymen against lawyers." *ABA Opinion* 144 (1935).

48. ABA CANONS OF PROFESSIONAL ETHICS, CANON 4 (1908) uses a slightly different test, saying, "A lawyer assigned as counsel for an indigent prisoner ought not to ask to be excused for any trivial reason . . . ."

49. *Cf.* ABA CANONS OF PROFESSIONAL ETHICS, CANON 7 (1908).

50. *See* ABA CANONS OF PROFESSIONAL ETHICS, CANON 5 (1908).

51. Dr. Johnson's reply to Boswell upon being asked what he thought of "supporting a cause which you know to be bad" was: "Sir, you do not know it to be good or bad till the Judge determines it. I have said that you are to state facts fairly; so that your thinking, or what you call knowing, a cause to be bad, must be from reasoning, must be from supposing your arguments to be weak and inconclusive. But, Sir, that is not enough. An argument which does not convince yourself, may convince the Judge to whom you urge it: and if it does convince him, why, then, Sir, you are wrong, and he is right." 2 BOSWELL, THE LIFE OF JOHNSON 47-48 (Hill ed. 1887).

52. "The lawyer deciding whether to undertake a case must be able to judge objectively whether he is capable of handling it and whether he can assume its burdens without prejudice to previous commitments . . . ." *Professional Responsibility: Report of the Joint Conference*, 44 A.B.A. J. 1158, 1218 (1958).

53. "The lawyer must decline to conduct a civil cause or to make a defense when convinced that it is intended merely to harass or to injure the opposite party or to work oppression or wrong. ABA CANONS OF PROFESSIONAL ETHICS, CANON 30 (1908).

54. *See* ABA CANONS OF PROFESSIONAL ETHICS, CANON 7 (1908).

55. *Id.*

"From the facts stated we assume that the client has discharged the first attorney and given notice of the discharge. Such being the case, the second attorney may properly accept employment. Canon 7; Opinions 10, 130, 149." *ABA Opinion* 209 (1941).

56. *See* ABA CANONS OF PROFESSIONAL ETHICS, CANON 44 (1908).

"I will carefully consider, before taking a case, whether it appears that I can fully represent the client within the framework of law. If the decision is in the affirmative then it will take extreme circumstances to cause me to decide later that I cannot so represent him." Thode, *The Ethical Standard for the Advocate,* 39 TEXAS L. REV. 575, 592 (1961) (from "A Proper Oath for Advocates").

57. *ABA Opinion* 314 (l965) held that a lawyer should not disassociate himself from a cause when "it is obvious that the very act of disassociation would have the effect of violating Canon 37."

58. ABA CANON 44 enumerates instances in which " . . . the lawyer may be warranted in withdrawing on due notice to the client, allowing him time to employ another lawyer."

59. *See* ABA CANONS OF PROFESSIONAL ETHICS, CANON 44 (1908).

60. Amended, February 1975, House Informational Report No. 110.

61. Amended, August 1978, House Informational Report No. 130.

62. *Id.*

63. Amended, February 1976, House Informational Report No. 100.

64. *See ABA Opinion* 301(1961).

65. "[I]t has become commonplace for many lawyers to participate in government service; to deny them the right, upon their return to private practice, to refer to their prior employment in a brief and dignified manner, would place an undue limitation upon a large element of our profession. It is entirely proper for a member of the profession to explain his absence from private practice, where such is the primary purpose of the announcement, by a brief and dignified reference to the prior employment.

". . . [A]ny such announcement should be limited to the immediate past connection of the lawyer with the government, made upon his leaving that position to enter private practice." *ABA Opinion* 301 (1961).

66. *See ABA Opinion* 251 (1943).

67. "Those lawyers who are working for an individual lawyer or a law firm may be designated on the letterhead and in other appropriate places as 'associates.'" *ABA Opinion* 310 (1963).

68. *See* ABA CANONS OF PROFESSIONAL ETHICS, CANON 33 (1908).

69. *But see ABA Opinion* 285 (1951).

70. *See* ABA CANONS OF PROFESSIONAL ETHICS, CANON 33 (1908); *cf. ABA Opinions* 318 (1967), 267 (1945), 219 (1941), 208 (1940). 192 (1939), 97 (1933), and 6 (1925).

71. *ABA Opinion* 318 (1967) held, "anything to the contrary in Formal Opinion 315 or in the other opinions cited notwithstanding that: "Where a partner whose name appears in the name of a law firm is elected or appointed to high local, state or federal office, which office he intends to occupy only temporarily, at the end of which time he intends to return to his position with the firm, and provided that he is not precluded by holding such office from engaging in the practice of law and does not in fact sever his relationship with the firm but only takes a leave of absence, and provided that there is no local law, statute or custom to the contrary, his name may be retained in the firm name during his term or terms of office, but only if proper precautions are taken not to mislead the public as to his degree of participation in the firm's affairs."

Cf. ABA Opinion 143 (1935), NewYork County Opinion 67, and NewYork City Opinions 36 and 798; but *cf. ABA Opinion* 192 (1939) and Michigan Opinion 164.

72. *Cf.* ABA CANONS OF PROFESSIONAL ETHICS, CANON 33 (1908).

73. Amended, February 1979, House Informational Report No. 123.

74. *See ABA Opinion* 277 (1948); *cf.* ABA Canon of Professional Ethics, Canon 33 (1908) and *ABA Opinions* 318 (1967), 126 (1935), 115 (1934), 106 (1934), and 1383 (1977).

75. *See ABA Opinions* 318 (1967) and 316 (1967); *cf.* ABA CANONS OF PROFESSIONAL ETHICS, CANON 33 (1908).

76. DR 2-102(E) was deleted and DR 2-102(F) was redesignated as DR 2-102(E) in February 1980, House Informational Report No. 107.

77. *Cf.* ABA CANONS OF PROFESSIONAL ETHICS, CANON 28 (1908).

78. "We think it clear that a lawyer's seeking employment in an ordinary law office, or appointment to a civil service position, is not prohibited by . . . [Canon 27]." *ABA Opinion* 197 (1939).

79. "[A] lawyer may not seek from persons not his clients the opportunity to perform . . . a [legal] check-up." *ABA Opinion* 307 (1962).

80. *Cf. ABA Opinion* 78 (1932).

81. "No financial connection of any kind between the Brotherhood and any lawyer is permissible. No lawyer can properly pay any amount whatsoever to the Brotherhood or any of its departments, officers or members as compensation, reimbursement of expenses or gratuity in connection with the procurement of a case.'" In re Brotherhood of R. R. Trainmen, 13 111. 2d 391, 398, 150 N. E. 2d 163, 167 (1958), *quoted in* In re Ratner, 194 Kan. 362, 372, 399 P.2d 865, 873 (1965).

See ABA Opinion 147 (1935).

82. Amended, February 1975, House Informational Report No. 110.

83. "This Court has condemned the practice of ambulance chasing through the media of runners and touters. In similar fashion we have with equal emphasis condemned the practice of direct solicitation by a lawyer. We have classified both offenses as serious breaches of the Canons of Ethics demanding severe treatment of the offending lawyer." State v. Dawson, 111 So. 2d 427, 431 (Fla. 1959).

84. "Registrants [of a lawyer referral plan] may be required to contribute to the expense of operating it by a reasonable registration charge or by a reasonable percentage of fees collected by them." *ABA Opinion* 291 (1956). *Cf. ABA Opinion* 227 (1941).

85. Amended, February 1975, House Informational Report No. 110.

86. *Cf. ABA Opinion* 148 (1935).

87. United Mine Workers v. Ill. State Bar Ass'n., 389 U.S. 217, 19 L. Ed. 2d 426, 88 S. Ct. 353 (1967); Brotherhood of R.R. Trainmen v. Virginia, 371 U.S. 1, 12 L. Ed. 2d 89, 84 S. Ct. 1113 (1964); NAACP v. Button, 371 U.S. 415, 9 L. Ed. 2d 405, 83 S. Ct. 328 (1963). *Also see ABA Opinions* 332 (1973) and 333 (1973).

88. Amended, February 1975, House Informational Report No. 110.

89. "If a bar association has embarked on a program of institutional advertising for an annual legal check-up and provides brochures and reprints, it is not improper to have these available in the lawyers office for persons to read and take." *ABA Opinion* 307 (1962).

Cf. ABA Opinion 121 (1934).

90. ABA CANONS OF PROFESSIONAL ETHICS, CANON 28 (1908).

91. *Cf. ABA Opinions* 229 (1941) and 173 (1937).

92. "It certainly is not improper for a lawyer to advise his regular clients of new statutes, court decisions, and administrative rulings, which may affect the client's interests, provided the communication is strictly limited to such information . . . .

"When such communications go to concerns or individuals other than regular clients of the lawyer, they are thinly disguised advertisements for professional employment, and are obviously improper." *ABA Opinion* 213 (1941).

"It is our opinion that where the lawyer has no reason to believe that he has been supplanted by another lawyer, it is not only his right, but it might even be his duty to advise his client of any change of fact or law which might defeat the client's testamentary purpose as expressed in the will.

"Periodic notices might be sent to the client for whom a lawyer has drawn a will, suggesting that it might be wise for the client to reexamine his will to determine whether or not there has been any change in his situation requiring a modification of his will." *ABA Opinion* 210 (1941).

    Cf. ABA CANONS OF PROFESSIONAL ETHICS, CANON 28 (1908).

    93. Amended, March 1974, House Informational Report No. 127.

    94. Amended, February 1975, House Informational Report No. 110.

    95. *Cf. ABA Opinion* 168 (1937).

    96. *But cf. ABA Opinion* 111 (1934).

    97. *See* ABA CANONS OF PROFESSIONAL ETHICS, CANON 45 (1908); *cf.* ABA CANONS OF PROFESSIONAL ETHICS, CANONS 43, and 46 (1908).

    98. This provision is included to conform to action taken by the ABA House of Delegates at the Mid-Winter Meeting, January, 1969.

    99. *See* ABA CANONS OF PROFESSIONAL ETHICS, CANON 12 (1908).

    100. The charging of a "clearly excessive fee" is a ground for discipline. State ex rel. Nebraska State Bar Ass'n v. Richards, 165 Neb. 80, 90, 84 N.W.2d 136, 143 (1957).

    "An attorney has the right to contract for any fee he chooses so long as it is not excessive (see Opinion 190), and this Committee is not concerned with the amount of such fees unless so excessive as to constitute a misappropriation of the client's funds (see Opinion 27)." *ABA Opinion* 320 (1968).

    Cf. ABA Opinions 209 (1940), 190 (1939), and 27 (1930) and State ex rel. Lee v. Buchanan, 191 So. 2d 33 (Fla. 1966).

    101. *Cf.* ABA CANONS OF PROFESSIONAL ETHICS, CANON 13 (1908); see generally MACKINNON, CONTINGENT FEES FOR LEGAL SERVICES (1964) (a Report of the American Bar Foundation).

    102. "Contingent fees, whether in civil or criminal cases, are a special concern of the law . . . .

    "In criminal cases, the rule is stricter because of the danger of corrupting justice. The second part of Section 542 of the Restatement [of Contracts] reads: 'A bargain to conduct a criminal case . . . in consideration of a promise of a fee contingent on success is illegal . . . .'" Peyton v. Margiotti, 398 Pa. 86, 156 A.2d 865, 967 (1959).

    "The third area of practice in which the use of the contingent fee is generally considered to be prohibited is the prosecution and defense of criminal cases. However, there are so few cases, and these are predominantly old, that it is doubtful that there can be said to be any current law on the subject . . . . In the absence of cases on the validity of contingent fees for defense attorneys, it is necessary to rely on the consensus among commentators that such a fee is void as against public policy. The nature of criminal practice itself makes unlikely the use of contingent fee contracts." MACKINNON, CONTINGENT FEES FOR LEGAL SERVICES 52 (1964) (a Report of the American Bar Foundation).

    103. *See* ABA CANONS OF PROFESSIONAL ETHICS, CANON 34 (1908) and *ABA Opinions* 316 (1967) and 294 (1958); *see generally ABA Opinions* 265 (1945), 204 (1940), 190 (1939), 171 (1937), 153 (1936), 97 (1933), 63 (1932), 28 (1930), 27 (1930), and 18 (1930).

    104. "*Canon 12* contemplates that a lawyer's fee should not exceed the value of the services rendered . . . .

    "*Canon 12* applies, whether joint or separate fees are charged [by associate attorneys] . . . ." *ABA Opinion* 204 (1940).

    105. "[A] general covenant restricting an employed lawyer, after leaving the employment, from practicing; in the community for a stated period, appears to this Committee to be an unwarranted restriction on the right of a lawyer to choose where he will practice and inconsistent with our professional status. Accordingly, the Committee is of the opinion it would be improper for the employing lawyer to require the covenant and likewise for the employed lawyer to agree to it." *ABA Opinion* 300 (1961).

    106. *See* ABA CANONS OF PROFESSIONAL ETHICS, CANON 30 (1908).

"Rule 13 . . . . A member of the State Bar shall not accept employment to prosecute or defend a case solely out of spite, or solely for the purpose of harassing or delaying another . . . ." CAL. BUSINESS AND PROFESSIONS CODE § 6067 (West 1962).

107. *Cf.* ABA CANONS OF PROFESSIONAL ETHICS, CANON 44 (1908).

108. *See also* MODEL CODE OF PROFESSIONAL RESPONSIBILITY, DR 5-102 and DR 5-105.

109. *Cf.* ABA CANONS OF PROFESSIONAL ETHICS, CANON 4 (1908).

110. *Cf.* Anders v. California, 386 U.S. 738, 18 L. Ed. 2d 493, 87 S. Ct. 1396 (1967), *rehearing denied*, 388 U.S. 924, 18 L. Ed. 2d 1377, 87 S. Ct. 2094 (1967).

CANON 3
A Lawyer Should Assist in Preventing the Unauthorized Practice of Law

ETHICAL CONSIDERATIONS

EC 3-1   The prohibition against the practice of law by a layman is grounded in the need of the public for integrity and competence of those who undertake to render legal services. Because of the fiduciary and personal character of the lawyer-client relationship and the inherently complex nature of our legal system, the public can better be assured of the requisite responsibility and competence if the practice of law is confined to those who are subject to the requirements and regulations imposed upon members of the legal profession.

EC 3-2   The sensitive variations in the considerations that bear on legal determinations often make it difficult even for a lawyer to exercise appropriate professional judgment, and it is therefore essential that the personal nature of the relationship of client and lawyer be preserved. Competent professional judgment is the product of a trained familiarity with law and legal processes, a disciplined, analytical approach to legal problems, and a firm ethical commitment.

EC 3-3   A non-lawyer who undertakes to handle legal matters is not governed as to integrity or legal competence by the same rules that govern the conduct of a lawyer. A lawyer is not only subject to that regulation but also is committed to high standards of ethical conduct. The public interest is best served in legal matters by a regulated profession committed to such standards.[1] The Disciplinary Rules protect the public in that they prohibit a lawyer from seeking employment by improper overtures, from acting in cases of divided loyalties, and from submitting to the control of others in the exercise of his judgment. Moreover, a person who entrusts legal matters to a lawyer is protected by the attorney-client privilege and by the duty of the lawyer to hold inviolate the confidences and secrets of his client.

EC 3-4   A layman who seeks legal services often is not in a position to judge whether he will receive proper professional attention. The entrustment of a legal matter may well involve the confidences, the reputation, the property, the freedom, or even the life of the client. Proper protection of members of the public demands that no person be permitted to act in the confidential and demanding capacity of a lawyer unless he is subject to the regulations of the legal profession.

EC 3-5   It is neither necessary nor desirable to attempt the formulation of a single, specific definition of what constitutes the practice of law.[2] Functionally, the practice of law relates to the rendition of services for others that call for the professional judgment of a lawyer. The essence of the professional judgment of the lawyer is his educated ability to relate the general body and philosophy of law to a specific legal problem of a client; and thus, the public interest will be better served if only lawyers are permitted to act in matters involving professional judgment. Where this professional judgment is not involved, non-lawyers, such as court clerks, police officers, abstracters, and many governmental employees, may engage in occupations that require a special knowledge of law in certain areas. But the services of a lawyer are essential in the public interest whenever the exercise of professional legal judgment is required.

EC 3-6   A lawyer often delegates tasks to clerks, secretaries, and other lay persons. Such delegation is proper if the lawyer maintains a direct relationship with his client, supervises the delegated work, and has complete professional responsibility for the work product.[3] This delegation enables a lawyer to render legal service more economically and efficiently.

EC 3-7   The prohibition against a non-lawyer practicing law does not prevent a layman from representing himself, for then he is ordinarily exposing only himself to possible injury. The purpose of the legal profession is to make educated legal representation available to the public; but anyone who does not wish to avail himself of such representation is not required to do so. Even so, the legal profession should help members of the public to recognize legal problems and to understand why it may be unwise for them to act for themselves in matters having legal consequences.

EC 3-8   Since a lawyer should not aid or encourage a layman to practice law, he should not practice law in association with a layman or otherwise share legal fees with a layman.[4] This does not mean, however, that the pecuniary value of the interest of a deceased lawyer in his firm or practice may not be paid to his estate or specified persons such as his widow or heirs.[5] In like manner, profit-sharing retirement plans of a lawyer or law firm which include non-lawyer office employees are not improper.[6] These limited exceptions to the rule against sharing legal fees with laymen are permissible since they do not aid or encourage laymen to practice law.

EC 3-9 Regulation of the practice of law is accomplished principally by the respective states.[7] Authority to engage in the practice of law conferred in any jurisdiction is not per se a grant of the right to practice elsewhere, and it is improper for a lawyer to engage in practice where he is not permitted by law or by court order to do so. However, the demands of business and the mobility of our society pose distinct problems in the regulation of the practice of law by the states.[8] In furtherance of the public interest, the legal profession should discourage regulation that unreasonably imposes territorial limitations upon the right of a lawyer to handle the legal affairs of his client or upon the opportunity of a client to obtain the services of a lawyer of his choice in all matters including the presentation of a contested matter in a tribunal before which the lawyer is not permanently admitted to practice.[9]

DISCIPLINARY RULES

DR 3-101   Aiding Unauthorized Practice of Law.[10]

(A) A lawyer shall not aid a non-lawyer in the unauthorized practice of law.[11]

(B) A lawyer shall not practice law in a jurisdiction where to do so would be in violation of regulations of the profession in that jurisdiction.[12]

DR 3-102   Dividing Legal Fees with a Non-Lawyer.

(A) A lawyer or law firm shall not share legal fees with a non-lawyer,[13] except that:

(1) An agreement by a lawyer with his firm, partner, or associate may provide for the payment of money, over a reasonable period of time after his death, to his estate or to one or more specified persons.[14]

(2) A lawyer who undertakes to complete unfinished legal business of a deceased lawyer may pay to the estate of the deceased lawyer that proportion of the total compensation which fairly represents the services rendered by the deceased lawyer.

(3) A lawyer or law firm may include non-lawyer employees in a retirement plan, even though the plan is based in whole or in part on a profit-sharing arrangement,[15] providing such plan does not circumvent another Disciplinary Rule.[16, 17]

DR 3-103   Forming a Partnership with a Non-Lawyer.

(A) A lawyer shall not form a partnership with a non-lawyer if any of the activities of the partnership consist of the practice of law.[18]

NOTES

1. "The condemnation of the unauthorized practice of law is designed to protect the public from legal services by persons unskilled in the law. The prohibition of lay intermedi-

ABA Model
Code of
Professional
Responsibility

aries is intended to insure the loyalty of the lawyer to the client unimpaired by intervening and possibly conflicting interests." Cheatham, *Availability of Legal Services: The Responsibility of the Individual Lawyer and of the Organized Bar,* 12 U.C.L.A. L. REV. 438, 439 (1965).

2. "What constitutes unauthorized practice of the law in a particular jurisdiction is a matter for determination by the courts of that jurisdiction." *ABA Opinion* 198 (1939).

"In the light of the historical development of the lawyer's functions, it is impossible to lay down an exhaustive definition of 'the practice of law' by attempting to enumerate every conceivable act performed by lawyers in the normal course of their work." State Bar of Arizona v. Arizona Land Title & Trust Co., 90 Ariz., 76, 87, 366 P.2d 1, 8-9 (1961), *modified,* 91 Ariz. 293, 371 P.2d 1020 (1962).

3. "A lawyer can employ lay secretaries, lay investigators, lay detectives, lay researchers, accountants, lay scriveners, nonlawyer draftsmen or nonlawyer researchers. In fact, he may employ nonlawyers to do any task for him except counsel clients about law matters, engage directly in the practice of law, appear in court or appear in formal proceedings that are a part of the judicial process, so long as it is he who takes the work and vouches for it to the client and becomes responsible to the client." *ABA Opinion* 316 (1967).

ABA Opinion 316 (1967) also stated that if a lawyer practices law as part of a law firm which includes lawyers from several states, he may delegate tasks to firm members in other states so long as he "is the person who, on behalf of the firm, vouched for the work of all of the others and, with the client and in the courts, did the legal acts defined by that state as the practice of law."

"A lawyer cannot delegate his professional responsibility to a law student employed in his office. He may avail himself of the assistance of the student in many of the fields of the lawyer's work, such as examination of case law, finding and interviewing witnesses, making collections of claims, examining court records, delivering papers, conveying important messages, and other similar matters. But the student is not permitted, until he is admitted to the Bar, to perform the professional functions of a lawyer, such as conducting court trials, giving professional advice to clients or drawing legal documents for them. The student in all his work must act as agent for the lawyer employing him, who must supervise his work and be responsible for his good conduct." *ABA Opinion* 85 (1932).

4. "No division of fees for legal services is proper, except with another lawyer . . . ." ABA CANONS OF PROFESSIONAL ETHICS, CANON 34 (1908). Otherwise, according to *ABA Opinion* 316 (1967), "[t]he Canons of Ethics do not examine into the method by which such persons are remunerated by the lawyer . . . . They may be paid a salary, a per diem charge, a flat fee, a contract price, etc."

See ABA CANONS OF PROFESSIONAL ETHICS, CANONS 33 and 47 (1908).

5. "Many partnership agreements provide that the active partners, on the death of any one of them, are to make payments to the estate or to the nominee of a deceased partner on a predetermined formula. It is only where the effect of such an arrangement is to make the estate or nominee a member of the partnership along with the surviving partners that it is prohibited by Canon 34. Where the payments are made in accordance with a pre-existing agreement entered into by the deceased partner during his lifetime and providing for a fixed method for determining their amount based upon the value of services rendered during the partner's lifetime and providing for a fixed period over which the payments are to be made, this is not the case. Under these circumstances, whether the payments are considered to be delayed payment of compensation earned but withheld during the partner's lifetime, or whether they are considered to be an approximation of his interest in matters pending at the time of his death, is immaterial. In either event, as Henry S. Drinker says in his book, LEGAL ETHICS, at page 189: 'It would seem, however, that a reasonable agreement to pay the estate a proportion of the receipts for a reasonable period is a proper practical settlement for the lawyer's services to his retirement or death.'" *ABA Opinion* 308 (1963).

6. *Cf. ABA Opinion* 311 (1964).

7. "That the States have broad power to regulate the practice of law is, of course, beyond question." United Mine Workers v. Ill. State Bar Ass'n, 389 U.S. 217, 222 (1967).

"It is a matter of law, not of ethics, as to where an individual may practice law. Each state has its own rules." *ABA Opinion* 316 (1967).

8. "Much of clients' business crosses state lines. People are mobile, moving from state to state. Many metropolitan areas cross state lines. It is common today to have a single economic and social community involving more than one state. The business of a single client may involve legal problems in several states." *ABA Opinion* 316 (1967).

9. "[W]e reaffirmed the general principle that legal services to New Jersey residents with respect to New Jersey matters may ordinarily be furnished only by New Jersey counsel; but we pointed out that there may be multistate transactions where strict adherence to this thesis would not be in the public interest and that, under the circumstances, it would have been not only more costly to the client but also 'grossly impractical and inefficient' to have had the settlement negotiations conducted by separate lawyers from different states." In re Estate of Waring, 47 N.J. 367, 376, 221 A.2d 193, 197 (1966).

Cf. ABA Opinion 316 (1967).

10. Conduct permitted by Disciplinary Rules of Canons 2 and 5 does not violate DR 3-101.

11. *See* ABA CANONS OF PROFESSIONAL ETHICS, CANON 47 (1908).

12. It should be noted, however, that a lawyer may engage in conduct, otherwise prohibited by this Disciplinary Rule, where such conduct is authorized by preemptive federal legislation. *See* Sperry v. Florida, 373 U.S. 379, 10 L. Ed. 2d 428, 83 S. Ct. 1322 (1963).

13. *See* ABA CANONS OF PROFESSIONAL ETHICS, CANON 34 (1908) and *ABA Opinions* 316 (1967), 180 (1938), and 48 (1931).

"The receiving attorney shall not under any guise or form share his fee for legal services with a lay agency, personal or corporate, without prejudice, however, to the right of the lay forwarder to charge and collect from the creditor proper compensation for nonlegal services rendered by the law [sic] forwarder which are separate and apart from the services performed by the receiving attorney." *ABA Opinion* 294 (1958).

14. *See ABA Opinion* 266 (1945).

15. *Cf. ABA Opinion* 311 (1964).

16. *See ABA Opinion* 1440.

17. Amended, February 1980, House Informational Report No. 107.

18. *See* ABA CANONS OF PROFESSIONAL ETHICS, CANON 33 (1908); *cf. ABA Opinions* 239 (1942) and 201 (1940)

ABA Opinion 316 (1967) states that lawyers licensed in different jurisdictions may, under certain conditions, enter "into an arrangement for the practice of law" and that a lawyer licensed in State A is not, for such purpose, a layman in State B.

CANON 4
A Lawyer Should Preserve the
Confidences and Secrets of a Client

ETHICAL CONSIDERATIONS

EC 4-1   Both the fiduciary relationship existing between lawyer and client and the proper functioning of the legal system require the preservation by the lawyer of confidences and secrets of one who has employed or sought to employ him.[1] A client must feel free to discuss whatever he wishes with his

ABA Model Code of Professional Responsibility

ABA Model
Code of
Professional
Responsibility

lawyer and a lawyer must be equally free to obtain information beyond that volunteered by his client.[2] A lawyer should be fully informed of all the facts of the matter he is handling in order for his client to obtain the full advantage of our legal system. It is for the lawyer in the exercise of his independent professional judgment to separate the relevant and important from the irrelevant and unimportant. The observance of the ethical obligation of a lawyer to hold inviolate the confidences and secrets of his client not only facilitates the full development of facts essential to proper representation of the client but also encourages laymen to seek early legal assistance.

EC 4-2   The obligation to protect confidences and secrets obviously does not preclude a lawyer from revealing information when his client consents after full disclosure,[3] when necessary to perform his professional employment, when permitted by a Disciplinary Rule, or when required by law. Unless the client otherwise directs, a lawyer may disclose the affairs of his client to partners or associates of his firm. It is a matter of common knowledge that the normal operation of a law office exposes confidential professional information to non-lawyer employees of the office, particularly secretaries and those having access to the files; and this obligates a lawyer to exercise care in selecting and training his employees so that the sanctity of all confidences and secrets of his clients may be preserved. If the obligation extends to two or more clients as to the same information, a lawyer should obtain the permission of all before revealing the information. A lawyer must always be sensitive to the rights and wishes of his client and act scrupulously in the making of decisions which may involve the disclosure of information obtained in his professional relationship.[4] Thus, in the absence of consent of his client after full disclosure, a lawyer should not associate another lawyer in the handling of a matter; nor should he, in the absence of consent, seek counsel from another lawyer if there is a reasonable possibility that the identity of the client or his confidences or secrets would be revealed to such lawyer. Both social amenities and professional duty should cause a lawyer to shun indiscreet conversations concerning his clients.

EC 4-3   Unless the client otherwise directs, it is not improper for a lawyer to give limited information from his files to an outside agency necessary for statistical, bookkeeping, accounting, data processing, banking, printing, or other legitimate purposes, provided he exercises due care in the selection of the agency and warns the agency that the information must be kept confidential.

EC 4-4   The attorney-client privilege is more limited than the ethical obligation of a lawyer to guard the confidences and secrets of his client. This ethical precept, unlike the evidentiary privilege, exists without regard to the nature or source of information or the fact that others share the knowledge.

A lawyer should endeavor to act in a manner which preserves the evidentiary privilege; for example, he should avoid professional discussions in the presence of persons to whom the privilege does not extend. A lawyer owes an obligation to advise the client of the attorney-client privilege and timely to assert the privilege unless it is waived by the client.

EC 4-5   A lawyer should not use information acquired in the course of the representation of a client to the disadvantage of the client and a lawyer should not use, except with the consent of his client after full disclosure, such information for his own purposes.[5] Likewise, a lawyer should be diligent in his efforts to prevent the misuse of such information by his employees and associates.[6] Care should be exercised by a lawyer to prevent the disclosure of the confidences and secrets of one client to another,[7] and no employment should be accepted that might require such disclosure.

EC 4-6   The obligation of a lawyer to preserve the confidences and secrets of his client continues after the termination of his employment.[8] Thus a lawyer should not attempt to sell a law practice as a going business because, among other reasons, to do so would involve the disclosure of confidences and secrets.[9] A lawyer should also provide for the protection of the confidences and secrets of his client following the termination of the practice of the lawyer, whether termination is due to death, disability, or retirement. For example, a lawyer might provide for the personal papers of the client to be returned to him and for the papers of the lawyer to be delivered to another lawyer or to be destroyed. In determining the method of disposition, the instructions and wishes of the client should be a dominant consideration.

DISCIPLINARY RULES

DR 4-101   Preservation of Confidences and Secrets of a Client.[10]

(A) "Confidence" refers to information protected by the attorney-client privilege under applicable law, and "secret" refers to other information gained in the professional relationship that the client has requested be held inviolate or the disclosure of which would be embarrassing or would be likely to be detrimental to the client.

(B) Except when permitted under DR 4-101(C), a lawyer shall not knowingly:
   (1) Reveal a confidence or secret of his client.[11]
   (2) Use a confidence or secret of his client to the disadvantage of the client.
   (3) Use a confidence or secret of his client for the advantage of himself[12] or of a third person,[13] unless the client consents after full disclosure.

ABA Model
Code of
Professional
Responsibility

(C) A lawyer may reveal:

    (1) Confidences or secrets with the consent of the client or clients affected, but only after a full disclosure to them.[14]

    (2) Confidences or secrets when permitted under Disciplinary Rules or required by law or court order.[15]

    (3) The intention of his client to commit a crime[16] and the information necessary to prevent the crime.[17]

    (4) Confidences or secrets necessary to establish or collect his fee[18] or to defend himself or his employees or associates against an accusation of wrongful conduct.[19]

(D) A lawyer shall exercise reasonable care to prevent his employees, associates, and others whose services are utilized by him from disclosing or using confidences or secrets of a client, except that a lawyer may reveal the information allowed by DR 4-101(C) through an employee.

NOTES

1. *See* ABA CANONS OF PROFESSIONAL ETHICS, CANONS 6 and 37 (1908) and *ABA Opinion* 287 (1953).

"The reason underlying the rule with respect to confidential communications between attorney and client is well stated in Mechem on Agency, 2d Ed., Vol. 2, §2297, as follows: 'The purposes and necessities of the relation between a client and his attorney require, in many cases, on the part of the client, the fullest and freest disclosures to the attorney of the client's objects, motives and acts. This disclosure is made in the strictest confidence, relying upon the attorney's honor and fidelity. To permit the attorney to confidence, relying upon the attorney's honor and fidelity. To permit the attorney to reveal to others what is so disclosed, would be not only a gross violation of a sacred trust upon his part, but it would utterly destroy and prevent the usefulness and benefits to be derived from professional assistance. Based upon considerations of public policy, therefore, the law wisely declares that all confidential communications and disclosures, made by a client to his legal adviser for the purpose of obtaining his professional aid or advice shall be strictly privileged; -that the attorney shall not be permitted, without the consent of his client,-and much less will he be compelled-to reveal or disclose communications made to him under such circumstances.'" *ABA Opinion* 250(1943).

"While it is true that complete revelation of relevant facts should be encouraged for trial purposes, nevertheless an attorney's dealings with his client, if both are sincere, and if the dealings involve more than mere technical matters, should be immune to discovery proceedings. There must be freedom from fear of revealment of matters disclosed to an attorney because of the peculiarly intimate relationship existing." Ellis-Foster Co. v. Union Carbide & Carbon Corp., 159 F. Supp. 917, 919 (D.N.J. 1958).

Cf. ABA Opinions 314 (1965), 274 (1946) and 268 (1945).

2. "While it is the great purpose of law to ascertain the truth, there is the countervailing necessity of insuring the right of every person to freely and fully confer and confide in one having knowledge of the law, and skilled in its practice, in order that the former may have adequate advice and a proper defense. This assistance can be made safely and readily available only when the client is free from the consequences of apprehension of disclosure by reason of the subsequent statements of the skilled lawyer. Baird v. Koemer, 279 F.2d 623, 629-30 (9th Cir. 1960).

Cf. ABA Opinion 150 (1936).

3. "Where . . . [a client] knowingly and after full disclosure participates in a [legal fee]

ABA Model Code of Professional Responsibility

financing plan which requires the furnishing of certain information to the bank, clearly by his conduct he has waived any privilege as to that information." *ABA Opinion* 320 (1968)

4. "The lawyer must decide when he takes a case whether it is a suitable one for him to undertake and after this decision is made, he is not justified in turning against his client by exposing injurious evidence entrusted to him . . . . [D]oing something intrinsically regrettable, because the only alternative involves worse consequences, is a necessity in every profession. WILLISTON, LIFE AND LAW 271 (1940).

Cf. ABA Opinions 177 (1938) and 83 (1932).

5. *See* ABA CANONS OF PROFESSIONAL ETHICS, CANON 11 (1908).

6. *See* ABA CANONS OF PROFESSIONAL ETHICS, CANON 37 (1908).

7. *See* ABA CANONS OF PROFESSIONAL ETHICS, CANONS 6 and 37 (1908). "[A]n attorney must not accept professional employment against a client or a former client which will, or even may require him to use confidential information obtained by the attorney in the course of his professional relations with such client regarding the subject matter of the employment . . . ." *ABA Opinion* 165 (1936).

8. *See* ABA CANONS OF PROFESSIONAL ETHICS, CANON 37 (1908). "Confidential communications between an attorney and his client, made because of the relationship and concerning the subject-matter of the attorney's employment, are generally privileged from disclosure without the consent of the client, and this privilege outlasts the attorney's employment. Canon 37." *ABA Opinion* 154 (1936).

9. *Cf. ABA Opinion* 266 (1945).

10. *See* ABA CANONS OF PROFESSIONAL ETHICS, CANON 37 (1908); *cf.* ABA CANONS OF PROFESSIONAL ETHICS, CANON 6 (1908).

11. "§6068 . . . It is the duty of an attorney:

. . . .

"(e) To maintain inviolate the confidence, and at every peril to himself to preserve the secrets, of his client. CAL. BUSINESS AND PROFESSIONS CODE §6068 (West 1962). Virtually the same provision is found in the Oregon statutes. Ore. REV. Stats. ch. 9 §9.460(5).

"Communication between lawyer and client are privileged (WIGMORE ON EVIDENCE, 3d Ed., Vol. 8, §§2290-2329). The modern theory underlying the privilege is subjective and is to give the client freedom of apprehension in consulting his legal adviser (*ibid.*, §2290, p. 548). The privilege applies to communications made in seeking legal advice for any purpose (*ibid.*, §2294, p.563). The mere circumstance that the advice is given without charge therefor does not nullify the privilege (*ibid.*, §2303)." *ABA Opinion* 216 (1941).

"It is the duty of an attorney to maintain the confidence and preserve inviolate the secrets of his client . . . ." *ABA Opinion* 155 (1936).

12. *See* ABA CANONS OF PROFESSIONAL ETHICS, CANON 11 (1908).

"The provision respecting employment is in accord with the general rule announced in the adjudicated cases that a lawyer may not make use of knowledge or information acquired by him through his professional relations with his client, or in the conduct of his client's business, to his own advantage or profit (7 C.J.S., § 125, p. 958, Healy v. Gray, 184 Iowa 111, 168 N.W. 222; Baumgardner v. Hudson, D.C. App., 277 F. 552, Goodrum v. Clement, D.C. App., 277 F. 586)." *ABA Opinion* 250 (1943).

13. *See ABA Opinion* 177 (1938).

14. "[A lawyer] may not divulge confidential communications, information, and secrets imparted to him by the client or acquired during their professional relations unless he is authorized to do so by the client (People v. Gerold, 265 Ill. 448, 107 N.E. 165, 178; Murphy v. Riggs, 238 Mich. 151, 213 N.W. 110, 112; Opinion of this Committee, No. 91)." *ABA Opinion* 202 (1940).

Cf. ABA Opinion 91 (1933).

15. "A defendant in a criminal case when admitted to bail is not only regarded as in the custody of his bail, but he is also in the custody of the law, and admission to bail does

not deprive the court of its inherent power to deal with the person of the prisoner. Being in lawful custody, the defendant is guilty of an escape when he gains his liberty before he is delivered in due process of law, and is guilty of a separate offense for which he may be punished. In failing to disclose his client's whereabouts as a fugitive under these circumstances the attorney would not only be aiding his client to escape trial on the charge for which he was indicted, but would likewise be aiding him in evading prosecution for the additional offense of escape.

"It is the opinion of the committee that under such circumstances the attorney's knowledge of his client's whereabouts is not privileged, and that he may be disciplined for failing to disclose that information to the proper authorities . . . ." *ABA Opinion* 155 (1936).

"We held in Opinion 155 that a communication by a client to his attorney in respect to the future commission of an unlawful act or to a continuing wrong is not privileged from disclosure. Public policy forbids that the relation of attorney and client should be used to conceal wrongdoing on the part of the client.

. . . .

"When an attorney representing a defendant in a criminal case applies on his behalf for probation or suspension of sentence, he represents to the court, by implication at least that his client will abide by the terms and conditions of the court's order. When that attorney is later advised of a violation of that order, it is his duty to advise his client of the consequences of his act, and endeavor to prevent a continuance of the wrongdoing. If his client thereafter persists in violating the terms and conditions of his probation, it is the duty of the attorney as an officer of the court to advise the proper authorities concerning his client's conduct. Such information, even though coming to the attorney from the client in the course of his professional relations with respect to other matters in which he represents the defendant, is not privileged from disclosure . . . ."

See *ABA Opinion* 156 (1936).

16. *ABA Opinion* 314 (1965) indicates that a lawyer must disclose even the confidences of his clients if "the facts in the attorney's possession indicate beyond reasonable doubt that a crime will be committed." See *ABA Opinion* 155 (1936).

17. *See* ABA CANONS OF PROFESSIONAL ETHICS, CANON 37 (1908) and *ABA Opinion* 202 (1940).

18. *Cf. ABA Opinion* 250 (1943).

19. *See* ABA CANONS OF PROFESSIONAL ETHICS, CANON 37 (1908) and *ABA Opinions* 202 (1940) and 19 (1930).

"[T]he adjudicated cases recognize an exception to the rule [that a lawyer shall not reveal the confidences of his client], where disclosure is necessary to protect the attorney's interests arising out of the relation of attorney and client in which disclosure was made.

"The exception is stated in MECHEM ON AGENCY, 2d Ed., Vol. 2, §2313, as follows: 'But the attorney may disclose information received from the client when it becomes necessary for his own protection, as if the client should bring an action against the attorney for negligence or misconduct, and it became necessary for the attorney to show what his instructions were, or what was the nature of the duty which the client expected him to perform. So if it became necessary for the attorney to bring an action against the client, the client's privilege could not prevent the attorney from disclosing what was essential as a means of obtaining or defending his own rights.'

"Mr Jones, in his COMMENTARIES ON EVIDENCE, 2d Ed., Vol. 5, §2165, states the exception thus 'It has frequently been held that the rule as to privileged communications does not apply when litigation arises between attorney and client to the extent that their communications are relevant to the issue. In such cases, if the disclosure of privileged communications becomes necessary to protect the attorney's rights, he is released from those obligations of secrecy which the law places upon him. He should not, however disclose more than is necessary for his own protection. It would be a manifest injustice to allow the client to take advantage of the rule of exclusion as to professional confidence to the prejudice of his attorney, or that it should be carried to the extent of depriving the attorney of the means of obtaining or defending his own rights. In such cases the attorney is exempted from the obligations of secrecy.' " *ABA Opinion* 250 (1943).

CANON 5
A Lawyer Should Exercise Independent Professional Judgment on Behalf of a Client

ETHICAL CONSIDERATIONS

EC 5-1   The professional judgment of a lawyer should be exercised, within the bounds of the law, solely for the benefit of his client and free of compromising influences and loyalties.[1] Neither his personal interests, the interests of other clients, nor the desires of third persons should be permitted to dilute his loyalty to his client.

Interests of a Lawyer That May Affect His Judgment

EC 5-2   A lawyer should not accept proffered employment if his personal interests or desires will, or there is a reasonable probability that they will, affect adversely the advice to be given or services to be rendered the prospective client.[2] After accepting employment, a lawyer carefully should refrain from acquiring a property right or assuming a position that would tend to make his judgment less protective of the interests of his client.

EC 5-3   The self-interest of a lawyer resulting from his ownership of property in which his client also has an interest or which may affect property of his client may interfere with the exercise of free judgment on behalf of his client. If such interference would occur with respect to a prospective client, a lawyer should decline employment proffered by him. After accepting employment, a lawyer should not acquire property rights that would adversely affect his professional judgment in the representation of his client. Even if the property interests of a lawyer do not presently interfere with the exercise of his independent judgment, but the likelihood of interference can reasonably be foreseen by him, a lawyer should explain the situation to his client and should decline employment or withdraw unless the client consents to the continuance of the relationship after full disclosure. A lawyer should not seek to persuade his client to permit him to invest in an undertaking of his client nor make improper use of his professional relationship to influence his client to invest in an enterprise in which the lawyer is interested.

EC 5-4   If, in the course of his representation of a client, a lawyer is permitted to receive from his client a beneficial ownership in publication rights

ABA Model
Code of
Professional
Responsibility

relating to the subject matter of the employment, he may be tempted to subordinate the interests of his client to his own anticipated pecuniary gain. For example, a lawyer in a criminal case who obtains from his client television, radio, motion picture, newspaper, magazine, book, or other publication rights with respect to the case may be influenced, consciously or unconsciously, to a course of conduct that will enhance the value of his publication rights to the prejudice of his client. To prevent these potentially differing interests, such arrangements should be scrupulously avoided prior to the termination of all aspects of the matter giving rise to the employment, even though his employment has previously ended.

EC 5-5   A lawyer should not suggest to his client that a gift be made to himself or for his benefit. If a lawyer accepts a gift from his client, he is peculiarly susceptible to the charge that he unduly influenced or overreached the client. If a client voluntarily offers to make a gift to his lawyer, the lawyer may accept the gift, but before doing so, he should urge that his client secure disinterested advice from an independent, competent person who is cognizant of all the circumstances.[3] Other than in exceptional circumstances, a lawyer should insist that an instrument in which his client desires to name him beneficially be prepared by another lawyer selected by the client.[4]

EC 5-6   A lawyer should not consciously influence a client to name him as executor, trustee, or lawyer in an instrument. In those cases where a client wishes to name his lawyer as such, care should be taken by the lawyer to avoid even the appearance of impropriety.[5]

EC 5-7   The possibility of an adverse effect upon the exercise of free judgment by a lawyer on behalf of his client during litigation generally makes it undesirable for the lawyer to acquire a proprietary interest in the cause of his client or otherwise to become financially interested in the outcome of the litigation.[6] However, it is not improper for a lawyer to protect his right to collect a fee for his services by the assertion of legally permissible liens, even though by doing so he may acquire an interest in the outcome of litigation. Although a contingent fee arrangement[7] gives a lawyer a financial interest in the outcome of litigation, a reasonable contingent fee is permissible in civil cases because it may be the only means by which a layman can obtain the services of a lawyer of his choice. But a lawyer, because he is in a better position to evaluate a cause of action, should enter into a contingent fee arrangement only in those instances where the arrangement will be beneficial to the client.

EC 5-8   A financial interest in the outcome of litigation also results if monetary advances are made by the lawyer to his client.[8] Although this assistance generally is not encouraged, there are instances when it is not improper to make loans to a client. For example, the advancing or guaranteeing of payment of the costs and expenses of litigation by a lawyer may be the only way a client can enforce his cause of action,[9] but the ultimate liability for such costs and expenses must be that of the client.

EC 5-9   Occasionally a lawyer is called upon to decide in a particular case whether he will be a witness or an advocate. If a lawyer is both counsel and witness, he becomes more easily impeachable for interest and thus may be a less effective witness. Conversely, the opposing counsel may be handicapped in challenging the credibility of the lawyer when the lawyer also appears as an advocate in the case. An advocate who becomes a witness is in the unseemly and ineffective position of arguing his own credibility. The roles of an advocate and of a witness are inconsistent; the function of an advocate is to advance or argue the cause of another, while that of a witness is to state facts objectively.

EC 5-10   Problems incident to the lawyer-witness relationship arise at different stages; they relate either to whether a lawyer should accept employment or should withdraw from employment.[10] Regardless of when the problem arises, his decision is to be governed by the same basic considerations. It is not objectionable for a lawyer who is a potential witness to be an advocate if it is unlikely that he will be called as a witness because his testimony would be merely cumulative or if his testimony will relate only to an uncontested issue.[11] In the exceptional situation where it will be manifestly unfair to the client for the lawyer to refuse employment or to withdraw when he will likely be a witness on a contested issue, he may serve as advocate even though he may be a witness.[12] In making such decision, he should determine the personal or financial sacrifice of the client that may result from his refusal of employment or withdrawal therefrom, the materiality of his testimony, and the effectiveness of his representation in view of his personal involvement. In weighing these factors, it should be clear that refusal or withdrawal will impose an unreasonable hardship upon the client before the lawyer accepts or continues the employment.[13] Where the question arises, doubts should be resolved in favor of the lawyer testifying and against his becoming or continuing as an advocate.[14]

EC 5-11   A lawyer should not permit his personal interests to influence his advice relative to a suggestion by his client that additional counsel be employed.[15] In like manner, his personal interests should not deter him from suggesting that additional counsel be employed; on the contrary, he should be alert to the desirability of recommending additional counsel when, in his judgment, the proper representation of his client requires it. However, a lawyer should advise his client not to employ additional counsel suggested by the client if the lawyer believes that such employment would be a disservice to the client, and he should disclose the reasons for his belief.

ABA Model
Code of
Professional
Responsibility

EC 5-12 Inability of co-counsel to agree on a matter vital to the representation of their client requires that their disagreement be submitted by them jointly to their client for his resolution, and the decision of the client shall control the action to be taken.[16]

EC 5-13 A lawyer should not maintain membership in or be influenced by any organization of employees that undertakes to prescribe, direct, or suggest when or how he should fulfill his professional obligations to a person or organization that employs him as a lawyer. Although it is not necessarily improper for a lawyer employed by a corporation or similar entity to be a member of an organization of employees, he should be vigilant to safeguard his fidelity as a lawyer to his employer, free from outside influences.

Interests of Multiple Clients

EC 5-14 Maintaining the independence of professional judgment required of a lawyer precludes his acceptance or continuation of employment that will adversely affect his judgment on behalf of or dilute his loyalty to a client.[17] This problem arises whenever a lawyer is asked to represent two or more clients who may have differing interests, whether such interests be conflicting, inconsistent, diverse, or otherwise discordant.[18]

EC 5-15 If a lawyer is requested to undertake or to continue representation of multiple clients having potentially differing interests, he must weigh carefully the possibility that his judgment may be impaired or his loyalty divided if he accepts or continues the employment. He should resolve all doubts against the propriety of the representation. A lawyer should never represent in litigation multiple clients with differing interest;[19] and there are few situations in which he would be justified in representing in litigation multiple clients with potentially differing interests. If a lawyer accepted such employment and the interests did become actually differing, he would have to withdraw from employment with likelihood of resulting hardship on the clients; and for this reason it is preferable that he refuse the employment initially. On the other hand, there are many instances in which a lawyer may properly serve multiple clients having potentially differing interests in matters not involving litigation. If the interests vary only slightly, it is generally likely that the lawyer will not be subjected to an adverse influence and that he can retain his independent judgment on behalf of each client; and if the interests become differing, withdrawal is less likely to have a disruptive effect upon the causes of his clients.

EC 5-16 In those instances in which a lawyer is justified in representing two or more clients having differing interests, it is nevertheless essential that each client be given the opportunity to evaluate his need for representation free of any potential conflict and to obtain other counsel if he so desires.[20]

Thus before a lawyer may represent multiple clients, he should explain fully to each client the implications of the common representation and should accept or continue employment only if the clients consent.[21] If there are present other circumstances that might cause any of the multiple clients to question the undivided loyalty of the lawyer, he should also advise all of the clients of those circumstances.[22]

EC 5-17 Typically recurring situations involving potentially differing interests are those in which a lawyer is asked to represent co-defendants in a criminal case, co-plaintiffs in a personal injury case, an insured and his insurer,[23] and beneficiaries of the estate of a decedent. Whether a lawyer can fairly and adequately protect the interests of multiple clients in these and similar situations depends upon an analysis of each case. In certain circumstances, there may exist little chance of the judgment of the lawyer being adversely affected by the slight possibility that the interests will become actually differing; in other circumstances, the chance of adverse effect upon his judgment is not unlikely.

EC 5-18 A lawyer employed or retained by a corporation or similar entity owes his allegiance to the entity and not to a stockholder, director, officer, employee, representative, or other person connected with the entity. In advising the entity, a lawyer should keep paramount its interests and his professional judgment should not be influenced by the personal desires of any person or organization. Occasionally a lawyer for an entity is requested by a stockholder, director, officer, employee, representative, or other person connected with the entity to represent him in an individual capacity; in such case the lawyer may serve the individual only if the lawyer is convinced that differing interests are not present.

EC 5-19 A lawyer may represent several clients whose interests are not actually or potentially differing. Nevertheless, he should explain any circumstances that might cause a client to question his undivided loyalty.[24] Regardless of the belief of a lawyer that he may properly represent multiple clients, he must defer to a client who holds the contrary belief and withdraw from representation of that client.

EC 5-20 A lawyer is often asked to serve as an impartial arbitrator or mediator in matters which involve present or former clients. He may serve in either capacity if he first discloses such present or former relationships. After a lawyer has undertaken to act as an impartial arbitrator or mediator, he should not thereafter represent in the dispute any of the parties involved.

Desires of Third Persons

EC 5-21 The obligation of a lawyer to exercise professional judgment solely on behalf of his client requires that he disregard the desires of others that might impair his free judgment.[25] The desires of a third person will seldom adversely affect a lawyer unless that person is in a position to exert strong economic, political, or social pressures upon the lawyer. These influences are often subtle, and a lawyer must be alert to their existence. A lawyer subjected to outside pressures should make full disclosure of them to his client;[26] and if he or his client believes that the effectiveness of his representation has been or will be impaired thereby, the lawyer should take proper steps to withdraw from representation of his client.

EC 5-22   Economic, political, or social pressures by third persons are less likely to impinge upon the independent judgment of a lawyer in a matter in which he is compensated directly by his client and his professional work is exclusively with his client. On the other hand, if a lawyer is compensated from a source other than his client, he may feel a sense of responsibility to someone other than his client.

EC 5-23   A person or organization that pays or furnishes lawyers to represent others possesses a potential power to exert strong pressures against the independent judgment of those lawyers. Some employers may be interested in furthering their own economic, political, or social goals without regard to the professional responsibility of the lawyer to his individual client. Others may be far more concerned with establishment or extension of legal principles than in the immediate protection of the rights of the lawyer's individual client. On some occasions, decisions on priority of work may be made by the employer rather than the lawyer with the result that prosecution of work already undertaken for clients is postponed to their detriment. Similarly, an employer may seek, consciously or unconsciously, to further its own economic interests through the action of the lawyers employed by it. Since a lawyer must always be free to exercise his professional judgment without regard to the interests or motives of a third person, the lawyer who is employed by one to represent another must constantly guard against erosion of his professional freedom.[27]

EC 5-24   To assist a lawyer in preserving his professional independence, a number of courses are available to him. For example, a lawyer should not practice with or in the form of a professional legal corporation, even though the corporate form is permitted by law,[28] if any director, officer, or stockholder of it is a non-lawyer. Although a lawyer may be employed by a business corporation with non-lawyers serving as directors or officers, and they necessarily have the right to make decisions of business policy, a lawyer must decline to accept direction of his professional judgment from any layman. Various types of legal aid offices are administered by boards of directors composed of lawyers and laymen. A lawyer should not accept employment from such an organization unless the board sets only broad policies and there is no interference in the relationship of the lawyer and the individual client he serves. Where a lawyer is employed by an organization, a written agreement that defines the relationship between him and the organization and provides for his independence is desirable since it may serve to prevent misunderstanding as to their respective roles. Although other innovations in the means of supplying legal counsel may develop, the responsibility of the lawyer to maintain his professional independence remains constant, and the legal profession must insure that changing circumstances do not result in loss of the professional independence of the lawyer.

DISCIPLINARY RULES

DR 5-101   Refusing Employment When the Interests of the Lawyer May Impair His Independent Professional Judgment.

(A) Except with the consent of his client after full disclosure, a lawyer shall not accept employment if the exercise of his professional judgment on behalf of his client will be or reasonably may be affected by his own financial, business, property, or personal interests.[29]

(B) A lawyer shall not accept employment in contemplated or pending litigation if he knows or it is obvious that he or a lawyer in his firm ought to be called as a witness, except that he may undertake the employment and he or a lawyer in his firm may testify:

(1) If the testimony will relate solely to an uncontested matter.

(2) If the testimony will relate solely to a matter of formality and there is no reason to believe that substantial evidence will be offered in opposition to the testimony.

(3) If the testimony will relate solely to the nature and value of legal services rendered in the case by the lawyer or his firm to the client.

(4) As to any matter, if refusal would work a substantial hardship on the client because of the distinctive value of the lawyer or his firm as counsel in the particular case.

DR 5-102   Withdrawal as Counsel When the Lawyer Becomes a Witness.[30]

(A) If, after undertaking employment in contemplated or pending litigation, a lawyer learns or it is obvious that he or a lawyer in his firm ought to be called as a witness on behalf of his client, he shall withdraw from the conduct of the trial and his firm, if any, shall not continue the representation in the trial, except that he may continue the representation and he or a lawyer in his firm may testify in the circumstances enumerated in DR 5-101(B) (1) through (4).

(B) If, after undertaking employment in contemplated or pending litigation, a lawyer learns or it is obvious that he or a lawyer in his firm may be called as a witness other than on behalf of his client, he may continue the representation until it is apparent that his testimony is or may be prejudicial to his client.[31]

ABA Model
Code of
Professional
Responsibility

DR 5-103   Avoiding Acquisition of Interest in Litigation.

(A) A lawyer shall not acquire a proprietary interest in the cause of action or subject matter of litigation he is conducting for a client,[32] except that he may:

   (1) Acquire a lien granted by law to secure his fee or expenses.

   (2) Contract with a client for a reasonable contingent fee in a civil case.[33]

(B) While representing a client in connection with contemplated or pending litigation, a lawyer shall not advance or guarantee financial assistance to his client,[34] except that a lawyer may advance or guarantee the expenses of litigation, including court costs, expenses of investigation, expenses of medical examination, and costs of obtaining and presenting evidence, provided the client remains ultimately liable for such expenses.

DR 5-104   Limiting Business Relations with a Client.

(A) A lawyer shall not enter into a business transaction with a client if they have differing interests therein and if the client expects the lawyer to exercise his professional judgment therein for the protection of the client, unless the client has consented after full disclosure.

(B) Prior to conclusion of all aspects of the matter giving rise to his employment, a lawyer shall not enter into any arrangement or understanding with a client or a prospective client by which he acquires an interest in publication rights with respect to the subject matter of his employment or proposed employment.

DR 5-105   Refusing to Accept or Continue Employment If the Interests of Another Client May Impair the Independent Professional Judgment of the Lawyer.

(A) A lawyer shall decline proffered employment if the exercise of his independent professional judgment in behalf of a client will be or is likely to be adversely affected by the acceptance of the proffered employment,[35] or if it would likely to involve him in representing differing interests,[36] except to the extent permitted under DR 5-105(C).[37]

(B) A lawyer shall not continue multiple employment if the exercise of his independent professional judgment in behalf of a client will be or is likely to be adversely affected by his representation of another client, or if it would be likely to involve him in representing differing interests,[38] except to the extent permitted under DR 5-105(C).[39]

(C) In the situations covered by DR 5-105(A) and (B), a lawyer may represent multiple clients if it is obvious that he can adequately represent the interest of each and if each consents to the representation after full disclosure of the possible effect of such representation on the exercise of his independent professional judgment on behalf of each.

(D) If a lawyer is required to decline employment or to withdraw from employment under a Disciplinary Rule, no partner, or associate, or any other lawyer affiliated with him[40] or his firm, may accept or continue such employment.

DR 5-106   Settling Similar Claims of Clients.[41]

(A) A lawyer who represents two or more clients shall not make or participate in the making of an aggregate settlement of the claims of or against his clients, unless each client has consented to the settlement after being advised of the existence and nature of all the claims involved in the proposed settlement, of the total amount of the settlement, and of the participation of each person in the settlement.

DR 5-107   Avoiding Influence by Others than the Client.

(A) Except with the consent of his client after full disclosure, a lawyer shall not:

(1) Accept compensation for his legal services from one other than his client.

(2) Accept from one other than his client any thing of value related to his representation of or his employment by his client.[42]

(B) A lawyer shall not permit a person who recommends, employs, or pays him to render legal services for another to direct or regulate his professional judgment in rendering such legal services.[43]

(C) A lawyer shall not practice with or in the form of a professional corporation or association authorized to practice law for a profit, if:

(1) A non-lawyer owns any interest therein,[44] except that a fiduciary representative of the estate of a lawyer may hold the stock or interest of the lawyer for a reasonable time during administration;

(2) A non-lawyer is a corporate director or officer thereof;[45] or

(3) A non-lawyer has the right to direct or control the professional judgment of a lawyer.[46]

NOTES

1. *Cf.* ABA CANONS OF PROFESSIONAL ETHICS, CANON 35 (1908).

"[A lawyer's] fiduciary duty is of the highest order and he must not represent interests adverse to those of the client. It is true that because of his professional responsibility and the confidence and trust which his client may legitimately repose in him, he must adhere to a high standard of honesty, integrity and good faith in dealing with his client. He is not permitted to take advantage of his position or superior knowledge to impose upon the client; nor to conceal facts or law, nor in any way deceive him without being held responsible therefor." Smoot v. Lund, 13 Utah 2d 168, 172, 369 P.2d 933, 936 (1962).

"When a client engages the services of a lawyer in a given piece of business he is

ABA Model Code of Professional Responsibility

ABA Model Code of Professional Responsibility

entitled to feel that, until that business is finally disposed of in some manner, he has the undivided loyalty of the one upon whom he looks as his advocate and champion. If, as in this case, he is sued and his home attached by his own attorney, who is representing him in another matter, all feeling of loyalty is necessarily destroyed, and the profession is exposed to the charge that it is interested only in money." Grievance Comm. v. Rattner, 152 Conn. 59, 65, 203 A.2d 82, 84 (1964).

"One of the cardinal principles confronting every attorney in the representation of a client is the requirement of complete loyalty and service in good faith to the best of his ability. In a criminal case the client is entitled to a fair trail, but not a perfect one. These are fundamental requirements of due process under the Fourteenth Amendment . . . . The same principles are applicable in Sixth Amendment cases (not pertinent herein) and suggest that an attorney should have no conflict of interest and that he must devote his full and faithful efforts toward the defense of his client" Johns v. Smyth, 176 F. Supp. 949, 952 (E.D. Va. 1959), modified, United States ex rel Wilkins v. Banmiller, 205 F. Supp. 123, 128 n.5 (E.D. Pa. 1962), aff'd 325F.2d 514(3d Cir. 1963), *cert. denied*, 379 U.S. 847, 13 L. Ed. 2d 51, 85 S. Ct. 87 (1964).

2. "Attorneys must not allow their private interests to conflict with those of their clients . . . . They owe their entire devotion to the interests of their client" United States v. Anonymous, 215 F. Supp. 111, 113 (E.D. Tenn. 1963).

"[T]he court [below] concluded that a firm may not accept any action against a person whom they are presently representing even though there is no relationship between the two cases. In arriving at this conclusion, the court cites an opinion of the Committee on Professional Ethics of the New York County Lawyers'Association which stated in part: 'While under the circumstances . . . there may be no actual conflict of interest . . . "maintenance of public confidence in the Bar requires an attorney who has accepted representation of a client to decline, while representing such client, any employment from an adverse party in any matter even though wholly unrelated to the original retainer." See Question and Answer No. 350, N.Y. County L. Ass'n, Question and Answer No. 450 (June 21, 1956).'" Grievance Comm. v. Rattner, 152 Conn. 59, 65, 203 A.2d 82, 84 (1964).

3. "Courts of equity will scrutinize with jealous vigilance transactions between parties occupying fiduciary relations toward each other . . . . A deed will not be held invalid, however, if made by the grantor with full knowledge of its nature and effect, and because of the deliberate voluntary and intelligent desire of the grantor . . . . Where a fiduciary relation exists, the burden of proof is on the grantee of beneficiary of an instrument executed during the existence of such relationship to show the fairness of the transaction, that it was equitable and just and that it did not proceed from undue influence . . . . The same rule has application where an attorney engages in a transaction with a client during the existence of the relation and is benefited thereby . . . . Conversely, an attorney is not prohibited from dealing with his client or buying his property, and such contracts, if open, fair and honest, when deliberately made, are as valid as contracts between other parties . . . . [I]mportant factors in determining whether a transaction is fair include a showing by the fiduciary (1) that he made a full and frank disclosure of all the relevant information that he had; (2) that the consideration was adequate; and (3) that the principal had independent advice before completing the transaction." McFail v. Braden, 19 Ill. 2d 108, 117-18, 166 N.E.2d 46, 52 (1960).

4. *See* State ex rel. Nebraska State Bar Ass'n v. Richards, 165 Neb. 80, 94-95, 84 N.W.2d 136, 146 (1957).

5. *See* ABA CANONS OF PROFESSIONAL ETHICS, CANON 9(1908).

6. *See* ABA CANONS OF PROFESSIONAL ETHICS, CANON 10(1908).

7. *See* Model Code of Professional Responsibility, EC 2-20.

8. *See* ABA CANONS OF PROFESSIONAL ETHICS, CANON 42 (1908).

9. "Rule 3a . . . . A member of the State Bar shall not directly or indirectly pay or agree

to pay, or represent or sanction the representation that he will pay, medical hospital or nursing bills or other personal expenses incurred by or for a client, prospective or existing; provided this rule shall not prohibit a member:

"(1) with the consent of the client, from paying or agreeing to pay to third persons such expenses from funds collected or to be collected for the client; or

(2) after he has been employed, from lending money to his client upon the client's promise in writing to repay such loan; or

(3) from advancing the costs of prosecuting or defending a claim or action. Such costs within the meaning of this subparagraph (3) include all taxable costs or disbursements, costs of investigation and costs of obtaining and presenting evidence." CAL. BUSINESS AND PROFESSIONS CODE § 6076 (West Supp. 1967).

10. "When a lawyer knows, prior to trial, that he will be a necessary witness, except as to merely formal matters such as identification or custody of a document or the like, neither he nor his firm or associates should conduct the trial. If, during the trial, he discovers that the ends of justice require his testimony, he should, from that point on, if feasible and not prejudicial to his client's case, leave further conduct of the trial to other counsel. If circumstances do not permit withdrawal from the conduct of the trial to other counsel. If circumstances do not permit withdrawal from the conduct of the trial, the lawyer should not argue the credibility of his own testimony." *A Code of Trial Conduct: Promulgated by the American College of Trial Lawyers,* 43 A.B.A. J. 223,224-25 (1957).

11. *Cf.* ABA CANONS OF PROFESSIONAL ETHICS, CANON 19 (1908): "When a lawyer is a witness for his client, except as to merely formal matters, such as the attestation or custody of an instrument and the like, he should leave the trial of the case to other counsel."

12. "It is the general rule that a lawyer may not testify in ligation in which he is a advocate unless circumstances arise which could not be anticipated and it is necessary to prevent a miscarriage of justice. In those rare cases where the testimony of an attorney is needed to protect his client's interest, it is not only proper but mandatory that it be forthcoming." Schwartz v. Wenger, 267 Minn. 40, 43-44, 124 N.W.2d 489, 492 (1963).

13. "The great weight of authority in this country holds that the attorney who acts as counsel and witness, in behalf of his client, in the same cause on a material matter, not of merely formal character, and not in an emergency, but having knowledge that he would be required to be a witness in ample time to have secured other counsel and given up his service in the case, violates a highly important provision of the Code of Ethics and a rule of professional conduct, but does not commit a legal error in so testifying, as a result of which a new trial will be granted." Erwin M. Jennings Co. v. DiGenova, 107 Conn. 491, 499, 141 A. 866, 869(1928).

14. "[C]ases may arise, and in practice often do arise, in which there would be a failure of justice should the attorney withhold his testimony. In such a case it would be a vicious professional sentiment which would deprive the client of the benefit of his attorney's testimony." Connoly v. Straw, 53 Wis. 645, 649, 11 N.W. 17, 19 (1881). But see ABA CANONS OF PROFESSIONAL ETHICS, CANON 19 (1908): "Except when essential to the ends of justice, a lawyer should avoid testifying in court in behalf of his client."

15. *Cf.* ABA CANONS OF PROFESSIONAL ETHICS, CANON 7 (1908).

16. *See* ABA CANONS OF PROFESSIONAL ETHICS, CANON 7 (1908).

17. *See* ABA CANONS OF PROFESSIONAL ETHICS, CANON 6 (1908); *cf. ABA Opinions* 261 (1944), 242 (1942), 142 (1935), and 30 (1931).

18. The ABA Canons speak of "conflicting interests" rather than "differing interests" but make no attempt to define such other than the statement in Canon 6: "Within the meaning of this canon, a lawyer represents conflicting interests when, in behalf of one client, it is his duty to contend for that which duty to another client requires him to oppose."

19. "Canon 6 of the Canons of professional Ethics, adopted by the American Bar Association on September 30, 1937, and by the Pennsylvania Bar Association on January

7, 1938, provides in part that 'It is unprofessional to represent conflicting interests, except by express consent of all concerned given after a full disclosure of the facts. Within the meaning of this Canon, a lawyer represents conflicting interest when, in behalf of one client, it is his duty to contend for that which duty to another client requires him to oppose.' The full disclosure required by this canon contemplates that the possible adverse effect of the conflict be fully explained by the attorney to the client to be affected and by him thoroughly understood . . . .

"The foregoing canon applies to cases where the circumstances are such that possibly conflicting interests may permissibly be represented by the same attorney. But manifestly, there are instances where the conflicts of interest are so critically adverse as not to admit of one attorney's representing both sides. Such is the situation which this record presents. No one could conscionably contend that the same attorney may represent both the plaintiff and defendant in an adversary action. Yet, that is what is being done in this case." Jedwabny v. Philadelphia Transportation Co., 390 Pa. 231, 235, 135 A.2d 252, 254 (1957), *cert. denied*, 355 U.S. 966, 2 L. Ed. 2d 5431, 78 S. Ct. 557 (1958).

20. "Glasser wished the benefit of the undivided assistance of counsel of his own choice. We think that such a desire on the part of an accused should be respected. Irrespective of any conflict of interest, the additional burden of representing another party may conceivably impair counsel's effectiveness.

"To determine the precise degree of prejudice sustained by Glasser as a result of the court's appointment of Stewart as counsel for Kretske is at once difficult and unnecessary. The right to have the assistance of counsel is too fundamental and absolute to allow courts to indulge in nice calculations and to the amount of prejudice arising from its denial." Glasser v. United States, 315 U.S. 60, 75-76, 86 L. Ed. 680, 702 S. Ct. 457, 467 (1942).

21. *See* ABA CANONS OF PROFESSIONAL ETHICS, CANON 6 (1908).

22. *Id.*

23. *Cf. ABA Opinion* 282 (1950). "When counsel, although paid by the casualty company, undertakes to represent the policy holder and files his notice of appearance , he owes to his client, the assured, an undeviating and single allegiance. His fealty embraces the requirement to produce in court all witnesses, fact and expert, who are available and necessary for the proper protection of the rights of his client . . . .

". . . The Canons of Professional Ethics make it pellucid that there are not two standards, one applying to counsel privately retained by a client, and the other to counsel paid by an insurance carrier." American Employers Ins. Co. v. Goble Aircraft Specialties 205 Misc. 1066, 1075, 131 N.Y.S.2d 393, 401 (1954), *motion to withdraw appeal granted*, 1 App. Div. 2d 1008, 154 N.Y.S.2d 835 (1956).

"[C]ounsel, selected by State Farm to defend Dorothy Walker's suit for $50,000 damages, was apprised by Walker that his earlier version of the accident was untrue and that actually the accident occurred because he lost control of his car in passing a Cadillac just ahead. At that point, Walker's counsel should have refused to participate further in view of the conflict of interest between Walker and State Farm . . . . Instead he participated in the ensuing deposition of the Walkers, even took an ex parte sworn statement from Mr. Walker in order to advise State Farm what action it should take, and later used the statement against Walker in the District Court. This action appears to contravene an Indiana attorney's duty 'at every peril to himself, to preserve the secrets of his client'. . . ." State Farm Mut. Auto Ins. Co. v. Walker, 382 F.2d 548, 552 (1967), *cert. denied*, 389 U.S. 1045, 19 L. Ed. 2d 837, 88 S. Ct. 789 (1968).

24. *See* ABA CANONS OF PROFESSIONAL ETHICS, CANON 6 (1908).

25. *See* ABA CANONS OF PROFESSIONAL ETHICS, CANON 35 (1908). "Objection to the intervention of a lay intermediary, who may control litigation or otherwise interfere with the rendering of legal services in a confidential relationship, . . . derives from the element of pecuniary gain. Fearful of dangers thought to arise from that element, the courts of

several States have sustained regulations aimed at these activities. We intimate no view one way or the other as to the merits of those decisions with respect to the particular arrangements against which they are directed. It is enough that the superficial resemblance in form between those arrangements and that at bar cannot obscure the vital fact that here the entire arrangement employs constitutionally privileged means of expression to secure constitutionally guaranteed civil rights." NAACP v. Button, 371 U.S. 415, 441-42, 9 L. Ed. 2d 405, 423-24, 83 S. Ct. 328, 342-43 (1963).

26. *Cf.* ABA CANONS OF PROFESSIONAL ETHICS, CANON 38 (1908).

27. "Certainly it is true that 'the professional relationship between an attorney and his client is highly personal, involving an intimate appreciation of each individual client's particular problem.' And this Committee does not condone practices which interfere with that relationship. However, the mere fact the lawyer is actually paid by some entity other than the client does not affect that relationship, so long as the lawyer is selected by and is directly responsible to the client. See Informal Opinions 469 and 679. Of course, as the latter decision points out, there must be full disclosure of the arrangement by the attorney to the client . . . ." *ABA Opinion* 320 (1968).

"[A] third party may pay the cost of legal services as long as control remains in the client and the responsibility of the lawyer is solely to the client. Informal Opinions 469 ad [sic] 679. *See also* Opinion 237." *Id.*

28. *ABA Opinion* 303 (1961) recognized that "[s]tatutory provisions now exist in several states which are designed to make [the practice of law in a form that will be classified as a corporation for federal income tax purpose] legally possible, either as a result of lawyers incorporating or forming associations with various corporate characteristics."

29. *Cf.* ABA CANONS OF PROFESSIONAL ETHICS, CANON 6 (1908) and *ABA Opinions* 181(1938), 104 (1934), 103 (1933), 72 (1932), 50 (1931), 49 (1931), and 33 (1931). "New York County [Opinion] 203 . . . . [A lawyer] should not advise a client to employ an investment company in which he is interested, without informing him of this." DRINKER, LEGAL ETHICS 956 (1953).

"In Opinions 72 and 49 this Committee held: The relations of partners in a law firm are such that neither the firm nor any member or associate thereof, may accept any professional employment which any member of the firm cannot properly accept.

"In Opinion 16 this Committee held that a member of a law firm could not represent a defendant in a criminal case which was being prosecuted by another member of the firm who was public prosecuting attorney. The Opinion stated that it was clearly unethical for one member of the firm to oppose the interest of the state which another member represented those interests . . . . Since the prosecutor himself could not represent both the public and the defendant, no member of his law firm could either." *ABA Opinion* 296 (1959).

30. *Cf.* ABA CANONS OF PROFESSIONAL ETHICS, CANON 19 (1908) and *ABA Opinions* 220 (1941), 185 (1938), 50 (1931), and 33 (1931); *but cf.* Erwin M. Jennings Co. v. DiGenova, 107 Conn. 491, 498-99, 141 A. 866, 868 (1928).

31. This Canon [19] of Ethics needs no elaboration to be applied to the facts here. Apparently, the object of this precept is to avoid putting a lawyer in the obviously embarrassing predicament of testifying and then having to argue the credibility and effect of his own testimony. It was not designed to permit a lawyer to call opposing counsel as a witness and thereby disqualify him as counsel." Galarowicz v. Ward, 119 Utah 611, 620, 230 P.2d 576, 580 (1951).

32. ABA CANONS OF PROFESSIONAL ETHICS, CANON 10 (1908) and *ABA Opinions* 279 (1949), 246 (1942), and 176 (1938).

33. *See* Model Code of Professional Responsibility, DR 2-106(C).

34. *See* ABA CANONS OF PROFESSIONAL ETHICS, CANON 42 (1908); *cf. ABA Opinion* 288 (1954).

35. *See* ABA CANONS OF PROFESSIONAL ETHICS, CANON 6 (1908); *cf. ABA Opinions* 167 (1937), 60 (1931), and 40 (1931).

ABA Model
Code of
Professional
Responsibility

36. Amended, March 1974, House Informational Report No. 127.

37. *ABA Opinion* 247 (1942) held that an attorney could not investigate a night club shooting on behalf of one of the owner's liability insurers, obtaining the cooperation of the owner, and later represent the injured patron in an action against the owner and a different insurance company unless the attorney obtain the "express consent of all concerned given after a full disclosure of the facts," since to do so would be to represent conflicting interests.

See ABA Opinions 247 (1942), 224 (1941), 222 (1941), 218 (1941), 112 (1934), 86 (1932), and 83 (1932).

38. Amended, March 1974, House Information Report No. 127.

39. *Cf. ABA Opinions* 231 (1941) and 160 (1936).

40. Amended, March 1974, House Informational Report No. 127.

41. *Cf. ABA Opinion* 235 (1941).

42. *See* ABA CANONS OF PROFESSIONAL ETHICS, CANON 38 (1908).

"A lawyer who receives a commission (whether delayed or not) from a title insurance company or guaranty fund for recommending or selling the insurance to his client, or for work done for the client or the company, without either fully disclosing to the client his financial interest in the transaction, or crediting the client's bill with the amount thus received, is guilty of unethical conduct." *ABA Opinion* 304 (1962.

43. *See* ABA CANONS OF PROFESSIONAL ETHICS, CANON 35 (1908); *cf. ABA Opinion* 237 (1941).

"When the lay forwarder, as agent for the creditor, forwards a claim to an attorney, the direct relationship of attorney and client shall then exist between the attorney and the creditor, and the forwarder shall not interpose itself as an intermediary to control the activities of the attorney." *ABA Opinion* 294 (1958).

44. "Permanent beneficial and voting rights in the organization set up the practice law, whatever its form, must be restricted to lawyers while the organization is engaged in the practice of law." *ABA Opinion* 303 (1961).

45. "Canon 33 . . . promulgates underlying principles that must be observed no matter in what form of organization lawyers practice law. Its requirement that no person shall be admitted or held out as a practitioner or member who is not a member of the legal profession duly authorized to practice, and amenable to professional discipline, makes it clear that any centralized management must be in lawyers to avoid a violation of this Canon." *ABA Opinion* 303 (1961).

46. "There is no intervention of any lay agency between lawyer and client when centralized management provided only by lawyers may give guidance or direction to the services being rendered by a lawyer-member of the organization to a client. The language in Canon 35 that a lawyer should avoid all relations which direct the performance of his duties by or in the interest of an intermediary refers to lay intermediaries and not lawyer intermediaries with whom he is associated in the practice of law." *ABA Opinion* 303 (1961).

CANON 6
A Lawyer Should Represent
a Client Competently

ETHICAL CONSIDERATIONS

EC 6-1   Because of his vital role in the legal process, a lawyer should act with competence and proper care in representing clients. He should strive to become and remain proficient in his practice[1] and should accept employment only in matters which he is or intends to become competent to handle.

EC 6-2   A lawyer is aided in attaining and maintaining his competence by keeping abreast of current legal literature and developments, participating in continuing legal education programs,[2] concentrating in particular areas of the law, and by utilizing other available means. He has the additional ethical obligation to assist in improving the legal profession, and he may do so by participating in bar activities intended to advance the quality and standards of members of the profession. Of particular importance is the careful training of his younger associates and the giving of sound guidance to all lawyers who consult him. In short, a lawyer should strive at all levels to aid the legal profession in advancing the highest possible standards of integrity and competence and to meet those standards himself.

EC 6-3   While the licensing of a lawyer is evidence that he has met the standards then prevailing for admission to the bar, a lawyer generally should not accept employment in any area of the law in which he is not qualified.[3] However, he may accept such employment if in good faith he expects to become qualified through study and investigation, as long as such preparation would not result in unreasonable delay or expense to his client. Proper preparation and representation may require the association by the lawyer of professionals in other disciplines. A lawyer offered employment in a matter in which he is not and does not expect to become so qualified should either decline the employment or, with the consent of his client, accept the employment and associate a lawyer who is competent in the matter.

EC 6-4   Having undertaken representation, a lawyer should use proper care to safeguard the interests of his client. If a lawyer has accepted employment in a matter beyond his competence but in which he expected to become competent, he should diligently undertake the work and study necessary to qualify himself. In addition to being qualified to handle a particular matter, his obligation to his client requires him to prepare adequately for and give appropriate attention to his legal work.

EC 6-5   A lawyer should have pride in his professional endeavors. His obligation to act competently calls for higher motivation than that arising from fear of civil liability or disciplinary penalty.

EC 6-6   A lawyer should not seek, by contract or other means, to limit his individual liability to his client for his malpractice. A lawyer who handles the affairs of his client properly has no need to attempt to limit his liability for his professional activities and one who does not handle the affairs of his client properly should not be permitted to do so. A lawyer who is a stockholder in or is associated with a professional legal corporation may, however, limit his liability for malpractice of his associates in the corporation, but only to the extent permitted by law.[4]

DISCIPLINARY RULES

DR 6-101   Failing to Act Competently.

(A) A lawyer shall not:

    (1) Handle a legal matter which he knows or should know that he is not competent to handle, without associating with him a lawyer who is competent to handle it.

    (2) Handle a legal matter without preparation adequate in the circumstances.

    (3) Neglect a legal matter entrusted to him.[5]

DR 6-102   Limiting Liability to Client.

(A) A lawyer shall not attempt to exonerate himself from or limit his liability to his client for his personal malpractice.

NOTES

1. "[W]hen a citizen is faced with the need for a lawyer, he wants, and is entitled to, the best informed counsel he can obtain. Changing times produce changes in our laws and legal procedures. The natural complexities of law require continuing intensive study by a lawyer if he is to render his clients a maximum of efficient service. And, in so doing, he maintains the high standards of the legal profession; and he also increases respect and confidence by the general public." Rochelle & Payne, *The Struggle of Public Understanding,* 25 TEXAS B.J. 109, 160 (1962).

"We have undergone enormous changes in the last fifty years within the lives of most of the adults living today who may be seeking advice. Most of these changes have been accompanied by changes and developments in the law. . . . Every practicing lawyer encounters these problems and is often perplexed with his own inability to keep up, not only with changes in the law, but also with changes in the lives of his clients and their legal problems.

"To be sure, no client has a right to expect that his lawyer will have all of the answers at the end of his tongue or even in the back of his head at all times. But the client does have the right to expect that the lawyer will have devoted his time and energies to maintaining and improving his competence to know where to look for the answers to know how to deal with the problems, and to know how to advise to the best of his legal talents and abilities." Levy & Sprague, *Accounting and Law: Is Dual Practice in the Public Interest?*, 52 A.B.A. J. 1110, 1112 (1966).

2. "The whole purpose of continuing legal education, so enthusiastically supported by the ABA, is to make it possible for lawyers to make themselves better lawyers. But there are no nostrums for proficiency in the law; it must come through the hard work of the lawyer himself. To the extent that work, whether it be in attending institutes or lecture courses, in studying after hours or in the actual day in and day out practice of his profession, can be concentrated within a limited field, the greater the proficiency and expertness that can developed." *Report of the Special Committee on Specialization and Specialized Legal Education,* 79 A.B.A. REP. 582, 588 (1954).

3. "If the attorney is not competent to skillfully and properly perform the work, he should not undertake the service." Design v. Steinbrink, 202 App. Div. 477, 481, 195 N.Y.S. 810, 814 (1922), *aff'd mem.*, 236 N.Y. 669, 142 N.E. 328 (1923).

4. *See ABA Opinion* 303 (1961); *cf.* CODE OF PROFESSIONAL RESPONSIBILITY, EC 2-11.

5. The annual report for 1967-1968 of the Committee on Grievances of the Association

of the Bar of the City of New York showed a receipt of 2,232 complaints; of the 828 offenses against clients, 76 involved conversion, 49 involved "overreaching," and 452, or more than half of all such offenses, involved neglect. *Annual Report of the Committee on Grievances of the Association of the Bar of the City of New York*, N.Y. L .J., Sept 12, 1968, at 4, col. 5.

CANON 7
A Lawyer Should Represent a Client Zealously Within the Bounds of the Law

ETHICAL CONSIDERATIONS

EC 7-1   The duty of a lawyer, both to his client[1] and to the legal system, is to represent his client zealously[2] within the bounds of the law,[3] which includes Disciplinary Rules and enforceable professional regulations.[4] The professional responsibility of a lawyer derives from his membership in a profession which has the duty of assisting members of the public to secure and protect available legal rights and benefits. In our government of laws and not of men, each member of our society is entitled to have his conduct judged and regulated in accordance with the law;[5] to seek any lawful objective[6] through legally permissible means;[7] and to present for adjudication any lawful claim, issue, or defense.

EC 7-2   The bounds of the law in a given case are often difficult to ascertain.[8] The language of legislative enactments and judicial opinions may be uncertain as applied to varying factual situations. The limits and specific meaning of apparently relevant law may be made doubtful by changing or developing constitutional interpretations, inadequately expressed statutes or judicial opinions, and changing public and judicial attitudes. Certainty of law ranges from well-settled rules through areas of conflicting authority to areas without precedent.

EC 7-3   Where the bounds of law are uncertain, the action of a lawyer may depend on whether he is serving as advocate or adviser. A lawyer may serve simultaneously as both advocate and adviser, but the two roles are essentially different.[9] In asserting a position on behalf of his client, an advocate for the most part deals with past conduct and must take the facts as he finds them. By contrast, a lawyer serving as adviser primarily assists his client in determining the course of future conduct and relationships. While serving as advocate, a lawyer should resolve in favor of his client doubts as to the bounds of the law.[10] In serving a client as adviser, a lawyer in appropriate circumstances should give his professional opinion as to what the ultimate decisions of the courts would likely be as to the applicable law.

Duty of the Lawyer to a Client

ABA Model Code of Professional Responsibility

EC 7-4   The advocate may urge any permissible construction of the law favorable to his client, without regard to his professional opinion as to the likelihood that the construction will ultimately prevail.[11] His conduct is within the bounds of the law, and therefore permissible, if the position taken is supported by the law or is supportable by a good faith argument for an extension, modification, or reversal of the law. However, a lawyer is not justified in asserting a position in litigation that is frivolous.[12]

EC 7-5   A lawyer as adviser furthers the interest of his client by giving his professional opinion as to what he believes would likely be the ultimate decision of the courts on the matter at hand and by informing his client of the practical effect of such decision.[13] He may continue in the representation of his client even though his client has elected to pursue a course of conduct contrary to the advice of the lawyer so long as he does not thereby knowingly assist the client to engage in illegal conduct or to take a frivolous legal position. A lawyer should never encourage or aid his client to commit criminal acts or counsel his client on how to violate the law and avoid punishment therefor.[14]

EC 7-6   Whether the proposed action of a lawyer is within the bounds of the law may be a perplexing question when his client is contemplating a course of conduct having legal consequences that vary according to the client's intent, motive, or desires at the time of the action. Often a lawyer is asked to assist his client in developing evidence relevant to the state of mind of the client at a particular time. He may properly assist his client in the development and preservation of evidence of existing motive, intent, or desire; obviously, he may not do anything furthering the creation or preservation of false evidence. In many cases a lawyer may not be certain as to the state of mind of his client, and in those situations he should resolve reasonable doubts in favor of his client.

EC 7-7   In certain areas of legal representation not affecting the merits of the cause or substantially prejudicing the rights of a client, a lawyer is entitled to make decisions on his own. But otherwise the authority to make decisions is exclusively that of the client and, if made within the framework of the law, such decisions are binding on his lawyer. As typical examples in civil cases, it is for the client to decide whether he will accept a settlement offer or whether he will waive his right to plead an affirmative defense. A defense lawyer in a criminal case has the duty to advise his client fully on whether a particular plea to a charge appears to be desirable and as to the prospects of success on appeal, but it is for the client to decide what plea should be entered and whether an appeal should be taken.[15]

EC 7-8　A lawyer should exert his best efforts to insure that decisions of his client are made only after the client has been informed of relevant considerations. A lawyer ought to initiate this decision-making process if the client does not do so. Advice of a lawyer to his client need not be confined to purely legal considerations.[16] A lawyer should advise his client of the possible effect of each legal alternative.[17] A lawyer should bring to bear upon this decision-making process the fullness of his experience as well as his objective viewpoint.[18] In assisting his client to reach a proper decision, it is often desirable for a lawyer to point out those factors which may lead to a decision that is morally just as well as legally permissible.[19] He may emphasize the possibility of harsh consequences that might result from assertion of legally permissible positions. In the final analysis, however, the lawyer should always remember that the decision whether to forego legally available objectives or methods because of non-legal factors is ultimately for the client and not for himself. In the event that the client in a non-adjudicatory matter insists upon a course of conduct that is contrary to the judgment and advice of the lawyer but not prohibited by Disciplinary Rules, the lawyer may withdraw from the employment.[20]

EC 7-9　In the exercise of his professional judgment on those decisions which are for his determination in the handling of a legal matter,[21] a lawyer should always act in a manner consistent with the best interests of his client.[22] However, when an action in the best interest of his client seems to him to be unjust, he may ask his client for permission to forego such action.

EC 7-10　The duty of a lawyer to represent his client with zeal does not militate against his concurrent obligation to treat with consideration all persons involved in the legal process and to avoid the infliction of needless harm.

EC 7-11　The responsibilities of a lawyer may vary according to the intelligence, experience, mental condition or age of a client, the obligation of a public officer, or the nature of a particular proceeding. Examples include the representation of an illiterate or an incompetent, service as a public prosecutor or other government lawyer, and appearances before administrative and legislative bodies.

EC 7-12　Any mental or physical condition of a client that renders him incapable of making a considered judgment on his own behalf casts additional responsibilities upon his lawyer. Where an incompetent is acting through a guardian or other legal representative, a lawyer must look to such representative for those decisions which are normally the prerogative of the client to make. If a client under disability has no legal representative, his lawyer may be compelled in court proceedings to make decisions on behalf of the client. If the client is capable of understanding the matter in question or of contributing to the advancement of his interests, regardless of whether

ABA Model
Code of
Professional
Responsibility

he is legally disqualified from performing certain acts, the lawyer should obtain from him all possible aid. If the disability of a client and the lack of a legal representative compel the lawyer to make decisions for his client, the lawyer should consider all circumstances then prevailing and act with care to safeguard and advance the interests of his client. But obviously a lawyer cannot perform any act or make any decision which the law requires his client to perform or make, either acting for himself if competent, or by a duly constituted representative if legally incompetent.

EC 7-13　The responsibility of a public prosecutor differs from that of the usual advocate; his duty is to seek justice, not merely to convict.[23] This special duty exists because: (1) the prosecutor represents the sovereign and therefore should use restraint in the discretionary exercise of governmental powers, such as in the selection of cases to prosecute; (2) during trial the prosecutor is not only an advocate but he also may make decisions normally made by an individual client, and those affecting the public interest should be fair to all; and (3) in our system of criminal justice the accused is to be given the benefit of all reasonable doubts. With respect to evidence and witnesses, the prosecutor has responsibilities different from those of a lawyer in private practice: the prosecutor should make timely disclosure to the defense of available evidence, known to him, that tends to negate the guilt of the accused, mitigate the degree of the offense, or reduce the punishment. Further, a prosecutor should not intentionally avoid pursuit of evidence merely because he believes it will damage the prosecutor's case or aid the accused.

EC 7-14　A government lawyer who has discretionary power relative to litigation should refrain from instituting or continuing litigation that is obviously unfair. A government lawyer not having such discretionary power who believes there is lack of merit in a controversy submitted to him should so advise his superiors and recommend the avoidance of unfair litigation. A government lawyer in a civil action or administrative proceeding has the responsibility to seek justice and to develop a full and fair record, and he should not use his position or the economic power of the government to harass parties or to bring about unjust settlements or results.

EC 7-15　The nature and purpose of proceedings before administrative agencies vary widely. The proceedings may be legislative or quasi-judicial, or a combination of both. They may be ex parte in character, in which event they may originate either at the instance of the agency or upon motion of an interested party. The scope of an inquiry may be purely investigative or it may be truly adversary looking toward the adjudication of specific rights of a party or of classes of parties. The foregoing are but examples of some of the types of proceedings conducted by administrative agencies. A lawyer appearing before an administrative agency,[24] regardless of the nature of the proceeding it is conducting, has the continuing duty to advance the cause of his client within the bounds of the law.[25] Where the applicable rules of the agency impose specific obligations upon a lawyer, it is his duty to comply therewith, unless the lawyer has a legitimate basis for challenging the validity thereof. In all appearances before administrative agencies, a lawyer should identify himself, his client if identity of his client is not privileged[26] and the representative nature of his appearance. It is not improper, however, for a lawyer to seek from an agency information available to the public without identifying his client.

EC 7-16   The primary business of a legislative body is to enact laws rather than to adjudicate controversies, although on occasion the activities of a legislative body may take on the characteristics of an adversary proceeding, particularly in investigative and impeachment matters. The role of a lawyer supporting or opposing proposed legislation normally is quite different from his role in representing a person under investigation or on trial by a legislative body. When a lawyer appears in connection with proposed legislation, he seeks to affect the lawmaking process, but when he appears on behalf of a client in investigatory or impeachment proceedings, he is concerned with the protection of the rights of his client. In either event, he should identify himself and his client, if identity of his client is not privileged, and should comply with applicable laws and legislative rules.[27]

EC 7-17   The obligation of loyalty to his client applies only to a lawyer in the discharge of his professional duties and implies no obligation to adopt a personal viewpoint favorable to the interests or desires of his client.[28] While a lawyer must act always with circumspection in order that his conduct will not adversely affect the rights of a client in a matter he is then handling, he may take positions on public issues and espouse legal reforms he favors without regard to the individual views of any client.

EC 7-18   The legal system in its broadest sense functions best when persons in need of legal advice or assistance are represented by their own counsel. For this reason a lawyer should not communicate on the subject matter of the representation of his client with a person he knows to be represented in the matter by a lawyer, unless pursuant to law or rule of court or unless he has the consent of the lawyer for that person.[29] If one is not represented by counsel, a lawyer representing another may have to deal directly with the unrepresented person; in such an instance, a lawyer should not undertake to give advice to the person who is attempting to represent himself,[30] except that he may advise him to obtain a lawyer.

Duty of the Lawyer to the Adversary System of Justice

EC 7-19   Our legal system provides for the adjudication of disputes governed by the rules of substantive, evidentiary, and procedural law. An adver-

ABA Model
Code of
Professional
Responsibility

sary presentation counters the natural human tendency to judge too swiftly in terms of the familiar that which is not yet fully known,[31] the advocate, by his zealous preparation and presentation of fact and law, enables the tribunal to come to the hearing with an open and neutral mind and to render impartial judgments.[32] The duty of a lawyer to his client and his duty to the legal system are the same; to represent his client zealously within the bounds of the law.[33]

EC 7-20   In order to function properly, our adjudicative process requires an informed, impartial tribunal capable of administering justice promptly and efficiently[34] according to procedures that command public confidence and respect.[35] Not only must there be competent, adverse presentation of evidence and issues, but a tribunal must be aided by rules appropriate to an effective and dignified process. The procedures under which tribunals operate in our adversary system have been prescribed largely by legislative enactments, court rules and decisions, and administrative rules. Through the years certain concepts of proper professional conduct have become rules of law applicable to the adversary adjudicative process. Many of these concepts are the bases for standards of professional conduct set forth in the Disciplinary Rules.

EC 7-21   The civil adjudicative process is primarily designed for the settlement of disputes between parties, while the criminal process is designed for the protection of society as a whole. Threatening to use, or using, the criminal process to coerce adjustment of private civil claims or controversies is a subversion of that process;[36] further, the person against whom the criminal process is so misused may be deterred from asserting his legal rights and thus the usefulness of the civil process in settling private disputes is impaired. As in all cases of abuse of judicial process, the improper use of criminal process tends to diminish public confidence in our legal system.

EC 7-22   Respect for judicial rulings is essential to the proper administration of justice; however, a litigant or his lawyer may, in good faith and within the framework of the law, take steps to test the correctness of a ruling of a tribunal.[37]

EC 7-23   The complexity of law often makes it difficult for a tribunal to be fully informed unless the pertinent law is presented by the lawyers in the cause. A tribunal that is fully informed on the applicable law is better able to make a fair and accurate determination of the matter before it. The adversary system contemplates that each lawyer will present and argue the existing law in the light most favorable to his client.[38] Where a lawyer knows of legal authority in the controlling jurisdiction directly adverse to the position of his client, he should inform the tribunal of its existence unless his adversary has done so; but, having made such disclosure, he may challenge its soundness in whole or in part.[39]

EC 7-24 In order to bring about just and informed decisions, evidentiary and procedural rules have been established by tribunals to permit the inclusion of relevant evidence and argument and the exclusion of all other considerations. The expression by a lawyer of his personal opinion as to the justness of a cause, as to the credibility of a witness, as to the culpability of a civil litigant, or as to the guilt or innocence of an accused is not a proper subject for argument to the trier of fact.[40] It is improper as to factual matters because admissible evidence possessed by a lawyer should be presented only as sworn testimony. It is improper as to all other matters because, were the rule otherwise, the silence of a lawyer on a given occasion could be construed unfavorably to his client. However, a lawyer may argue, on his analysis of the evidence, for any position or conclusion with respect to any of the foregoing matters.

EC 7-25 Rules of evidence and procedure are designed to lead to just decisions and are part of the framework of the law. Thus while a lawyer may take steps in good faith and within the framework of the law to test the validity of rules, he is not justified in consciously violating such rules and he should be diligent in his efforts to guard against his unintentional violation of them.[41] As examples, a lawyer should subscribe to or verify only those pleadings that he believes are in compliance with applicable law and rules; a lawyer should not make any prefatory statement before a tribunal in regard to the purported facts of the case on trial unless he believes that his statement will be supported by admissible evidence; a lawyer should not ask a witness a question solely for the purpose of harassing or embarrassing him; and a lawyer should not by subterfuge put before a jury matters which it cannot properly consider.

EC 7-26 The law and Disciplinary Rules prohibit the use of fraudulent, false, or perjured testimony or evidence.[42] A lawyer who knowingly[43] participates in introduction of such testimony or evidence is subject to discipline. A lawyer should, however, present any admissible evidence his client desires to have presented unless he knows, or from facts within his knowledge should know, that such testimony or evidence is false, fraudulent, or perjured.[44]

EC 7-27 Because it interferes with the proper administration of justice, a lawyer should not suppress evidence that he or his client has a legal obligation to reveal or produce. In like manner, a lawyer should not advise or cause a person to secrete himself or to leave the jurisdiction of a tribunal for the purpose of making him unavailable as a witness therein.[45]

EC 7-28 Witnesses should always testify truthfully[46] and should be free from any financial inducements that might tempt them to do otherwise.[47] A lawyer should not pay or agree to pay a non-expert witness an amount in

ABA Model
Code of
Professional
Responsibility

excess of reimbursement for expenses and financial loss incident to his being a witness; however, a lawyer may pay or agree to pay an expert witness a reasonable fee for his services as an expert. But in no event should a lawyer pay or agree to pay a contingent fee to any witness. A lawyer should exercise reasonable diligence to see that his client and lay associates conform to these standards.[48]

EC 7-29 To safeguard the impartiality that is essential to the judicial process, veniremen and jurors should be protected against extraneous influences.[49] When impartiality is present, public confidence in the judicial system is enhanced. There should be no extrajudicial communication with veniremen prior to trial or with jurors during trial by or on behalf of a lawyer connected with the case. Furthermore, a lawyer who is not connected with the case should not communicate with or cause another to communicate with a venireman or a juror about the case. After the trial, communication by a lawyer with jurors is permitted so long as he refrains from asking questions or making comments that tend to harass or embarrass the juror[50] or to influence actions of the juror in future cases. Were a lawyer to be prohibited from communicating after trial with a juror, he could not ascertain if the verdict might be subject to legal challenge, in which event the invalidity of a verdict might go undetected.[51] When an extrajudicial communication by a lawyer with a juror is permitted by law, it should be made considerately and with deference to the personal feelings of the juror.

EC 7-30 Vexatious or harassing investigations of veniremen or jurors seriously impair the effectiveness of our jury system. For this reason, a lawyer or anyone on his behalf who conducts an investigation of veniremen or jurors should act with circumspection and restraint.

EC 7-31 Communications with or investigations of members of families of veniremen or jurors by a lawyer or by anyone on his behalf are subject to the restrictions imposed upon the lawyer with respect to his communications with or investigations of veniremen and jurors.

EC 7-32 Because of his duty to aid in preserving the integrity of the jury system, a lawyer who learns of improper conduct by or towards a venireman, a juror, or a member of the family of either should make a prompt report to the court regarding such conduct.

EC 7-33 A goal of our legal system is that each party shall have his case, criminal or civil, adjudicated by an impartial tribunal. The attainment of this goal may be defeated by dissemination of news or comments which tend to influence judge or jury.[52] Such news or comments may prevent prospective jurors from being impartial at the outset of the trial[53] and may also interfere with the obligation of jurors to base their verdict solely upon the evidence admitted in the trial.[54] The release by a lawyer of out-of-court statements regarding an anticipated or pending trial may improperly affect the impartiality of the tribunal.[55] For these reasons, standards for permissible and prohibited conduct of a lawyer with respect to trial publicity have been established.

EC 7-34 The impartiality of a public servant in our legal system may be impaired by the receipt of gifts or loans. A lawyer,[56] therefore, is never justified in making a gift or a loan to a judge, a hearing officer, or an official or employee of a tribunal except as permitted by Section C(4) of Canon 5 of the Code of Judicial Conduct, but a lawyer may make a contribution to the campaign fund of a candidate for judicial office in conformity with Section B(2) under Canon 7 of the Code of Judicial Conduct.[57, 58]

EC 7-35 All litigants and lawyers should have access to tribunals on an equal basis. Generally, in adversary proceedings a lawyer should not communicate with a judge relative to a matter pending before, or which is to be brought before, a tribunal over which he presides in circumstances which might have the effect or give the appearance of granting undue advantage to one party.[59] For example, a lawyer should not communicate with a tribunal by a writing unless a copy thereof is promptly delivered to opposing counsel or to the adverse party if he is not represented by a lawyer. Ordinarily an oral communication by a lawyer with a judge or hearing officer should be made only upon adequate notice to opposing counsel, or, if there is none, to the opposing party. A lawyer should not condone or lend himself to private importunities by another with a judge or hearing officer on behalf of himself or his client.

EC 7-36 Judicial hearings ought to be conducted through dignified and orderly procedures designed to protect the rights of all parties. Although a lawyer has the duty to represent his client zealously, he should not engage in any conduct that offends the dignity and decorum of proceedings.[60] While maintaining his independence, a lawyer should be respectful, courteous, and above-board in his relations with a judge or hearing officer before whom he appears.[61] He should avoid undue solicitude for the comfort or convenience of judge or jury and should avoid any other conduct calculated to gain special consideration.

EC 7-37 In adversary proceedings, clients are litigants and though ill feeling may exist between clients, such ill feeling should not influence a lawyer in his conduct, attitude, and demeanor towards opposing lawyers.[62] A lawyer should not make unfair or derogatory personal reference to opposing counsel. Haranguing and offensive tactics by lawyers interfere with the orderly administration of justice and have no proper place in our legal system.

ABA Model
Code of
Professional
Responsibility

EC 7-38 A lawyer should be courteous to opposing counsel and should accede to reasonable requests regarding court proceedings, settings, continuances, waiver of procedural formalities, and similar matters which do not prejudice the rights of his client.[63] He should follow local customs of courtesy or practice, unless he gives timely notice to opposing counsel of his intention not to do so.[64] A lawyer should be punctual in fulfilling all professional commitments.[65]

EC 7-39 In the final analysis, proper functioning of the adversary system depends upon cooperation between lawyers and tribunals in utilizing procedures which will preserve the impartiality of tribunals and make their decisional processes prompt and just, without impinging upon the obligation of lawyers to represent their clients zealously within the framework of the law.

DISCIPLINARY RULES

DR 7-101   Representing a Client Zealously.

(A) A lawyer shall not intentionally:[66]

    (1) Fail to seek the lawful objectives of his client through reasonably available means[67] permitted by law and the Disciplinary Rules, except as provided by DR 7-101(B). A lawyer does not violate this Disciplinary Rule, however, by acceding to reasonable requests of opposing counsel which do not prejudice the rights of his client, by being punctual in fulfilling all professional commitments, by avoiding offensive tactics, or by treating with courtesy and consideration all persons involved in the legal process.

    (2) Fail to carry out a contract of employment entered into with a client for professional services, but he may withdraw as permitted under DR 2-110, DR 5-102, and DR 5-105.

    (3) Prejudice or damage his client during the course of the professional relationship,[68] except as required under DR 7-102(B).

(B) In his representation of a client, a lawyer may:

    (1) Where permissible, exercise his professional judgment to waive or fail to assert a right or position of his client.

    (2) Refuse to aid or participate in conduct that he believes to be unlawful, even though there is some support for an argument that the conduct is legal.

DR 7-102   Representing a Client Within the Bounds of the Law.

(A) In his representation of a client, a lawyer shall not:

    (1) File a suit, assert a position, conduct a defense, delay a trial, or take other action on behalf of his client when he knows or when it is obvious that such action would serve merely to harass or maliciously injure another.[69]

(2) Knowingly advance a claim or defense that is unwarranted under existing law, except that he may advance such claim or defense if it can be supported by good faith argument for an extension, modification, or reversal of existing law.

(3) Conceal or knowingly fail to disclose that which he is required by law to reveal.

(4) Knowingly use perjured testimony or false evidence.[70]

(5) Knowingly make a false statement of law or fact.

(6) Participate in the creation or preservation of evidence when he knows or it is obvious that the evidence is false.

(7) Counsel or assist his client in conduct that the lawyer knows to be illegal or fraudulent.

(8) Knowingly engage in other illegal conduct or conduct contrary to a Disciplinary Rule.

(B) A lawyer who receives information clearly establishing that:

(1) His client has, in the course of the representation, perpetrated a fraud upon a person or tribunal shall promptly call upon his client to rectify the same, and if his client refuses or is unable to do so, he shall reveal the fraud to the affected person or tribunal, except when the information is protected as a privileged communication.[71, 72]

(2) A person other than his client has perpetrated a fraud upon a tribunal shall promptly reveal the fraud to the tribunal.[73]

DR 7-103 Performing the Duty of Public Prosecutor or Other Government Lawyer.[74]

(A) A public prosecutor or other government lawyer shall not institute or cause to be instituted criminal charges when he knows or it is obvious that the charges are not supported by probable cause.

(B) A public prosecutor or other government lawyer in criminal litigation shall make timely disclosure to counsel for the defendant, or to the defendant if he has no counsel, of the existence of evidence, known to the prosecutor or other government lawyer, that tends to negate the guilt of the accused, mitigate the degree of the offense, or reduce the punishment.

DR 7-104 Communicating With One of Adverse Interest.[75]

(A) During the course of his representation of a client a lawyer shall not:

(1) Communicate or cause another to communicate on the subject of the representation with a party he knows to be represented by a lawyer in that matter unless he has the prior consent of the lawyer representing such other party[76] or is authorized by law to do so.

(2) Give advice to a person who is not represented by a lawyer, other than the advice to secure counsel,[77] if the interests of such person

ABA Model
Code of
Professional
Responsibility

are or have a reasonable possibility of being in conflict with the interests of his client.[78]

DR 7-105   Threatening Criminal Prosecution.

(A) A lawyer shall not present, participate in presenting, or threaten to present criminal charges solely to obtain an advantage in a civil matter.

DR 7-106   Trial Conduct.

(A) A lawyer shall not disregard or advise his client to disregard a standing rule of a tribunal or a ruling of a tribunal made in the course of a proceeding, but he may take appropriate steps in good faith to test the validity of such rule or ruling.

(B) In presenting a matter to a tribunal, a lawyer shall disclose:[79]

   (1) Legal authority in the controlling jurisdiction known to him to be directly adverse to the position of his client and which is not disclosed by opposing counsel.[80]

   (2) Unless privileged or irrelevant, the identities of the clients he represents and of the persons who employed him.[81]

(C) In appearing in his professional capacity before a tribunal, a lawyer shall not:

   (1) State or allude to any matter that he has no reasonable basis to believe is relevant to the case or that will not be supported by admissible evidence.[82]

   (2) Ask any question that he has no reasonable basis to believe is relevant to the case and that is intended to degrade a witness or other person.[83]

   (3) Assert his personal knowledge of the facts in issue, except when testifying as a witness.

   (4) Assert his personal opinion as to the justness of a cause, as to the credibility of a witness, as to the culpability of a civil litigant, or as to the guilt or innocence of an accused;[84] but he may argue, on his analysis of the evidence, for any position or conclusion with respect to the matters stated herein.

   (5) Fail to comply with known local customs of courtesy or practice of the bar or a particular tribunal without giving to opposing counsel timely notice of his intent not to comply.[85]

   (6) Engage in undignified or discourteous conduct which is degrading to a tribunal.

   (7) Intentionally or habitually violate any established rule of procedure or of evidence.

DR 7-107   Trial Publicity.[86]

(A) A lawyer participating in or associated with the investigation of a criminal matter shall not make or participate in making an extrajudicial statement that a reasonable person would expect to be disseminated by means of public communication and that does more than state without elaboration:

(1) Information contained in a public record.

(2) That the investigation is in progress.

(3) The general scope of the investigation including a description of the offense and, if permitted by law, the identity of the victim.

(4) A request for assistance in apprehending a suspect or assistance in other matters and the information necessary thereto.

(5) A warning to the public of any dangers.

(B) A lawyer or law firm associated with the prosecution or defense of a criminal matter shall not, from the time of the filing of a complaint, information, or indictment, the issuance of an arrest warrant, or arrest until the commencement of the trial or disposition without trial, make or participate in making an extrajudicial statement that a reasonable person would expect to be disseminated by means of public communication and that relates to:

(1) The character, reputation, or prior criminal record (including arrests, indictments, or other charges of crime) of the accused.

(2) The possibility of a plea of guilty to the offense charged or to a lesser offense.

(3) The existence or contents of any confession, admission, or statement given by the accused or his refusal or failure to make a statement.

(4) The performance or results of any examinations or tests or the refusal or failure of the accused to submit to examinations or tests.

(5) The identity, testimony, or credibility of a prospective witness.

(6) Any opinion as to the guilt or innocence of the accused, the evidence, or the merits of the case.

(C) DR 7-107(B) does not preclude a lawyer during such period from announcing:

(1) The name, age, residence, occupation, and family status of the accused.

(2) If the accused has not been apprehended, any information necessary to aid in his apprehension or to warn the public of any dangers he may present.

(3) A request for assistance in obtaining evidence.

(4) The identity of the victim of the crime.

(5) The fact, time, and place of arrest, resistance, pursuit, and use of weapons.

(6) The identity of investigating and arresting officers or agencies and the length of the investigation.

ABA Model Code of Professional Responsibility

(7) At the time of seizure, a description of the physical evidence seized, other than a confession, admission, or statement.

(8) The nature, substance, or text of the charge.

(9) Quotations from or references to public records of the court in the case.

(10) The scheduling or result of any step in the judicial proceedings.

(11) That the accused denies the charges made against him.

(D) During the selection of a jury or the trial of a criminal matter, a lawyer or law firm associated with the prosecution or defense of a criminal matter shall not make or participate in making an extra-judicial statement that a reasonable person would expect to be disseminated by means of public communication and that relates to the trial, parties, or issues in the trial or other matters that are reasonably likely to interfere with a fair trial, except that he may quote from or refer without comment to public records of the court in the case.

(E) After the completion of a trial or disposition without trial of a criminal matter and prior to the imposition of sentence, a lawyer or law firm associated with the prosecution or defense shall not make or participate in making an extrajudicial statement that a reasonable person would expect to be disseminated by public communication and that is reasonably likely to affect the imposition of sentence.

(F) The foregoing provisions of DR 7-107 also apply to professional disciplinary proceedings and juvenile disciplinary proceedings when pertinent and consistent with other law applicable to such proceedings.

(G) A lawyer or law firm associated with a civil action shall not during its investigation or litigation make or participate in making an extrajudicial statement, other than a quotation from or reference to public records, that a reasonable person would expect to be disseminated by means of public communication and that relates to:

(1) Evidence regarding the occurrence or transaction involved.

(2) The character, credibility, or criminal record of a party, witness, or prospective witness.

(3) The performance or results of any examinations or tests or the refusal or failure of a party to submit to such.

(4) His opinion as to the merits of the claims or defenses of a party, except as required by law or administrative rule.

(5) Any other matter reasonably likely to interfere with a fair trial of the action.

(H) During the pendency of an administrative proceeding, a lawyer or law firm associated therewith shall not make or participate in making a statement, other than a quotation from or reference to public records, that a reasonable person would expect to be disseminated by means of public communication if it is made outside the official course of the proceeding and relates to:

(1) Evidence regarding the occurrence or transaction involved.

(2) The character, credibility, or criminal record of a party, witness, or prospective witness.

(3) Physical evidence or the performance or results of any examinations or tests or the refusal or failure of a party to submit to such.

(4) His opinion as to the merits of the claims, defenses, or positions of an interested person.

(5) Any other matter reasonably likely to interfere with a fair hearing.

(I) The foregoing provisions of DR 7-107 do not preclude a lawyer from replying to charges of misconduct publicly made against him or from participating in the proceedings of legislative, administrative, or other investigative bodies.

(J) A lawyer shall exercise reasonable care to prevent his employees and associates from making an extrajudicial statement that he would be prohibited from making under DR 7-107.

DR 7-108 Communication with or Investigation of Jurors.

(A) Before the trial of a case a lawyer connected therewith shall not communicate with or cause another to communicate with anyone he knows to be a member of the venire from which the jury will be selected for the trial of the case.

(B) During the trial of a case:

(1) A lawyer connected therewith shall not communicate with or cause another to communicate with any member of the jury.[87]

(2) A lawyer who is not connected therewith shall not communicate with or cause another to communicate with a juror concerning the case.

(C) DR 7-108(A) and (B) do not prohibit a lawyer from communicating with veniremen or jurors in the course of official proceedings.

(D) After discharge of the jury from further consideration of a case with which the lawyer was connected, the lawyer shall not ask questions of or make comments to a member of that jury that are calculated merely to harass or embarrass the juror or to influence his actions in future jury service.[88]

(E) A lawyer shall not conduct or cause, by financial support or otherwise, another to conduct a vexatious or harassing investigation of either a venireman or a juror.

(F) All restrictions imposed by DR 7-108 upon a lawyer also apply to communications with or investigations of members of a family of a venireman or a juror.

(G) A lawyer shall reveal promptly to the court improper conduct by a venireman or a juror, or by another toward a venireman or a juror or a member of his family, of which the lawyer has knowledge.

DR 7-109   Contact with Witnesses.

(A) A lawyer shall not suppress any evidence that he or his client has a legal obligation to reveal or produce.[89]

(B) A lawyer shall not advise or cause a person to secrete himself or to leave the jurisdiction of a tribunal for the purpose of making him unavailable as a witness therein.[90]

(C) A lawyer shall not pay, offer to pay, or acquiesce in the payment of compensation to a witness contingent upon the content of his testimony or the outcome of the case.[91] But a lawyer may advance, guarantee, or acquiesce in the payment of:

　(1)　Expenses reasonably incurred by a witness in attending or testifying.

　(2)　Reasonable compensation to a witness for his loss of time in attending or testifying.

　(3)　A reasonable fee for the professional services of an expert witness.

DR 7-110   Contact with Officials.[92]

(A) A lawyer shall not give or lend any thing of value to a judge, official, or employee of a tribunal except as permitted by Section C(4) of Canon 5 of the Code of Judicial Conduct, but a lawyer may make a contribution to the campaign fund of a candidate for judicial office in conformity with Section B(2) under Canon 7 of the Code of Judicial Conduct.[93]

(B) In an adversary proceeding, a lawyer shall not communicate, or cause another to communicate, as to the merits of the cause with a judge or an official before whom the proceeding is pending, except:

　(1)　In the course of official proceedings in the cause.*

　(2)　In writing if he promptly delivers a copy of the writing to opposing counsel or to the adverse party if he is not represented by a lawyer.

　(3)　Orally upon adequate notice to opposing counsel or to the adverse party if he is not represented by a lawyer.

　(4)　As otherwise authorized by law, or by Section A(4) under Canon 3 of the Code of Judicial Conduct.[94, 95]

NOTES

　1. "The right to be heard would be, in many cases, of little avail if it did not comprehend the right to be heard by counsel. Even intelligent and educated layman has small and sometimes no skill in the science of law." Powell v. Alabama, 287 U.S. 45, 68-69, 77 L. Ed. 158, 170, 53 S. Ct. 55,64 (1932).

2. *Cf.* ABA CANONS OF PROFESSIONAL ETHICS, CANON 4 (1908).

"At times . . . . [the tax lawyer] will be wise to discard some argument and he should exercise discretion to emphasize the arguments which in his judgment are most likely to be persuasive. But this process involves legal judgment rather than moral attitudes. The tax lawyer should put aside private disagreements with Congressional and Treasury policies. His own notions of policy, and his personal view of what the law should be, are irrelevant. The job entrusted to him by his client is to use all his learning and ability to protect his client's rights, not to help in the process of promoting a better tax system. The tax lawyer need not accept his client's economic and social opinions, but the client is paying for the technical attention and undivided concentration upon his affairs. He is equally entitled to performance unfettered by his attorney's economic and social predilections." Paul, *The Lawyer as a Tax Adviser*, 25 ROCKY MT. L. REV. 412, 418 (1953).

3. *See* ABA CANONS OF PROFESSIONAL ETHICS, CANONS 15 and 32 (1908).

ABA Canon 5, although only speaking of one accused of crime, imposes a similar obligation on the lawyer: "[T]he lawyer is bound, by all fair and honorable means, to present every defense that the law of the land permits, to the end that no person may be deprived of life liberty, but by due process of law."

"Any persuasion of pressure on the advocate which deters him from planning and carrying out the litigation on the basis of 'what, within the framework of the law, is best for my client's interest?' interferes with the obligation to represent the client fully within the law.

"This obligation, in it fullest sense, is the heart of the adversary process. Each attorney, as an advocate, acts for and seeks that which in his judgment is best for his client, within the bounds authoritatively established. The advocate does not decide what is just in this case—he would be usurping the function of the judge and jury—he acts for and seeks for his client that which he is entitled to under the law. He can do no less and properly represent the client." Thode, *The Ethical Standard for the Advocate*, 39 TEXAS L. REV. 575, 584 (1961).

"The [Texas public opinion] survey indicates that distrust of the lawyer can be traced directly to certain factors. Foremost of these is a basis misunderstanding of the function of the lawyer as an advocate in an adversary system.

"Lawyers are accused of taking advantage of 'loopholes' and 'technicalities' to win. Person who make this charge are unaware, or do not understand, that the lawyer is hired to win, and if he does not exercise every legitimate effort in his client's behalf, then he is betraying a sacred trust." Rochelle & Payne, *The Struggle for Public Understanding*, 25 TEXAS B.J. 109, 159 (1962).

"The importance of the attorney's undivided allegiance and faithful service to one accused of crime, irrespective of the attorney's personal opinion as to the guilt of his client, lies in Canon 5 of the American Bar Association Canon of Ethics.

"The difficulty lies, of course, in ascertaining whether the attorney has been guilty of an error of judgment, such as an election with respect to trial tactics, or has otherwise been actuated by his conscience or belief that his client should be convicted in any event. All too frequently courts are called upon to review actions of defense counsel which are at the most, errors of judgment, not properly reviewable or habeas corpus unless the trial is a farce and a mockery of justice which requires the court to intervene . . . . But when defense counsel, in a truly adverse proceeding, admits that his conscience would not permit him to adopt certain customary trial procedures, this extends beyond the realm of judgment and strongly suggests an invasion of constitutional rights." Johns v. Smyth, 176 F. Supp. 949, 952 (E.D. Va. 1959), *modified*, United States ex rel. Wilkins v. Banmiller, 205 F. Supp. 123, 128, n.5 (E.D. Pa. 1962), *aff'd*, 325 F.2d 514 (3d Cir. 1963), *cert. denied*, 279 U.S. 847, 13 L. Ed. 2d 51, 85 S. Ct. 87 (1964).

"The adversary system in law administration bears a striking resemblance to the competitive economic system. In each we assume that the individual through partisanship or through self-interest will strive mightily for his side, and that kind of striving we must have. But neither system would be tolerable without restraints and modifications, and at times without outright departures from the system itself. Since the legal profession is entrusted with the system of law administration, a part of its task is to develop in its members appropriate restraints without impairing the values of partisan striving. An accompanying task is to aid in the modification of the adversary system or departure from it in areas to which the system is unsuited." Cheatham, *The Lawyer's Role and Surroundings,* 25 ROCK MT. L. REV. 405, 410 (1953).

4. "Rule 4.15 prohibits, in the pursuit of a client's cause, 'any manner of fraud or chicane'; Rule 4.22 requires 'candor and fairness' in the conduct of the lawyer, and forbids the making of knowing misquotations; Rule 4.47 provides that a lawyer 'should always maintain his integrity,' and generally forbids all misconduct injurious to the interests of the public, the courts, or his clients, and acts contrary to 'justice, honesty, modesty or good morals.' Our Commissioner has accurately paraphrased these rules as follows: 'An attorney does not have the duty to do all and whatever he can that may enable him to win his client's cause or to further his client's interest. His duty and efforts in these respects, although they should be prompted by his "entire devotion" to the interest of his client, must be within and not without the bounds of the law.' " In re Wines, 370 S.W.2d 328, 333 (Mo. 1963).

See Note, 38 TEXAS L. REV. 107,110 (1959).

5. "Under our system of government the process of adjudication is surrounded by safeguards evolved from centuries of experience. These safeguards are not designed merely to lend formality and decorum to the trial of causes. They are predicated on the assumption that to secure for any controversy a truly informed and dispassionate decision is a difficult thing, requiring for its achievement a special summoning and organization of human effort and the adoption of measures to exclude the biases and prejudgments that have free play outside the courtroom. All of this goes for naught if the man with an unpopular cause is unable to find a competent lawyer courageous enough to represent him. His chance to have his day in court loses much of its meaning if his case is handicapped from the outset by the very kind of prejudgment our rules of evidence and procedure are intended to prevent." *Professional Responsibility: Report of the Joint Conference,* 44 A.B.A. J. 1159, 1216 (1958).

6. "[I]t is . . . [the tax lawyer's] positive duty to show the client how to avail himself to the full of what the law permits. He is not the keeper of the Congressional conscience." Paul, *The Lawyer as a Tax Adviser,* 25 ROCKY MT. L. REV. 412, 418 (1953).

7. *See* ABA CANONS OF PROFESSIONAL ETHICS, CANONS 15 and 30 (1908).

8. "The fact that it desired to evade the law, as it is called, is immaterial, because the very meaning of a line in the law is that you intentionally may go as close to it as you can if you do not pass it . . . . It is a matter of proximity and degree as to which minds will differ . . . ." Justice Holmes, in Superior Oil Co. v. Mississippi, 280 U.S. 390, 395-96, 74 L. Ed. 504, 508, 50 S. Ct. 169, 170 (1930).

9. "Today's lawyers perform two distinct types of functions, and our ethical standards should, but in the main do not, recognize these two functions. Judge Philbrick McCoy recently reported to the American Bar Association the need for a reappraisal of the Canons in light of the new and distinct function of counselor, as distinguished from advocate, which today predominates in the legal profession . . . .

". . . In the first place, any revision of the canons must take into account and speak to this new and now predominant function of the lawyer . . . . It is beyond the scope of this paper to discuss the ethical standards to be applied to the counselor except to state that in my opinion such standards should require a greater recognition and protection for the interest of the public generally than is presently expressed in the canons. Also, the counselor's obligation should extend to requiring him to inform and to impress upon the client a just solution of the problem, considering all interests involved." Thode, *The Ethical Standard for the Advocate*, 39 Texas L. Rev. 575, 578-79 (1961).

"The man who has been called into court to answer for his own actions is entitled to fair hearing. Partisan advocacy plays its essential part in such a hearing, and the lawyer pleading his client's case may properly present it in the most favorable light. A similar resolution of doubts in one direction becomes inappropriate when the lawyer acts as counselor. The reasons that justify and even require partisan advocacy in the trial of a cause do not grant any license to the lawyer to participate as legal advisor in a line of conduct that is immoral, unfair, or of doubtful legality. In saving himself from this unworthy involvement, the lawyer cannot be guided solely by an unreflective inner sense of good faith; he must be at pains to preserve a sufficient detachment from his client's interests so that he remains capable of a sound and objective appraisal of the propriety of what his client proposes to do." *Professional Responsibility: Report of the Joint Conference*, 4 A.B.A. J. 1159, 1161 (1958).

10. "[A] lawyer who is asked to advise his client . . . may freely urge the statement of positions most favorable to the client just as long as there is reasonable basis for those positions." *ABA Opinion* 314 (1965).

11. "The lawyer . . . is not an umpire, but an advocate. He is under no duty to refrain from making every proper argument in support of any legal point because he is not convinced of its inherent soundness . . . . His personal belief in the soundness of his cause or of the authorities supporting it, is irrelevant." *ABA Opinion* 280 (1949).

"Counsel apparently misconceived his role. It was his duty to honorably present his client's contentions in the light most favorable to his client. Instead he presumed to advise the court as to the validity and sufficiency of prisoner's motion, by letter. We therefore conclude that prisoner had no effective assistance of counsel and remand this case to the District Court with instructions to set aside the Judgment, appoint new counsel to represent the prisoner if he makes no objection thereto, and proceed anew." McCartney v. United States, 343 F. 2d 471, 472 (9th Cir. 1965).

12. "Here the court-appointed counsel had the transcript but refused to proceed with the appeal because he found no merit in it . . . . We cannot say that there was a finding of frivolity by either of the California courts or that counsel acted in any greater capacity than merely as amicus curiae which was condemned in Ellis, supra. Hence California's procedure did not furnish petitioner with counsel acting in the role of an advocate nor did it provide that full consideration and resolution of the matter as is obtained when counsel is acting in the capacity . . . .

"The constitutional requirement of substantial equality and fair process can only be attained where counsel acts in the rule of an active advocate in behalf of his client, as opposed to that of amicus curiae. The no-merit letter and the procedure it triggers do not reach that dignity. Counsel should, and can with honor and without conflict, be of more assistance to his client and to the court. His role as advocate requires that he support his client's appeal to the best of his ability. Of course, if counsel finds his case to be wholly frivolous, after a conscientious examination of it, he should so advise the court and request permission to withdraw. That request must, however, be accompanies by a brief referring to anything in the record that might arguably support the appeal. A copy of counsel's brief should be furnished the indigent and time allowed him to raise any points that he chooses; the court—not counsel—then proceeds, after a full examination of all the proceedings, to decide whether the case is wholly frivolous. If it so finds it may grant counsel's request to withdraw and dismiss the appeal insofar as federal requirements are concerned, or proceed to a decision of the merits, if state law so requires. On the other hand, if it finds any of the legal points argule on their merits (and therefore not frivolous) it must, prior to decision, afford the indigent the assistance of counsel to argue the appeal." Anders v. California, 386 U.S. 738, 744, 18 L. Ed. 2d 493, 498, 87 S. Ct. 1396, 1399-1400 (1967), *rehearing denied*, 388 U.S. 924, 18 L. Ed. 2d 1377, 87 S. Ct. 2094 (1967).

ABA Model
Code of
Professional
Responsibility

See Paul, *The Lawyer as a Tax Adviser*, 25 ROCKY MT. L. REV. 412, 432 (1953).

13. *See* ABA CANONS OF PROFESSIONAL ETHICS, CANON 32 (1908).

14. "For a lawyer to represent a syndicate notroriously engaged in the violation of the law for the purpose of advising the members how to break the law and at the same time escape it, is manifestly improper. While a lawyer may see to it that anyone accused of crime, no matter how serious and flagrant, has a fair trial, and present all available defenses, he may not co-operate in planning violations of the law. There is a sharp distinction, of course, between advising what can lawfully be done and advising how unlawful acts can be done in a way to avoid conviction. Where a lawyer accepts a retainer from an organization, known to be unlawful, and agrees in advance to defend its members when from time to time they are accused of crime arising out of its unlawful activities, this is equally improper."

"*See also Opinion* 155." *ABA Opinion* 281 (1952).

15. *See* ABA Special Committee on Minimum Standards for the Administration of Criminal Justice, *Standards Relating to Pleas of Guilty*, pp. 69-70 (1968).

16. "First of all, a truly great lawyer is a wise counselor to all manner of men in the varied crises of their lives when they most need disinterested advice. Effective counseling necessarily involves a thoroughgoing knowledge of the principles of the law not merely as they appear in the books but as they actually operate in action." Vanderbilt, *The Five Functions of the Lawyer: Service to Client and the Public,* 40 A.B.A. J. 31 (1954).

17. "A lawyer should endeavor to obtain full knowledge of his client's cause before advising theron . . . ."ABA CANONS OF PROFESSIONAL ETHICS, CANON 8 (1908).

18. "[I]n devising charters of collaborative effort the lawyer often acts where all of the affected parties are present as participants. But the lawyer also performs a similar function in situations where this is not so, as, for example, in planning estates and drafting wills. Here the instrument defining the terms of collaborating may affect persons not present and often not born. Yet here, too, the good lawyer does not serve merely as a legal conduit for his client's desires, but as a wise counselor, experienced in the art of devising arrangements that will put in workable order the entangled affairs and interests of human beings." *Professional Responsibility: Report of the Joint Conference,* 44 A.B.A .J. 1159, 1162 (1958).

19. *See* ABA CANONS OF PROFESSIONAL ETHICS, CANON 8 (1908).

"Vital as is the lawyer's role in adjudication, it should not be thought that it is only as an advocate pleading in open court that he contributes to the administration of the law. The most effective realization of the law's aims often takes place in the attorney's office, where litigation is forestalled by anticipating its outcome, where the lawyer's quit counsel takes the place of public force. Contrary to popular belief, the compliance with the law thus brought about is not generally lip-serving and narrow, for by reminding him of its long-run costs the lawyer often deters his client from a course of conduct technically permissible under existing law, though inconsistent with its underlying spirit and purpose." *Professional Responsibility: Report of the Joint Conference,* 44 A.B.A. J. 1159, 1161 (1958).

20. "My summation of Judge Sharswood's view of the advocate's duty to the client is that he owes to the client the duty to use all legal means in support of the client's case. However, at the same time Judge Sharswood recognized that many advocates would find this obligation unbearable if applicable without exception. Therefore, the individual lawyer is given the choice of representing his client fully within the bounds set by the law or of telling his client that he cannot do so, so that the client may obtain another attorney if he wishes." Thode, *The Ethical Standard of the Advocate,* 39 TEXAS L. REV. 575, 582 (1961).

Cf. MODEL CODE OF PROF'L RESPONSIBILITY, DR 2-110(C).

21. *See* ABA CANONS OF PROFESSIONAL ETHICS, CANON 24 (1908).

22. Thode, *The Ethical Standard of the Advocate,* 39 TEXAS L. REV. 575, 592 (1961).

23. *See* ABA CANONS OF PROFESSIONAL ETHICS, CANON 5 (1908) and Berger v. United States, 295 U.S.78, 79 L. Ed. 1314, 55 S. Ct. 629(1935).

"The public prosecutor cannot take as a guide for the conduct of his office the standards of an attorney appearing on behalf of an individual client. The freedom elsewhere wisely granted to a partisan advocate must ge severely curtailed if the prosector's duties are to be properly discharged. The public prosecutor must recall that he occupies a dual role, being obligated, on the one hand, to furnish that adversary element essential to the informed decision of any controversy, but being possessed, on the other, of important governmental power that are pledge to the accomplishment of one objective only, that of impartial justice. Where the prosecutor is recreant to the trust implicit in his office, he undermines confidence, not only in his profession, but in government and the very ideal of justice itself." *Professional Responsibility: Report of the Joint Conference*, 44 A.B.A. J. 1159, 1218 (1958).

"The Prosecuting attorney is the attorney of the state, and it is his primary duty not to convict but to see that justice is done." *ABA Opinion* 150 (1936).

24. As to appearance before a department of government, ABA CANONS OF PROFESSIONAL ETHICS, CANON 26 (1908) provides: "A lawyer openly . . . may render professional services . . . in advocacy of claims before department of government upon the same principles of ethics which justify his appearance before the Courts . . . ."

25. "But as an advocate before a service which itself represents the adversary point of view, where his client's case is fairly arguable, a lawyer is under no duty to disclose its weaknesses, any more than he would be to make such a disclosure to a brother lawyer. The limitations within which he must operate are best expressed in Canon 22 . . . ." *ABA Opinion* 314 (1965).

26. *See Baird v. Koerner*, 279 F.2d 623 (9th Cir. 1960).

27. *See* ABA CANONS OF PROFESSIONAL ETHICS, CANON 26 (1908).

28. "Law should be so practiced that the lawyer remains free to make up his own mind how he will vote, what causes he will support, what economic and political philosophy he will espouse. It is one of the glories of the profession that it admits of his freedom. Distinguished examples can be cited of lawyers whose views were at variance from those of their clients, lawyers whose skill and wisdom makes them valued advisers to those who had little sympathy with their views as citizens." *Professional Responsibility: Report of the Joint Conference*, 44 A.B.A. J. 1159, 1217 (1958).

"No doubt some tax lawyers feel constrained to abstain from activities on behalf of a better tax system because they think that their clients may object. Clients have no right to object if the tax adviser handles their affairs competently and faithfully and independently of his private views as to tax policy. They buy his expert services, not his private opinions or his silence on issues that gravely affect the public interest." Paul, *The Lawyer as a Tax Adviser*, 25 ROCKY MT. L. REV. 412, 434 (1953).

29. *See* ABA CANONS OF PROFESSIONAL ETHICS, CANON 9 (1908).

30. *Id.*

31. *See Professional Responsibility: Report of the Joint Conference*, 44 A.B.A. J. 1159, 1160 (1958).

32. "Without the participation of someone who can act responsibly for each of the parties, this essential narrowing of the issues [by exchange of written pleading or stipulation of counsel] becomes impossible. But here again the true significance of partisan advocacy lies deeper, touching once more the integrity of the adjudicative process itself. It is only through the advocate's participation that the hearing may remain in fact what it purports to be in theory; a public trial of the facts and issues. Each advocate comes to the hearing prepared to present his proofs and arguments, knowing at the same time that his arguments may fail to persuade and that his proof may be rejected as inadequate . . . . The deciding tribunal, on the other hand, comes to the hearing uncommitted. It has not represented to the public that any fact can be proved, that any argument is sound, or that any particular way of stating a litigant's case is the most effective expression of its merits." *Professional Responsibility: Report of the Joint Conference*, 44 A.B.A. J. 1159, 1160-61 (1958).

33. *Cf.* ABA CANONS OF PROFESSIONAL ETHICS, CANONS 15 and 32 (1908).

34. *Cf.* ABA CANONS OF PROFESSIONAL ETHICS, CANON 21 (1908).

35. *See Professional Responsibility: Report of the Joint Conference*, 44 A.B.A. J. 1159, 1216 (1958).

36. "We are of the opinion that the letter in question was improper, and that in writing and sending it respondent was guilty of unprofessional conduct. This court has heretofore expressed its disapproval of using threats of criminal prosecution as a means of forcing settlement of civil claims . . . .

"Respondent has been guilty of a violation of a principle which condemns any confusion of threats of criminal prosecution with the enforcement of the civil claims. For this misconduct he should be severely censured." Matter of Gelman, 230 App. Div. 524, 527, N.Y.S. 416, 419 (1930).

37. "An attorney has the duty to protect the interests of his client. He has a right to press legitimate argument and to protest an erroneous ruling." Galagher v. Municpal Court, 31 Cal. 2d 784, 796, 192 P.2d 905, 913 (1948).

"There must be protection, however, in the far more frequent case of the attorney who stands on his rights and combats the order in good faith and without disrespect believing with good cause that it is void, for it is here that the independence of the bar becomes valuable." Note, 39 COLUM .L. REV. 433, 438 (1939).

38. "Too many do not understand that accomplishment of the layman's abstract ideas of justice is the function of the judge and jury, and that it is the lawyer's sworn duty to portray his client's case in its most favorable light." Rochelle & Payne, *The Struggle for Public Understanding*, 25 TEXAS B.J. 109, 159 (1962).

39. "We are of the opinion that this Canon requires the lawyer to disclose such decisions [that are adverse to his client's contentions] to the court. He may, of course, after doing so, challenge the soundness of the decisions or present reasons which he believes would warrant the court in not following them in the pending case." *ABA Opinion* 146 (1935).

Cf. ABA Opinion 280 (1949) and Thode, *The Ethical Standard for the Advocate*, 39 TEXAS L. REV. 575, 585-86 (1961).

40. *See* ABA CANONS OF PROFESSIONAL ETHICS, CANON 15 (1908).

"The traditional duty of an advocate is that he honorably uphold the contentions of his client. He should not voluntarily undermine them." Harders v. State of California, 373 F.2d 839, 842 (9th Cir. 1967).

41. *See* ABA CANONS OF PROFESSIONAL ETHICS, CANON 22 (1908).

42. *Id.; cf.* ABA CANONS OF PROFESSIONAL ETHICS, CANON 41 (1908).

43. *See* generally *ABA Opinion* 287 (1953) as to a lawyer's duty when he unknowingly participates in introducing perjured testimony.

44. "Under any standard of proper ethical conduct an attorney would not sit by silently and permit his client to commit what may have been perjury, and which certainly would mislead the court and opposing party on a matter vital to the issue under consideration . . . .
. . . .

"Respondent next urges that it was his duty to observe the utmost good faith toward his client, and therefore he could not divulge any confidential information. This duty to the client of course does not extend to the point of authorizing collaboration with him in the commission of fraud." In re Carrol, 244 S.W.2d 474, 474-75 (Ky. 1951).

45. *See* ABA CANONS OF PROFESSIONAL ETHICS, CANON 5 (1908); *cf. ABA Opinion* 131 (1935).

46. *Cf.* ABA CANONS OF PROFESSIONAL ETHICS, CANON 39 (1908).

47. "The prevalence of perjury is a serious menace to the administration of justice, to prevent which no means have as yet been satisfactorily devised. But there certainly can be no greater incentive to perjury than to allow a party to make payments to it opponent's witnesses under any guise or on any excuse, and at least attorneys who are officers of the court to aid in the administration of justice, must keep themselves clear of any connection

which in the slightest degree tends to induce witness to testify in favor of their clients." In re Robinson, 151 App. Div. 589, 600, 136 N.Y.S. 548, 556-57 (1912), *aff'd*, 209 N.Y. 354, 103 N.E. 160 (1913).

48. "It will not do for an attorney who seeks to justify himself against charges of this kind to show that he has escaped criminal responsibility under the Penal Law, nor can he blindly shut his eyes to a system which tends to suborn witnesses, to produce perjured testimony, and to suppress the truth. He has an active affirmative duty to protect the administration of justice from perjury and fraud, and that duty is not performed by allowing his subordinates and assistants to attempt to subvert justice and procure results for his clients based upon false testimony and perjured witnesses." *Id.*, 151 App. Div. at 592, 136 N.Y.S. at 551.

49. *See* ABA CANONS OF PROFESSIONAL ETHICS, CANON 23 (1908).

50. "[I]t is unfair to jurors to permit a disappointed litigant to pick over their private associations in search of something to discredit them and their verdict. And it would be unfair to the public too if jurors should understand that they cannot convict a man of means without risking an inquiry of that kind by paid investigators, with, to boot, the distortions an inquiry of that kind can produce." State v. LaFera, 42 N.J. 97, 107, 199 A.2d 630, 636 (1964).

51. *ABA Opinion* 319 (1968) points out that "[m]any courts today, and the trend is in this direction, allow the testimony of jurors as to all irregularities in and out of the court-room except those irregularities whose existence can be determined only by exploring the consciousness of a single particular juror, New Jersey v. Kociolek, 20 N.J. 92, 118 A.2d 812 (1955). Model Code of Evidence Rule 301. Certainly as to states in which the testimony and affidavits of jurors may be received in support of or against a motion for new trial, a lawyer, in his obligation to protect his client, must have the tools for ascertaining whether or not grounds for a new trial exist and it is not unethical for him to take to and question jurors."

52. *Generally see* ABA ADVISORY COMMITTEE ON FAIR TRIAL AND FREE PRESS, STANDARDS RELATING TO FAIR TRIAL AND FREE PRESS (1966).

"[T]he trial court might well have proscribed extrajudicial statements by any lawyer, party, witness, or court official which divulged prejudicial matters . . . . See state v. Van Dwyne. 43 N.J. 369, 389, 204 A.2d 841, 852 (1964), in which the court interpreted Canon 20 of the American Bar Association's Canons of Professional Ethics to prohibit such statements. Being advised of the great pubic interest in the case, the mass coverage of the press, and the potential prejudicial impact of publicity, the court could also have request the appropriate city and county officials to promulgate a regulation with respect to dissemination of information about the case by their employees. In addition, reporters who wrote or broadcast prejudicial stories, could have been warned as to the impropriety of publishing material not introduced in the proceedings . . . . In this manner, Sheppard's right to a trial free from outside interference would have been given added protection without corresponding curtailment of the news media. Had the judge, the other officers of the court, and the police placed in the interest of justice first, the news media would have soon learned to be content with the task of reporting the case as it unfolded in the courtroom—not pieced together from extrajudicial statements." Sheppard v. Maxwell, 384 U.S. 333, 361-62, 16 L. Ed. 2d 600, 619-20, 86 S. Ct. 1507, 1521-22 (1966).

"Court proceedings are held for the solemn purpose of endeavoring to ascertain the truth which is the sine qua non of a fair trial. Over the centuries Anglo-American courts have devised careful safeguards by rule and otherwise to protect and facilitate the performance of this high function. As a result, at this time those safeguards do not permit the televising and photographing of a criminal trial, save in two States and there only under restrictions. The federal courts prohibit it by specific rule. This is weighty evidence that our concepts of a fair trial do not tolerate such an indulgence. We have always held that the atmosphere essential to the preservation of a fair trial-the most fundamental of all

ABA Model Code of Professional Responsibility

freedoms-must be maintained at all costs." Estes v. State of Texas, 381 U.S. 532, 540, 14 L. Ed. 2d 543, 549, 85 S. Ct. 1628, 1631-32 (1965), *rehearing denied*, 382 U.S. 875, 15 L. Ed. 2d 118, 86 S. Ct. 18 (1965).

53. "Pretrial can create a major problem for the defendant in a criminal case. Indeed, it may be more harmful than publicity during the trial for it may well set the community opinion as to guilt or innocence . . . . The trial witnesses present at the hearing, as well as the original jury panel, were undoubtedly made aware of the peculiar public importance of the case by the press and television coverage being provided, and by the fact that they themselves were televised live and their pictures rebroadcast on the evening show." *Id.*, 381 U.S. at 536-37, 14 L. Ed. 2d at 546-47, 85 S. Ct. at 1629-30.

54. "The undeviating rule of this Court was expressed by Mr. Justice Holmes over half a century ago in Patterson v. Colorado, 205 U.S. 454, 462 (1907):

The theory of our system is that the conclusions to be reached in a case will be induced only by evidence and argument in open court, and not by any outside influence, whether of private talk or public print."

Sheppard v. Maxwell, 384 U.S. 333, 351, 16 L. Ed. 2d 600, 614, 86 S. Ct. 1507, 1516 (1966).

"The trial judge has a large discretion in ruling on the issue of prejudice resulting from the reading by jurors of news articles concerning the trial . . . . Generalizations beyond that statement are not profitable, because each case must turn on its special facts. We have here the exposure of jurors to information of a character which the trial judge ruled was so prejudicial it could not be directly offered as evidence. The prejudice to the defendant is almost certain to be as great when that evidence reaches the jury through news accounts as when it is part of the prosecution's evidence . . . . It may indeed be greater for it is then not tempered by protective procedures." Marshall v. United States, 360 U.S. 310, 312-13, 3 L. Ed. 2d 1252, 79 S. Ct. 1171, 1173 (1959).

"The experience trial lawyer knows that an adverse public opinion is a tremendous disadvantage to the defense of his client. Although grand jurors conduct their deliberation in secret, they are selected from the body of the public. They are likely to know what the general public knows and to reflect the public attitude. Trials are open to the public, and aroused pubic opinion respecting the merits of a legal controversy creates a court room atmosphere which, without any vocal expression in the presence of the petit jury, makes itself felt and has its effect upon the action of the petit jury. Our fundamental concepts of justice and our American sense of fair play requires that the petit jury shall be composed of person with fair and impartial minds and without preconceived views as to the merits of the controversy, and that it shall determine the issues presented to it solely upon the evidence adduced at the trial and according to the law given in the instructions of the trial judge.

"While we may doubt that the effect of public opinion would sway or bias the judgment of the trial judge in an equity proceeding, the defendant should not be called upon to run that risk and the trial court should not have his work made more difficult by any dissemination of statements to the public that would be calculated to create a public demand for a particular judgment in a prospective or pending case." *ABA Opinion* 199 (1940).

Cf. Estes v. State of Texas, 381 U.S. 532, 544-45, 144 L. Ed. 2d 543, 551, 85 S. Ct. 1628, 1634 (1965), *rehearing denied*, 381 U.S. 875, 15 L. Ed. 2d 118, 86 S. Ct. 18 (1965).

55. *See* ABA CANONS OF PROFESSIONAL ETHICS, CANON 20 (1908).

56. Canon 3 observes that a lawyer "deserves rebuke and denunciation for any device or attempt to gain from a Judge special personal consideration or favor." *See* ABA CANONS OF PROFESSIONAL ETHICS, CANON 32 (1908).

57. "Judicial Canon 32 provides:

A judge should not accept any present or favors from litigants, or from lawyers practicing before him or from other whose interests are likely to be submitted to him for judgment.

The language of this Canon is perhaps broad enough to prohibit campaign contributions by lawyers, practicing before the court upon which the candidate hopes to sit. However, we do not think it was intended to prohibit such contributions when the candidate is obligated, by force of circumstances over which he has no control, to conduct a campaign, the expense of which exceeds that which he should reasonably be expected to personally bear!" *ABA Opinion* 226 (1941).

58. Amended, March 1974, House Informational Report No. 127.

59. *See* ABA CANONS OF PROFESSIONAL ETHICS, CANONS 3 and 32 (1908).

60. *Cf.* ABA CANONS OF PROFESSIONAL ETHICS, CANON 18 (1908).

61. *See* ABA CANONS OF PROFESSIONAL ETHICS, CANONS 1 and 3 (1908).

62. *See* ABA CANONS OF PROFESSIONAL ETHICS, CANON 17 (1908).

63. *See* ABA CANONS OF PROFESSIONAL ETHICS, CANON 24 (1908).

64. *See* ABA CANONS OF PROFESSIONAL ETHICS, CANON 25 (1908).

65. *See* ABA CANONS OF PROFESSIONAL ETHICS, CANON 21 (1908).

66. *See* ABA CANONS OF PROFESSIONAL ETHICS, CANON 15 (1908).

67. *See* ABA CANONS OF PROFESSIONAL ETHICS, CANONS 5 and 15 (1908). *cf.* ABA Canons 4 and 32 (1908).

68. *Cf.* ABA CANONS OF PROFESSIONAL ETHICS, CANON 24 (1908).

69. *Cf.* ABA CANONS OF PROFESSIONAL ETHICS, CANON 30 (1908).

70. *Cf.* ABA CANONS OF PROFESSIONAL ETHICS, CANONS 22 and 29 (1908).

71. *Cf. See* ABA CANONS OF PROFESSIONAL ETHICS, CANON 41 (1908); *cf.* Hinds v. State Bar, 19 Cal. 2d 87, 92-93, 119 P.2d 134, 137 (1941); *but see ABA Opinion* 287 (1953) and Texas Canon 38. *Also see* MODEL CODE OF PROFESSIONAL RESPONSIBILITY, DR 4-101(C)(2).

72. Amended, March 1974, House Informational Report No. 127.

73. *See* Precision Inst. Mfg. Co. v. Automotive M.M. Co., 324 U.S. 806, 89 L. Ed. 1381, 65 S. Ct. 993 (1945).

74. *Cf.* ABA CANONS OF PROFESSIONAL ETHICS, CANON 5 (1908).

75. "*Rule 12* . . . . A member of the State Bar shall not communicate with a party represented by counsel upon a subject of controversy, in the absence and without the consent of such counsel. This rule shall not apply to communications with a public officer, board committee or body." CAL. BUS. AND PROF. CODE § 6076 (West 1962).

76. *See* ABA CANONS OF PROFESSIONAL ETHICS, CANON 9 (1908); *cf. ABA Opinions* 124 (1934), 108 (1935), 95 (1933), and 75 (1932); *also see* In re Schwabe, 242 Or. 169, 174-75, 408 P.2d 922, 924 (1965).

"It is clear from the earlier opinions of this committee that Canon 9 is to be construed literally and does not allow a communication with an opposing party, without the consent of his counsel, though the purpose merely be to investigate the facts. Opinions 117, 55, 66," *ABA Opinion* 187 (1938).

77. *Cf. ABA Opinion* 102 (1933).

78. *Cf.* ABA CANONS OF PROFESSIONAL ETHICS, CANON 9 (1908) and *ABA Opinion* 58 (1931).

79. *Cf.* Note, 38 TEXAS L. REV. 107, 108-09 (1959).

80. "In the brief summary in the 1947 edition of the Committee's decisions (p. 17), Opinion 146 was thus summarized: Opinion 146—A lawyer should disclose to the court a decision directly adverse to his client's case that is unknown to his adversary.

. . . .

"We would not confine the Opinion to 'controlling authorities'—i.e., those decisive of the pending case—but, in accordance with the tests hereafter suggested, would apply it to a decision directly adverse to any proposition of law on which the lawyer expressly relies, which would reasonably be considered important by the judge sitting on the case.

. . . .

". . . The test in every case should be: Is the decision which opposing counsel has over-

ABA Model
Code of
Professional
Responsibility

looked one which the court should clearly consider in deciding the case? Would a reasonable judge properly feel that a lawyer who advanced, as the law, a proposition adverse to the undisclosed decision, was lacking in candor and fairness to him? Might the judge consider himself misled by an implied representation that the lawyer knew of no adverse authority?" *ABA Opinion* 280 (1949).

81. "The authorities are substantially uniform against any privilege as applied to the fact of retainer or identity of the client. The privilege is limited to confidential communications, and a retainer is not a confidential communication, although it cannot come into existence without some communication between the attorney and the—at that stage prospective—client." United States v. Pape; 144 F.2d 778, 782 (2d Cir. 1944), *cert. denied*, 323 U.S. 752, 89 L. Ed. 2d 602, 65 S. Ct. 86 (1944).

"To be sure, there may be circumstances under which the identification of a client may amount to the prejudicial disclosure of a confidential communication, as where the substance of a disclosure has already been revealed but not its source." Colton v. United States, 306 F.2d 633, 637 (2d Cir. 1962).

82. *See* ABA CANONS OF PROFESSIONAL ETHICS, CANON 22 (1908); *cf.* ABA CANONS OF PROFESSIONAL ETHICS, CANON 17 (1908).

"The rule allowing counsel when addressing the jury the widest latitude in discussing the evidence and presenting the client's theories falls far short of authorizing the statement by counsel of matter not in evidence, or indulging in argument founded on no proof, or demanding verdicts for purposes other than the just settlement of the matters at issue between the litigants, or appealing to prejudice or passion. The rule confining counsel to legitimate argument is not based on etiquette, but on justice. Its violation is not merely an overstepping of the bounds of property, but a violation of a party's rights. The jurors must determine the issues upon the evidence. Counsel's address should help them do this, not tend to lead them astray." Cherry Creek Nat. Bank v. Fidelity & Cas. Co., 207 App. Div. 787, 790-91, 202 N.Y.S. 611, 614 (1924).

83. *Cf.* ABA CANONS OF PROFESSIONAL ETHICS, CANON 18 (1908).

§6068 . . . . It is the duty of an attorney . . . .

"(f) To abstain from all offensive personality, and to advance no fact prejudicial to the honor or reputation of a party or witness unless required by the justice of the cause with which he is charged." CAL. BUS. AND PROF. CODE § 6068 (West 1962).

84. "The record in the case at bar was silent concerning the qualities and character of the deceased. It is especially improper, in addressing the jury in a murder case, for the prosecuting attorney to make reference to his knowledge of the good qualities of the deceased where there is no evidence in the record bearing upon his character.... A prosecutor should never inject into his argument evidence not introduced at the trial." People v. Dukes, 12 Ill. 2d 334, 341, 146 N.E.2d 14, 17-18 (1957).

85. "A lawyer should not ignore known customs or practice of the Bar or of a particular Court, even when the law permits, without giving timely notice to the opposing counsel." ABA CANONS OF PROFESSIONAL ETHICS, CANON 25 (1908).

86. The provisions of Section (A), (B), (C), and (D) of this Disciplinary Rule incorporate the fair trial-free press standards which apply to lawyers as adopted by the ABA House of Delegates, Feb. 19, 1968, upon the recommendation of the Fair Trial and Free Press Advisory Committee of the ABA Special Committee on Minimum Standards for the Administration of Criminal Justice.

Cf. ABA CANONS OF PROFESSIONAL ETHICS, CANON 20 (1908); *see generally* ABA ADVISORY COMMITTEE ON FAIR TRIAL AND FREE PRESS, STANDARDS RELATING TO FAIR TRIAL AND FREE PRESS (1966).

"From the cases coming here we note that unfair and prejudicial news comment on pending trials has become increasingly prevalent. Due process requires that the accused receive a trial by an impartial jury free from outside influences. Given the pervasiveness of modern communications and the difficulty of effacing prejudicial publicity from the minds of the jurors, the trial courts must take strong measures to ensure that the balance is never weighed against the accused. And appellate tribunals have the duty to malice an independent evaluation of the circumstances. Of course, there is nothing that prescribes the press from reporting events that transpire in the courtroom. But where there is a reasonable likelihood that prejudicial news prior to trial will prevent a fair trial the judge should continue the case until the threat abates, or transfer it to another County not so permeated with publicity . . . . The courts must take such steps by rule and regulation that will protect their processes from prejudicial outside interferences. Neither prosecutors, counsel for defense, the accused, witnesses, court staff nor enforcement officers coming under the jurisdiction of the court should be permitted to frustrate its function. Collaboration between counsel and the press as to information affecting the fairness of criminal trial is not only subject to regulation, but is highly censurable and worthy of disciplinary measures." Sheppard v. Maxwell, 384 U.S. 333, 362-63, 16 L. Ed. 2d 600, 620, 86 S. Ct. 1507, 1522 (1966).

87. *See* ABA CANONS OF PROFESSIONAL ETHICS, CANON 23 (1908).

88. "[I]t would be unethical for a lawyer to harass, entice, induce or exert influence on a juror to obtain his testimony." *ABA Opinion* 319 (1968).

89. *See* ABA CANONS OF PROFESSIONAL ETHICS, CANON 5 (1908).

90. *Cf.* ABA CANONS OF PROFESSIONAL ETHICS, CANON 5 (1908).

"Rule 15 . . . . A member of the State Bar shall not advise a person, whose testimony could establish or tend to establish a material fact, to avoid service of process, or secrete himself, or otherwise to make his testimony unavailable." CAL. BUS. AND PROF. CODE §6076 (West 1962).

91. *See* In re O'Keefe, 49 Mont. 369, 142 P. 638 (1914).

92. *Cf.* ABA CANONS OF PROFESSIONAL ETHICS, CANON 3 (1908).

93. Amended, March 1974, House Informational Report No. 127.

94. "Rule 16 . . . . A member of the State Bar shall not, in the absence of opposing counsel, communicate with or argue to a judge or judicial officer except in open court upon the merits of a contested matter pending before such judge or judicial officer; nor shall he, without finishing opposing counsel with a copy thereof, address a written communication to a judge or judicial officer concerning the merits of a contested matter pending before such judge or judicial officer. This rule shall not apply to ex parte matters." CAL. BUS. AND PROF. CODE § 6076 (West 1962).

95. Amended, March 1974, House Informational Report No. 127.

CANON 8
A Lawyer Should Assist in
Improving the Legal System

ETHICAL CONSIDERATIONS

EC 8-1   Changes in human affairs and imperfections in human institutions make necessary constant efforts to maintain and improve our legal system.[1] This system should function in a manner that commands public respect and fosters the use of legal remedies to achieve redress of grievances. By reason of education and experience, lawyers are especially qualified to recognize deficiencies in the legal system and to initiate corrective measures

ABA Model
Code of
Professional
Responsibility

therein. Thus they should participate in proposing and supporting legislation and programs to improve the system,[2] without regard to the general interests or desires of clients or former clients.[3]

EC 8-2   Rules of law are deficient if they are not just, understandable, and responsive to the needs of society. If a lawyer believes that the existence or absence of a rule of law, substantive or procedural, causes or contributes to an unjust result, he should endeavor by lawful means to obtain appropriate changes in the law. He should encourage the simplification of laws and the repeal or amendment of laws that are outmoded.[4] Likewise, legal procedures should be improved whenever experience indicates a change is needed.

EC 8-3   The fair administration of justice requires the availability of competent lawyers. Members of the public should be educated to recognize the existence of legal problems and the resultant need for legal services, and should be provided methods for intelligent selection of counsel. Those persons unable to pay for legal services should be provided needed services. Clients and lawyers should not be penalized by undue geographical restraints upon representation in legal matters, and the bar should address itself to improvements in licensing, reciprocity, and admission procedures consistent with the needs of modern commerce.

EC 8-4   Whenever a lawyer seeks legislative or administrative changes, he should identify the capacity in which he appears, whether on behalf of himself, a client, or the public.[5] A lawyer may advocate such changes on behalf of a client even though he does not agree with them. But when a lawyer purports to act on behalf of the public, he should espouse only those changes which he conscientiously believes to be in the public interest.

EC 8-5   Fraudulent, deceptive, or otherwise illegal conduct by a participant in a proceeding before a tribunal or legislative body is inconsistent with fair administration of justice, and it should never be participated in or condoned by lawyers. Unless constrained by his obligation to preserve the confidences and secrets of his client, a lawyer should reveal to appropriate authorities any knowledge he may have of such improper conduct.

EC 8-6   Judges and administrative officials having adjudicatory powers ought to be persons of integrity, competence, and suitable temperament. Generally, lawyers are qualified, by personal observation or investigation, to evaluate the qualifications of persons seeking or being considered for such public offices, and for this reason they have a special responsibility to aid in the selection of only those who are qualified.[6] It is the duty of lawyers to endeavor to prevent political considerations from outweighing judicial fitness in the selection of judges. Lawyers should protest earnestly against the appointment or election of those who are unsuited for the bench and should strive to have elected[7] or appointed thereto only those who are willing to forego pursuits, whether of a business, political, or other nature, that may interfere with the free and fair consideration of questions presented for adjudication. Adjudicatory officials, not being wholly free to defend themselves, are entitled to receive the support of the bar against unjust criticism.[8] While a lawyer as a citizen has a right to criticize such officials publicly,[9] he should be certain of the merit of his complaint, use appropriate language, and avoid petty criticisms, for unrestrained and intemperate statements tend to lessen public confidence in our legal system.[10] Criticisms motivated by reasons other than a desire to improve the legal system are not justified.

EC 8-7   Since lawyers are a vital part of the legal system, they should be persons of integrity, of professional skill, and of dedication to the improvement of the system. Thus a lawyer should aid in establishing, as well as enforcing, standards of conduct adequate to protect the public by insuring that those who practice law are qualified to do so.

EC 8-8   Lawyers often serve as legislators or as holders of other public offices. This is highly desirable, as lawyers are uniquely qualified to make significant contributions to the improvement of the legal system. A lawyer who is a public officer, whether full or part-time, should not engage in activities in which his personal or professional interests are or foreseeably may be in conflict with his official duties.[11]

EC 8-9   The advancement of our legal system is of vital importance in maintaining the rule of law and in facilitating orderly changes; therefore, lawyers should encourage, and should aid in making, needed changes and improvements.

DISCIPLINARY RULES

DR 8-101   Action as a Public Official.

(A) A lawyer who holds public office shall not:

    (1) Use his public position to obtain, or attempt to obtain, a special advantage in legislative matters for himself or for a client under circumstances where he knows or it is obvious that such action is not in the public interest.

    (2) Use his public position to influence, or attempt to influence, a tribunal to act in favor of himself or of a client.

    (3) Accept any thing of value from any person when the lawyer knows or it is obvious that the offer is for the purpose of influencing his action as a public official.

DR 8-102   Statements Concerning Judges and Other Adjudicatory Officers.[12]

(A) A lawyer shall not knowingly make false statements of fact concerning the qualifications of a candidate for election or appointment to a judicial office.

(B) A lawyer shall not knowingly make false accusations against a judge or other adjudicatory officer.

DR 8-103   Lawyer Candidate for Judicial Office.

(A) A lawyer who is a candidate for judicial office shall comply with the applicable provisions of Canon 7 of the Code of Judicial Conduct.[13]

NOTES

1. ". . . . [Another] task: of the great lawyer is to do his part individually and as a member of the organized bar to improve his profession, the courts, and the law. As President Theodore Roosevelt aptly put it, 'Every man owes some of his time to the up building of the profession to which he belongs. Indeed, this obligation is one of the great things which distinguishes a profession from a business. The soundness and the necessity of President Roosevelt's admonition insofar as it relates to the legal profession cannot be doubted. The advances in natural science and technology are so startling and the velocity of change in business and in social life is so great that the law along with the other social sciences, and even human life itself, is in grave danger of being extinguished by new gods of its own invention if it does not awake from its lethargy." Vanderbilt, *The Five Functions of the Lawyer: Service to Client and the Public*, 40 A.B.A. J. 31, 31-32

2. *See* ABA CANONS OF PROFESSIONAL ETHICS, CANON 29 (1908); *cf.* Cheatham, *The Lawyer's Role and Surroundings*, 25 ROCKY MT. L. REV. 405, 406-07 (1953).

"The lawyer tempted by repose should recall the heavy costs paid by his profession when needed legal reform has to be accomplished though the initiative of public-spirited laymen. Where change must be thrust from without upon an unwilling Bar, the public's least flattering picture of the lawyer seems confirmed. The lawyer concerned for the standing of his profession will therefor interest himself actively in the improvement of the law. In doing so he will not only help to maintain confidence in the Bar, but will have the satisfaction of meeting a responsibility inhering in the nature of his calling." *Professional Responsibility: Report of the Joint Conference*, 44 A.B.A. J. I 59, 1217 (1958).

3. *See* Stayton, CUM HONOR OFFICIUM, 19 Tex B.J. 76S, 766 (1956); *Professional Responsibility: Report of the Joint Conference*, 44 A.B.A. J. I 1159, 1162 (1958); and Paul, *The Lawyer as a Tax Adviser*, 25 ROCKY MT. L. REV. 412, 433-34 (1953).

4. "There are few great figures in the history of the Bar who have not concerned themselves with the reform and improvement of the law. The special obligation of the profession with respect to legal reform rests on considerations too obvious to require enumeration. Certainly it is the lawyer who has both the best chance to know when the law is working badly and the special competence to put it in order." *Professional Responsibility: Report of the Joint Conference*, 44 A.B.A. J. 1159, 1217 (1958).

5. "Rule 14 . . . . A member of the State Bar shall not communicate with, or appear before, a public officer, board, committee or body, in his professional capacity, without first disclosing that he is an attorney representing interests that may be affected by action of such officer, board, committee or body." CAL. BUS. AND PROF. § 6076 (West 1962).

6. *See* ABA CANONS OF PROFESSIONAL ETHICS, CANON 2 (1908).

"Lawyers are better able than laymen to appraise accurately the qualifications of candidates for judicial office. It is proper that they should make that appraisal known to the voters in a proper and dignified manner. A lawyer may with propriety endorse a candidate for judicial office and seek like endorsement from other lawyers. But the lawyer who endorses a judicial candidate or seeks that endorsement from other lawyer should

ABA Model Code of Professional Responsibility

be actuated by a sincere belief in the superior qualifications of the candidate for judicial service and not by personal or selfish motives; and a lawyer should not use or attempt to use the power or prestige of the judicial office to secure such endorsement. On the other hand, the lawyer whose endorsement is sought, if he believes the candidate lacks the essential qualifications for the office or believes the opposing candidate is better qualified, should have the courage and moral stamina to refuse the request for endorsement." *ABA Opinion* 189 (1938).

7. "[W]e are of the opinion that, whenever a candidate for judicial office merits the endorsement and support of lawyers, the lawyers may make financial contributions toward the campaign if its cost, when reasonably conducted, exceeds that which the candidate would be expected to bear personally." *ABA Opinion* 226 (1941).

8. *See* ABA CANONS OF PROFESSIONAL ETHICS, CANON 1 (1908).

9. "Citizens have a right under our constitutional system to criticize governmental officials and agencies. Courts are not, and should not be, immune to such criticism." Konigsberg v. State Bar of California, 353 U.S. 252, 269 (1957).

10. "[E]very lawyer, worthy of respect, realizes that public confidence in our courts is the cornerstone of our governmental structure, and will refrain from unjustified attack on the character of the judges, while recognizing the duty to denounce and expose a corrupt or dishonest judge." Kentucky State Bar Ass'n v. Lewis, 282 S.W. 2d 321, 326 (Ky. 1955).

"We should be the last to deny that Mr. Meeker has the right to uphold the honor of the profession and to expose without fear or favor corrupt or dishonest conduct in the profession, whether the conduct be that of a judge or not . . . . However, this Canon [29] does not permit one to make charges which are false and untrue and unfounded in fact. When one's fancy leads him to make false charges, attacking the character and integrity of others, he does so at his peril. He should not do so without adequate proof of his charges and he is certainly not authorized to make careless, untruthful and vile charges against his professional brethren." In re Meeker, 76 N.M. 354, 364-65, 414 P.2d 862, 869 (1966), *appeal dismissed,* 385 U.S. 449, 17 L. Ed. 2d 510, 87 S. Ct. 613 (1967).

11. "Opinions 16, 30, 34, 77, 118 and 134 relate to Canon 6, and pass on questions concerning the property of the conduct of an attorney who is a public officer, in representing private interests adverse to those of the public body which he represents. The principle applied in those opinions is that an attorney holding public office should avoid all conduct which might lead the layman to conclude that the attorney is utilizing his public position to further his professional success or personal interests." *ABA Opinion* 192 (1939).

"The next question is whether a lawyer-member of a legislative body may appear as counsel or co-counsel at hearings before a zoning board of appeals, or similar tribunal, created by the legislative group of which he is a member. We are of the opinion that he may practice before fact-finding officers, hearing bodies and commissioners, since under our views he may appear as counsel in the courts where his municipality is a party. Decisions made at such hearings are usually subject to administrative review by the courts upon the record there made. It would be inconsistent to say that a lawyer-member of a legislative body could not participate in a hearing at which the record is made, but could appear thereafter when the cause is heard by the court on administrative review. This is subject to an important exception. He should not appear as counsel where the matter is subject to review by the legislature body of which he is a member . . . . We are of the opinion that where a lawyer does so appear there would be conflict of interests between his duty as an advocate for his client on the one hand and the obligation to his governmental unit on the other hand." In re Becker, 16 Ill. 2d 488, 494-95, 158 N.E. 2d 753, 756-57 (1959).

Cf. ABA *Opinions* 186 (1938), 136 (1935), 118 (1934) and 77 (1932).

12. *Cf.* ABA CANONS OF PROFESSIONAL ETHICS, CANONS 1 and 2 (1908).

13. Amended, March 1974, House Informational Report No. 127.

CANON 9
A Lawyer Should Avoid
Even the Appearance of
Professional Impropriety

ABA Model
Code of
Professional
Responsibility

ETHICAL CONSIDERATIONS

EC 9-1   Continuation of the American concept that we are to be governed by rules of law requires that the people have faith that justice can be obtained through our legal system.[1] A lawyer should promote public confidence in our system and in the legal profession.[2]

EC 9-2   Public confidence in law and lawyers may be eroded by irresponsible or improper conduct of a lawyer. On occasion, ethical conduct of a lawyer may appear to laymen to be unethical. In order to avoid misunderstandings and hence to maintain confidence, a lawyer should fully and promptly inform his client of material developments in the matters being handled for the client. While a lawyer should guard against otherwise proper conduct that has a tendency to diminish public confidence in the legal system or in the legal profession, his duty to clients or to the public should never be subordinate merely because the full discharge of his obligation may be misunderstood or may tend to subject him or the legal profession to criticism. When explicit ethical guidance does not exist, a lawyer should determine his conduct by acting in a manner that promotes public confidence in the integrity and efficiency of the legal system and the legal profession.[3]

EC 9-3   After a lawyer leaves judicial office or other public employment, he should not accept employment in connection with any matter in which he had substantial responsibility prior to his leaving, since to accept employment would give the appearance of impropriety even if none exists.[4]

EC 9-4   Because the very essence of the legal system is to provide procedures by which matters can be presented in an impartial manner so that they may be decided solely upon the merits, any statement or suggestion by a lawyer that he can or would attempt to circumvent those procedures is detrimental to the legal system and tends to undermine public confidence in it.

EC 9-5   Separation of the funds of a client from those of his lawyer not only serves to protect the client but also avoids even the appearance of impropriety, and therefore commingling of such funds should be avoided.

EC 9-6   Every lawyer owes a solemn duty to uphold the integrity and honor of his profession; to encourage respect for the law and for the courts and the judges thereof; to observe the Code of Professional Responsibility; to act as a member of a learned profession, one dedicated to public service; to cooperate with his brother lawyers in supporting the organized bar through the devoting of his time, efforts, and financial support as his professional standing and ability reasonably permit; to conduct himself so as to reflect credit on the legal profession and to inspire the confidence, respect, and trust of his clients and of the public; and to strive to avoid not only professional impropriety but also the appearance of impropriety.[5]

EC 9-7   A lawyer has an obligation to the public to participate in collective efforts of the bar to reimburse persons who have lost money or property as a result of the misappropriation or defalcation of another lawyer, and contribution to a client's security fund is an acceptable method of meeting this obligation.[6]

DISCIPLINARY RULES

DR 9-101   Avoiding Even the Appearance of Impropriety.[7]

(A) A lawyer shall not accept private employment in a matter upon the merits of which he has acted in a judicial capacity.[8]

(B) A lawyer shall not accept private employment in a matter in which he had substantial responsibility while he was a public employee.[9]

(C) A lawyer shall not state or imply that he is able to influence improperly or upon irrelevant grounds any tribunal, legislative body,[10] or public official.

DR 9-102   Preserving Identity of Funds and Property of a Client.[11]

(A) All funds of clients paid to a lawyer or law firm, other than advances for costs and expenses, shall be deposited in one or more identifiable bank accounts maintained in the state in which the law office is situated and no funds belonging to the lawyer or law firm shall be deposited therein except as follows:

(1) Funds reasonably sufficient to pay bank charges may be deposited therein.

(2) Funds belonging in part to a client and in part presently or potentially to the lawyer or law firm must be deposited therein, but the portion belonging to the lawyer or law firm may be withdrawn when due unless the right of the lawyer or law firm to receive it is disputed by the client, in which event the disputed portion shall not be withdrawn until the dispute is finally resolved.

(B) A lawyer shall:

(1) Promptly notify a client of the receipt of his funds, securities, or other properties.

(2) Identify and label securities and properties of a client promptly upon receipt and place them in a safe deposit box or other place of safekeeping as soon as practicable.

ABA Model
Code of
Professional
Responsibility

(3) Maintain complete records of all funds, securities, and other properties of a client coming into the possession of the lawyer and render appropriate accounts to his client regarding them.

(4) Promptly pay or deliver to the client as requested by a client the funds, securities, or other properties in the possession of the lawyer which the client is entitled to receive.

NOTES

1. "Integrity is the very breath of justice. Confidence in our law, our courts, and in the administration of justice is our supreme interest. No practice must be permitted to prevail which invites towards the administration of justice a doubt or distrust of its integrity." Erwin M. Jennings Co. v DiGenova, 107 Conn. 491, 499, 141 A. 866, 868 (1928).

2. "A lawyer should never be reluctant or too proud to answer unjustified criticism of his profession, of himself, or of his brother lawyer. He should guard the reputation of his profession and of his brother as zealously as he guards his own." Rochelle & Payne, *The Struggle for Public Understanding*, 25 TEXAS B.J. 109, 162 (1962).

3. *See* ABA CANONS OF PROFESSIONAL ETHICS, CANON 29 (1908).

4. *See* ABA CANONS OF PROFESSIONAL ETHICS, CANON 36 (1908).

5. "As said in Opinion 49, of the Committee on Professional Ethics and Grievances of the American Bar Association, page 134: 'An attorney should not only avoid impropriety but should avoid the appearance of impropriety.'" State ex rel. Nebraska State Bar Ass'n v. Richards, 165 Neb. 80, 93, 84 N.W. 2d 136, 145 (1957).

"It would also be preferable that such contribution [to the campaign of a candidate for judicial office] be made to a campaign committee rather than to the candidate personally. In so doing, possible appearances of impropriety would be reduced to a minimum" *ABA Opinion* 226 (1941).

"The lawyer assumes high duties, and has imposed upon him grave responsibilities. He may be the means of much good or much mischief. Interests of vast magnitude are entrusted to him; confidence is reposed in him; life, liberty, character and property should be protected by him. He should guard, with jealous watchfulness his own reputation, as well as that of his profession." People ex rel. Cutler v Ford, 54 III. 520, 522 (1870), and also quoted in State Board of Law Examiners v. Sheldon, 43 Wyo. 522, 526, 7 P.2d 226, 227 (1932).

See ABA Opinion 150 (1936).

6. Amended, February 1980, House Informational Report No. 105.

7. *Cf.* MODEL CODE OF PROFESSIONAL RESPONSIBILITY, EC 5-6.

8. *See* ABA CANONS OF PROFESSIONAL ETHICS, CANON 36 (1908).

"It is the duty of the judge to rule on questions of law and evidence in misdemeanor cases and examinations in felony cases. That duty calls for impartial and uninfluenced judgement, regardless of the effect on those immediately involved or others who may, directly or indirectly, be affected. Discharge of that duty might be greatly interfered with if the judge, in another capacity, were permitted to hold himself out to employment by those who are to be, or who may be, brought to trial in felony cases, even though he did not conduct the examination. His private interests as a lawyer in building up his clientele, his duty as such zealously to espouse the cause of his private clients and to defend against charges of crime brought by law enforcement agencies of which he is a part, might prevent, or even destroy, that unbiased judicial judgement which is so essential in the administration of justice.

"In our opinion, acceptance of a judgeship with the duties of conducting misdemeanor trials, and examinations in felony cases to determine whether those accused should be bound over for trial in a higher court, ethically bars the judge from acting as attorney for the defendants upon such trial, whether they were examined by him or by some other judge. Such a practice would not only diminish public confidence in the administration of justice in both courts, but would produce serious conflict between the private interests of the judge as a lawyer, and of his clients, and his duties as a judge in adjudicating important phases of criminal processes in other cases. The public and private duties would be incompatible. The prestige of judicial office would be diverted to private benefit, and the judicial office would be demeaned thereby," *ABA Opinion* 242 (1942).

"A lawyer, who has previously occupied a judicial position or acted in a judicial capacity, should refrain from accepting employment in any matter involving the same facts as were involved in any specific question which he acted upon in a judicial capacity and, for the same reasons, should also refrain from accepting any employment which might reasonably appear to involve the same facts." *ABA Opinion* 49 (1931).

See *ABA Opinion* 110 (1934).

9. See *ABA Opinions* 135 (1935) and 134 (1935); *cf.* ABA CANONS OF PROFESSIONAL ETHICS, CANON 36 (1980) and *ABA Opinions* 39 (1931) and 26 (1930). *But see ABA Opinion* 37 (1931).

10. "[A statement by a governmental department or agency with regard to a lawyer resigning from its staff that includes a laudation of his legal ability] carries implications, probably not founded in fact, that the lawyer's acquaintance and previous relations with the personnel of the administrative agencies of the government place him in an advantageous position in practicing before such agencies. So to imply would not only represent what probably is untrue, but would be highly reprehensible." *ABA Opinion* 184 (1938).

11. See ABA CANONS OF PROFESSIONAL ETHICS, CANON 11 (1908).

"Rule 9. . . . A member of the State Bar shall not commingle the money or other property of a client with his own; and he shall promptly report to the client the receipt by him of all money and other property belonging to such client. Unless the client otherwise directs in writing, he shall promptly deposit his client's funds in a bank or trust company . . . in a bank account separate from his own account and clearly designated as 'Clients' Funds Account' or 'Trust Funds Account' or words of similar import. Unless the client otherwise directs in writing, securities of a client in bearer form shall be kept by the attorney in a safe deposit box at a bank or trust company . . . which safe deposit box shall be clearly designated as 'Clients'Account' or 'Trust Account' or words of similar import, and be separate from the attorney's own safe deposit box."CAL. BUS. AND PROF. § 6076 (West 1962).

"[C]ommingling is committed when a client's money is intermingled with that of his attorney and its separate identity lost so that it may be used for the attorney's personal expenses or subjected to claims of his creditors . . . . The rule against commingling was adopted to provide against the probability in some cases, the possibility in many cases, and the danger in all cases that such commingling will result in the loss of clients' money.'" Black v. State Bar, 57 Cal. 2d 219, 225-26, 368 P.2d 118, 122, 18 Cal. Rptr. 518, 522 (1962).

DEFINITIONS*

As used in the Disciplinary Rules of the Model Code of Professional Responsibility:

1. "Differing interests" include every interest that will adversely affect either the judgment or the loyalty of a lawyer to a client, whether it be a conflicting, inconsistent, diverse, or other interest.
2. "Law firm" includes a professional legal corporation.
3. "Person" includes a corporation, an association, a trust, a partnership, and any other organization or legal entity.

4. "Professional legal corporation" means a corporation, or an association treated as a corporation, authorized by law to practice law for profit.
5. "State" includes the District of Columbia, Puerto Rico, and other federal territories and possessions.
6. "Tribunal" includes all courts and all other adjudicatory bodies.
7. "A Bar association" includes a bar association of specialists as referred to in DR 2-105(A)(1) or (4).[1]
8. "Qualified legal assistance organization" means an office or organization of one of the four types listed in DR 2-103(D)(1)-(4), inclusive, that meets all the requirements thereof.[2]

NOTES

* "Confidence" and "secret" are defined in DR 4-101(A).
1. Amended, February 1975, House Informational Report No. 110.
2. *Id.*

INDEX

B

Bank accounts for clients' funds, EC 9-5, DR 9-102

Bank charges on clients' accounts, EC 9-5, DR 9-102

Bar applicant. *See* Admission to practice.

bar examiners, assisting, EC 1-2

Bar associations

disciplinary authority, assisting, EC 1-4, DR 1-103

educational activities, EC 6-2

lawyer referral service, DR 2-103(C)(1), DR 2-103(D)(3)

legal aid office, DR 2-103(D)(1)(d)

Barratry. *See* Advice by lawyer to secure legal services; Recommendation of professional employment.

Bequest by client to lawyer, EC 5-5

Best efforts. *See* Zeal

Bounds of law

difficulty of ascertaining, EC 7-2, 7-3, 7-4, 7-6

duty to observe, EC 7-1, DR 7-102

generally, Canon 7

Bribes. *See* Gifts to tribunal officer or employee by lawyer.

Building directory. *See* Advertising, building directory.

Business card. *See* Advertising, cards, professional.

C

Calling card. *See* Advertising, cards, professional.

Candidate. *See* Political activity.

Canons, purpose and function of, Preamble & Preliminary Statement

Cards. *See* Advertising, cards.

Change of office address. *See* Advertising, announcement of change of office address.

Change of association. *See* Advertising, announcement of change of association.

Change of firm name. *See* Advertising, announcement of change of firm name.

Character requirements, EC 1-3

Class action. *See* Advice by lawyer to secure legal services, parties to legal action.

Clients. *See also* Employment; Adverse effect on professional judgment of lawyer; Fee for legal services; Indigent parties, representation of; Unpopular party, representation of, appearance as witness for, EC 5-9, EC 5-10, DR 5-101(B), DR 5-102

attorney-client privilege, Canon 4

commingling of funds of, EC 9-5, DR 9-102

confidence of, Canon 4

counseling, EC 7-5, EC 7-7, EC 7-8, EC 7-9, EC 7-12, DR 7-102(A)(7), (B)(1), DR 7-109(B)

Clients' security fund, EC 9-7

Co-counsel. *See also* Association of counsel.

division of fee with, DR 2-107

inability to work with, DR 2-110(C)(3)

Commercial publicity. *See* Advertising, commercial publicity.

Commingling of funds, EC 9-5, DR 9-102

Communications with one of adverse interests, DR 7-104

judicial officers, EC 7-34, EC 7-35, EC 7-36, DR 7-110

jurors, EC 7-29, EC 7-31, DR 7-108

opposing party, DR 7-104

veniremen, EC 7-29, EC 7-31, DR 7-108

witnesses, EC 7-28, DR 7-109

ABA Model
Code of
Professional
Responsibility

ABA Model
Code of
Professional
Responsibility

ABA Model
Code of
Professional
Responsibility

ABA Model
Code of
Professional
Responsibility

labor required, DR 2-106(B)(1)

nature of employment, EC 2-18

question involved, difficulty and novelty of, DR 2-106(B)(1)

relationship with client, professional, EC 2-17, DR 2-106(B)(6)

reputation of lawyer, EC 2-18, DR 2-106(7)

responsibility assumed by lawyer, EC 2-18

results obtained, EC 2-18, DR 2-106(B)(4)

skill requisite to services, EC 2-18

time required, EC 2-18, DR 2-106(B)(1)

type of fee, fixed or contingent, EC 2-18, DR 2-106(B)(8)

division of, EC 2-22, DR 2-107, DR 3-102

establishment of fee, use of client's confidences and secrets, DR 4-101(C)(4)

excessive fee, EC 2-17, DR 2-106(A)

explanation of, EC 2-17, EC 2-18

illegal fee, prohibition against, DR 2-106(A)

persons able to pay reasonable fee, EC 2-17, EC 2-18

persons only able to pay a partial fee, EC 2-16

persons without means to pay a fee, EC 2-24, EC 2-25

reasonable fee, rationale against overcharging EC 2-17

refund of unearned portion to client, DR 2-110 (A)(3)

Felony. See Discipline of lawyer, grounds for, illegal conduct.

Firm name. See Name, use of, firm name.

Framework of law. See Bounds of law.

Frivolous position, avoiding, EC 7-4, DR 7-102 (A) (1)

Funds of client, protection of, EC 9-5, DR 9-102

Future conduct of client, counseling as to. See Clients, counseling.

G

"General Counsel" designation, DR 2-102(A)(4)

Gift to lawyer by client, EC 5-5

Gifts to tribunal officer or employee by lawyer, DR 7-110(A)

Government legal agencies, working with, DR 2-103(C)(2), DR 2-103 (D)(1)(C)

Grievance committee. See Bar associations, disciplinary authority, assisting.

Guaranteeing payment of client's cost and expenses, EC 5-8, DR 5-103(B)

H

Harassment, duty to avoid litigation, involving, EC 2-30, DR 2-109(A)(1), DR 7-102(A)(1)

as limiting practice, EC 2-8, EC 2-14, DR 2-101(B)(2), DR 2-105

as partnership, EC 2-13, DR 2-102(C)

as specialist, EC 2-8, EC 2-14, DR 2-101(B)(2), DR 2-105

I

Identity of client, duty to reveal, EC 7-16, EC 8-5

Illegal conduct, as cause for discipline, EC 1-5, DR 1-102(A)(3), DR 7-102(A)(7)

Impartiality of tribunal, aiding in the, Canon 7

Instability, mental or emotional of bar applicant, EC 1-6, EC 1-6, DR 2-110(B)(3), DR 2-110(C)(4)

recognition of rehabilitation, EC 1-6

Improper influences, gift or loan to judicial officer, EC 7-34, DR 7-110(A)

on judgment of lawyer. *See* Adverse effect on professional judgment of lawyer.

Improvement of legal system, EC 8-1, EC 8-2, EC 8-9

Incompetence, mental. *See* Instability, mental or emotional; Mental competence of client.

Incompetence, professional. *See* Competence, professional.

Independent professional judgment, duty to preserve, Canon 5

Indigent parties

provisions of legal services to, EC 2-24, EC 2-25

representation of, EC 2-25

Integrity of legal profession, maintaining

Preamble, EC 1-1, EC 1-4, DR 1-101, EC 8-7

Intent of client, as factor in giving advice, EC 7-5, EC 7-6, DR 7-102

Interests of lawyer. *See* Adverse effect on professional judgment of lawyer, interests of lawyer.

Interests of other client. *See* Adverse effect on professional judgment of lawyer, interests of other clients.

Interests of third person. *See* Adverse effect on professional judgment of lawyer, desires of third persons.

Intermediary, prohibition against use of, EC 5-21, EC 5-23, EC 5-24, DR 5-107(A), (B)

Interview,

with opposing party, DR 7-104

with news media EC-7-33, DR 7-107

with witness, EC 7-28, DR 7-109

Investigation expenses, advancing or guaranteeing payment, EC 5-8, DR 5-103(B)

J

Judges,

false statements concerning DR 8-102

improper influences on gifts to EC 7-34, DR 7-110(A)

private communication with, EC 7-39, DR 7-110(B)

misconduct toward,

criticisms of, EC 8-6

disobedience of orders, EC 7-36, DR 7-106(A)

false statement regarding, DR 8-102

name in partnership, use of, EC 2-12, DR 2-102(B)

retirement from bench, EC 9-3

selection of, EC 8-6

Judgment of lawyer. *See* Adverse effect on professional judgment of lawyer.

Jury,

arguments before, EC 7-25, DR 7-102(A)(4), (5), (6)

investigation of members EC 7-30, DR 7-108(E)

misconduct of, duty to reveal, EC 7-32, DR 7-108(G)

questioning members of after their dismissal, EC 7-29, DR 7-108(D)

K

Knowledge of intended crime, revealing, DR 4-101(C)(3)

L

Law firm. *See* Partnership.

Law office. *See* Partnership

Law School, working with legal aid office or public defender office sponsored by, DR 2-103(D)(1)(a)

Lawyer-client privilege. *See* Attorney-client privilege.

ABA Model Code of Professional Responsibility

ABA Model Code of Professional Responsibility

Office building directory. *See* advertising, building directory.

Office sign, DR 2-102(A)(3)

Opposing counsel, EC 5-9, EC 7-20, EC 7-23, EC 735, EC 7-37, EC 7-38, DR 7104, DR 7-106(C)(5), DR 7110(B)(2), (3)

Opposing party, communications with, EC 7-18, DR 7-104

P

Partnership,

advertising, *See* Advertising conflicts of interest DR 5-105

deceased member,

payments to estate of, EC 3-8

use of name, EC 2-11, DR 2-102(A)(4), (B)

dissolved, use of name of, EC 2-11, EC 2-12, EC 2-13, DR 2-102(A)(4), (B), (C)

holding out as, falsely, EC 2-13, DR 2-102(B), (C)

members licensed in different jurisdictions, DR 2-102(D)

name, EC 2-11, EC 2-12, DR 2-102(B)

nonexistent, holding out falsely, EC 2-13, DR 2-102(B), (C)

non-lawyer, with, EC 3-8, DR 3-103

professional corporation, with, DR 2-102(C)

recommending professional employment of, EC 2-9

Patent practitioner, EC 2-14, DR 2-105-105(A)(1)

Payment to obtain recommendation or employment, prohibition against, EC 2-8, DR 2-103(B), (D)

Pending litigation, discussion of in media, EC 7-33, DR 7-107

Perjury, EC 7-5, EC 7-6, EC 7-26, EC 728, DR 7-102(A)(4), (6), (7), DR 7-102(B)

Personal interests of lawyer. *See* Adverse effect on professional judgment of lawyer, interests of lawyer.

Personal opinion of client's cause, EC 2-27, EC 2-28, EC 2-29, EC 7-24, DR 7-106(C)(4)

Political activity, EC 8-8, DR 8-101, DR 8-103

Political considerations in selection of judges, EC 8-6, DR 8-103

Potentially differing interests. *See* Adverse effect on professional judgment of lawyer.

Practice of law, unauthorized, Canon 3

Prejudice to right of client, duty to avoid, EC 2-32, DR 2-110(A)(2), (C)(3), (C)(4), DR 7-101(A)(3)

Preservation of confidences of client, Canon 4

Preservation of secrets of client, Canon 4

Pressure on lawyer by third person. *See* Adverse effect on professional judgment of lawyer.

Privilege, attorney-client. *See* Attorney-client privilege.

Procedures, duty to help improve, EC 8-1, EC 8-2, EC 8-9

Professional card of lawyer. *See* Advertising, cards, professional.

Professional impropriety, avoiding appearance of, EC 5-1, Canon 9

Professional judgment, duty to protect independence of, Canon 5

Professional legal corporations, Definitions (2), (4), DR 2102(B), EC 5-24, DR 5-107(C)

Professional notices. *See* Advertising.

Professional status, responsibility not to mislead concerning, EC 2-11, EC 2-12, EC 2-14, DR 2-102(B), (C), (D)

ABA Model Code of Professional Responsibility

ABA Model Code of Professional Responsibility

S

Sanction for violating disciplinary rules, Preliminary statement

Secrets of client, Canon 4

Selection of lawyer, EC 2-6, EC 2-7, EC 2-8, EC 2-9, EC 2-11, EC 2-14, EC 2-15, DR 2-101

Selection of judges, duty of lawyers, EC 8-6, DR 8-102(A)

Self interest of lawyer. *See* Adverse effect on professional judgment of lawyer, interests of lawyer.

Self-representation, privilege of, EC 3-7

Settlement agreement, DR 5-106

Solicitation of business.
See Advertising; Recommendation of professional employment.

Specialist, holding out as, EC 2-14, DR 2-105

Specialization,

admiralty, EC 2-14,

holding out as having, EC 2-14, DR 2-105

patents, EC 2-14, DR 2-105(A)(1)

trademark, EC 2-14, DR 2-105(A)(1)

Speeches to lay groups, EC 2-2, EC 2-5

State of mind of client, effect of in advising him, EC 7-11, EC 7-12

State's attorney. *See* Prosecuting attorney.

"Stirring up litigation."
See Advertising; Advice by lawyer to secure legal services; Recommendation of professional employment.

Stockholders of corporation, corporate counsel's allegiance to, EC 5-18

Suit to harass another, duty to avoid, EC 2-30, DR 2-109(A)(1), EC 710, EC 7-14, DR 7-102(A)(1)

Suit to maliciously harm another duty, to avoid, EC 2-30, DR 2-109(A)(1), EC 710, EC 7-14, DR 7-102(A)(1)

Suggested fee schedule. *See* Fee for legal services, determination of minimum fee schedule.

Suggestion of need for legal services. *See* Advice by lawyer to secure legal services.

Suppression of evidence, EC 7-27, DR 7-102(A)(2), DR 7-103(B), DR 7-106(C)(7)

T

Technical and professional licenses, DR 2-101(B)(12), DR 2-102(E)

Termination of employment.
See Confidences of client; Employment, withdrawal from.

Third persons, desires of.
See adverse effect on professional judgment of lawyer, desire of third persons.

Threatening criminal process, EC 7-21, DR 7-105(A)

Trademark practitioner, EC 2-14, DR 2-105(A)(1)

Trade name. *See* Name, use of trade name.

Trial publicity, EC 7-33, DR 7-107

Trial tactics, Canon 7

Tribunal, representation of client before, Canon 7

Trustee, client naming lawyer as, EC 5-6

U

Unauthorized practice of law.
See also Division of legal fees; Partnership, non-lawyer, with.
aiding a layman in the, prohibited, EC 3-8, DR 3-101(A)

distinguished from delegation of tasks to subprofessionals, EC 3-5, EC 3-6, DR 3-102(A)(3)

ABA Model
Code of
Professional
Responsibility

ABA Model Code of Judicial Conduct

*The Model Code of Judicial Conduct was adopted by the
House of Delegates of the American Bar Association on
August 7, 1990 and amended on August 6, 1997, August 10, 1999,
August 12, 2003, February 12, 2007, and August 10, 2010.*

ABA
Model Code
of Judicial
Conduct

Contents

A JUDGE SHALL UPHOLD AND PROMOTE THE INDEPENDENCE,
INTEGRITY, AND IMPARTIALITY OF THE JUDICIARY, AND SHALL
AVOID IMPROPRIETY AND THE APPEARANCE OF IMPROPRIETY.

A JUDGE SHALL PERFORM THE DUTIES OF JUDICIAL
OFFICE IMPARTIALLY, COMPETENTLY, AND DILIGENTLY.

Canon 3 375

A JUDGE SHALL CONDUCT THE JUDGE'S PERSONAL AND EXTRAJUDICIAL ACTIVITIES TO MINIMIZE THE RISK OF CONFLICT WITH THE OBLIGATIONS OF JUDICIAL OFFICE.

Rule

Acknowledgments

The publication by the American Bar Association Center for Professional Responsibility of the 2007 Model Code of Judicial Conduct was the culmination of a multi-year national effort to conduct a comprehensive review of the Model Code in light of the dynamics of modern law practice and changes in the role of the judiciary.

The Center expresses its gratitude to Mark I. Harrison, under whose distinguished leadership the Commission completed its study with excellence and professionalism. The abiding commitment, good will and tireless efforts of the Commission members, advisors, counsel and staff have been exceptional. The Association is especially indebted to its reporters, Professor Charles G. Geyh and Professor Emeritus W. William Hodes, whose outstanding efforts have advanced the cause of professional responsibility law.

Special gratitude is expressed to The Joyce Foundation of Chicago, Illinois, whose generous funding made possible this entire endeavor. The unwavering support of Joyce Foundation Vice President Lawrence Hansen is greatly appreciated.

The Center for Professional Responsibility also thanks the West Publishing Corporation for its generous gift of the West Professional Responsibility Law Library, the resource for much of the research reflected in this publication.

The American Bar Association is proud of the work of the Joint Commission to Evaluate the Model Code of Judicial Conduct and trusts that the judiciary, the legal profession and the public will be enriched by their efforts.

Jeanne P. Gray, Director
Center for Professional Responsibility

Preface

In 1924, the American Bar Association adopted the Canons of Judicial Ethics that, according to Chief Justice William Howard Taft, who chaired the ABA Committee on Judicial Ethics, were intended to be a "guide and reminder to the judiciary."[1] The 1924 Canons of Judicial Ethics consisted of 36 provisions that included both generalized, hortatory admonitions and specific rules of proscribed conduct. The 1924 Canons were not intended to be a basis for disciplinary action. Many states, however, adopted this "guide" as a set of substantive rules, giving the Canons in those states the force of law with the added persuasion of sanctions for violations.[2]

Answering criticism that the 1924 Canons engaged in "moral posturing" that was more "hortatory than helpful in providing firm guidance for the solution of difficult questions,"[3] the ABA appointed a Special Committee on Standards of Judicial Conduct in 1969 to develop new ethics rules for judges. California Supreme Court Justice Roger J. Traynor chaired the Special Committee. After three years of work by the Special Committee, the Code of Judicial Conduct was adopted by unanimous vote of the ABA House of Delegates on August 16, 1972.[4] The 1972 Code was designed to be enforceable and was intended to preserve the integrity and independence of the judiciary.[5]

In 1986, the American Bar Association Standing Committee on Ethics and Professional Responsibility, with jurisdiction over the Code, conducted a survey that led to the conclusion that, in general, the Code was serving its purposes well, but that a comprehensive review of the Code was desirable. That review was conducted from 1987 to 1990 by the Standing Committee on Ethics and Professional Responsibility and its Judicial Code Subcommittee composed of several members and former members of the Ethics Committee and several members of the judiciary. This national effort was funded by the Josephson Institute for the Advancement of Ethics, the State Justice Institute, and the American Bar Association.

In the revision process, the Association sought and considered the views of members of the judiciary, the bar and the general public. The Committee

---

1. *See* Randall T. Shepard, *Campaign Speech: Restraint and Liberty in Judicial Ethics*, 9 GEO. J. LEGAL ETHICS 1059, 1065 n. 26 (1996) (citing the *Final Report and Proposed Canons of Judicial Ethics*, 9 A.B.A.J. 449, 449 (1923)).

2. *Id.* (citing Robert Martineau, *Enforcement of the Code of Judicial Conduct*, 1972 UTAH L. REV. 410, 410).

3. Robert McKay, *Judges, the Code of Judicial Conduct, and Nonjudicial Activities*, 1972 UTAH L. REV. 391, 391.

4. American Bar Association, *Report of the Special Committee on Standards of Judicial Conduct*, 96 REP. OF THE A.B.A. 733-34 (1971).

5. *See* E. WAYNE THODE, REPORTER'S NOTES TO THE CODE OF JUDICIAL CONDUCT (1973).

was aware that the 1972 Canons, apart from their subsections, were used widely as a basis for discipline. Therefore, the Committee declined to replace the black letter language with descriptive headings and determined that the Code, consisting of statements of norms denominated Canons, specific Sections, and explanatory Commentary, stated the appropriate ethical obligations of judges.[6]

On August 7, 1990, the House of Delegates of the American Bar Association adopted the Model Code of Judicial Conduct. In the 1990 Code, a Preamble and a Terminology section were added, and an Application section followed the Canons. The 1990 Code was amended three times: on August 6, 1997; August 10, 1999; and August 12, 2003.

In September 2003, with a grant from The Joyce Foundation of Chicago, Illinois, the American Bar Association announced the appointment of the Joint Commission to Evaluate the Model Code of Judicial Conduct under the auspices of the ABA Standing Committee on Ethics and Professional Responsibility and the ABA Standing Committee on Judicial Independence. The mandate of the Commission was to review the 1990 Code and to recommend revisions for possible adoption. The eleven-member Commission was composed of judges, experts in the field of judicial and legal ethics and a public member and was supported by two reporters, ten advisors and counsel from the American Bar Association.

Over the course of three and one half years, the Commission conducted a comprehensive examination of the standards for the ethical conduct of judges and judicial candidates that promote the independence, integrity and impartiality of the judiciary. This examination was prompted, in part, by the collective experience of judges and judicial regulators who had worked with the 1990 Code for more than a decade and by the emergence of new types of courts and courts processes, the increasing frequency of pro se representation, and the utilization of diverse methods in the judicial selection process. This national effort culminated in the adoption of the revised Model Code of Judicial Conduct by the ABA House of Delegates on February 12, 2007.

The 2007 Code proposed both format and substantive changes to the 1990 Code. Following a format similar to the ABA Model Rules of Professional Conduct, the 2007 Code preserved the Canons, which state overarching principles of judicial conduct, followed by enforceable black letter Rules, and Comments that provide both aspirational statements and guidance in interpreting and applying the Rules. The four Canons and their numbered Rules and Comments were reorganized to provide topics under a functional arrangement. Canon 1 addresses the paramount obligations of judges to

---

6. *See* LISA L. MILORD, THE DEVELOPMENT OF THE ABA JUDICIAL CODE at 8 (1992).

uphold the independence, integrity and impartiality of the judiciary and to avoid impropriety and its appearance; Canon 2 addresses solely the judge's professional duties as a judge; Canon 3 addresses extrajudicial and personal conduct; and Canon 4 addresses the political conduct of judges and judicial candidates. Also included are four sections that precede the Canons: a Preamble, which states the objectives of the Model Code; a new Scope section, which describes the manner in which the Canons and their Rules and Comments are to be interpreted, used for guidance, and enforced; a Terminology section, which provides definitional guidance, and an Application section, which establishes when the various Rules apply to a judge or judicial candidate.

This publication presents several informative appendixes that are not part of the Code. Appendix A contains Correlation Tables to the *ABA Model Code of Judicial Conduct* that compare the provisions of the 2007 Code with those of the predecessor 1990 Code. Appendix B reproduces the August 2010 Report to the House of Delegates that amended the Application section of the Code. Appendix C provides information on establishing judicial ethics advisory committees. Appendix D explains the jurisdiction and procedures of the ABA Standing Committee on Ethics and Professional Responsibility. Appendix E contains the most recent ABA judicial ethics opinion. A separate publication, the *Reporter's Notes to the Model Code of Judicial Conduct*, by Charles G. Geyh and W. William Hodes, provides detailed information regarding the drafting of the 2007 Code.

The American Bar Association continues to pursue its goal of assuring the highest standards of professional competence and ethical conduct. The Standing Committee on Ethics and Professional Responsibility, charged with interpreting the professional standards of the Association and recommending appropriate amendments and clarifications, issues opinions interpreting the Model Rules of Professional Conduct and the Model Code of Judicial Conduct. The opinions of the Committee are published by the American Bar Association.

JOINT COMMISSION TO EVALUATE THE MODEL CODE OF JUDICIAL CONDUCT
Chair's Introduction

On September 23, 2003, American Bar Association President Dennis W. Archer, Jr., announced the appointment of a Joint Commission to Evaluate the Model Code of Judicial Conduct under the auspices of the Standing Committee on Ethics and Professional Responsibility and the Standing Committee on Judicial Independence. The last Model Code revision occurred in 1990 and, although specific provisions of the Model Code were amended in the intervening years, there was a need for a comprehensive evaluation and revision in light of societal changes, as well as changes in the role of judges. The Model Code revision project was funded almost entirely by the Joyce Foundation, which provides resources for countless projects that contribute to the betterment of our society.

The unanimous approval of the revised Model Code of Judicial Conduct by the ABA House of Delegates on February 12, 2007 culminated a three and one-half year effort by a group comprised of distinguished judges, lawyers, academicians and a public member. The work of the Joint Commission was significantly enhanced by the active participation of an advisory group comprised of representatives of the organizations principally involved in the work of the judiciary and in the enforcement of the rules governing judicial conduct, and the invaluable assistance of two able Reporters and Center for Professional Responsibility counsel and professional staff.

The revised Model Code is the product of a transparent process during which the Joint Commission held nine public hearings, met in-person twenty times, had more than thirty teleconferences, and regularly posted its work on its website with requests for feedback and comment. Although the Commission set out to preserve as much of the 1990 Code as it could, consistent with the process of overall evaluation, it carefully considered all submitted suggestions and criticism and incorporated many of the suggested changes into the revised Model Code that was adopted by the House of Delegates.

At the time of its adoption, the revised Model Code had the support of the Conference of Chief Justices and the co-sponsorship of the Judicial Division of the ABA, the ABA Standing Committees on Ethics and Professional Responsibility; Professional Discipline and on Judicial Independence, the ABA Sections of Litigation and Dispute Resolution, and the American Judicature Society. In light of this significant support from the judiciary and the profession, the Joint Commission expects that the highest court in each state will adopt the revised Model Code, thereby improving and clarifying the standards of conduct for the judiciary throughout the nation and creating national uniformity.

An independent, impartial judiciary is indispensable to our system of justice. Equally important is the confidence of the public in the independence, integrity and impartiality of our judiciary as an institution. In fulfilling its mission, the Joint Commission took great care to adhere to those principles as it worked to provide sound, clear, and reasoned guidance to judges faced with difficult issues involving their conduct. The end result is a Model Code that should serve both judges and the public well for many years to come.

Mark I. Harrison
April 2007

ABA MODEL CODE OF JUDICIAL CONDUCT

Preamble

[1] An independent, fair and impartial judiciary is indispensable to our system of justice. The United States legal system is based upon the principle that an independent, impartial, and competent judiciary, composed of men and women of integrity, will interpret and apply the law that governs our society. Thus, the judiciary plays a central role in preserving the principles of justice and the rule of law. Inherent in all the Rules contained in this Code are the precepts that judges, individually and collectively, must respect and honor the judicial office as a public trust and strive to maintain and enhance confidence in the legal system.

[2] Judges should maintain the dignity of judicial office at all times, and avoid both impropriety and the appearance of impropriety in their professional and personal lives. They should aspire at all times to conduct that ensures the greatest possible public confidence in their independence, impartiality, integrity, and competence.

[3] The Model Code of Judicial Conduct establishes standards for the ethical conduct of judges and judicial candidates. It is not intended as an exhaustive guide for the conduct of judges and judicial candidates, who are governed in their judicial and personal conduct by general ethical standards as well as by the Code. The Code is intended, however, to provide guidance and assist judges in maintaining the highest standards of judicial and personal conduct, and to provide a basis for regulating their conduct through disciplinary agencies.

Scope

[1] The Model Code of Judicial Conduct consists of four Canons, numbered Rules under each Canon, and Comments that generally follow and explain each Rule. Scope and Terminology sections provide additional guidance in interpreting and applying the Code. An Application section establishes when the various Rules apply to a judge or judicial candidate.

[2] The Canons state overarching principles of judicial ethics that all judges must observe. Although a judge may be disciplined only for violating a Rule, the Canons provide important guidance in interpreting the Rules. Where a Rule contains a permissive term, such as "may" or "should," the conduct being addressed is committed to the personal and professional discretion of the judge or candidate in question, and no disciplinary action should be taken for action or inaction within the bounds of such discretion.

[3] The Comments that accompany the Rules serve two functions. First, they provide guidance regarding the purpose, meaning, and proper application of the Rules. They contain explanatory material and, in some instances, provide examples of permitted or prohibited conduct. Comments neither add to nor subtract from the binding obligations set forth in the Rules. Therefore, when a Comment contains the term "must," it does not mean that the Comment itself is binding or enforceable; it signifies that the Rule in question, properly understood, is obligatory as to the conduct at issue.

[4] Second, the Comments identify aspirational goals for judges. To implement fully the principles of this Code as articulated in the Canons, judges should strive to exceed the standards of conduct established by the Rules, holding themselves to the highest ethical standards and seeking to achieve those aspirational goals, thereby enhancing the dignity of the judicial office.

[5] The Rules of the Model Code of Judicial Conduct are rules of reason that should be applied consistent with constitutional requirements, statutes, other court rules, and decisional law, and with due regard for all relevant circumstances. The Rules should not be interpreted to impinge upon the essential independence of judges in making judicial decisions.

[6] Although the black letter of the Rules is binding and enforceable, it is not contemplated that every transgression will result in the imposition of discipline. Whether discipline should be imposed should be determined through a reasonable and reasoned application of the Rules, and should depend upon factors such as the seriousness of the transgression, the facts and circumstances that existed at the time of the transgression, the extent of any pattern of improper activity, whether there have been previous violations, and the effect of the improper activity upon the judicial system or others.

[7] The Code is not designed or intended as a basis for civil or criminal liability. Neither is it intended to be the basis for litigants to seek collateral remedies against each other or to obtain tactical advantages in proceedings before a court.

Terminology

The first time any term listed below is used in a Rule in its defined sense, it is followed by an asterisk (*).

"**Aggregate**," in relation to contributions for a candidate, means not only contributions in cash or in kind made directly to a candidate's campaign committee, but also all contributions made indirectly with the understanding that they will be used to support the election of a candidate or to oppose the election of the candidate's opponent. See Rules 2.11 and 4.4.

"**Appropriate authority**" means the authority having responsibility for initiation of disciplinary process in connection with the violation to be reported. See Rules 2.14 and 2.15.

"**Contribution**" means both financial and in-kind contributions, such as goods, professional or volunteer services, advertising, and other types of assistance, which, if obtained by the recipient otherwise, would require a financial expenditure. See Rules 2.11, 2.13, 3.7, 4.1, and 4.4.

"**De minimis**," in the context of interests pertaining to disqualification of a judge, means an insignificant interest that could not raise a reasonable question regarding the judge's impartiality. See Rule 2.11.

"**Domestic partner**" means a person with whom another person maintains a household and an intimate relationship, other than a person to whom he or she is legally married. See Rules 2.11, 2.13, 3.13, and 3.14.

"**Economic interest**" means ownership of more than a de minimis legal or equitable interest. Except for situations in which the judge participates in the management of such a legal or equitable interest, or the interest could be substantially affected by the outcome of a proceeding before a judge, it does not include:

    (1) an interest in the individual holdings within a mutual or common investment fund;

    (2) an interest in securities held by an educational, religious, charitable, fraternal, or civic organization in which the judge or the judge's spouse, domestic partner, parent, or child serves as a director, an officer, an advisor, or other participant;

    (3) a deposit in a financial institution or deposits or proprietary interests the judge may maintain as a member of a mutual savings association or credit union, or similar proprietary interests; or

    (4) an interest in the issuer of government securities held by the judge. See Rules 1.3 and 2.11.

"**Fiduciary**" includes relationships such as executor, administrator, trustee, or guardian. See Rules 2.11, 3.2, and 3.8.

ABA
Model Code
of Judicial
Conduct

"Impartial," "impartiality," and **"impartially"** mean absence of bias or prejudice in favor of, or against, particular parties or classes of parties, as well as maintenance of an open mind in considering issues that may come before a judge. See Canons 1, 2, and 4, and Rules 1.2, 2.2, 2.10, 2.11, 2.13, 3.1, 3.12, 3.13, 4.1, and 4.2.

"Impending matter" is a matter that is imminent or expected to occur in the near future. See Rules 2.9, 2.10, 3.13, and 4.1.

"Impropriety" includes conduct that violates the law, court rules, or provisions of this Code, and conduct that undermines a judge's independence, integrity, or impartiality. See Canon 1 and Rule 1.2.

"Independence" means a judge's freedom from influence or controls other than those established by law. See Canons 1 and 4, and Rules 1.2, 3.1, 3.12, 3.13, and 4.2.

"Integrity" means probity, fairness, honesty, uprightness, and soundness of character. See Canons 1 and 4 and Rules 1.2, 3.1, 3.12, 3.13, and 4.2.

"Judicial candidate" means any person, including a sitting judge, who is seeking selection for or retention in judicial office by election or appointment. A person becomes a candidate for judicial office as soon as he or she makes a public announcement of candidacy, declares or files as a candidate with the election or appointment authority, authorizes or, where permitted, engages in solicitation or acceptance of contributions or support, or is nominated for election or appointment to office. See Rules 2.11, 4.1, 4.2, and 4.4.

"Knowingly," "knowledge," "known," and **"knows"** mean actual knowledge of the fact in question. A person's knowledge may be inferred from circumstances. See Rules 2.11, 2.13, 2.15, 2.16, 3.6, and 4.1.

"Law" encompasses court rules as well as statutes, constitutional provisions, and decisional law. See Rules 1.1, 2.1, 2.2, 2.6, 2.7, 2.9, 3.1, 3.4, 3.9, 3.12, 3.13, 3.14, 3.15, 4.1, 4.2, 4.4, and 4.5.

"Member of the candidate's family" means a spouse, domestic partner, child, grandchild, parent, grandparent, or other relative or person with whom the candidate maintains a close familial relationship.

"Member of the judge's family" means a spouse, domestic partner, child, grandchild, parent, grandparent, or other relative or person with whom the judge maintains a close familial relationship. See Rules 3.7, 3.8, 3.10, and 3.11.

"Member of a judge's family residing in the judge's household" means any relative of a judge by blood or marriage, or a person treated by a judge as a member of the judge's family, who resides in the judge's household. See Rules 2.11 and 3.13.

"Nonpublic information" means information that is not available to the public. Nonpublic information may include, but is not limited to, information that is sealed by statute or court order or impounded or communicated in camera, and information offered in grand jury proceedings, presentencing reports, dependency cases, or psychiatric reports. See Rule 3.5.

"Pending matter" is a matter that has commenced. A matter continues to be pending through any appellate process until final disposition. See Rules 2.9, 2.10, 3.13, and 4.1.

"Personally solicit" means a direct request made by a judge or a judicial candidate for financial support or in-kind services, whether made by letter, telephone, or any other means of communication. See Rules 3.7, and 4.1.

"Political organization" means a political party or other group sponsored by or affiliated with a political party or candidate, the principal purpose of which is to further the election or appointment of candidates for political office. For purposes of this Code, the term does not include a judicial candidate's campaign committee created as authorized by Rule 4.4. See Rules 4.1 and 4.2.

"Public election" includes primary and general elections, partisan elections, nonpartisan elections, and retention elections. See Rules 4.2 and 4.4.

"Third degree of relationship" includes the following persons: great-grandparent, grandparent, parent, uncle, aunt, brother, sister, child, grandchild, great-grandchild, nephew, and niece. See Rule 2.11.

ABA
Model Code
of Judicial
Conduct

ABA
Model Code
of Judicial
Conduct

Application

The Application section establishes when the various Rules apply to a judge or judicial candidate.

I. Applicability of This Code

(A) The provisions of the Code apply to all full-time judges. Parts II through V of this section identify provisions that apply to four categories of part-time judges only while they are serving as judges, and provisions that do not apply to part-time judges at any time. All other Rules are therefore applicable to part-time judges at all times. The four categories of judicial service in other than a full-time capacity are necessarily defined in general terms because of the widely varying forms of judicial service. Canon 4 applies to judicial candidates.

(B) A judge, within the meaning of this Code, is anyone who is authorized to perform judicial functions, including an officer such as a justice of the peace, magistrate, court commissioner, special master, referee, or member of the administrative law judiciary.[1]

Comment

[1] The Rules in this Code have been formulated to address the ethical obligations of any person who serves a judicial function, and are premised upon the supposition that a uniform system of ethical principles should apply to all those authorized to perform judicial functions.

[2] The determination of which category and, accordingly, which specific Rules apply to an individual judicial officer, depends upon the facts of the particular judicial service.

[3] In recent years many jurisdictions have created what are often called "problem solving" courts, in which judges are authorized by court rules to act in nontraditional ways. For example, judges presiding in drug courts and monitoring the progress of participants in those courts' programs may be authorized and even encouraged to communicate directly with social workers,

---

1. Each jurisdiction should consider the characteristics of particular positions within the administrative law judiciary in adopting, adapting, applying, and enforcing the Code for the administrative law judiciary. *See, e.g.*, Model Code of Judicial Conduct for Federal Administrative Law Judges (1989) and Model Code of Judicial Conduct for State Administrative Law Judges (1995). Both Model Codes are endorsed by the ABA National Conference of Administrative Law Judiciary.

probation officers, and others outside the context of their usual judicial role as independent decision makers on issues of fact and law. When local rules specifically authorize conduct not otherwise permitted under these Rules, they take precedence over the provisions set forth in the Code. Nevertheless, judges serving on "problem solving" courts shall comply with this Code except to the extent local rules provide and permit otherwise.

II. Retired Judge Subject to Recall

A retired judge subject to recall for service, who by law is not permitted to practice law, is not required to comply:

(A) with Rule 3.9 (Service as Arbitrator or Mediator), except while serving as a judge.

(B) at any time with Rule 3.8(A) (Appointments to Fiduciary Positions).

Comment

[1] For the purposes of this section, as long as a retired judge is subject to being recalled for service, the judge is considered to "perform judicial functions."

III. Continuing Part-Time Judge

A judge who serves repeatedly on a part-time basis by election or under a continuing appointment, including a retired judge subject to recall who is permitted to practice law ("continuing part-time judge"),

(A) is not required to comply:

(1) with Rule 4.1 (Political and Campaign Activities of Judges and Judicial Candidates in General) (A)(1) through (7), except while serving as a judge; or

(2) at any time with Rules 3.4 (Appointments to Governmental Positions), 3.8(A) (Appointments to Fiduciary Positions), 3.9 (Service as Arbitrator or Mediator), 3.10 (Practice of Law), and 3.11(B) (Financial, Business, or Remunerative Activities); and

(B) shall not practice law in the court on which the judge serves or in any court subject to the appellate jurisdiction of the court on which the judge serves, and shall not act as a lawyer in a proceeding in which the judge has served as a judge or in any other proceeding related thereto.

Comment

[1] When a person who has been a continuing part-time judge is no longer a continuing part-time judge, including a retired judge no longer subject

to recall, that person may act as a lawyer in a proceeding in which he or she has served as a judge or in any other proceeding related thereto only with the informed consent of all parties, and pursuant to any applicable Model Rules of Professional Conduct. An adopting jurisdiction should substitute a reference to its applicable rule.

IV. Periodic Part-Time Judge

A periodic part-time judge who serves or expects to serve repeatedly on a part-time basis, but under a separate appointment for each limited period of service or for each matter,

    (A) is not required to comply:

        (1) with Rule 4.1 (Political and Campaign Activities of Judges and Judicial Candidates in General) (A)(1) through (7), except while serving as a judge; or

        (2) at any time with Rules 3.4 (Appointments to Governmental Positions), 3.8(A) (Appointments to Fiduciary Positions), 3.9 (Service as Arbitrator or Mediator), 3.10 (Practice of Law), and 3.11(B) (Financial, Business, or Remunerative Activities); and

    (B) shall not practice law in the court on which the judge serves or in any court subject to the appellate jurisdiction of the court on which the judge serves, and shall not act as a lawyer in a proceeding in which the judge has served as a judge or in any other proceeding related thereto.

V. Pro Tempore Part-Time Judge

A pro tempore part-time judge who serves or expects to serve once or only sporadically on a part-time basis under a separate appointment for each period of service or for each case heard is not required to comply:

    (A) except while serving as a judge, with Rules 2.4 (External Influences on Judicial Conduct), 3.2 (Appearances before Governmental Bodies and Consultation with Government Officials), and 4.1 (Political and Campaign Activities of Judges and Judicial Candidates in General) (A)(1) through (7); or

    (B) at any time with Rules 3.4 (Appointments to Governmental Positions), 3.8(A) (Appointments to Fiduciary Positions), 3.9 (Service as Arbitrator or Mediator), 3.10 (Practice of Law), and 3.11(B) (Financial, Business, or Remunerative Activities).

VI. Time for Compliance

A person to whom this Code becomes applicable shall comply immediately with its provisions, except that those judges to whom Rules 3.8 (Appointments to Fiduciary Positions) and 3.11 (Financial, Business, or Remunerative Activities) apply shall comply with those Rules as soon as reasonably possible, but in no event later than one year after the Code becomes applicable to the judge.

Comment

[1] If serving as a fiduciary when selected as judge, a new judge may, notwithstanding the prohibitions in Rule 3.8, continue to serve as fiduciary, but only for that period of time necessary to avoid serious adverse consequences to the beneficiaries of the fiduciary relationship and in no event longer than one year. Similarly, if engaged at the time of judicial selection in a business activity, a new judge may, notwithstanding the prohibitions in Rule 3.11, continue in that activity for a reasonable period but in no event longer than one year.

ABA
Model Code
of Judicial
Conduct

Canon 1

A JUDGE SHALL UPHOLD AND PROMOTE THE INDEPENDENCE, INTEGRITY, AND IMPARTIALITY OF THE JUDICIARY, AND SHALL AVOID IMPROPRIETY AND THE APPEARANCE OF IMPROPRIETY.

Rule 1.1: Compliance with the Law

A judge shall comply with the law,* including the Code of Judicial Conduct.

Rule 1.2: Promoting Confidence in the Judiciary

A judge shall act at all times in a manner that promotes public confidence in the independence,* integrity,* and impartiality* of the judiciary, and shall avoid impropriety* and the appearance of impropriety.

Comment

[1] Public confidence in the judiciary is eroded by improper conduct and conduct that creates the appearance of impropriety. This principle applies to both the professional and personal conduct of a judge.

[2] A judge should expect to be the subject of public scrutiny that might be viewed as burdensome if applied to other citizens, and must accept the restrictions imposed by the Code.

[3] Conduct that compromises or appears to compromise the independence, integrity, and impartiality of a judge undermines public confidence in the judiciary. Because it is not practicable to list all such conduct, the Rule is necessarily cast in general terms.

[4] Judges should participate in activities that promote ethical conduct among judges and lawyers, support professionalism within the judiciary and the legal profession, and promote access to justice for all.

[5] Actual improprieties include violations of law, court rules or provisions of this Code. The test for appearance of impropriety is whether the conduct would create in reasonable minds a perception that the judge violated this Code or engaged in other conduct that reflects adversely on the judge's honesty, impartiality, temperament, or fitness to serve as a judge.

[6] A judge should initiate and participate in community outreach activities for the purpose of promoting public understanding of and confidence in the administration of justice. In conducting such activities, the judge must act in a manner consistent with this Code.

Rule 1.3: Avoiding Abuse of the
Prestige of Judicial Office

A judge shall not abuse the prestige of judicial office to advance the personal or economic interests* of the judge or others, or allow others to do so.

Comment

[1] It is improper for a judge to use or attempt to use his or her position to gain personal advantage or deferential treatment of any kind. For example, it would be improper for a judge to allude to his or her judicial status to gain favorable treatment in encounters with traffic officials. Similarly, a judge must not use judicial letterhead to gain an advantage in conducting his or her personal business.

[2] A judge may provide a reference or recommendation for an individual based upon the judge's personal knowledge. The judge may use official letterhead if the judge indicates that the reference is personal and if there is no likelihood that the use of the letterhead would reasonably be perceived as an attempt to exert pressure by reason of the judicial office.

[3] Judges may participate in the process of judicial selection by cooperating with appointing authorities and screening committees, and by responding to inquiries from such entities concerning the professional qualifications of a person being considered for judicial office.

[4] Special considerations arise when judges write or contribute to publications of for-profit entities, whether related or unrelated to the law. A judge should not permit anyone associated with the publication of such materials to exploit the judge's office in a manner that violates this Rule or other applicable law. In contracts for publication of a judge's writing, the judge should retain sufficient control over the advertising to avoid such exploitation.

Canon 2

A JUDGE SHALL PERFORM THE DUTIES OF JUDICIAL
OFFICE IMPARTIALLY, COMPETENTLY, AND DILIGENTLY.

Rule 2.1: Giving Precedence to the
Duties of Judicial Office

The duties of judicial office, as prescribed by law,* shall take precedence over all of a judge's personal and extrajudicial activities.

ABA
Model Code
of Judicial
Conduct

Comment

[1] To ensure that judges are available to fulfill their judicial duties, judges must conduct their personal and extrajudicial activities to minimize the risk of conflicts that would result in frequent disqualification. See Canon 3.

[2] Although it is not a duty of judicial office unless prescribed by law, judges are encouraged to participate in activities that promote public understanding of and confidence in the justice system.

Rule 2.2: Impartiality and Fairness

A judge shall uphold and apply the law,* and shall perform all duties of judicial office fairly and impartially.*

Comment

[1] To ensure impartiality and fairness to all parties, a judge must be objective and open-minded.

[2] Although each judge comes to the bench with a unique background and personal philosophy, a judge must interpret and apply the law without regard to whether the judge approves or disapproves of the law in question.

[3] When applying and interpreting the law, a judge sometimes may make good-faith errors of fact or law. Errors of this kind do not violate this Rule.

[4] It is not a violation of this Rule for a judge to make reasonable accommodations to ensure pro se litigants the opportunity to have their matters fairly heard.

Rule 2.3: Bias, Prejudice, and Harassment

(A) A judge shall perform the duties of judicial office, including administrative duties, without bias or prejudice.

(B) A judge shall not, in the performance of judicial duties, by words or conduct manifest bias or prejudice, or engage in harassment, including but not limited to bias, prejudice, or harassment based upon race, sex, gender, religion, national origin, ethnicity, disability, age, sexual orientation, marital status, socioeconomic status, or political affiliation, and shall not permit court staff, court officials, or others subject to the judge's direction and control to do so.

(C) A judge shall require lawyers in proceedings before the court to refrain from manifesting bias or prejudice, or engaging in harassment, based upon attributes including but not limited to race, sex, gender, religion, national origin, ethnicity, disability, age, sexual orientation, marital

status, socioeconomic status, or political affiliation, against parties, witnesses, lawyers, or others.

(D) The restrictions of paragraphs (B) and (C) do not preclude judges or lawyers from making legitimate reference to the listed factors, or similar factors, when they are relevant to an issue in a proceeding.

Comment

[1] A judge who manifests bias or prejudice in a proceeding impairs the fairness of the proceeding and brings the judiciary into disrepute.

[2] Examples of manifestations of bias or prejudice include but are not limited to epithets; slurs; demeaning nicknames; negative stereotyping; attempted humor based upon stereotypes; threatening, intimidating, or hostile acts; suggestions of connections between race, ethnicity, or nationality and crime; and irrelevant references to personal characteristics. Even facial expressions and body language can convey to parties and lawyers in the proceeding, jurors, the media, and others an appearance of bias or prejudice. A judge must avoid conduct that may reasonably be perceived as prejudiced or biased.

[3] Harassment, as referred to in paragraphs (B) and (C), is verbal or physical conduct that denigrates or shows hostility or aversion toward a person on bases such as race, sex, gender, religion, national origin, ethnicity, disability, age, sexual orientation, marital status, socioeconomic status, or political affiliation.

[4] Sexual harassment includes but is not limited to sexual advances, requests for sexual favors, and other verbal or physical conduct of a sexual nature that is unwelcome.

Rule 2.4: External Influences on Judicial Conduct

(A) A judge shall not be swayed by public clamor or fear of criticism.

(B) A judge shall not permit family, social, political, financial, or other interests or relationships to influence the judge's judicial conduct or judgment.

(C) A judge shall not convey or permit others to convey the impression that any person or organization is in a position to influence the judge.

Comment

[1] An independent judiciary requires that judges decide cases according to the law and facts, without regard to whether particular laws or litigants are popular or unpopular with the public, the media, government officials, or the judge's friends or family. Confidence in the judiciary is eroded if

judicial decision making is perceived to be subject to inappropriate outside influences.

Rule 2.5: Competence, Diligence, and Cooperation

(A) A judge shall perform judicial and administrative duties, competently and diligently.

(B) A judge shall cooperate with other judges and court officials in the administration of court business.

Comment

[1] Competence in the performance of judicial duties requires the legal knowledge, skill, thoroughness, and preparation reasonably necessary to perform a judge's responsibilities of judicial office.

[2] A judge should seek the necessary docket time, court staff, expertise, and resources to discharge all adjudicative and administrative responsibilities.

[3] Prompt disposition of the court's business requires a judge to devote adequate time to judicial duties, to be punctual in attending court and expeditious in determining matters under submission, and to take reasonable measures to ensure that court officials, litigants, and their lawyers cooperate with the judge to that end.

[4] In disposing of matters promptly and efficiently, a judge must demonstrate due regard for the rights of parties to be heard and to have issues resolved without unnecessary cost or delay. A judge should monitor and supervise cases in ways that reduce or eliminate dilatory practices, avoidable delays, and unnecessary costs.

Rule 2.6: Ensuring the Right to Be Heard

(A) A judge shall accord to every person who has a legal interest in a proceeding, or that person's lawyer, the right to be heard according to law.*

(B) A judge may encourage parties to a proceeding and their lawyers to settle matters in dispute but shall not act in a manner that coerces any party into settlement.

Comment

[1] The right to be heard is an essential component of a fair and impartial system of justice. Substantive rights of litigants can be protected only if procedures protecting the right to be heard are observed.

[2] The judge plays an important role in overseeing the settlement of disputes, but should be careful that efforts to further settlement do not undermine any party's right to be heard according to law. The judge should keep in mind

the effect that the judge's participation in settlement discussions may have, not only on the judge's own views of the case, but also on the perceptions of the lawyers and the parties if the case remains with the judge after settlement efforts are unsuccessful. Among the factors that a judge should consider when deciding upon an appropriate settlement practice for a case are (1) whether the parties have requested or voluntarily consented to a certain level of participation by the judge in settlement discussions, (2) whether the parties and their counsel are relatively sophisticated in legal matters, (3) whether the case will be tried by the judge or a jury, (4) whether the parties participate with their counsel in settlement discussions, (5) whether any parties are unrepresented by counsel, and (6) whether the matter is civil or criminal.

[3] Judges must be mindful of the effect settlement discussions can have, not only on their objectivity and impartiality, but also on the appearance of their objectivity and impartiality. Despite a judge's best efforts, there may be instances when information obtained during settlement discussions could influence a judge's decision making during trial, and, in such instances, the judge should consider whether disqualification may be appropriate. See Rule 2.11(A)(1).

Rule 2.7: Responsibility to Decide

A judge shall hear and decide matters assigned to the judge, except when disqualification is required by Rule 2.11 or other law.*

Comment

[1] Judges must be available to decide the matters that come before the court. Although there are times when disqualification is necessary to protect the rights of litigants and preserve public confidence in the independence, integrity, and impartiality of the judiciary, judges must be available to decide matters that come before the courts. Unwarranted disqualification may bring public disfavor to the court and to the judge personally. The dignity of the court, the judge's respect for fulfillment of judicial duties, and a proper concern for the burdens that may be imposed upon the judge's colleagues require that a judge not use disqualification to avoid cases that present difficult, controversial, or unpopular issues.

Rule 2.8: Decorum, Demeanor, and Communication with Jurors

(A) A judge shall require order and decorum in proceedings before the court.

(B) A judge shall be patient, dignified, and courteous to litigants, jurors, witnesses, lawyers, court staff, court officials, and others with whom

the judge deals in an official capacity, and shall require similar conduct of lawyers, court staff, court officials, and others subject to the judge's direction and control.

(C) A judge shall not commend or criticize jurors for their verdict other than in a court order or opinion in a proceeding.

Comment

[1] The duty to hear all proceedings with patience and courtesy is not inconsistent with the duty imposed in Rule 2.5 to dispose promptly of the business of the court. Judges can be efficient and businesslike while being patient and deliberate.

[2] Commending or criticizing jurors for their verdict may imply a judicial expectation in future cases and may impair a juror's ability to be fair and impartial in a subsequent case.

[3] A judge who is not otherwise prohibited by law from doing so may meet with jurors who choose to remain after trial but should be careful not to discuss the merits of the case.

Rule 2.9: Ex Parte Communications

(A) A judge shall not initiate, permit, or consider ex parte communications, or consider other communications made to the judge outside the presence of the parties or their lawyers, concerning a pending* or impending matter,* except as follows:

(1) When circumstances require it, ex parte communication for scheduling, administrative, or emergency purposes, which does not address substantive matters, is permitted, provided:

(a) the judge reasonably believes that no party will gain a procedural, substantive, or tactical advantage as a result of the ex parte communication; and

(b) the judge makes provision promptly to notify all other parties of the substance of the ex parte communication, and gives the parties an opportunity to respond.

(2) A judge may obtain the written advice of a disinterested expert on the law applicable to a proceeding before the judge, if the judge gives advance notice to the parties of the person to be consulted and the subject matter of the advice to be solicited, and affords the parties a reasonable opportunity to object and respond to the notice and to the advice received.

(3) A judge may consult with court staff and court officials whose functions are to aid the judge in carrying out the judge's adjudicative responsibilities, or with other judges, provided the

judge makes reasonable efforts to avoid receiving factual information that is not part of the record, and does not abrogate the responsibility personally to decide the matter.

(4) A judge may, with the consent of the parties, confer separately with the parties and their lawyers in an effort to settle matters pending before the judge.

(5) A judge may initiate, permit, or consider any ex parte communication when expressly authorized by law* to do so.

(B) If a judge inadvertently receives an unauthorized ex parte communication bearing upon the substance of a matter, the judge shall make provision promptly to notify the parties of the substance of the communication and provide the parties with an opportunity to respond.

(C) A judge shall not investigate facts in a matter independently, and shall consider only the evidence presented and any facts that may properly be judicially noticed.

(D) A judge shall make reasonable efforts, including providing appropriate supervision, to ensure that this Rule is not violated by court staff, court officials, and others subject to the judge's direction and control.

Comment

[1] To the extent reasonably possible, all parties or their lawyers shall be included in communications with a judge.

[2] Whenever the presence of a party or notice to a party is required by this Rule, it is the party's lawyer, or if the party is unrepresented, the party, who is to be present or to whom notice is to be given.

[3] The proscription against communications concerning a proceeding includes communications with lawyers, law teachers, and other persons who are not participants in the proceeding, except to the limited extent permitted by this Rule.

[4] A judge may initiate, permit, or consider ex parte communications expressly authorized by law, such as when serving on therapeutic or problem-solving courts, mental health courts, or drug courts. In this capacity, judges may assume a more interactive role with parties, treatment providers, probation officers, social workers, and others.

[5] A judge may consult with other judges on pending matters, but must avoid ex parte discussions of a case with judges who have previously been disqualified from hearing the matter, and with judges who have appellate jurisdiction over the matter.

[6] The prohibition against a judge investigating the facts in a matter extends to information available in all mediums, including electronic.

[7] A judge may consult ethics advisory committees, outside counsel, or

legal experts concerning the judge's compliance with this Code. Such consultations are not subject to the restrictions of paragraph (A)(2).

Rule 2.10: Judicial Statements on Pending and Impending Cases

(A) A judge shall not make any public statement that might reasonably be expected to affect the outcome or impair the fairness of a matter pending* or impending* in any court, or make any nonpublic statement that might substantially interfere with a fair trial or hearing.

(B) A judge shall not, in connection with cases, controversies, or issues that are likely to come before the court, make pledges, promises, or commitments that are inconsistent with the impartial* performance of the adjudicative duties of judicial office.

(C) A judge shall require court staff, court officials, and others subject to the judge's direction and control to refrain from making statements that the judge would be prohibited from making by paragraphs (A) and (B).

(D) Notwithstanding the restrictions in paragraph (A), a judge may make public statements in the course of official duties, may explain court procedures, and may comment on any proceeding in which the judge is a litigant in a personal capacity.

(E) Subject to the requirements of paragraph (A), a judge may respond directly or through a third party to allegations in the media or elsewhere concerning the judge's conduct in a matter.

Comment

[1] This Rule's restrictions on judicial speech are essential to the maintenance of the independence, integrity, and impartiality of the judiciary.

[2] This Rule does not prohibit a judge from commenting on proceedings in which the judge is a litigant in a personal capacity, or represents a client as permitted by these Rules. In cases in which the judge is a litigant in an official capacity, such as a writ of mandamus, the judge must not comment publicly.

[3] Depending upon the circumstances, the judge should consider whether it may be preferable for a third party, rather than the judge, to respond or issue statements in connection with allegations concerning the judge's conduct in a matter.

Rule 2.11: Disqualification

(A) A judge shall disqualify himself or herself in any proceeding in which the judge's impartiality* might reasonably be questioned, including but not limited to the following circumstances:

(1) The judge has a personal bias or prejudice concerning a party or a party's lawyer, or personal knowledge* of facts that are in dispute in the proceeding.

(2) The judge knows* that the judge, the judge's spouse or domestic partner,* or a person within the third degree of relationship* to either of them, or the spouse or domestic partner of such a person is:

   (a) a party to the proceeding, or an officer, director, general partner, managing member, or trustee of a party;

   (b) acting as a lawyer in the proceeding;

   (c) a person who has more than a de minimis* interest that could be substantially affected by the proceeding; or

   (d) likely to be a material witness in the proceeding.

(3) The judge knows that he or she, individually or as a fiduciary,* or the judge's spouse, domestic partner, parent, or child, or any other member of the judge's family residing in the judge's household,* has an economic interest* in the subject matter in controversy or in a party to the proceeding.

(4) The judge knows or learns by means of a timely motion that a party, a party's lawyer, or the law firm of a party's lawyer has within the previous [insert number] year[s] made aggregate* contributions* to the judge's campaign in an amount that [is greater than $[insert amount] for an individual or $[insert amount] for an entity] [is reasonable and appropriate for an individual or an entity].

(5) The judge, while a judge or a judicial candidate,* has made a public statement, other than in a court proceeding, judicial decision, or opinion, that commits or appears to commit the judge to reach a particular result or rule in a particular way in the proceeding or controversy.

(6) The judge:

   (a) served as a lawyer in the matter in controversy, or was associated with a lawyer who participated substantially as a lawyer in the matter during such association;

   (b) served in governmental employment, and in such capacity participated personally and substantially as a lawyer or public official concerning the proceeding, or has publicly expressed in such capacity an opinion concerning the merits of the particular matter in controversy;

   (c) was a material witness concerning the matter; or

   (d) previously presided as a judge over the matter in another court.

(B) A judge shall keep informed about the judge's personal and fiduciary economic interests, and make a reasonable effort to keep informed about the personal economic interests of the judge's spouse or domestic partner and minor children residing in the judge's household.

(C) A judge subject to disqualification under this Rule, other than for bias or prejudice under paragraph (A)(1), may disclose on the record the basis of the judge's disqualification and may ask the parties and their lawyers to consider, outside the presence of the judge and court personnel, whether to waive disqualification. If, following the disclosure, the parties and lawyers agree, without participation by the judge or court personnel, that the judge should not be disqualified, the judge may participate in the proceeding. The agreement shall be incorporated into the record of the proceeding.

Comment

[1] Under this Rule, a judge is disqualified whenever the judge's impartiality might reasonably be questioned, regardless of whether any of the specific provisions of paragraphs (A)(1) through (6) apply. In many jurisdictions, the term "recusal" is used interchangeably with the term "disqualification."

[2] A judge's obligation not to hear or decide matters in which disqualification is required applies regardless of whether a motion to disqualify is filed.

[3] The rule of necessity may override the rule of disqualification. For example, a judge might be required to participate in judicial review of a judicial salary statute, or might be the only judge available in a matter requiring immediate judicial action, such as a hearing on probable cause or a temporary restraining order. In matters that require immediate action, the judge must disclose on the record the basis for possible disqualification and make reasonable efforts to transfer the matter to another judge as soon as practicable.

[4] The fact that a lawyer in a proceeding is affiliated with a law firm with which a relative of the judge is affiliated does not itself disqualify the judge. If, however, the judge's impartiality might reasonably be questioned under paragraph (A), or the relative is known by the judge to have an interest in the law firm that could be substantially affected by the proceeding under paragraph (A)(2)(c), the judge's disqualification is required.

[5] A judge should disclose on the record information that the judge believes the parties or their lawyers might reasonably consider relevant to a possible motion for disqualification, even if the judge believes there is no basis for disqualification.

[6] "Economic interest," as set forth in the Terminology section, means

ownership of more than a de minimis legal or equitable interest. Except for situations in which a judge participates in the management of such a legal or equitable interest, or the interest could be substantially affected by the outcome of a proceeding before a judge, it does not include:

(1) an interest in the individual holdings within a mutual or common investment fund;

(2) an interest in securities held by an educational, religious, charitable, fraternal, or civic organization in which the judge or the judge's spouse, domestic partner, parent, or child serves as a director, officer, advisor, or other participant;

(3) a deposit in a financial institution or deposits or proprietary interests the judge may maintain as a member of a mutual savings association or credit union, or similar proprietary interests; or

(4) an interest in the issuer of government securities held by the judge.

Rule 2.12: Supervisory Duties

(A) A judge shall require court staff, court officials, and others subject to the judge's direction and control to act in a manner consistent with the judge's obligations under this Code.

(B) A judge with supervisory authority for the performance of other judges shall take reasonable measures to ensure that those judges properly discharge their judicial responsibilities, including the prompt disposition of matters before them.

Comment

[1] A judge is responsible for his or her own conduct and for the conduct of others, such as staff, when those persons are acting at the judge's direction or control. A judge may not direct court personnel to engage in conduct on the judge's behalf or as the judge's representative when such conduct would violate the Code if undertaken by the judge.

[2] Public confidence in the judicial system depends upon timely justice. To promote the efficient administration of justice, a judge with supervisory authority must take the steps needed to ensure that judges under his or her supervision administer their workloads promptly.

Rule 2.13: Administrative Appointments

(A) In making administrative appointments, a judge:

(1) shall exercise the power of appointment impartially* and on the basis of merit; and

(2) shall avoid nepotism, favoritism, and unnecessary appointments.

(B) A judge shall not appoint a lawyer to a position if the judge either knows* that the lawyer, or the lawyer's spouse or domestic partner,* has contributed more than $[insert amount] within the prior [insert number] year[s] to the judge's election campaign, or learns of such a contribution* by means of a timely motion by a party or other person properly interested in the matter, unless:

(1) the position is substantially uncompensated;

(2) the lawyer has been selected in rotation from a list of qualified and available lawyers compiled without regard to their having made political contributions; or

(3) the judge or another presiding or administrative judge affirmatively finds that no other lawyer is willing, competent, and able to accept the position.

(C) A judge shall not approve compensation of appointees beyond the fair value of services rendered.

Comment

[1] Appointees of a judge include assigned counsel, officials such as referees, commissioners, special masters, receivers, and guardians, and personnel such as clerks, secretaries, and bailiffs. Consent by the parties to an appointment or an award of compensation does not relieve the judge of the obligation prescribed by paragraph (A).

[2] Unless otherwise defined by law, nepotism is the appointment or hiring of any relative within the third degree of relationship of either the judge or the judge's spouse or domestic partner, or the spouse or domestic partner of such relative.

[3] The rule against making administrative appointments of lawyers who have contributed in excess of a specified dollar amount to a judge's election campaign includes an exception for positions that are substantially uncompensated, such as those for which the lawyer's compensation is limited to reimbursement for out-of-pocket expenses.

Rule 2.14: Disability and Impairment

A judge having a reasonable belief that the performance of a lawyer or another judge is impaired by drugs or alcohol, or by a mental, emotional, or physical condition, shall take appropriate action, which may include a confidential referral to a lawyer or judicial assistance program.

Comment

[1] "Appropriate action" means action intended and reasonably likely to help the judge or lawyer in question address the problem and prevent harm

ABA
Model Code
of Judicial
Conduct

to the justice system. Depending upon the circumstances, appropriate action may include but is not limited to speaking directly to the impaired person, notifying an individual with supervisory responsibility over the impaired person, or making a referral to an assistance program.

[2] Taking or initiating corrective action by way of referral to an assistance program may satisfy a judge's responsibility under this Rule. Assistance programs have many approaches for offering help to impaired judges and lawyers, such as intervention, counseling, or referral to appropriate health care professionals. Depending upon the gravity of the conduct that has come to the judge's attention, however, the judge may be required to take other action, such as reporting the impaired judge or lawyer to the appropriate authority, agency, or body. See Rule 2.15.

Rule 2.15: Responding to
Judicial and Lawyer Misconduct

(A) A judge having knowledge* that another judge has committed a violation of this Code that raises a substantial question regarding the judge's honesty, trustworthiness, or fitness as a judge in other respects shall inform the appropriate authority.*

(B) A judge having knowledge that a lawyer has committed a violation of the Rules of Professional Conduct that raises a substantial question regarding the lawyer's honesty, trustworthiness, or fitness as a lawyer in other respects shall inform the appropriate authority.

(C) A judge who receives information indicating a substantial likelihood that another judge has committed a violation of this Code shall take appropriate action.

(D) A judge who receives information indicating a substantial likelihood that a lawyer has committed a violation of the Rules of Professional Conduct shall take appropriate action.

Comment

[1] Taking action to address known misconduct is a judge's obligation. Paragraphs (A) and (B) impose an obligation on the judge to report to the appropriate disciplinary authority the known misconduct of another judge or a lawyer that raises a substantial question regarding the honesty, trustworthiness, or fitness of that judge or lawyer. Ignoring or denying known misconduct among one's judicial colleagues or members of the legal profession undermines a judge's responsibility to participate in efforts to ensure public respect for the justice system. This Rule limits the reporting obligation to those offenses that an independent judiciary must vigorously endeavor to prevent.

[2] A judge who does not have actual knowledge that another judge or a lawyer may have committed misconduct, but receives information indicating a substantial likelihood of such misconduct, is required to take appropriate action under paragraphs (C) and (D). Appropriate action may include, but is not limited to, communicating directly with the judge who may have violated this Code, communicating with a supervising judge, or reporting the suspected violation to the appropriate authority or other agency or body. Similarly, actions to be taken in response to information indicating that a lawyer has committed a violation of the Rules of Professional Conduct may include but are not limited to communicating directly with the lawyer who may have committed the violation, or reporting the suspected violation to the appropriate authority or other agency or body.

Rule 2.16: Cooperation with Disciplinary Authorities

(A) A judge shall cooperate and be candid and honest with judicial and lawyer disciplinary agencies.

(B) A judge shall not retaliate, directly or indirectly, against a person known* or suspected to have assisted or cooperated with an investigation of a judge or a lawyer.

Comment

[1] Cooperation with investigations and proceedings of judicial and lawyer discipline agencies, as required in paragraph (A), instills confidence in judges' commitment to the integrity of the judicial system and the protection of the public.

Canon 3

A JUDGE SHALL CONDUCT THE JUDGE'S PERSONAL AND EXTRAJUDICIAL ACTIVITIES TO MINIMIZE THE RISK OF CONFLICT WITH THE OBLIGATIONS OF JUDICIAL OFFICE.

Rule 3.1: Extrajudicial Activities in General

A judge may engage in extrajudicial activities, except as prohibited by law* or this Code. However, when engaging in extrajudicial activities, a judge shall not:

(A) participate in activities that will interfere with the proper performance of the judge's judicial duties;

(B) participate in activities that will lead to frequent disqualification of the judge;

(C) participate in activities that would appear to a reasonable person to undermine the judge's independence,* integrity,* or impartiality;*

(D) engage in conduct that would appear to a reasonable person to be coercive; or

(E) make use of court premises, staff, stationery, equipment, or other resources, except for incidental use for activities that concern the law, the legal system, or the administration of justice, or unless such additional use is permitted by law.

Comment

[1] To the extent that time permits, and judicial independence and impartiality are not compromised, judges are encouraged to engage in appropriate extrajudicial activities. Judges are uniquely qualified to engage in extrajudicial activities that concern the law, the legal system, and the administration of justice, such as by speaking, writing, teaching, or participating in scholarly research projects. In addition, judges are permitted and encouraged to engage in educational, religious, charitable, fraternal or civic extrajudicial activities not conducted for profit, even when the activities do not involve the law. See Rule 3.7.

[2] Participation in both law-related and other extrajudicial activities helps integrate judges into their communities, and furthers public understanding of and respect for courts and the judicial system.

[3] Discriminatory actions and expressions of bias or prejudice by a judge, even outside the judge's official or judicial actions, are likely to appear to a reasonable person to call into question the judge's integrity and impartiality. Examples include jokes or other remarks that demean individuals based upon their race, sex, gender, religion, national origin, ethnicity, disability, age, sexual orientation, or socioeconomic status. For the same reason, a judge's extrajudicial activities must not be conducted in connection or affiliation with an organization that practices invidious discrimination. See Rule 3.6.

[4] While engaged in permitted extrajudicial activities, judges must not coerce others or take action that would reasonably be perceived as coercive. For example, depending upon the circumstances, a judge's solicitation of contributions or memberships for an organization, even as permitted by Rule 3.7(A), might create the risk that the person solicited would feel obligated to respond favorably, or would do so to curry favor with the judge.

Rule 3.2: Appearances before Governmental Bodies and Consultation with Government Officials

A judge shall not appear voluntarily at a public hearing before, or otherwise consult with, an executive or a legislative body or official, except:

(A) in connection with matters concerning the law, the legal system, or the administration of justice;

(B) in connection with matters about which the judge acquired knowledge or expertise in the course of the judge's judicial duties; or

(C) when the judge is acting pro se in a matter involving the judge's legal or economic interests, or when the judge is acting in a fiduciary* capacity.

Comment

[1] Judges possess special expertise in matters of law, the legal system, and the administration of justice, and may properly share that expertise with governmental bodies and executive or legislative branch officials.

[2] In appearing before governmental bodies or consulting with government officials, judges must be mindful that they remain subject to other provisions of this Code, such as Rule 1.3, prohibiting judges from using the prestige of office to advance their own or others' interests, Rule 2.10, governing public comment on pending and impending matters, and Rule 3.1(C), prohibiting judges from engaging in extrajudicial activities that would appear to a reasonable person to undermine the judge's independence, integrity, or impartiality.

[3] In general, it would be an unnecessary and unfair burden to prohibit judges from appearing before governmental bodies or consulting with government officials on matters that are likely to affect them as private citizens, such as zoning proposals affecting their real property. In engaging in such activities, however, judges must not refer to their judicial positions, and must otherwise exercise caution to avoid using the prestige of judicial office.

Rule 3.3: Testifying as a Character Witness

A judge shall not testify as a character witness in a judicial, administrative, or other adjudicatory proceeding or otherwise vouch for the character of a person in a legal proceeding, except when duly summoned.

Comment

[1] A judge who, without being subpoenaed, testifies as a character witness abuses the prestige of judicial office to advance the interests of another. See Rule 1.3. Except in unusual circumstances where the demands of justice require, a judge should discourage a party from requiring the judge to testify as a character witness.

Rule 3.4: Appointments to Governmental Positions

A judge shall not accept appointment to a governmental committee, board, commission, or other governmental position, unless it is one that concerns the law,* the legal system, or the administration of justice.

Comment

[1] Rule 3.4 implicitly acknowledges the value of judges accepting appointments to entities that concern the law, the legal system, or the administration of justice. Even in such instances, however, a judge should assess the appropriateness of accepting an appointment, paying particular attention to the subject matter of the appointment and the availability and allocation of judicial resources, including the judge's time commitments, and giving due regard to the requirements of the independence and impartiality of the judiciary.

[2] A judge may represent his or her country, state, or locality on ceremonial occasions or in connection with historical, educational, or cultural activities. Such representation does not constitute acceptance of a government position.

Rule 3.5: Use of Nonpublic Information

A judge shall not intentionally disclose or use nonpublic information* acquired in a judicial capacity for any purpose unrelated to the judge's judicial duties.

Comment

[1] In the course of performing judicial duties, a judge may acquire information of commercial or other value that is unavailable to the public. The judge must not reveal or use such information for personal gain or for any purpose unrelated to his or her judicial duties.

[2] This rule is not intended, however, to affect a judge's ability to act on information as necessary to protect the health or safety of the judge or a member of a judge's family, court personnel, or other judicial officers if consistent with other provisions of this Code.

Rule 3.6: Affiliation with Discriminatory Organizations

(A) A judge shall not hold membership in any organization that practices invidious discrimination on the basis of race, sex, gender, religion, national origin, ethnicity, or sexual orientation.

(B) A judge shall not use the benefits or facilities of an organization if

ABA
Model Code
of Judicial
Conduct

the judge knows* or should know that the organization practices invidi-ous discrimination on one or more of the bases identified in paragraph (A). A judge's attendance at an event in a facility of an organization that the judge is not permitted to join is not a violation of this Rule when the judge's attendance is an isolated event that could not reasonably be per-ceived as an endorsement of the organization's practices.

Comment

[1] A judge's public manifestation of approval of invidious discrimi-nation on any basis gives rise to the appearance of impropriety and di-minishes public confidence in the integrity and impartiality of the judiciary. A judge's membership in an organization that practices invidious discrimi-nation creates the perception that the judge's impartiality is impaired.

[2] An organization is generally said to discriminate invidiously if it arbitrarily excludes from membership on the basis of race, sex, gender, re-ligion, national origin, ethnicity, or sexual orientation persons who would otherwise be eligible for admission. Whether an organization practices in-vidious discrimination is a complex question to which judges should be attentive. The answer cannot be determined from a mere examination of an organization's current membership rolls, but rather, depends upon how the organization selects members, as well as other relevant factors, such as whether the organization is dedicated to the preservation of religious, ethnic, or cultural values of legitimate common interest to its members, or whether it is an intimate, purely private organization whose membership limitations could not constitutionally be prohibited.

[3] When a judge learns that an organization to which the judge belongs engages in invidious discrimination, the judge must resign immediately from the organization.

[4] A judge's membership in a religious organization as a lawful exercise of the freedom of religion is not a violation of this Rule.

[5] This Rule does not apply to national or state military service.

Rule 3.7: Participation in Educational, Religious, Charitable, Fraternal, or Civic Organizations and Activities

(A) Subject to the requirements of Rule 3.1, a judge may participate in activities sponsored by organizations or governmental entities concerned with the law, the legal system, or the administration of justice, and those sponsored by or on behalf of educational, religious, charitable, fraternal, or civic organizations not conducted for profit, including but not limited to the following activities:

ABA
Model Code
of Judicial
Conduct

(1) assisting such an organization or entity in planning related to fund-raising, and participating in the management and investment of the organization's or entity's funds;

(2) soliciting* contributions* for such an organization or entity, but only from members of the judge's family,* or from judges over whom the judge does not exercise supervisory or appellate authority;

(3) soliciting membership for such an organization or entity, even though the membership dues or fees generated may be used to support the objectives of the organization or entity, but only if the organization or entity is concerned with the law, the legal system, or the administration of justice;

(4) appearing or speaking at, receiving an award or other recognition at, being featured on the program of, and permitting his or her title to be used in connection with an event of such an organization or entity, but if the event serves a fund-raising purpose, the judge may participate only if the event concerns the law, the legal system, or the administration of justice;

(5) making recommendations to such a public or private fund-granting organization or entity in connection with its programs and activities, but only if the organization or entity is concerned with the law, the legal system, or the administration of justice; and

(6) serving as an officer, director, trustee, or nonlegal advisor of such an organization or entity, unless it is likely that the organization or entity:

(a) will be engaged in proceedings that would ordinarily come before the judge; or

(b) will frequently be engaged in adversary proceedings in the court of which the judge is a member, or in any court subject to the appellate jurisdiction of the court of which the judge is a member.

(B) A judge may encourage lawyers to provide pro bono publico legal services.

Comment

[1] The activities permitted by paragraph (A) generally include those sponsored by or undertaken on behalf of public or private not-for-profit educational institutions, and other not-for-profit organizations, including law-related, charitable, and other organizations.

[2] Even for law-related organizations, a judge should consider whether

the membership and purposes of the organization, or the nature of the judge's participation in or association with the organization, would conflict with the judge's obligation to refrain from activities that reflect adversely upon a judge's independence, integrity, and impartiality.

[3] Mere attendance at an event, whether or not the event serves a fund-raising purpose, does not constitute a violation of paragraph (A)(4). It is also generally permissible for a judge to serve as an usher or a food server or preparer, or to perform similar functions, at fund-raising events sponsored by educational, religious, charitable, fraternal, or civic organizations. Such activities are not solicitation and do not present an element of coercion or abuse the prestige of judicial office.

[4] Identification of a judge's position in educational, religious, charitable, fraternal, or civic organizations on letterhead used for fund-raising or membership solicitation does not violate this Rule. The letterhead may list the judge's title or judicial office if comparable designations are used for other persons.

[5] In addition to appointing lawyers to serve as counsel for indigent parties in individual cases, a judge may promote broader access to justice by encouraging lawyers to participate in pro bono publico legal services, if in doing so the judge does not employ coercion, or abuse the prestige of judicial office. Such encouragement may take many forms, including providing lists of available programs, training lawyers to do pro bono publico legal work, and participating in events recognizing lawyers who have done pro bono publico work.

Rule 3.8: Appointments to Fiduciary Positions

(A) A judge shall not accept appointment to serve in a fiduciary* position, such as executor, administrator, trustee, guardian, attorney in fact, or other personal representative, except for the estate, trust, or person of a member of the judge's family,* and then only if such service will not interfere with the proper performance of judicial duties.

(B) A judge shall not serve in a fiduciary position if the judge as fiduciary will likely be engaged in proceedings that would ordinarily come before the judge, or if the estate, trust, or ward becomes involved in adversary proceedings in the court on which the judge serves, or one under its appellate jurisdiction.

(C) A judge acting in a fiduciary capacity shall be subject to the same restrictions on engaging in financial activities that apply to a judge personally.

(D) If a person who is serving in a fiduciary position becomes a judge, he or she must comply with this Rule as soon as reasonably practicable, but in no event later than [one year] after becoming a judge.

Comment

[1] A judge should recognize that other restrictions imposed by this Code may conflict with a judge's obligations as a fiduciary; in such circumstances, a judge should resign as fiduciary. For example, serving as a fiduciary might require frequent disqualification of a judge under Rule 2.11 because a judge is deemed to have an economic interest in shares of stock held by a trust if the amount of stock held is more than de minimis.

ABA
Model Code
of Judicial
Conduct

Rule 3.9: Service as Arbitrator or Mediator

A judge shall not act as an arbitrator or a mediator or perform other judicial functions apart from the judge's official duties unless expressly authorized by law.*

Comment

[1] This Rule does not prohibit a judge from participating in arbitration, mediation, or settlement conferences performed as part of assigned judicial duties. Rendering dispute resolution services apart from those duties, whether or not for economic gain, is prohibited unless it is expressly authorized by law.

Rule 3.10: Practice of Law

A judge shall not practice law. A judge may act pro se and may, without compensation, give legal advice to and draft or review documents for a member of the judge's family,* but is prohibited from serving as the family member's lawyer in any forum.

Comment

[1] A judge may act pro se in all legal matters, including matters involving litigation and matters involving appearances before or other dealings with governmental bodies. A judge must not use the prestige of office to advance the judge's personal or family interests. See Rule 1.3.

Rule 3.11: Financial, Business, or Remunerative Activities

(A) A judge may hold and manage investments of the judge and members of the judge's family.*

(B) A judge shall not serve as an officer, director, manager, general partner, advisor, or employee of any business entity except that a judge may manage or participate in:

    (1) a business closely held by the judge or members of the judge's family; or

(2) a business entity primarily engaged in investment of the finan-
       cial resources of the judge or members of the judge's family.
   (C) A judge shall not engage in financial activities permitted under
paragraphs (A) and (B) if they will:
   (1) interfere with the proper performance of judicial duties;
   (2) lead to frequent disqualification of the judge;
   (3) involve the judge in frequent transactions or continuing busi-
       ness relationships with lawyers or other persons likely to come
       before the court on which the judge serves; or
   (4) result in violation of other provisions of this Code.

Comment

[1] Judges are generally permitted to engage in financial activities, including managing real estate and other investments for themselves or for
members of their families. Participation in these activities, like participation
in other extrajudicial activities, is subject to the requirements of this Code.
For example, it would be improper for a judge to spend so much time on
business activities that it interferes with the performance of judicial duties.
See Rule 2.1. Similarly, it would be improper for a judge to use his or her
official title or appear in judicial robes in business advertising, or to conduct
his or her business or financial affairs in such a way that disqualification is
frequently required. See Rules 1.3 and 2.11.

[2] As soon as practicable without serious financial detriment, the judge
must divest himself or herself of investments and other financial interests
that might require frequent disqualification or otherwise violate this Rule.

Rule 3.12: Compensation for Extrajudicial Activities

A judge may accept reasonable compensation for extrajudicial activities
permitted by this Code or other law* unless such acceptance would appear
to a reasonable person to undermine the judge's independence,* integrity,* or impartiality.*

Comment

[1] A judge is permitted to accept honoraria, stipends, fees, wages, sala-
ries, royalties, or other compensation for speaking, teaching, writing, and other
extrajudicial activities, provided the compensation is reasonable and commen-
surate with the task performed. The judge should be mindful, however, that
judicial duties must take precedence over other activities. See Rule 2.1.

[2] Compensation derived from extrajudicial activities may be subject to
public reporting. See Rule 3.15.

Rule 3.13: Acceptance and Reporting of Gifts, Loans, Bequests, Benefits, or Other Things of Value

(A) A judge shall not accept any gifts, loans, bequests, benefits, or other things of value, if acceptance is prohibited by law* or would appear to a reasonable person to undermine the judge's independence,* integrity,* or impartiality.*

(B) Unless otherwise prohibited by law, or by paragraph (A), a judge may accept the following without publicly reporting such acceptance:

(1) items with little intrinsic value, such as plaques, certificates, trophies, and greeting cards;

(2) gifts, loans, bequests, benefits, or other things of value from friends, relatives, or other persons, including lawyers, whose appearance or interest in a proceeding pending* or impending* before the judge would in any event require disqualification of the judge under Rule 2.11;

(3) ordinary social hospitality;

(4) commercial or financial opportunities and benefits, including special pricing and discounts, and loans from lending institutions in their regular course of business, if the same opportunities and benefits or loans are made available on the same terms to similarly situated persons who are not judges;

(5) rewards and prizes given to competitors or participants in random drawings, contests, or other events that are open to persons who are not judges;

(6) scholarships, fellowships, and similar benefits or awards, if they are available to similarly situated persons who are not judges, based upon the same terms and criteria;

(7) books, magazines, journals, audiovisual materials, and other resource materials supplied by publishers on a complimentary basis for official use; or

(8) gifts, awards, or benefits associated with the business, profession, or other separate activity of a spouse, a domestic partner,* or other family member of a judge residing in the judge's household,* but that incidentally benefit the judge.

(C) Unless otherwise prohibited by law or by paragraph (A), a judge may accept the following items, and must report such acceptance to the extent required by Rule 3.15:

(1) gifts incident to a public testimonial;

(2) invitations to the judge and the judge's spouse, domestic partner, or guest to attend without charge:

   (a) an event associated with a bar-related function or other activity relating to the law, the legal system, or the administration of justice; or

   (b) an event associated with any of the judge's educational, religious, charitable, fraternal or civic activities permitted by this Code, if the same invitation is offered to nonjudges who are engaged in similar ways in the activity as is the judge; and

  (3) gifts, loans, bequests, benefits, or other things of value, if the source is a party or other person, including a lawyer, who has come or is likely to come before the judge, or whose interests have come or are likely to come before the judge.

Comment

[1] Whenever a judge accepts a gift or other thing of value without paying fair market value, there is a risk that the benefit might be viewed as intended to influence the judge's decision in a case. Rule 3.13 imposes restrictions upon the acceptance of such benefits, according to the magnitude of the risk. Paragraph (B) identifies circumstances in which the risk that the acceptance would appear to undermine the judge's independence, integrity, or impartiality is low, and explicitly provides that such items need not be publicly reported. As the value of the benefit or the likelihood that the source of the benefit will appear before the judge increases, the judge is either prohibited under paragraph (A) from accepting the gift, or required under paragraph (C) to publicly report it.

[2] Gift-giving between friends and relatives is a common occurrence, and ordinarily does not create an appearance of impropriety or cause reasonable persons to believe that the judge's independence, integrity, or impartiality has been compromised. In addition, when the appearance of friends or relatives in a case would require the judge's disqualification under Rule 2.11, there would be no opportunity for a gift to influence the judge's decision making. Paragraph (B)(2) places no restrictions upon the ability of a judge to accept gifts or other things of value from friends or relatives under these circumstances, and does not require public reporting.

[3] Businesses and financial institutions frequently make available special pricing, discounts, and other benefits, either in connection with a temporary promotion or for preferred customers, based upon longevity of the relationship, volume of business transacted, and other factors. A judge may freely accept such benefits if they are available to the general public, or if the judge qualifies for the special price or discount according to the same criteria as are applied to persons who are not judges. As an example, loans

provided at generally prevailing interest rates are not gifts, but a judge could not accept a loan from a financial institution at below-market interest rates unless the same rate was being made available to the general public for a certain period of time or only to borrowers with specified qualifications that the judge also possesses.

[4] Rule 3.13 applies only to acceptance of gifts or other things of value by a judge. Nonetheless, if a gift or other benefit is given to the judge's spouse, domestic partner, or member of the judge's family residing in the judge's household, it may be viewed as an attempt to evade Rule 3.13 and influence the judge indirectly. Where the gift or benefit is being made primarily to such other persons, and the judge is merely an incidental beneficiary, this concern is reduced. A judge should, however, remind family and household members of the restrictions imposed upon judges, and urge them to take these restrictions into account when making decisions about accepting such gifts or benefits.

[5] Rule 3.13 does not apply to contributions to a judge's campaign for judicial office. Such contributions are governed by other Rules of this Code, including Rules 4.3 and 4.4.

Rule 3.14: Reimbursement of Expenses and Waivers of Fees or Charges

(A) Unless otherwise prohibited by Rules 3.1 and 3.13(A) or other law,* a judge may accept reimbursement of necessary and reasonable expenses for travel, food, lodging, or other incidental expenses, or a waiver or partial waiver of fees or charges for registration, tuition, and similar items, from sources other than the judge's employing entity, if the expenses or charges are associated with the judge's participation in extrajudicial activities permitted by this Code.

(B) Reimbursement of expenses for necessary travel, food, lodging, or other incidental expenses shall be limited to the actual costs reasonably incurred by the judge and, when appropriate to the occasion, by the judge's spouse, domestic partner,* or guest.

(C) A judge who accepts reimbursement of expenses or waivers or partial waivers of fees or charges on behalf of the judge or the judge's spouse, domestic partner, or guest shall publicly report such acceptance as required by Rule 3.15.

Comment

[1] Educational, civic, religious, fraternal, and charitable organizations often sponsor meetings, seminars, symposia, dinners, awards ceremonies, and similar events. Judges are encouraged to attend educational programs,

as both teachers and participants, in law-related and academic disciplines, in furtherance of their duty to remain competent in the law. Participation in a variety of other extrajudicial activity is also permitted and encouraged by this Code.

[2] Not infrequently, sponsoring organizations invite certain judges to attend seminars or other events on a fee-waived or partial-fee-waived basis, and sometimes include reimbursement for necessary travel, food, lodging, or other incidental expenses. A judge's decision whether to accept reimbursement of expenses or a waiver or partial waiver of fees or charges in connection with these or other extrajudicial activities must be based upon an assessment of all the circumstances. The judge must undertake a reasonable inquiry to obtain the information necessary to make an informed judgment about whether acceptance would be consistent with the requirements of this Code.

[3] A judge must assure himself or herself that acceptance of reimbursement or fee waivers would not appear to a reasonable person to undermine the judge's independence, integrity, or impartiality. The factors that a judge should consider when deciding whether to accept reimbursement or a fee waiver for attendance at a particular activity include:

(a) whether the sponsor is an accredited educational institution or bar association rather than a trade association or a for-profit entity;

(b) whether the funding comes largely from numerous contributors rather than from a single entity and is earmarked for programs with specific content;

(c) whether the content is related or unrelated to the subject matter of litigation pending or impending before the judge, or to matters that are likely to come before the judge;

(d) whether the activity is primarily educational rather than recreational, and whether the costs of the event are reasonable and comparable to those associated with similar events sponsored by the judiciary, bar associations, or similar groups;

(e) whether information concerning the activity and its funding sources is available upon inquiry;

(f) whether the sponsor or source of funding is generally associated with particular parties or interests currently appearing or likely to appear in the judge's court, thus possibly requiring disqualification of the judge under Rule 2.11;

(g) whether differing viewpoints are presented; and

(h) whether a broad range of judicial and nonjudicial participants are invited, whether a large number of participants are invited, and whether the program is designed specifically for judges.

Rule 3.15: Reporting Requirements

(A) A judge shall publicly report the amount or value of:

    (1) compensation received for extrajudicial activities as permitted by Rule 3.12;

    (2) gifts and other things of value as permitted by Rule 3.13(C), unless the value of such items, alone or in the aggregate with other items received from the same source in the same calendar year, does not exceed $[insert amount]; and

    (3) reimbursement of expenses and waiver of fees or charges permitted by Rule 3.14(A), unless the amount of reimbursement or waiver, alone or in the aggregate with other reimbursements or waivers received from the same source in the same calendar year, does not exceed $[insert amount].

(B) When public reporting is required by paragraph (A), a judge shall report the date, place, and nature of the activity for which the judge received any compensation; the description of any gift, loan, bequest, benefit, or other thing of value accepted; and the source of reimbursement of expenses or waiver or partial waiver of fees or charges.

(C) The public report required by paragraph (A) shall be made at least annually, except that for reimbursement of expenses and waiver or partial waiver of fees or charges, the report shall be made within thirty days following the conclusion of the event or program.

(D) Reports made in compliance with this Rule shall be filed as public documents in the office of the clerk of the court on which the judge serves or other office designated by law,* and, when technically feasible, posted by the court or office personnel on the court's website.

Canon 4

A JUDGE OR CANDIDATE FOR JUDICIAL OFFICE SHALL NOT ENGAGE IN POLITICAL OR CAMPAIGN ACTIVITY THAT IS INCONSISTENT WITH THE INDEPENDENCE, INTEGRITY, OR IMPARTIALITY OF THE JUDICIARY.

Rule 4.1: Political and Campaign Activities of Judges and Judicial Candidates in General

(A) Except as permitted by law,* or by Rules 4.2, 4.3, and 4.4, a judge or a judicial candidate* shall not:

    (1) act as a leader in, or hold an office in, a political organization;*

    (2) make speeches on behalf of a political organization;

(3) publicly endorse or oppose a candidate for any public office;

(4) solicit funds for, pay an assessment to, or make a contribution* to a political organization or a candidate for public office;

(5) attend or purchase tickets for dinners or other events sponsored by a political organization or a candidate for public office;

(6) publicly identify himself or herself as a candidate of a political organization;

(7) seek, accept, or use endorsements from a political organization;

(8) personally solicit* or accept campaign contributions other than through a campaign committee authorized by Rule 4.4;

(9) use or permit the use of campaign contributions for the private benefit of the judge, the candidate, or others;

(10) use court staff, facilities, or other court resources in a campaign for judicial office;

(11) knowingly,* or with reckless disregard for the truth, make any false or misleading statement;

(12) make any statement that would reasonably be expected to affect the outcome or impair the fairness of a matter pending* or impending* in any court; or

(13) in connection with cases, controversies, or issues that are likely to come before the court, make pledges, promises, or commitments that are inconsistent with the impartial* performance of the adjudicative duties of judicial office.

(B) A judge or judicial candidate shall take reasonable measures to ensure that other persons do not undertake, on behalf of the judge or judicial candidate, any activities prohibited under paragraph (A).

Comment

General Considerations

[1] Even when subject to public election, a judge plays a role different from that of a legislator or executive branch official. Rather than making decisions based upon the expressed views or preferences of the electorate, a judge makes decisions based upon the law and the facts of every case. Therefore, in furtherance of this interest, judges and judicial candidates must, to the greatest extent possible, be free and appear to be free from political influence and political pressure. This Canon imposes narrowly tailored restrictions upon the political and campaign activities of all judges and judicial candidates, taking into account the various methods of selecting judges.

[2] When a person becomes a judicial candidate, this Canon becomes applicable to his or her conduct.

Participation in Political Activities

[3] Public confidence in the independence and impartiality of the judiciary is eroded if judges or judicial candidates are perceived to be subject to political influence. Although judges and judicial candidates may register to vote as members of a political party, they are prohibited by paragraph (A) (1) from assuming leadership roles in political organizations.

[4] Paragraphs (A)(2) and (A)(3) prohibit judges and judicial candidates from making speeches on behalf of political organizations or publicly endorsing or opposing candidates for public office, respectively, to prevent them from abusing the prestige of judicial office to advance the interests of others. See Rule 1.3. These Rules do not prohibit candidates from campaigning on their own behalf, or from endorsing or opposing candidates for the same judicial office for which they are running. See Rules 4.2(B)(2) and 4.2(B) (3).

[5] Although members of the families of judges and judicial candidates are free to engage in their own political activity, including running for public office, there is no "family exception" to the prohibition in paragraph (A)(3) against a judge or candidate publicly endorsing candidates for public office. A judge or judicial candidate must not become involved in, or publicly associated with, a family member's political activity or campaign for public office. To avoid public misunderstanding, judges and judicial candidates should take, and should urge members of their families to take, reasonable steps to avoid any implication that they endorse any family member's candidacy or other political activity.

[6] Judges and judicial candidates retain the right to participate in the political process as voters in both primary and general elections. For purposes of this Canon, participation in a caucus-type election procedure does not constitute public support for or endorsement of a political organization or candidate, and is not prohibited by paragraphs (A)(2) or (A)(3).

Statements and Comments Made during a Campaign for Judicial Office

[7] Judicial candidates must be scrupulously fair and accurate in all statements made by them and by their campaign committees. Paragraph (A)(11) obligates candidates and their committees to refrain from making statements that are false or misleading, or that omit facts necessary to make the communication considered as a whole not materially misleading.

[8] Judicial candidates are sometimes the subject of false, misleading, or unfair allegations made by opposing candidates, third parties, or the media. For example, false or misleading statements might be made regarding the identity, present position, experience, qualifications, or judicial rulings of a

ABA
Model Code
of Judicial
Conduct

candidate. In other situations, false or misleading allegations may be made that bear upon a candidate's integrity or fitness for judicial office. As long as the candidate does not violate paragraphs (A)(11), (A)(12), or (A)(13), the candidate may make a factually accurate public response. In addition, when an independent third party has made unwarranted attacks on a candidate's opponent, the candidate may disavow the attacks, and request the third party to cease and desist.

[9] Subject to paragraph (A)(12), a judicial candidate is permitted to respond directly to false, misleading, or unfair allegations made against him or her during a campaign, although it is preferable for someone else to respond if the allegations relate to a pending case.

[10] Paragraph (A)(12) prohibits judicial candidates from making comments that might impair the fairness of pending or impending judicial proceedings. This provision does not restrict arguments or statements to the court or jury by a lawyer who is a judicial candidate, or rulings, statements, or instructions by a judge that may appropriately affect the outcome of a matter.

Pledges, Promises, or Commitments
Inconsistent with Impartial Performance
of the Adjudicative Duties of Judicial Office

[11] The role of a judge is different from that of a legislator or executive branch official, even when the judge is subject to public election. Campaigns for judicial office must be conducted differently from campaigns for other offices. The narrowly drafted restrictions upon political and campaign activities of judicial candidates provided in Canon 4 allow candidates to conduct campaigns that provide voters with sufficient information to permit them to distinguish between candidates and make informed electoral choices.

[12] Paragraph (A)(13) makes applicable to both judges and judicial candidates the prohibition that applies to judges in Rule 2.10(B), relating to pledges, promises, or commitments that are inconsistent with the impartial performance of the adjudicative duties of judicial office.

[13] The making of a pledge, promise, or commitment is not dependent upon, or limited to, the use of any specific words or phrases; instead, the totality of the statement must be examined to determine if a reasonable person would believe that the candidate for judicial office has specifically undertaken to reach a particular result. Pledges, promises, or commitments must be contrasted with statements or announcements of personal views on legal, political, or other issues, which are not prohibited. When making such statements, a judge should acknowledge the overarching judicial obligation to apply and uphold the law, without regard to his or her personal views.

[14] A judicial candidate may make campaign promises related to judicial organization, administration, and court management, such as a promise to dispose of a backlog of cases, start court sessions on time, or avoid favoritism in appointments and hiring. A candidate may also pledge to take action outside the courtroom, such as working toward an improved jury selection system, or advocating for more funds to improve the physical plant and amenities of the courthouse.

[15] Judicial candidates may receive questionnaires or requests for interviews from the media and from issue advocacy or other community organizations that seek to learn their views on disputed or controversial legal or political issues. Paragraph (A)(13) does not specifically address judicial responses to such inquiries. Depending upon the wording and format of such questionnaires, candidates' responses might be viewed as pledges, promises, or commitments to perform the adjudicative duties of office other than in an impartial way. To avoid violating paragraph (A)(13), therefore, candidates who respond to media and other inquiries should also give assurances that they will keep an open mind and will carry out their adjudicative duties faithfully and impartially if elected. Candidates who do not respond may state their reasons for not responding, such as the danger that answering might be perceived by a reasonable person as undermining a successful candidate's independence or impartiality, or that it might lead to frequent disqualification. See Rule 2.11.

Rule 4.2: Political and Campaign Activities of Judicial Candidates in Public Elections

(A) A judicial candidate* in a partisan, nonpartisan, or retention public election* shall:

    (1) act at all times in a manner consistent with the independence,* integrity,* and impartiality* of the judiciary;

    (2) comply with all applicable election, election campaign, and election campaign fund-raising laws and regulations of this jurisdiction;

    (3) review and approve the content of all campaign statements and materials produced by the candidate or his or her campaign committee, as authorized by Rule 4.4, before their dissemination; and

    (4) take reasonable measures to ensure that other persons do not undertake on behalf of the candidate activities, other than those described in Rule 4.4, that the candidate is prohibited from doing by Rule 4.1.

(B) A candidate for elective judicial office may, unless prohibited by law,* and not earlier than [insert amount of time] before the first applicable primary election, caucus, or general or retention election:

    (1) establish a campaign committee pursuant to the provisions of Rule 4.4;

    (2) speak on behalf of his or her candidacy through any medium, including but not limited to advertisements, websites, or other campaign literature;

    (3) publicly endorse or oppose candidates for the same judicial office for which he or she is running;

    (4) attend or purchase tickets for dinners or other events sponsored by a political organization* or a candidate for public office;

    (5) seek, accept, or use endorsements from any person or organization other than a partisan political organization; and

    (6) contribute to a political organization or candidate for public office, but not more than $[insert amount] to any one organization or candidate.

(C) A judicial candidate in a partisan public election may, unless prohibited by law, and not earlier than [insert amount of time] before the first applicable primary election, caucus, or general election:

    (1) identify himself or herself as a candidate of a political organization; and

    (2) seek, accept, and use endorsements of a political organization.

Comment

[1] Paragraphs (B) and (C) permit judicial candidates in public elections to engage in some political and campaign activities otherwise prohibited by Rule 4.1. Candidates may not engage in these activities earlier than [insert amount of time] before the first applicable electoral event, such as a caucus or a primary election.

[2] Despite paragraphs (B) and (C), judicial candidates for public election remain subject to many of the provisions of Rule 4.1. For example, a candidate continues to be prohibited from soliciting funds for a political organization, knowingly making false or misleading statements during a campaign, or making certain promises, pledges, or commitments related to future adjudicative duties. See Rule 4.1(A), paragraphs (4), (11), and (13).

[3] In partisan public elections for judicial office, a candidate may be nominated by, affiliated with, or otherwise publicly identified or associated with a political organization, including a political party. This relationship may be maintained throughout the period of the public campaign, and may include use of political party or similar designations on campaign literature and on the ballot.

[4] In nonpartisan public elections or retention elections, paragraph (B) (5) prohibits a candidate from seeking, accepting, or using nominations or endorsements from a partisan political organization.

[5] Judicial candidates are permitted to attend or purchase tickets for dinners and other events sponsored by political organizations.

[6] For purposes of paragraph (B)(3), candidates are considered to be running for the same judicial office if they are competing for a single judgeship or if several judgeships on the same court are to be filled as a result of the election. In endorsing or opposing another candidate for a position on the same court, a judicial candidate must abide by the same rules governing campaign conduct and speech as apply to the candidate's own campaign.

[7] Although judicial candidates in nonpartisan public elections are prohibited from running on a ticket or slate associated with a political organization, they may group themselves into slates or other alliances to conduct their campaigns more effectively. Candidates who have grouped themselves together are considered to be running for the same judicial office if they satisfy the conditions described in Comment [6].

Rule 4.3: Activities of Candidates for Appointive Judicial Office

A candidate for appointment to judicial office may:

(A) communicate with the appointing or confirming authority, including any selection, screening, or nominating commission or similar agency; and

(B) seek endorsements for the appointment from any person or organization other than a partisan political organization.

Comment

[1] When seeking support or endorsement, or when communicating directly with an appointing or confirming authority, a candidate for appointive judicial office must not make any pledges, promises, or commitments that are inconsistent with the impartial performance of the adjudicative duties of the office. See Rule 4.1(A)(13).

Rule 4.4: Campaign Committees

(A) A judicial candidate* subject to public election* may establish a campaign committee to manage and conduct a campaign for the candidate, subject to the provisions of this Code. The candidate is responsible for ensuring that his or her campaign committee complies with applicable provisions of this Code and other applicable law.*

(B) A judicial candidate subject to public election shall direct his or her campaign committee:

(1) to solicit and accept only such campaign contributions* as are reasonable, in any event not to exceed, in the aggregate,* $[insert amount] from any individual or $[insert amount] from any entity or organization;

(2) not to solicit or accept contributions for a candidate's current campaign more than [insert amount of time] before the applicable primary election, caucus, or general or retention election, nor more than [insert number] days after the last election in which the candidate participated; and

(3) to comply with all applicable statutory requirements for disclosure and divestiture of campaign contributions, and to file with [name of appropriate regulatory authority] a report stating the name, address, occupation, and employer of each person who has made campaign contributions to the committee in an aggregate value exceeding $[insert amount]. The report must be filed within [insert number] days following an election, or within such other period as is provided by law.

Comment

[1] Judicial candidates are prohibited from personally soliciting campaign contributions or personally accepting campaign contributions. See Rule 4.1(A)(8). This Rule recognizes that in many jurisdictions, judicial candidates must raise campaign funds to support their candidacies, and permits candidates, other than candidates for appointive judicial office, to establish campaign committees to solicit and accept reasonable financial contributions or in-kind contributions.

[2] Campaign committees may solicit and accept campaign contributions, manage the expenditure of campaign funds, and generally conduct campaigns. Candidates are responsible for compliance with the requirements of election law and other applicable law, and for the activities of their campaign committees.

[3] At the start of a campaign, the candidate must instruct the campaign committee to solicit or accept only such contributions as are reasonable in amount, appropriate under the circumstances, and in conformity with applicable law. Although lawyers and others who might appear before a successful candidate for judicial office are permitted to make campaign contributions, the candidate should instruct his or her campaign committee to be especially cautious in connection with such contributions, so they do not create grounds for disqualification if the candidate is elected to judicial office. See Rule 2.11.

Rule 4.5: Activities of Judges Who Become Candidates for Nonjudicial Office

(A) Upon becoming a candidate for a nonjudicial elective office, a judge shall resign from judicial office, unless permitted by law* to continue to hold judicial office.

(B) Upon becoming a candidate for a nonjudicial appointive office, a judge is not required to resign from judicial office, provided that the judge complies with the other provisions of this Code.

ABA
Model Code
of Judicial
Conduct

Comment

[1] In campaigns for nonjudicial elective public office, candidates may make pledges, promises, or commitments related to positions they would take and ways they would act if elected to office. Although appropriate in nonjudicial campaigns, this manner of campaigning is inconsistent with the role of a judge, who must remain fair and impartial to all who come before him or her. The potential for misuse of the judicial office, and the political promises that the judge would be compelled to make in the course of campaigning for nonjudicial elective office, together dictate that a judge who wishes to run for such an office must resign upon becoming a candidate.

[2] The "resign to run" rule set forth in paragraph (A) ensures that a judge cannot use the judicial office to promote his or her candidacy, and prevents post-campaign retaliation from the judge in the event the judge is defeated in the election. When a judge is seeking appointive nonjudicial office, however, the dangers are not sufficient to warrant imposing the "resign to run" rule.

ABA Model Code of Judicial Conduct Correlation Tables

1990 CODE TO 2007 CODE

1990 CODE	2007 CODE
Preamble	Preamble and Scope
Terminology	Terminology
Canon 1	Canon 1 (partial)
Canon 1A	Preamble [1]
Canon 2	Canon 1 (partial) and Rule 1.2 (partial)
Canon 2A	Rules 1.1 and 1.2 (partial)
Canon 2B	Rules 1.3, 2.4(B) and (C), 3.1(E) and 3.3
Canon 2C	Rule 3.6(A)
Performing the Duties of Judicial Office	
1990 CODE	2007 CODE
Canon 3	Canon 2
Judicial Duties in General	
1990 CODE	2007 CODE
Canon 3A	Rule 2.1
Adjudicative Responsibilities	
1990 CODE	2007 CODE
Canon 3B(1)	Rule 2.7
Canon 3B(2)	Rules 2.2 (partial), 2.4(A) and 2.5(A) (partial)
Canon 3B(3)	Rule 2.8(A)
Canon 3B(4)	Rule 2.8(B)
Canon 3B(5)	Rule 2.3(A) and (B)
Canon 3B(6)	Rule 2.3(C) and (D)
Canon 3B(7)	Rules 2.6(A) and 2.9(A)
Canon 3B(7)(a)	Rule 2.9(A)(1)
Canon 3B(7)(a)(i)	Rule 2.9(A)(1)(a)
Canon 3B(7)(a)(ii)	Rule 2.9(A)(1)(b)
Canon 3B(7)(b)	Rule 2.9(A)(2)
Canon 3B(7)(c)	Rule 2.9(A)(3)
Canon 3B(7)(d)	Rule 2.9(A)(4)

Adjudicative Responsibilities (*continued*)	
1990 CODE	2007 CODE
Canon 3B(7)(e)	Rule 2.9(A)(5)
Canon 3B(8)	Rule 2.2 (partial), 2.5(A)
Canon 3B(9)	Rule 2.10(A), (C) and (D)
Canon 3B(10)	Rule 2.10(B)
Canon 3B(11)	Rule 2.8(C)
Canon 3B(12)	Rule 3.5
Administrative Responsibilities	
1990 CODE	2007 CODE
Canon 3C(1)	Rule 2.5(A) and (B)
Canon 3C(2)	Rule 2.12(A)
Canon 3C(3)	Rule 2.12(B)
Canon 3C(4)	Rule 2.13(A), (A)(1), (A)(2) and (C)
Canon 3C(5)	Rule 2.13(B)
Canon 3C(5)(a)	Rule 2.13(B)(1)
Canon 3C(5)(b)	Rule 2.13(B)(2)
Canon 3C(5)(c)	Rule 2.13(B)(3)
Disciplinary Responsibilities	
1990 CODE	2007 CODE
Canon 3D(1)	Rule 2.15(A) and (C)
Canon 3D(2)	Rule 2.15(B) and (D)
Canon 3D(3)	Deleted (See REC to Rule 2.15)
Disqualification	
1990 CODE	2007 CODE
Canon 3E(1)	Rule 2.11(A)
Canon 3E(1)(a)	Rule 2.11(A)(1)
Canon 3E(1)(b)	Rule 2.11(A)(6), (A)(6)(a) and (A)(6)(c)
Canon 3E(1)(c)	Rule 2.11(A)(3)
Canon 3E(1)(d)	Rule 2.11(A)(2)
Canon 3E(1)(d)(i)	Rule 2.11(A)(2)(a)
Canon 3E(1)(d)(ii)	Rule 2.11(A)(2)(b)
Canon 3E(1)(d)(iii)	Rule 2.11(A)(2)(c)
Canon 3E(1)(d)(iv)	Rule 2.11(A)(2)(d)
Canon 3E(1)(e)	Rule 2.11(A)(4)
Canon 3E(1)(f)	Rule 2.11(A)(5)
Canon 3E(2)	Rule 2.11(B)

Remittal of Disqualification	
1990 CODE	2007 CODE
Canon 3F	2.11(C)

Personal and Extrajudicial Activities	
1990 CODE	2007 CODE
Canon 4	Canon 3

Extrajudicial Activities in General	
1990 CODE	2007 CODE
Canon 4A	Rule 3.1
Canon 4A(1)	Rule 3.1(C)
Canon 4A(2)	Deleted
Canon 4A(3)	Rule 3.1(A)

Avocational Activities	
1990 CODE	2007 CODE
Canon 4B	Deleted (See REC to Comment [1] of Rule 3.1)

Governmental, Civic or Charitable Activities	
1990 CODE	2007 CODE
Canon 4C(1)	Rules 3.2 and 3.2(A) and (C)
Canon 4C(2)	Rule 3.4
Canon 4C(3)	Rule 3.7(A)
Canon 4C(3)(a)	Rule 3.7(A)(6)
Canon 4C(3)(a)(i)	Rule 3.7(A)(6)(a)
Canon 4C(3)(a)(ii)	Rule 3.7(A)(6)(b)
Canon 4C(3)(b)(i)	Rule 3.7(A)(1) and (2)
Canon 4C(3)(b)(ii)	Rule 3.7(A)(5)
Canon 4C(3)(b)(iii)	Rule 3.7(A)(3)
Canon 4C(3)(b)(iv)	Deleted

Financial Activities	
1990 CODE	2007 CODE
Canon 4D(1)	Rule 3.11(C)
Canon 4D(1)(a)	Deleted (See REC to Rule 3.11)
Canon 4D(1)(b)	Rule 3.11(C)(3)
Canon 4D(2)	Rule 3.11(A) (partial)
Canon 4D(3)	Rule 3.11(B)
Canon 4D(3)(a)	Rule 3.11(B)(1)
Canon 4D(3)(b)	Rule 3.11(B)(2)

ABA
Model Code
of Judicial
Conduct

Financial Activities (*continued*)	
1990 CODE	2007 CODE
Canon 4D(4)	Rule 3.11(C)(2)(3) and Comment [2]
Canon 4D(5)	Rule 3.13(A), (B) and (C)
Canon 4D(5)(a)	Rule 3.13(B)(7), (C)(1), (C)(2) and (C)(2)(a)
Canon 4D(5)(b)	Rule 3.13(B)(8)
Canon 4D(5)(c)	Rule 3.13(B)(3)
Canon 4D(5)(d)	Rule 3.13 Comment [2]
Canon 4D(5)(e)	Rule 3.13(B)(2)
Canon 4D(5)(f)	Rule 3.13(B)(4)
Canon 4D(5)(g)	Rule 3.13(B)(6)
Canon 4D(5)(h)	Rule 3.13(C)(3)
Fiduciary Activities	
1990 CODE	2007 CODE
Canon 4E(1)	Rule 3.8(A)
Canon 4E(2)	Rule 3.8(B)
Canon 4E(3)	Rule 3.8(C)
Service as Arbitrator or Mediator	
1990 CODE	2007 CODE
Canon 4F	Rule 3.9
Practice of Law	
1990 CODE	2007 CODE
Canon 4G	Rule 3.10
Compensation, Reimbursement and Reporting	
1990 CODE	2007 CODE
Canon 4H(1)	Rules 3.12 (partial) and 3.14(A)
Canon 4H(1)(a)	Rule 3.12
Canon 4H(1)(b)	Rule 3.14(B)
Canon 4H(2)	Rules 3.14(C) and 3.15
Canon 4I	Deleted (See REC to Rule 3.15)
Political and Campaign Activity	
1990 CODE	2007 CODE
Canon 5	Canon 4

All Judges and Candidates	
1990 CODE	2007 CODE
Canon 5A(1)	Rule 4.1(A)
Canon 5A(1)(a)	Rule 4.1(A)(1)
Canon 5A(1)(b)	Rule 4.1(A)(3)
Canon 5A(1)(c)	Rule 4.1(A)(2)
Canon 5A(1)(d)	Deleted (See REC to Rule 4.1)
Canon 5A(1)(e)	Rule 4.1(A)(4) and (5)
Canon 5A(2)	Rule 4.5(A) and (B)
Canon 5A(3)(a)	Rules 4.1(B), 4.2(A)(1) and (4)
Canon 5A(3)(b)	Rules 4.1(B) and 4.2(A)(4)
Canon 5A(3)(c)	Rule 4.2(A)(4)
Canon 5A(3)(d)	Rule 4.1(A)(13)
Canon 5A(3)(d)(i)	Rule 4.1(A)(13)
Canon 5A(3)(d)(ii)	Rule 4.1(A)(11) (partial)
Canon 5A(3)(e)	Rule 4.1 Comments [8] and [9]

Candidates Seeking Appointment to Judicial or Other Governmental Office	
1990 CODE	2007 CODE
Canon 5B	Rule 4.3
Canon 5B(2)	Deleted
Canon 5B(2)(a)(i)	Rule 4.3(A)
Canon 5B(2)(a)(ii)	Rule 4.3(B)
Canon 5B(2)(a)(iii)	Deleted
Canon 5B(2)(b)	Deleted

Judges and Candidates Subject to Public Election	
1990 CODE	2007 CODE
Canon 5C(1)	Rule 4.2(A) and (C)
Canon 5C(1)(a)(i)	Rule 4.2(B)(4)
Canon 5C(1)(a)(ii)	Rule 4.2(C)(1)
Canon 5C(1)(a)(iii)	Rule 4.2(B)(6)
Canon 5C(1)(b)(i)	Rule 4.2(B)(2) (partial)
Canon 5C(1)(b)(ii)	Rule 4.2(B)(2) (partial)
Canon 5C(1)(b)(iii)	Rule 4.2(B)(2) (partial)
Canon 5C(1)(b)(iv)	Rule 4.2(B)(3)
Canon 5C(2)	Rules 4.1(A)(8) and (9), 4.2(B) and (B)(1) and 4.4(A), (B), (B)(1) (partial) and (B)(2)

ABA
Model Code
of Judicial
Conduct

Judges and Candidates Subject to Public Election *(continued)*	
1990 CODE	2007 CODE
Canon 5C(3)	Rule 4.4(B)(1)
Canon 5C(4)	Rule 4.4(A) and (B)(3) (partial) and Comments [2] and [3]
Canon 5C(5)	Rule 4.2(B)(3) (partial)
Incumbent Judges	
1990 CODE	2007 CODE
Canon 5D	Deleted
Applicability	
1990 CODE	2007 CODE
Canon 5E	Deleted
Application	Application

ABA
Model Code
of Judicial
Conduct

2007 CODE TO 1990 CODE

2007 CODE	1990 CODE
Preamble	Preamble (partial) and Canon 1A
Scope	Preamble (partial)
Terminology	Terminology
Application	Application
Canon 1	Canons 1 and 2

Compliance with the Law

2007 CODE	1990 CODE
Rule 1.1	Canon 2A (partial)

Promoting Confidence in the Judiciary

2007 CODE	1990 CODE
Rule 1.2	Canons 2 and 2A (partial)

Avoiding Abuse of the Prestige of Judicial Office

2007 CODE	1990 CODE
Rule 1.3	Canon 2B (partial)

Performing the Duties of Judicial Office

2007 CODE	1990 CODE
Canon 2	Canon 3

Giving Precedence to the Duties of Judicial Office

2007 CODE	1990 CODE
Rule 2.1	Canon 3A

Impartiality and Fairness

2007 CODE	1990 CODE
Rule 2.2	Canons 3B(2) (partial) and 3B(8)

Bias, Prejudice, and Harassment

2007 CODE	1990 CODE
Rule 2.3(A)	Canon 3B(5) (partial)
Rule 2.3(B)	Canon 3B(5) (partial)
Rule 2.3(C)	Canon 3B(6) (partial)
Rule 2.3(D)	Canon 3B(6) (partial)

ABA
Model Code
of Judicial
Conduct

ABA
Model Code
of Judicial
Conduct

External Influences on Judicial Conduct	
2007 CODE	1990 CODE
Rule 2.4(A)	Canon 3B(2) (partial)
Rule 2.4(B)	Canon 2B (partial)
Rule 2.4(C)	Canon 2B (partial)
Competence, Diligence, and Cooperation	
2007 CODE	1990 CODE
Rule 2.5(A)	Canons 3B(2) (partial) and 3C(1) (partial) and 3B(8)
Rule 2.5(B)	3C(1) (partial)
Ensuring the Right to Be Heard	
2007 CODE	1990 CODE
Rule 2.6(A)	Canon 3B(7) (partial)
Rule 2.6(B)	Canon 3B(8) Commentary
Responsibility to Decide	
2007 CODE	1990 CODE
Rule 2.7	Canon 3B(1)
Decorum, Demeanor, and Communication with Jurors	
2007 CODE	1990 CODE
Rule 2.8(A)	Canon 3B(3)
Rule 2.8(B)	Canon 3B(4)
Rule 2.8(C)	Canon 3B(11)
Ex Parte Communication	
2007 CODE	1990 CODE
Rule 2.9(A)	Canon 3B(7) (partial)
Rule 2.9(A)(1)	Canon 3B(7)(a)
Rule 2.9(A)(1)(a)	Canon 3B(7)(a)(i)
Rule 2.9(A)(1)(b)	Canon 3B(7)(a)(ii)
Rule 2.9(A)(2)	Canon 3B(7)(b)
Rule 2.9(A)(3)	Canon 3B(7)(c)
Rule 2.9(A)(4)	Canon 3B(7)(d)
Rule 2.9(A)(5)	Canon 3B(7)(e)
Rule 2.9(B)	New
Rule 2.9(C)	Canon 3B(7) Commentary
Rule 2.9(D)	Canon 3B(7) Commentary

Judicial Statements on Pending and Impending Cases	
2007 CODE	1990 CODE
Rule 2.10(A)	Canon 3B(9) (partial)
Rule 2.10(B)	Canon 3B(10)
Rule 2.10(C)	Canon 3B(9) (partial)
Rule 2.10(D)	Canon 3B(9) (partial)
Rule 2.10(E)	New

Disqualification	
2007 CODE	1990 CODE
Rule 2.11(A)	Canon 3E(1)
Rule 2.11(A)(1)	Canon 3E(1)(a)
Rule 2.11(A)(2)	Canon 3E(1)(d)
Rule 2.11(A)(2)(a)	Canon 3E(1)(d)(i)
Rule 2.11(A)(2)(b)	Canon 3E(1)(d)(ii)
Rule 2.11(A)(2)(c)	Canon 3E(1)(d)(iii)
Rule 2.11(A)(2)(d)	Canon 3E(1)(d)(iv)
Rule 2.11(A)(3)	Canon 3E(1)(c)
Rule 2.11(A)(4)	Canon 3E(1)(e)
Rule 2.11(A)(5)	Canon 3E(1)(f)
Rule 2.11(A)(6)	Canon 3E(1)(b) (partial)
Rule 2.11(A)(6)(a)	Canon 3E(1)(b) (partial)
Rule 2.11(A)(6)(b)	Canon 3E(1)(b) Commentary
Rule 2.11(A)(6)(c)	Canon 3E(1)(b) (partial)
Rule 2.11(A)(6)(d)	New
Rule 2.11(B)	Canon 3E(2)
Rule 2.11(C)	Canon 3F

Supervisory Duties	
2007 CODE	1990 CODE
Rule 2.12(A)	Canon 3C(2)
Rule 2.12(B)	Canon 3C(3)

Administrative Appointments	
2007 CODE	1990 CODE
Rule 2.13(A)	Canon 3C(4) (partial)
Rule 2.13(A)(1)	Canon 3C(4) (partial)
Rule 2.13(A)(2)	Canon 3C(4) (partial)
Rule 2.13(B)	Canon 3C(5)
Rule 2.13(B)(1)	Canon 3C(5)(a)

ABA Model Code of Judicial Conduct

ABA
Model Code
of Judicial
Conduct

Administrative Appointments *continued*	
2007 CODE	1990 CODE
Rule 2.13(B)(2)	Canon 3C(5)(b)
Rule 2.13(B)(3)	Canon 3C(5)(c)
Rule 2.13(C)	Canon 3C(4) (partial)
Disability and Impairment	
2007 CODE	1990 CODE
Rule 2.14	New
Responding to Judicial and Lawyer Misconduct	
2007 CODE	1990 CODE
Rule 2.15(A)	Canon 3D(1) (partial)
Rule 2.15(B)	Canon 3D(2) (partial)
Rule 2.15(C)	Canon 3D(1) (partial)
Rule 2.15(D)	Canon 3D(2) (partial)
Cooperation with Disciplinary Authorities	
2007 CODE	1990 CODE
Rule 2.16(A)	New
Rule 2.16(B)	New
Personal and Extrajudicial Activities	
2007 CODE	1990 CODE
Canon 3	Canon 4
Extrajudicial Activities in General	
2007 CODE	1990 CODE
Rule 3.1	Canon 4A
Rule 3.1(A)	Canon 4A(3)
Rule 3.1(B)	New (but derived from Canon 4(A)(3)
Rule 3.1(C)	Canon 4A(1)
Rule 3.1(D)	New
Rule 3.1(E)	Canon 2B (partial)
Appearances before Governmental Bodies and Consultation with Government Officials	
2007 CODE	1990 CODE
Rule 3.2	Canon 4C(1) (partial)
Rule 3.2(A)	Canon 4C(1) (partial)
Rule 3.2(B)	New
Rule 3.2(C)	Canon 4C(1) (partial)

Testifying as a Character Witness	
2007 CODE	1990 CODE
Rule 3.3	Canon 2B (partial)

Appointments to Governmental Positions	
2007 CODE	1990 CODE
Rule 3.4	Canon 4C(2)

Use of Nonpublic Information	
2007 CODE	1990 CODE
Rule 3.5	Canon 3B(12)

Affiliation with Discriminatory Organizations	
2007 CODE	1990 CODE
Rule 3.6(A)	Canon 2C
Rule 3.6(B)	Canon 2C Commentary

Participation in Educational, Religious, Charitable, Fraternal, or Civic Organizations and Activities	
2007 CODE	1990 CODE
Rule 3.7(A)	Canon 4C(3)
Rule 3.7(A)(1)	Canon 4C(3)(b)(i) (partial)
Rule 3.7(A)(2)	Canon 4C(3)(b)(i) (partial)
Rule 3.7(A)(3)	Canon 4C(3)(b)(iii)
Rule 3.7(A)(4)	New
Rule 3.7(A)(5)	Canon 4C(3)(b)(ii)
Rule 3.7(A)(6)	Canon 4C(3)(a)
Rule 3.7(A)(6)(a)	Canon 4C(3)(a)(i)
Rule 3.7(A)(6)(b)	Canon 4C(3)(a)(ii)
Rule 3.7(B)	New

Appointments to Fiduciary Positions	
2007 CODE	1990 CODE
Rule 3.8(A)	Canon 4E(1)
Rule 3.8(B)	Canon 4E(2)
Rule 3.8(C)	Canon 4E(3)
Rule 3.8(D)	Canon 4E Commentary

Service as Arbitrator or Mediator	
2007 CODE	1990 CODE
Rule 3.9	Canon 4F

ABA Model Code of Judicial Conduct

Practice of Law	
2007 CODE	1990 CODE
Rule 3.10	Canon 4G

Financial, Business, or Remunerative Activities	
2007 CODE	1990 CODE
Rule 3.11(A)	Canon 4D(2)
Rule 3.11(B)	Canon 4D(3)
Rule 3.11(B)(1)	Canon 4D(3)(a)
Rule 3.11(B)(2)	Canon 4D(3)(b)
Rule 3.11(C)	Canon 4D(1)
Rule 3.11(C)(1)	Canon 4D(1) Commentary
Rule 3.11(C)(2)	Canon 4D(4)
Rule 3.11(C)(3)	Canon 4D(1)(b)
Rule 3.11(C)(4)	New

Compensation for Extrajudicial Activities	
2007 CODE	1990 CODE
Rule 3.12	Canons 4H(1) (partial) and 4H(1)(a)

Acceptance and Reporting of Gifts, Loans, Bequests, Benefits, or Other Things of Value	
2007 CODE	1990 CODE
Rule 3.13(A)	Canon 4D(5) (partial)
Rule 3.13(B)	Canon 4D(5) (partial)
Rule 3.13(B)(1)	Canon 4D(5)(h) (partial)
Rule 3.13(B)(2)	Canon 4D(5)(e)
Rule 3.13(B)(3)	Canon 4D(5)(c)
Rule 3.13(B)(4)	Canon 4D(5)(f)
Rule 3.13(B)(5)	New
Rule 3.13(B)(6)	Canon 4D(5)(g)
Rule 3.13(B)(7)	Canon 4D(5)(a) (partial)
Rule 3.13(B)(8)	Canon 4D(5)(b)
Rule 3.13(C)	Canon 4D(5) (partial)
Rule 3.13(C)(1)	Canon 4D(5)(a) (partial)
Rule 3.13(C)(2)	Canon 4D(5)(a) (partial)
Rule 3.13(C)(2)(a)	Canon 4D(5)(a) (partial)
Rule 3.13(C)(2)(b)	New
Rule 3.13(C)(3)	Canon 4D(5)(h)

Reimbursement of Expenses and Waivers of Fees or Charges	
2007 CODE	1990 CODE
Rule 3.14(A)	Canon 4H(1) (partial)
Rule 3.14(B)	Canon 4H(1)(b)
Rule 3.14(C)	Canon 4H(2)
Reporting Requirements	
2007 CODE	1990 CODE
Rule 3.15(A)	Canon 4H(2) (partial)
Rule 3.15(A)(1)	Canon 4H(2) (partial)
Rule 3.15(A)(2)	Canon 4H(2) (partial)
Rule 3.15(A)(3)	Canon 4H(2) (partial)
Rule 3.15(B)	Canon 4H(2) (partial)
Rule 3.15(C)	Canon 4H(2) (partial)
Rule 3.15(D)	Canon 4H(2) (partial)
Political and Campaign Activity	
2007 CODE	1990 CODE
Canon 4	Canon 5
Political and Campaign Activities of Judges and Judicial Candidates in General	
2007 CODE	1990 CODE
Rule 4.1(A)	Canon 5A(1)
Rule 4.1(A)(1)	Canon 5A(1)(a)
Rule 4.1(A)(2)	Canon 5A(1)(c)
Rule 4.1(A)(3)	Canon 5A(1)(b)
Rule 4.1(A)(4)	Canon 5A(1)(e) (partial)
Rule 4.1(A)(5)	Canon 5A(1)(e) (partial)
Rule 4.1(A)(6)	New
Rule 4.1(A)(7)	New
Rule 4.1(A)(8)	Canon 5C(2) (partial)
Rule 4.1(A)(9)	Canon 5C(2) (partial)
Rule 4.1(A)(10)	New
Rule 4.1(A)(11)	Canon 5A(3)(d)(ii)
Rule 4.1(A)(12)	Canon 3B(9) (partial)
Rule 4.1(A)(13)	Canon 5A(3)(d) and (d)(i)
Rule 4.1(B)	Canon 5A(3)(b)

ABA
Model Code
of Judicial
Conduct

Political and Campaign Activities of Judicial Candidates in Public Elections	
2007 CODE	1990 CODE
Rule 4.2(A)	Canon 5C(1)
Rule 4.2(A)(1)	Canon 5A(3)(a)
Rule 4.2(A)(2)	New
Rule 4.2(A)(3)	New
Rule 4.2(A)(4)	Canon 5A(3)(c)
Rule 4.2(B)	Canon 5C(2) (partial)
Rule 4.2(B)(1)	Canon 5C(2) (partial)
Rule 4.2(B)(2)	Canons 5C(1)(b)(i) – (iii)
Rule 4.2(B)(3)	Canon 5C(1)(b)(iv)
Rule 4.2(B)(4)	Canon 5C(1)(a)(i)
Rule 4.2(B)(5)	New
Rule 4.2(B)(6)	Canon 5C(1)(a)(iii)
Rule 4.2(C)	Canon 5C(1)
Rule 4.2(C)(1)	Canon 5C(1)(a)(ii)
Rule 4.2(C)(2)	New
Activities of Candidates for Appointive Judicial Office	
2007 CODE	1990 CODE
Rule 4.3	Canon 5B
Rule 4.3(A)	Canon 5B(2)(a)(i)
Rule 4.3(B)	Canon 5B(2)(a)(ii)
Campaign Committees	
2007 CODE	1990 CODE
Rule 4.4(A)	Canon 5C(2) (partial)
Rule 4.4(B)	Canon 5C(2) (partial)
Rule 4.4(B)(1)	Canons 5C(2) (partial) and 5C(3)
Rule 4.4(B)(2)	Canon 5C(2) (partial)
Rule 4.4(B)(3)	Canon 5C(4)
Activities of Judges Who Become Candidates for Non-Judicial Office	
2007 CODE	1990 CODE
Rule 4.5(A)	Canon 5A(2)
Rule 4.5(B)	New (but implicit in and derived from Canon 5A(2))

APPENDIX B

Judicial Ethics Committee

A. The [chief judge of the highest court of the jurisdiction] shall appoint a Judicial Ethics Committee consisting of [nine] members. [Five] members shall be judges; [two] members shall be non-judge lawyers; and [two] members shall be public members. Of the judicial members, one member shall be appointed from each of [the highest court, the intermediate levels of courts, and the trial courts.] The remaining judicial members shall be judges appointed from any of the above courts, but not from the [highest court of the jurisdiction]. The [chief judge] shall designate on of the members as chairperson. Members shall serve three-year terms; terms shall be staggered; and no individual shall serve for more than two consecutive terms.

B. The Judicial Ethics Committee so established shall have the authority to:

(1) by the concurrence of a majority of its members, express its opinion on proper judicial conduct with respect to the provisions of [the code of judicial conduct adopted by the jurisdiction and any other specified sections of law of the jurisdiction regarding the judiciary , such as financial reporting requirements], either on its own initiative, at the request of a judge or candidate for judicial office, or at the request of a court or an agency charged with the administration of judicial discipline in the jurisdiction, provided that an opinion may not be issued on a matter that is pending before a court or before such an agency except on request of the court or agency:

(2) make recommendations to [the highest court of the jurisdiction] for amendment of the Code of Judicial Conduct for the jurisdiction]; and

(3) adopt rules relating to the procedures to be used in expressing opinions, including rules to assure a timely response to inquiries.

C. A judge or candidate for judicial office as defined in the terminology Section of this Code who has requested and relied upon an opinion may not be disciplined for conduct conforming to that opinion.

D. An opinion issues pursuant to this rule shall be filed with [appropriate official of the judicial conference of the jurisdiction]. Such an opinion is confidential and not public information unless [the highest court of the jurisdiction] otherwise directs. However, the [appropriate official of the judicial conference of the jurisdiction] shall caused an edited version of each opinion to be prepared, in which the identity and geographic location of the person who has requested the opinion, the specific court involved, and the identity of other individuals, organizations or groups mentioned in the opinion are not disclosed. Opinions so edited shall be published periodically in the manner [the appropriate official of the judicial conference of the jurisdiction] deems proper.

Index

ABA Model Code of Judicial Conduct

ABA
Model Code
of Judicial
Conduct

ABA Model Code of Judicial Conduct

ABA
Model Code
of Judicial
Conduct

ABA Model Code of Judicial Conduct

ABA Canons of Professional Ethics

The Canons of Professional Ethics, to and including Canon 32,
were adopted by the American Bar Association at its
31st Annual Meeting on August 27, 1908.
Canon 28 was amended and Canons 33 to 45
adopted at the 51st Annual Meeting on July 26, 1928.
Canons 11, 13, 34, 35, and 43 were amended and Canon 46
was adopted at the 56th Annual Meeting, on August 31, 1933.
Canons 7, 11, 12, 27, 31, 33, 34, 37, 39, and 43 were amended
and Canon 47 adopted on September 30, 1937;
Canon 27 was amended on September 11, 1940;
Canons 27 and 43 were amended on August 27, 1942;
Canon 27 on August 25, 1943, and on September 19, 1951;
Canon 46 rewritten on February 21, 1956.

Preamble

In America, where the stability of Courts and of all departments of government rests upon the approval of the people, it is peculiarly essential that the system for establishing and dispensing Justice be developed to a high point of efficiency and so maintained that the public shall have absolute confidence in the integrity and impartiality of its administration. The future of the Republic, to a great extent, depends upon our maintenance of Justice pure and unsullied. It cannot be so maintained unless the conduct and the motives of the members of our profession are such as to merit the approval of all just men.

No code or set of rules can be framed, which will particularize all the duties of the lawyer in the varying phases of litigation or in all the relations of professional life. The following canons of ethics are adopted by the American Bar Association as a general guide, yet the enumeration of particular duties should not be construed as a denial of the existence of others equally imperative, though not specifically mentioned.

ABA
Canons of
Professional
Ethics

Canon 1. The Duty of the Lawyer to the Courts.

It is the duty of the lawyer to maintain towards the Courts a respectful attitude, not for the sake of the temporary incumbent of the judicial office, but for the maintenance of its supreme importance. Judges, not being wholly free to defend themselves, are peculiarly entitled to receive the support of the Bar against unjust criticism and clamor. Whenever there is proper ground for serious complaint of a judicial officer, it is the right and duty of the lawyer to submit his grievances to the proper authorities. In such cases, but not otherwise, such charges should be encouraged and the person making them should be protected.

Canon 2. The Selection of Judges.

It is the duty of the Bar to endeavor to prevent political considerations from outweighing judicial fitness in the selections of Judges. It should protect earnestly and actively against the appointment or election of those who are unsuitable for the Bench; and it should strive to have elevated thereto only those willing to forego other employments, whether of a business, political or other character, which may embarrass their free and fair consideration of questions before them for decision. The aspiration of lawyers for judicial positions should be governed by an impartial estimate of their ability to add honor to the office and not by a desire for the distinction the position may bring to themselves.

Canon 3. Attempts to Exert Personal Influence on the Court.

Marked attention and unusual hospitality on the part of a lawyer to a Judge, uncalled for by the personal relations of the parties, subject both the Judge and the lawyer to misconstructions of motive and should be avoided. A lawyer should not communicate or argue privately with the Judge as to the merits of a pending cause, and he deserves rebuke and denunciation for any device or attempt to gain from a Judge special personal consideration or favor. A self-respecting independence in the discharge of professional duty, without denial or diminution of the courtesy and respect due the Judge's station, is the only proper foundation for cordial personal and official relations between Bench and Bar.

Canon 4. When Counsel for an Indigent Prisoner.

A lawyer assigned as counsel for an indigent prisoner ought not to ask to be excused for any trivial reason, and should always exert his best efforts in his behalf.

Canon 5. The Defense of Prosecution of Those Accused of Crime.

It is the right of the lawyer to undertake the defense of a person accused of crime, regardless of his personal opinion as to the guilt of the accused;

ABA Canons of Professional Ethics

otherwise, innocent persons, victims only of suspicious circumstances, might be denied proper defense. Having undertaken such defense, the lawyer is bound by all fair and honorable means to present every defense that the law of the land permits, to the end that no person may be deprived of life or liberty, but by due process of law.

The primary duty of a lawyer engaged in public prosecution is not to convict, but to see that justice is done. The suppression of facts or the secreting of witnesses capable of establishing the innocence of the accused is highly reprehensible.

Canon 6. Adverse Influences and Conflicting Interests.

It is the duty of a lawyer at the time of retainer to disclose to the client all the circumstances of his relations to the parties, and any interest in or connection with the controversy, which might influence the client in the selection of counsel.

It is unprofessional to represent conflicting interests, except by express consent of all concerned given after a full disclosure of the facts. Within the meaning of this canon, a lawyer represents conflicting interests when, in behalf of one client, it is his duty to contend for that which duty to another client requires him to oppose.

The obligation to represent the client with undivided fidelity and not to divulge his secrets or confidences forbids also the subsequent acceptance of retainers or employment from others in matters adversely affecting any interest of the client with respect to which confidence has been reposed.

Canon 7. Professional Colleagues and Conflicts of Opinion.

A client's proffer of assistance of additional counsel should not be regarded as evidence of want of confidence, but the matter should be left to the determination of the client. A lawyer should decline association as colleague if it is objectionable to the original counsel, but if the lawyer first retained is relieved, another may come into the case.

When lawyers jointly associated in a cause cannot agree as to any matter vital to the interest of the client, the conflict of opinion should be frankly stated to him for his final determination. His decision should be accepted unless the nature of the difference makes it impracticable for the lawyer whose judgment has been overruled to co-operate effectively. In this event it is his duty to ask the client to relieve him.

Efforts, direct or indirect, in any way to encroach upon the business of another lawyer, are unworthy of those who should be brethren at the Bar; but, nevertheless, it is the right of any lawyer, without fear or favor, to give proper advice to those seeking relief against unfaithful or neglectful counsel, generally after communication with the lawyer of whom the complaint is made.

Canon 8. Advising Upon the Merits of a Client's Cause.

A lawyer should endeavor to obtain full knowledge of his client's cause before advising thereon, and he is bound to give a candid opinion of the merits and probable result of pending or contemplated litigation. The miscarriages to which justice is subject, by reason of surprises and disappointments in evidence and witnesses, and through mistakes of juries and errors of Courts, even though only occasional, admonish lawyers to beware of bold and confident assurances to clients, especially where the employment may depend upon such assurance. Whenever the controversy will admit of fair adjustment, the client should be advised to avoid or to end the litigation.

Canon 9. Negotiations with Opposite Party.

A lawyer should not in any way communicate upon the subject of controversy with a party represented by counsel; much less should he undertake to negotiate or compromise the matter with him, but should deal only with his counsel. It is incumbent upon the lawyer most particularly to avoid everything that may tend to mislead a party not represented by counsel, and he should not undertake to advise him as to the law.

Canon 10. Acquiring Interest in Litigation.

The lawyer should not purchase any interest in the subject matter of the litigation which he is conducting.

Canon 11. Dealing with Trust Property.[1]

The lawyer should refrain from any action whereby for his personal benefit or gain he abuses or takes advantage of the confidence reposed in him by his client.

Money of the client or collected for the client or other just property coming into the possession of the lawyer should be reported and accounted for promptly, and should not under any circumstances be commingled with his own or be used by him.

Canon 12. Fixing the Amount of the Fee.[2]

In fixing fees, lawyers should avoid charges which overestimate their advice and services, as well as those which undervalue them. A client's ability to pay cannot justify a charge in excess of the value of the service, though his poverty may require a less charge, or even none at all. The reasonable requests of brother lawyers, and of their widows and orphans without ample means, should receive special and kindly consideration.

---

1. Canon 11 was amended at the Fifty-sixth Annual Meeting in 1933.
2. Canon 12 was amended on September 30, 1937.

In determining the amount of the fee, it is proper to consider: (1) the time and labor required, the novelty and difficulty of the questions involved and the skill requisite properly to conduct the cause; (2) whether the acceptance of employment in the particular case will preclude the lawyer's appearance for others in cases likely to arise out of the transaction, and in which there is a reasonable expectation that otherwise he would be employed, or will involve the loss of other employment while employed in the particular case or antagonisms with other clients; (3) the customary charges of the Bar for similar services; (4) the amount involved in the controversy and the benefits resulting to the client from the services; (5) the contingency or the certainty of the compensation; and (6) the character of the employment, whether casual or for an established and constant client. No one of these considerations in itself is controlling. They are mere guides in ascertaining the real value of the service.

In determining the customary charges of the Bar for similar services, it is proper for a lawyer to consider a schedule of minimum fees adopted by a Bar Association, but no lawyer should permit himself to be controlled thereby or to follow it as his sole guide in determining the amount of his fee.

In fixing fees it should never be forgotten that the profession is a branch of the administration of justice and not a mere money-getting trade.

Canon 13. Contingent Fees.[3]

A contract for a contingent fee where sanctioned by law, should be reasonable under all the circumstances of the case, including the risk and uncertainty of the compensation, but should always be subject to the supervision of a Court, as to its reasonableness.

Canon 14. Suing a Client for a Fee.

Controversies with clients concerning compensation are to be avoided by the lawyer so far as shall be compatible with his self-respect and with his right to receive reasonable recompense for his services; and lawsuits with clients should be resorted to only to prevent injustice, imposition or fraud.

Canon 15. How Far a Lawyer May Go in Supporting a Client's Cause.

Nothing operates more certainly to create or to foster popular prejudice against lawyers as a class, and to deprive the profession of that full measure of public esteem and confidence which belongs to the proper discharge of its duties than does the false claim, often set up by the unscrupulous in defense of questionable transactions, that it is the duty of the lawyer to do whatever may enable him to succeed in winning his client's cause.

---

3. Canon 13 was amended at the Fifty-sixth Annual Meeting in 1933.

It is improper for a lawyer to assert in argument his personal belief in his client's innocence or in the justice of his cause.

The lawyer owes entire devotion to the interest of the client, warm zeal in the maintenance and defense of his rights and the exertion of his utmost learning and ability, to the end that nothing be taken or be withheld from him, save by the rules of law, legally applied. No fear of judicial disfavor or public unpopularity should restrain him from the full discharge of his duty. In the judicial forum the client is entitled to the benefit of any and every remedy and defense that is authorized by the law of the land, and he may expect his lawyer to assert every such remedy or defense. But it is steadfastly to be borne in the mind that the great trust of the lawyer is to be performed within and not without the bounds of the law. The office of attorney does not permit, much less does it demand of him for any client, violation of law or any manner of fraud or chicane. He must obey his own conscience and not that of his client.

Canon 16. Restraining Clients From Improprieties.

A lawyer should use his best efforts to restrain and to prevent his clients from doing those things which the lawyer himself ought not to do, particularly with reference to their conduct towards Courts, judicial officers, jurors, witnesses and suitors. If a client persists in such wrongdoing the lawyer should terminate their relation.

Canon 17. Ill Feeling and Personalities Between Advocates.

Clients, not lawyers, are the litigants. Whatever may be the ill-feeling existing between clients, it should not be allowed to influence counsel in their conduct and demeanor toward each other or toward suitors in the cause. All personalities between counsel should be scrupulously avoided. In the trial of a cause it is indecent to allude to the personal history or the personal peculiarities and idiosyncrasies of counsel on the other side. Personal colloquies between counsel which cause delay and promote unseemly wrangling should also be carefully avoided.

Canon 18. Treatment of Witnesses and Litigants.

A lawyer should always treat adverse witnesses and suitors with fairness and due consideration, and he should never minister to the malevolence or prejudices of a client in the trial or conduct of a cause. The client cannot be made the keeper of the lawyer's conscience in professional matters. He has no right to demand that his counsel shall abuse the opposite party or indulge in offensive personalities. Improper speech is not excusable on the ground that it is what the client would say if speaking in his own behalf.

ABA
Canons of
Professional
Ethics

Canon 19. Appearance of Lawyer
as Witness for His Client.

When a lawyer is a witness for his client, except as to merely formal matters, such as the attestation or custody of an instrument and the like, he should leave the trial of the case to other counsel. Except when essential to the ends of justice, a lawyer should avoid testifying in court in behalf of his client.

Canon 20. Newspaper Discussion
of Pending Litigation.

Newspaper publications by a lawyer as to pending or anticipated litigation may interfere with a fair trial in the Courts and otherwise prejudice the due administration of justice. Generally they are to be condemned. If the extreme circumstances of a particular case justify a statement to the public, it is unprofessional to make it anonymously. An ex parte reference to the facts should not go beyond quotation from the records and papers on file in the court; but even in extreme cases it is better to avoid any ex parte statement.

Canon 21. Punctuality and Expedition.

It is the duty of the lawyer not only to his client, but also to the Court and to the public to be punctual in attendance, and to be concise and direct in the trial and disposition of causes.

Canon 22. Candor and Fairness.

The conduct of the lawyer before the Court and with other lawyers should be characterized by candor and fairness.

It is not candid or fair for the lawyer knowingly to misquote the contents of a paper, the testimony of a witness, the language or the argument of opposing counsel, or the language of a decision or a textbook; or with knowledge of its invalidity, to cite as authority a decision that has been overruled, or a statute that has been repealed; or in argument to assert as a fact that which has not been proved, or in those jurisdictions where a side has the opening and closing arguments to mislead his opponent by concealing or withholding positions in his opening argument upon which his side then intends to rely.

It is unprofessional and dishonorable to deal other than candidly with the facts in taking the statements of witnesses, in drawing affidavits and other documents, and in the presentation of causes.

A lawyer should not offer evidence which he knows the Court should reject, in order to get the same before the jury by argument for its admissibility, nor should he address to the Judge arguments upon any point not properly calling for determination by him. Neither should he introduce into an argument, addressed to the court, remarks or statements intended to influence the jury or bystanders.

These and all kindred practices are unprofessional and unworthy of an officer of the law charged, as is the lawyer, with the duty of aiding in the administration of justice.

Canon 23. Attitude Toward Jury.

All attempts to curry favor with juries by fawning, flattery or pretended solicitude for their personal comfort are unprofessional. Suggestions of counsel, looking to the comfort or convenience of jurors, and propositions to dispense with argument, should be made to the Court out of the jury's hearing. A lawyer must never converse privately with jurors about the case; and both before and during the trial he should avoid communicating with them, even as to matters foreign to the cause.

Canon 24. Right of Lawyer to Control the Incidents of the Trial.

As to incidental matters pending the trial, not affecting the merits of the cause, or working substantial prejudice to the rights of the client, such as forcing the opposite lawyer to trial when he is under affliction or bereavement; forcing the trial on a particular day to the injury of the opposite lawyer when no harm will result from a trial at a different time; agreeing to an extension of time for signing a bill of exceptions, cross interrogatories and the like, the lawyer must be allowed to judge. In such matters no client has a right to demand that his counsel shall be illiberal, or that he do anything therein repugnant to his own sense of honor and propriety.

Canon 25. Taking Technical Advantage of Opposite Counsel; Agreements with Him.

A lawyer should not ignore known customs or practice of the Bar or of a particular Court, even when the law permits, without giving timely notice to the opposing counsel. As far as possible, important agreements, affecting the rights of clients, should be reduced to writing; but it is dishonorable to avoid performance of an agreement fairly made because it is not reduced to writing, as required by rules of Court.

Canon 26. Professional Advocacy Other Than Before Courts.

A lawyer openly, and in his true character, may render professional services before legislative or other bodies, regarding proposed legislation and in advocacy of claims before departments of government, upon the same principles of ethics which justify his appearance before the Courts; but it is unprofessional for a lawyer so engaged to conceal his attorneyship, or to employ secret personal solicitations, or to use means other than those addressed to the reason and understanding, to influence action.

Canon 27. Advertising, Direct or Indirect[4]

It is unprofessional to solicit professional employment by circulars, advertisements, through touters or by personal communications or interviews not warranted by personal relations. Indirect advertisements for professional employment such as furnishing or inspiring newspaper comments, or procuring his photograph to be published in connection with causes in which the lawyer has been or is engaged or concerning the manner of their conduct, the magnitude of the interest involved, the importance of the lawyer's position, and all other like self-laudation, offend the traditions and lower the tone of our profession and are reprehensible; but the customary use of simple professional cards is not improper.

Publication in reputable law lists in a manner consistent with the standards of conduct imposed by these canons of brief biographical and informative data is permissible. Such data must not be misleading and may include only a statement of the lawyer's name and the names of his professional associates; addresses, telephone numbers, cable addresses; branches of the profession practiced; date and place of birth and admission to the bar; schools attended, with dates of graduation, degrees and other educational distinctions; public or quasi-public offices; posts of honor; legal authorships; legal teaching positions; memberships and offices in bar associations and committees thereof, in legal and scientific societies and legal fraternities; the fact of listings in other reputable law lists; the names and addresses of references; and, with their written consent, the names of clients regularly represented. A certificate of compliance with the Rules and Standards issued by the Special Committee on Law Lists may be treated as evidence that such list is reputable.

It is not improper for a lawyer who is admitted to practice as proctor in admiralty to use that designation on his letterhead or shingle or for a lawyer who has complied with the statutory requirements of admission to practice before the patent office to so use the designation "patent attorney" or "patent lawyer" or "trademark attorney" or "trademark lawyer" or any combination of those terms.

Canon 28. Stirring Up Litigation, Directly or Through Agents.[5]

It is unprofessional for a lawyer to volunteer advice to bring a lawsuit, except in rare cases where ties of blood, relationship or trust make it his duty to do so. Stirring up strife and litigation is not only unprofessional, but it is indictable at common law. It is disreputable to hunt up defects in titles or other causes of action and inform thereof in order to be employed

---

4. Canon 27 was amended to its present form at the annual meeting on August 25, 1943. The last paragraph was added by the amendment of September, 1951.

5. Canon 28 was amended to its present form at this Annual Meeting on July 26, 1928, by inserting the words "or collect judgment" in the 5th line as printed above.

to bring suit or collect judgment, or to breed litigation by seeking out those with claims for personal injuries or those having any other grounds of action in order to secure them as clients, or to employ agents or runners for like purposes, or to pay or reward, directly or indirectly, those who bring or influence the bringing of such cases to his office, or to remunerate policemen, court or prison officials, physicians, hospital attaches or others who may succeed, under the guise of giving disinterested friendly advice, in influencing the criminal, the sick and the injured, the ignorant or other, to seek his professional services. A duty to the public and to the profession devolves upon every member of the Bar having knowledge of such practices upon the part of any practitioner immediately to inform thereof, to the end that the offender may be disbarred.

ABA
Canons of
Professional
Ethics

Canon 29. Upholding the Honor of the Profession.

Lawyers should expose without fear or favor before the proper tribunals corrupt or dishonest conduct in the profession, and should accept without hesitation employment against a member of the Bar who has wronged his client. The counsel upon the trial of a cause in which perjury has been committed owes it to the profession and to the public to bring the matter to the knowledge of the prosecuting authorities. The lawyer should aid in guarding the Bar against the admission to the profession of candidates unfit or unqualified because deficient in either moral character or education. He should strive at all times to uphold the honor and to maintain the dignity of the profession and to improve not only the law but the administration of justice.

Canon 30. Justifiable and Unjustifiable Litigation.

The lawyer must decline to conduct a civil cause or to make a defense when convinced that it is intended merely to harass or to injure the opposite party or to work oppression or wrong. But otherwise it is his right, and, having accepted retainer, it becomes his duty to insist upon the judgment of the Court as to the legal merits of his client's claim. His appearance in Court should be deemed equivalent to an assertion on his honor that in his opinion his client's cause is one proper for judicial determination.

Canon 31. Responsibility for Litigation.[6]

No lawyer is obliged to act either as adviser or advocate for every person who may wish to become his client. He has the right to decline employment. Every lawyer upon his own responsibility must decide what employment he will accept as counsel, what causes he will bring into Court for plaintiffs, what causes he will contest in Court for defendants. The responsibility for

---

6. Canon 31 was amended on September 30, 1937, by substituting the word "employment" on line 3, for "business."

advising as to questionable transactions, for bringing questionable suits, for urging questionable defenses, is the lawyer's responsibility. He cannot escape it by urging as an excuse that he is only following his client's instructions.

Canon 32. The Lawyer's Duty in Its Last Analysis.

No client, corporate or individual, however powerful, nor any cause, civil or political, however important, is entitled to receive nor should any lawyer render any service or advice involving disloyalty to the law whose ministers we are, or disrespect of the judicial office, which we are bound to uphold, or corruption of any person or persons exercising a public office or private trust, or deception or betrayal of the public. When rendering any such improper service or advice, the lawyer invites and merits stern and just condemnation. Correspondingly, he advances the honor of his profession and the best interests of his client when he renders service or gives advice tending to impress upon the client and his undertaking exact compliance with the strictest principles of moral law. He must also observe and advise his client to observe the statute law, though until a statute shall have been construed and interpreted by competent adjudication, he is free and is entitled to advise as to its validity and as to what he conscientiously believes to be its just meaning and extent. But above all a lawyer will find his highest honor in a deserved reputation for fidelity to private trust and to public duty, as an honest man and as a patriotic and loyal citizen.

Canon 33. Partnerships—Names.[7]

Partnerships among lawyers for the practice of their profession are very common and are not to be condemned. In the formation of partnerships and the use of partnership names care should be taken not to violate any law, custom, or rule of court locally applicable. Where partnerships are formed between lawyers who are not all admitted to practice in the courts of the state, care should be taken to avoid any misleading name or representation which would create a false impression as to the professional position or privileges of the member not locally admitted. In the formation of partnerships for the practice of law, no person should be admitted or held out as a practitioner or member who is not a member of the legal profession duly authorized to practice, and amenable to professional discipline. In the selection and use of a firm name, no false, misleading, assumed or trade name should be used. The continued use of the name of a deceased or former partner, when permissible by local custom, is not unethical, but care should be taken that no imposition or deception is practiced through this use. When a member of the firm, on becoming a judge, is precluded from practising law, his name should not be continued in the firm name.

---

7. Canon 33 was amended September 30, 1937.

Partnerships between lawyers and members of other professions or non-professional persons should not be formed or permitted where any part of the partnership's employment consists of the practice of law.

Canon 34. Division of Fees.[8]

No division of fees for legal services is proper, except with another lawyer, based upon a division of service or responsibility.

Canon 35. Intermediaries.[9]

The professional services of a lawyer should not be controlled or exploited by any lay agency, personal or corporate, which intervenes between client and lawyer. A lawyer's responsibilities and qualifications are individual. He should avoid all relations which direct the performance of his duties by or in the interest of such intermediary. A lawyer's relation to his client should be personal, and the responsibility should be direct to the client. Charitable societies rendering aid to the indigent are not deemed such intermediaries.

A lawyer may accept employment from any organization, such as an association, club or trade organization, to render legal services in any matter in which the organization, as an entity, is interested, but this employment should not include the rendering of legal services to the members of such an organization in respect to their individual affairs.

"The established custom of receiving commercial collections through a law agency is not condemned hereby."

Canon 36. Retirement from Judicial Position or Public Employment.

A lawyer should not accept employment as an advocate in any matter upon the merits of which he has previously acted in a judicial capacity.

A lawyer, having once held public office or having been in the public employ, should not after his retirement accept employment in connection with any matter which he has investigated or passed upon while in such office or employ.

Canon 37. Confidences of a Client.[10]

It is the duty of a lawyer to preserve his client's confidences. This duty outlasts the lawyer's employment, and extends as well to his employees; and neither of them should accept employment which involves or may involve the disclosure or use of these confidences, either for the private advantage of

---

8. Canon 34 was amended September 30, 1937.

9. Canon 35 was amended August 31, 1933.

10. As amended September 30, 1937.

the lawyer or his employees or to the disadvantage of the client, without his knowledge and consent, and even though there are other available sources of such information. A lawyer should not continue employment when he discovers that this obligation prevents the performance of his full duty to his former or to his new client.

If a lawyer is accused by his client, he is not precluded from disclosing the truth in respect to the accusation. The announced intention of a client to commit a crime is not included within the confidences which he is bound to respect. He may properly make such disclosures as may be necessary to prevent the act or protect those against whom it is threatened.

Canon 38. Compensation, Commissions and Rebates.

A lawyer should accept no compensation, commission, rebates or other advantages from others without the knowledge and consent of his client after full disclosure.

Canon 39. Witnesses.[11]

A lawyer may properly interview any witness or prospective witness for the opposing side in any civil or criminal action without the consent of opposing counsel or party. In doing so, however, he should scrupulously avoid any suggestion calculated to induce the witness to suppress or deviate from the truth, or in any degree to affect his free and untrammeled conduct when appearing at the trial or on the witness stand.

Canon 40. Newspapers.

A lawyer may with propriety write articles for publications in which he gives information upon the law; but he should not accept employment from such publications to advise inquirers in respect to their individual rights.

Canon 41. Discovery of Imposition and Deception.

When a lawyer discovers that some fraud or deception has been practiced, which has unjustly imposed upon the court or a party, he should endeavor to rectify it; at first by advising his client, and if his client refuses to forego the advantage thus unjustly gained, he should promptly inform the injured person or his counsel, so that they may take appropriate steps.

Canon 42. Expenses of Litigation.

A lawyer may not properly agree with a client that the lawyer shall pay or bear the expenses of litigation; he may in good faith advance expenses as a matter of convenience, but subject to reimbursement.

---

11. Canon 39 was amended on September 30, 1937.

Canon 43. Approved Law Lists.[12]

It is improper for a lawyer to permit his name to be published in a law list the conduct, management or contents of which are calculated or likely to deceive or injure the public or the profession, or to lower the dignity or standing of the profession.

Canon 44. Withdrawal from Employment as Attorney or Counsel.

The right of an attorney or counsel to withdraw from employment, once assumed, arises only from good cause. Even the desire or consent of the client is not always sufficient. The lawyer should not throw up the unfinished task to the detriment of his client except for reasons of honor or self-respect. If the client insists upon an unjust or immoral course in the conduct of his case, or if he persists over the attorney's remonstrance in presenting frivolous defenses, or if he deliberately disregards an agreement or obligation as to fees or expenses, the lawyer may be warranted in withdrawing on due notice to the client, allowing him time to employ another lawyer. So also when a lawyer discovers that his client has no case and the client is determined to continue it; or even if the lawyer finds himself incapable of conducting the case effectively. Sundry other instances may arise in which withdrawal is to be justified. Upon withdrawing from a case after a retainer has been paid, the attorney should refund such part of the retainer as has not been clearly earned.

Canon 45. Specialists.

The canons of the American Bar Association apply to all branches of the legal profession; specialists in particular branches are not to be considered as exempt from the application of these principles.

Canon 46. Notice to Local Lawyers.[13]

A lawyer available to act as an associate of other lawyers in a particular branch of the law or legal service may send to local lawyers only and publish in his local legal journal a brief and dignified announcement of his availability to serve other lawyers in connection therewith. The announcement should be in a form which does not constitute a statement or representation of special experience or expertness.

Canon 47. Aiding the Unauthorized Practice of Law.[14]

No lawyer shall permit his professional services, or his name, to be used in aid of, or to make possible, the unauthorized practice of law by any lay agency, personal or corporate.

---

12. Canon 43, with its title, was amended on August 27, 1942.
13. Canon 46 was amended on February 21, 1956.
14. Adopted September 30, 1937.

ABA Standards for Imposing Lawyer Sanctions

As approved February 10, 1986, and as amended February 4, 1992.

ABA Standards
for Imposing
Lawyer
Sanctions

Contents

ABA Standards for Imposing Lawyer Sanctions

ABA Standards
for Imposing
Lawyer
Sanctions

I. Preface

A. Background

In 1979, the American Bar Association published the *Standards for Lawyer Discipline and Disability Proceedings*.[1] That book was a result of work by the Joint Committee on Professional Discipline of the American Bar Association. The Joint Committee was composed of members of the Judicial Administration Division and the Standing Committee on Professional Discipline of the American Bar Association. The task of the Joint Committee was to prepare standards for enforcement of discipline in the legal community.

The 1979 standards have been most helpful, and have been used by numerous jurisdictions as a frame of reference against which to compare their own disciplinary systems. Many jurisdictions have modified their procedures to comport with these suggested standards, and the Standing Committee on Professional Discipline of the American Bar Association has assisted state disciplinary systems in evaluating their programs in light of the approved standards.

It became evident that additional analysis was necessary in one important area—that of *appropriate sanctions* for lawyer misconduct. The American Bar Association *Standards for Lawyer Discipline and Disability Proceedings* (hereinafter "Standards for Lawyer Discipline") do not attempt to recommend the type of discipline to be imposed in any particular case. The Standards merely state that the discipline to be imposed "should depend upon the facts and circumstances of the case, should be fashioned in light of the purpose of lawyer discipline, and may take into account aggravating or mitigating circumstances" (Standard 7.1).

For lawyer discipline to be truly effective, sanctions must be based on clearly developed standards. Inappropriate sanctions can undermine the goals of lawyer discipline: sanctions which are too lenient fail to adequately deter misconduct and thus lower public confidence in the profession; sanctions which are too onerous may impair confidence in the system and deter lawyers from reporting ethical violations on the part of other lawyers. Inconsistent sanctions, either within a jurisdiction or among jurisdictions, cast doubt on the efficiency and the basic fairness of all disciplinary systems.

As an example of this problem of inconsistent sanctions, consider the range in levels of sanctions imposed for a conviction for failure to file federal income taxes. In one jurisdiction, in 1979, a lawyer who failed to file income tax returns for one year was suspended for one year,[2] while, in 1980,

---

1. Model Rules for Lawyer Disciplinary Enforcement (American Bar Association Standing Committee on Professional Discipline, 1989).
2. In re Gold, 77 Ill. 2d 224, 396 N.E.2d 25 (1979).

a lawyer who failed to file income tax returns for two years was merely censured.[3]

Within a two-year period, the sanctions imposed on lawyers who converted their clients' funds included disbarment,[4] suspension,[5] and censure.[6] The inconsistency of sanctions imposed by different jurisdictions for the same misconduct is even greater.

An examination of these cases illustrates the need for a comprehensive system of sanctions. In many cases, different sanctions are imposed for the same acts of misconduct, and the courts rarely provide any explanation for the selection of sanctions. In other cases, the courts may give reasons for their decisions, but their statements are too general to be useful. In still other cases, the courts may list specific factors to support a certain result, but they do not state whether these factors must be considered in every discipline case, nor do they explain whether these factors are entitled to equal weight.

The Joint Committee on Professional Sanctions (hereinafter "Sanctions Committee") was formed to address these problems by formulating standards to be used in imposing sanctions for lawyer misconduct. The Sanctions Committee was composed of members from the Judicial Administration Division and the Standing Committee on Professional Discipline. The mandate given was ambitious: the Committee was to examine the current range of sanctions imposed and to formulate standards for the imposition of appropriate sanctions.

In addressing this task, the Sanctions Committee recognized that any proposed standards should serve as a model which sets forth a comprehensive system of sanctions, but which leaves room for flexibility and creativity in assigning sanctions in particular cases of lawyer misconduct. These standards are designed to promote thorough, rational consideration of all factors relevant to imposing a sanction in an individual case. The standards attempt to ensure that such factors are given appropriate weight in light of the stated goals of lawyer discipline, and that only relevant aggravating and mitigating circumstances are considered at the appropriate time. Finally, the standards should help achieve the degree of consistency in the imposition of lawyer discipline necessary for fairness to the public and the bar.

While these standards will improve the operation of lawyer discipline systems, there is an additional factor which, though not the focus of this report, cannot be overlooked. In discussing sanctions for lawyer misconduct, this report assumes that all instances of unethical conduct will be brought to

ABA Standards for Imposing Lawyer Sanctions

---

3. In re Oliver, M.R. 2454, 79-CH-6 (1980).
4. In re Smith, 63 Ill. 2d 250, 347 N.E.2d 133 (1976).
5. In re DiBella, 58 Ill. 2d 5, 316 N.E.2d 771 (1974).
6. In re Sherman, 60 Ill. 2d 590, 328 N.E.2d 553 (1975).

the attention of the disciplinary system. Experience indicates that such is not the case. In 1970, the ABA Special Committee on Evaluation of Disciplinary Enforcement (the Clark Committee) was charged with the responsibility for evaluating the effectiveness of disciplinary enforcement systems. The Clark Committee concluded that one of the most significant problems in lawyer discipline was the reluctance of lawyers and judges to report misconduct.[7] That same problem exists today. It cannot be emphasized strongly enough that lawyers and judges must report unethical conduct to the appropriate disciplinary agency.[8] Failure to render such reports is a disservice to the public and the legal profession.

Judges in particular should be reminded of their obligation to report unethical conduct to the disciplinary agencies. Under the ABA Model Code of Judicial Conduct, a judge is obligated to "take or initiate appropriate disciplinary measures against a judge or lawyer for unprofessional conduct of which the judge may become aware."[9] Frequently, judges take the position that there is no such need and that errant behavior of lawyers can be remedied solely by use of contempt proceedings and other alternative means. It must be emphasized that the goals of lawyer discipline are not properly and fully served if the judge who observes unethical conduct simply deals with it on an ad hoc basis. It may be proper and wise for a judge to use contempt powers in order to assure that the court maintains control of the proceeding and punishes a lawyer for abusive or obstreperous conduct in the court's presence. However, the lawyer discipline system is in addition to and serves purposes different from contempt powers and other mechanisms available to the judge. Only if all lawyer misconduct is in fact reported to the appropriate disciplinary agency can the legal profession have confidence that consistent sanctions are imposed for similar misconduct.

Consistency of sanctions depends on reporting of other types as well. The American Bar Association Center for Professional Responsibility has established a "National Discipline Data Bank" which collects statistics on the nature of ethical violations and sanctions imposed in lawyer discipline cases in all jurisdictions. The information available from the data bank is only as good as the reports which reach it. It is vital that the data bank promptly receive complete, accurate and detailed information with regard to all discipline cases.

---

7. PROBLEMS AND RECOMMENDATIONS IN DISCIPLINARY ENFORCEMENT (Chicago: American Bar Association, Special Committee on Evaluation of Disciplinary Enforcement, 1970), at 167.

8. Lawyers have a duty to report ethical misconduct of other lawyers under Rule 8.3 of the MODEL RULES OF PROFESSIONAL CONDUCT (American Bar Association, 1983) and under DR 1-103 of the MODEL RULES OF PROFESSIONAL RESPONSIBILITY (American Bar Association, 1981). Judges have a similar duty under the MODEL CODE OF JUDICIAL CONDUCT, Canon 3(D)(2) (American Bar Association, 1990).

9. Id., MODEL CODE OF JUDICIAL CONDUCT.

Finally, the purposes of lawyer sanctions can best be served, and the consistency of those sanctions enhanced, if courts and disciplinary agencies throughout the country articulate the reasons for sanctions imposed. Courts of record that impose lawyer discipline do a valuable service to the legal profession and the public when they issue opinions in lawyer discipline cases that explain the imposition of a specific sanction. The effort of the Sanctions Committee was made easier by the well-reasoned judicial opinions that were available. At the same time, the Sanctions Committee was frustrated by the fact that many jurisdictions do not publish lawyer discipline decisions, and that even published decisions are often summary in nature, failing to articulate the justification for the sanctions imposed.

The *Standards for Imposing Lawyer Sanctions* were amended by the ABA House of Delegates on February 4, 1992. The amendments were proposed by the ABA Standing Committee on Professional Discipline as a result of its ongoing review of the courts' use of the Standards in lawyer disciplinary cases to assure their consistency with the developing case law.

B. Methodology

The *Standards for Imposing Lawyer Sanctions* have been developed after an examination of all reported lawyer discipline cases from 1980 to June 1984, where public discipline was imposed.[10] In addition, eight jurisdictions, which represent a variety of disciplinary systems as well as diversity in geography and population size, were examined in depth. In these jurisdictions— Arizona, California, the District of Columbia, Florida, Illinois, New Jersey, North Dakota, and Utah—all published disciplinary cases from January, 1974 through June 1984 were analyzed. In each case, data were collected concern-

---

10. See Appendix 3 for a listing of the actual number of reported cases from each jurisdiction. The differences in the number of reported cases among the jurisdictions is a function not only of the differences in lawyer populations, but in the operation of the state discipline systems. States differ dramatically in the sophistication of their disciplinary systems; most importantly for this study, states vary in the extent to which disciplinary orders are published. In those jurisdictions where disciplinary decisions are not published in the regional reporters, summaries in state bar publications or unreported cases (supplied by bar counsel) were examined. (To obtain copies of unreported decisions, contact the ABA Center for Professional Responsibility.) The states in which only reported cases were examined were: Alabama, Alaska, Arkansas, Colorado, Connecticut, Delaware, Georgia, Hawaii, Idaho, Indiana, Iowa, Kansas, Louisiana, Maryland, Minnesota, Mississippi, Missouri, Montana, Nebraska, Nevada, New Jersey, New Mexico, North Carolina, Ohio, Oklahoma, Oregon, Rhode Island, South Carolina, South Dakota, Utah, Vermont, Washington, West Virginia, and Wisconsin. In the following jurisdictions both reported and unreported cases were examined: Arizona, California, District of Columbia, Florida, Illinois, Kentucky, Massachusetts, New York, Pennsylvania, Tennessee, Virginia, and Wyoming. In the following jurisdictions, all data were collected from unreported decisions (supplied by bar counsel or taken from case summaries in bar publications): Maine, Michigan, New Hampshire, and Texas.

ing the type of offense, the sanction imposed, the policy considerations identified, and aggravating or mitigating circumstances noted by the court.[11]

These data were examined to identify the patterns that currently exist among courts imposing sanctions and the policy considerations that guide the courts. In general, the courts were consistent in identifying the following policy considerations: protecting the public, ensuring the administration of justice, and maintaining the integrity of the profession. In the words of the California Supreme Court: "The purpose of a disciplinary proceeding is not punitive but to inquire into the fitness of the lawyer to continue in that capacity for the protection of the public, the courts, and the legal profession."[12] However, the courts failed to articulate any theoretical framework for use in imposing sanctions.

In attempting to develop such a framework, the Sanctions Committee considered a number of options. The Committee considered the obvious possibility of identifying each and every type of misconduct in which a lawyer could engage, then suggesting either a recommended sanction or a range of recommended sanctions to deal with that particular misconduct. The Sanctions Committee unanimously rejected that option as being both theoretically simplistic and administratively cumbersome.[13]

The Sanctions Committee next considered an approach that dealt with general categories of lawyer misconduct and applied recommended sanctions to those types of misconduct depending on whether or not—and to what extent—the misconduct resulted from intentional or malicious acts of the lawyer. There is some merit in that approach; certainly, the intentional or unintentional conduct of the lawyer is a relevant factor. Nonetheless, that approach was also abandoned after the Sanctions Committee carefully reviewed the purposes of lawyer sanctions. Solely focusing on the intent of the lawyer is not sufficient, and proposed standards must also consider

---

11. Because of the difficulty in getting complete factual statements, the report does not include cases which were the result of consent orders, or cases in which reciprocal discipline was imposed.

12. Ballard v. State Bar of California, 35 Cal. 3d 274, 673 P.2d 226, 197 Cal. Rptr. 556 (1983).

13. An example of the problems which would be encountered in such an approach will suffice to demonstrate why that approach was rejected. It is improper for a lawyer to neglect a legal matter entrusted to him (Rule 1.3/DR 6-101 (A)(3)). Sanctions which are imposed for violations of this ethical rule vary dramatically. Such conduct may be an intentional violation of the rule (as where a lawyer takes a client's money never intending to perform the services requested), or it may result from negligence (as where an overworked or inexperienced lawyer does not meet a deadline relating to some aspect of the representation). The Sanctions Committee felt that a listing of sanctions based merely on the type of lawyer misconduct would not adequately differentiate between conduct which has an extremely deleterious effect on the client, the public, the legal system, and the profession, and conduct which has only a minimal effect. In short, the Sanctions Committee concluded that an approach that reviewed each type of misconduct would result in nothing more than a general statement that the individual circumstances of a case dictate the type of sanction which ought to be imposed.

the damage which the lawyer's misconduct causes to the client, the public, the legal system, and the profession. An approach which looked only at the extent of injury was also rejected as being too narrow.

The Committee adopted a model that looks first at the ethical duty and to whom it is owed, and then at the lawyer's mental state and the amount of injury caused by the lawyer's misconduct. (See Theoretical Framework, p. 5, for a detailed discussion of this approach.) Thus, one will look in vain for a section of this report which recommends a specific sanction for, say, improper contact with opposing parties who are represented by counsel [Rule 4.2/DR 7-104(A)(1)],[14] or for any other specific misconduct. What one will find, however, is an organizational framework that provides recommendations as to the type of sanction that should be imposed based on violations of duties owed to clients, the public, the legal system, and the profession.

To provide support for this approach, the Sanctions Committee has offered as much specific data and guidance as possible from reported cases.[15] Thus, with regard to each category of misconduct, the report provides the following:

- discussion of what types of sanctions have been imposed for similar misconduct in reported cases;
- discussion of policy reasons which are articulated in reported cases to support such sanctions; and,
- finally, a recommendation as to the level of sanction imposed for the given misconduct, absent aggravating or mitigating circumstances.

While it is recognized that any individual case may present aggravating or mitigating factors which would lead to the imposition of a sanction different from that recommended, these standards present a model which can be used initially to categorize misconduct and to identify the appropriate sanction. The decision as to the effect of any aggravating or mitigating factors should come only after this initial determination of the sanction.

The Sanctions Committee also recognized that the imposition of a sanction of suspension or disbarment does not conclude the matter. Typically, disciplined lawyers will request reinstatement or readmission. While this report does not include an in-depth study of reinstatement and readmission cases, a general recommendation concerning standards for reinstatement and readmission appears as Standard 2.10.

---

14. Although the House of Delegates of the American Bar Association adopted the MODEL RULES OF PROFESSIONAL CONDUCT on August 2, 1983, as the ethical standards for the legal profession, references to the CODE OF PROFESSIONAL RESPONSIBILITY are included here because some states' ethical standards still follow the Code in both form and substance.

15. While it is not possible to discuss in detail each of the 2,991 cases which have been examined in preparing this report, statistical summaries are available from the American Bar Association Center for Professional Responsibility.

II. Theoretical Framework

These standards are based on an analysis of the nature of the professional relationship. Historically, being a member of a profession has meant that an individual is some type of expert, possessing knowledge of high instrumental value such that the members of the community give the professional the power to make decisions for them. In the legal profession, the community has allowed the profession the right of self-regulation. As stated in the Preamble to the ABA Model Rules of Professional Conduct (hereinafter "Model Rules"), "[t]he legal profession's relative autonomy carries with it special responsibilities of self-government. The profession has a responsibility to assure that its regulations are conceived in the public interest and not in furtherance of parochial or self-interested concerns of the bar."[16]

This view of the professional relationship requires lawyers to observe the ethical requirements that are set out in the Model Rules (or applicable standard in the jurisdiction where the lawyer is licensed). While the Model Rules define the ethical guidelines for lawyers, they do not provide any method for assigning sanctions for ethical violations. The Committee developed a model which requires a court imposing sanctions to answer each of the following questions:

(1) What ethical duty did the lawyer violate? (A duty to a client, the public, the legal system, or the profession?)

(2) What was the lawyer's mental state? (Did the lawyer act intentionally, knowingly, or negligently?)

(3) What was the extent of the actual or potential injury caused by the lawyer's misconduct? (Was there a serious or potentially serious injury?) and

(4) Are there any aggravating or mitigating circumstances?

In determining the nature of the ethical duty violated, the standards assume that the most important ethical duties are those obligations which a lawyer owes to clients. These include:

(a) the duty of loyalty which (in the terms of the Model Rules and Code of Professional Responsibility) includes the duties to:

   (i) preserve the property of a client [Rule 1.15/DR 9-102],

   (ii) maintain client confidences [Rule 1.6/DR 4-101], and

   (iii) avoid conflicts of interest [Rules 1.7 through 1.13, 2.2, 3.7, 5.4(c) and 6.3/ DR 5-101 through DR 5-105, DR 9-101];

(b) the duty of diligence [Rules 1.2, 1.3, 1.4/DR 6-101(A)(3)];

(c) the duty of competence [Rule 1.1/DR 6-101(A)(1) & (2)]; and

(d) the duty of candor [Rule 8.4(c)/DR 1-102(A)(4) & DR 7-101(A)(3)].

---

16. Preamble to Model Rules, paragraph 11, *supra* note 8.

In addition to duties owed to clients, the lawyer also owes duties to the general public. Members of the public are entitled to be able to trust lawyers to protect their property, liberty, and their lives. The community expects lawyers to exhibit the highest standards of honesty and integrity, and lawyers have a duty not to engage in conduct involving dishonesty, fraud, or interference with the administration of justice [Rules 8.2, 8.4(b)&(c)/DR 1-102(A)(3) (4)&(5), DR 8101 through DR 8-103, DR 9-101(c)].

Lawyers also owe duties to the legal system. Lawyers are officers of the court, and must abide by the rules of substance and procedure which shape the administration of justice. Lawyers must always operate within the bounds of the law, and cannot create or use false evidence, or engage in any other illegal or improper conduct [Rules 3.1 through 3.6, 3.9, 4.1 through 4.4, 8.2, 8.4(d)(e) & (f)/DR 7-102 through DR 7-110].

Finally, lawyers owe duties to the legal profession. Unlike the obligations mentioned above, these duties are not inherent in the relationship between the professional and the community. These duties do not concern the lawyer's basic responsibilities in representing clients, serving as an officer of the court, or maintaining the public trust, but include other duties relating to the profession. These ethical rules concern:

(a) restrictions on advertising and recommending employment [Rules 7.1 through 7.5/DR 2-101 through 2-104];

(b) fees [Rules 1.5, 5.4 and 5.6/DR 2-106, DR 2-107, and DR 3-102];

(c) assisting unauthorized practice [Rule 5.5/DR 3-101 through DR3-103];

(d) accepting, declining, or terminating representation [Rules 1.2, 1.14, 1.16/ DR 2-110]; and

(e) maintaining the integrity of the profession [Rules 8.1&8.3/DR 1-101 and DR 1-103].

The mental states used in this model are defined as follows. The most culpable mental state is that of intent, when the lawyer acts with the conscious objective or purpose to accomplish a particular result. The next most culpable mental state is that of knowledge, when the lawyer acts with conscious awareness of the nature or attendant circumstances of his or her conduct both without the conscious objective or purpose to accomplish a particular result. The least culpable mental state is negligence, when a lawyer fails to be aware of a substantial risk that circumstances exist or that a result will follow, which failure is a deviation from the standard of care that a reasonable lawyer would exercise in the situation.

The extent of the injury is defined by the type of duty violated and the extent of actual or potential harm. For example, in a conversion case, the injury is determined by examining the extent of the client's actual or potential loss. In a case where a lawyer tampers with a witness, the injury is measured by evaluating the level of interference or potential interference with the legal proceeding. In this model, the standards refer to various levels of injury: "serious injury," "injury," and "little or no injury." A reference to "injury" alone indicates any level of injury greater than "little or no" injury.

As an example of how this model works, consider two cases of conversion of a client's property. After concluding that the lawyers engaged in ethical misconduct, it is necessary to determine what duties were breached. In these cases, each lawyer breached the duty of loyalty owed to clients. To assign a sanction, however, it is necessary to go further, and to examine each lawyer's mental state and the extent of the injuries caused by the lawyers' actions.

In the first case, assume that the client gave the lawyer $100 as an advance against the costs of investigation. The lawyer took the money, deposited it in a personal checking account, and used it for personal expenses. In this case, where the lawyer acted intentionally and the client actually suffered an injury, the most severe sanction—disbarment—would be appropriate.

Contrast this with the case of a second lawyer, whose client delivered $100 to be held in a trust account. The lawyer, in a hurry to get to court, neglected to inform the secretary what to do with these funds and they were erroneously deposited into the lawyer's general office account. When the lawyer needed additional funds he drew against the general account. The lawyer discovered the mistake, and immediately replaced the money. In this case, where there was no actual injury and a potential for only minor injury, and where the lawyer was merely negligent, a less serious sanction should be imposed. The appropriate sanction would be either reprimand or admonition.

In each case, after making the initial determination as to the appropriate sanction, the court would then consider any relevant aggravating or mitigating factors (Standard 9). For example, the presence of aggravating factors, such as vulnerability of the victim or refusal to comply with an order to appear before the disciplinary agency, could increase the appropriate sanction. The presence of mitigating factors, such as absence of prior discipline or inexperience in the practice of law, could make a lesser sanction appropriate.

While there may be particular cases of lawyer misconduct that are not easily categorized, the standards are not designed to propose a specific sanction for each of the myriad of fact patterns in cases of lawyer misconduct. Rather, the standards provide a theoretical framework to guide the courts in imposing sanctions. The ultimate sanction imposed will depend on the presence of any aggravating or mitigating factors in that particular situation. The standards thus are not analogous to criminal determinate sentences, but are guidelines which give courts the flexibility to select the appropriate sanction in each particular case of lawyer misconduct.

The standards do not account for multiple charges of misconduct. The ultimate sanction imposed should at least be consistent with the sanction for the most serious instance of misconduct among a number of violations; it might well be and generally should be greater than the sanction for the most serious misconduct. Either a pattern of misconduct or multiple instances of misconduct should be considered as aggravating factors (see Standard 9.22).

III. STANDARDS FOR IMPOSING LAWYER SANCTIONS: BLACK LETTER RULES

Definitions

"Injury" is harm to a client, the public, the legal system, or the profession which results from a lawyer's misconduct. The level of injury can range from "serious" injury to "little or no" injury; a reference to "injury" alone indicates any level of injury greater than "little or no" injury.

"Intent" is the conscious objective or purpose to accomplish a particular result.

"Knowledge" is the conscious awareness of the nature or attendant circumstances of the conduct but without the conscious objective or purpose to accomplish a particular result.

"Negligence" is the failure of a lawyer to heed a substantial risk that circumstances exist or that a result will follow, which failure is a deviation from the standard of care that a reasonable lawyer would exercise in the situation.

"Potential injury" is the harm to a client, the public, the legal system or the profession that is reasonably foreseeable at the time of the lawyer's misconduct, and which, but for some intervening factor or event, would probably have resulted from the lawyer's misconduct.

A. Purpose and Nature of Sanctions

1.1 *Purpose of Lawyer Discipline Proceedings.*

The purpose of lawyer discipline proceedings is to protect the public and the administration of justice from lawyers who have not discharged, will not discharge, or are unlikely properly to discharge their professional duties to clients, the public, the legal system, and the legal profession.

1.2 *Public Nature of Lawyer Discipline.*

Upon the filing and service of formal charges, lawyer discipline proceedings should be public, and disposition of lawyer discipline should be public in cases of disbarment, suspension, and reprimand. Only in cases of minor misconduct, when there is little or no injury to a client, the public, the legal

452

system, or the profession, and when there is little likelihood of repetition by the lawyer, should private discipline be imposed.

1.3 *Purpose of These Standards.*

These standards are designed for use in imposing a sanction or sanctions following a determination by clear and convincing evidence that a member of the legal profession has violated a provision of the Model Rules of Professional Conduct (or applicable standard under the laws of the jurisdiction where the proceeding is brought). Descriptions in these standards of substantive disciplinary offenses are not intended to create grounds for determining culpability independent of the Model Rules. The Standards constitute a model, setting forth a comprehensive system for determining sanctions, permitting flexibility and creativity in assigning sanctions in particular cases of lawyer misconduct. They are designed to promote: (1) consideration of all factors relevant to imposing the appropriate level of sanction in an individual case; (2) consideration of the appropriate weight of such factors in light of the stated goals of lawyer discipline; (3) consistency in the imposition of disciplinary sanctions for the same or similar offenses within and among jurisdictions.

B. Sanctions

2.1 *Scope*

A disciplinary sanction is imposed on a lawyer upon a finding or acknowledgment that the lawyer has engaged in professional misconduct.

2.2 *Disbarment*

Disbarment terminates the individual's status as a lawyer. Where disbarment is not permanent, procedures should be established for a lawyer who has been disbarred to apply for readmission, provided that:

(1) no application should be considered for five years from the effective date of disbarment; and

(2) the petitioner must show by clear and convincing evidence:

(a) successful completion of the bar examination;

(b) compliance with all applicable discipline or disability orders and rules; and

(c) rehabilitation and fitness to practice law.

2.3 *Suspension*

Suspension is the removal of a lawyer from the practice of law for a specified minimum period of time. Generally, suspension should be for a period of time equal to or greater than six months, but in no event should the time period prior to application for reinstatement be more than three years. Procedures should be established to allow a suspended lawyer to apply for reinstatement, but a lawyer who has been suspended should not be permitted to return to practice until he has completed a reinstatement process demonstrating rehabilitation, compliance with all applicable discipline or disability orders and rules, and fitness to practice law.

2.4 *Interim Suspension*

Interim suspension is the temporary suspension of a lawyer from the practice of law pending imposition of final discipline. Interim suspension includes:
(a) suspension upon conviction of a "serious crime" or,
(b) suspension when the lawyer's continuing conduct is or is likely to cause immediate and serious injury to a client or the public.

2.5 *Reprimand*

Reprimand, also known as censure or public censure, is a form of public discipline which declares the conduct of the lawyer improper, but does not limit the lawyer's right to practice.

2.6 *Admonition*

Admonition, also known as private reprimand, is a form of non-public discipline which declares the conduct of the lawyer improper, but does not limit the lawyer's right to practice.

2.7 *Probation*

Probation is a sanction that allows a lawyer to practice law under specified conditions. Probation can be imposed alone or in conjunction with a reprimand, an admonition or immediately following a suspension. Probation can also be imposed as a condition of readmission or reinstatement.

2.8 *Other Sanctions and Remedies*

Other sanctions and remedies which may be imposed include:
(a) restitution,
(b) assessment of costs,
(c) limitation upon practice,
(d) appointment of a receiver,
(e) requirement that the lawyer take the bar examination or professional responsibility examination,
(f) requirement that the lawyer attend continuing education courses, and
(g) other requirements that the state's highest court or disciplinary board deems consistent with the purposes of lawyer sanctions.

2.9 *Reciprocal Discipline*

Reciprocal discipline is the imposition of a disciplinary sanction on a lawyer who has been disciplined in another jurisdiction.

2.10 *Readmission and Reinstatement*

In jurisdictions where disbarment is not permanent, procedures should be established.

C. Factors to be Considered in Imposing Sanctions

3.0 *Generally*

In imposing a sanction after a finding of lawyer misconduct, a court should consider the following factors:

(a) the duty violated;

(b) the lawyer's mental state;

(c) the potential or actual injury caused by the lawyer's misconduct; and

(d) the existence of aggravating or mitigating factors.

4.0 *Violations of Duties Owed to Clients*

4.1 *Failure to Preserve the Client's Property*

Absent aggravating or mitigating circumstances, upon application of the factors set out in 3.0, the following sanctions are generally appropriate in cases involving the failure to preserve client property.

4.11 Disbarment is generally appropriate when a lawyer knowingly converts client property and causes injury or potential injury to a client.

4.12 Suspension is generally appropriate when a lawyer knows or should know that he is dealing improperly with client property and causes injury or potential injury to a client.

4.13 Reprimand is generally appropriate when a lawyer is negligent in dealing with client property and causes injury or potential injury to a client.

4.14 Admonition is generally appropriate when a lawyer is negligent in dealing with client property and causes little or no actual or potential injury to a client.

4.2 *Failure to Preserve the Client's Confidences*

Absent aggravating or mitigating circumstances, upon application of the factors set out in 3.0, the following sanctions are generally appropriate in cases involving improper revelation of information relating to representation of a client:

4.21 Disbarment is generally appropriate when a lawyer, with the intent to benefit the lawyer or another, knowingly reveals information relating to representation of a client not otherwise lawfully permitted to be disclosed, and this disclosure causes injury or potential injury to a client.

4.22 Suspension is generally appropriate when a lawyer knowingly reveals information relating to the representation of a client not otherwise lawfully permitted to be disclosed, and this disclosure causes injury or potential injury to a client.

4.23 Reprimand is generally appropriate when a lawyer negligently reveals information relating to representation of a client not otherwise lawfully permitted to be disclosed and this disclosure causes injury or potential injury to a client.

4.24 Admonition is generally appropriate when a lawyer negligently reveals information relating to representation of a client not otherwise lawfully permitted to be disclosed and this disclosure causes little or no actual or potential injury to a client.

4.3 *Failure to Avoid Conflicts of Interest*

Absent aggravating or mitigating circumstances, upon application of the factors set out in Standard 3.0, the following sanctions are generally appropriate in cases involving conflicts of interest:

4.31 Disbarment is generally appropriate when a lawyer, without the informed consent of client(s):

(a) engages in representation of a client knowing that the lawyer's interests are adverse to the client's with the intent to benefit the lawyer or another, and causes serious or potentially serious injury to the client; or

(b) simultaneously represents clients that the lawyer knows have adverse interests with the intent to benefit the lawyer or another, and causes serious or potentially serious injury to a client; or

(c) represents a client in a matter substantially related to a matter in which the interests of a present or former client are materially adverse, and knowingly uses information relating to the representation of a client with the intent to benefit the lawyer or another, and causes serious or potentially serious injury to a client.

4.32 Suspension is generally appropriate when a lawyer knows of a conflict of interest and does not fully disclose to a client the possible effect of that conflict, and causes injury or potential injury to a client.

4.33 Reprimand is generally appropriate when a lawyer is negligent in determining whether the representation of a client may be materially affected by the lawyer's own interests, or whether the representation will adversely affect another client, and causes injury or potential injury to a client.

4.34 Admonition is generally appropriate when a lawyer engages in an isolated instance of negligence in determining whether the representation of a client may be materially affected by the lawyer's own interests, or whether the representation will adversely affect another client, and causes little or no actual or potential injury to a client.

4.4 *Lack of Diligence*

Absent aggravating or mitigating circumstances, upon application of the factors set out in Standard 3.0, the following sanctions are generally appropriate in cases involving a failure to act with reasonable diligence and promptness in representing a client:

4.41 Disbarment is generally appropriate when:

(a) a lawyer abandons the practice and causes serious or potentially serious injury to a client; or

(b) a lawyer knowingly fails to perform services for a client and causes serious or potentially serious injury to a client; or

(c) a lawyer engages in a pattern of neglect with respect to client matters and causes serious or potentially serious injury to a client.

4.42 Suspension is generally appropriate when:

(a) a lawyer knowingly fails to perform services for a client and causes injury or potential injury to a client, or

(b) a lawyer engages in a pattern of neglect and causes injury or potential injury to a client.

4.43 Reprimand is generally appropriate when a lawyer is negligent and does not act with reasonable diligence in representing a client, and causes injury or potential injury to a client.

4.44 Admonition is generally appropriate when a lawyer is negligent and does not act with reasonable diligence in representing a client, and causes little or no actual or potential injury to a client.

4.5 *Lack of Competence*

Absent aggravating or mitigating circumstances, upon application of the factors set out in Standard 3.0, the following sanctions are generally appropriate in cases involving failure to provide competent representation to a client:

4.51 Disbarment is generally appropriate when a lawyer's course of conduct demonstrates that the lawyer does not understand the most fundamental legal doctrines or procedures, and the lawyer's conduct causes injury or potential injury to a client.

4.52 Suspension is generally appropriate when a lawyer engages in an area of practice in which the lawyer knows he or she is not competent, and causes injury or potential injury to a client.

4.53 Reprimand is generally appropriate when a lawyer:

(a) demonstrates failure to understand relevant legal doctrines or procedures and causes injury or potential injury to a client; or

(b) is negligent in determining whether he or she is competent to handle a legal matter and causes injury or potential injury to a client.

4.54 Admonition is generally appropriate when a lawyer engages in an isolated instance of negligence in determining whether he or she is competent to handle a legal matter, and causes little or no actual or potential injury to a client.

4.6 Lack of Candor

Absent aggravating or mitigating circumstances, upon application of the factors set out in Standard 3.0, the following sanctions are generally appropriate in cases where the lawyer engages in fraud, deceit, or misrepresentation directed toward a client:

4.61 Disbarment is generally appropriate when a lawyer knowingly deceives a client with the intent to benefit the lawyer or another, and causes serious injury or potential serious injury to a client.

4.62 Suspension is generally appropriate when a lawyer knowingly deceives a client, and causes injury or potential injury to the client.

4.63 Reprimand is generally appropriate when a lawyer negligently fails to provide a client with accurate or complete information, and causes injury or potential injury to the client.

4.64 Admonition is generally appropriate when a lawyer engages in an isolated instance of negligence in failing to provide a client with accurate or complete information, and causes little or no actual or potential injury to the client.

5.0 Violations of Duties Owed to the Public

5.1 Failure to Maintain Personal Integrity

Absent aggravating or mitigating circumstances, upon application of the factors set out in Standard 3.0, the following sanctions are generally appropriate in cases involving commission of a criminal act that reflects adversely on the lawyer's honesty, trustworthiness, or fitness as a lawyer in other respects, or in cases with conduct involving dishonesty, fraud, deceit, or misrepresentation:

5.11 Disbarment is generally appropriate when:

(a) a lawyer engages in serious criminal conduct, a necessary element of which includes intentional interference with the administration of justice, false swearing, misrepresentation, fraud, extortion, misappropriation, or theft; or the sale, distribution or importation of controlled substances; or the intentional killing of another; or an attempt or conspiracy or solicitation of another to commit any of these offenses; or

(b) a lawyer engages in any other intentional conduct involving

ABA Standards for Imposing Lawyer Sanctions

dishonesty, fraud, deceit, or misrepresentation that seriously adversely reflects on the lawyer's fitness to practice.

5.12 Suspension is generally appropriate when a lawyer knowingly engages in criminal conduct which does not contain the elements listed in Standard 5.11 and that seriously adversely reflects on the lawyer's fitness to practice.

5.13 Reprimand is generally appropriate when a lawyer knowingly engages in any other conduct that involves dishonesty, fraud, deceit, or misrepresentation and that adversely reflects on the lawyer's fitness to practice law.

5.14 Admonition is generally appropriate when a lawyer engages in any other conduct that reflects adversely on the lawyer's fitness to practice law.

5.2 Failure to Maintain the Public Trust

Absent aggravating or mitigating circumstances, upon application of the factors set out in Standard 3.0, the following sanctions are generally appropriate in cases involving public officials who engage in conduct that is prejudicial to the administration of justice or who state or imply an ability to influence improperly a government agency or official:

5.21 Disbarment is generally appropriate when a lawyer in an official or governmental position knowingly misuses the position with the intent to obtain a significant benefit or advantage for himself or another, or with the intent to cause serious or potentially serious injury to a party or to the integrity of the legal process.

5.22 Suspension is generally appropriate when a lawyer in an official or governmental position knowingly fails to follow proper procedures or rules, and causes injury or potential injury to a party or to the integrity of the legal process.

5.23 Reprimand is generally appropriate when a lawyer in an official or governmental position negligently fails to follow proper procedures or rules, and causes injury or potential injury to a party or to the integrity of the legal process.

5.24 Admonition is generally appropriate when a lawyer in an official or governmental position engages in an isolated instance of negligence in not following proper procedures or rules, and causes little or no actual or potential injury to a party or to the integrity of the legal process.

6.0 Violations of Duties Owed to the Legal System

6.1 False Statements, Fraud, and Misrepresentation

Absent aggravating or mitigating circumstances, upon application of the factors set out in Standard 3.0, the following sanctions are generally appropriate in cases involving conduct that is prejudicial to the administration of justice or that involves dishonesty, fraud, deceit, or misrepresentation to a court:

6.11   Disbarment is generally appropriate when a lawyer, with the intent to deceive the court, makes a false statement, submits a false document, or improperly withholds material information, and causes serious or potentially serious injury to a party, or causes a significant or potentially significant adverse effect on the legal proceeding.

6.12   Suspension is generally appropriate when a lawyer knows that false statements or documents are being submitted to the court or that material information is improperly being withheld, and takes no remedial action, and causes injury or potential injury to a party to the legal proceeding, or causes an adverse or potentially adverse effect on the legal proceeding.

6.13   Reprimand is generally appropriate when a lawyer is negligent either in determining whether statements or documents are false or in taking remedial action when material information is being withheld, and causes injury or potential injury to a party to the legal proceeding, or causes an adverse or potentially adverse effect on the legal proceeding.

6.14   Admonition is generally appropriate when a lawyer engages in isolated instance of neglect in determining whether submitted statements or documents are false or in failing to disclose material information upon learning of its falsity, and causes little or no actual or potential injury to a party, or causes little or no adverse or potentially adverse effect on the legal proceeding.

6.2 *Abuse of the Legal Process*

Absent aggravating or mitigating circumstances, upon application of the factors set out in Standard 3.0, the following sanctions are generally appropriate in cases involving failure to expedite litigation or bring a meritorious claim, or failure to obey any obligation under the rules of a tribunal except for an open refusal based on an assertion that no valid obligation exists:

6.21   Disbarment is generally appropriate when a lawyer knowingly violates a court order or rule with the intent to obtain a benefit for the lawyer or another, and causes serious injury or potentially serious injury to a party or causes serious or potentially serious interference with a legal proceeding.

6.22   Suspension is generally appropriate when a lawyer knows that he or she is violating a court order or rule, and causes injury or potential injury to a client or a party, or causes interference or potential interference with a legal proceeding.

6.23 Reprimand is generally appropriate when a lawyer negligently fails to comply with a court order or rule, and causes injury or potential injury to a client or other party, or causes interference or potential interference with a legal proceeding.

6.24 Admonition is generally appropriate when a lawyer engages in an isolated instance of negligence in complying with a court order or rule, and causes little or no actual or potential injury to a party, or causes little or no actual or potential interference with a legal proceeding.

6.3 *Improper Communications with Individuals in the Legal System*

Absent aggravating or mitigating circumstances, upon application of the factors set out in Standard 3.0, the following sanctions are generally appropriate in cases involving attempts to influence a judge, juror, prospective juror or other official by means prohibited by law:

6.31 Disbarment is generally appropriate when a lawyer:

(a) intentionally tampers with a witness and causes serious or potentially serious injury to a party, or causes significant or potentially significant interference with the outcome of the legal proceeding; or

(b) makes an ex parte communication with a judge or juror with intent to affect the outcome of the proceeding, and causes serious or potentially serious injury to a party, or causes significant or potentially significant interference with the outcome of the legal proceeding; or

(c) improperly communicates with someone in the legal system other than a witness, judge, or juror with the intent to influence or affect the outcome of the proceeding, and causes significant or potentially significant interference with the outcome of the legal proceeding.

6.32 Suspension is generally appropriate when a lawyer engages in communication with an individual in the legal system when the lawyer knows that such communication is improper, and causes injury or potential injury to a party or causes interference or potential interference with the outcome of the legal proceeding.

6.33 Reprimand is generally appropriate when a lawyer is negligent in determining whether it is proper to engage in communication with an individual in the legal system, and causes injury or potential injury to a party or interference or potential interference with the outcome of the legal proceeding.

6.34 Admonition is generally appropriate when a lawyer engages in an isolated instance of negligence in improperly communicating with an individual in the legal system, and causes little or no actual or potential injury to a party, or causes little or no actual or potential interference with the outcome of the legal proceeding.

7.0 *Violations of Other Duties Owed as a Professional*

Absent aggravating or mitigating circumstances, upon application of the factors set out in Standard 3.0, the following sanctions are generally appropriate in cases involving false or misleading communication about the lawyer or the lawyer's services, improper communication of fields of practice, improper solicitation of professional employment from a prospective client, unreasonable or improper fees, unauthorized practice of law, improper withdrawal from representation, or failure to report professional misconduct.

7.1　Disbarment is generally appropriate when a lawyer knowingly engages in conduct that is a violation of a duty owed as a professional with the intent to obtain a benefit for the lawyer or another, and causes serious or potentially serious injury to a client, the public, or the legal system.

7.2　Suspension is generally appropriate when a lawyer knowingly engages in conduct that is a violation of a duty owed as a professional and causes injury or potential injury to a client, the public, or the legal system.

7.3　Reprimand is generally appropriate when a lawyer negligently engages in conduct that is a violation of a duty owed as a professional and causes injury or potential injury to a client, the public, or the legal system.

7.4　Admonition is generally appropriate when a lawyer engages in an isolated instance of negligence that is a violation of a duty owed as a professional, and causes little or no actual or potential injury to a client, the public, or the legal system.

8.0 *Prior Discipline Orders*

Absent aggravating or mitigating circumstances, upon application of the factors set out in Standard 3.0, the following sanctions are generally appropriate in cases involving prior discipline.

8.1　Disbarment is generally appropriate when a lawyer:

(a) intentionally or knowingly violates the terms of a prior disciplinary order and such violation causes injury or potential injury to a client, the public, the legal system, or the profession; or

(b) has been suspended for the same or similar misconduct, and intentionally or knowingly engages in further similar acts of misconduct that cause injury or potential injury to a client, the public, the legal system, or the profession.

8.2   Suspension is generally appropriate when a lawyer has been reprimanded for the same or similar misconduct and engages in further similar acts of misconduct that cause injury or potential injury to a client, the public, the legal system, or the profession.

8.3   Reprimand is generally appropriate when a lawyer:

(a) negligently violates the terms of a prior disciplinary order and such violation causes injury or potential injury to a client, the public, the legal system, or the profession; or

(b) has received an admonition for the same or similar misconduct and engages in further similar acts of misconduct that cause injury or potential injury to a client, the public, the legal system, or the profession.

8.4   An admonition is generally not an appropriate sanction when a lawyer violates the terms of a prior disciplinary order or when a lawyer has engaged in the same or similar misconduct in the past.

9.0 *Aggravation and Mitigation*

9.1 *Generally*

After misconduct has been established, aggravating and mitigating circumstances may be considered in deciding what sanction to impose.

9.2 *Aggravation*

9.21   *Definition.* Aggravation or aggravating circumstances are any considerations or factors that may justify an increase in the degree of discipline to be imposed.

9.22   *Factors which may be considered in aggravation.* Aggravating factors include:

(a) prior disciplinary offenses;

(b) dishonest or selfish motive;

(c) a pattern of misconduct;

(d) multiple offenses;

(e) bad faith obstruction of the disciplinary proceeding by intentionally failing to comply with rules or orders of the disciplinary agency;

(f) submission of false evidence, false statements, or other deceptive practices during the disciplinary process;

(g) refusal to acknowledge wrongful nature of conduct;

(h) vulnerability of victim;

(i) substantial experience in the practice of law;

(j) indifference to making restitution.

(k) illegal conduct, including that involving the use of controlled substances.

9.3 *Mitigation*

9.31 *Definition.* Mitigation or mitigating circumstances are any considerations or factors that may justify a reduction in the degree of discipline to be imposed.

9.32 *Factors which may be considered in mitigation.* Mitigating factors include:

(a) absence of a prior disciplinary record;

(b) absence of a dishonest or selfish motive;

(c) personal or emotional problems;

(d) timely good faith effort to make restitution or to rectify consequences of misconduct;

(e) full and free disclosure to disciplinary board or cooperative attitude toward proceedings;

(f) inexperience in the practice of law;

(g) character or reputation;

(h) physical disability;

(i) mental disability or chemical dependency including alcoholism or drug abuse when:

(1) there is medical evidence that the respondent is affected by a chemical dependency or mental disability;

(2) the chemical dependency or mental disability caused the misconduct;

(3) the respondent's recovery from the chemical dependency or mental disability is demonstrated by a meaningful and sustained period of successful rehabilitation; and

(4) the recovery arrested the misconduct and recurrence of that misconduct is unlikely.

(j) delay in disciplinary proceedings;

(k) imposition of other penalties or sanctions;

(l) remorse;

(m) remoteness of prior offenses.

9.4 *Factors Which Are Neither Aggravating nor Mitigating.*

The following factors should not be considered as either aggravating or mitigating:

(a) forced or compelled restitution;

(b) agreeing to the client's demand for certain improper behavior or result;

(c) withdrawal of complaint against the lawyer;

(d) resignation prior to completion of disciplinary proceedings;

(e) complainant's recommendation as to sanction;

(f) failure of injured client to complain.

APPENDIX 1

Cross-Reference Table:
ABA Model Rules of Professional Conduct
and Standards for Imposing Sanctions

ABA Model Rules of Professional Conduct	*Standards for Imposing Sanctions*
Competence	
Rule 1.1	Standard 4.5
Scope of Representation	
Rule 1.2(a), (b), (c), (e)	Standard 4.4
Rule 1.2(d)	Standard 6.1
Diligence	
Rule 1.3	Standard 4.4
Communication	
Rule 1.4	Standard 4.4
Fees	
Rule 1.5	Standards 4.6 & 7.0
Confidentiality of Information	
Rule 1.6	Standard 4.2
Conflict of Interest	
Rule 1.7	Standard 4.3
Prohibited Transactions	
Rule 1.8	Standard 4.3
Former Client	
Rule 1.9	Standard 4.3
Imputed Disqualification	
Rule 1.10	Standard 4.3
Successive Government and Private Employment	
Rule 1.11	Standard 4.3
Former Judge or Arbitrator	
Rule 1.12	Standard 4.3
Organization as Client	
Rule 1.13	Standard 4.3
Disabled Client	
Rule 1.14	Standard 7.0
Safekeeping Property	
Rule 1.15	Standard 4.1
Declining or Terminating Representation	
Rule 1.16	Standard 7.0
Advisor	
Rule 2.1	Standard 7.0

ABA Standards for Imposing Lawyer Sanctions

ABA Model Rules of Professional Conduct	*Standards for Imposing Sanctions*
Unauthorized Practice of Law	
Rule 5.5	Standard 7.0
Restrictions on Right to Practice	
Rule 5.6	Standard 7.0
Responsibilities Regarding Law-related Services	
Rule 5.7	No Applicable Standard
Pro Bono Publico Service	
Rule 6.1	No Applicable Standard
Accepting Appointments	
Rule 6.2	Standard 7.0
Membership in Legal Services Organization	
Rule 6.3	Standard 4.3
Law Reform Activities Affecting Client Interests	
Rule 6.4	Standard 5.2
Communication Concerning Lawyer's Services	
Rule 7.1	Standard 7.0
Advertising	
Rule 7.2	Standard 7.0
Direct Contact with Prospective Clients	
Rule 7.3	Standard 7.0
Communication of Fields of Practice	
Rule 7.4	Standard 7.0
Firm Names and Letterheads	
Rule 7.5	Standard 7.0
Bar Admission and Disciplinary Matters	
Rule 8.1	Standards 5.1, 7.0
Judges and Legal Officials	
Rule 8.2	Standard 6.1
Reporting Professional Misconduct	
Rule 8.3	Standard 7.0
Misconduct	
Rule 8.4(a)	Standards 4.0, 5.0, 6.0, 7.0
Rule 8.4(b)	Standard 5.1
Rule 8.4(c)	Standards 4.6, 5.1
Rule 8.4(d)	Standard 6.0
Rule 8.4(e), (f)	Standard 6.2
Jurisdiction Rule 8.5	None

APPENDIX 2

Cross-Reference Table:
ABA Code of Professional Responsibility
and Standards for Imposing Sanctions

ABA Model Rules of Professional Responsibility   *Standards for Imposing Sanctions*

Canon 1: Integrity of Profession
DR 1-101.. Standard 7.0
DR 1-102.. Standards 4.6, 5.1, 6.2
DR 1-103.. Standard 7.0

Canon 2: Making Counsel Available
DR 2-101.. Standard 7.0
DR 2-102.. Standard 7.0
DR 2-103.. Standard 7.0
DR 2-104.. Standard 7.0
DR 2-105.. Standard 7.0
DR 2-106.. Standard 7.0
DR 2-107.. Standard 7.0
DR 2-108.. Standard 7.0
DR 2-109.. Standard 7.0
DR 2-110.. Standard 7.0

Canon 3: Unauthorized Practice
DR 3-101(A) .... Standard 7.0
DR 3-101(B)... Standard 8.0
DR 3-102.. Standard 7.0
DR 3-103.. Standard 7.0

Canon 4: Confidences and Secrets
DR 4-101.. Standard 4.2

Canon 5: Independent Judgment
DR 5-101.. Standard 4.3
DR 5-102.. Standard 4.3
DR 5-103.. Standard 4.3
DR 5-104.. Standard 4.3
DR 5-105.. Standard 4.3
DR 5-106.. Standard 4.3
DR 5-107.. Standard 4.3

ABA Standards for Imposing Lawyer Sanctions

ABA Model Rules
Related to
Multijurisdictional Practice

ABA Model
Rules Related to
Multijurisdictional
Practice

ABA Model Rule on Practice Pending Admission

ABA Model Rule on Practice Pending Admission

1. A lawyer currently holding an active license to practice law in another U.S. jurisdiction and who has been engaged in the active practice of law for three of the last five years, may provide legal services in this jurisdiction through an office or other systematic and continuous presence for no more than [365] days, provided that the lawyer:

    a. is not disbarred or suspended from practice in any jurisdiction and is not currently subject to discipline or a pending disciplinary matter in any jurisdiction;

    b. has not previously been denied admission to practice in this jurisdiction or failed this jurisdiction's bar examination;

    c. notifies Disciplinary Counsel and the Admissions Authority in writing prior to initiating practice in this jurisdiction that the lawyer will be doing so pursuant to the authority in this Rule;

    d. submits within [45] days of first establishing an office or other systematic and continuous presence for the practice of law in this jurisdiction a complete application for admission by motion or by examination;

    e. reasonably expects to fulfill all of this jurisdiction's requirements for that form of admission;

    f. associates with a lawyer who is admitted to practice in this jurisdiction;

    g. complies with Rules 7.1 and 7.5 of the Model Rules of Professional Conduct [or jurisdictional equivalent] in all communications with the public and clients regarding the nature and scope of the lawyer's practice authority in this jurisdiction; and

    h. pays any annual client protection fund assessment.

2. A lawyer currently licensed as a foreign legal consultant in another U.S. jurisdiction may provide legal services in this jurisdiction through an office or other systematic and continuous presence for no more than [365] days, provided that the lawyer:

    a. provides services that are limited to those that may be provided in this jurisdiction by foreign legal consultants;

    b. is a member in good standing of a recognized legal profession in the foreign jurisdiction, the members of which are admitted to practice as lawyers or counselors at law or the equivalent, and are subject to effective regulation and discipline by a duly constituted professional body or a public authority;

    c. submits within [45] days of first establishing an office or other systematic and continuous presence for the practice of law in this juris-

ABA Model
Rules Related to
Multijurisdictional
Practice

diction a complete application for admission to practice as a foreign legal consultant;

d. reasonably expects to fulfill all of this jurisdiction's requirements for admission as a foreign legal consultant; and

e. meets the requirements of paragraphs 1(a), (b), (c), (f), (g), and (h) of this Rule.

3. Prior to admission by motion, through examination, or as a foreign legal consultant, the lawyer may not appear before a tribunal in this jurisdiction that requires pro hac vice admission unless the lawyer is granted such admission.

4. The lawyer must immediately notify Disciplinary Counsel and the Admissions Authority in this jurisdiction if the lawyer becomes subject to a disciplinary matter or disciplinary sanctions in any other jurisdiction at any time during the [365] days of practice authorized by this Rule. The Admissions Authority shall take into account such information in determining whether to grant the lawyer's application for admission to this jurisdiction.

5. The authority in this Rule shall terminate immediately if:

a. the lawyer withdraws the application for admission by motion, by examination, or as a foreign legal consultant, or if such application is denied, prior to the expiration of [365] days;

b. the lawyer fails to file the application for admission within [45] days of first establishing an office or other systematic and continuous presence for the practice of law in this jurisdiction;

c. the lawyer fails to remain in compliance with Paragraph 1 of this Rule;

d. the lawyer is disbarred or suspended in any other jurisdiction in which the lawyer is licensed to practice law; or

e. the lawyer has not complied with the notification requirements of Paragraph 4 of this Rule.

6. Upon the termination of authority pursuant to Paragraph 5, the lawyer, within [30] days, shall:

a. cease to occupy an office or other systematic and continuous presence for the practice of law in this jurisdiction unless authorized to do so pursuant to another Rule;

b. notify all clients being represented in pending matters, and opposing counsel or co-counsel of the termination of the lawyer's authority to practice pursuant to this Rule;

c. not undertake any new representation that would require the lawyer to be admitted to practice law in this jurisdiction; and

    d. take all other necessary steps to protect the interests of the lawyer's clients.

7. Upon the denial of the lawyer's application for admission by motion, by examination, or as a foreign legal consultant, the Admissions Authority shall immediately notify Disciplinary Counsel that the authority granted by this Rule has terminated.

8. The Court, in its discretion, may extend the time limits set forth in this Rule for good cause shown.

Comment

[1] This Rule recognizes that a lawyer admitted in another jurisdiction may need to relocate to or commence practice in this jurisdiction, sometimes on short notice. The admissions process can take considerable time, thus placing a lawyer at risk of engaging in the unauthorized practice of law and leaving the lawyer's clients without the benefit of their chosen counsel. This Rule closes this gap by authorizing the lawyer to practice in this jurisdiction for a limited period of time, up to 365 days, subject to restrictions, while the lawyer diligently seeks admission. The practice authority provided pursuant to this Rule commences immediately upon the lawyer's establishment of an office or other systematic and continuous presence for the practice of law.

[2] Paragraph 1(f) requires a lawyer practicing in this jurisdiction pursuant to the authority granted under this Rule to associate with a lawyer who is admitted to practice law in this jurisdiction. The association between the incoming lawyer and the lawyer licensed in this jurisdiction is akin to that between a local lawyer and a lawyer practicing in a jurisdiction on a temporary basis pursuant to Model Rule of Professional Conduct 5.5(c)(1).

[3] While exercising practice authority pursuant to this Rule, a lawyer cannot hold out to the public or otherwise represent that the lawyer is admitted to practice in this jurisdiction. See Model Rule of Professional Conduct 5.5(b)(2). Because such a lawyer will typically be assumed to be admitted to practice in this jurisdiction, that lawyer must disclose the limited practice authority and jurisdiction of licensure in all communications with potential clients, such as on business cards, websites, and letterhead. Further, the lawyer must disclose the limited practice authority to all potential clients before agreeing to represent them. See Model Rules 7.1 and 7.5(b).

[4] The provisions of paragraph 5 (a) through (d) of this Rule are necessary to avoid prejudicing the rights of existing clients or other parties. Thirty days should be sufficient for the lawyer to wind up his or her practice in this jurisdiction in an orderly manner.

Adopted August 6, 2012 by the ABA House of Delegates.

ABA Model Rule on Pro Hac Vice Admission

ABA Model
Rules Related to
Multijurisdictional
Practice

ABA Model Rule on Pro Hac Vice Admission

I. Admission In Pending Litigation Before A Court Or Agency

A. Definitions

1. An "out-of-state" lawyer is a person not admitted to practice law in this state but who is admitted in another state or territory of the United States or of the District of Columbia, and not disbarred or suspended from practice in any jurisdiction.

2. An out-of-state lawyer is "eligible" for admission pro hac vice if that lawyer:

   a. lawfully practices solely on behalf of the lawyer's employer and its commonly owned organizational affiliates, regardless of where such lawyer may reside or work; or

   b. neither resides nor is regularly employed at an office in this state; or

   c. resides in this state but (i) lawfully practices from offices in one or more other states and (ii) practices no more than temporarily in this state, whether pursuant to admission pro hac vice or in other lawful ways.

3. A "client" is a person or entity for whom the out-of-state lawyer has rendered services or by whom the lawyer has been retained prior to the lawyer's performance of services in this state.

4. An "alternative dispute resolution" ("ADR") proceeding includes all types of arbitration or mediation, and all other forms of alternative dispute resolution, whether arranged by the parties or otherwise.

5. "This state" refers to [state or other U.S. jurisdiction promulgating this Rule]. This Rule does not govern proceedings before a federal court or federal agency located in this state unless that body adopts or incorporates this Rule.

B. Authority of Court or Agency To Permit Appearance By Out-of-State Lawyer

1. Court Proceeding. A court of this state may, in its discretion, admit an eligible out-of-state lawyer retained to appear in a particular proceeding pending before such court to appear pro hac vice as counsel in that proceeding.

2. Administrative Agency Proceeding. If practice before an agency of this state is limited to lawyers, the agency may, using the same standards and procedures as a court, admit an eligible out-of-state lawyer who has been retained to appear in a particular agency proceeding to appear as counsel in that proceeding pro hac vice.

ABA Model Rules Related to Multijurisdictional Practice

C. In-State Lawyer's Duties. When an out-of-state lawyer appears for a client in a proceeding pending in this state, either in the role of co-counsel of record with the in-state lawyer, or in an advisory or consultative role, the in-state lawyer who is co-counsel or counsel of record for that client in the proceeding remains responsible to the client and responsible for the conduct of the proceeding before the court or agency. It is the duty of the in-state lawyer to advise the client of the in-state lawyer's independent judgment on contemplated actions in the proceeding if that judgment differs from that of the out-of-state lawyer.

D. Application Procedure

1. Verified Application. An eligible out-of-state lawyer seeking to appear in a proceeding pending in this state as counsel pro hac vice shall file a verified application with the court where the proceeding is filed. The application shall be served on all parties who have appeared in the case and the [Disciplinary Counsel]. The application shall include proof of service. The court has the discretion to grant or deny the application summarily if there is no opposition.

2. Objection to Application. The [Disciplinary Counsel] or a party to the proceeding may file an objection to the application or seek the court's imposition of conditions to its being granted. The [Disciplinary Counsel] or objecting party must file with its objection a verified affidavit containing or describing information establishing a factual basis for the objection. The [Disciplinary Counsel] or objecting party may seek denial of the application or modification of it. If the application has already been granted, the [Disciplinary Counsel] or objecting party may move that the pro hac vice admission be withdrawn.

3. Standard for Admission and Revocation of Admission. The courts and agencies of this state have discretion as to whether to grant applications for admission pro hac vice. An application ordinarily should be granted unless the court or agency finds reason to believe that such admission:

a. may be detrimental to the prompt, fair and efficient administration of justice,

b. may be detrimental to legitimate interests of parties to the proceedings other than the client(s) the applicant proposes to represent,

c. one or more of the clients the applicant proposes to represent may be at risk of receiving inadequate representation and cannot adequately appreciate that risk, or

d. the applicant has engaged in such frequent appearances as to constitute regular practice in this state.

ABA Model
Rules Related to
Multijurisdictional
Practice

ABA Model
Rules Related to
Multijurisdictional
Practice

4. Revocation of Admission. Admission to appear as counsel pro hac vice in a proceeding may be revoked for any of the reasons listed in Section I(D)(3) above.

E. Verified Application and Fees:

1. Required Information. An application shall state the information listed on Appendix A to this Rule. The applicant may also include any other matters supporting admission pro hac vice.

2. Application Fee. An applicant for permission to appear as counsel pro hac vice under this Rule shall pay a non-refundable fee as set by the [court or other proper authority] at the time of filing the application. The [court or other proper authority] shall determine for what purpose or purposes these fees shall be used.

3. Exemption for Pro Bono Representation. An applicant shall not be required to pay the fee established by I(E)(2) above if the applicant will not charge an attorney fee to the client(s) and is:

   a. employed or associated with a pro bono project or nonprofit legal services organization in a civil case involving the client(s) of such programs: or

   b. involved in a criminal case or a habeas proceeding for an indigent defendant.

4. Lawyers' Fund for Client Protection. Upon the granting of a request to appear as counsel pro hac vice under this Rule, the lawyer shall pay any required assessments to the lawyers' fund for client protection. This assessment is in addition to the application fee referred to in Section (E)(2) above.

F. Authority of the [Disciplinary Counsel], the Court: Application of Rules of Professional Conduct, Rules of Disciplinary Enforcement, Contempt, and Sanctions

1. Authority Over Out-of-State Lawyer and Applicant.

   a. During pendency of an application for admission pro hac vice and upon the granting of such application, an out-of-state lawyer submits to the authority of the courts and the jurisdiction of [Disciplinary Counsel] of this state for all conduct arising out of or relating in any way to the application or proceeding in which the out-of-state lawyer seeks to appear, regardless of where the conduct occurs. An applicant or out-of-state lawyer who has pro hac vice authority for a proceeding may be disciplined in the same manner as an in-state lawyer.

   b. The court's and the [Disciplinary Counsel's] authority includes, without limitation, the court's and the [Disciplinary Counsel's] rules of professional conduct, rules of disciplinary enforcement,

contempt and sanctions orders, local court rules, and court policies and procedures.

2. **Familiarity With Rules.** An applicant shall become familiar with all
applicable rules of professional conduct, rules of disciplinary enforcement, local court rules, and policies and procedures of the court
before which the applicant seeks to practice.

II. Out-of-State Proceedings, Potential In-State and Out-of-State Proceedings, and All ADR

A. In-State Ancillary Proceeding Related to Pending Out-of-State Proceeding. In connection with proceedings pending outside this state, an out-
of-state lawyer admitted to appear in that proceeding may render in this
state legal services regarding or in aid of such proceeding.

B. Consultation by Out-of-State Lawyer

1. Consultation with In-State Lawyer. An out-of-state lawyer may consult in this state with an in-state lawyer concerning the in-state's lawyer's client's pending or potential proceeding in this state.

2. Consultation with Potential Client. At the request of a person in this
state contemplating a proceeding or involved in a pending proceeding, irrespective of where the proceeding is located, an out-of-state
lawyer may consult in this state with that person about that person's
possible retention of the out-of-state lawyer in connection with the
proceeding.

C. Preparation for In-State Proceeding. On behalf of a client in this state or
elsewhere, the out-of-state lawyer may render legal services in this state
in preparation for a potential proceeding to be filed in this state, provided that the out-of-state lawyer reasonably believes he is eligible for
admission pro hac vice in this state.

D. Preparation for Out-of-State Proceeding. In connection with a potential
proceeding to be filed outside this state, an out-of-state lawyer may render legal services in this state for a client or potential client located in
this state, provided that the out-of-state lawyer is admitted or reasonably believes the lawyer is eligible for admission generally or pro hac
vice in the jurisdiction where the proceeding is anticipated to be filed.

E. Services Rendered Outside This State for In-State Client. An out-of-state
lawyer may render legal services while the lawyer is physically outside
this state when requested by a client located within this state in connection with a potential or pending proceeding filed in or outside this
state.

F. Alternative Dispute Resolution ("ADR") Procedures. An out-of-state
lawyer may render legal services in this state to prepare for and partici-

ABA Model
Rules Related to
Multijurisdictional
Practice

pate in an ADR procedure regardless of where the ADR procedure is expected to take or actually takes place.

G. No Solicitation. An out-of-state lawyer rendering services in this state in compliance with this Rule or here for other reasons is not authorized by anything in this Rule to hold out to the public or otherwise represent that the lawyer is admitted to practice in this jurisdiction. Nothing in this Rule authorizes out-of-state lawyers to solicit, advertise, or otherwise hold themselves out in publications as available to assist in litigation in this state.

H. Temporary Practice. An out-of-state lawyer will be eligible for admission pro hac vice or to practice in another lawful way only on a temporary basis.

I. Authorized Services. The foregoing services may be undertaken by the out-of-state lawyer in connection with a potential proceeding in which the lawyer reasonably expects to be admitted pro hac vice, even if ultimately no proceeding is filed or if pro hac vice admission is denied.

III. Admission of Foreign Lawyer in Pending Litigation Before a Court or Agency

A. A foreign lawyer is a person admitted in a non-United States jurisdiction and who is a member of a recognized legal profession in that jurisdiction, the members of which are admitted to practice as lawyers or counselors at law or the equivalent and are subject to effective regulation and discipline by a duly constituted professional body or a public authority, and who is not disbarred, suspended or the equivalent thereof from practice in any jurisdiction.

B. The definitions of "client" and "state" in paragraphs I(A)(3) and (5) are incorporated by reference in this Paragraph III.

C. A court or agency of this state may, in its discretion, admit a foreign lawyer in a particular proceeding pending before such court or agency to appear pro hac vice in a defined role as a lawyer, advisor or consultant in that proceeding with an in-state lawyer, provided that the in-state lawyer is responsible to the client, responsible for the conduct of the proceeding, responsible for independently advising the client on the substantive law of a United States jurisdiction and procedural issues in the proceeding, and for advising the client whether the in-state lawyer's judgment differs from that of the foreign lawyer. See paragraph III(E).

D. In addition to the factors listed in paragraph I(D)(3) above, a court or agency in ruling on an application to admit a foreign lawyer pro hac vice, as a lawyer, advisor, or consultant, or in an advisory or consultative role, shall weigh factors, including:

1. the legal training and experience of the foreign lawyer including in matters similar to the matter before the court or agency;
2. the extent to which the matter will include the application of:
   a. the law of the jurisdiction in which the foreign lawyer is admitted or
   b. international law or other law with which the foreign lawyer has a demonstrated expertise;
3. the foreign lawyer's familiarity with the law of a United States jurisdiction applicable to the matter before the court or agency;
4. the extent to which the foreign lawyer's relationship and familiarity with the client or with the facts and circumstances of the matter will facilitate the fair and efficient resolution of the matter;
5. the foreign lawyer's English language ability; and
6. the extent to which it is possible to define the scope of the foreign lawyer's authority in the matter as described in paragraph III(F) so as to facilitate its fair and efficient resolution, including by a limitation on the foreign lawyer's authority to advise the client on the law of a United States jurisdiction except in consultation with the in-state lawyer.

E. The court or agency shall limit the activities of the foreign lawyer or require further action by the in-state lawyer, as appropriate in its discretion in light of paragraph III(D). It may, for example, require the in-state lawyer to sign all pleadings and other documents submitted to the court or to other parties, to be present at all depositions and conferences among counsel, or to attend all proceedings before the court or agency.

F. The provisions of section I, paragraphs (D), (E), and (F) and Section II, paragraphs (G) and (H), applicable to out-of-state lawyers, also apply to foreign lawyers for purposes of the requirements of Paragraph III of this Rule.

Appendix A

The out-of-state or foreign lawyer's verified application for admission pro hac vice shall include:

1. the applicant's residence and business address, telephone number(s), and e-mail address(es);
2. the name, address, telephone number(s), and e-mail address(es) of each client sought to be represented;
3. the U.S. and foreign jurisdictions in, and agencies and courts before which the applicant has been admitted to practice, the contact information for each, and the respective period(s) of admission;
4. the name and address of each court or agency and a full identification of each proceeding in which the applicant has filed an application to appear pro hac vice in this state within the preceding two years and the date of each application;

5. a statement as to whether, within the last [five (5)] years, the applicant (a) has been denied admission pro hac vice in any jurisdiction, U.S. or foreign, including this state, (b) has ever had admission pro hac vice revoked in any jurisdiction, U.S. or foreign, including this state, or (c) has ever been disciplined or sanctioned by any court or agency in any jurisdiction, U.S. or foreign, including this state. If so, specify the nature of the allegations; the name of the authority bringing such proceedings; the caption of the proceedings, the date filed, and what findings were made and what action was taken in connection with those proceedings. A certified copy of the written finding or order shall be attached to the application. If the written finding or order is not in English, the applicant shall submit an English translation and satisfactory proof of the accuracy of the translation;
6. whether any disciplinary proceeding has ever been brought against the applicant by a disciplinary counsel or analogous foreign regulatory authority in any jurisdiction within the last [five (5)] years and, as to each such proceeding: the nature of the allegations; the date the proceedings were initiated, which, if any, of the proceedings are still pending, and, for those proceedings that are not still pending, the dates upon which the proceedings were concluded; the caption of the proceedings; and the findings made and actions taken in connection with those proceedings, including exoneration from any charges. A certified copy of any written order or findings shall be attached to the application. If the written order or findings is not in English, the applicant shall submit an English translation and satisfactory proof of the accuracy of the translation.

ABA Model Rules Related to Multijurisdictional Practice

7. whether the applicant has been held in contempt by any court in a written order in the last [five (5)] years, and, if so: the nature of the allegations; the name of the court before which such proceedings were conducted; the date of the contempt order, the caption of the proceedings, and the substance of the court's rulings. A copy of the written order or transcript of the oral rulings shall be attached to the application. If the written finding or order is not in English, the applicant shall submit an English translation and satisfactory proof of the accuracy of the translation;

8. an averment as to the applicant's familiarity with the rules of professional conduct, rules of disciplinary enforcement, local or agency rules, and policies and procedures of the court or agency before which the applicant seeks to practice; and

9. the name, address, telephone number(s), e-mail address(es), and bar number of the active member in good standing of the bar of this state who supports the applicant's pro hac vice request, who shall appear of record together with the out-of-state lawyer, and who shall remain ultimately responsible to the client as set forth in Paragraph C of this Rule.

10. for applicants admitted in a foreign jurisdiction, an averment by the in-state lawyer referred to in Paragraph 9 above and by the lawyer admitted in a foreign jurisdiction that, if the application for pro hac vice admission is granted, service of any documents by a party or Disciplinary Counsel upon that foreign lawyer shall be accomplished by service upon the in-state lawyer or that in-state lawyer's agent.

11. Optional: the applicant's prior or continuing representation in other matters of one or more of the clients the applicant proposes to represent and any relationship between such other matter(s) and the proceeding for which applicant seeks admission.

12. Optional: any special experience, expertise, or other factor deemed to make it particularly desirable that the applicant be permitted to represent the client(s) the applicant proposes to represent in the particular cause.

Adopted August 12, 2012 by the ABA House of Delegates.
Amended February 11, 2013.

ABA Model Rules Related to Multijurisdictional Practice

ABA Model Rule on Admission by Motion

ABA Model Rule on Admission by Motion

1. An applicant who meets the requirements of (a) through (h) of this Rule may, upon motion, be admitted to the practice of law in this jurisdiction. The applicant shall:

   (a) have been admitted to practice law in another state, territory, or the District of Columbia;

   (b) hold a J.D. or LL.B. degree from a law school approved by the Council of the Section of Legal Education and Admissions to the Bar of the American Bar Association at the time the applicant matriculated or graduated;

   (c) have been primarily engaged in the active practice of law in one or more states, territories or the District of Columbia for three of the five years immediately preceding the date upon which the application is filed;

   (d) establish that the applicant is currently a member in good standing in all jurisdictions where admitted;

   (e) establish that the applicant is not currently subject to lawyer discipline or the subject of a pending disciplinary matter in any jurisdiction;

   (f) establish that the applicant possesses the character and fitness to practice law in this jurisdiction; and

   (g) designate the Clerk of the jurisdiction's highest court for service of process.

2. For the purposes of this Rule, the "active practice of law" shall include the following activities, if performed in a jurisdiction in which the applicant is admitted and authorized to practice, or if performed in a jurisdiction that affirmatively permits such activity by a lawyer not admitted in that jurisdiction; however, in no event shall any activities that were performed pursuant to the Model Rule on Practice Pending Admission in advance of bar admission in some state, territory, or the District of Columbia be accepted toward the durational requirement:

   (a) Representation of one or more clients in the practice of law;

   (b) Service as a lawyer with a local, state, or federal agency, including military service;

   (c) Teaching law at a law school approved by the Council of the Section of Legal Education and Admissions to the Bar of the American Bar Association;

   (d) Service as a judge in a federal, state, territorial or local court of record;

   (e) Service as a judicial law clerk; or

   (f) Service as in-house counsel provided to the lawyer's employer or its organizational affiliates.

3. For the purposes of this Rule, the active practice of law shall not include work that, as undertaken, constituted the unauthorized practice of law in the jurisdiction in which it was performed or in the jurisdiction in which the clients receiving the unauthorized services were located.
4. An applicant who has failed a bar examination administered in this jurisdiction within five years of the date of filing an application under this rule shall not be eligible for admission on motion.

Adopted August 12, 2002 by the ABA House of Delegates.
Amended February 14, 2011 and August 6, 2012.

ABA Model
Rules Related to
Multijurisdictional
Practice

ABA Model Rule
for Temporary Practice
by Foreign Lawyers

ABA Model Rule for Temporary Practice by Foreign Lawyers

(a) A lawyer who is admitted only in a non-United States jurisdiction shall not, except as authorized by this Rule or other law, establish an office or other systematic and continuous presence in this jurisdiction for the practice of law, or hold out to the public or otherwise represent that the lawyer is admitted to practice law in this jurisdiction. Such a lawyer does not engage in the unauthorized practice of law in this jurisdiction when on a temporary basis the lawyer performs services in this jurisdiction that:

  (1) are undertaken in association with a lawyer who is admitted to practice in this jurisdiction and who actively participates in the matter;

  (2) are in or reasonably related to a pending or potential proceeding before a tribunal held or to be held in a jurisdiction outside the United States if the lawyer, or a person the lawyer is assisting, is authorized by law or by order of the tribunal to appear in such proceeding or reasonably expects to be so authorized;

  (3) are in or reasonably related to a pending or potential arbitration, mediation or other alternative dispute resolution proceeding held or to be held in this or another jurisdiction, if the services arise out of or are reasonably related to the lawyer's practice in a jurisdiction in which the lawyer is admitted to practice;

  (4) are not within paragraphs (2) or (3) and

    (i) are performed for a client who resides or has an office in a jurisdiction in which the lawyer is authorized to practice to the extent of that authorization; or

    (ii) arise out of or are reasonably related to a matter that has a substantial connection to a jurisdiction in which the lawyer is authorized to practice to the extent of that authorization; or

  (5) are governed primarily by international law or the law of a non-United States jurisdiction.

(b) For purposes of this grant of authority, the lawyer must be a member in good standing of a recognized legal profession in a foreign jurisdiction, the members of which are admitted to practice as lawyers or counselors at law or the equivalent and subject to effective regulation and discipline by a duly constituted professional body or a public authority.

Adopted August 12, 2002 by the ABA House of Delegates.

ABA Model Rule for the Licensing and Practice of Foreign Legal Consultants

ABA Model Rule for the Licensing and Practice of Foreign Legal Consultants

§ 1. General Regulation as to Licensing

In its discretion, the [name of court] may license to practice in this United States jurisdiction as a foreign legal consultant, without examination, an applicant who:

(a) is, and for at least five years has been, a member in good standing of a recognized legal profession in a foreign country, the members of which are admitted to practice as lawyers or counselors at law or the equivalent and are subject to effective regulation and discipline by a duly constituted professional body or a public authority;

(b) for at least five years preceding his or her application has been a member in good standing of such legal profession and has been lawfully engaged in the practice of law in the foreign country or elsewhere substantially involving or relating to the rendering of advice or the provision of legal services concerning the law of the foreign country; [1]

(c) possesses the good moral character and general fitness requisite for a member of the bar of this jurisdiction; and

(d) intends to practice as a foreign legal consultant in this jurisdiction and to maintain an office in this jurisdiction for that purpose.

§ 2. Application

An applicant under this Rule shall file an application for a foreign legal consultant license, which shall include all of the following:

(a) a certificate from the professional body or public authority having final jurisdiction over professional discipline in the foreign country in which the applicant is admitted, certifying the applicant's admission to practice, date of admission, and good standing as a lawyer or counselor at law or the equivalent;

(b) a letter of recommendation from one of the members of the executive body of such professional body or public authority or from one of the judges of the highest law court or court of original jurisdiction in the foreign country in which the applicant is admitted;

(c) duly authenticated English translations of the certificate required by Section 2(a) of this Rule and the letter required by Section 2(b) of this Rule if they are not in English;

---

1. Section 1(b) is optional; it may be included as written, modified through the substitution of shorter periods than five and seven years, respectively, or omitted entirely.

(d) other evidence as the [name of court] may require regarding the applicant's educational and professional qualifications, good moral character and general fitness, and compliance with the requirements of Section 1 of this Rule;

(e) an application fee as set by the [name of court].

§ 3. Scope of Practice

A person licensed to practice as a foreign legal consultant under this Rule may render legal services in this jurisdiction but shall not be considered admitted to practice law in this jurisdiction, or in any way hold himself or herself out as a member of the bar of this jurisdiction, or, do any of the following:

(a) appear as a lawyer on behalf of another person in any court, or before any magistrate or other judicial officer, in this jurisdiction (except when admitted pro hac vice pursuant to [citation of applicable rule]);

(b) prepare any instrument effecting the transfer or registration of title to real estate located in the United States of America;

(c) prepare:

    (i) any will or trust instrument effecting the disposition on death of any property located and owned by a resident of the United States of America, or

    (ii) any instrument relating to the administration of a decedent's estate in the United States of America;

(d) prepare any instrument in respect of the marital or parental relations, rights or duties of a resident of the United States of America, or the custody or care of the children of such a resident;

(e) render professional legal advice on the law of this jurisdiction or of the United States of America (whether rendered incident to the preparation of legal instruments or otherwise) except on the basis of advice from a person duly qualified and entitled (other than by virtue of having been licensed under this Rule) to render professional legal advice in this jurisdiction;

(f) carry on a practice under, or utilize in connection with such practice, any name, title or designation other than one or more of the following:

    (i) the foreign legal consultant's own name;

    (ii) the name of the law firm with which the foreign legal consultant is affiliated;

    (iii) the foreign legal consultant's authorized title in the foreign country of his or her admission to practice, which may be used in conjunction with the name of that country; and

(iv) the title "foreign legal consultant," which may be used in conjunction with the words "admitted to the practice of law in [name of the foreign country of his or her admission to practice]".

[(g) render legal services in this jurisdiction pursuant to the Model Rule for the Temporary Practice by Foreign Lawyers.]

§ 4. Practice by a Foreign Legal Consultant in Another United States Jurisdiction

[A person licensed as a foreign legal consultant in another United States jurisdiction may provide legal services in this jurisdiction on a temporary basis pursuant to the Model Rule for Temporary Practice by Foreign Lawyers. A person licensed as a foreign legal consultant in another United States jurisdiction shall not establish an office or otherwise engage in a systematic and continuous practice in this jurisdiction or hold out to the public or otherwise represent that the foreign legal consultant is licensed as a foreign legal consultant in this jurisdiction.]

§ 5. Rights and Obligations

Subject to the limitations listed in Section 3 of this Rule, a person licensed under this Rule shall be considered a foreign legal consultant affiliated with the bar of this jurisdiction and shall be entitled and subject to:

(a) the rights and obligations set forth in the [Rules] [Code] of Professional [Conduct] [Responsibility] of [citation] or arising from the other conditions and requirements that apply to a member of the bar of this jurisdiction under the [rules of court governing members of the bar, including ethics]; and

(b) the rights and obligations of a member of the bar of this jurisdiction with respect to:

    (i) affiliation in the same law firm with one or more members of the bar of this jurisdiction, including by:

        (A) employing one or more members of the bar of this jurisdiction;

        (B) being employed by one or more members of the bar of this jurisdiction or by any partnership [or professional corporation] that includes members of the bar of this jurisdiction or that maintains an office in this jurisdiction; and

        (C) being a partner in any partnership [or shareholder in any professional corporation] that includes members of the bar of this jurisdiction or that maintains an office in this jurisdiction; and

    (ii) attorney-client privilege, work-product privilege and similar professional privileges.

ABA Model Rules Related to Multijurisdictional Practice

§ 6. Discipline

A person licensed to practice as a foreign legal consultant under this Rule shall be subject to professional discipline in the same manner and to the same extent as members of the bar of this jurisdiction. To this end:

    (a) Every person licensed to practice as a foreign legal consultant under this Rule:

        (i)   shall be subject to the jurisdiction of the [name of court] and to censure, suspension, removal or revocation of his or her license to practice by the [name of court] and shall otherwise be governed by [citation of applicable rules]; and

        (ii) shall execute and file with the [name of court], in the form and manner as the court may prescribe:

            (A) a commitment to observe the [Rules] [Code] of Professional [Conduct] [Responsibility] of [citation] and the [rules of court governing members of the bar] to the extent applicable to the legal services authorized under Section 3 of this Rule;

            (B) an undertaking or appropriate evidence of professional liability insurance, in an amount as the court may prescribe, to assure the foreign legal consultant's proper professional conduct and responsibility;

            (C) a written undertaking to notify the court of any change in the foreign legal consultant's good standing as a member of the foreign legal profession referred to in Section 1(a) of this Rule and of any final action of the professional body or public authority referred to in Section 2(a) of this Rule imposing any disciplinary censure, suspension, or other sanction upon the foreign legal consultant; and

            (D) a duly acknowledged instrument in writing, providing the foreign legal consultant's address in this jurisdiction and designating the clerk of [name of court] as his or her agent for service of process. The foreign legal consultant shall keep the clerk advised in writing of any changes of address in this jurisdiction. In any action or proceeding brought against the foreign legal consultant and arising out of or based upon any legal services rendered or offered to be rendered by the foreign legal consultant within or to residents of this jurisdiction, service shall first be attempted upon the foreign legal consultant at the most recent address filed with the clerk. Whenever after due diligence service cannot be made upon the foreign legal consultant at that address, service may be made upon the clerk. Service made upon the clerk in accor-

ABA Model Rules Related to Multijurisdictional Practice

dance with this provision is effective as if service had been made personally upon the foreign legal consultant.

(b) Service of process on the clerk under Section 5(a)(ii)(D) of this Rule shall be made by personally delivering to the clerk's office, and leaving with the clerk, or with a deputy or assistant authorized by the clerk to receive service, duplicate copies of the process together with a fee as set by the [name of court]. The clerk shall promptly send one copy of the process to the foreign legal consultant to whom the process is directed, by certified mail, return receipt requested, addressed to the foreign legal consultant at the most recent address provided in accordance with section 5(a)(ii)(D).

§ 7. Annual Fee

A person licensed as a foreign legal consultant shall pay an annual fee as set by the [name of court].

§ 8. Revocation of License

If the [name of court] determines that a person licensed as a foreign legal consultant under this Rule no longer meets the requirements for licensure set forth in Section 1(a) or Section 1(b) of this Rule, it shall revoke the foreign legal consultant's license.

§ 9. Admission to Bar

If a person licensed as a foreign legal consultant under this Rule is subsequently admitted as a member of the bar of this jurisdiction under the Rules governing admission, that person's foreign legal consultant license shall be deemed superseded by the license to practice law as a member of the bar of this jurisdiction.

§ 10. Application for Waiver of Provisions

The [name of court], upon written application, may waive any provision or vary the application of this Rule where strict compliance will cause undue hardship to the applicant. An application for waiver shall be in the form of a verified petition setting forth the applicant's name, age and residence address, the facts relied upon and a prayer for relief.

Adopted August 10-11, 1993 by the ABA House of Delegates.
Amended, August 7-8, 2006.

ABA Model
Rules Related to
Multijurisdictional
Practice

ABA Model Court Rule on Provision of Legal Services Following Determination of Major Disaster

ABA Model Court Rule on Provision of Legal Services Following Determination of Major Disaster

(Adopted February 12, 2007)

Rule ___. Provision of Legal Services Following Determination of Major Disaster

(a) *Determination of existence of major disaster.* Solely for purposes of this Rule, this Court shall determine when an emergency affecting the justice system, as a result of a natural or other major disaster has occurred in:

(1) this jurisdiction and whether the emergency caused by the major disaster affects the entirety or only a part of this jurisdiction, or

(2) another jurisdiction but only after such a determination and its geographical scope have been made by the highest court of that jurisdiction. The authority to engage in the temporary practice of law in this jurisdiction pursuant to paragraph (c) shall extend only to lawyers who principally practice in the area of such other jurisdiction determined to have suffered a major disaster causing an emergency affecting the justice system and the provision of legal services.

(b) *Temporary practice in this jurisdiction following major disaster.* Following the determination of an emergency affecting the justice system in this jurisdiction pursuant to paragraph (a) of this Rule, or a determination that persons displaced by a major disaster in another jurisdiction and residing in this jurisdiction are in need of pro bono services and the assistance of lawyers from outside of this jurisdiction is required to help provide such assistance, a lawyer authorized to practice law in another United States jurisdiction, and not disbarred, suspended from practice or otherwise restricted from practice in any jurisdiction, may provide legal services in this jurisdiction on a temporary basis. Such legal services must be provided on a pro bono basis without compensation, expectation of compensation or other direct or indirect pecuniary gain to the lawyer. Such legal services shall be assigned and supervised through an established not-for-profit bar association, pro bono program or legal services program or through such organization(s) specifically designated by this Court.

(c) *Temporary practice in this jurisdiction following major disaster in another jurisdiction.* Following the determination of a major disaster in another United States jurisdiction, a lawyer who is authorized to practice law and who principally practices in that affected jurisdiction, and who is not disbarred, suspended from practice or otherwise restricted from practice in any jurisdiction, may provide legal services in this jurisdiction on a temporary basis. Those legal services must arise out of and be reasonably related to that lawyer's practice of law in the jurisdiction, or area of such other jurisdiction, where the major disaster occurred.

(d) *Duration of authority for temporary practice.* The authority to practice law in this jurisdiction granted by paragraph (b) of this Rule shall end when this Court determines that the conditions caused by the major disaster in this jurisdiction have ended except that a lawyer then representing clients in this jurisdiction pursuant to paragraph (b) is authorized to continue the provision of legal services for such time as is reasonably necessary to complete the representation, but the lawyer shall not thereafter accept new clients. The authority to practice law in this jurisdiction granted by paragraph (c) of this Rule shall end [60] days after this Court declares that the conditions caused by the major disaster in the affected jurisdiction have ended.

(e) *Court appearances.* The authority granted by this Rule does not include appearances in court except:

(1) pursuant to that court's *pro hac vice* admission rule and, if such authority is granted, any fees for such admission shall be waived; or

(2) if this Court, in any determination made under paragraph (a), grants blanket permission to appear in all or designated courts of this jurisdiction to lawyers providing legal services pursuant to paragraph (b). If such an authorization is included, any pro hac vice admission fees shall be waived.

(f) *Disciplinary authority and registration requirement.* Lawyers providing legal services in this jurisdiction pursuant to paragraphs (b) or (c) are subject to this Court's disciplinary authority and the *Rules of Professional Conduct* of this jurisdiction as provided in Rule 8.5 of the *Rules of Professional Conduct.* Lawyers providing legal services in this jurisdiction under paragraphs (b) or (c) shall, within 30 days from the commencement of the provision of legal services, file a registration statement with the Clerk of this Court. The registration statement shall be in a form prescribed by this Court. Any lawyer who provides legal services pursuant to this Rule shall not be considered to be engaged in the unlawful practice of law in this jurisdiction.

(g) *Notification to clients.* Lawyers authorized to practice law in another United States jurisdiction who provide legal services pursuant to this Rule shall inform clients in this jurisdiction of the jurisdiction in which they are authorized to practice law, any limits of that authorization, and that they are not authorized to practice law in this jurisdiction except as permitted by this Rule. They shall not state or imply to any person that they are otherwise authorized to practice law in this jurisdiction.

Comment

[1] A major disaster in this or another jurisdiction may cause an emergency affecting the justice system with respect to the provision of legal services for a sustained period of time interfering with the ability of lawyers admitted and practicing in the affected jurisdiction to continue to represent clients until the disaster has ended. When this happens, lawyers from the affected jurisdiction may need to provide legal services to their clients, on a temporary basis, from an office outside their home jurisdiction. In addition, lawyers in an unaffected jurisdiction may be willing to serve residents of the affected jurisdiction who have unmet legal needs as a result of the disaster or, though independent of the disaster, whose legal needs temporarily are unmet because of disruption to the practices of local lawyers. Lawyers from unaffected jurisdictions may offer to provide these legal services either by traveling to the affected jurisdiction or from their own offices or both, provided the legal services are provided on a pro bono basis through an authorized not-for-profit entity or such other organization(s) specifically designated by this Court. A major disaster includes, for example, a hurricane, earthquake, flood, wildfire, tornado, public health emergency or an event caused by terrorists or acts of war.

[2] Under paragraph (a)(1), this Court shall determine whether a major disaster causing an emergency affecting the justice system has occurred in this jurisdiction, or in a part of this jurisdiction, for purposes of triggering paragraph (b) of this Rule. This Court may, for example, determine that the entirety of this jurisdiction has suffered a disruption in the provision of legal services or that only certain areas have suffered such an event. The authority granted by paragraph (b) shall extend only to lawyers authorized to practice law and not disbarred, suspended from practice or otherwise restricted from practice in any other manner in any other jurisdiction.

[3] Paragraph (b) permits lawyers authorized to practice law in an unaffected jurisdiction, and not disbarred, suspended from practice or otherwise restricted from practicing law in any other manner in any other jurisdiction, to provide pro bono legal services to residents of the affected jurisdiction following determination of an emergency caused by a major disaster; notwithstanding that they are not otherwise authorized to practice law in the affected jurisdiction. Other restrictions on a lawyer's license to practice law that would prohibit that lawyer from providing legal services pursuant to this Rule include, but are not limited to, probation, inactive status, disability inactive status or a non-disciplinary administrative suspension for failure to complete continuing legal education or other requirements. Lawyers on probation may be subject to monitoring and specific limitations on their practices. Lawyers on inactive status, despite being characterized in many

ABA Model Rules Related to Multijurisdictional Practice

jurisdictions as being "in good standing," and lawyers on disability inactive status are not permitted to practice law. Public protection warrants exclusion of these lawyers from the authority to provide legal services as defined in this Rule. Lawyers permitted to provide legal services pursuant to this Rule must do so without fee or other compensation, or expectation thereof. Their service must be provided through an established not-for-profit organization that is authorized to provide legal services either in its own name or that provides representation of clients through employed or cooperating lawyers. Alternatively, this court may instead designate other specific organization(s) through which these legal services may be rendered. Under paragraph (b), an emeritus lawyer from another United State jurisdiction may provide pro bono legal services on a temporary basis in this jurisdiction provided that the emeritus lawyer is authorized to provide pro bono legal services in that jurisdiction pursuant to that jurisdiction's emeritus or pro bono practice rule. Lawyers may also be authorized to provide legal services in this jurisdiction on a temporary basis under Rule 5.5(c) of the *Rules of Professional Conduct*.

[4] Lawyers authorized to practice law in another jurisdiction, who principally practice in the area of such other jurisdiction determined by this Court to have suffered a major disaster, and whose practices are disrupted by a major disaster there, and who are not disbarred, suspended from practice or otherwise restricted from practicing law in any other manner in any other jurisdiction, are authorized under paragraph (c) to provide legal services on a temporary basis in this jurisdiction. Those legal services must arise out of and be reasonably related to the lawyer's practice of law in the affected jurisdiction. For purposes of this Rule, the determination of a major disaster in another jurisdiction should first be made by the highest court of appellate jurisdiction in that jurisdiction. For the meaning of "arise out of and reasonably related to," see Rule 5.5 Comment [14], *Rules of Professional Conduct*.

[5] Emergency conditions created by major disasters end, and when they do, the authority created by paragraphs (b) and (c) also ends with appropriate notice to enable lawyers to plan and to complete pending legal matters. Under paragraph (d), this Court determines when those conditions end only for purposes of this Rule. The authority granted under paragraph (b) shall end upon such determination except that lawyers assisting residents of this jurisdiction under paragraph (b) may continue to do so for such longer period as is reasonably necessary to complete the representation. The authority created by paragraph (c) will end [60] days after this Court makes such a determination with regard to an affected jurisdiction.

[6] Paragraphs (b) and (c) do not authorize lawyers to appear in the courts of this jurisdiction. Court appearances are subject to the pro hac vice admission rules of the particular court. This Court may, in a determination

ABA Model
Rules Related to
Multijurisdictional
Practice

made under paragraph (e)(2), include authorization for lawyers who provide legal services in this jurisdiction under paragraph (b) to appear in all or designated courts of this jurisdiction without need for such pro hac vice admission. If such an authorization is included, any pro hac vice admission fees shall be waived. A lawyer who has appeared in the courts of this jurisdiction pursuant to para-graph (e) may continue to appear in any such matter notwithstanding a declaration under paragraph (d) that the conditions created by major disaster have ended. Furthermore, withdrawal from a court appearance is subject to Rule 1.16 of the *Rules of Professional Conduct.*

[7] Authorization to practice law as a foreign legal consultant or in-house counsel in a United States jurisdiction offers lawyers a limited scope of permitted practice and may therefore restrict that person's ability to provide legal services under this Rule.

[8] The ABA National Lawyer Regulatory Data Bank is available to help determine whether any lawyer seeking to practice in this jurisdiction pursuant to paragraphs (b) or (c) of this Rule is disbarred, suspended from practice or otherwise subject to a public disciplinary sanction that would restrict the lawyer's ability to practice law in any other jurisdiction.

ABA Model
Rules Related to
Multijurisdictional
Practice

ABA Model Rule
for Registration of
In-House Counsel

ABA Model Rule for
Registration of In-House Counsel

GENERAL PROVISIONS:

A. A lawyer who is admitted to the practice of law in another United States jurisdiction or is a foreign lawyer, who is employed as a lawyer and has a continuous presence in this jurisdiction by an organization, the business of which is lawful and consists of activities other than the practice of law or the provision of legal services, and who has a systematic and continuous presence in this jurisdiction as permitted pursuant to Rule 5.5(d)(1) of the Model Rules of Professional Conduct, shall register as in-house counsel within [180 days] of the commencement of employment as a lawyer or if currently so employed then within [180 days] of the effective date of this Rule, by submitting to the [registration authority] the following:

1) A completed application in the form prescribed by the [registration authority];
2) A fee in the amount determined by the [registration authority];
3) Documents proving admission to practice law and current good standing in all jurisdictions, U.S. and foreign, in which the lawyer is admitted to practice law.
4) If the jurisdiction is foreign and the documents are not in English, the lawyer shall submit an English translation and satisfactory proof of the accuracy of the translation; and
5) An affidavit from an officer, director, or general counsel of the employing entity attesting to the lawyer's employment by the entity and the capacity in which the lawyer is so employed, and stating that the employment conforms to the requirements of this Rule.

For purposes of this Rule, a "foreign lawyer" is a member in good standing of a recognized legal profession in a foreign jurisdiction, the members of which are admitted to practice as lawyers or counselors at law or the equivalent and subject to effective regulation and discipline by a duly constituted professional body or a public authority. For purposes of this Rule, the [state's highest court of appellate jurisdiction] may, in its discretion, allow a lawyer lawfully practicing as in-house counsel in a foreign jurisdiction who does not meet the above requirements to register as an in-house counsel after consideration of other criteria, including the lawyer's legal education, references, and experience.

SCOPE OF AUTHORITY OF REGISTERED LAWYER:

B. A lawyer registered under this Rule shall have the rights and privileges otherwise applicable to members of the bar of this jurisdiction with the following restrictions:

1. The registered lawyer is authorized to provide legal services to the entity client or its organizational affiliates, including entities that control, are controlled by, or are under common control with the employer, and for employees, officers and directors of such entities, but only on matters directly related to their work for the entity and only to the extent consistent with Rule 1.7 of the Model Rules of Professional Conduct [or jurisdictional equivalent];

2. The registered lawyer shall not:

    a. Except as otherwise permitted by the rules of this jurisdiction, appear before a court or any other tribunal as defined in Rule 1.0(m) of the Model Rules of Professional Conduct [or jurisdictional equivalent]; or

    b. Offer or provide legal services or advice to any person other than as described in paragraph B.1., or hold himself or herself out as being authorized to practice law in this jurisdiction other than as described in paragraph B.1; and

    c. If a foreign lawyer, provide advice on the law of this or another jurisdiction of the United States except on the basis of advice from a lawyer who is duly licensed and authorized to provide such advice.

PRO BONO PRACTICE:

C. Notwithstanding the provisions of paragraph B above, a lawyer registered under this Rule is authorized to provide pro bono legal services through an established not-for-profit bar association, pro bono program or legal services program or through such 60 organization(s) specifically authorized in this jurisdiction.

OBLIGATIONS:

D. A lawyer registered under this Rule shall:

1. Pay an annual fee in the amount of $_____;

2. Pay any annual client protection fund assessment;

3. Fulfill the continuing legal education requirements that are required of active members of the bar in this jurisdiction;

4. Report within [___] days to the jurisdiction the following:

    a. Termination of the lawyer's employment as described in paragraph A.5.;

    b. Whether or not public, any change in the lawyer's license status in another jurisdiction, whether U.S. or foreign, including by the lawyer's resignation;

c. Whether or not public, any disciplinary charge, finding, or sanction concerning the lawyer by any disciplinary authority, court, or other tribunal in any jurisdiction, U.S. or foreign.

LOCAL DISCIPLINE:

E. A registered lawyer under this Rule shall be subject to the [jurisdiction's Rules of Professional Conduct], [jurisdiction's Rules of Lawyer Disciplinary Enforcement], and all other laws and rules governing lawyers admitted to the active practice of law in this jurisdiction. The [jurisdiction's disciplinary counsel] has and shall retain jurisdiction over the registered lawyer with respect to the conduct of the lawyer in this or another jurisdiction to the same extent as it has over lawyers generally admitted in this jurisdiction.

ABA Model Rules Related to Multijurisdictional Practice

AUTOMATIC TERMINATION:

F. A registered lawyer's rights and privileges under this Rule automatically terminate when:

1. The lawyer's employment terminates;
2. The lawyer is suspended or disbarred or the equivalent thereof in any jurisdiction or any court or agency before which the lawyer is admitted, U.S. or foreign; or
3. The lawyer fails to maintain active status in at least one jurisdiction, U.S. or foreign.

REINSTATEMENT:

G. A registered lawyer whose registration is terminated under paragraph F.1. above, may be reinstated within [___] months of termination upon submission to the [registration authority] of the following:

1. An application for reinstatement in a form prescribed by the [registration authority];
2. A reinstatement fee in the amount of $_____;
3. An affidavit from the current employing entity as prescribed in paragraph A.5.

SANCTIONS:

H. A lawyer under this Rule who fails to register shall be:

1. Subject to professional discipline in this jurisdiction;
2. Ineligible for admission on motion in this jurisdiction;
3. Referred by the [registration authority] to this [jurisdiction's bar admissions authority]; and

4. Referred by the [registration authority] to the disciplinary authority or to any duly constituted organization overseeing the lawyer's profession, or that granted authority to practice law in the jurisdictions of licensure, U.S. and/or foreign.

Comment

[1] Paragraph A of this Rule provides that the [state's highest court of appellate jurisdiction] may, in its discretion, allow someone who does not meet the Rule's other definitional requirements of a foreign lawyer, but who is lawfully practicing as in-house counsel in their home foreign jurisdiction, to register. The exercise of such discretion by the court may be necessary, because some foreign jurisdictions may not permit otherwise qualified in-house counsel to be members of or admitted to the bar. Lawyers in such foreign jurisdictions who are employed as in-house counsel may be required to relinquish any bar membership or admission while so employed or they may never have obtained such admission or membership status.

[2] Paragraph F of this Rule sets forth three circumstances that result in automatic termination of in-house counsel's registrations status. In situations where a court has exercised its discretion pursuant to Paragraph A of this Rule, a registered foreign in-house counsel lacking bar admission or licensure in that individual's home country cannot "fail to maintain active status" as set forth in Paragraph F(3). There is no active status in existence. Absent the circumstances set forth in Paragraph F(2), the triggering event to terminate registration status of such foreign in-house counsel would be the termination of employment of that individual by the employer as set forth in Paragraph F(1).

Adopted August 11, 2008 by the ABA House of Delegates.
Amended February 11, 2013, and February 8, 2016.

ABA Model Rules Related to Multijurisdictional Practice

ABA Model Rules
for Client Protection
(Selected)

ABA Model
Rules for Client
Protection
(Selected)

ABA Model Rules for Trust Account Overdraft Notification

*Adopted by the American Bar Association
House of Delegates on February 9, 1988.*

AMERICAN BAR ASSOCIATION
STANDING COMMITTEE ON
LAWYERS' RESPONSIBILITY FOR CLIENT PROTECTION
1987-1988

Honorable William R. Robie, *Chair*
Falls Church, Virginia

Robert L. Burkett
Los Angeles, California

Gail A. Lione
Baltimore, Maryland

Isaac Hecht
Baltimore, Maryland

Frederick Miller
Albany, New York

I.S. Leevy Johnson
Columbia, South Carolina

Herbert M. Rosenthal
San Francisco, California

Paul M. Larson
Yakima, Washington

Harry Zukernick
Miami, Florida

Honorable William R. Goldberg, *Liaison*
ABA Board of Governors
Providence, Rhode Island

AMERICAN BAR ASSOCIATION
ADVISORY COMMISSION ON CLIENT SECURITY FUNDS
1987-1988

Kenneth J. Bossong, *Chair*
Trenton, New Jersey

Bobby E. James
Raleigh, North Carolina

William D. Ricker, Jr.
Fort Lauderdale, Florida

Jerome F. O'Rourke
Flint, Michigan

Sarah Singer
Boston, Massachusetts

Richard Reimers
Scottsdale, Arizona

Kiyoko Tatsui
Los Angeles, California

CENTER FOR PROFESSIONAL RESPONSIBILITY

Director
Jeanne P. Gray

Assistant Client Protection Counsel
Gilbert A. Webb

Model Rules for Trust Account Overdraft Notification

PREFACE

The rules of professional conduct mandate and the lawyer disciplinary systems enforce the standard of safekeeping of client property as a fundamental fiduciary obligation of lawyers. The dishonor of drafts for insufficient funds drawn from client trust accounts is an "early warning" that a lawyer is engaging in conduct likely to injure clients. An overdraft notification program has the potential to reduce significantly the level of lawyer defalcations across the country. By requiring financial institutions which maintain lawyer trust accounts to notify the highest court or lawyer disciplinary agency of overdrafts the appropriate disciplinary authorities are able to intervene before major losses occur and significant number of clients are harmed. The rule also enables authorities to counsel errant lawyers to take corrective action before the lawyer's misconduct becomes so egregious as to mandate serious sanction. Participation by financial institutions is a prerequisite to their continued eligibility to hold lawyer trust accounts. The costs of providing notification can be assessed against the lawyer who caused the overdraft. An effective overdraft notification program should conserve substantial resources for both clients and lawyers' funds for client protection.

Rule 1. CLEARLY IDENTIFIED TRUST ACCOUNTS REQUIRED

Lawyers who practice law in this jurisdiction shall deposit all funds held in trust in this jurisdiction in accordance with [Rule 1.15(a) of the ABA *Model Rules of Professional Conduct***] in accounts clearly identified as "trust" or "escrow" accounts, referred to herein as "trust accounts," and shall take all steps necessary to inform the depository institution of the purpose and identity of such accounts. Funds held in trust include funds held in any fiduciary capacity in connection with a representation, whether as trustee, agent, guardian, executor or otherwise. Lawyer trust accounts shall be maintained only in financial institutions approved by the highest court of the jurisdiction or the state lawyer discipline agency.**

Comment

Under Rule 1.15(a) of the ABA Model Rules of Professional Conduct or its equivalent, a lawyer must maintain client funds in an account separate from the lawyer's own property. Trust funds for a lawyer's own spouse or minor child and a lawyer's own funds properly held in a non-fiduciary capacity, such as funds in a business or personal account, do not fall under this rule.

It should be noted that although Rule 1.15 generally requires that trust accounts be maintained in the state where the lawyer's office is situated, trust property may be held outside the lawyer's home jurisdiction upon consent of the client. The overdraft notification rule governs funds held within the adopting state. A lawyer's obligation to deposit trust funds in an approved institution will arise upon adoption of the overdraft notification rule in a state where the lawyer deposits trust funds, whether that state is the state wherein the lawyer's office is situated or some other state.

Rule 2. OVERDRAFT NOTIFICATION AGREEMENT REQUIRED

A financial institution shall be approved as a depository for lawyer trust accounts if it shall file with the highest court of the jurisdiction or the state lawyer disciplinary agency an agreement, in a form provided by the court or disciplinary agency, to report to the disciplinary agency in the event any properly payable instrument is presented against a lawyer trust account containing insufficient funds, irrespective of whether or not the instrument is honored. The court or disciplinary agency shall establish rules governing approval and termination of approved status for financial institutions, and shall annually publish a list of approved financial institutions.

No trust account shall be maintained in any financial institution which does not agree to make such reports. Any such agreement shall apply to all branches of the financial institution and shall not be canceled except upon [30] days notice in writing to the court or disciplinary agency.

Comment

For purposes of this rule, each financial institution wishing to be approved as a depository of client trust funds must file an overdraft notification agreement with the highest court or the jurisdiction. In some jurisdictions, the court may wish to delegate to the state bar or some other agency the duty to enter into overdraft notification agreements with financial institutions and to publish a list of approved institutions.

The overdraft notification agreement requires that all overdrafts be reported to the state lawyer disciplinary agency, irrespective of whether or not the instrument is honored. In light of the purposes of this rule, and the ethical proscriptions concerning the preservation of client funds and commingling of client and lawyer funds, it would be improper for a lawyer to accept "overdraft privileges" or any other arrangement for a personal loan on a lawyer trust account.

Denial of discretion to financial institutions serves two important purposes. First, it makes notification by a financial institution an administra-

ABA Model Rules for Client Protection (Selected)

tively simple matter. An institution which receives an instrument for payment against insufficient funds need not evaluate whether circumstances require that notification be given; it merely provides notice. It then becomes the responsibility of the lawyer disciplinary agency to determine whether further action is warranted.

Second, mandatory notification shields the financial institution from potential tort claims by the lawyer's clients for failure to report overdrafts. Liability for negligence in reporting overdrafts could be alleged by a person, injured by such failure to report, who falls within the zone of foreseeability and for whose benefit the duty to report was instituted. Arguably, a financial institution could owe a duty to the lawyer's clients who supplied the funds, and to the lawyers' fund for client protection if a pay-out is made in the event of theft of those funds. If an institution reports all overdrafts, its potential liability for negligent failure to report is minimized. In cases where a bounced check or overdrafts is a result of an accounting error (caused by either the lawyer or the financial institution), but notification has already been sent to the state agency, the institution should provide the lawyer with a written explanation (preferably, an affidavit from an officer of the institution) which the lawyer can then submit to the agency to verify the error. In the event of financial institution error no record need be kept by the agency.

The rule calls for the highest court of the jurisdiction (or lawyer disciplinary agency, where the court has so delegated) to establish rules governing approval of financial institutions' holding of client trust funds, and termination of such approved status. These rules should specify under what circumstances approved status will be withdrawn. For instance, the court's rules might state that approved status may be revoked where the institution demonstrates "a pattern of neglect or a showing of bad faith" rather than an occasional or negligent failure to report an overdraft.

Rule 3. OVERDRAFT REPORTS

The overdraft notification agreement shall provide that all reports made by the financial institution shall be in the following format:

(1) In the case of a dishonored instrument, the report shall be identical to the overdraft notice customarily forwarded to the depositor, and should include a copy of the dishonored instrument, if such a copy is normally provided to depositors; and

(2) In the case of instruments that are presented against insufficient funds but which instruments are honored, the report shall identify the financial institution, the lawyer or law firm, the account number, the date of presentation for payment and the date paid, as well as the amount of overdraft created thereby.

Such reports shall be made simultaneously with, and within the time provided by law for, notice of dishonor, if any. If an instrument presented against insufficient funds is honored, then the report shall be made within [5] banking days of the date of presentation for payment against insufficient funds.

Comment

The rule provides the proper format for overdraft reports, distinguishing between dishonored instruments and instruments that are presented against insufficient funds but honored. Where instruments are dishonored, a copy of the notice of dishonor is sufficient. Where instruments are presented against insufficient funds but paid, the rule specifies the information that the institution should provide.

Ordinarily, a financial institution gives notice of an overdraft to a depositor before midnight of the next banking day following receipt of the item or notice. See Uniform Commercial Code (U.L.A.) § 3-503(c) (Revised Article 3, 1990) or Uniform Commercial Code (U.L.A.) § 3-508(2) (Prior Article 3, pre-1990). This is the same time period in which overdraft notification is to be given to the state lawyer disciplinary agency. Where an instrument presented against insufficient funds is honored, the rule recommends that the financial institution send overdraft notification to the agency within 5 days of the date of presentation.

The rule contemplates that the lawyer disciplinary agency, upon receipt of the overdraft notification, will contact the lawyer or law firm by telephone and request an explanation for the overdraft. A letter, requesting a documented explanation, may also be sent. If the overdraft is an accounting error, the lawyer or law firm will submit a written, documented explanation to substantiate the error.

Where the lawyer or law firm cannot supply an adequate or complete explanation for the overdraft, other action may be taken, including an audit or a demand for production of the lawyer's books and records.

Rule 4. CONSENT BY LAWYERS

Every lawyer practicing or admitted to practice in this jurisdiction shall, as a condition thereof, be conclusively deemed to have consented to the reporting and production requirements mandated by this rule.

Comment

The rule establishes that consent to the reporting and production requirements mandated by the rule is a condition of the privilege to practice law in the jurisdiction which has adopted the rule. As a consequence, financial institutions are protected from claims by lawyer-depositors based on

ABA Model Rules for Client Protection (Selected)

disclosures made in accordance with the rule, although the only parties to an overdraft notification agreement are the court and the financial institution.

Rule 5. COSTS

Nothing herein shall preclude a financial institution from charging a particular lawyer or law firm for the reasonable cost of producing the reports and records required by this rule.

Comment

In addition to normal monthly maintenance fees on each account, the lawyer or law firm can anticipate that financial institutions will charge additional fees for reporting overdrafts in accordance with this rule.

Financial institutions, however, already flag overdrafts and returned checks, and, thus, it is only slightly more burdensome for the institution to forward a copy to the state lawyer disciplinary agency. The additional cost to the lawyer should be insignificant.

Rule 5 should not be interpreted to allow a lawyer to permit trust account funds to be reduced through deductions made by a financial institution to cover costs of overdraft notification. Notification costs, if charged, should not be borne by clients.

ABA Model Rules for Client Protection (Selected)

Rule 6. DEFINITIONS

"Financial institution" includes banks, savings and loan associations, credit unions, savings banks and any other business or person which accepts for deposit funds held in trust by lawyers.

"Properly payable" refers to an instrument which, if presented in the normal course of business, is in a form requiring payment under the laws of this jurisdiction.

"Notice of dishonor" refers to the notice which a financial institution is required to give, under the laws of this jurisdiction, upon presentation of an instrument which the institution dishonors.

Comment

Under the laws of most jurisdictions, the definition of "properly payable" will be contained in Uniform Commercial Code (U.L.A.) § 4-401(a) (Amended Article 4, 1990) ("An item is properly payable if it is authorized by the customer and is in accordance with any agreement between the customer and bank.") or its predecessor, Uniform Commercial Code (U.L.A.) § 4-104(i) (Prior Article 4, pre-1990) ("Properly payable' includes the availability of funds for payment at the time of decision to pay or dishonor").

Under the laws of most jurisdictions, the definition of "notice of dishonor" will be determined by reference to Uniform Commercial Code

(U.L.A.) § 3503(c) (Revised Article 3, 1990), under which notice must be given by a collecting bank before midnight of the next banking day following the banking day on which the bank receives notice of dishonor or by any other person within 30 days following the day on which the person receives notice of dishonor, or its predecessor, Uniform Commercial Code (U.L.A) § 3-508(2) (Prior Article 3, pre-1990), which states any necessary notice must be given by a bank before its midnight deadline and by any other person before midnight of the third business day after dishonor or receipt of notice of dishonor.

ABA Model Rules
for Client Trust
Account Records

Adopted by the American Bar Association
House of Delegates on August 9, 2010.

Model Rules for Client Trust Account Records

Rule 1: RECORDKEEPING GENERALLY

A lawyer who practices in this jurisdiction shall maintain current financial records as provided in these Rules and required by [Rule 1.15 of the Model Rules of Professional Conduct], and shall retain the following records for a period of [five years] after termination of the representation:

(a) receipt and disbursement journals containing a record of deposits to and withdrawals from client trust accounts, specifically identifying the date, source, and description of each item deposited, as well as the date, payee and purpose of each disbursement;

(b) ledger records for all client trust accounts showing, for each separate trust client or beneficiary, the source of all funds deposited, the names of all persons for whom the funds are or were held, the amount of such funds, the descriptions and amounts of charges or withdrawals, and the names of all persons or entities to whom such funds were disbursed;

(c) copies of retainer and compensation agreements with clients [as required by Rule 1.5 of the Model Rules of Professional Conduct];

(d) copies of accountings to clients or third persons showing the disbursement of funds to them or on their behalf;

(e) copies of bills for legal fees and expenses rendered to clients;

(f) copies of records showing disbursements on behalf of clients;

(g) the physical or electronic equivalents of all checkbook registers, bank statements, records of deposit, pre-numbered canceled checks, and substitute checks provided by a financial institution;

(h) records of all electronic transfers from client trust accounts, including the name of the person authorizing transfer, the date of transfer, the name of the recipient and confirmation from the financial institution of the trust account number from which money was withdrawn and the date and the time the transfer was completed;

(i) copies of [monthly] trial balances and [quarterly] reconciliations of the client trust accounts maintained by the lawyer; and

(j) copies of those portions of client files that are reasonably related to client trust account transactions.

Comment

[1] Rule 1 enumerates the basic financial records that a lawyer must maintain with regard to all trust accounts of a law firm. These include the standard books of account, and the supporting records that are necessary to safeguard and account for the receipt and disbursement of client or third person funds as required by Rule 1.15 of the Model Rules of Professional

Conduct or its equivalent. Consistent with Rule 1.15, this Rule proposes that lawyers maintain client trust account records for a period of five years after termination of each particular legal engagement or representation. Although these Model Rules address the accepted use of a client trust account by a lawyer when holding client or third person funds, some jurisdictions may permit a lawyer to deposit certain advance fees for legal services into the lawyer's business or operating account. In those situations, the lawyer should still be guided by the standards contained in these Model Rules.

[2] Rule 1(g) requires that the physical or electronic equivalents of all checkbook registers, bank statements, records of deposit, pre-numbered canceled checks, and substitute checks be maintained for a period of five years after termination of each legal engagement or representation. The "Check Clearing for the 21st Century Act" or "Check 21 Act", codified at 12 U.S.C.§5001 *et. seq.*, recognizes "substitute checks" as the legal equivalent of an original check. A "substitute check" is defined at 12 U.S.C. §5002(16) as "paper reproduction of the original check that contains an image of the front and back of the original check; bears a magnetic ink character recognition ("MICR") line containing all the information appearing on the MICR line of the original check; conforms with generally applicable industry standards for substitute checks; and is suitable for automated processing in the same manner as the original check. Banks, as defined in 12 U.S.C. §5002(2), are not required to return to customers the original canceled checks. Most banks now provide electronic images of checks to customers who have access to their accounts on internet-based websites. It is the lawyer's responsibility to download electronic images. Electronic images shall be maintained for the requisite number of years and shall be readily available for printing upon request or shall be printed and maintained for the requisite number of years.

[3] The ACH (Automated Clearing House) Network is an electronic funds transfer or payment system that primarily provides for the inter-bank clearing of electronic payments between originating and receiving participating financial institutions. ACH transactions are payment instructions to either debit or credit a deposit account. ACH payments are used in a variety of payment environments including bill payments, business-to-business payments, and government payments (e.g. tax refunds.) In addition to the primary use of ACH transactions, retailers and third parties use the ACH system for other types of transactions including electronic check conversion (ECC). ECC is the process of transmitting MICR information from the bottom of a check, converting check payments to ACH transactions depending upon the authorization given by the account holder at the point-of-purchase. In this type of transaction, the lawyer should be careful to comply with the requirements of Rule 1(h).

[4] There are five types of check conversions where a lawyer should be careful to comply with the requirements of Rule 1(h). First, in a "point-of-purchase conversion," a paper check is converted into a debit at the point of purchase and the paper check is returned to the issuer. Second, in a "back-office conversion," a paper check is presented at the point of purchase and is later converted into a debit and the paper check is destroyed. Third, in an "account-receivable conversion," a paper check is converted into a debit and the paper check is destroyed. Fourth, in a "telephone-initiated debit" or "check-by-phone" conversion, bank account information is provided via the telephone and the information is converted to a debit. Fifth, in a "web-initiated debit," an electronic payment is initiated through a secure web environment. Rule 1(h) applies to each of the type of electronic funds transfers described. All electronic funds transfers shall be recorded and a lawyer should not re-use a check number which has been previously used in an electronic transfer transaction.

[5] The potential of these records to serve as safeguards is realized only if the procedures set forth in Rule 1(i) are regularly performed. The trial balance is the sum of balances of each client's ledger card (or the electronic equivalent). Its value lies in comparing it on a monthly basis to a control balance. The control balance starts with the previous month's balance, then adds receipts from the Trust Receipts Journal and subtracts disbursements from the Trust Disbursements Journal. Once the total matches the trial balance, the reconciliation readily follows by adding amounts of any outstanding checks and subtracting any deposits not credited by the bank at month's end. This balance should agree with the bank statement. Quarterly reconciliation is recommended only as a minimum requirement; monthly reconciliation is the preferred practice given the difficulty of identifying an error (whether by the lawyer or the bank) among three months' transactions.

[6] In some situations, documentation in addition to that listed in paragraphs (a) through (i) of Rule 1 is necessary for a complete understanding of a trust account transaction. The type of document that a lawyer must retain under paragraph (j) because it is "reasonably related" to a client trust transaction will vary depending on the nature of the transaction and the significance of the document in shedding light on the transaction. Examples of documents that typically must be retained under this paragraph include correspondence between the client and lawyer relating to a disagreement over fees or costs or the distribution of proceeds, settlement agreements contemplating payment of funds, settlement statements issued to the client, documentation relating to sharing litigation costs and attorney fees for subrogated claims, agreements for division of fees between lawyers, guarantees of payment to third parties out of proceeds recovered on behalf of a client,

ABA Model Rules for Client Protection (Selected)

and copies of bills, receipts or correspondence related to any payments to third parties on behalf of a client (whether made from the client's funds or from the lawyer's funds advanced for the benefit of the client).

Rule 2: CLIENT TRUST ACCOUNT SAFEGUARDS

With respect to client trust accounts required by [Rule 1.15 of the Model Rules of Professional Conduct]:

(a) only a lawyer admitted to practice law in this jurisdiction or a person under the direct supervision of the lawyer shall be an authorized signatory or authorize transfers from a client trust account;

(b) receipts shall be deposited intact and records of deposit should be sufficiently detailed to identify each item; and

(c) withdrawals shall be made only by check payable to a named payee and not to cash, or by authorized electronic transfer.

Comment

[1] Rule 2 enumerates minimal accounting controls for client trust accounts. It also enunciates the requirement that only a lawyer admitted to the practice of law in the jurisdiction or a person who is under the direct supervision of the lawyer shall be the authorized signatory or authorize electronic transfers from a client trust account. While it is permissible to grant limited nonlawyer access to a client trust account, such access should be limited and closely monitored by the lawyer. The lawyer has a non-delegable duty to protect and preserve the funds in a client trust account and can be disciplined for failure to supervise subordinates who misappropriate client funds. See, Rules 5.1 and 5.3 of the Model Rules of Professional Conduct.

[2] Authorized electronic transfers shall be limited to (1) money required for payment to a client or third person on behalf of a client; (2) expenses properly incurred on behalf of a client, such as filing fees or payment to third persons for services rendered in connection with the representation; or (3) money transferred to the lawyer for fees that are earned in connection with the representation and are not in dispute; or (4) money transferred from one client trust account to another client trust account.

[3] The requirements in paragraph (b) that receipts shall be deposited intact mean that a lawyer cannot deposit one check or negotiable instrument into two or more accounts at the same time, a practice commonly known as a split deposit.

Rule 3: AVAILABILITY OF RECORDS

Records required by Rule 1 may be maintained by electronic, photographic, or other media provided that they otherwise comply with these

Rules and that printed copies can be produced. These records shall be readily accessible to the lawyer.

Comment

[1] Rule 3 allows the use of alternative media for the maintenance of client trust account records if printed copies of necessary reports can be produced. If trust records are computerized, a system of regular and frequent (preferably daily) back-up procedures is essential. If a lawyer uses third-party electronic or internet based file storage, the lawyer must make reasonable efforts to ensure that the company has in place, or will establish reasonable procedures to protect the confidentiality of client information. See, ABA Formal Ethics Opinion 398 (1995). Records required by Rule 1 shall be readily accessible and shall be readily available to be produced upon request by the client or third person who has an interest as provided in Model Rule 1.15, or by the official request of a disciplinary authority, including but not limited to, a subpoena duces tecum. Personally identifying information in records produced upon request by the client or third person or by disciplinary authority shall remain confidential and shall be disclosed only in a manner to ensure client confidentiality as otherwise required by law or court rule.

[2] Rule 28 of the Model Rules for Lawyer Disciplinary Enforcement provides for the preservation of a lawyer's client trust account records in the event that the lawyer is transferred to disability inactive status, suspended, disbarred, disappears, or dies.

Rule 4: DISSOLUTION OF LAW FIRM

Upon dissolution of a law firm or of any legal professional corporation, the partners shall make reasonable arrangements for the maintenance of client trust account records specified in Rule 1.

Comment

[1] Rules 4 and 5 provide for the preservation of a lawyer's client trust account records in the event of dissolution or sale of a law practice. Regardless of the arrangements the partners or shareholders make among themselves for maintenance of the client trust records, each partner may be held responsible for ensuring the availability of these records. For the purposes of these Rules, the terms "law firm," "partner," and "reasonable" are defined in accordance with Rules 1.0(c),(g), and (h) of the Model Rules of Professional Conduct.

Rule 5: SALE OF LAW PRACTICE

Upon the sale of a law practice, the seller shall make reasonable arrangements for the maintenance of records specified in Rule 1.

ABA Model Rules for Client Protection (Selected)

ABA Model Court Rule on Insurance Disclosure

*Adopted by the American Bar Association
House of Delegates on August 10, 2004.*

ABA Model
Rules for Client
Protection
(Selected)

Model Court Rule
on Insurance Disclosure

PREFACE

The ABA Model Court Rule on Insurance Disclosure requires lawyers to disclose on their annual registration statements whether they maintain professional liability insurance. The Model Court Rule excludes from the Rule's reporting requirement those lawyers who are not engaged in the active practice of law and those who are engaged in the practice of law as full-time government lawyers or as counsel employed by an organizational client and do not represent clients outside that capacity. The Model Court Rule places an affirmative duty upon lawyers to notify the highest court whenever the insurance policy covering the lawyer's conduct lapses or is terminated. This ensures that the information reported to the highest court is accurate during the entire reporting period. Lawyers who do not comply with the Model Court Rule are not authorized to practice law until they comply.

The purpose of the Model Court Rule is to provide a potential client with access to relevant information related to a lawyer's representation in order to make an informed decision about whether to hire a particular lawyer. The Model Court Rule is a balanced standard that allows potential clients to obtain relevant information about a lawyer if they initiate an inquiry, while placing a modest annual reporting requirement on lawyers. The information submitted by lawyers will be made available by such means as designated by the highest court in the jurisdiction.

Rule ___. Insurance Disclosure

A. Each lawyer admitted to the active practice of law shall certify to the [highest court of the jurisdiction] on or before [December 31 of each year]: 1) whether the lawyer is engaged in the private practice of law; 2) if engaged in the private practice of law, whether the lawyer is currently covered by professional liability insurance; 3) whether the lawyer intends to maintain insurance during the period of time the lawyer is engaged in the private practice of law; and 4) whether the lawyer is exempt from the provisions of this Rule because the lawyer is engaged in the practice of law as a full-time government lawyer or is counsel employed by an organizational client and does not represent clients outside that capacity. Each lawyer admitted to the active practice of law in this jurisdiction who reports being covered by professional liability insurance shall notify [the highest court in the jurisdiction] in writing within 30 days if the insurance policy providing coverage lapses, is no longer in effect or terminates for any reason.

B. The foregoing shall be certified by each lawyer admitted to the active practice of law in this jurisdiction in such form as may be prescribed by the [highest court of the jurisdiction]. The information submitted pursuant to this Rule will be made available to the public by such means as may be designated by the [highest court of the jurisdiction].

C. Any lawyer admitted to the active practice of law who fails to comply with this Rule in a timely fashion, as defined by the [highest court in the jurisdiction], may be suspended from the practice of law until such time as the lawyer complies. Supplying false information in response to this Rule shall subject the lawyer to appropriate disciplinary action.

ABA Model
Rules for Client
Protection
(Selected)

ABA Model
Rules for Client
Protection
(Selected)

ABA Professionalism
Codes and Creeds

ABA
Professionalism
Codes and
Creeds

American Bar Association
Young Lawyers Division
(Annual Meeting 1988)

The Division's second recommendation was amended by the proponents and approved by voice vote. As approved, it reads:

BE IT RESOLVED, That the American Bar Association authorizes the dissemination to the profession of the following "Lawyers' Pledge of Professionalism."

LAWYERS' PLEDGE OF PROFESSIONALISM

1. I will remember that the practice of law is first and foremost a profession, and I will subordinate business concerns to professionalism concerns.
2. I will encourage respect for the law and our legal system through my words and actions.
3. I will remember my responsibilities to serve as an officer of the court and protector of individual rights.
4. I will contribute time and resources to public service, public education, charitable, and pro bono activities in my community.
5. I will work with the other participants in the legal system, including judges, opposing counsel and those whose practices are different from mine, to make our legal system more accessible and responsive.
6. I will resolve matters expeditiously and without unnecessary expense.
7. I will resolve disputes through negotiation whenever possible.
8. I will keep my clients well-informed and involved in making the decisions that affect them.
9. I will continue to expand my knowledge of the law.
10. I will achieve and maintain proficiency in my practice.
11. I will be courteous to those with whom I come into contact during the course of my work.
12. I will honor the spirit and intent, as well as the requirements, of the applicable rules or code of professional conduct for my jurisdiction, and I will encourage others to do the same.

American Bar Association
Section of Tort, Trial and Insurance Practice
(Annual Meeting 1988)

The Section's second recommendation was amended by the proponents and approved by voice vote. As approved, it reads:

BE IT RESOLVED, That the American Bar Association recommend to state and local bar associations that they encourage their members to accept as a guide for the individual conduct, and to comply with, a lawyer's creed of professionalism.

BE IT FURTHER RESOLVED, That nothing contained in such a creed shall be deemed to supersede or in any way amend the Model Rules of Professional Conduct or other disciplinary codes, alter existing standards of conduct against which lawyer negligence might be judged or become a basis for the imposition of civil liability of any kind.

LAWYER'S CREED OF PROFESSIONALISM

Preamble

As a lawyer I must strive to make our system of justice work fairly and efficiently. In order to carry out that responsibility, not only will I comply with the letter and spirit of the disciplinary standards applicable to all lawyers, but I will also conduct myself in accordance with the following Creed of Professionalism when dealing with my client, opposing parties, their counsel, the courts and the general public.

A. With respect to my client:
1. I will be loyal and committed to my client's cause, but I will not permit that loyalty and commitment to interfere with my ability to provide my client with objective and independent advice;
2. I will endeavor to achieve my client's lawful objectives in business transactions and in litigation as expeditiously and economically as possible;
3. In appropriate cases, I will counsel my client with respect to mediation, arbitration and other alternative methods of resolving disputes;
4. I will advise my client against pursuing litigation (or any other course of action) that is without merit and against insisting on tactics which are intended to delay resolution of the matter or to harass or drain the financial resources of the opposing party;

5. I will advise my client that civility and courtesy are not to be equated with weakness;

6. While I must abide by my client's decision concerning the objectives of the representation, I nevertheless will counsel my client that a willingness to initiate or engage in settlement discussions is consistent with zealous and effective representation.

B. With respect to opposing parties and their counsel:

1. I will endeavor to be courteous and civil, both in oral and in written communications;

2. I will not knowingly make statements of fact or of law that are untrue;

3. In litigation proceedings I will agree to reasonable requests for extensions of time or for waiver of procedural formalities when the legitimate interests of my client will not be adversely affected;

4. I will endeavor to consult with opposing counsel before scheduling depositions and meetings and before re-scheduling hearings, and I will cooperate with opposing counsel when scheduling changes are requested;

5. I will refrain from utilizing litigation or any other course of conduct to harass the opposing party;

6. I will refrain from engaging in excessive and abusive discovery, and I will comply with all reasonable discovery requests;

7. I will refrain from utilizing delaying tactics;

8. In depositions and other proceedings, and in negotiations, I will conduct myself with dignity, avoid making groundless objections and refrain from engaging in acts of rudeness or disrespect;

9. I will not serve motions and pleadings on the other party, or his counsel, at such a time or in such a manner as will unfairly limit the other party's opportunity to respond;

10. In business transactions I will not quarrel over matters of form or style, but will concentrate on matters of substance and content;

11. I will clearly identify, for other counsel or parties, all changes that I have made in documents submitted to me for review.

C. With respect to the courts and other tribunals:

1. I will be a vigorous and zealous advocate on behalf of my client, while recognizing, as an officer of the court, that excessive zeal may be detrimental to my client's interests as well as to the proper function of our system of justice;

2. Where consistent with my client's interests, I will communicate with opposing counsel in an effort to avoid litigation and to resolve litigation that has actually commenced;

ABA Professionalism Codes and Creeds

3. I will voluntarily withdraw claims or defenses when it becomes apparent that they do not have merit or are superfluous;

4. I will refrain from filing frivolous motions;

5. I will make every effort to agree with other counsel, as early as possible on a voluntary exchange of information and on a plan for discovery;

6. I will attempt to resolve, by agreement, my objections to matters contained in my opponent's pleadings and discovery requests;

7. When scheduling hearings or depositions have to be canceled, I will notify opposing counsel, and, if appropriate, the court (or other tribunal) as early as possible;

8. Before dates for hearings or trials are set—or if that is not feasible, immediately after such dates have been set—I will attempt to verify the availability of key participants and witnesses so that I can promptly notify the court (or other tribunal) and opposing counsel of any likely problem in that regard;

9. In civil matters, I will stipulate to facts as to which there is no genuine dispute;

10. I will endeavor to be punctual in attending court hearings, conferences and depositions;

11. I will at all times be candid with the court.

D. With respect to the public and to our system of justice:

1. I will remember that, in addition to commitment to my client's cause, my responsibilities as a lawyer include a devotion to the public good;

2. I will endeavor to keep myself current in the areas in which I practice and, when necessary, will associate with, or refer my client to, counsel knowledgeable in anther field of practice;

3. I will be mindful of the fact that, as a member of a self-regulating profession, it is incumbent on me to report violations by fellow lawyers of any disciplinary rule;

4. I will be mindful of the need to protect the image of the legal profession in the eyes of the public and will be so guided when considering methods and content of advertising;

5. I will be mindful that the law is a learned profession and that among its desirable goals are devotion to public service, improvement of administration of justice, and the contribution of uncompensated time and civic influence on behalf of those persons who cannot afford adequate legal assistance.

ABA
Professionalism
Codes and
Creeds

American Bar Association
Standing Committee on Professionalism
(Annual Meeting 1995)

RECOMMENDATION

RESOLVED, That the American Bar Association encourages federal, state, territorial and local bar associations and courts to adopt standards of civility, courtesy and conduct as aspirational goals to promote professionalism of lawyers and judges.

REPORT

In 1988 the following recommendation of the American Bar Association Section of Tort and Insurance Practice was approved by the House of Delegates:

BE IT RESOLVED, That the American Bar Association recommend to state and local bar associations that they encourage their members to accept as a guide for their individual conduct, and to comply with, a Lawyer's Creed of Professionalism.

BE IT FURTHER RESOLVED, That nothing in such a creed shall be deemed to supersede or in any way amend the Model Rules of Professional Conduct or other disciplinary codes, alter existing standards of conduct against which lawyer negligence might be judged or become a basis for the imposition of civil liability of any kind.

The purpose of this recommendation is to build upon the good work that has been generated by that recommendation (with its accompanying example of a Lawyer's Creed of Professionalism), and the contemporaneous authorization by the House of Delegates of the dissemination of the Lawyers' Pledge of Professionalism proposed by the American Bar Association Young Lawyers Division, by particularly encouraging the courts and those bar associations that have not heretofore provided aspirational standards of civility, courtesy and conduct to their members as a guide, to adopt such standards.

The files of the American Bar Association Center for Professional Responsibility presently show that 88 state and local bar associations and organizations in 38 states, as well as one American Bar Association Section, one American Bar Association division and one Federal Judicial Circuit, have adopted standards of professional conduct in some form.

These standards address and respond to concerns over deteriorating

ABA Professionalism Codes and Creeds

professionalism, a fear that in pursuing the interests of clients or their own self interests, lawyers' regard for the dignity of the justice system and the trust among counsel and the courts engendered to principles of integrity, courtesy and mutual respect may lessen.

The common principles of such standards are:

- A lawyer's duty to represent each client zealously within the bounds of the law is a duty to be honored consistent with the lawyer's responsibility to a justice system;
- In addition to the duties of candor, honesty and diligence that a lawyer owes to the judiciary under rules of professional conduct, a lawyer owes to the judiciary a duty of respect;
- A judge owes to the practicing bar a duty of attentiveness, courtesy, respect and a dedication to the proper administration of the courts;
- A lawyer owes opposing counsel, parties and the courts a duty of courtesy, fairness and cooperation;
- A lawyer owes to the profession adherence to a higher level of conduct than observance of rules of professional conduct.

No documentation of the degree to which regard for the legal profession both among the public and among lawyers and judges has fallen is available, but the observation is virtually uniform. To the extent that lawyers and judges are responsible for the problem, they can take action to correct it.

Adoption of aspirational standards to improve professional conduct of each of us is one measure that the profession can take to address a troublesome issue. The promotion of such standards of conduct demonstrates this Association's concern and its desire to advance the ideals of professionalism.

The recommendation does not attempt to provide a model code of professionalism, of which many splendid examples exist. Rather, the recommendation encourages practicing lawyers and the judiciary to identify standards that go beyond the mere upholding of law and ethics rules and codes that sanction misconduct. The development of codes at the local and state bar levels, judicial circuits and among specialty bars is a healthy and powerful demonstration of a commitment to professionalism.

ABA
Professionalism
Codes and
Creeds

ABA Practice Guidelines

ABA
Practice
Guidelines

ABA Guidelines for Litigation Conduct

ABA
Practice
Guidelines

Introduction

The widely-perceived, accelerating decline in professionalism—often denominated "civility"—has been the subject of increasing concern to the profession for many years. Twice since 1988, the American Bar Association has urged adoption of, and adherence to, civility codes. What has been lacking, however, is an ABA-endorsed model code. The Guidelines for Litigation Conduct fill that void.

These Guidelines are consensus-driven and state nothing novel or revolutionary. They are purely aspirational and are not to be used as a basis for litigation, liability, discipline, sanctions or penalties of any type. The Guidelines are designed not to promote punishment but rather to elevate the tenor of practice—to set a voluntary, higher standard, "in the hope that," in the words of former ABA President John J. Curtin, "some progress might be made towards greater professional satisfaction."

The Guidelines for Litigation Conduct are modeled on the Standards for Professional Conduct adopted by the United States Court of Appeals for the Seventh Circuit, a set of proven aspirational standards. Chief United States District Judge Marvin E. Aspen of Chicago, architect of the Seventh Circuit Standards, has accurately observed that civility in the legal profession is inextricably linked to the manner in which lawyers are perceived by the public—and, therefore, to the deteriorating public confidence that our system of justice enjoys.

Deteriorating civility, in former ABA President Lee Cooper's words, "interrupts the administration of justice. It makes the practice of law less rewarding. It robs a lawyer of the sense of dignity and self-worth that should come from a learned profession. Not least of all, it . . . brings with it all the problems . . . that accompany low public regard for lawyers and lack of confidence in the justice system."

The problem of incivility is more pervasive, and insidious, than its impact on the legal profession alone. As Justice Anthony M. Kennedy has stressed:

> Civility is the mark of an accomplished and superb professional, but it is more even than this. It is an end in itself. Civility has deep roots in the idea of respect for the individual.

The decline in civility is not limited to the legal profession, but this profession has been in the forefront of those addressing this problem. These Guidelines are offered in this spirit.

Gregory P. Joseph
Chair, 1997-1998
Section of Litigation
American Bar Association

American Bar Association
GUIDELINES FOR LITIGATION CONDUCT
August 1998

Preamble

A lawyer's conduct should be characterized at all times by personal courtesy and professional integrity in the fullest sense of those terms. In fulfilling our duty to represent a client vigorously as lawyers, we will be mindful of our obligations to the administration of justice, which is a truth-seeking process designed to resolve human and societal problems in a rational, peaceful, and efficient manner.

A judge's conduct should be characterized at all times by courtesy and patience toward all participants. As judges we owe to all participants in a legal proceeding respect, diligence, punctuality, and protection against unjust and improper criticism or attack.

Conduct that may be characterized as uncivil, abrasive, abusive, hostile, or obstructive impedes the fundamental goal of resolving disputes rationally, peacefully, and efficiently. Such conduct tends to delay and often to deny justice.

The following Guidelines are designed to encourage us, judges and lawyers, to meet our obligations to each other, to litigants and to the system of justice, and thereby achieve the twin goals of civility and professionalism, both of which, are hallmarks of a learned profession dedicated to public service.

We encourage judges, lawyers and clients to make a mutual and firm commitment to these Guidelines.

We support the principles espoused in the following Guidelines, but under no circumstances should these Guidelines be used as a basis for litigation or for sanctions or penalties.

Lawyers' Duties to Other Counsel

1. We will practice our profession with a continuing awareness that our role is to zealously advance the legitimate interests of our clients. In our dealings with others we will not reflect the ill feelings of our clients. We will treat all other counsel, parties, and witnesses in a civil and courteous manner, not only in court, but also in all other written and oral communications. We will refrain from acting upon or manifesting bias or prejudice based upon race, sex, religion, national origin, disability, age, sexual orientation or socioeconomic status toward any participant in the legal process.

ABA
Practice
Guidelines

2. We will not, even when called upon by a client to do so, abuse or indulge in offensive conduct directed to other counsel, parties, or witnesses. We will abstain from disparaging personal remarks or acrimony toward other counsel, parties, or witnesses. We will treat adverse witnesses and parties with fair consideration.

3. We will not encourage or knowingly authorize any person under our control to engage in conduct that would be improper if we were to engage in such conduct.

4. We will not, absent good cause, attribute bad motives or improper conduct to other counsel.

5. We will not lightly seek court sanctions.

6. We will in good faith adhere to all express promises and to agreements with other counsel, whether oral or in writing, and to all agreements implied by the circumstances or local customs.

7. When we reach an oral understanding on a proposed agreement or a stipulation and decide to commit it to writing, the drafter will endeavor in good faith to state the oral understanding accurately and completely. The drafter will provide other counsel the opportunity to review the writing. As drafts are exchanged between or among counsel, changes from prior drafts will be identified in the draft or otherwise explicitly brought to other counsel's attention. We will not include in a draft matters to which there has been no agreement without explicitly advising other counsel in writing of the addition.

8. We will endeavor to confer early with other counsel to assess settlement possibilities. We will not falsely hold out the possibility of settlement to obtain unfair advantage.

9. In civil actions, we will stipulate to relevant matters if they are undisputed and if no good faith advocacy basis exists for not stipulating.

10. We will not use any form of discovery or discovery scheduling as a means of harassment.

11. Whenever circumstances allow, we will make good faith efforts to resolve by agreement objections before presenting them to the court.

12. We will not time the filing or service of motions or pleadings in any way that unfairly limits another party's opportunity to respond.

13. We will not request an extension of time solely for the purpose of unjustified delay or to obtain unfair advantage.

14. We will consult other counsel regarding scheduling matters in a good faith effort to avoid scheduling conflicts.

15. We will endeavor to accommodate previously scheduled dates for hearings, depositions, meetings, conferences, vacations, seminars, or other functions that produce good faith calendar conflicts on the part of other counsel.

16. We will promptly notify other counsel and, if appropriate, the court or other persons, when hearings, depositions, meetings, or conferences are to be canceled or postponed.

17. We will agree to reasonable requests for extensions of time and for waiver of procedural formalities, provided our clients' legitimate rights will not be materially or adversely affected.

18. We will not cause any default or dismissal to be entered without first notifying opposing counsel, when we know his or her identity, unless the rules provide otherwise.

19. We will take depositions only when actually needed. We will not take depositions for the purposes of harassment or other improper purpose.

20. We will not engage in any conduct during a deposition that would not be appropriate in the presence of a judge.

21. We will not obstruct questioning during a deposition or object to deposition questions unless permitted under applicable law.

22. During depositions we will ask only those questions we reasonably believe are necessary, and appropriate, for the prosecution or defense of an action.

23. We will carefully craft document production requests so they are limited to those documents we reasonably believe are necessary, and appropriate, for the prosecution or defense of an action. We will not design production requests to place an undue burden or expense on a party, or for any other improper purpose.

24. We will respond to document requests reasonably and not strain to interpret requests in an artificially restrictive manner to avoid disclosure of relevant and nonprivileged documents. We will not produce documents in a manner designed to hide or obscure the existence of particular documents, or to accomplish any other improper purpose.

25. We will carefully craft interrogatories so they are limited to those matters we reasonably believe are necessary, and appropriate, for the prosecution or defense of an action, and we will not design them to place an undue burden or expense on a party, or for any other improper purpose.

26. We will respond to interrogatories reasonably and will not strain to interpret them in an artificially restrictive manner to avoid disclosure of relevant and non-privileged information, or for any other improper purpose.

27. We will base our discovery objections on a good faith belief in their merit and will not object solely for the purpose of withholding or delaying the disclosure of relevant information, or for any other improper purpose.

28. When a draft order is to be prepared by counsel to reflect a court ruling, we will draft an order that accurately and completely reflects the court's

ABA
Practice
Guidelines

ruling. We will promptly prepare and submit a proposed order to other counsel and attempt to reconcile any differences before the draft order is presented to the court.

29. We will not ascribe a position to another counsel that counsel has not taken.

30. Unless permitted or invited by the court, we will not send copies of correspondence between counsel to the court.

31. Nothing contained in these Guidelines is intended or shall be construed to inhibit vigorous advocacy, including vigorous cross-examination.

Lawyers' Duties to the Court

1. We will speak and write civilly and respectfully in all communications with the court.

2. We will be punctual and prepared for all court appearances so that all hearings, conferences, and trials may commence on time; if delayed, we will notify the court and counsel, if possible.

3. We will be considerate of the time constraints and pressures on the court and court staff inherent in their efforts to administer justice.

4. We will not engage in any conduct that brings disorder or disruption to the courtroom. We will advise our clients and witnesses appearing in court of the proper conduct expected and required there and, to the best of our ability, prevent our clients and witnesses from creating disorder or disruption.

5. We will not knowingly misrepresent, mischaracterize, misquote, or miscite facts or authorities in any oral or written communication to the court.

6. We will not write letters to the court in connection with a pending action, unless invited or permitted by the court.

7. Before dates for hearings or trials are set, or if that is not feasible, immediately after such date has been set, we will attempt to verify the availability of necessary participants and witnesses so we can promptly notify the court of any likely problems.

8. We will act and speak civilly* to court marshals, clerks, court reporters, secretaries, and law clerks with an awareness that they, too, are an integral part of the judicial system.

Courts' Duties to Lawyers

1. We will be courteous, respectful, and civil to lawyers, parties, and witnesses. We will maintain control of the proceedings, recognizing that judges have both the obligation and the authority to insure that all litigation proceedings are conducted in a civil manner.

2. We will not employ hostile, demeaning, or humiliating words in opinions or in written or oral communications with lawyers, parties, or witnesses.

3. We will be punctual in convening all hearings, meetings, and conferences; if delayed, we will notify counsel, if possible.

4. In scheduling all hearings, meetings and conferences we will be considerate of time schedules of lawyers, parties, and witnesses.

5. We will make all reasonable efforts to decide promptly all matters presented to us for decision.

6. We will give the issues in controversy deliberate, impartial, and studied analysis and consideration.

7. While endeavoring to resolve disputes efficiently, we will be considerate of the time constraints and pressures imposed on lawyers by the exigencies of litigation practice.

8. We recognize that a lawyer has a right and a duty to present a cause fully and properly, and that a litigant has a right to a fair and impartial hearing. Within the practical limits of time, we will allow lawyers to present proper arguments and to make a complete and accurate record.

9. We will not impugn the integrity or professionalism of any lawyer on the basis of the clients whom or the causes which a lawyer represents.

10. We will do our best to insure that court personnel act civilly toward lawyers, parties, and witnesses.

11. We will not adopt procedures that needlessly increase litigation expense.

12. We will bring to lawyers' attention uncivil conduct which we observe.

Judges' Duties to Each Other

1. We will be courteous, respectful, and civil in opinions, ever mindful that a position articulated by another judge is the result of that judge's earnest effort to interpret the law and the facts correctly.

2. In all written and oral communications, we will abstain from disparaging personal remarks or criticisms, or sarcastic or demeaning comments about another judge.

3. We will endeavor to work with other judges in an effort to foster a spirit of cooperation in our mutual goal of enhancing the administration of justice.

ABA
Practice
Guidelines

ABA
Practice
Guidelines

ABA Best Practice Guidelines for Legal Information Web Site Providers

ABA Best Practice Guidelines
for Legal Information
Web Site Providers

An increasing number of sites on the web provide legal information. Government departments, non-profit community organizations, private companies, educational institutions, individuals, and law firms publish sites. Users of these sites have varying levels of knowledge of the law and the Internet. Therefore, it is essential that legal web sites providers give users sufficient information to make assessments about the accuracy and the quality of the legal information that is published.

The goal of these guidelines is to promote the development of quality legal web sites and to provide guidance to legal web site developers. The purpose of the guidelines is to establish "best practices" for both lawyers and other web site providers who offer legal information, documents and other services to the public, but the guidelines do not address the additional requirements that would be applicable to individual lawyers and law firm sites that provide legal advice. Individual lawyers and law firms should also consider whether the rules of professional responsibility apply to any aspect of their operation of a legal information website. When providers adopt and follow the guidelines, users will be less likely to be misled.

However, it is important to understand that compliance with these guidelines does not constitute approval or certification by the American Bar Association of the content and operation of the web site and no one is authorized to represent that it does. Instead, the guidelines encourage publishers of legal web sites to provide information about the legal content of their sites that assists a user in making a judgment on the quality of the legal information that appears on the site.

1. *Contact Information*—A web site providing legal information should provide full and accurate information on the identity and contact details of the provider of the site. The person(s) or organization(s) responsible for the information on a site is (are) clearly indicated on all pages of the site. Providers should include full contact details, including name, mailing address, telephone, and/or e-mail address. A government agency or court with limited resources to reply may choose to omit a telephone contact or e-mail address, but as a minimum should list a mailing address.

Comment:

Given that anyone may publish on the web, the ability to identify providers helps users make judgments about the authority of the legal information and advice they encounter within a site. Authority can be implied when the information comes from a recognized organization, such as government department or community legal center. When the information comes from an individual or less well known organization, stating the credentials of contributing authors will assist users in judging authority. This can be achieved simply by including qualifications or position held with an author's name. Sometimes search engines take users directly to pages within a site. Providing authorship details on every page ensures users can ascertain the organization or person responsible for the information.

2. *Dating Material*—Web site providers should include information about the dates on which the substantive content on their sites was prepared or last reviewed.

Comment:

Laws and information about legal matters change frequently and at any given time. Users of web sites that provide legal information should be able to determine the age of the substantive content and should not be misled into believing out-dated material is current. A provider should avoid the use of an automated dating mechanism if it may lead to confusion about the date on which the content was posted or changed.

3. *Jurisdiction*—Web site providers should avoid misleading users about the jurisdiction to which the site's content relates. If the legal content is clearly state-specific, the jurisdiction in which the law applies should be identified within the content of the information or otherwise.

Comment:

Lay people often have little or no understanding of the legal concept of jurisdiction. They may be unaware that laws can vary from state to state or in some cases from country to country. If a web site displays generic legal content, the provider should make it clear this legal content may not apply in the user's jurisdiction. The same guideline applies when a legal web site offers form documents. Providers should consider providing information about jurisdiction within the site's terms and conditions section if that helps avoid confusion or misrepresentations.

ABA
Practice
Guidelines

4. *Limits of Legal Information*—When a site provides only legal information, the provider should give users conspicuous notice that legal information does not constitute legal advice.

Comment:

Sites providing only legal information should include a notice on the site that explains the differences between legal information and legal advice and warns the user that the site does not constitute legal advice and is not a substitute for the professional judgment of an attorney. Legal information by itself is often insufficient to resolve legal problems. Users often need specific legal advice that applies to their facts and only lawyers who are members of the bar in the user's jurisdiction can provide legal advice.

Some web sites advertise that the user can contact a lawyer through the site without making it clear to the user that the lawyer is providing general legal information only and not specific legal advice. Lay persons are often unaware that only a lawyer who is a member of a state bar can provide legal advice and the lawyer is only qualified to provide specific legal advice about the law in the state in which he or she is admitted to practice. Therefore, users may believe that an exchange with a lawyer is the equivalent of receiving specific legal advice when it is not.

Similarly, when a web site offers document preparation services, the provider should clarify whether the site is offering legal services and under what specific conditions, or whether the document preparation service is provided by a lay person and therefore without the protection of the attorney/client relationship. In some jurisdictions, document preparation by a lay person may constitute the unauthorized practice of law.

5. *Links*—Sites should link to other resources that are likely to assist users with their problems.

Comment:

The web is an open medium and its power is based on the capacity of the user to move from one web site to another easily. Users should be encouraged to move from one legal web site to another when the other web site may have additional current, relevant, and in-depth information.

Accordingly, sites should contain links to other sites and sources that contain information related to the user's problems and concerns. An annotation that briefly indicates the authorship, content or relevance of these sites enhances the usefulness of these links and limits the possibility that the user will believe that the linked site is also sponsored by the web site provider.

Framing (as opposed to linking to) the content provided by another web site can create problems. When a site is "framed," the URL of the external

ABA Practice Guidelines

site does not appear in the location box, which may cause users to wrongly assume that the information within the frame belongs to the original site. It also makes it difficult for users to determine the true source of the information they are viewing. Moreover, the act of copying the content of the framed site and republishing it on the provider's own site may result in a copyright violation.

6. *Legal Citations*—When appropriate, sites should contain links to relevant case law and legislation.

Comment:

Frequently people use legal information web sites to research solutions to their legal matters. Ready access to legal authority facilitates this research and helps validate the accuracy of the legal content displayed on the web site. Because of limitations on linking to proprietary sites, however, not every legal service web site will be able to achieve this guideline. Nevertheless, it is worthwhile to have links when the information is readily available.

7. *Referrals*—Where appropriate, sites should provide users with information on how and where to obtain legal advice and further information.

Comment:

One purpose of these guidelines is to remind users that legal information by itself is often insufficient in terms of problems solving. Users often need specific legal advice that applies to their facts and only lawyers who are members of the bar in the user's jurisdiction can provide that advice. Therefore, providers of sites are encouraged to link to other sites, such as http://www.findlegalhelp.org, that may provide the resources to help resolve the user's issues.

8. *Permissions*—Providers should obtain permission to use content from other providers.

Comment:

Web site providers should have all appropriate permissions to use content sourced from other providers since the unauthorized republication of such content may infringe upon the proprietor's copyright. In addition, the source of the content should be acknowledged.

Unless the content is acknowledged users may have a difficult time assessing the integrity of the content based on authorship. Users may also erroneously believe that the material was authored by the site provider.

ABA
Practice
Guidelines

9. *Terms and Conditions*—Sites should clearly and conspicuously provide users with information about the provider's terms and conditions of use.

Comment:

"Terms and Conditions" or "Terms of Service" define the terms under which a user is authorized to use the web site and/or to purchase products or services from the web site. Typical provisions include disclaimers of implied warranties, limitations on damages, and dispute resolution provisions.

A link to terms and conditions should be located in a conspicuous manner and should advise the user that the use of the site is subject to the terms and conditions. Even with such measures, however, the case law is not settled that electronically-posted terms and conditions will create a binding contract unless the user clearly manifests assent, such as by clicking "I agree."

10. *Privacy Statement*—Sites should clearly and conspicuously provide users with their privacy policies and policies on security of communications

Comment:

The site should have clearly worded privacy policies that address the provider's use of personal information of users and visitors, including the sale or transfer of information to third parties.

When users communicate with web sites, the user should be notified whether that communication is secured.

Approved on February 10, 2003 by the ABA House of Delegates.

ABA
Practice
Guidelines

Federal Rules
and Standards
(Selected)

Federal Rules
and Standards
(Selected)

Code of Federal Regulations

Title 17—Commodity and Securities Exchanges

CHAPTER II—SECURITIES AND EXCHANGE COMMISSION

PART 205 – STANDARDS OF PROFESSIONAL CONDUCT FOR ATTORNEYS APPEARING AND PRACTICING BEFORE THE COMMISSION IN THE REPRESENTATION OF AN ISSUER

Authority: 15 U.S.C. 77s, 78d-3, 78w, 80a-37, 80a-38, 80b-11, 7202, 7245, and 7262.

§ 205.1 Purpose and scope.

This part sets forth minimum standards of professional conduct for attorneys appearing and practicing before the Commission in the representation of an issuer. These standards supplement applicable standards of any jurisdiction where an attorney is admitted or practices and are not intended to limit the ability of any jurisdiction to impose additional obligations on an attorney not inconsistent with the application of this part. Where the standards of a state or other United States jurisdiction where an attorney is admitted or practices conflict with this part, this part shall govern.

§ 205.2 Definitions.

For purposes of this part, the following definitions apply:

(a) Appearing and practicing before the Commission:

(1) Means:

(i) Transacting any business with the Commission, including communications in any form;

(ii) Representing an issuer in a Commission administrative proceeding or in connection with any Commission investigation, inquiry, information request, or subpoena;

Federal Rules
and Standards
(Selected)

(iii) Providing advice in respect of the United States securities laws or the Commission's rules or regulations thereunder regarding any document that the attorney has notice will be filed with or submitted to, or incorporated into any document that will be filed with or submitted to, the Commission, including the provision of such advice in the context of preparing, or participating in the preparation of, any such document; or

(iv) Advising an issuer as to whether information or a statement, opinion, or other writing is required under the United States securities laws or the Commission's rules or regulations thereunder to be filed with or submitted to, or incorporated into any document that will be filed with or submitted to, the Commission; but

(2) Does not include an attorney who:

(i) Conducts the activities in paragraphs (a)(1)(i) through (a)(1)(iv) of this section other than in the context of providing legal services to an issuer with whom the attorney has an attorney-client relationship; or

(ii) Is a non-appearing foreign attorney.

(b) Appropriate response means a response to an attorney regarding reported evidence of a material violation as a result of which the attorney reasonably believes:

(1) That no material violation, as defined in paragraph (i) of this section, has occurred, is ongoing, or is about to occur;

(2) That the issuer has, as necessary, adopted appropriate remedial measures, including appropriate steps or sanctions to stop any material violations that are ongoing, to prevent any material violation that has yet to occur, and to remedy or otherwise appropriately address any material violation that has already occurred and to minimize the likelihood of its recurrence; or

(3) That the issuer, with the consent of the issuer's board of directors, a committee thereof to whom a report could be made pursuant to §205.3(b)(3), or a qualified legal compliance committee, has retained or directed an attorney to review the reported evidence of a material violation and either:

(i) Has substantially implemented any remedial recommendations made by such attorney after a reasonable investigation and evaluation of the reported evidence; or

(ii) Has been advised that such attorney may, consistent with his or her professional obligations, assert a colorable defense on behalf of the issuer (or the issuer's officer, director, employee, or agent, as the case may be) in any investigation or judicial or administrative proceeding relating to the reported evidence of a material violation.

(c) Attorney means any person who is admitted, licensed, or otherwise qualified to practice law in any jurisdiction, domestic or foreign, or who holds himself or herself out as admitted, licensed, or otherwise qualified to practice law.

(d) Breach of fiduciary duty refers to any breach of fiduciary or similar duty to the issuer recognized under an applicable federal or state statute or at common law, including but not limited to misfeasance, nonfeasance, abdication of duty, abuse of trust, and approval of unlawful transactions.

(e) Evidence of a material violation means credible evidence, based upon which it would be unreasonable, under the circumstances, for a prudent and competent attorney not to conclude that it is reasonably likely that a material violation has occurred, is ongoing, or is about to occur.

(f) Foreign government issuer means a foreign issuer as defined in 17 CFR 230.405 eligible to register securities on Schedule B of the Securities Act of 1933 (15 U.S.C. 77a et seq., Schedule B).

(g) In the representation of an issuer means providing legal services as an attorney for an issuer, regardless of whether the attorney is employed or retained by the issuer.

(h) Issuer means an issuer (as defined in section 3 of the Securities Exchange Act of 1934 (15 U.S.C. 78c)), the securities of which are registered under section 12 of that Act (15 U.S.C. 78l), or that is required to file reports under section 15(d) of that Act (15 U.S.C. 78o(d)), or that files or has filed a registration statement that has not yet become effective under the Securities Act of 1933 (15 U.S.C. 77a et seq.), and that it has not withdrawn, but does not include a foreign government issuer. For purposes of paragraphs (a) and (g) of this section, the term "issuer" includes any person controlled by an issuer, where an attorney provides legal services to such person on behalf of, or at the behest, or for the benefit of the issuer, regardless of whether the attorney is employed or retained by the issuer.

(i) Material violation means a material violation of an applicable United States federal or state securities law, a material breach of fiduciary duty arising under United States federal or state law, or a similar material violation of any United States federal or state law.

(j) Non-appearing foreign attorney means an attorney:

(1) Who is admitted to practice law in a jurisdiction outside the United States;

(2) Who does not hold himself or herself out as practicing, and does not give legal advice regarding, United States federal or state securities or other laws (except as provided in paragraph (j)(3)(ii) of this section); and

(3) Who:

(i) Conducts activities that would constitute appearing and prac-

Federal Rules and Standards (Selected)

ticing before the Commission only incidentally to, and in the ordinary course of, the practice of law in a jurisdiction outside the United States; or

(ii) Is appearing and practicing before the Commission only in consultation with counsel, other than a non-appearing foreign attorney, admitted or licensed to practice in a state or other United States jurisdiction.

(k) Qualified legal compliance committee means a committee of an issuer (which also may be an audit or other committee of the issuer) that:

(1) Consists of at least one member of the issuer's audit committee (or, if the issuer has no audit committee, one member from an equivalent committee of independent directors) and two or more members of the issuer's board of directors who are not employed, directly or indirectly, by the issuer and who are not, in the case of a registered investment company, "interested persons" as defined in section 2(a)(19) of the Investment Company Act of 1940 (15 U.S.C. 80a-2(a)(19));

(2) Has adopted written procedures for the confidential receipt, retention, and consideration of any report of evidence of a material violation under §205.3;

(3) Has been duly established by the issuer's board of directors, with the authority and responsibility:

(i) To inform the issuer's chief legal officer and chief executive officer (or the equivalents thereof) of any report of evidence of a material violation (except in the circumstances described in §205.3(b)(4));

(ii) To determine whether an investigation is necessary regarding any report of evidence of a material violation by the issuer, its officers, directors, employees or agents and, if it determines an investigation is necessary or appropriate, to:

(A) Notify the audit committee or the full board of directors;

(B) Initiate an investigation, which may be conducted either by the chief legal officer (or the equivalent thereof) or by outside attorneys; and

(C) Retain such additional expert personnel as the committee deems necessary; and

(iii) At the conclusion of any such investigation, to:

(A) Recommend, by majority vote, that the issuer implement an appropriate response to evidence of a material violation; and

(B) Inform the chief legal officer and the chief executive officer (or the equivalents thereof) and the board of directors of the results of any such investigation under this section and the appropriate remedial measures to be adopted; and

(4) Has the authority and responsibility, acting by majority vote, to

Federal Rules and Standards (Selected)

take all other appropriate action, including the authority to notify the Commission in the event that the issuer fails in any material respect to implement an appropriate response that the qualified legal compliance committee has recommended the issuer to take.

(l) Reasonable or reasonably denotes, with respect to the actions of an attorney, conduct that would not be unreasonable for a prudent and competent attorney.

(m) Reasonably believes means that an attorney believes the matter in question and that the circumstances are such that the belief is not unreasonable.

(n) Report means to make known to directly, either in person, by telephone, by e-mail, electronically, or in writing.

§ 205.3 Issuer as client.

(a) Representing an issuer. An attorney appearing and practicing before the Commission in the representation of an issuer owes his or her professional and ethical duties to the issuer as an organization. That the attorney may work with and advise the issuer's officers, directors, or employees in the course of representing the issuer does not make such individuals the attorney's clients.

(b) Duty to report evidence of a material violation.

(1) If an attorney, appearing and practicing before the Commission in the representation of an issuer, becomes aware of evidence of a material violation by the issuer or by any officer, director, employee, or agent of the issuer, the attorney shall report such evidence to the issuer's chief legal officer (or the equivalent thereof) or to both the issuer's chief legal officer and its chief executive officer (or the equivalents thereof) forthwith. By communicating such information to the issuer's officers or directors, an attorney does not reveal client confidences or secrets or privileged or otherwise protected information related to the attorney's representation of an issuer.

(2) The chief legal officer (or the equivalent thereof) shall cause such inquiry into the evidence of a material violation as he or she reasonably believes is appropriate to determine whether the material violation described in the report has occurred, is ongoing, or is about to occur. If the chief legal officer (or the equivalent thereof) determines no material violation has occurred, is ongoing, or is about to occur, he or she shall notify the reporting attorney and advise the reporting attorney of the basis for such determination. Unless the chief legal officer (or the equivalent thereof) reasonably believes that no material violation has occurred, is ongoing, or is about to occur, he or she shall take all reasonable steps to cause the issuer to adopt an appropriate response, and shall advise

the reporting attorney thereof. In lieu of causing an inquiry under this paragraph (b), a chief legal officer (or the equivalent thereof) may refer a report of evidence of a material violation to a qualified legal compliance committee under paragraph (c)(2) of this section if the issuer has duly established a qualified legal compliance committee prior to the report of evidence of a material violation.

(3) Unless an attorney who has made a report under paragraph (b)(1) of this section reasonably believes that the chief legal officer or the chief executive officer of the issuer (or the equivalent thereof) has provided an appropriate response within a reasonable time, the attorney shall report the evidence of a material violation to:

(i) The audit committee of the issuer's board of directors;

(ii) Another committee of the issuer's board of directors consisting solely of directors who are not employed, directly or indirectly, by the issuer and are not, in the case of a registered investment company, "interested persons" as defined in section 2(a)(19) of the Investment Company Act of 1940 (15 U.S.C. 80a-2(a)(19)) (if the issuer's board of directors has no audit committee); or

(iii) The issuer's board of directors (if the issuer's board of directors has no committee consisting solely of directors who are not employed, directly or indirectly, by the issuer and are not, in the case of a registered investment company, "interested persons" as defined in section 2(a)(19) of the Investment Company Act of 1940 (15 U.S.C. 80a-2(a)(19))).

(4) If an attorney reasonably believes that it would be futile to report evidence of a material violation to the issuer's chief legal officer and chief executive officer (or the equivalents thereof) under paragraph (b)(1) of this section, the attorney may report such evidence as provided under paragraph (b)(3) of this section.

(5) An attorney retained or directed by an issuer to investigate evidence of a material violation reported under paragraph (b)(1), (b)(3), or (b)(4) of this section shall be deemed to be appearing and practicing before the Commission. Directing or retaining an attorney to investigate reported evidence of a material violation does not relieve an officer or director of the issuer to whom such evidence has been reported under paragraph (b)(1), (b)(3), or (b)(4) of this section from a duty to respond to the reporting attorney.

(6) An attorney shall not have any obligation to report evidence of a material violation under this paragraph (b) if:

(i) The attorney was retained or directed by the issuer's chief legal officer (or the equivalent thereof) to investigate such evidence of a material violation and:

(A) The attorney reports the results of such investigation to the chief legal officer (or the equivalent thereof); and

(B) Except where the attorney and the chief legal officer (or the equivalent thereof) each reasonably believes that no material violation has occurred, is ongoing, or is about to occur, the chief legal officer (or the equivalent thereof) reports the results of the investigation to the issuer's board of directors, a committee thereof to whom a report could be made pursuant to paragraph (b)(3) of this section, or a qualified legal compliance committee; or

(ii) The attorney was retained or directed by the chief legal officer (or the equivalent thereof) to assert, consistent with his or her professional obligations, a colorable defense on behalf of the issuer (or the issuer's officer, director, employee, or agent, as the case may be) in any investigation or judicial or administrative proceeding relating to such evidence of a material violation, and the chief legal officer (or the equivalent thereof) provides reasonable and timely reports on the progress and outcome of such proceeding to the issuer's board of directors, a committee thereof to whom a report could be made pursuant to paragraph (b)(3) of this section, or a qualified legal compliance committee.

(7) An attorney shall not have any obligation to report evidence of a material violation under this paragraph (b) if such attorney was retained or directed by a qualified legal compliance committee:

(i) To investigate such evidence of a material violation; or

(ii) To assert, consistent with his or her professional obligations, a colorable defense on behalf of the issuer (or the issuer's officer, director, employee, or agent, as the case may be) in any investigation or judicial or administrative proceeding relating to such evidence of a material violation.

(8) An attorney who receives what he or she reasonably believes is an appropriate and timely response to a report he or she has made pursuant to paragraph (b)(1), (b)(3), or (b)(4) of this section need do nothing more under this section with respect to his or her report.

(9) An attorney who does not reasonably believe that the issuer has made an appropriate response within a reasonable time to the report or reports made pursuant to paragraph (b)(1), (b)(3), or (b)(4) of this section shall explain his or her reasons therefor to the chief legal officer (or the equivalent thereof), the chief executive officer (or the equivalent thereof), and directors to whom the attorney reported the evidence of a material violation pursuant to paragraph (b)(1), (b)(3), or (b)(4) of this section.

(10) An attorney formerly employed or retained by an issuer who has reported evidence of a material violation under this part and reasonably

Federal Rules and Standards (Selected)

believes that he or she has been discharged for so doing may notify the issuer's board of directors or any committee thereof that he or she believes that he or she has been discharged for reporting evidence of a material violation under this section.

(c) Alternative reporting procedures for attorneys retained or employed by an issuer that has established a qualified legal compliance committee.

(1) If an attorney, appearing and practicing before the Commission in the representation of an issuer, becomes aware of evidence of a material violation by the issuer or by any officer, director, employee, or agent of the issuer, the attorney may, as an alternative to the reporting requirements of paragraph (b) of this section, report such evidence to a qualified legal compliance committee, if the issuer has previously formed such a committee. An attorney who reports evidence of a material violation to such a qualified legal compliance committee has satisfied his or her obligation to report such evidence and is not required to assess the issuer's response to the reported evidence of a material violation.

(2) A chief legal officer (or the equivalent thereof) may refer a report of evidence of a material violation to a previously established qualified legal compliance committee in lieu of causing an inquiry to be conducted under paragraph (b)(2) of this section. The chief legal officer (or the equivalent thereof) shall inform the reporting attorney that the report has been referred to a qualified legal compliance committee. Thereafter, pursuant to the requirements under §205.2(k), the qualified legal compliance committee shall be responsible for responding to the evidence of a material violation reported to it under this paragraph (c).

(d) Issuer confidences.

(1) Any report under this section (or the contemporaneous record thereof) or any response thereto (or the contemporaneous record thereof) may be used by an attorney in connection with any investigation, proceeding, or litigation in which the attorney's compliance with this part is in issue.

(2) An attorney appearing and practicing before the Commission in the representation of an issuer may reveal to the Commission, without the issuer's consent, confidential information related to the representation to the extent the attorney reasonably believes necessary:

(i) To prevent the issuer from committing a material violation that is likely to cause substantial injury to the financial interest or property of the issuer or investors;

(ii) To prevent the issuer, in a Commission investigation or administrative proceeding from committing perjury, proscribed in 18 U.S.C. 1621; suborning perjury, proscribed in 18 U.S.C. 1622; or committing any act proscribed in 18 U.S.C. 1001 that is likely to perpetrate a fraud upon the Commission; or

Federal Rules and Standards (Selected)

(iii) To rectify the consequences of a material violation by the issuer that caused, or may cause, substantial injury to the financial interest or property of the issuer or investors in the furtherance of which the attorney's services were used.

§ 205.4 Responsibilities of supervisory attorneys.

(a) An attorney supervising or directing another attorney who is appearing and practicing before the Commission in the representation of an issuer is a supervisory attorney. An issuer's chief legal officer (or the equivalent thereof) is a supervisory attorney under this section.

(b) A supervisory attorney shall make reasonable efforts to ensure that a subordinate attorney, as defined in §205.5(a), that he or she supervises or directs conforms to this part. To the extent a subordinate attorney appears and practices before the Commission in the representation of an issuer, that subordinate attorney's supervisory attorneys also appear and practice before the Commission.

(c) A supervisory attorney is responsible for complying with the reporting requirements in §205.3 when a subordinate attorney has reported to the supervisory attorney evidence of a material violation.

(d) A supervisory attorney who has received a report of evidence of a material violation from a subordinate attorney under §205.3 may report such evidence to the issuer's qualified legal compliance committee if the issuer has duly formed such a committee.

§ 205.5 Responsibilities of a subordinate attorney.

(a) An attorney who appears and practices before the Commission in the representation of an issuer on a matter under the supervision or direction of another attorney (other than under the direct supervision or direction of the issuer's chief legal officer (or the equivalent thereof)) is a subordinate attorney.

(b) A subordinate attorney shall comply with this part notwithstanding that the subordinate attorney acted at the direction of or under the supervision of another person.

(c) A subordinate attorney complies with §205.3 if the subordinate attorney reports to his or her supervising attorney under §205.3(b) evidence of a material violation of which the subordinate attorney has become aware in appearing and practicing before the Commission.

(d) A subordinate attorney may take the steps permitted or required by §205.3(b) or (c) if the subordinate attorney reasonably believes that a supervisory attorney to whom he or she has reported evidence of a material violation under §205.3(b) has failed to comply with §205.3.

§ 205.6 Sanctions and discipline.

(a) A violation of this part by any attorney appearing and practicing before the Commission in the representation of an issuer shall subject such attorney to the civil penalties and remedies for a violation of the federal securities laws available to the Commission in an action brought by the Commission thereunder.

(b) An attorney appearing and practicing before the Commission who violates any provision of this part is subject to the disciplinary authority of the Commission, regardless of whether the attorney may also be subject to discipline for the same conduct in a jurisdiction where the attorney is admitted or practices. An administrative disciplinary proceeding initiated by the Commission for violation of this part may result in an attorney being censured, or being temporarily or permanently denied the privilege of appearing or practicing before the Commission.

(c) An attorney who complies in good faith with the provisions of this part shall not be subject to discipline or otherwise liable under inconsistent standards imposed by any state or other United States jurisdiction where the attorney is admitted or practices.

(d) An attorney practicing outside the United States shall not be required to comply with the requirements of this part to the extent that such compliance is prohibited by applicable foreign law.

§ 205.7 No private right of action.

(a) Nothing in this part is intended to, or does, create a private right of action against any attorney, law firm, or issuer based upon compliance or noncompliance with its provisions.

(b) Authority to enforce compliance with this part is vested exclusively in the Commission.

By the Commission.
Jill M. Peterson
Assistant Secretary
Date: January 29, 2003

Treasury Department
Circular No. 230
(excerpted version)
(Rev. 6-2014)

Regulations Governing Practice
before the Internal Revenue Service

Department of the Treasury
Internal Revenue Service

Title 31 Code of Federal Regulations,
Subtitle A, Part 10, revised as of June 12, 2014

PART 10—PRACTICE BEFORE THE INTERNAL REVENUE SERVICE

Subpart C—Sanctions for Violation of the Regulations

* * * *

Subpart D—Rules Applicable to Disciplinary Proceedings

* * * *

Subpart E—General Provisions

* * * *

§ 10.0 Scope of part.

(a) This part contains rules governing the recognition of attorneys, certified public accountants, enrolled agents, enrolled retirement plan agents, registered tax return preparers, and other persons representing taxpayers before the Internal Revenue Service. Subpart A of this part sets forth rules relating to the authority to practice before the Internal Revenue Service; subpart B of this part prescribes the duties and restrictions relating to such practice; subpart C of this part prescribes the sanctions for violating the regulations; subpart D of this part contains the rules applicable to disciplinary proceedings; and subpart E of this part contains general provisions relating to the availability of official records.

(b) *Effective/applicability date.* This section is applicable beginning August 2, 2011.

Subpart A—Rules Governing Authority to Practice

§ 10.1 Offices

(a) *Establishment of office(s).* The Commissioner shall establish the Office of Professional Responsibility and any other office(s) within the Internal Revenue Service necessary to administer and enforce this part. The Com-

Federal Rules
and Standards
(Selected)

missioner shall appoint the Director of the Office of Professional Responsibility and any other Internal Revenue official(s) to manage and direct any office(s) established to administer or enforce this part. Offices established under this part include, but are not limited to:

(1) The Office of Professional Responsibility, which shall generally have responsibility for matters related to practitioner conduct and shall have exclusive responsibility for discipline, including disciplinary proceedings and sanctions; and

(2) An office with responsibility for matters related to authority to practice before the Internal Revenue Service, including acting on applications for enrollment to practice before the Internal Revenue Service and administering competency testing and continuing education.

(b) Officers and employees within any office established under this part may perform acts necessary or appropriate to carry out the responsibilities of their office(s) under this part or as otherwise prescribed by the Commissioner.

(c) *Acting.* The Commissioner will designate an officer or employee of the Internal Revenue Service to perform the duties of an individual appointed under paragraph (a) of this section in the absence of that officer or employee or during a vacancy in that office.

(d) *Effective/applicability date.* This section is applicable beginning August 2, 2011, except that paragraph (a)(1) is applicable beginning June 12, 2014.

§ 10.2 Definitions.

(a) As used in this part, except where the text provides otherwise —

(1) *Attorney* means any person who is a member in good standing of the bar of the highest court of any state, territory, or possession of the United States, including a Commonwealth, or the District of Columbia.

(2) *Certified public accountant* means any person who is duly qualified to practice as a certified public accountant in any state, territory, or possession of the United States, including a Commonwealth, or the District of Columbia.

(3) *Commissioner* refers to the Commissioner of Internal Revenue.

(4) *Practice before the Internal Revenue Service* comprehends all matters connected with a presentation to the Internal Revenue Service or any of its officers or employees relating to a taxpayer's rights, privileges, or liabilities under laws or regulations administered by the Internal Revenue Service. Such presentations include, but are not limited to, preparing documents; filing documents; corresponding and communicating with the Internal Revenue Service; rendering written advice with respect to any entity, transaction, plan or arrangement, or other plan or arrangement having a potential for tax avoidance or evasion; and representing a client at conferences, hearings, and meetings.

(5) *Practitioner* means any individual described in paragraphs (a), (b), (c), (d), (e), or (f) of §10.3.

(6) A *tax return* includes an amended tax return and a claim for refund.

(7) *Service* means the Internal Revenue Service.

(8) *Tax return preparer* means any individual within the meaning of section 7701(a)(36) and 26 CFR 301.7701-15.

(b) *Effective/applicability date.* This section is applicable on August 2, 2011.

§ 10.3 Who may practice.

(a) *Attorneys.* Any attorney who is not currently under suspension or disbarment from practice before the Internal Revenue Service may practice before Internal Revenue Service by filing with the Internal Revenue Service a written declaration that the attorney is currently qualified as an attorney and is authorized to represent the party or parties. Notwithstanding the preceding sentence, attorneys who are not currently under suspension or disbarment from practice before the Internal Revenue Service are not required to file a written declaration with the IRS before rendering written advice covered under §10.37, but their rendering of this advice is practice before the Internal Revenue Service.

* * * *

Subpart B—Duties and Restrictions Relating to Practice Before the Internal Revenue Service

§ 10.20 Information to be furnished

(a) *To the Internal Revenue Service*

(1) A practitioner must, on a proper and lawful request by a duly authorized officer or employee of the Internal Revenue Service, promptly submit records or information in any matter before the Internal Revenue Service unless the practitioner believes in good faith and on reasonable grounds that the records or information are privileged.

(2) Where the requested records or information are not in the possession of, or subject to the control of, the practitioner or the practitioner's client, the practitioner must promptly notify the requesting Internal Revenue Service officer or employee and the practitioner must provide any information that the practitioner has regarding the identity of any person who the practitioner believes may have possession or control of the requested records or information. The practitioner must make reasonable inquiry of his or her client regarding the identity of any person who may have possession or control of the requested records or information, but the practitioner is not required to make inquiry of any other person

Federal Rules and Standards (Selected)

or independently verify any information provided by the practitioner's client regarding the identity of such persons.

(3) When a proper and lawful request is made by a duly authorized officer or employee of the Internal Revenue Service, concerning an inquiry into an alleged violation of the regulations in this part, a practitioner must provide any information the practitioner has concerning the alleged violation and testify regarding this information in any proceeding instituted under this part, unless the practitioner believes in good faith and on reasonable grounds that the information is privileged.

(b) *Interference with a proper and lawful request for records or information.* A practitioner may not interfere, or attempt to interfere, with any proper and lawful effort by the Internal Revenue Service, its officers or employees, to obtain any record or information unless the practitioner believes in good faith and on reasonable grounds that the record or information is privileged.

(c) *Effective/applicability date.* This section is applicable beginning August 2, 2011.

§ 10.21 Knowledge of client's omission.

A practitioner who, having been retained by a client with respect to a matter administered by the Internal Revenue Service, knows that the client has not complied with the revenue laws of the United States or has made an error in or omission from any return, document, affidavit, or other paper which the client submitted or executed under the revenue laws of the United States, must advise the client promptly of the fact of such noncompliance, error, or omission. The practitioner must advise the client of the consequences as provided under the Code and regulations of such noncompliance, error, or omission.

§ 10.22 Diligence as to accuracy.

(a) *In general.* A practitioner must exercise due diligence—

(1) In preparing or assisting in the preparation of, approving, and filing tax returns, documents, affidavits, and other papers relating to Internal Revenue Service matters;

(2) In determining the correctness of oral or written representations made by the practitioner to the Department of the Treasury; and

(3) In determining the correctness of oral or written representations made by the practitioner to clients with reference to any matter administered by the Internal Revenue Service.

(b) *Reliance on others.* Except as provided in §§ 10.34 and 10.37, a practitioner will be presumed to have exercised due diligence for purposes of this section if the practitioner relies on the work product of another person and the practitioner used reasonable care in engaging, supervising, training, and evaluating the person, taking proper account of the nature of the relationship between the practitioner and the person.

§ 10.23 Prompt disposition of pending matters.

A practitioner may not unreasonably delay the prompt disposition of any matter before the Internal Revenue Service.

§ 10.24 Assistance from or to disbarred or suspended persons and former Internal Revenue Service employees.

A practitioner may not, knowingly and directly or indirectly:

(a) Accept assistance from or assist any person who is under disbarment or suspension from practice before the Internal Revenue Service if the assistance relates to a matter or matters constituting practice before the Internal Revenue Service.

(b) Accept assistance from any former government employee where the provisions of § 10.25 or any Federal law would be violated.

§ 10.25 Practice by former Government employees, their partners and their associates.

(a) *Definitions.* For purposes of this section—

(1) Assist means to act in such a way as to advise, furnish information to, or otherwise aid another person, directly or indirectly.

(2) Government employee is an officer or employee of the United States or any agency of the United States, including a special government employee as defined in 18 U.S.C. 202(a), or of the District of Columbia, or of any State, or a member of Congress or of any State legislature.

(3) Member of a firm is a sole practitioner or an employee or associate thereof, or a partner, stockholder, associate, affiliate or employee of a partnership, joint venture, corporation, professional association or other affiliation of two or more practitioners who represent nongovernmental parties.

(4) Practitioner includes any individual described in paragraph (f) of § 10.2.

(5) Official responsibility means the direct administrative or operating authority, whether intermediate or final, and either exercisable alone or with others, and either personally or through subordinates, to approve, disapprove, or otherwise direct Government action, with or without knowledge of the action.

(6) Participate or participation means substantial involvement as a Government employee by making decisions, or preparing or reviewing documents with or without the right to exercise a judgment of approval

Federal Rules and Standards (Selected)

or disapproval, or participating in conferences or investigations, or rendering advice of a substantial nature.

(7) Rule includes Treasury Regulations, whether issued or under preparation for issuance as Notices of Proposed Rule Making or as Treasury Decisions; revenue rulings; and revenue procedures published in the Internal Revenue Bulletin. Rule does not include a transaction as defined in paragraph (a)(8) of this section.

(8) Transaction means any decision, determination, finding, letter ruling, technical advice, Chief Counsel advice, or contract or the approval or disapproval thereof, relating to a particular factual situation or situations involving a specific party or parties whose rights, privileges, or liabilities under laws or regulations administered by the Internal Revenue Service, or other legal rights, are determined or immediately affected therein and to which the United States is a party or in which it has a direct and substantial interest, whether or not the same taxable periods are involved. Transaction does not include rule as defined in paragraph (a)(7) of this section.

(b) *General rules.*

(1) No former Government employee may, subsequent to his or her Government employment, represent anyone in any matter administered by the Internal Revenue Service if the representation would violate 18 U.S.C. 207 or any other laws of the United States.

(2) No former Government employee who participated in a transaction may, subsequent to his or her Government employment, represent or knowingly assist, in that transaction, any person who is or was a specific party to that transaction.

(3) A former Government employee who within a period of one year prior to the termination of Government employment had official responsibility for a transaction may not, within two years after his or her Government employment is ended, represent or knowingly assist in that transaction any person who is or was a specific party to that transaction.

(4) No former Government employee may, within one year after his or her Government employment is ended, appear before any employee of the Treasury Department in connection with the publication, withdrawal, amendment, modification, or interpretation of a rule in the development of which the former Government employee participated or for which, within a period of one year prior to the termination of his or her Government employment, he or she had official responsibility. This paragraph (b)(4) does not, however, preclude such former employee from appearing on his or her own behalf or from representing a taxpayer before the Internal Revenue Service in connection with a transaction involving the application or interpretation of such a rule with respect to

that transaction, provided that such former employee does not utilize or disclose any confidential information acquired by the former employee in the development of the rule.

(c) *Firm representation.*

(1) No member of a firm of which a former Government employee is a member may represent or knowingly assist a person who was or is a specific party in any transaction with respect to which the restrictions of paragraph (b)(2) or (3) of this section apply to the former Government employee, in that transaction, unless the firm isolates the former Government employee in such a way to ensure that the former Government employee cannot assist in the representation.

(2) When isolation of a former Government employee is required under paragraph (c)(1) of this section, a statement affirming the fact of such isolation must be executed under oath by the former Government employee and by another member of the firm acting on behalf of the firm. The statement must be retained by the firm and, upon request, provided to the office(s) of the Internal Revenue Service administering or enforcing this part.

(d) *Pending representation.* The provisions of this regulation will govern practice by former Government employees, their partners and associates with respect to representation in particular matters involving specific parties where actual representation commenced before the effective date of this regulation.

(e) *Effective/applicability date.* This section is applicable beginning August 2, 2011.

§ 10.26 Notaries.

A practitioner may not take acknowledgments, administer oaths, certify papers, or perform any official act as a notary public with respect to any matter administered by the Internal Revenue Service and for which he or she is employed as counsel, attorney, or agent, or in which he or she may be in any way interested.

§ 10.27 Fees.

(a) *Generally.* A practitioner may not charge an unconscionable fee for representing a client in a matter before the Internal Revenue Service.

(b) *Contingent fees.*

(1) For purposes of this section, a contingent fee is any fee that is based, in whole or in part, on whether or not a position taken on a tax return or other filing avoids challenge by the Internal Revenue Service or is sustained either by the Internal Revenue Service or in litigation. A contingent fee includes any fee arrangement in which the practitioner

will reimburse the client for all or a portion of the client's fee in the event that a position taken on a tax return or other filing is challenged by the Internal Revenue Service or is not sustained, whether pursuant to an indemnity agreement, a guarantee, rescission rights, or any other arrangement with a similar effect.

(2) A practitioner may not charge a contingent fee for preparing an original tax return or for any advice rendered in connection with a position taken or to be taken on an original tax return.

(3) A contingent fee may be charged for preparation of or advice in connection with an amended tax return or a claim for refund (other than a claim for refund made on an original tax return), but only if the practitioner reasonably anticipates at the time the fee arrangement is entered into that the amended tax return or refund claim will receive substantive review by the Internal Revenue Service.

§ 10.28 Return of client's records.

(a) In general, a practitioner must, at the request of a client, promptly return any and all records of the client that are necessary for the client to comply with his or her Federal tax obligations. The practitioner may retain copies of the records returned to a client. The existence of a dispute over fees generally does not relieve the practitioner of his or her responsibility under this section. Nevertheless, if applicable state law allows or permits the retention of a client's records by a practitioner in the case of a dispute over fees for services rendered, the practitioner need only return those records that must be attached to the taxpayer's return. The practitioner, however, must provide the client with reasonable access to review and copy any additional records of the client retained by the practitioner under state law that are necessary for the client to comply with his or her Federal tax obligations.

(b) For purposes of this section—Records of the client include all documents or written or electronic materials provided to the practitioner, or obtained by the practitioner in the course of the practitioner's representation of the client, that preexisted the retention of the practitioner by the client. The term also includes materials that were prepared by the client or a third party (not including an employee or agent of the practitioner) at any time and provided to the practitioner with respect to the subject matter of the representation. The term also includes any return, claim for refund, schedule, affidavit, appraisal or any other document prepared by the practitioner, or his or her employee or agent, that was presented to the client with respect to a prior representation if such document is necessary for the taxpayer to comply with his or her current Federal tax obligations. The term does not include any return, claim for refund, schedule, affidavit, appraisal or any

Federal Rules and Standards (Selected)

other document prepared by the practitioner or the practitioner's firm, employees or agents if the practitioner is withholding such document pending the client's performance of its contractual obligation to pay fees with respect to such document.

§ 10.29 Conflicting interests.

(a) Except as provided by paragraph (b) of this section, a practitioner shall not represent a client in his or her practice before the Internal Revenue Service if the representation involves a conflict of interest. A conflict of interest exists if:

(1) The representation of one client will be directly adverse to another client; or

(2) There is a significant risk that the representation of one or more clients will be materially limited by the practitioner's responsibilities to another client, a former client or a third person or by a personal interest of the practitioner.

(b) Notwithstanding the existence of a conflict of interest under paragraph (a) of this section, the practitioner may represent a client if:

(1) The practitioner reasonably believes that the practitioner will be able to provide competent and diligent representation to each affected client;

(2) The representation is not prohibited by law;

(3) Each affected client gives informed consent, confirmed in writing.

(c) Copies of the written consents must be retained by the practitioner for at least 36 months from the date of the conclusion of the representation of the affected clients and the written consents must be provided to any officer or employee of the Internal Revenue Service on request.

(Approved by the Office of Management and Budget under Control No. 1545-1726)

§ 10.30 Solicitation.

(a) *Advertising and solicitation restrictions.*

(1) A practitioner may not, with respect to any Internal Revenue Service matter, in any way use or participate in the use of any form of public communication or private solicitation containing a false, fraudulent, or coercive statement or claim; or a misleading or deceptive statement or claim. Enrolled agents, enrolled retirement plan agents, or registered tax return preparers, in describing their professional designation, may not utilize the term "certified" or imply an employer/employee relationship with the Internal Revenue Service. Examples of acceptable descriptions for enrolled agents are "enrolled to represent taxpayers before the Internal Revenue Service," "enrolled to practice before the Internal Revenue Service," and

Federal Rules and Standards (Selected)

"admitted to practice before the Internal Revenue Service." Similarly, examples of acceptable descriptions for enrolled retirement plan agents are "enrolled to represent taxpayers before the Internal Revenue Service as a retirement plan agent" and "enrolled to practice before the Internal Revenue Service as a retirement plan agent." An example of an acceptable description for registered tax return preparers is "designated as a registered tax return preparer by the Internal Revenue Service."

(2) A practitioner may not make, directly or indirectly, an uninvited written or oral solicitation of employment in matters related to the Internal Revenue Service if the solicitation violates Federal or State law or other applicable rule, e.g., attorneys are precluded from making a solicitation that is prohibited by conduct rules applicable to all attorneys in their State(s) of licensure. Any lawful solicitation made by or on behalf of a practitioner eligible to practice before the Internal Revenue Service must, nevertheless, clearly identify the solicitation as such and, if applicable, identify the source of the information used in choosing the recipient.

(b) *Fee information.*(1)(i) A practitioner may publish the availability of a written schedule of fees and disseminate the following fee information—(A) Fixed fees for specific routine services.(B) Hourly rates.(C) Range of fees for particular services.(D) Fee charged for an initial consultation.(ii) Any statement of fee information concerning matters in which costs may be incurred must include a statement disclosing whether clients will be responsible for such costs.(2) A practitioner may charge no more than the rate(s) published under paragraph (b)(1) of this section for at least 30 calendar days after the last date on which the schedule of fees was published.

(c) *Communication of fee information.* Fee information may be communicated in professional lists, telephone directories, print media, mailings, and electronic mail, facsimile, hand delivered flyers, radio, television, and any other method. The method chosen, however, must not cause the communication to become untruthful, deceptive, or otherwise in violation of this part. A practitioner may not persist in attempting to contact a prospective client if the prospective client has made it known to the practitioner that he or she does not desire to be solicited. In the case of radio and television broadcasting, the broadcast must be recorded and the practitioner must retain a recording of the actual transmission. In the case of direct mail and e-commerce communications, the practitioner must retain a copy of the actual communication, along with a list or other description of persons to whom the communication was mailed or otherwise distributed. The copy must be retained by the practitioner for a period of at least 36 months from the date of the last transmission or use.

(d) *Improper associations.* A practitioner may not, in matters related to the Internal Revenue Service, assist, or accept assistance from, any person or en-

Federal Rules and Standards (Selected)

tity who, to the knowledge of the practitioner, obtains clients or otherwise practices in a manner forbidden under this section.

(e) *Effective/applicability date.* This section is applicable beginning August 2, 2011.

(Approved by the Office of Management and Budget under Control No. 1545-1726)

§ 10.31 Negotiation of taxpayer checks.

(a) A practitioner may not endorse or otherwise negotiate any check (including directing or accepting payment by any means, electronic or otherwise, into an account owned or controlled by the practitioner or any firm or other entity with whom the practitioner is associated) issued to a client by the government in respect of a Federal tax liability.

(b) Effective/applicability date. This section is applicable beginning June 12, 2014.

§ 10.32 Practice of law.

Nothing in the regulations in this part may be construed as authorizing persons not members of the bar to practice law.

§ 10.33 Best practices for tax advisors.

(a) *Best practices.* Tax advisors should provide clients with the highest quality representation concerning Federal tax issues by adhering to best practices in providing advice and in preparing or assisting in the preparation of a submission to the Internal Revenue Service. In addition to compliance with the standards of practice provided elsewhere in this part, best practices include the following:

(1) Communicating clearly with the client regarding the terms of the engagement. For example, the advisor should determine the client's expected purpose for and use of the advice and should have a clear understanding with the client regarding the form and scope of the advice or assistance to be rendered.

(2) Establishing the facts, determining which facts are relevant, evaluating the reasonableness of any assumptions or representations, relating the applicable law (including potentially applicable judicial doctrines) to the relevant facts, and arriving at a conclusion supported by the law and the facts.

(3) Advising the client regarding the import of the conclusions reached, including, for example, whether a taxpayer may avoid accuracy-related penalties under the Internal Revenue Code if a taxpayer acts in reliance on the advice.

Federal Rules and Standards (Selected)

(4) Acting fairly and with integrity in practice before the Internal Revenue Service.

(b) *Procedures to ensure best practices for tax advisors.* Tax advisors with responsibility for overseeing a firm's practice of providing advice concerning Federal tax issues or of preparing or assisting in the preparation of submissions to the Internal Revenue Service should take reasonable steps to ensure that the firm's procedures for all members, associates, and employees are consistent with the best practices set forth in paragraph (a) of this section.

(c) *Applicability date.* This section is effective after June 20, 2005.

§ 10.34 Standards with respect to tax returns and documents, affidavits and other papers.

(a) *Tax returns.*

(1) A practitioner may not willfully, recklessly, or through gross incompetence —

(i) Sign a tax return or claim for refund that the practitioner knows or reasonably should know contains a position that —

(A) Lacks a reasonable basis;

(B) Is an unreasonable position as described in section 6694(a)(2) of the Internal Revenue Code (Code) (including the related regulations and other published guidance); or

(C) Is a willful attempt by the practitioner to understate the liability for tax or a reckless or intentional disregard of rules or regulations by the practitioner as described in section 6694(b)(2) of the Code (including the related regulations and other published guidance).

(ii) Advise a client to take a position on a tax return or claim for refund, or prepare a portion of a tax return or claim for refund containing a position, that —

(A) Lacks a reasonable basis;

(B) Is an unreasonable position as described in section 6694(a)(2) of the Code (including the related regulations and other published guidance); or

(C) Is a willful attempt by the practitioner to understate the liability for tax or a reckless or intentional disregard of rules or regulations by the practitioner as described in section 6694(b)(2) of the Code (including the related regulations and other published guidance).

(2) A pattern of conduct is a factor that will be taken into account in determining whether a practitioner acted willfully, recklessly, or through gross incompetence.

(b) *Documents, affidavits and other papers*—

(1) A practitioner may not advise a client to take a position on a document, affidavit or other paper submitted to the Internal Revenue Service unless the position is not frivolous.

(2) A practitioner may not advise a client to submit a document, affidavit or other paper to the Internal Revenue Service—

(i) The purpose of which is to delay or impede the administration of the Federal tax laws;

(ii) That is frivolous; or

(iii) That contains or omits information in a manner that demonstrates an intentional disregard of a rule or regulation unless the practitioner also advises the client to submit a document that evidences a good faith challenge to the rule or regulation.

(c) *Advising clients on potential penalties*—

(1) A practitioner must inform a client of any penalties that are reasonably likely to apply to the client with respect to—

(i) A position taken on a tax return if—

(A) The practitioner advised the client with respect to the position; or

(B) The practitioner prepared or signed the tax return; and

(ii) Any document, affidavit or other paper submitted to the Internal Revenue Service.

(2) The practitioner also must inform the client of any opportunity to avoid any such penalties by disclosure, if relevant, and of the requirements for adequate disclosure.(3) This paragraph (c) applies even if the practitioner is not subject to a penalty under the Internal Revenue Code with respect to the position or with respect to the document, affidavit or other paper submitted.

(d) *Relying on information furnished by clients.* A practitioner advising a client to take a position on a tax return, document, affidavit or other paper submitted to the Internal Revenue Service, or preparing or signing a tax return as a preparer, generally may rely in good faith without verification upon information furnished by the client. The practitioner may not, however, ignore the implications of information furnished to, or actually known by, the practitioner, and must make reasonable inquiries if the information as furnished appears to be incorrect, inconsistent with an important fact or another factual assumption, or incomplete.

(e) *Effective/applicability date.* Paragraph (a) of this section is applicable for returns or claims for refund filed, or advice provided, beginning August 2, 2011. Paragraphs (b) through (d) of this section are applicable to tax returns, documents, affidavits, and other papers filed on or after September 26, 2007.

§ 10.35 Competence.

(a) A practitioner must possess the necessary competence to engage in practice before the Internal Revenue Service. Competent practice requires the appropriate level of knowledge, skill, thoroughness, and preparation necessary for the matter for which the practitioner is engaged. A practitioner may become competent for the matter for which the practitioner has been engaged through various methods, such as consulting with experts in the relevant area or studying the relevant law.

(b) *Effective/applicability date.* This section is applicable beginning June 12, 2014.

§ 10.36 Procedures to ensure compliance.

(a) Any individual subject to the provisions of this part who has (or individuals who have or share) principal authority and responsibility for overseeing a firm's practice governed by this part, including the provision of advice concerning Federal tax matters and preparation of tax returns, claims for refund, or other documents for submission to the Internal Revenue Service, must take reasonable steps to ensure that the firm has adequate procedures in effect for all members, associates, and employees for purposes of complying with subparts A, B, and C of this part, as applicable. In the absence of a person or persons identified by the firm as having the principal authority and responsibility described in this paragraph, the Internal Revenue Service may identify one or more individuals subject to the provisions of this part responsible for compliance with the requirements of this section.

(b) Any such individual who has (or such individuals who have or share) principal authority as described in paragraph (a) of this section will be subject to discipline for failing to comply with the requirements of this section if—

(1) The individual through willfulness, recklessness, or gross incompetence does not take reasonable steps to ensure that the firm has adequate procedures to comply with this part, as applicable, and one or more individuals who are members of, associated with, or employed by, the firm are, or have, engaged in a pattern or practice, in connection with their practice with the firm, of failing to comply with this part, as applicable;

(2) The individual through willfulness, recklessness, or gross incompetence does not take reasonable steps to ensure that firm procedures in effect are properly followed, and one or more individuals who are members of, associated with, or employed by, the firm are, or have, engaged in a pattern or practice, in connection with their practice with the firm, of failing to comply with this part, as applicable; or

(3) The individual knows or should know that one or more individuals who are members of, associated with, or employed by, the firm are, or have, engaged in a pattern or practice, in connection with their practice with the firm, that does not comply with this part, as applicable, and the individual, through willfulness, recklessness, or gross incompetence fails to take prompt action to correct the noncompliance.

(c) *Effective/applicability date.* This section is applicable beginning June 12, 2014.

§10.37 Requirements for written advice.

(a) *Requirements.* (1) A practitioner may give written advice (including by means of electronic communication) concerning one or more Federal tax matters subject to the requirements in paragraph (a)(2) of this section. Government submissions on matters of general policy are not considered written advice on a Federal tax matter for purposes of this section. Continuing education presentations provided to an audience solely for the purpose of enhancing practitioners' professional knowledge on Federal tax matters are not considered written advice on a Federal tax matter for purposes of this section. The preceding sentence does not apply to presentations marketing or promoting transactions.

(2) The practitioner must—

(i) Base the written advice on reasonable factual and legal assumptions (including assumptions as to future events);

(ii) Reasonably consider all relevant facts and circumstances that the practitioner knows or reasonably should know;

(iii) Use reasonable efforts to identify and ascertain the facts relevant to written advice on each Federal tax matter;

(iv) Not rely upon representations, statements, findings, or agreements (including projections, financial forecasts, or appraisals) of the taxpayer or any other person if reliance on them would be unreasonable;

(v) Relate applicable law and authorities to facts; and

(vi) Not, in evaluating a Federal tax matter, take into account the possibility that a tax return will not be audited or that a matter will not be raised on audit.

(3) Reliance on representations, statements, findings, or agreements is unreasonable if the practitioner knows or reasonably should know that one or more representations or assumptions on which any representation is based are incorrect, incomplete, or inconsistent.

(b) *Reliance on advice of others.* A practitioner may only rely on the advice of another person if the advice was reasonable and the reliance is in good faith considering all the facts and circumstances. Reliance is not reasonable when—

(1) The practitioner knows or reasonably should know that the opinion of the other person should not be relied on;

(2) The practitioner knows or reasonably should know that the other person is not competent or lacks the necessary qualifications to provide the advice; or

(3) The practitioner knows or reasonably should know that the other person has a conflict of interest in violation of the rules described in this part.

(c) *Standard of review.*

(1) In evaluating whether a practitioner giving written advice concerning one or more Federal tax matters complied with the requirements of this section, the Commissioner, or delegate, will apply a reasonable practitioner standard, considering all facts and circumstances, including, but not limited to, the scope of the engagement and the type and specificity of the advice sought by the client.

(2) In the case of an opinion the practitioner knows or has reason to know will be used or referred to by a person other than the practitioner (or a person who is a member of, associated with, or employed by the practitioner's firm) in promoting, marketing, or recommending to one or more taxpayers a partnership or other entity, investment plan or arrangement a significant purpose of which is the avoidance or evasion of any tax imposed by the Internal Revenue Code, the Commissioner, or delegate, will apply a reasonable practitioner standard, considering all facts and circumstances, with emphasis given to the additional risk caused by the practitioner's lack of knowledge of the taxpayer's particular circumstances, when determining whether a practitioner has failed to comply with this section.

(d) *Federal tax matter.* A Federal tax matter, as used in this section, is any matter concerning the application or interpretation of—

(1) A revenue provision as defined in section 6110(i)(1)(B) of the Internal Revenue Code;

(2) Any provision of law impacting a person's obligations under the internal revenue laws and regulations, including but not limited to the person's liability to pay tax or obligation to file returns; or

(3) Any other law or regulation administered by the Internal Revenue Service.

(e) *Effective/applicability date.* This section is applicable to written advice rendered after June 12, 2014.

§10.38 Establishment of advisory committees.

(a) *Advisory committees.* To promote and maintain the public's confidence in tax advisors, the Internal Revenue Service is authorized to establish one or more advisory committees composed of at least six individuals authorized to practice before the Internal Revenue Service. Membership of an advisory committee must be balanced among those who practice as attorneys, accountants, enrolled agents, enrolled actuaries, enrolled retirement plan agents, and registered tax return preparers. Under procedures prescribed by the Internal Revenue Service, an advisory committee may review and make general recommendations regarding the practices, procedures, and policies of the offices described in §10.1.

(b) *Effective date.* This section is applicable beginning August 2, 2011.

* * * *

Subpart C—Sanctions for Violation of the Regulations

§10.50 Sanctions.

(a) *Authority to censure, suspend, or disbar.* The Secretary of the Treasury, or his or her delegate, after notice and an opportunity for a proceeding, may censure, suspend or disbar any practitioner from practice before the Internal Revenue Service if the practitioner is shown to be incompetent or disreputable, fails to comply with any regulation in this part, or with intent to defraud, willfully and knowingly misleads or threatens a client or prospective client. Censure is a public reprimand.

(b) *Authority to disqualify.* The Secretary of the Treasury, or his or her delegate, after due notice and opportunity for hearing, may disqualify any appraiser with respect to whom a penalty has been assessed under section 6701(a) of the Internal Revenue Code.

(1) If any appraiser is disqualified pursuant to this subpart C, such appraiser is barred from presenting evidence or testimony in any administrative proceeding before the Department of Treasury or the Internal Revenue Service, unless and until authorized to do so by the Director of Practice pursuant to §10.81, regardless of whether such evidence or testimony would pertain to an appraisal made prior to or after such date.

(2) Any appraisal made by a disqualified appraiser after the effective date of disqualification will not have any probative effect in any administrative proceeding before the Department of the Treasury or the Internal Revenue Service. An appraisal otherwise barred from admission into evidence pursuant to this section may be admitted into evidence solely for the purpose of determining the taxpayer's reliance in good faith on such appraisal.

§ 10.51 Incompetence and disreputable conduct.

(a) *Incompetence and disreputable conduct.* Incompetence and disreputable conduct for which a practitioner may be sanctioned under §10.50 includes, but is not limited to—

(1) Conviction of any criminal offense under the Federal tax laws.

(2) Conviction of any criminal offense involving dishonesty or breach of trust.

(3) Conviction of any felony under Federal or State law for which the conduct involved renders the practitioner unfit to practice before the Internal Revenue Service.

(4) Giving false or misleading information, or participating in any way in the giving of false or misleading information to the Department of the Treasury or any officer or employee thereof, or to any tribunal authorized to pass upon Federal tax matters, in connection with any matter pending or likely to be pending before them, knowing the information to be false or misleading. Facts or other matters contained in testimony, Federal tax returns, financial statements, applications for enrollment, affidavits, declarations, and any other document or statement, written or oral, are included in the term "information."

(5) Solicitation of employment as prohibited under §10.30, the use of false or misleading representations with intent to deceive a client or prospective client in order to procure employment, or intimating that the practitioner is able improperly to obtain special consideration or action from the Internal Revenue Service or any officer or employee thereof.

(6) Willfully failing to make a Federal tax return in violation of the Federal tax laws, or willfully evading, attempting to evade, or participating in any way in evading or attempting to evade any assessment or payment of any Federal tax.

(7) Willfully assisting, counseling, encouraging a client or prospective client in violating, or suggesting to a client or prospective client to violate, any Federal tax law, or knowingly counseling or suggesting to a client or prospective client an illegal plan to evade Federal taxes or payment thereof.

(8) Misappropriation of, or failure properly or promptly to remit, funds received from a client for the purpose of payment of taxes or other obligations due the United States.

(9) Directly or indirectly attempting to influence, or offering or agreeing to attempt to influence, the official action of any officer or employee of the Internal Revenue Service by the use of threats, false accusations, duress or coercion, by the offer of any special inducement or promise of an advantage or by the bestowing of any gift, favor or thing of value.

(10) Disbarment or suspension from practice as an attorney, certified public accountant, public accountant, or actuary by any duly constituted authority of any State, territory, or possession of the United States, in-

cluding a Commonwealth, or the District of Columbia, any Federal court of record or any Federal agency, body or board.

(11) Knowingly aiding and abetting another person to practice before the Internal Revenue Service during a period of suspension, disbarment or ineligibility of such other person.

(12) Contemptuous conduct in connection with practice before the Internal Revenue Service, including the use of abusive language, making false accusations or statements, knowing them to be false, or circulating or publishing malicious or libelous matter.

(13) Giving a false opinion, knowingly, recklessly, or through gross incompetence, including an opinion which is intentionally or recklessly misleading, or engaging in a pattern of providing incompetent opinions on questions arising under the Federal tax laws. False opinions described in this paragraph (a)(13) include those which reflect or result from a knowing misstatement of fact or law, from an assertion of a position known to be unwarranted under existing law, from counseling or assisting in conduct known to be illegal or fraudulent, from concealing matters required by law to be revealed, or from consciously disregarding information indicating that material facts expressed in the opinion or offering material are false or misleading. For purposes of this paragraph (a)(13), reckless conduct is a highly unreasonable omission or misrepresentation involving an extreme departure from the standards of ordinary care that a practitioner should observe under the circumstances. A pattern of conduct is a factor that will be taken into account in determining whether a practitioner acted knowingly, recklessly, or through gross incompetence. Gross incompetence includes conduct that reflects gross indifference, preparation which is grossly inadequate under the circumstances, and a consistent failure to perform obligations to the client.

(14) Willfully failing to sign a tax return prepared by the practitioner when the practitioner's signature is required by Federal tax laws unless the failure is due to reasonable cause and not due to willful neglect.

(15) Willfully disclosing or otherwise using a tax return or tax return information in a manner not authorized by the Internal Revenue Code, contrary to the order of a court of competent jurisdiction, or contrary to the order of an administrative law judge in a proceeding instituted under §10.60.

(16) Willfully failing to file on magnetic or other electronic media a tax return prepared by the practitioner when the practitioner is required to do so by the Federal tax laws unless the failure is due to reasonable cause and not due to willful neglect.

(17) Willfully preparing all or substantially all of, or signing, a tax return or claim for refund when the practitioner does not possess a cur-

Federal Rules and Standards (Selected)

rent or otherwise valid preparer tax identification number or other prescribed identifying number.

(18) Willfully representing a taxpayer before an officer or employee of the Internal Revenue Service unless the practitioner is authorized to do so pursuant to this part.

(b) *Effective/applicability date.* This section is applicable beginning August 2, 2011.

§10.52 Violation of regulations.

(a) *Prohibited conduct.* A practitioner may be censured, suspended or disbarred from practice before the Internal Revenue Service for any of the following:

(1) Willfully violating any of the regulations (other than §10.33) contained in this part.

(2) Recklessly or through gross incompetence (within the meaning of §10.51(l)) violating §§ 10.34, 10.35, 10.36 or 10.37.

(b) *Effective date.* This section applies after June 20, 2005.

Federal Rules
and Standards
(Selected)

Selected Federal Rules of Civil Procedure

Rule 11. Signing Pleadings, Motions, and Other Papers; Representations to the Court; Sanctions

(As amended, effective December 1, 2007)

(a) Signature. Every pleading, written motion, and other paper must be signed by at least one attorney of record in the attorney's name—or by a party personally if the party is unrepresented. The paper must state the signer's address, e-mail address, and telephone number. Unless a rule or statute specifically states otherwise, a pleading need not be verified or accompanied by an affidavit. The court must strike an unsigned paper unless the omission is promptly corrected after being called to the attorney's or party's attention.

(b) Representations to the Court. By presenting to the court a pleading, written motion, or other paper—whether by signing, filing, submitting, or later advocating it—an attorney or unrepresented party certifies that to the best of the person's knowledge, information, and belief, formed after an inquiry reasonable under the circumstances:

(1) it is not being presented for any improper purpose, such as to harass, cause unnecessary delay, or needlessly increase the cost of litigation;

(2) the claims, defenses, and other legal contentions are warranted by existing law or by a nonfrivolous argument for extending, modifying, or reversing existing law or for establishing new law;

(3) the factual contentions have evidentiary support or, if specifically so identified, will likely have evidentiary support after a reasonable opportunity for further investigation or discovery; and

(4) the denials of factual contentions are warranted on the evidence or, if specifically so identified, are reasonably based on belief or a lack of information.

(c) Sanctions.

(1) *In General.* If, after notice and a reasonable opportunity to respond, the court determines that Rule 11(b) has been violated, the court may impose an appropriate sanction on any attorney, law firm, or party that violated the rule or is responsible for the violation. Absent exceptional circumstances, a law firm must be held jointly responsible for a violation committed by its partner, associate, or employee.

(2) *Motion for Sanctions.* A motion for sanctions must be made separately from any other motion and must describe the specific conduct that allegedly violates Rule 11(b). The motion must be served under Rule

Federal Rules and Standards (Selected)

5, but it must not be filed or be presented to the court if the challenged paper, claim, defense, contention, or denial is withdrawn or appropriately corrected within 21 days after service or within another time the court sets. If warranted, the court may award to the prevailing party the reasonable expenses, including attorney's fees, incurred for the motion.

(3) *On the Court's Initiative.* On its own, the court may order an attorney, law firm, or party to show cause why conduct specifically described in the order has not violated Rule 11(b).

(4) *Nature of a Sanction.* A sanction imposed under this rule must be limited to what suffices to deter repetition of the conduct or comparable conduct by others similarly situated. The sanction may include nonmonetary directives; an order to pay a penalty into court; or, if imposed on motion and warranted for effective deterrence, an order directing payment to the movant of part or all of the reasonable attorney's fees and other expenses directly resulting from the violation.

(5) *Limitations on Monetary Sanctions.* The court must not impose a monetary sanction:

(A) against a represented party for violating Rule 11(b)(2); or

(B) on its own, unless it issued the show-cause order under Rule 11(c)(3) before voluntary dismissal or settlement of the claims made by or against the party that is, or whose attorneys are, to be sanctioned.

(6) *Requirements for an Order.* An order imposing a sanction must describe the sanctioned conduct and explain the basis for the sanction.

(d) **Inapplicability to Discovery.** This rule does not apply to disclosures and discovery requests, responses, objections, and motions under Rules 26 through 37.

Rule 26. Duty to Disclose;
General Provisions Governing Discovery

(As amended, April 29, 2015 effective December 1, 2015)

(a) Required Disclosures.

  (1) *Initial Disclosure.*

    (A) *In General.* Except as exempted by Rule 26(a)(1)(B) or as otherwise stipulated or ordered by the court, a party must, without awaiting a discovery request, provide to the other parties:

      (i)   the name and, if known, the address and telephone number of each individual likely to have discoverable information—along with the subjects of that information—that the disclosing party may use to support its claims or defenses, unless the use would be solely for impeachment;

      (ii)   a copy—or a description by category and location—of all documents, electronically stored information, and tangible things that the disclosing party has in its possession, custody, or control and may use to support its claims or defenses, unless the use would be solely for impeachment;

      (iii)   a computation of each category of damages claimed by the disclosing party—who must also make available for inspection and copying as under Rule 34 the documents or other evidentiary material, unless privileged or protected from disclosure, on which each computation is based, including materials bearing on the nature and extent of injuries suffered; and

      (iv)   for inspection and copying as under Rule 34, any insurance agreement under which an insurance business may be liable to satisfy all or part of a possible judgment in the action or to indemnify or reimburse for payments made to satisfy the judgment.

    (B) *Proceedings Exempt from Initial Disclosure.* The following proceedings are exempt from initial disclosure:

      (i)   an action for review on an administrative record;

      (ii)   a forfeiture action in rem arising from a federal statute;

      (iii)   a petition for habeas corpus or any other proceeding to challenge a criminal conviction or sentence;

      (iv)   an action brought without an attorney by a person in the custody of the United States, a state, or a state subdivision;

      (v)   an action to enforce or quash an administrative summons or subpoena;

      (vi)   an action by the United States to recover benefit payments;

Federal Rules and Standards (Selected)

    (vii) an action by the United States to collect on a student loan guaranteed by the United States;

    (viii) a proceeding ancillary to a proceeding in another court; and

    (ix) an action to enforce an arbitration award.

(C) *Time for Initial Disclosures—In General.* A party must make the initial disclosures at or within 14 days after the parties' Rule 26(f) conference unless a different time is set by stipulation or court order, or unless a party objects during the conference that initial disclosures are not appropriate in this action and states the objection in the proposed discovery plan. In ruling on the objection, the court must determine what disclosures, if any, are to be made and must set the time for disclosure.

(D) *Time for Initial Disclosures—For Parties Served or Joined Later.* A party that is first served or otherwise joined after the Rule 26(f) conference must make the initial disclosures within 30 days after being served or joined, unless a different time is set by stipulation or court order.

(E) *Basis for Initial Disclosure; Unacceptable Excuses.* A party must make its initial disclosures based on the information then reasonably available to it. A party is not excused from making its disclosures because it has not fully investigated the case or because it challenges the sufficiency of another party's disclosures or because another party has not made its disclosures.

(2) Disclosure of Expert Testimony.

(A) *In General.* In addition to the disclosures required by Rule 26(a)(1), a party must disclose to the other parties the identity of any witness it may use at trial to present evidence under Federal Rule of Evidence 702, 703, or 705.

(B) *Witnesses Who Must Provide a Written Report.* Unless otherwise stipulated or ordered by the court, this disclosure must be accompanied by a written report—prepared and signed by the witness—if the witness is one retained or specially employed to provide expert testimony in the case or one whose duties as the party's employee regularly involve giving expert testimony. The report must contain:

    (i) a complete statement of all opinions the witness will express and the basis and reasons for them;

    (ii) the facts or data considered by the witness in forming them;

    (iii) any exhibits that will be used to summarize or support them;

    (iv) the witness's qualifications, including a list of all publications authored in the previous 10 years;

    (v) a list of all other cases in which, during the previous 4 years, the witness testified as an expert at trial or by deposition; and

Federal Rules and Standards (Selected)

(vi)   a statement of the compensation to be paid for the study and testimony in the case.

(C) *Witnesses Who Do Not Provide a Written Report.* Unless otherwise stipulated or ordered by the court, if the witness is not required to provide a written report, this disclosure must state:

(i)   the subject matter on which the witness is expected to present evidence under Federal Rule of Evidence 702, 703, or 705; and

(ii)   a summary of the facts and opinions to which the witness is expected to testify.

(D) *Time to Disclose Expert Testimony.* A party must make these disclosures at the times and in the sequence that the court orders. Absent a stipulation or a court order, the disclosures must be made:

(i)   at least 90 days before the date set for trial or for the case to be ready for trial; or

(ii)   if the evidence is intended solely to contradict or rebut evidence on the same subject matter identified by another party under Rule 26(a)(2)(B) or (C), within 30 days after the other party's disclosure.

(E) *Supplementing the Disclosure.* The parties must supplement these disclosures when required under Rule 26(e).

(3) Pretrial Disclosures.

(A) *In General.* In addition to the disclosures required by Rule 26(a)(1) and (2), a party must provide to the other parties and promptly file the following information about the evidence that it may present at trial other than solely for impeachment:

(i)   the name and, if not previously provided, the address and telephone number of each witness—separately identifying those the party expects to present and those it may call if the need arises;

(ii)   the designation of those witnesses whose testimony the party expects to present by deposition and, if not taken stenographically, a transcript of the pertinent parts of the deposition; and

(iii)   an identification of each document or other exhibit, including summaries of other evidence—separately identifying those items the party expects to offer and those it may offer if the need arises.

(B) *Time for Pretrial Disclosures; Objections.* Unless the court orders otherwise, these disclosures must be made at least 30 days before trial. Within 14 days after they are made, unless the court sets a different time, a party may serve and promptly file a list of the following objections: any objections to the use under Rule 32(a) of a deposition designated by another party under Rule 26(a)(3)(A)(ii); and any objection, together with the grounds for it, that may be made to the admissibility of materials

Federal Rules and Standards (Selected)

identified under Rule 26(a)(3)(A)(iii). An objection not so made—except for one under Federal Rule of Evidence 402 or 403—is waived unless excused by the court for good cause.

(4) *Form of Disclosures.* Unless the court orders otherwise, all disclosures under Rule 26(a) must be in writing, signed, and served.

(b) Discovery Scope and Limits.

(1) *Scope in General.* Unless otherwise limited by court order, the scope of discovery is as follows: Parties may obtain discovery regarding any non-privileged matter that is relevant to any party's claim or defense and proportional to the needs of the case, considering the importance of the issues at stake in the action, the amount in controversy, the parties' relative access to relevant information, the parties' resources, the importance of the discovery in resolving the issues, and whether the burden or expense of the proposed discovery outweighs its likely benefit. Information within this scope of discovery need not be admissible in evidence to be discoverable.

(2) *Limitations on Frequency and Extent.*

(A) *When Permitted.* By order, the court may alter the limits in these rules on the number of depositions and interrogatories or on the length of depositions under Rule 30. By order or local rule, the court may also limit the number of requests under Rule 36.

(B) *Specific Limitations on Electronically Stored Information.* A party need not provide discovery of electronically stored information from sources that the party identifies as not reasonably accessible because of undue burden or cost. On motion to compel discovery or for a protective order, the party from whom discovery is sought must show that the information is not reasonably accessible because of undue burden or cost. If that showing is made, the court may nonetheless order discovery from such sources if the requesting party shows good cause, considering the limitations of Rule 26(b)(2)(C). The court may specify conditions for the discovery.

(C) *When Required.* On motion or on its own, the court must limit the frequency or extent of discovery otherwise allowed by these rules or by local rule if it determines that:

(i) the discovery sought is unreasonably cumulative or duplicative, or can be obtained from some other source that is more convenient, less burdensome, or less expensive;

(ii) the party seeking discovery has had ample opportunity to obtain the information by discovery in the action; or

(iii) the proposed discovery is outside the scope permitted by Rule 26(b)(1).

(3) *Trial Preparation: Materials.*

(A) *Documents and Tangible Things.* Ordinarily, a party may not discover documents and tangible things that are prepared in anticipation of litigation or for trial by or for another party or its representative (including the other party's attorney, consultant, surety, indemnitor, insurer, or agent). But, subject to Rule 26(b)(4), those materials may be discovered if:

    (i)   they are otherwise discoverable under Rule 26(b)(1); and

    (ii)   the party shows that it has substantial need for the materials to prepare its case and cannot, without undue hardship, obtain their substantial equivalent by other means.

(B) *Protection Against Disclosure.* If the court orders discovery of those materials, it must protect against disclosure of the mental impressions, conclusions, opinions, or legal theories of a party's attorney or other representative concerning the litigation.

(C) *Previous Statement.* Any party or other person may, on request and without the required showing, obtain the person's own previous statement about the action or its subject matter. If the request is refused, the person may move for a court order, and Rule 37(a)(5) applies to the award of expenses. A previous statement is either:

    (i)   a written statement that the person has signed or otherwise adopted or approved; or

    (ii)   a contemporaneous stenographic, mechanical, electrical, or other recording—or a transcription of it—that recites substantially verbatim the person's oral statement.

(4) *Trial Preparation: Experts.*

(A) *Deposition of an Expert Who May Testify.* A party may depose any person who has been identified as an expert whose opinions may be presented at trial. If Rule 26(a)(2)(B) requires a report from the expert, the deposition may be conducted only after the report is provided.

(B) *Trial-Preparation Protection for Draft Reports or Disclosures.* Rules 26(b)(3)(A) and (B) protect drafts of any report or disclosure required under Rule 26(a)(2), regardless of the form in which the draft is recorded.

(C) *Trial-Preparation Protection for Communications Between a Party's Attorney and Expert Witnesses.* Rules 26(b)(3)(A) and (B) protect communications between the party's attorney and any witness required to provide a report under Rule 26(a)(2)(B), regardless of the form of the communications, except to the extent that the communications:

    (i)   relate to compensation for the expert's study or testimony;

    (ii)   identify facts or data that the party's attorney provided and that the expert considered in forming the opinions to be expressed; or

Federal Rules and Standards (Selected)

(iii)   identify assumptions that the party's attorney provided and that the expert relied on in forming the opinions to be expressed.

(D) *Expert Employed Only for Trial Preparation.* Ordinarily, a party may not, by interrogatories or deposition, discover facts known or opinions held by an expert who has been retained or specially employed by another party in anticipation of litigation or to prepare for trial and who is not expected to be called as a witness at trial. But a party may do so only:

(i)   as provided in Rule 35(b); or

(ii)   on showing exceptional circumstances under which it is impracticable for the party to obtain facts or opinions on the same subject by other means.

(E) *Payment.* Unless manifest injustice would result, the court must require that the party seeking discovery:

(i)   pay the expert a reasonable fee for time spent in responding to discovery under Rule 26(b)(4)(A) or (D); and

(ii)   for discovery under (D), also pay the other party a fair portion of the fees and expenses it reasonably incurred in obtaining the expert's facts and opinions.

(5) *Claiming Privilege or Protecting Trial-Preparation Materials.*

(A) *Information Withheld.* When a party withholds information otherwise discoverable by claiming that the information is privileged or subject to protection as trial-preparation material, the party must:

(i)   expressly make the claim; and

(ii)   describe the nature of the documents, communications, or tangible things not produced or disclosed—and do so in a manner that, without revealing information itself privileged or protected, will enable other parties to assess the claim.

(B) *Information Produced.* If information produced in discovery is subject to a claim of privilege or of protection as trial-preparation material, the party making the claim may notify any party that received the information of the claim and the basis for it. After being notified, a party must promptly return, sequester, or destroy the specified information and any copies it has; must not use or disclose the information until the claim is resolved; must take reasonable steps to retrieve the information if the party disclosed it before being notified; and may promptly present the information to the court under seal for a determination of the claim. The producing party must preserve the information until the claim is resolved.

(c) Protective Orders.

(1) *In General.* A party or any person from whom discovery is sought may move for a protective order in the court where the action is pending—

Federal Rules and Standards (Selected)

or as an alternative on matters relating to a deposition, in the court for the district where the deposition will be taken. The motion must include a certification that the movant has in good faith conferred or attempted to confer with other affected parties in an effort to resolve the dispute without court action. The court may, for good cause, issue an order to protect a party or person from annoyance, embarrassment, oppression, or undue burden or expense, including one or more of the following:

(A) *forbidding the disclosure or discovery;*

(B) *specifying terms, including time and place or the allocation of expenses, for the disclosure or discovery;*

(C) *prescribing a discovery method other than the one selected by the party seeking discovery;*

(D) *forbidding inquiry into certain matters, or limiting the scope of disclosure or discovery to certain matters;*

(E) *designating the persons who may be present while the discovery is conducted;*

(F) *requiring that a deposition be sealed and opened only on court order;*

(G) *requiring that a trade secret or other confidential research, development, or commercial information not be revealed or be revealed only in a specified way; and*

(H) *requiring that the parties simultaneously file specified documents or information in sealed envelopes, to be opened as the court directs.*

(2) **Ordering Discovery.** If a motion for a protective order is wholly or partly denied, the court may, on just terms, order that any party or person provide or permit discovery.

(3) **Awarding Expenses.** Rule 37(a)(5) applies to the award of expenses.

(d) Timing and Sequence of Discovery.

(1) **Timing.** A party may not seek discovery from any source before the parties have conferred as required by Rule 26(f), except in a proceeding exempted from initial disclosure under Rule 26(a)(1)(B), or when authorized by these rules, by stipulation, or by court order.

(2) **Early Rule 34 Requests.**

(A) *Time to Deliver.* More than 21 days after the summons and complaint are served on a party, a request under Rule 34 may be delivered:

(i)   to that party by any other party, and

(ii)   by that party to any plaintiff or to any other party that has been served.

(B) *When Considered Served.* The request is considered to have been served at the first Rule 26(f) conference.

(3) *Sequence.* Unless the parties stipulate or the court orders otherwise for the parties' and witnesses' convenience and in the interests of justice:

    (A) methods of discovery may be used in any sequence; and

    (B) discovery by one party does not require any other party to delay its discovery.

(e) Supplementing Disclosures and Responses.

    (1) *In General.* A party who has made a disclosure under Rule 26(a)—or who has responded to an interrogatory, request for production, or request for admission—must supplement or correct its disclosure or response:

        (A) in a timely manner if the party learns that in some material respect the disclosure or response is incomplete or incorrect, and if the additional or corrective information has not otherwise been made known to the other parties during the discovery process or in writing; or

        (B) as ordered by the court.

    (2) *Expert Witness.* For an expert whose report must be disclosed under Rule 26(a)(2)(B), the party's duty to supplement extends both to information included in the report and to information given during the expert's deposition. Any additions or changes to this information must be disclosed by the time the party's pretrial disclosures under Rule 26(a)(3) are due.

(f) Conference of the Parties; Planning for Discovery.

    (1) *Conference Timing.* Except in a proceeding exempted from initial disclosure under Rule 26(a)(1)(B) or when the court orders otherwise, the parties must confer as soon as practicable—and in any event at least 21 days before a scheduling conference is to be held or a scheduling order is due under Rule 16(b).

    (2) *Conference Content; Parties' Responsibilities.* In conferring, the parties must consider the nature and basis of their claims and defenses and the possibilities for promptly settling or resolving the case; make or arrange for the disclosures required by Rule 26(a)(1); discuss any issues about preserving discoverable information; and develop a proposed discovery plan. The attorneys of record and all unrepresented parties that have appeared in the case are jointly responsible for arranging the conference, for attempting in good faith to agree on the proposed discovery plan, and for submitting to the court within 14 days after the conference a written report outlining the plan. The court may order the parties or attorneys to attend the conference in person.

    (3) *Discovery Plan.* A discovery plan must state the parties' views and proposals on:

Federal Rules and Standards (Selected)

(A) what changes should be made in the timing, form, or requirement for disclosures under Rule 26(a), including a statement of when initial disclosures were made or will be made;

(B) the subjects on which discovery may be needed, when discovery should be completed, and whether discovery should be conducted in phases or be limited to or focused on particular issues;

(C) any issues about disclosure, discovery, or preservation of electronically stored information, including the form or forms in which it should be produced;

(D) any issues about claims of privilege or of protection as trial-preparation materials, including—if the parties agree on a procedure to assert these claims after production—whether to ask the court to include their agreement in an order under Federal Rule of Evidence 502;

(E) what changes should be made in the limitations on discovery imposed under these rules or by local rule, and what other limitations should be imposed; and

(F) any other orders that the court should issue under Rule 26(c) or under Rule 16(b) and (c).

(4) *Expedited Schedule.* If necessary to comply with its expedited schedule for Rule 16(b) conferences, a court may by local rule:

(A) require the parties' conference to occur less than 21 days before the scheduling conference is held or a scheduling order is due under Rule 16(b); and

(B) require the written report outlining the discovery plan to be filed less than 14 days after the parties' conference, or excuse the parties from submitting a written report and permit them to report orally on their discovery plan at the Rule 16(b) conference.

(g) Signing Disclosures and Discovery Requests, Responses, and Objections.

(1) *Signature Required; Effect of Signature.* Every disclosure under Rule 26(a)(1) or (a)(3) and every discovery request, response, or objection must be signed by at least one attorney of record in the attorney's own name—or by the party personally, if unrepresented—and must state the signer's address, e-mail address, and telephone number. By signing, an attorney or party certifies that to the best of the person's knowledge, information, and belief formed after a reasonable inquiry:

(A) with respect to a disclosure, it is complete and correct as of the time it is made; and

(B) with respect to a discovery request, response, or objection, it is:

(i) consistent with these rules and warranted by existing law or by a nonfrivolous argument for extending, modifying, or reversing existing law, or for establishing new law;

(ii) not interposed for any improper purpose, such as to harass, cause unnecessary delay, or needlessly increase the cost of litigation; and

(iii) neither unreasonable nor unduly burdensome or expensive, considering the needs of the case, prior discovery in the case, the amount in controversy, and the importance of the issues at stake in the action.

(2) *Failure to Sign.* Other parties have no duty to act on an unsigned disclosure, request, response, or objection until it is signed, and the court must strike it unless a signature is promptly supplied after the omission is called to the attorney's or party's attention.

(3) *Sanction for Improper Certification.* If a certification violates this rule without substantial justification, the court, on motion or on its own, must impose an appropriate sanction on the signer, the party on whose behalf the signer was acting, or both. The sanction may include an order to pay the reasonable expenses, including attorney's fees, caused by the violation.

Rule 37. Failure to Make Disclosures or to Cooperate in Discovery; Sanctions

(As amended, effective December 1, 2015)

(a) Motion for an Order Compelling Disclosure or Discovery.

(1) *In General.* On notice to other parties and all affected persons, a party may move for an order compelling disclosure or discovery. The motion must include a certification that the movant has in good faith conferred or attempted to confer with the person or party failing to make disclosure or discovery in an effort to obtain it without court action.

(2) *Appropriate Court.* A motion for an order to a party must be made in the court where the action is pending. A motion for an order to a nonparty must be made in the court where the discovery is or will be taken.

(3) *Specific Motions.*

(A) *To Compel Disclosure.* If a party fails to make a disclosure required by Rule 26(a), any other party may move to compel disclosure and for appropriate sanctions.

(B) *To Compel a Discovery Response.* A party seeking discovery may move for an order compelling an answer, designation, production, or inspection. This motion may be made if:

(i)   a deponent fails to answer a question asked under Rule 30 or 31;

(ii)   a corporation or other entity fails to make a designation under Rule 30(b)(6) or 31(a)(4);

(iii)   a party fails to answer an interrogatory submitted under Rule 33; or

(iv)   a party fails to produce documents or fails to respond that inspection will be permitted—or fails to permit inspection—as requested under Rule 34.

(C) *Related to a Deposition.* When taking an oral deposition, the party asking a question may complete or adjourn the examination before moving for an order.

(4) *Evasive or Incomplete Disclosure, Answer, or Response.* For purposes of this subdivision (a), an evasive or incomplete disclosure, answer, or response must be treated as a failure to disclose, answer, or respond.

(5) *Payment of Expenses; Protective Orders.*

(A) *If the Motion Is Granted (or Disclosure or Discovery Is Provided After Filing).* If the motion is granted—or if the disclosure or requested discovery is provided after the motion was filed—the court must, after giving an opportunity to be heard, require the party or deponent whose conduct necessitated the motion, the party or attorney advising that conduct, or both to pay the movant's reasonable expenses in-

Federal Rules
and Standards
(Selected)

601

curred in making the motion, including attorney's fees. But the court must not order this payment if:

(i)   the movant filed the motion before attempting in good faith to obtain the disclosure or discovery without court action;

(ii)   the opposing party's nondisclosure, response, or objection was substantially justified; or

(iii)   other circumstances make an award of expenses unjust.

(B) *If the Motion Is Denied.* If the motion is denied, the court may issue any protective order authorized under Rule 26(c) and must, after giving an opportunity to be heard, require the movant, the attorney filing the motion, or both to pay the party or deponent who opposed the motion its reasonable expenses incurred in opposing the motion, including attorney's fees. But the court must not order this payment if the motion was substantially justified or other circumstances make an award of expenses unjust.

(C) *If the Motion Is Granted in Part and Denied in Part.* If the motion is granted in part and denied in part, the court may issue any protective order authorized under Rule 26(c) and may, after giving an opportunity to be heard, apportion the reasonable expenses for the motion.

(b) Failure to Comply with a Court Order.

(1) *Sanctions Sought in the District Where the Deposition Is Taken.* If the court where the discovery is taken orders a deponent to be sworn or to answer a question and the deponent fails to obey, the failure may be treated as contempt of court. If a deposition-related motion is transferred to the court where the action is pending, and that court orders a deponent to be sworn or to answer a question and the deponent fails to obey, the failure may be treated as contempt of either the court where the discovery is taken or the court where the action is pending.

(2) *Sanctions Sought in the District Where the Action Is Pending.*

(A) *For Not Obeying a Discovery Order.* If a party or a party's officer, director, or managing agent—or a witness designated under Rule 30(b)(6) or 31(a)(4)—fails to obey an order to provide or permit discovery, including an order under Rule 26(f), 35, or 37(a), the court where the action is pending may issue further just orders. They may include the following:

(i)   directing that the matters embraced in the order or other designated facts be taken as established for purposes of the action, as the prevailing party claims;

(ii)   prohibiting the disobedient party from supporting or opposing designated claims or defenses, or from introducing designated matters in evidence;

(iii) striking pleadings in whole or in part;

(iv) staying further proceedings until the order is obeyed;

(v) dismissing the action or proceeding in whole or in part;

(vi) rendering a default judgment against the disobedient party; or

(vii) treating as contempt of court the failure to obey any order except an order to submit to a physical or mental examination.

(B) *For Not Producing a Person for Examination.* If a party fails to comply with an order under Rule 35(a) requiring it to produce another person for examination, the court may issue any of the orders listed in Rule 37(b)(2)(A)(i)-(vi), unless the disobedient party shows that it cannot produce the other person.

(C) *Payment of Expenses.* Instead of or in addition to the orders above, the court must order the disobedient party, the attorney advising that party, or both to pay the reasonable expenses, including attorney's fees, caused by the failure, unless the failure was substantially justified or other circumstances make an award of expenses unjust.

(c) **Failure to Disclose, to Supplement an Earlier Response, or to Admit.**

(1) *Failure to Disclose or Supplement.* If a party fails to provide information or identify a witness as required by Rule 26(a) or (e), the party is not allowed to use that information or witness to supply evidence on a motion, at a hearing, or at a trial, unless the failure was substantially justified or is harmless. In addition to or instead of this sanction, the court, on motion and after giving an opportunity to be heard:

(A) may order payment of the reasonable expenses, including attorney's fees, caused by the failure;

(B) may inform the jury of the party's failure; and

(C) may impose other appropriate sanctions, including any of the orders listed in Rule 37(b)(2)(A)(i)-(vi).

(2) *Failure to Admit.* If a party fails to admit what is requested under Rule 36 and if the requesting party later proves a document to be genuine or the matter true, the requesting party may move that the party who failed to admit pay the reasonable expenses, including attorney's fees, incurred in making that proof. The court must so order unless:

(A) the request was held objectionable under Rule 36(a);

(B) the admission sought was of no substantial importance;

(C) the party failing to admit had a reasonable ground to believe that it might prevail on the matter; or

(D) there was other good reason for the failure to admit.

Federal Rules and Standards (Selected)

(d) Party's Failure to Attend Its Own Deposition, Serve Answers to Interrogatories, or Respond to a Request for Inspection.

(1) *In General.*

(A) *Motion; Grounds for Sanctions.* The court where the action is pending may, on motion, order sanctions if:

(i) a party or a party's officer, director, or managing agent—or a person designated under Rule 30(b)(6) or 31(a)(4)—fails, after being served with proper notice, to appear for that person's deposition; or

(ii) a party, after being properly served with interrogatories under Rule 33 or a request for inspection under Rule 34, fails to serve its answers, objections, or written response.

(B) *Certification.* A motion for sanctions for failing to answer or respond must include a certification that the movant has in good faith conferred or attempted to confer with the party failing to act in an effort to obtain the answer or response without court action.

(2) *Unacceptable Excuse for Failing to Act.* A failure described in Rule 37(d)(1)(A) is not excused on the ground that the discovery sought was objectionable, unless the party failing to act has a pending motion for a protective order under Rule 26(c).

(3) *Types of Sanctions.* Sanctions may include any of the orders listed in Rule 37(b)(2)(A)(i)-(vi). Instead of or in addition to these sanctions, the court must require the party failing to act, the attorney advising that party, or both to pay the reasonable expenses, including attorney's fees, caused by the failure, unless the failure was substantially justified or other circumstances make an award of expenses unjust.

(e) Failure to Preserve Electronically Stored Information. If electronically stored information that should have been preserved in the anticipation or conduct of litigation is lost because a party failed to take reasonable steps to preserve it, and it cannot be restored or replaced through additional discovery, the court:

(1) upon finding prejudice to another party from loss of the information, may order measures no greater than necessary to cure the prejudice; or

(2) only upon finding that the party acted with the intent to deprive another party of the information's use in the litigation may:

(A) presume that the lost information was unfavorable to the party;

(B) instruct the jury that it may or must presume the information was unfavorable to the party; or

(C) dismiss the action or enter a default judgment.

Federal Rules and Standards (Selected)

(f) Failure to Participate in Framing a Discovery Plan. If a party or its attorney fails to participate in good faith in developing and submitting a proposed discovery plan as required by Rule 26(f), the court may, after giving an opportunity to be heard, require that party or attorney to pay to any other party the reasonable expenses, including attorney's fees, caused by the failure.

Federal Rules of Appellate Procedure

[Effective December 1, 1998]

Rule 38. Frivolous Appeal—Damages and Costs

If a court of appeals determines that an appeal is frivolous, it may, after a separately filed motion or notice from the court and reasonable opportunity to respond, award just damages and single or double costs to the appellee.

Rule 46. Attorneys

(a) Admission to the Bar.

(1) *Eligibility.* An attorney is eligible for admission to the bar of a court of appeals if that attorney is of good moral and professional character and is admitted to practice before the Supreme Court of the United States, the highest court of a state, another United States court of appeals, or a United States district court (including the district courts for Guam, the Northern Mariana Islands, and the Virgin Islands).

(2) *Application.* An applicant must file an application for admission, on a form approved by the court that contains the applicant's personal statement showing eligibility for membership. The applicant must subscribe to the following oath or affirmation: "I, _____, do solemnly swear [or affirm] that I will conduct myself as an attorney and counselor of this court, uprightly and according to law; and that I will support the Constitution of the United States."

(3) *Admission Procedures.* On written or oral motion of a member of the court's bar, the court will act on the application. An applicant may be admitted by oral motion in open court. But, unless the court orders otherwise, an applicant need not appear before the court to be admitted. Upon admission, an applicant must pay the clerk the fee prescribed by local rule or court order.

(b) Suspension or Disbarment.

(1) *Standard.* A member of the court's bar is subject to suspension or disbarment by the court if the member:

(A) has been suspended or disbarred from practice in any other court; or

(B) is guilty of conduct unbecoming a member of the court's bar.

(2) *Procedure.* The member must be given an opportunity to show good cause, within the time prescribed by the court, why the member should not be suspended or disbarred.

(3) *Order.* The court must enter an appropriate order after the member responds and a hearing is held, if requested, or after the time prescribed for a response expires, if no response is made.

(c) Discipline. A court of appeals may discipline an attorney who practices before it for conduct unbecoming a member of the bar or for failure to comply with any court rule. First, however, the court must afford the attorney reasonable notice, an opportunity to show cause to the contrary, and, if requested, a hearing.

Federal Rules of Evidence

Rule 502. Attorney-Client Privilege and Work Product; Limitations on Waiver

The following provisions apply, in the circumstances set out, to disclosure of a communication or information covered by the attorney-client privilege or work-product protection.

(a) DISCLOSURE MADE IN A FEDERAL PROCEEDING OR TO A FEDERAL OFFICE OR AGENCY; SCOPE OF A WAIVER. When the disclosure is made in a federal proceeding or to a federal office or agency and waives the attorney-client privilege or work-product protection, the waiver extends to an undisclosed communication or information in a federal or state proceeding only if:

(1) the waiver is intentional;

(2) the disclosed and undisclosed communications or information concern the same subject matter; and

(3) they ought in fairness to be considered together.

(b) INADVERTENT DISCLOSURE. When made in a federal proceeding or to a federal office or agency, the disclosure does not operate as a waiver in a federal or state proceeding if:

(1) the disclosure is inadvertent;

(2) the holder of the privilege or protection took reasonable steps to prevent disclosure; and

(3) the holder promptly took reasonable steps to rectify the error, including (if applicable) following Federal Rule of Civil Procedure 26(b)(5)(B).

(c) DISCLOSURE MADE IN A STATE PROCEEDING. When the disclosure is made in a state proceeding and is not the subject of a state-court order concerning waiver, the disclosure does not operate as a waiver in a federal proceeding if the disclosure:

(1) would not be a waiver under this rule if it had been made in a federal proceeding; or

(2) is not a waiver under the law of the state where the disclosure occurred.

(d) CONTROLLING EFFECT OF A COURT ORDER. A federal court may order that the privilege or protection is not waived by disclosure connected with the litigation pending before the court—in which event the disclosure is also not a waiver in any other federal or state proceeding.

(e) CONTROLLING EFFECT OF A PARTY AGREEMENT. An agreement on the effect of disclosure in a federal proceeding is binding only on the parties to the agreement, unless it is incorporated into a court order.

(f) CONTROLLING EFFECT OF THIS RULE. Notwithstanding Rules 101 and 1101, this rule applies to state proceedings and to federal court-annexed and federal court-mandated arbitration proceedings, in the circumstances set out in the rule. And notwithstanding Rule 501, this rule applies even if state law provides the rule of decision.

(g) DEFINITIONS. In this rule:
　　(1) "attorney-client privilege" means the protection that applicable law provides for confidential attorney-client communications; and
　　(2) "work-product protection" means the protection that applicable law provides for tangible material (or its intangible equivalent) prepared in anticipation of litigation or for trial.

Added Sept. 19, 2008, eff. Sept. 19, 2008, amended Apr. 26, 2011, eff. Dec. 1, 2011.

Explanatory Note on Evidence Rule 502
Prepared by the Judicial Conference Advisory Committee
on Evidence Rules (Revised 11/28/2007)

This new rule has two major purposes:

1) It resolves some longstanding disputes in the courts about the effect of certain disclosures of communications or information protected by the attorney-client privilege or as work product—specifically those disputes involving inadvertent disclosure and subject matter waiver.

2) It responds to the widespread complaint that litigation costs necessary to protect against waiver of attorney-client privilege or work product have become prohibitive due to the concern that any disclosure (however innocent or minimal) will operate as a subject matter waiver of all protected communications or information. This concern is especially troubling in cases involving electronic discovery. See, e.g., Hopson v. City of Baltimore, 232 F.R.D. 228, 244 (D.Md. 2005) (electronic discovery may encompass "millions of documents" and to insist upon "record-by-record pre-production privilege review, on pain of subject matter waiver, would impose upon parties costs of production that bear no proportionality to what is at stake in the litigation").

The rule seeks to provide a predictable, uniform set of standards under which parties can determine the consequences of a disclosure of a communication or information covered by the attorney-client privilege or work-product protection. Parties to litigation need to know, for example, that if they exchange privileged information pursuant to a confidentiality order, the court's order will be enforceable. Moreover, if a federal court's confidentiality order is not enforceable in a state court then the burdensome costs of privilege review and retention are unlikely to be reduced.

The rule makes no attempt to alter federal or state law on whether a communication or information is protected under the attorney-client privilege or work-product immunity as an initial matter. Moreover, while establishing some exceptions to waiver, the rule does not purport to supplant applicable waiver doctrine generally.

The rule governs only certain waivers by disclosure. Other common-law waiver doctrines may result in a finding of waiver even where there is no disclosure of privileged information or work product. See, e.g., Nguyen v. Excel Corp., 197 F.3d 200 (5th Cir. 1999) (reliance on an advice of counsel defense waives the privilege with respect to attorney-client communications pertinent to that defense); Ryers v. Burleson, 100 F.R.D. 436 (D.D.C. 1983) (allegation of lawyer malpractice constituted a waiver of confidential communications under the circumstances). The rule is not intended to displace or modify federal common law concerning waiver of privilege or work product where no disclosure has been made.

Subdivision (a). The rule provides that a voluntary disclosure in a federal proceeding or to a federal office or agency, if a waiver, generally results in a waiver only of the communication or information disclosed; a subject matter waiver (of either privilege or work product) is reserved for those unusual situations in which fairness requires a further disclosure of related, protected information, in order to prevent a selective and misleading presentation of evidence to the disadvantage of the adversary. See, e.g., In re United Mine Workers of America Employee Benefit Plans Litig., 159 F.R.D. 307, 312 (D.D.C. 1994) (waiver of work product limited to materials actually disclosed, because the party did not deliberately disclose documents in an attempt to gain a tactical advantage). Thus, subject matter waiver is limited to situations in which a party intentionally puts protected information into the litigation in a selective, misleading and unfair manner. It follows that an inadvertent disclosure of protected information can never result in a subject matter waiver. See Rule 502(b). The rule rejects the result in In re Sealed Case, 877 F.2d 976 (D.C.Cir. 1989), which held that inadvertent disclosure of documents during discovery automatically constituted a subject matter waiver.

Federal Rules and Standards (Selected)

The language concerning subject matter waiver—"ought in fairness"—is taken from Rule 106, because the animating principle is the same. Under both Rules, a party that makes a selective, misleading presentation that is unfair to the adversary opens itself to a more complete and accurate presentation.

To assure protection and predictability, the rule provides that if a disclosure is made at the federal level, the federal rule on subject matter waiver governs subsequent state court determinations on the scope of the waiver by that disclosure.

Subdivision (b). Courts are in conflict over whether an inadvertent disclosure of a communication or information protected as privileged or work product constitutes a waiver. A few courts find that a disclosure must be intentional to be a waiver. Most courts find a waiver only if the disclosing party acted carelessly in disclosing the communication or information and failed to request its return in a timely manner. And a few courts hold that any inadvertent disclosure of a communication or information protected under the attorney-client privilege or as work product constitutes a waiver without regard to the protections taken to avoid such a disclosure. See generally Hopson v. City of Baltimore, 232 F.R.D. 228 (D.Md. 2005), for a discussion of this case law.

The rule opts for the middle ground: inadvertent disclosure of protected communications or information in connection with a federal proceeding or to a federal office or agency does not constitute a waiver if the holder took reasonable steps to prevent disclosure and also promptly took reasonable steps to rectify the error. This position is in accord with the majority view on whether inadvertent disclosure is a waiver.

Cases such as Lois Sportswear, U.S.A., Inc. v. Levi Strauss & Co., 104 103, 105 (S.D.N.Y. 1985) and Hartford Fire Ins. Co. v. Garvey, 109 323, 332 (N.D.Cal. 1985), set out a multifactor test for determining whether inadvertent disclosure is a waiver. The stated factors (none of which is dispositive) are the reasonableness of precautions taken, the time taken to rectify the error, the scope of discovery, the extent of disclosure and the overriding issue of fairness. The rule does not explicitly codify that test, because it is really a set of non-determinative guidelines that vary from case to case. The rule is flexible enough to accommodate any of those listed factors. Other considerations bearing on the reasonableness of a producing party's efforts include the number of documents to be reviewed and the time constraints for production. Depending on the circumstances, a party that uses advanced analytical software applications and linguistic tools in screening for privilege and work product may be found to have taken "reasonable steps" to prevent

Federal Rules and Standards (Selected)

inadvertent disclosure. The implementation of an efficient system of records management before litigation may also be relevant.

The rule does not require the producing party to engage in a postproduction review to determine whether any protected communication or information has been produced by mistake. But the rule does require the producing party to follow up on any obvious indications that a protected communication or information has been produced inadvertently.

The rule applies to inadvertent disclosures made to a federal office or agency, including but not limited to an office or agency that is acting in the course of its regulatory, investigative or enforcement authority. The consequences of waiver, and the concomitant costs of pre-production privilege review, can be as great with respect to disclosures to offices and agencies as they are in litigation.

Subdivision (c). Difficult questions can arise when 1) a disclosure of a communication or information protected by the attorney-client privilege or as work product is made in a state proceeding, 2) the communication or information is offered in a subsequent federal proceeding on the ground that the disclosure waived the privilege or protection, and 3) the state and federal laws are in conflict on the question of waiver. The Committee determined that the proper solution for the federal court is to apply the law that is most protective of privilege and work product. If the state law is more protective (such as where the state law is that an inadvertent disclosure can never be a waiver), the holder of the privilege or protection may well have relied on that law when making the disclosure in the state proceeding. Moreover, applying a more restrictive federal law of waiver could impair the state objective of preserving the privilege or work-product protection for disclosures made in state proceedings. On the other hand, if the federal law is more protective, applying the state law of waiver to determine admissibility in federal court is likely to undermine the federal objective of limiting the costs of production.

The rule does not address the enforceability of a state court confidentiality order in a federal proceeding, as that question is covered both by statutory law and principles of federalism and comity. See 28 U.S.C. § 1738 (providing that state judicial proceedings "shall have the same full faith and credit in every court within the United States . . . as they have by law or usage in the courts of such State . . . from which they are taken"). See also Tucker v. Ohtsu Tire & Rubber Co., 191 F.R.D. 495, 499 (D.Md. 2000) (noting that a federal court considering the enforceability of a state confidentiality order is "constrained by principles of comity, courtesy, and . . . federalism"). Thus, a state court order finding no waiver in connection with a disclosure made in a state court proceeding is enforceable under existing law in subsequent federal proceedings.

Subdivision (d). Confidentiality orders are becoming increasingly important in limiting the costs of privilege review and retention, especially in cases involving electronic discovery. But the utility of a confidentiality order in reducing discovery costs is substantially diminished if it provides no protection outside the particular litigation in which the order is entered. Parties are unlikely to be able to reduce the costs of pre-production review for privilege and work product if the consequence of disclosure is that the communications or information could be used by non-parties to the litigation.

There is some dispute on whether a confidentiality order entered in one case is enforceable in other proceedings. See generally Hopson v. City of Baltimore, 232 F.R.D. 228 (D.Md. 2005), for a discussion of this case law. The rule provides that when a confidentiality order governing the consequences of disclosure in that case is entered in a federal proceeding, its terms are enforceable against non-parties in any federal or state proceeding. For example, the court order may provide for return of documents without waiver irrespective of the care taken by the disclosing party; the rule contemplates enforcement of "claw-back" and "quick peek" arrangements as a way to avoid the excessive costs of pre-production review for privilege and work product. See Zubulake v. UBS Warburg LLC, 216 F.R.D. 280, 290 (S.D.N.Y. 2003) (noting that parties may enter into "so-called 'claw-back' agreements that allow the parties to forego privilege review altogether in favor of an agreement to return inadvertently produced privilege documents"). The rule provides a party with a predictable protection from a court order—predictability that is needed to allow the party to plan in advance to limit the prohibitive costs of privilege and work product review and retention.

Under the rule, a confidentiality order is enforceable whether or not it memorializes an agreement among the parties to the litigation. Party agreement should not be a condition of enforceability of a federal court's order.

Under subdivision (d), a federal court may order that disclosure of privileged or protected information "in connection with" a federal proceeding does not result in waiver. But subdivision (d) does not allow the federal court to enter an order determining the waiver effects of a separate disclosure of the same information in other proceedings, state or federal. If a disclosure has been made in a state proceeding (and is not the subject of a state-court order on waiver), then subdivision (d) is inapplicable. Subdivision (c) would govern the federal court's determination whether the state-court disclosure waived the privilege or protection in the federal proceeding.

Subdivision (e). Subdivision (e) codifies the well-established proposition that parties can enter an agreement to limit the effect of waiver by disclosure between or among them. Of course such an agreement can bind only the parties to the agreement. The rule makes clear that if parties want protection against non-parties from a finding of waiver by disclosure, the agreement must be made part of a court order.

Subdivision (f). The protections against waiver provided by Rule 502 must be applicable when protected communications or information disclosed in federal proceedings are subsequently offered in state proceedings. Otherwise the holders of protected communications and information, and their lawyers, could not rely on the protections provided by the Rule, and the goal of limiting costs in discovery would be substantially undermined. Rule 502(f) is intended to resolve any potential tension between the provisions of Rule 502 that apply to state proceedings and the possible limitations on the applicability of the Federal Rules of Evidence otherwise provided by Rules 101 and 1101.

The rule is intended to apply in all federal court proceedings, including court-annexed and court-ordered arbitrations, without regard to any possible limitations of Rules 101 and 1101. This provision is not intended to raise an inference about the applicability of any other rule of evidence in arbitration proceedings more generally.

The costs of discovery can be equally high for state and federal causes of action, and the rule seeks to limit those costs in all federal proceedings, regardless of whether the claim arises under state or federal law. Accordingly, the rule applies to state law causes of action brought in federal court.

Subdivision (g). The rule's coverage is limited to attorneyclient privilege and work product. The operation of waiver by disclosure, as applied to other evidentiary privileges, remains a question of federal common law. Nor does the rule purport to apply to the Fifth Amendment privilege against compelled selfincrimination. The definition of work product "materials" is intended to include both tangible and intangible information. See In re Cendant Corp. Sec. Litig., 343 F.3d 658, 662 (3d Cir. 2003) ("work product protection extends to both tangible and intangible work product").

Federal Rules
and Standards
(Selected)

ABA Formal Ethics Opinions (Selected)

ABA Formal
Ethics Opinions
(Selected)

Formal Opinion 93-379   December 6, 1993
Billing for Professional Fees,
Disbursements and Other Expenses

*Consistent with the Model Rules of Professional Conduct, a lawyer must dis-
close to a client the basis on which the client is to be billed for both professional
time and any other charges. Absent a contrary understanding, any invoice for
professional services should fairly reflect the basis on which the client's charges
have been determined. In matters where the client has agreed to have the fee
determined with reference to the time expended by the lawyer, a lawyer may
not bill more time than she actually spends on a matter, except to the extent
that she rounds up to minimum time periods (such as one-quarter or one-tenth
of an hour). A lawyer may not charge a client for overhead expenses generally
associated with properly maintaining, staffing and equipping an office; however, the lawyer may recoup expenses reasonably incurred in connection with
the client's matter for services performed in-house, such as photocopying, long
distance telephone calls, computer research, special deliveries, secretarial over-
time, and other similar services, so long as the charge reasonably reflects the
lawyer's actual cost for the services rendered. A lawyer may not charge a client
more than her disbursements for services provided by third parties like court
reporters, travel agents or expert witnesses, except to the extent that the lawyer incurs costs additional to the direct cost of the third-party services.*

The legal profession has dedicated a substantial amount of time and energy to
developing elaborate sets of ethical guidelines for the benefit of its clients. Similarly, the profession has spent extraordinary resources on interpreting, teaching
and enforcing these ethics rules. Yet, ironically, lawyers are not generally regarded by the public as particularly ethical. One major contributing factor to
the discouraging public opinion of the legal profession appears to be the billing
practices of some of its members.

It is a common perception that pressure on lawyers to bill a minimum number of hours and on law firms to maintain or improve profits may have led some
lawyers to engage in problematic billing practices. These include charges to
more than one client for the same work or the same hours, surcharges on services contracted with outside vendors, and charges beyond reasonable costs
for in-house services like photocopying and computer searches. Moreover, the
bases on which these charges are to be assessed often are not disclosed in advance or are disguised in cryptic invoices so that the client does not fully understand exactly what costs are being charged to him.

The Model Rules of Professional Conduct provide important principles applicable to the billing of clients, principles which, if followed, would ameliorate many
of the problems noted above. The Committee has decided to address several practices that are the subject of frequent inquiry, with the goal of helping the profession
adhere to its ethical obligations to its clients despite economic pressures.

The first set of practices involves billing more than one client for the same hours spent. In one illustrative situation, a lawyer finds it possible to schedule court appearances for three clients on the same day. He spends a total of four hours at the courthouse, the amount of time he would have spent on behalf of each client had it not been for the fortuitous circumstance that all three cases were scheduled on the same day. May he bill each of the three clients, who otherwise understand that they will be billed on the basis of time spent, for the four hours he spent on them collectively? In another scenario, a lawyer is flying cross-country to attend a deposition on behalf of one client, expending travel time she would ordinarily bill to that client. If she decides not to watch the movie or read her novel, but to work instead on drafting a motion for another client, may she charge both clients, each of whom agreed to hourly billing, for the time during which she was traveling on behalf of one and drafting a document on behalf of the other? A third situation involves research on a particular topic for one client that later turns out to be relevant to an inquiry from a second client. May the firm bill the second client, who agreed to be charged on the basis of time spent on his case, the same amount for the recycled work product that it charged the first client?

The second set of practices involves billing for expenses and disbursements, and is exemplified by the situation in which a firm contracts for the expert witness services of an economist at an hourly rate of $200. May the firm bill the client for the expert's time at the rate of $250 per hour? Similarly, may the firm add a surcharge to the cost of computer-assisted research if the per-minute total charged by the computer company does not include the cost of purchasing the computers or staffing their operation?

The questions presented to the Committee require us to determine what constitute reasonable billing procedures; that is, what are the services and costs for which a lawyer may legitimately charge, both generally and with regard to the specific scenarios? This inquiry requires an elucidation of the Rule of Professional Conduct 1.5,[1] and the Model Code of Professional Responsibility DR 2-106.[2]

ABA Formal
Ethics Opinions
(Selected)

---

1. Rule 1.5 states in relevant part:
    (a) A lawyer's fee shall be reasonable. The factors to be considered in determining the reasonableness of a fee include the following:
    (1) the time and labor required, the novelty and difficulty of the questions involved, and the skill requisite to perform the legal service properly;
    (2) the likelihood, if apparent to the client, that the acceptance of the particular employment will preclude other employment by the lawyer;
    (3) the fee customarily charged in the locality for similar legal services;
    (4) the amount involved and the results obtained;
    (5) the time limitations imposed by the client or by the circumstances;
    (6) the nature and length of the professional relationship with the client;
    (7) the experience, reputation, and ability of the lawyer or lawyers performing the services; and
    (8) whether the fee is fixed or contingent.

Disclosure of the Bases of the Amounts to Be Charged

At the outset of the representation the lawyer should make disclosure of the basis for the fee and any other charges to the client. This is a two-fold duty, including not only an explanation at the beginning of engagement of the basis on which fees and other charges will be billed, but also a sufficient explanation in the statement so that the client may reasonably be expected to understand what fees and other charges the client is actually being billed.

Authority for the obligation to make disclosure at the beginning of a representation is found in the interplay among a number of rules. Rule 1.5(b) provides that

When the lawyer has not regularly represented the client, the basis or rate of the fee shall be communicated to the client, preferably in writing, before or within a reasonable time after commencing the representation.

The Comment to Rule 1.5 gives guidance on how to execute the duty to communicate the basis of the fee:

In a new client-lawyer relationship . . . an understanding as to the fee should be promptly established. It is not necessary to recite all the factors that underlie the basis of the fee, but only those that are directly involved in its computation. It is sufficient, for example, to state that the basic rate is an hourly charge or a fixed amount or an estimated amount, or to identify the factors that may be taken into account in finally fixing the fee. When developments occur during the representation that render an earlier estimate substantially inaccurate, a revised estimate should be provided to the client. A written statement concerning the fee reduces the possibility of misunderstanding. Furnishing the client with a simple memorandum or a copy of the lawyer's customary fee schedule is sufficient if the basis or rate of the fee is set forth.

This obligation is reinforced by reference to Model Rule 1.4(b) which provides that

A lawyer shall explain a matter to the extent reasonably necessary to permit the client to make informed decisions regarding the representation.

While the Comment to this Rule suggests its obvious applicability to negotiations or litigation with adverse parties, its important principle should be equally applicable to the lawyer's obligation to explain the basis on which the lawyer expects to be compensated, so the client can make one of the more important decisions "regarding the representation."

ABA Formal
Ethics Opinions
(Selected)

(b) When the lawyer has not regularly represented the client, the basis or rate of the fee shall be communicated to the client, preferably in writing, before or within a reasonable time after commencing the representation.

2. DR 2-106 contains substantially the same factors listed in Rule 1.5 to determine reasonableness, but does not require that the basis of the fee be communicated to the client "preferably in writing" as Rule 1.5 does.

An obligation of disclosure is also supported by Model Rule 7.1, which addresses communications concerning a lawyer's services, including the basis on which fees would be charged. The rule provides:

A lawyer shall not make a false or misleading communication about the lawyer or the lawyer's services. A communication is false or misleading if it:

(a) contains a material misrepresentation of fact or law, or omits a fact necessary to make the statement considered as a whole not materially misleading.

It is clear under Model Rule 7.1 that in offering to perform services for prospective clients it is critical that lawyers avoid making any statements about fees that are not complete. If it is true that a lawyer when advertising for new clients must disclose, for example, that costs are the responsibility of the client, Zauderer v. Office of Disciplinary Counsel, 471 U.S. 626 (1985), it necessarily follows that in entering into an actual client relationship a lawyer must make fair disclosure of the basis on which fees will be assessed.

A corollary of the obligation to disclose the basis for future billing is a duty to render statements to the client that adequately apprise the client as to how that basis for billing has been applied. In an engagement in which the client has agreed to compensate the lawyer on the basis of time expended at regular hourly rates, a bill setting out no more than a total dollar figure for unidentified professional services will often be insufficient to tell the client what he or she needs to know in order to understand how the amount was determined. By the same token, billing other charges without breaking the charges down by type would not provide the client with the information the client needs to understand the basis for the charges.

Initial disclosure of the basis for the fee arrangement fosters communication that will promote the attorney-client relationship. The relationship will be similarly benefitted if the statement for services explicitly reflects the basis for the charges so that the client understands how the fee bill was determined.

Professional Obligations Regarding the Reasonableness of Fees

Implicit in the Model Rules and their antecedents is the notion that the attorney-client relationship is not necessarily one of equals, that it is built on trust, and that the client is encouraged to be dependent on the lawyer, who is dealing with matters of great moment to the client. The client should only be charged a reasonable fee for the legal services performed. Rule 1.5 explicitly addresses the reasonableness of legal fees. The rule deals not only with the determination of a reasonable hourly rate, but also with total cost to the client. The Comment to the rule states, for example, that "[a] lawyer should not exploit a fee arrangement based primarily on hourly charges by using wasteful procedures." The goal should be solely to compensate the lawyer fully for time reasonably expended, an approach that if followed will not take advantage of the client.

ABA Formal
Ethics Opinions
(Selected)

Ethical Consideration 2-17 of the Model Code of Professional Responsibility provides a framework for balancing the interests between the lawyer and client in determining the reasonableness of a fee arrangement:

> The determination of a proper fee requires consideration of the interests of both client and lawyer. A lawyer should not charge more than a reasonable fee, for excessive cost of legal service would deter laymen from utilizing the legal system in protection of their rights. Furthermore, an excessive charge abuses the professional relationship between lawyer and client. On the other hand, adequate compensation is necessary in order to enable the lawyer to serve his client effectively and to preserve the integrity and independence of the profession.

The lawyer's conduct should be such as to promote the client's trust of the lawyer and of the legal profession. This means acting as the advocate for the client to the extent necessary to complete a project thoroughly. Only through careful attention to detail is the lawyer able to manage a client's case properly. An unreasonable limitation on the hours a lawyer may spend on a client should be avoided as a threat to the lawyer's ability to fulfill her obligation under Model Rule 1.1 to "provide competent representation to a client." Competent representation requires the legal knowledge, skill, thoroughness and preparation necessary for the representation." Model Rule 1.1. Certainly either a willingness on the part of the lawyer, or a demand by the client, to circumscribe the lawyer's efforts, to compromise the lawyer's ability to be as thorough and as prepared as necessary, is not in the best interests of the client and may lead to a violation of Model Rule 1.1 if it means the lawyer is unable to provide competent representation. The Comment to Model Rule 1.2, while observing that "the scope of services provided by a lawyer may be limited by agreement," also notes that an agreement "concerning the scope of representation must accord with the Rules.... Thus, the client may not be asked to agree to representation so limited in scope as to violate Rule 1.1. ...." [3]

On the other hand, the lawyer who has agreed to bill on the basis of hours expended does not fulfill her ethical duty if she bills the client for more time than she actually spent on the client's behalf.[4] In addressing the hypotheticals regarding (a) simultaneous appearance on behalf of three clients, (b) the airplane flight on behalf of one client while working on another client's matters and (c) recycled work product, it is helpful to consider these questions, not from the perspective

ABA Formal
Ethics Opinions
(Selected)

---

3. Beyond the scope of this opinion is the question whether a lawyer, with full disclo- sure to a sophisticated client of the risks involved, can agree to undertake at the request of the client only ten hours of research, when the lawyer knows that the resulting work product does not fulfill the competent representation requirement of Model Rule 1.1.

4. Rule 1.5 clearly contemplates that there are bases for billing clients other than the time expended. This opinion, however, only addresses issues raised when it is under- stood that the client will be charged on the basis of time expended.

of what a client could be forced to pay, but rather from the perspective of what the lawyer actually earned. A lawyer who spends four hours of time on behalf of three clients has not earned twelve billable hours. A lawyer who flies for six hours for one client, while working for five hours on behalf of another, has not earned eleven billable hours. A lawyer who is able to reuse old work product has not re-earned the hours previously billed and compensated when the work product was first generated. Rather than looking to profit from the fortuity of coincidental scheduling, the desire to get work done rather than watch a movie, or the luck of being asked the identical question twice, the lawyer who has agreed to bill solely on the basis of time spent is obliged to pass the benefits of these economies on to the client. The practice of billing several clients for the same time or work product, since it results in the earning of an unreasonable fee, therefore is contrary to the mandate of the Model Rules. Model Rule 1.5.

Moreover, continuous toil on or overstaffing a project for the purpose of churning out hours is also not properly considered "earning" one's fees. One job of a lawyer is to expedite the legal process. Model Rule 3.2. Just as a lawyer is expected to discharge a matter on summary judgment if possible rather than proceed to trial, so too is the lawyer expected to complete other projects for a client efficiently. A lawyer should take as much time as is reasonably required to complete a project, and should certainly never be motivated by anything other than the best interests of the client when determining how to staff or how much time to spend on any particular project.

It goes without saying that a lawyer who has undertaken to bill on an hourly basis is never justified in charging a client for hours not actually expended. If a lawyer has agreed to charge the client on this basis and it turns out that the lawyer is particularly efficient in accomplishing a given result, it nonetheless will not be permissible to charge the client for more hours than were actually expended on the matter. When that basis for billing the client has been agreed to, the economies associated with the result must inure to the benefit of the client, not give rise to an opportunity to bill a client phantom hours. This is not to say that the lawyer who agreed to hourly compensation is not free, with full disclosure, to suggest additional compensation because of a particularly efficient or outstanding result, or because the lawyer was able to reuse prior work product on the client's behalf. The point here is that fee enhancement cannot be accomplished simply by presenting the client with a statement reflecting more billable hours than were actually expended. On the other hand, if a matter turns out to be more difficult to accomplish than first anticipated and more hours are required than were originally estimated, the lawyer is fully entitled (though not required) to bill those hours unless the client agreement turned the original estimate into a cap on the fees to be charged.

Charges Other Than Professional Fees

In addition to charging clients fees for professional services, lawyers typically charge their clients for certain additional items which are often referred to vari-

ABA Formal Ethics Opinions (Selected)

ously as disbursements, out-of-pocket expenses or additional charges. Inquiries to the Committee demonstrate that the profession has encountered difficulties in conforming to the ethical standards in this area as well. The Rules provide no specific guidance on the issue of how much a lawyer may charge a client for costs incurred over and above her own fee. However, we believe that the reasonableness standard explicitly applicable to fees under Rule 1.5(a) should be applicable to these charges as well.

The Committee, in trying to sort out the issues related to these charges, has identified three different questions which must be addressed. First, which items are properly subject to additional charges? Second, to what extent, if at all, may clients be charged for more than actual out-of-pocket disbursements? Third, on what basis may clients be charged for the provision of in-house services? We shall address these one at a time.

A. General Overhead

When a client has engaged a lawyer to provide professional services for a fee (whether calculated on the basis of the number of hours expended, a flat fee, a contingent percentage of the amount recovered or otherwise) the client would be justifiably disturbed if the lawyer submitted a bill to the client which included, beyond the professional fee, additional charges for general office overhead. In the absence of disclosure to the client in advance of the engagement to the contrary, the client should reasonably expect that the lawyer's cost in maintaining a library, securing malpractice insurance, renting of office space, purchasing utilities and the like would be subsumed within the charges the lawyer is making for professional services.

B. Disbursements

At the beginning of the engagement lawyers typically tell their clients that they will be charged for disbursements. When that term is used clients justifiably should expect that the lawyer will be passing on to the client those actual payments of funds made by the lawyer on the client's behalf. Thus, if the lawyer hires a court stenographer to transcribe a deposition, the client can reasonably expect to be billed as a disbursement the amount the lawyer pays to the court reporting service. Similarly, if the lawyer flies to Los Angeles for the client, the client can reasonably expect to be billed as a disbursement the amount of the airfare, taxicabs, meals and hotel room.

It is the view of the Committee that, in the absence of disclosure to the contrary, it would be improper if the lawyer assessed a surcharge on these disbursements over and above the amount actually incurred unless the lawyer herself incurred additional expenses beyond the actual cost of the disbursement item. In the same regard, if a lawyer receives a discounted rate from a third-party provider, it would be improper if she did not pass along the benefit of the discount to her client rather than charge the client the full rate and reserve the profit to herself. Clients quite properly could view these practices as an attempt to create

ABA Formal
Ethics Opinions
(Selected)

additional undisclosed profit centers when the client had been told he would be billed for disbursements.

C. In-House Provision of Services

Perhaps the most difficult issue is the handling of charges to clients for the provision of in-house services. In this connection the Committee has in view charges for photocopying, computer research, on-site meals, deliveries and other similar items. Like professional fees, it seems clear that lawyers may pass on reasonable charges for these services. Thus, in the view of the Committee, the lawyer and the client may agree in advance that, for example, photocopying will be charged at $.15 per page, or messenger services will be provided at $5.00 per mile. However, the question arises what may be charged to the client, in the absence of a specific agreement to the contrary, when the client has simply been told that costs for these items will be charged to the client. We conclude that under those circumstances the lawyer is obliged to charge the client no more than the direct cost associated with the service (i.e., the actual cost of making a copy on the photocopy machine) plus a reasonable allocation of overhead expenses directly associated with the provision of the service (e.g., the salary of a photocopy machine operator).

It is not appropriate for the Committee, in addressing ethical standards, to opine on the various accounting issues as to how one calculates direct cost and what may or may not be included in allocated overhead. These are questions which properly should be reserved for our colleagues in the accounting profession. Rather, it is the responsibility of the Committee to explain the principles it draws from the mandate of Model Rule 1.5's injunction that fees be reasonable. Any reasonable calculation of direct costs as well as any reasonable allocation of related overhead should pass ethical muster. On the other hand, in the absence of an agreement to the contrary, it is impermissible for a lawyer to create an additional source of profit for the law firm beyond that which is contained in the provision of professional services themselves. The lawyer's stock in trade is the sale of legal services, not photocopy paper, tuna fish sandwiches, computer time or messenger services.

Conclusion

As the foregoing demonstrates, the subject of fees for professional services and other charges is one that is fraught with tension between the lawyer and the client. Nonetheless, if the principles outlined in this opinion are followed, the ethical resolution of these issues can be achieved.

ABA Formal
Ethics Opinions
(Selected)

Formal Opinion 95-390
Conflicts of Interest in the Corporate Family Context

January 25, 1995

*A lawyer who represents a corporate client is not by that fact alone neces-
sarily barred from a representation that is adverse to a corporate affiliate
of that client in an unrelated matter. However, a lawyer may not accept
such a representation without consent of the corporate client if the circumstances are such that the affiliate should also be considered a client of the
lawyer; or if there is an understanding between the lawyer and the corporate client that the lawyer will avoid representations adverse to the client's
corporate affiliates; or if the lawyer's obligations to either the corporate client or the new, adverse client, will materially limit the lawyer's representation of the other client. Even if the circumstances are such that client
consent is not ethically required, as a matter of prudence and good practice
a lawyer who contemplates undertaking a representation adverse to a corporate affiliate of a client will be well advised to discuss the matter with the
client before undertaking the representation.*

The Committee has been asked whether a lawyer who represents a corporate client may undertake a representation that is adverse to a corporate
affiliate of the client in an unrelated matter, without obtaining the client's
consent.

The issue is one that has arisen with increasing frequency because of "[t]
he proliferation of national or multi-national public corporations owning or
partially owning subsidiaries which may also be national or multi-national
[and] the spawning of varied types of corporate affiliates...." Pennwalt
Corp. v. Plough, Inc., (D.Del.1980). Although, in the sense described in Pennwalt, the problem has been "created" by modern corporations, the onus is
squarely on the lawyer to anticipate and resolve conflicts of interest involving corporate affiliates. As stated in the Comment to Rule 1.7 of the Model
Rules of Professional Conduct (1983, amended 1994):

> The lawyer should adopt reasonable procedures, appropriate for
> the size and type of firm and practice, to determine in both litigation
> and non-litigation matters the parties and issues involved and to
> determine whether there are actual or potential conflicts of interest.

In addition to the ethical questions that a lawyer may face in undertaking a representation adverse to an affiliate of an existing corporate client,

the lawyer also faces a potential motion to disqualify. Indeed, these circumstances have been considered most often in the context of such a motion.[1]

Clearly, the best solution to the problems that may arise by reason of clients' corporate affiliations is to have a clear understanding between lawyer and client, at the very start of the representation, as to which entity or entities in the corporate family are to be the lawyer's clients, or are to be so treated for conflicts purposes. This Opinion is principally addressed to those circumstances where there are not such clear governing terms to the engagement. Such circumstances will frequently obtain simply because the relationship with the client is of long standing, antedating the time when letters of engagement came into common use; or because there is a change in the identity or the corporate affiliations of the client, through acquisitions, mergers and the like.

Even in circumstances where there is no established understanding about the lawyer's obligations toward affiliates of the client, considerations of client relations will ordinarily dictate the lawyer's course of action, without the occasion even arising to consider whether the Model Rules forbid the contemplated new representation. Nonetheless, there will sometimes be circumstances where the requirements of the Model Rules rather than considerations of client relations will govern: for example, where by virtue of merger or acquisition the corporate affiliation of the client changes.

It is the Committee's opinion that the Model Rules of Professional Conduct do not prohibit a lawyer from representing a party adverse to a particular corporation merely because the lawyer (or another lawyer in the same firm) represents, in an unrelated matter, another corporation that owns the potentially adverse corporation, or is owned by it, or is, together with the adverse corporation, owned by a third entity.[2] The fact of corporate affili-

ABA Formal Ethics Opinions (Selected)

1. E.g., Vanderveer Group, Inc. v. Petruny, No. Civ.A. 93-3677, 1993 WL 308720 (E.D.Pa. Aug. 13, 1993); Stratagem Dev. Corp. v. Heron Int'l N.V., 756 F.Supp. 789 (S.D.N.Y.1991); Teradyne, Inc. v. Hewlett-Packard Co., 20 U.S.P.Q.2d (BNA) 1143 (N.D.Cal.1991); Gould, Inc. v. Mitsui Mining & Smelting Co., 738 F.Supp. 1121 (N.D.Ohio 1990); Hartford Accident & Indem. Co. v. RJR Nabisco, Inc., 721 F.Supp.534 (S.D.N.Y.1989); Pennwalt Corp. v. Plough, Inc., 85 F.R.D. 264 (D.Del.1980).

2. We here principally address, for simplicity of analysis, situations where the sub- sidiaries in the corporate family are wholly owned by the corporate parent. Corporate affiliations involving lesser degrees of ownership may of course present the same issues, and involve in some degree the same analysis, as those involving whole owner- ship. The circumstance of only partial ownership, however, is a variable that may affect the result in a particular case. E.g., Whiting Corp. v. White Mach. Corp., 567 F.2d 713, 714-15 (7th Cir.1977) (court refused to disqualify counsel where counsel represented both plaintiff and a corporation that owned 20% of the defendant corpora- tion's stock and had the right to elect 40% of its board of directors); see also Vanderveer Group, Inc. v. Petruny, No. Civ.A 93-3677, 1993 WL 308720 (E.D.Pa. Aug. 13, 1993) (a law firm's representation of defendant company's 51%-owned subsidiary does not require the firm's disqualification from representing the plaintiff; the decision does not, however, rely on the degree of ownership).

ation, without more, does not make all of a corporate client's affiliates into clients as well. Nonetheless, the circumstances of a particular representation may be such that the corporate client has a reasonable expectation that the affiliates will be treated as clients, either generally or for purposes of avoidance of conflicts, and the lawyer is aware of the expectation.

In any event, although the ethical propriety of a given representation will depend on the particular circumstances, the Committee believes that as a general matter, in the absence of a clear understanding otherwise, the better course is for a lawyer to obtain the corporate client's consent before the lawyer undertakes a representation adverse to its affiliate.

The Requirements of Rule 1.7

The key provision of the Model Rules is Rule 1.7, which provides in pertinent part as follows:

> (a) A lawyer shall not represent a client if the representation of that client will be directly adverse to another client, unless:
> (1) the lawyer reasonably believes the representation will not adversely affect the relationship with the other client; and
> (2) each client consents after consultation.
> (b) A lawyer shall not represent a client if the representation of that client may be materially limited by the lawyer's responsibilities to another client or to a third person ... unless:
> (1) the lawyer reasonably believes the representation will not be adversely affected; and
> (2) the client consents after consultation.

Rule 1.7 is a rule of general applicability, governing lawyers' conduct whether they represent individuals or entities. The touchstone of the Rule, as the Comment to it makes clear, is loyalty to the client.

When requested to undertake a new representation that may adversely affect the interests of an existing client, a lawyer must first consider Rule 1.7(a). Under that provision, representation of a party "directly adverse to another client" is prohibited unless a lawyer concludes that his relationship with the existing client will not be "adversely affected" by the new representation, and both clients consent. The use of the term "directly adverse" in Rule 1.7(a) clearly differentiates the more general or indirect adverseness which is addressed in paragraph (b) of the Rule, discussed below. The Comment to Rule 1.7 confirms this interpretation of the term "directly," noting that "a lawyer ordinarily may not act as advocate against a person the lawyer represents in some other matter, even if it is wholly unrelated," but "simultaneous representation in unrelated matters of clients whose interests are only generally adverse, such as competing economic enterprises, does not require consent of the respective clients."

Where there is direct adverseness, so that Rule 1.7(a) applies, the lawyer may not take on the new representation unless two tests are met. First, the lawyer must reasonably believe that his new assignment will not adversely affect his relationship with his existing client. The lawyer's subjective judgment is not necessarily dispositive: his belief must be a reasonable one. See Clay v. Doherty, (N.D.Ill.1985); Charles W. Wolfram, Modern Legal Ethics § 7.2.3 (Student ed. 1986).

Second, both clients must consent after "consultation," which means that there has been "communication of information reasonably sufficient to permit the client to appreciate the significance of the matter in question." Model Rules, Terminology.

If the provisions of Rule 1.7(a) do not apply because the affiliate is not a client, the lawyer must nonetheless consider, under Rule 1.7(b), whether either the subsisting representation or the prospective one may be "materially limited by the lawyer's responsibilities to another client or to a third person." Loyalty to a client is impaired not only when a lawyer undertakes a representation directly adverse to the client, but also "when a lawyer cannot consider, recommend or carry out an appropriate course of action for the client because of the lawyer's other responsibilities or interests." Comment to Model Rule 1.7. Where the new representation will be materially limited by the lawyer's responsibilities to an existing client, the new representation is prohibited by Rule 1.7(b) unless the lawyer reasonably believes that the new representation will not be "adversely affected" by the limitations flowing from his duties to another client or third person, and the new client consents. Conversely, the lawyer must also consider under Rule 1.7(b) whether the lawyer's representation of his existing client would be materially limited by his duties to the new client.[3] By its terms, Rule 1.7(b) requires the consent only of the client whose representation may be materially limited by the lawyer's other duties, but the lawyer must consider the effect of the simultaneous representation of two clients on each of them, and obtain consent where required by the Rule.

* * *

The application of these provisions in the circumstances before us can best be addressed in relation to three questions: (1) Is the corporate client's affiliate also a client, or entitled to be so treated for purposes of Rule 1.7? (2) If

---

3. As the Comment makes clear, Rule 1.7 applies not merely to new representa- tions but also to conflicts arising after a representation has commenced.

ABA Formal
Ethics Opinions
(Selected)

the affiliate is not a client, is the representation adverse to the affiliate also "directly adverse" to the corporate client, so as to bring it under Rule 1.7(a)? (3) If Rule 1.7(a) is not applicable, will the lawyer's responsibilities to one or the other client nonetheless materially limit the lawyer's representation so as to bring Rule 1.7(b) into play?

(1) Is the Corporate Client's Affiliate Also a Client?

Since a lawyer owes a duty of loyalty only to the lawyer's client, it is necessary to determine at the outset of analysis whether the affiliate of the lawyer's corporate client is also a client. As explained below, we conclude that the fact of corporate affiliation, without more, does not necessarily make the affiliate of a corporate client also a client. Nonetheless, the particular circumstances may be such that the affiliate also should be considered a client. It may also be the case that the corporate client has an expectation, binding on the lawyer in the circumstances, that its affiliates will be treated as clients for purposes of addressing conflicts under Rule 1.7, even though there is not a full-fledged client-lawyer relationship with the affiliates.

As to whether the fact of corporate affiliation ipso facto creates a client-lawyer relationship with every member of a corporate family when one of its members is formally represented by the lawyer, the Model Rules are silent. It is possible to read the following passage in the Comment to Rule 1.7 as assuming that such a relationship necessarily exists:

> Ordinarily, a lawyer may not act as advocate against a client the lawyer represents in some other matter, even if the other matter is wholly unrelated. However, there are circumstances in which a lawyer may act as advocate against a client. For example, *a lawyer representing an enterprise with diverse operations may accept employment as an advocate against the enterprise in an unrelated matter if doing so will not adversely affect the lawyer's relationship with the enterprise ... and if both clients consent upon consultation.* (Emphasis added.)

The statement that a representation adverse to "an enterprise with diverse operations" requires the consent of both clients may be taken to imply that a lawyer who represents a corporation represents all of its affiliates, since in this context the term "enterprise" can be understood as referring not merely to a corporation with various divisions or product lines but also to a family of corporations. However, the use of "enterprise" in this connection does not refer to a corporate conglomerate; the term is used in the Model Rules, in distinction from "corporation" and "organization," to denote profit-making entities, which may include not only corporations but also partnerships, joint ventures and the like.[4]

Moreover, Rule 1.13 squarely states that when a lawyer represents an "organization"—a term that clearly includes corporations—it is the organization that is the lawyer's client. Its constituents, including its stockholders, are not also the lawyer's clients solely because of their relationship to the client. Rule 1.13(e) contemplates that a client-lawyer relationship between a constituent, including a stockholder, and corporate counsel, must be specifically formed, rather than arising automatically by virtue of the client-lawyer relationship with the organization.[5]

To be sure, Rule 1.13 does not directly address the question of when an affiliate of a corporate client is also a client, for the thrust of the Rule is to require the lawyer to distinguish between the corporation or other organization, which is his client, and the human representatives of the corporation, with whom the lawyer works and often forms personal relationships.[6]

Nonetheless, in light of the general proposition embodied in Model Rule 1.13, that an organization is separate from its constituents, construing the Comment to Rule 1.7 as establishing that all of a corporate client's affiliates should be considered clients of a lawyer is unwarranted. No court or ethics committee that has considered the general question of representation of corporate affiliates has given this construction to the Comment to Rule 1.7.

We conclude, therefore, that whether a lawyer represents a corporate affiliate of his client, for purposes of Rule 1.7, depends not upon any clear-cut per se rule but rather upon the particular circumstances.

ABA Formal
Ethics Opinions
(Selected)

4. See Comments to Rule 1.5, Rule 2.2, and Rule 5.1. Where a generic term including not only corporations and other profit-making enterprises but non-profit entities as well is called for, the term "organization" is used in the Model Rules: see, e.g., Rule 1.13.

5. Rule 1.13(e) provides:
A lawyer representing an organization may also represent any of its directors, officers, employees, members, shareholders or other constituents, subject to the provisions of Rule 1.7. If the organization's consent to the dual representation is required by Rule 1.7, the consent shall be given by an appropriate official of the organization other than the individual who is to be represented, or by the shareholders.

6. See ABA/BNA Lawyers' Manual on Professional Conduct 91:2002 (1994):
Because a lawyer who represents a corporation necessarily must deal with individuals—be they directors, officers and other employees, or shareholders—it is tempting to view some of them, or all of them collectively, as clients. Absent special circumstances, however, the rule of law applied by the courts, and the rule of professional responsibility that guides disciplinary authorities, is that the lawyer must view the cor- poration itself as the client, and in his or her representation must work for the best interest of the corporation.

The Model Rules do not directly address the question of when or how a client-lawyer relationship has been established: that is a matter governed by substantive law outside the Model Rules. See Model Rules, Scope Section:

> [F]or purposes of determining the lawyer's authority and responsibility, principles of substantive law external to these Rules determine whether a client-lawyer relationship exists.... Whether a client-lawyer relationship exists for any specific purpose can depend on the circumstances and may be a question of fact.

The client-lawyer relationship is principally a matter of contract, and the contract may be either express or implied. Thus, the entities within a corporate family that are to be considered clients may have been expressly identified as clients, or they may have become entitled to be so treated by reason of the way the representation of one of the members of the corporate family has been handled. In addition, it may be one of the terms of the engagement that the corporate client expects some or all of its affiliates to be treated as clients for purposes of Rule 1.7—i.e., that the lawyer will not accept engagements that would be prohibited by that Rule if the affiliates were clients.[7]

Clearly, a corporate affiliate must be treated as a client, whether generally or only for purposes of Rule 1.7, if the lawyer has agreed so to treat it, regardless of whether any actual work has been or is to be performed for the affiliate. Clearly also, it is important that lawyer and client share an understanding as to whether the client expects the lawyer to observe obligations to persons or entities other than the client itself, for that information is necessary for the lawyer to make the appropriate inquiries under Model Rule 1.7 to determine whether he can undertake the representation. Moreover, a client that has such an expectation has an obligation to keep the lawyer apprised of changes in the composition of the corporate family. While competent general counsel can be expected to be familiar with the corporate family and the expectations of one member as to the treatment of other members, outside lawyers who are performing only a limited role for a single aspect of the business, no matter how well-intentioned, should not be expected to be current on all of the names, relationships and ownership interests among a client's varied and sometimes far-flung business interests. A lawyer who has no reason to know that his potential adversary is

ABA Formal
Ethics Opinions
(Selected)

---

7. Such an understanding between the lawyer and the corporate client that the lawyer will refrain from representations adverse to the corporate affiliates of the client does not in itself establish a full-fledged client-lawyer relationship with the affiliates.

an affiliate of his client will not necessarily violate Rule 1.7 by accepting the new representation without his client's consent. See, e.g., Pennwalt Corp. v. Plough, Inc., (D.Del.1980).

A client-lawyer relationship does not, however, require an explicit agreement, let alone a written letter of engagement: it may come into being as a result of reasonable expectations and a failure of the lawyer to dispel those expectations. See Restatement (Third) of The Law Governing Lawyers ßß 26 (Tent.Draft No. 5, 1992):

ß 26. Formation of a Client-Lawyer Relationship

A relationship of client and lawyer arises when:

(1) *A person manifests to a lawyer the person's intent that the lawyer provide legal services for the person; and*

(2) (a) The lawyer manifests to the person consent to do so, or (b) *fails to manifest lack of consent to do so, when the lawyer knows or reasonably should know that the person reasonably relies on the lawyer to provide the services,* or (c) a tribunal with power to do so appoints the lawyer to provide the services. (Emphasis added.)

See also Westinghouse Elec. Corp. v. Kerr-McGee Corp., (7th Cir.), cert. denied, (1978):

> [A]n attorney-client relationship does not arise only in the agency manner such as when the parties expressly or impliedly consent to its formation.... [It] is not dependent upon the payment of fees [or] ... upon the execution of a formal contract.

Thus, when a lawyer is considering whether he can assume the representation adverse to a corporate affiliate of a client, he must consider not merely the terms of his engagement to that client but in addition whether the circumstances are such that the affiliate has reason to believe, on the basis of the nature of the lawyer's dealings with it, that it has a client-lawyer relationship with the lawyer.

Our Formal Opinions 91-361 (Representation of a Partnership) (1991) and 92-365 (Trade Associations as Clients) (1992) identify some of the circumstances that will bear on whether an affiliate of a lawyer's corporate client must also be considered a client of the lawyer.

In Formal Opinion 91-361, we considered whether a lawyer who represents a partnership also represents the individual partners. We concluded that the lawyer does not represent the partners merely because he represents the partnership, but that in particular circumstances the lawyer might be found to represent individual partners as well. We stated:

ABA Formal
Ethics Opinions
(Selected)

Whether such a relationship has been created almost always will depend on an analysis of the specific facts involved. The analysis may include such factors as whether the lawyer affirmatively assumed a duty of representation to the individual partner, whether the partner was separately represented by other counsel when the partnership was created or in connection with its affairs, whether the lawyer had represented an individual partner before undertaking to represent the partnership, and whether there was evidence of reliance by the individual partner on the lawyer as his or her separate counsel, or evidence of the partner's expectation of personal representation.

Similarly, in Formal Opinion 92-365, we opined that a lawyer who represents a trade association does not merely by reason of that fact have a client-lawyer relationship with individual members of the association. We stated:

> [D]etermining whether and to what extent the individual member has become a client requires careful examination of all of the circumstances of the lawyer's relationship to and representation of the trade association. Particularly important is an inquiry into what the member may have disclosed to the lawyer, under what circumstances and with what expectations.

* * *

> A fiduciary relationship may result because of the nature of the work performed and the circumstances under which confidential information is divulged.

The analysis in those Opinions is equally applicable here. Thus, the nature of the lawyer's dealings with affiliates of the corporate client may be such that they have become clients as well. This may be the case, for example, where the lawyer's work for the corporate parent—say, on a stock issue or bank financing—is intended to benefit all subsidiaries, and involves collecting confidential information from all of them.

Even if the subject matter of the lawyer's representation of the corporate client does not involve the affiliate at all, however, the lawyer's relationship with the corporate affiliate may lead the affiliate reasonably to believe that it is a client of the lawyer. For example, the fact that a lawyer for a subsidiary was engaged by and reports to an officer or general counsel for its parent may support the inference that the corporate parent reasonably expects to be treated as a client. See, e.g., Teradyne, Inc. v. Hewlett-Packard Co., (N.D.Cal.1991); Hartford Accident & Indem. Co. v. RJR Nabisco, Inc., (S.D.N.Y.1989).

A client-lawyer relationship with the affiliate may also arise because the affiliate imparted confidential information to the lawyer with the expecta-

635

tion that the lawyer would use it in representing the affiliate. See, e.g., Westinghouse Elec. Corp. v. Kerr-McGee Corp., (7th Cir.), cert. denied, (1978). Additionally, even if the affiliate confiding information does not expect that the lawyer will be representing the affiliate, there may well be a reasonable view on the part of the client that the information was imparted in furtherance of the representation, creating an ethically binding obligation that the lawyer will not use the information against the interests of any member of the corporate family.

Finally, the relationship of the corporate client to its affiliate may be such that the lawyer is required to regard the affiliate as his client. This would clearly be true where one corporation is the alter ego of the other. It is not necessary, however, for one corporation to be the alter ego of the other as a matter of law in order for both to be considered clients. A disregard of corporate formalities and/or a complete identity of managements and boards of directors could call for treating the two corporations as one. As stated by the court in Teradyne, supra (quoting Formal Opinion No. 1989-113 of the State Bar of California Standing Committee on Professional Responsibility and Conduct):

> In determining whether there is a sufficient unity of interests to require an attorney to disregard separate corporate entities for conflict purposes, the attorney should evaluate whether corporate formalities are observed, the extent to which each entity has distinct and independent managements and boards of directors and whether, for legal purposes, one entity could be considered the alter ego of the other.

The fact that the corporate client wholly owns, or is wholly owned by, its affiliate does not in itself make them alter egos. However, whole ownership may well entail not merely a shared legal department but a management so intertwined that all members of the corporate family effectively operate as a single entity; and in those circumstances representing one member of the family may effectively mean representing all the others as well. Conversely, where two corporations are related only through stock ownership, the ownership is less than a controlling interest and the lawyer has had no dealing whatever with the affiliate, there will rarely be any reason to conclude that the affiliate is the lawyer's client.[8]

---

8. Cf. Whiting Corp. v. White Mach. Corp., 567 F.2d 713, 714-15 (7th Cir.1977) (court refused to disqualify counsel where counsel represented both plaintiff and a cor- poration which owned 20% of the defendant corporation and had the power to appoint 40 percent of its Board).

(2) Is the Representation Affecting the Affiliate "Directly Adverse" to the Client?

Even though the corporation against which the lawyer is considering an adverse representation clearly is not the lawyer's client (or entitled for purposes of Rule 1.7 to be treated as such), the corporation that is a client may argue that the representation is nonetheless "directly adverse" to it, because any potential economic impact on the affiliate entails an impact on the corporation itself.

The paradigm situation here is presented by a lawyer's bringing a lawsuit, unrelated in substance to the lawyer's representation of a corporate client, seeking substantial money damages against a wholly owned subsidiary of the client: if the suit is successful, this will affect adversely not only the subsidiary but the parent as well, in the sense that one of its assets is the equity in the subsidiary, and its consolidated financial statements may (unless the subsidiary has applicable insurance coverage) reflect the impact of material adverse judgments against the subsidiary. See Stratagem Dev. Corp. v. Heron Int'l N.V., (S.D.N.Y.1991) ("the liabilities of a subsidiary corporation directly affect the bottom line of the corporate parent.").[9] It may also be the case, although less often, that a suit against a parent corporation will have a similarly direct economic impact on a wholly owned subsidiary (absent an "alter ego" situation),[10] or that a corporation will be directly affected by a suit against a sibling corporation.[11]

The critical question is whether, in any of the situations referred to above, the representation is, as to the corporate client, directly adverse, so as to fall under Rule 1.7(a); or only indirectly adverse, so that Rule 1.7(b) is the only potentially applicable provision. Although there is room for dispute on the point, we believe the better view is that the adverseness in such circumstances is indirect, and not direct.

This Committee has not previously addressed this question, although it has considered the general issue of direct and indirect adverseness in two recent opinions. In Formal Opinion 92-367 (Lawyer Examining a Client as an Adverse Witness (1992), or Conducting Third Party Discovery of the Client), we addressed the question whether a lawyer representing a client in

---

9. See also Telesat Cable Television, Inc. v. Opryland, USA, Inc., No. 90-137-CIV-ORL-19, 1990 WL 303150 (M.D.Fla. July 25, 1990) (holding impermissible a representation adverse to the interests of a third-tier subsidiary of a client).

10. Cf. Vanderveer Group, Inc. v. Petruny, No. Civ.A. 93-3677, 1993 WL 308720 at *3 (E.D.Pa. Aug. 13, 1993) (rejecting claim that suit against corporate parent of a client was "directly adverse" to the client).

11. Cf. Pennwalt Corp. v. Plough, Inc., 85 F.R.D. 264 (D.Del1980) (declining to disqualify a firm from a representation adverse to a sibling of the firm's corporate client).

litigation in which another client is a nonparty witness may cross-examine, or seek nonparty discovery from, that other client. We opined that the general circumstances (two clients involved in the same litigation, but one as a party and the other as a nonparty witness) might involve either direct or indirect adverseness, so as to fall under either Rule 1.7(a) or 1.7(b). If the representation involved attacking the conduct or credibility of the second client, or seeking to compel resisted discovery from the client, we concluded that the representation would be "directly adverse" to the witness client, because "any advantage gained by the lawyer in representation of the litigation client necessarily entails some concrete disadvantage to the [witness] client." In Formal Opinion 93-377 (Positional Conflicts) (1993), on the other hand, we held that representation of two clients in different suits, where one suit may create a legal precedent that materially undercuts the position being advanced for the client in the other suit, presents a conflict under Rule 1.7(b), not a "directly adverse" representation under Rule 1.7(a). We there explained (in footnote 4):

> Where there is such a conflict between separate representations, in the Committee's view the provision of Rule 1.7 that is potentially applicable is not paragraph (a), but paragraph (b). The former, in referring to a representation that is "directly adverse" to another client, contemplates litigating, or maintaining a position, in a given matter, on behalf of one client against a person or entity which is a client of the lawyer (or her firm) in another matter. The test under paragraph (b), on the other hand, is whether the representation of a client in one matter may be "materially limited" by the lawyer's responsibilities to another client in another matter, and the Committee views the impairment of a representation as a material limitation within the meaning of that paragraph.

Thus, we have interpreted "directly adverse" to refer not merely to the practical impact (on the adversely affected client) but also to the circumstances in which the conflict arises, and specifically the closeness of the connection between the lawyer's actions and the adverse effect on the client. As a prominent treatise observes in this connection:

> The direct-remote distinction ... calls attention not simply to the clients' general economic interests, but specifically to the transactions in which the clients employ the lawyer's services.

> 1 Geoffrey C. Hazard & William W. Hodes, The Law of Lawyering § 1.7.203 (2d ed. 1990).[12]

We conclude, then, that although in situations involving an unrelated suit against an affiliate of a corporate client, the client may be adversely affected, that adverseness is, for purposes of Rule 1.7, indirect rather than direct, since its immediate impact is on the affiliate, and only derivatively upon the client. The phrasing of Rule 1.7(a) is not ambiguous: the reference to a representation that is "directly adverse" clearly draws a distinction between direct and indirect adverseness, and thereby draws a bright line striking a balance between the interests of lawyer and client. If the proposed representation is directly adverse to a client, the client may veto its opponent's choice of counsel. A lawyer may not undertake litigation against a client without that client's consent, and the client may decline consent for any reason or no reason at all. Rule 1.7(a) thus establishes a per se rule, but its reach is appropriately limited to cases in which a lawyer is asked to undertake a matter that is "directly adverse" to an existing client. In all other cases, the client's only recourse is to fire the lawyer who undertakes a matter that displeases the client. Moreover, we see no principled way otherwise to draw a line short of the point where any discernible economic impact on a client arising from another representation (however slight or remote) must be treated as direct adverseness, requiring application of Rule 1.7(a) rather than Rule 1.7(b).

We recognize that there is some authority for a broader reading of "directly adverse."[13] However, we think the foregoing analysis represents a sounder approach to Rule 1.7.

(3) If Rule 1.7(a) Is Not Applicable, Is the Representation Nonetheless Barred by Rule 1.7(b)?

As has been discussed above, even if it is determined that Rule 1.7(a) does not bar a particular representation adverse to an affiliate of a corporate client, because the affiliate is not also a client and the representation is not directly adverse to the corporate client, the lawyer must also be sure that the representation does not fall afoul of Rule 1.7(b). The lawyer must consider whether the representation that is adverse to the affiliate may be materially

ABA Formal
Ethics Opinions
(Selected)

---

12. See also Annotated Model Rules of Professional Conduct Rule 1.7 at 112- 13 (2d ed. 1992).

13. See, e.g., North Star Hotels Corp. v. Mid-City Hotel Associates, 118 F.R.D. 109 (D.Minn.1987), (Law firm disqualified from suing a limited partnership when a general partner of that partnership, who would have personal liability, was also a gen- eral partner in two other partnerships that were represented by the law firm); Cincinnati Bell, Inc. v. Anizter Bros., Inc., No. C-1-93-0871 (S.D.Ohio, June 27, 1994) (law firm disqualified for representation of opponent's sister corporation in an unrelated matter); Telesat Cable Television, cited in note 9, supra.

limited by the lawyer's responsibilities to the corporate client, or, correlatively, the representation of the corporate client may be materially limited by the representation of the client adverse to the affiliate; and if so in either case, the lawyer may not take on the adverse representation unless the lawyer reasonably concludes that the representation will not be adversely affected, and the potentially affected client consents.

What triggers Rule 1.7(b) is a lawyer's recognition of the possibility that a particular representation may be materially limited by the lawyer's responsibilities to another client. As the Comment to the Rule makes clear, the reference is to situations "when a lawyer cannot consider, recommend or carry out an appropriate course of action for the client because of the lawyer's other responsibilities or interests." Such a material limitation on the lawyer's ability properly to represent a client could arise, for example, if the lawyer's concern for remaining in the good graces of client A was likely to impair the independence of judgment or the zeal that the lawyer could bring to bear on behalf of client B. Thus, Rule 1.7(b) might come into play if the lawyer had reason to believe that, even though there was no understanding as to how the corporate client's affiliates were to be treated, nonetheless the corporate client would resent the lawyer's undertaking any representation that threatened, even indirectly, any adverse effect on either the financial well-being or the programmatic purposes of the corporate client; and if, because of this belief, there was a significant risk that the lawyer's diligence or judgment on behalf of his new client would be adversely affected by his awareness of the corporate client's displeasure.

The foregoing discussion recognizes that Rule 1.7(b) must be considered by the lawyer whenever a representation adverse to a corporate client is considered; it should not, of course, be taken to imply that Rule 1.7(b) requires the lawyer to seek consent from either the new client or the existing corporate client whenever a proposed representation is adverse to an affiliate of a corporate client. It is only when there is a threat of material limitation on the lawyer's ability properly to represent a client because of his responsibilities to another client that the Rule requires the lawyer to seek consent.

Conclusion

The provisions of both paragraphs of Rule 1.7 emphasize the paramount importance of preserving a lawyer's relationship with his client. In that light, doubts about whether one or another requirement of the Rule applies should be resolved by a presumption that favors the client who will be adversely affected by the prospective representation.

ABA Formal
Ethics Opinions
(Selected)

A lawyer should not strain to conclude that a proposed representation will not adversely affect his relationship with that client.[14] Where it is difficult to ascertain whether a matter will be directly adverse to an existing client, or to judge whether taking on the matter will affect the lawyer's relationship with the client, a lawyer ordinarily would be well advised as a matter of prudence and good practice to discuss the matter with his existing client before undertaking a representation adverse to an affiliate of the client, even though consent may not be ethically required. We hasten to add that the fact that the lawyer has as a matter of prudence and good practice sought consent where consent was not ethically required does not make the lawyer's undertaking the new representation in the absence of consent a disciplinable ethical violation. However, in any instance where the lawyer concludes that no client consent is required, under either paragraph of Rule 1.7, the lawyer should be prepared to show how he was able to make the various determinations required without contacting the client for information or consent—particularly determinations (a) that the client does not have an expectation that the corporate affiliate will be treated as a client, and (b) that the proposed representation adverse to the affiliate will not have a material adverse effect on the representation of the client.

Assuming that obtaining client consent is the preferable course would have several practical benefits. Loyalty is an essential element in a lawyer's representation of any client. Disloyalty is easily perceived by a client, whether or not that perception is well-founded. As this Committee noted in Formal Opinion 91-361 (Representation of a Partnership) (1991), if a lawyer explains the implications of a dual representation and obtains the informed consent of both parties, "the likelihood of perceived ethical impropriety on the part of the lawyer should be significantly reduced."

Concurring in Part and Dissenting in Part

I dissent from that portion of the Committee's opinion which concludes that consultation with a client is solely a matter of prudence—not ethics— when a lawyer has difficulty making any of the judgments which are required by Rule 1.7. There are many such judgments, including whether the adverse

ABA Formal
Ethics Opinions
(Selected)

---

14. Lawyers who have taken an overly narrow view of what is "directly adverse" have found themselves disqualified in reported cases--e.g., Fund of Funds, Ltd. v. Arthur Andersen & Co., 567 F.2d 225 (2d Cir.1977); Stratagem Dev. Corp. v. Heron Int'l N.V., 756 F.Supp. 789 (S.D.N.Y.1991); North Star Hotels Corp. v. Mid-City Hotel Assoc., 118 F.R.D. 109, 111 (D.Minn.1987). Where disqualification is not avail- able, of course, a client can simply choose to discharge counsel.

party in the new matter is, or should be, treated as an existing client, and whether a lawyer's accepting the new matter will adversely affect the lawyer's relationship with his corporate client. Indeed, the issue of whether or not an action against a corporate affiliate would be "directly adverse" to a corporate client is a very difficult one, and the Committee's opinion, while announcing a decision on this point, hardly settles the matter, as my Colleagues' dissents well illustrate.

There is no doubt that accepting a new engagement adverse to an affiliate of a corporate client, without consultation with and the consent of that client, is business folly. This fact alone should impel most practitioners to call their clients before accepting such work. However, I submit that a lawyer has an ethical duty to consult with his client, and obtain consent, whenever the extent of the lawyer's representation of one or more members of a corporate family has not been clearly limited by prior agreement between the lawyer and client or circumstances known to and reasonably understood by both lawyer and client.

A lawyer's unilateral decision to take on a matter adverse to an affiliate of an existing client, made on the basis of imperfect information about how his client will regard that decision, can easily have significant ethical repercussions. Rule 1.4 states that "A lawyer shall explain a matter to the extent reasonably necessary to permit the client to make informed decisions regarding the representation." A lawyer's failure to consult his client about a new representation adverse to its affiliate deprives the client of the ability freely to make an "informed decision regarding the representation." Instead, the client is forced to decide between discharging the lawyer, even if such discharge will have a material adverse effect on its interests (a circumstance in which the lawyer would not have been permitted to withdraw), or acquiescing in the lawyer's continuing to represent it, with whatever impairment of communication, cooperation and diligence, and whatever threat to confidentiality, results. It cannot be consistent with a lawyer's ethical duties for a lawyer to force his client to such a decision.

Deborah A. Coleman

DISSENTS

This Committee has struggled for more than two years to formulate an answer to the submission which a majority of the Committee can agree upon. What the majority of this Committee has finally agreed upon is a departure from its tradition of interpreting the Model Rules in an aspirational manner.

The majority view, when reduced to its most simplistic terms, is as follows: XYZ Corporation is represented by the law firm of Roe & Doe. XYZ

ABA Formal
Ethics Opinions
(Selected)

has a number of subsidiaries which the majority characterizes as "corporate affiliates." One of them is about to be sued by another client of Roe & Doe in an "unrelated matter." In such a case, the majority opines that even if the suit threatens to adversely impact XYZ's economic interest, the conflict is governed not by Model Rule 1.7(a) which would require the consent of XYZ, but by Model Rule 1.7(b) which does not require the consent of XYZ, thus depriving it of a veto power which would prevent Roe & Doe from suing its subsidiary.

It may very well be that in the rarified Fortune 500 world, a suit against a subsidiary might be considered as having only a derivative impact upon the parent, but outside those elevated precincts most parent companies would view such a suit as outrageous and a clear conflict of interest. The majority suggests that the parent corporation might avoid this unhappy situation by arriving at an "understanding" with their lawyers that they "will avoid representations adverse to the client's corporate affiliates." In the most elementary terms, what the majority is doing is shifting the lawyer's burden or protecting the client to the client, who must now protect itself against its own lawyer. If there is one clear message to be drawn from the majority opinion, it is that all corporate in-house counsel and all corporate officers having responsibility for their company's relationship with their attorneys, should promptly review their retainer agreements and amend them in order to protect their "corporate affiliates" from their own lawyers.

The majority's repeated use of the term "corporate affiliate" must be viewed as an elevation of form over substance. Even the majority doesn't go so far as to suggest that if the XYZ Corporation had a number of divisions under its corporate umbrella, a suit brought by its lawyers, Roe & Doe, against one of those divisions would be indirectly adverse. [Rule 1.7(b)]. What they do say is that because XYZ chose to or was by law required to operate via corporate subsidiaries, if a profitable case against XYZ's subsidiary comes to Roe & Doe, it is free to make a business decision to take that case without XYZ's consent and the only recourse XYZ has is to discharge Roe & Doe or move to disqualify it. This "solution" ignores the fact that XYZ may be represented by Roe & Doe in other matters where the involvement in time and money makes it economically unrealistic to terminate the relationship. Thus, XYZ may be economically bound to a law firm which is suing its subsidiary—with both the law firm and the client unhappy with the relationship.

The majority is of the view that while the claim against the subsidiary is direct, the adverseness against the parent is "for the purpose of Rule 1.7, indirect rather than direct, since its immediate impact is upon the affiliate and only derivatively upon the client." I am hard put to understand what that means in the real world. I assume that if XYZ is maintaining a subsidiary, it does so with the expectancy that the subsidiary's profits will add to the bottom line of XYZ's annual report and that the subsidiary's reputation will add to the luster of XYZ's reputation. From XYZ's point of view, the suit against the subsidiary will always have a direct impact on it and no matter what the majority opines, will be a conflict of interest.

In the conclusion of the opinion, an effort is made to palliate the impact in the interest of "preserving a lawyer's relationship with his client." Doubts as to whether Rule 1.7(a) or 1.7(b) applies "should be resolved by a presumption that favors the client who will be adversely affected by the prospective representation."

Then, the majority suggests, if it is difficult to ascertain "whether a matter will be directly adverse to an existing client or to judge whether taking on the matter will affect the lawyer's relationship with the client," Roe & Doe "ordinarily would be well advised as a matter of prudence and good practice" to discuss the matter with XYZ "before assuming a representation adverse to an affiliate" of XYZ "even though such consent may not be ethically required." The majority "hastens to add" that the fact that Roe & Doe sought XYZ's consent "where such consent was not ethically required" (relying upon the majority opinion) does not subject Roe & Doe to a "disciplinable ethical violation" if it proceeds with the new representation without out XYZ's consent.

The foregoing invites a visit to the following scenario. Roe calls XYZ's President and says "Remember that little company you purchased a few years ago? We have just been retained by a major client to sue it for unfair competition. I hope you don't mind." XYZ's President explodes saying there is no way his Board of Directors is going to stand still for its lawyers suing its subsidiary and suggests that Roe & Doe are in a conflict of interest situation. Roe responds that their ethics partners have carefully reviewed the situation and in reliance upon an opinion of the American Bar Association's Standing Committee on Ethics and Professional Responsibility (handing XYZ's President a copy of the majority opinion appropriately underlined), Roe & Doe need not obtain XYZ's consent and the fact that they asked for it but didn't get it and proceeded with the action is not ethically disciplinable. So much for client relations—so much for enhancing the reputation of the profession.

Conclusion

The majority opinion fails to furnish bright line guidance in the complex and confused area of conflicts of interest. Stripped of its elegant verbiage, the opinion opens a Pandora's Box of unintended consequences which most assuredly will return to vex us in the future. Admittedly, Model Rule 1.7 problems do not always fit into precise categories, but to paraphrase an oft quoted sentence from a Supreme Court opinion, I may have difficulty defining a conflict but I know one when I see one. The majority opinion sends our profession the wrong message at the wrong time. For the foregoing reasons, I respectfully dissent therefrom.

Richard L. Amster

* * *

This Standing Committee on Ethics and Professional Responsibility has wrestled with the issues of conflict of interest in the corporate family context for years. Now it issues an opinion which, I am sad to report, prompts this member's first dissent. What makes this doubly sad is the fact that the opinion contains so much laudable practical advice regarding the lawyer's better course of action, what should be done when lawyers confront representations adverse to corporate affiliates of corporate clients, and how considerations of client relations will ordinarily dictate proper conduct. All of this "advice" would be ethically mandated as well, if the majority had not strained the meaning of Model Rule 1.7 to permit what everyone on this Committee agrees is ill-advised: suits against corporate affiliates of corporate clients.

Yet when the Committee's opinion is distilled and the hortatory language is removed, we learn that it is the opinion of the majority that when a lawyer represents less than all members of a corporate family that lawyer is free to take a position adverse to those non-client members of the corporate family without contacting the client member on the ground that the adverse effect of such representation on the client member is "indirect rather than direct, since its immediate impact is on the affiliate, and only derivatively upon the client." Op. at 21. Thus, in one unfortunate opinion the majority has turned a Rule of Professional Conduct designed to protect clients into one that can be used to permit lawyers freely, and without consultation, to take positions which destroy traditional notions of client loyalty and client concern.

The majority's opinion starts from a premise that is so flawed it can only be explained by the fact that its proponents imagine its conclusion only to apply to the largest of America's corporate conglomerates; then the majority compounds this error by assuming that companies that are part of these very large conglomerates do not very much care what happens to other members of the corporate family who are in different lines of business or in different geographical areas or led by different management, but just happen to be part of the same corporate enterprise.

The first problem with this approach is that the opinion as written applies to all corporate families regardless of their size or the nature of their

ABA Formal
Ethics Opinions
(Selected)

businesses. Thus, even if one could imagine a special rule for "nasty" big companies, a possibility this writer rejects out of hand, that is not what the majority has crafted. The second problem is that the majority opinion fails to recognize the fact that corporate families are financially totally inter-dependent and that the sole purpose for the existence of these corporate families is economic success. Thus, when the majority opinion argues that an event economically adverse to subsidiary "A" only indirectly affects subsidiary "B,"[15] it clearly ignores the fact that for members of a corporate family the location of a corporate family's losses are totally irrelevant to the impact on the bottom line. Parents are directly dependent on the health of their subsidiaries; subsidiaries are directly dependent on the health of the parent; and subsidiaries are directly dependent on the health of other subsidiaries. For the last proposition one need look no further than the drastic effects on General Electric Credit Corporation of the widely publicized events at Kidder, Peabody.

All members of this Committee agree that a lawyer may never take a position directly adverse to a client corporation no matter how minor the matter and no matter how distant geographically, by industry or by personnel, the new proposed representation is from the original one the lawyer is handling. Not only is that the rule, but that is what the rule should be. If the client wishes to consent to the representation because of those factors or because it otherwise wishes to accommodate the lawyer's desire to take on the new representation, that is something for the client to decide, giving the client the full protection of the rules governing conflicts of interest.

But today the majority announces a rule that would result in no call to the client, no request for a waiver of a conflict, no opportunity to determine what the client thinks about the proposed representation adverse to an affiliate of the client, no opportunity to condition the representation on reasonable safeguards like voluntary screening or an agreement not to sue for punitive damages. Rather, the majority empowers the lawyer at precisely the time when the lawyer's objectivity can be seen to be the most compromised, simply to take a position adverse to the client's corporate affiliate on the ground that as a matter of ethics and, therefore, as a matter not requiring any further inquiry, the effect on the client is merely indirect.

ABA Formal
Ethics Opinions
(Selected)

---

15. The "directly adverse/indirectly adverse" distinction is at the heart of this dispute since, if the proposed representation is directly adverse to the client, Model Rule 1.7(a), with its requirement that the client consent, is triggered. Under Model Rule 1.7(b) only the new client that is taking a position adverse to a corporate affiliate of the old client need consent

The invalidity of this result can be seen in a hypothetical: A lawyer regularly defends dealer termination litigation for the Lincoln Mercury Division of the Ford Motor Company. She receives a call from a friend whose mother-in-law was just injured in an automobile accident. She was driving a Jaguar, the friend relates, and the brakes failed. The mother-in-law wants to sue the manufacturer claiming faulty brake design. Lawyer consults a recent annual report of Ford and this Committee's majority opinion and replies that, since Jaguar is a subsidiary of Ford, she can take the case because any impact on her present client, Ford, will be at best indirect.

Two days later the same friend calls to tell lawyer that his mother-in-law has just been released from the hospital, her delusions of grandeur have disappeared and she now remembers that she was, in fact, driving a Ford Escort at the time of the accident. The friend wants confirmation that lawyer will still take the case. Lawyer again consults the majority opinion and replies that now, since Ford is a division of Ford Motors, she cannot take the case because the adverse effect of the representation will now be direct. Friend, a non-lawyer, asks for an explanation of the different results and when he is told the distinction the ABA Ethics Committee drew between subsidiaries of clients and divisions of clients in drafting its corporate family opinion, the friend remarks that the result exalts form over substance.

The friend is quite correct. Taking the profession where no prior opinion has ever tread, the majority today condones lawyers taking positions adverse to the parents, subsidiaries and siblings of their corporate clients on the ground that doing so is only indirectly adverse because it involves economic harm to a subsidiary, parent or sibling. The sole reason for corporate existence is the maximization of economic success. Thus, when a corporation is harmed economically it is being hurt in the only way that counts. Yet somehow because the corporation has decided to, been forced to or, indeed, been counseled by its own lawyer to conduct its affairs through subsidiaries, it has lost the protection the majority concedes it would enjoy if its various businesses were organized as divisions. Why a corporation with subsidiaries may be so "punished" is nowhere explained by the majority. Nor is it explained why the suit against the Ford Division of Ford, even if it is for $100, results in direct adverseness while the suit against Jaguar, even if it is for $100,000,000, is indirect.

It is the conclusion of the majority opinion that the way a client chooses, is advised or is forced to organize its business is determinative of how the company should be treated for conflict of interest purposes. Yet every lawyer knows that there will be almost no cases where, from the client's perspective, that should be so. And it is clients, not lawyers, that the conflict of interest rules are supposed to protect.

ABA Formal Ethics Opinions (Selected)

The existence of subsidiaries often reflects regulatory requirements, historical accidents or considerations of limiting liability. They will almost never reflect a client judgment that what happens to the subsidiary, parent or sibling is not a matter that it cares about very much indeed. Just as Ford undoubtedly cares as much about what happens at its Jaguar subsidiary as it does about what happens at its Lincoln Mercury Division, so, too, is this the case in virtually every wholly owned corporate family. In the final analysis the enterprise is simply one economic conglomerate whose sole reason for being is earning profits for its shareholders.

The majority's reliance on Formal Opinions 91-361 (Representation of a Partnership) (1991) and 92-365 (Trade Association as Clients) (1992) is clearly misplaced. In each of those cases the Committee considered whether an individual partner of a multi-partner partnership or an individual member of a multi-member trade association would become a client of the lawyer who represented, respectively, the partnership or the trade association. The author of this dissent agrees that in those two situations a careful analysis of other facts is required to determine whether the partner or the member become clients. But here we are talking about a wholly owned corporate family. The only analogies that would be apt here are a single partner partnership or a single member trade association. In each of those cases, there is no doubt that the lone partner or the lone member must either be considered a client of the lawyer or, at a minimum, a person who would suffer a direct adverse effect if any action were taken adverse to the partnership or trade association.

It is also surprising that the majority relies on Formal Opinion 92-367 (Lawyer Examining a Client as an Adverse Witness, or Conducting Third Party Discovery of the Client) (1992) in support of its position. In that opinion this Committee concluded that the cross examination of one's client, a non-party witness, in a case on behalf of another client, would be "directly adverse" to the client non-party witness because "any advantage gathered by the lawyer in representation of the litigation client necessarily entails some concrete disadvantage to the [witness] client." If attacking the credibility of a witness, who is not a party, is said to entail a concrete disadvantage then suing the subsidiary of a client for damages surely entails an even greater and more concrete disadvantage. In the former case, by definition, the witness has no stake in the litigation and so at worst some feelings get bruised or one's reputation tarnished; but in the latter the lawyer who is suing the subsidiary of a parent client is literally putting her hand in her client's pocketbook. Short of physical injury, it does not get more concrete than that.

One of the biggest problems with the majority approach is that those clients that are the most sophisticated and the least in need of protection,

ABA Formal Ethics Opinions (Selected)

the very independent Fortune 500 companies that the majority thinks are indifferent to lawsuits against corporate family affiliates, will be able to protect themselves from this opinion by sending each lawyer the company engages a letter telling the lawyer to treat all of the corporate affiliates listed on an annexed chart as clients for purposes of Rule 1.7. It is only the unsophisticated, those corporate families which do not have legions of in-house lawyers, who will be caught in the trap this opinion creates. It is they who will naively hire a lawyer, assume total loyalty and find out much to their surprise that the lawyer feels completely free to sue another member of the corporate family simply because the economic impact on the "client" was indirect.

The majority, of course, thinks this conflict result can be ameliorated because the client who learns its lawyer is suing a member of the corporate family can simply fire the lawyer for this unfortunate conduct. Op. at 22. However, as all lawyers recognize, firing one's counsel is rarely a satisfactory solution and often an impossibility, given the pressures of time and the extraordinary costs associated with hiring new counsel. Moreover, the last thing this Committee should ever condone is a device which would permit lawyers, who wish to take on a new, more lucrative engagement from which they are precluded because of some conflict, to place their clients in a position where they have a Hobson's choice of waiving the conflict or firing their lawyers.

The final ironic infirmity in the majority opinion is its recognition that the lawyer might run afoul of Model Rule 1.7(b)'s material limitation language because the client might "resent the lawyer's undertaking any representation that threatened, even indirectly, any adverse effect on ... the financial well being ... of the corporate client," while at the same time the opinion fails to recognize how much the client might resent far more the fact that the lawyer, according to the majority, is not even required to call the client before undertaking the "indirectly adverse" representation. The truth is both slights will be resented and justifiably so. Yet the majority deliberately eschews the only way that client resentment can be avoided: for the lawyer to be required to notify the client and then use all her advocacy power to persuade the client she should be allowed to undertake the adverse representation. If she succeeds, fine; if she fails, client loyalty will be preserved. Nothing less should be required.

Conclusion

It is the view of this writer that the majority opinion misinterprets Model Rule 1.7(a) when it concludes that the rule's interdiction of conduct directly adverse to a client does not include taking a position directly adverse to a corporate affiliate of the client. Perhaps another Standing Committee on Ethics and Professional Responsibility on another day will see the error of the majority's ways and correct it. Until then, this dissent is offered as a call to the profession to follow the dissent's bright line rule whenever the profession approaches conflicts of interest in the corporate family context. The last thing our profession needs is another black eye caused by jettisoned client loyalty in the name of economic expediency.

Lawrence J. Fox

* * *

I concur in the dissents of Messrs. Amster and Fox.

Kim Taylor-Thompson

ABA Formal Ethics Opinions (Selected)

Formal Opinion 96-402   August 2, 1996
Propriety of Payments to Occurrence Witnesses

> *A lawyer, acting on her client's behalf, may compensate a non-expert witness for time spent in attending a deposition or trial or in meeting with the lawyer preparatory to such testimony, provided that the payment is not conditioned on the content of the testimony and provided further that the payment does not violate the law of the jurisdiction.*

The Committee has been asked whether, under the Model Rules of Professional Conduct (1983, as amended), it is proper for a lawyer to compensate a non-expert witness for the reasonable value of the time expended by the witness while preparing for or giving testimony at a deposition or at a trial.

Model Rule 3.4 (Fairness to Opposing Party and Counsel) states that a lawyer shall not "(b) falsify evidence, counsel or assist a witness to testify falsely, or offer an inducement to a witness that is prohibited by law." Comment [3] to this Rule explains that "it is not improper to pay a witness's expenses or to compensate an expert witness on terms permitted by law," but that the "common law rule in most jurisdictions is that it is improper to pay an occurrence witness any fee for testifying."

Reading Comment [3] literally, compensating a witness for loss of time which he could have devoted to other pursuits does not constitute payment of an "expense" incurred by the witness. Nor, on the other hand, does compensating a witness for his loss of time amount to paying him a "fee for testifying." Indeed, the precursor of Model Rule 3.4, DR7-109 of the Model Code of Professional Responsibility, expressly permitted "[r]easonable compensation to a witness for his loss of time in attending or testifying,"[1] and there is nothing in the history of Rule 3.4 to indicate that the drafters of the Model Rules intended to negate this concept by using the language that they did. In addition, such compensation is implicitly authorized by certain statutes and court decisions. See, for example, 18 U.S.C. Section 201(j), which provides that payments to lay witnesses for "the reasonable value of time lost in atten- dance at any such trial, hearing or proceeding" do not violate federal bribery statutes. The Committee therefore concludes that payment for loss of time is not prohibited by Model Rule 3.4.

The Committee also sees no reason to draw a distinction between (a) compensating a witness for time spent in actually attending a deposition or a trial and (b) compensating the witness for time spent in pretrial interviews with the

ABA Formal
Ethics Opinions
(Selected)

---

1. DR 7-109(C) of the Model Code of Professional Responsibility stated:
    A lawyer shall not pay, offer to pay, or acquiesce in the payment of compensation to a witness contingent upon the content of his testimony or the outcome of the case. But a lawyer may advance, guarantee or acquiesce in the payment of:
    (1) Expenses reasonably incurred by a witness in attending or testifying.
    (2) Reasonable compensation to a witness for his loss of time in amending or testifying.
    (3) A reasonable fee for the professional services of an expert witness.

lawyer in preparation for testifying, as long as the lawyer makes it clear to the witness that the payment is not being made for the substance (or efficacy) of the witness's testimony or as an inducement to "tell the truth."[2] The Committee is further of the view that the witness may also be compensated for time spent in reviewing and researching records that are germane to his or her testimony, provided, of course, that such compensation is not barred by local law.

The Committee notes that this particular question was raised in Pennsylvania Bar Association Committee on Legal Ethics and Professional Responsibility Opinion 95-126 (1995). Pennsylvania Rule 3.4(b) is based on DR 7-109(C) and permits both the payment of expenses "reasonably incurred by a witness in attending or testifying" and "reasonable compensation to a witness for the witness' loss of time in attending or testifying." The Pennsylvania Committee concluded that, while the Pennsylvania rule does not expressly forbid payments to fact witnesses for preparatory work such as reviewing documents before testimony, that rule "can be read to disfavor compensation to non-expert witnesses for time invested in preparing for testimony."

The Committee does not construe Model Rule 3.4 that narrowly. As long as it is made clear to the witness that the payment is not being made for the substance or efficacy of the witness's testimony, and is being made solely for the purpose of compensating the witness for the time the witness has lost in order to give testimony in litigation in which the witness is not a party, the Committee is of the view that such payments do not violate the Model Rules.[3]

Nevertheless, the amount of such compensation must be reasonable, so as to avoid affecting, even unintentionally, the content of a witness's testimony. What is a reasonable amount is relatively easy to determine in situations where the witness can demonstrate to the lawyer that he has sustained a direct loss of income because of his time away from work--as, for example, loss of hourly wages or professional fees. In situations, however, where the witness has not sustained any direct loss of income in connection with giving, or preparing to give, testimony--as, for example, where the witness is retired or unemployed-- the lawyer must determine the reasonable value of the witness's time based on all relevant circumstances. Once that determination has been made, nothing in the Model Rules prohibits a lawyer from making payments to an occurrence witness as discussed herein.

ABA Formal
Ethics Opinions
(Selected)

---

2. Compare, in this regard, Prosecution Function, Standard 3-3.2 of the ABA Criminal Justice Standards, which states in relevant part:

(a) A prosecutor should not compensate a witness, other than an expert, for giving testimony, but it is not improper to reimburse an ordinary witness for the reasonable expens- es of attendance upon court, attendance for depositions pursuant to statute or court rule, or attendance for pretrial interview. Payments to a witness may be for transportation and loss of income provided there is no attempt to conceal the fact of reimbursements.

3. In addition, the witness is entitled to be reimbursed for his or her travel expenses, including lodging when an overnight stay is required. Compare 28 U.S.C. ß 1821, which permits a prevailing party to tax such costs for witnesses appearing in federal courts.

Formal Opinion 99-414
Ethical Obligations When
a Lawyer Changes Firms

September 8, 1999

A lawyer's ethical obligations upon withdrawal from one firm to join another derive from the concepts that clients' interests must be protected and that each client has the right to choose the departing lawyer or the firm, or another lawyer to represent him. The departing lawyer and the responsible members of her firm who remain must take reasonable measures to assure that the withdrawal is accomplished without material adverse effect on the interests of clients with active matters upon which the lawyer currently is working. The departing lawyer and responsible members of the law firm who remain have an ethical obligation to assure that prompt notice is given to clients on whose active matters she currently is working. The departing lawyer and responsible members of the law firm who remain also have ethical obligations to protect client information, files, and other client property. The departing lawyer is prohibited by ethical rules, and may be prohibited by other law, from making in-person contact prior to her departure with clients with whom she has no family or client-lawyer relationship. After she has left the firm, she may contact any firm client by letter.

When a lawyer ceases to practice at a law firm, both the departing lawyer and the responsible members of the firm who remain have ethical responsibilities to clients on whose active matters the lawyer currently is working to assure, to the extent reasonably practicable, that their representation is not adversely affected by the lawyer's departure. In this Opinion, the Committee addresses obligations under the Model Rules of Professional Conduct that a lawyer has when she leaves one law firm for another, including the following: (1) disclosing her pending departure in a timely fashion to clients for whose active matters she currently is responsible or plays a principal role in the current delivery of legal services (sometimes referred to in this Opinion as "current clients"); (2) assuring that client matters to be transferred with the lawyer to her new law firm do not create conflicts of interest in the new firm and can be competently managed there; (3) protecting client files and property and assuring that, to the extent reasonably practicable, no client matters are adversely affected as a result of her withdrawal; (4) avoiding conduct involving dishonesty, fraud, deceit, or misrepresentation in connection with her planned withdrawal; and (5) maintaining confidentiality and avoiding conflicts of interest in her new affiliation respecting client matters remaining in the lawyer's former firm.[1]

The departing lawyer also must consider legal obligations other than ethics rules that apply to her conduct when changing firms, as well as her fiduciary duties owed the former firm. The law of agency, partnership, property, contracts, and unfair competition impose obligations that are not addressed directly by the Model Rules. These obligations may affect the permissible timing, recipients, and content of communications with clients, and which files, documents, and other property the departing lawyer lawfully may copy or take with her from the firm. Although the Committee does not advise upon issues of law beyond the Model Rules, we must take account of other law in construing the Rules; so must the departing lawyer before determining an appropriate course of action.

Notification to Current Clients Is Required

The impending departure of a lawyer who is responsible for the client's representation or who plays a principal role in the law firm's delivery of legal services currently in a matter (i.e., the lawyer's current clients), is information that may affect the status of a client's matter as contemplated by Rule 1.4.[2] A lawyer who is departing one law firm for another has an ethi-

---

1. This Opinion addresses mainly the obligations of the departing lawyer. Nevertheless, the firm members remaining, and especially those with supervisory responsibility, have an obligation under the Rules of Professional Conduct, and may have obligations as well under other law, to assure to the extent reasonable practicable that the withdrawal from the firm is accomplished without material adverse effect on any clients' interests, especially clients on whose active matters the departing lawyer currently is working. *Cf.* ABA Informal Opinion 1428 (1979), decided under the former Model Code of Professional Responsibility, and California Bar Ethics Op. No. 1985-86,1985 WL 57193 *2 (Cal. St. Bar. Comm. Prof. Resp. 1985), both of which place the responsibility of notifying clients upon the departing lawyer and her firm. Among remaining firm members' ethical obligations are to make reasonable efforts to ensure that there are in effect measures: (1) to keep clients informed pursuant to Rule 1.4(b) of the impending departure of a lawyer having substantial responsibility for the clients' active matters; (2) to make clear to those clients and others for whom the departing lawyer has worked and who inquire that the clients may choose to be represented by the departing lawyer, the firm or neither (see RESTATEMENT (THIRD) OF THE LAW GOVERNING LAWYERS § 26 cmt. h (Proposed Official Draft 1998); (3) to assure that active matters on which the departing lawyer has been working continue to be managed by remaining lawyers with competence and diligence pursuant to Rules 1.1 and 1.3; and (4) to assure that, upon the firm's withdrawal from representation of any client, the firm takes reasonable steps to protect the client's interests pursuant to Rule 1.16(d). *See infra,* n.4 and accompanying text. This Opinion does not address the issue of a division of fees between the departing lawyer and her law firm.

2. Rule 1.4 (Communication) states:

   (a) A lawyer shall keep a client reasonably informed about the status of a matter and promptly comply with reasonable requests for information.

ABA Formal
Ethics Opinions
(Selected)

cal obligation, along with responsible members of the law firm who remain, to assure that those clients are informed that she is leaving the firm. This can be accomplished by the lawyer herself, the responsible members of the firm, or the lawyer and those members jointly. Because a client has the ultimate right to select counsel of his choice,[3] information that the lawyer is leaving and where she will be practicing will assist the client in determining whether his legal work should remain with the law firm, be transferred with the lawyer to her new firm, or be transferred elsewhere. Accordingly, informing the client of the lawyer's departure in a timely manner is critical to allowing the client to decide who will represent him.[4]

Notification of Current Clients is Not Impermissible Solicitation

Because she has a present professional relationship with her current clients, a departing lawyer does not violate Model Rule 7.3(a)[5] by notifying those clients that she is leaving for a new affiliation. Under Rule 7.3(a), the departing lawyer is, however, prohibited from making in-person contact with firm clients with whom she does not have a prior professional or family relationship. A lawyer does not have a prior professional relationship with a client sufficient to permit in-person or live telephone solicitation solely by having worked on a matter for the client along with other lawyers

---

(b) A lawyer shall explain a matter to the extent reasonably necessary to permit the client to make informed decisions regarding the representation.

Comment [1] to Rule 1.4 provides that "the client should have sufficient information to participate intelligently in decisions concerning . . . the means by which they [the objectives of the representation] are to be pursued . . . ."

3. Rule 1.16 (Declining Or Terminating Representation) in paragraph (a)(3) states in pertinent part that a lawyer "shall withdraw from the representation of a client if . . .the lawyer is discharged." *See also* Comment [4]; Restatement § 26 cmt h, *supra* n.1.

4. State ethics opinions also have determined that, under the Model Rules, a departing lawyer has an ethical duty to inform current clients that she is leaving the firm. *See, e.g.,* District of Columbia Bar Legal Ethics Committee Op. No. 273 (1997); State Bar of Michigan Std. Com. on Prof. and Jud. Ethics Op. No. RI-224, 1995 WL68957 (Mich. Prof. Jud. Eth. 1995). *See also* Rule 1.16(d), *infra* n.8. The ABA Committee gave approval under the former Model Code of Professional Responsibility for a partner or associate who is leaving one firm for another to send an announcement soon after departure to those clients for whose active, open, and pending matters the lawyer had been directly responsible immediately before resignation. Informal Opinions 1457 (1980) and 1466 (1981). These opinions did not, however, address the question whether the departing lawyer might send notices to any clients before resigning.

5. Model Rule 7.3(a) states:

A lawyer shall not by in-person or live telephone contact solicit professional employment from a prospective client with whom the lawyer has no family or prior professional relationship when a significant motive for the lawyer's doing so is the lawyer's pecuniary gain.

in a way that afforded little or no direct contact with the client.[6] The departing lawyer nevertheless may contact the client through written or oral recorded communication pursuant to Rule 7.2(a), subject to the limitations in Rules 7.1, 7.3(b), and 7.3(c), at least after the lawyer has departed the firm and joined the new firm.[7]

The Committee also is of the opinion that a departing lawyer must, under Rule 1.16(d),[8] take steps to the extent practicable to protect her current clients' interests. Moreover, the responsible members of the former firm must themselves comply with Rule 1.16(d) respecting all clients who select the departing lawyer to represent them, whether or not they are current clients of the departing lawyer.[9]

A lawyer's duty to inform her current clients of her impending departure is similar to a lawyer's obligation to inform clients if the lawyer will be unavailable to provide legal services to them for an extended period because

---

6. The rationale for the prohibition is that "there is a potential for abuse inherent indirect in-person or live telephone contact by a lawyer with a prospective client known to be in need of legal services." Rule 7.3, Comment [1]. The rationale for the exception is that "[t]here is far less likelihood that a lawyer would engage in abusive practices against an individual with whom the lawyer has a prior personal (sic) or professional relationship . . . ." Rule 7.3, Comment [4]. The Committee views the exception under Rule 7.3(a) to permit in-person solicitation only of those current clients of the firm with whom the lawyer personally has had sufficient professional conduct to afford the client an opportunity to judge the professional qualifications of the lawyer and as not extending beyond the text of the Rule to apply to firm clients with whom her relationship is solely personal and not professional. *See, e.g.,* N.C. Bar Opinion 200, 1994 WL899607 (N.C. St. Bar 1994) (lawyer after departure may contact clients of firm for whom he has been responsible); Arizona Comm. on Rules of Professional Conduct Op. No. 91-17 (June 10, 1991) (permissible before departure to notify clients with whom he had a personal, professional relationship); Kentucky Bar Opinion E-317 (1987) (permissible before departure to notify clients whom he personally represented of his impending departure).

7. Lawyers are permitted, subject to certain limitations, "to make known their services not only through reputation but also through organized information campaigns. Rule 7.2, Comment [1]. Rule 7.2 permits not only general advertising, but also targeted "written or recorded communication."

8. Model Rule 1.16(d) states: Upon termination of representation, a lawyer shall take steps to the extent reasonably practicable to protect a client's interests, such as giving reasonable notice to the client, allowing time for employment of other counsel, surrendering papers and property to which the client is entitled and refunding any advance payment of fee that has not been earned. The lawyer may retain papers relating to the client to the extent permitted by other law.

9. If a current client chooses to remain with the firm or to move with the departing lawyer to her new firm, the lawyer(s) selected must continue the representation unless withdrawal is necessary under Rule 1.16(a) or permissible under Rule 1.16(b). In the Committee's opinion, "other good cause for withdrawal" does not exist under Rule 1.16(b) (6) solely because the client's matter is difficult or time consuming or has little chance of success, so long as no other enumerated predicate for withdrawal exists.

ABA Formal
Ethics Opinions
(Selected)

of major surgery or an extended vacation.[10] In all of these situations, the clients have a right to know of the impending absence so that they can make informed decisions about future representation, even though the lawyer who temporarily will be unavailable is likely to believe that other lawyers in the firm are fully capable of handling the clients' matters during her absence.

The Initial Notice Must Fairly Describe the Client's Alternatives

Any initial in-person or written notice informing clients of the departing lawyer's new affiliation that is sent before the lawyer's resigning from the firm generally should conform to the following:

1) the notice should be limited to clients whose active matters the lawyer has direct professional responsibility at the time of the notice (i.e., the current clients);

2) the departing lawyer should not urge the client to sever its relationship with the firm, but may indicate the lawyer's willingness and ability to continue her responsibility for the matters upon which she currently is working;

3) the departing lawyer must make clear that the client has the ultimate right to decide who will complete or continue the matters; and

4) the departing lawyer must not disparage the lawyer's former firm.[11]

The Departing Lawyer Should Provide Additional Information

In order to provide each current client with the information needed to make a choice of counsel, the departing lawyer also may inform the cli-

---

10. Cf. Passanante v. Yormack, 138 N.J. Super. 233, 238, 350 A. 2d 497, 500 (N.J. 1975), *cert. denied*, 704 N.J. 144, 358 A.2d 199 (N.J. 1976) (lawyer has implicit obligation to inform clients of failure to act for whatever cause to permit clients to engage another lawyer).

11. ABA Informal Opinion 1457 (1980) found consistent with the Model Code of Professional Responsibility the timing, content, and choice of recipients of a form letter announcement by a lawyer that he had resigned from a law firm to become a member of another firm sent "soon after making the change to clients (and only those clients) for whose active, open, and pending matters he was directly responsible as a member of the ABC law firm immediately before his resignation." The form letter stated that the client had a right to decide how and by whom the pending matters would be handled and did not urge the client to choose the departing lawyer over the firm. In ABA Informal Opinion 1466 (1981), Opinion 1457 was extended to include associates, assuming the same fact pattern. The Committee there noted it "does not determine or advise upon issues of law," but then distinguished the facts presented to the Committee from the facts shown in Adler v. Epstein, 393 A.2d 1175 (Pa. 1978), *cert. denied*, 442 U.S. 907 (1979) (departing group of associates enjoined from actively soliciting clients of old firm as part of pre-departure efforts to borrow money on the basis of the clients). Today we reject any implication of Informal Opinions 1457 or 1466 that the notices to current clients and discussions as a matter of ethics must await departure from the firm.

ABA Formal Ethics Opinions (Selected)

ent whether she will be able to continue the representation at her new law firm.[12] If the client requests further information about the departing lawyer's new firm, the lawyer should provide whatever is reasonably necessary to assist the client in making an informed decision about future representation, including, for example, billing rates and a description of the resources available at the new firm to handle the client matter.[13] The departing lawyer nevertheless must continue to make clear in these discussions that the client has the right to choose whether the firm, the departing lawyer and her new firm, or some other lawyer will continue the representation.

Joint Notification By the Lawyer and the Firm is Preferred

Far the better course to protect clients' interests is for the departing lawyer and her law firm to give joint notice of the lawyer's impending departure to all clients for whom the lawyer has performed significant professional services while at the firm, or at least notice to the current clients.[14] Unfortunately, this is not always feasible when the departure is not amicable. In some instances, the lawyer's mere notice to the firm might prompt her immediate termination. When the departing lawyer reasonably anticipates that the firm will not cooperate on providing such a joint notice, she herself

---

ABA Formal
Ethics Opinions
(Selected)

12. The departing lawyer must ensure that her new firm would have no disqualifying conflict of interest in representing the client in a matter under Rule 1.7, or other Rules, and has the competence to undertake the representation. In order to do so, she may need to disclose to the new firm certain limited information relating to this representation. When discussing an association with another firm, the departing lawyer also must mindful of potentially disqualifying conflicts of interest in her old firm if the new firm currently represents any client with interests adverse to a client of the old firm. Should such a client be identified, the departing lawyer may need to be screened within the old firm no later than the commencement of serious discussions with the new firm. *See* ABA Formal Opinion 96-400. Lastly, the departing lawyer also might find that her work in her former firm would, upon her arrival at the new firm, create a conflict of interest under Rule 1.9 with one of her new firm's clients requiring the creation of a screen that, subject to the affected clients' consents in most jurisdictions, would avoid imputation her individual conflict of interest to her new firm under Model Rule 1.10(a).

13. In this respect, we agree with D.C. Bar Legal Ethics Opinion 273 (1997), "Ethical Considerations of Lawyers Moving From One Private Firm Another."

14. Cal. Bar Ethics Op. No. 1985-86, 1985 WL57193 at *2, *supra*, n.1, interprets the California Rule to require both the departing lawyer and the law firm to provide fair and adequate notice of the withdrawal to the client sufficient to allow a client opportunity to make an informed choice of counsel, and states that, where practical, the notice should be made jointly. ABA Informal Opinion 1428 (1979) suggested that, under the Model Code, both the departing lawyer and the law firm had an obligation give the client "the choice as to whether or not the client wishes the firm to continue handling the matter or whether the client wishes to choose another lawyer or legal services firm." *See also* Cleveland Bar Opinion 89-5 (under the Model Code, either the departing lawyer or the law firm must give due notice to those clients of the former firm for whose active, open, and pending matters the lawyer is directly responsible).

must provide notice to those clients for whose active matters she currently is responsible or plays a principal role in the delivery of legal services, in the manner described above, and preferably should confirm the conversations in writing so as to memorialize the details of the communication and her compliance with Model Rules 7.3 and 7.1.[15]

Law Other Than the Model Rules Applies to the Departure

In addition to satisfying her ethical obligations, the departing lawyer also must recognize the requirements of other principles of law as she prepares to leave, especially if she notifies her current clients before telling her firm she is leaving. For example, the departing lawyer may avoid charges of engaging in unfair competition and appropriation of trade secrets if she does not use any client lists or other proprietary information in advising clients of her new association, but uses instead only publicly available information and what she personally knows about the clients' matters.[16]

Charges of breach of fiduciary and other duties owed the former firm also might be avoided if the departing lawyer and her new firm go no further than the permissible conduct noted in Graubard Mollen v. Moskovitz[17]

---

15. The responsible members of the law firm must not take actions that frustrate the departing lawyer's current clients' right to choose their counsel under Rule 1.16(a) and Comment [4] by denying access to the clients' files or otherwise. To do so may violate the responsible members' ethical obligations under Rules 1.16(d) and 5.1.

16. *See, e.g.,* Siegel v. Arter & Hadden, 85 Ohio St. 3d 171, 707 N.E.2d 853 (Ohio Sup. Ct. 1999) (unresolved fact issues precluded summary judgment on unfair competition and trade secret counts because of departing lawyer's use of client list with names, addresses, telephone numbers and matters and fee information, despite notice to firm before notice to clients). *See also* Shein v. Myers, 394 Pa. Super. 549, 552, 576 A.2d 985, 986 (Pa. 1990), appeal denied, 533 Pa. 600, 617 A.2d 1274 (Pa. 1991) ("breakaway" lawyers tortiously interfered with contract between their former firm and its clients by taking 400 client files, making scurrilous statements about the firm, and sending misleading letters to firm clients). In a joint opinion, the Pennsylvania and Philadelphia Bars warned that notice to clients before advising the firm of her intended departure "may be construed as an attempt to lure clients away in violation of the lawyer's fiduciary duties to the firm, or as tortious interference with the firm's relationships with its clients." Pa. Bar Ass'n Comm. on Legal Ethics and Prof. Resp. Joint Op. No. 99-100,1999 WL239079 *2. (Pa. Bar. Assn. Comm. Leg. Eth. Prof. Resp. 1999). The Committee also noted that the "prudent approach" is for the departing lawyer not to notify her clients before advising the firm of her intention to leave to join another firm. *Id.*

17. 86 N.Y.2d 112, 653 N.E.2d 1179 (1995). The Court stated that a departing lawyer's efforts to locate alternative space and affiliations would not violate his fiduciary duties to his firm because those actions obviously require confidentiality. Also, informing firm clients with whom the departing lawyer has a prior professional relationship about his impending withdrawal and reminding them of their right to retain counsel of their choice is permissible. *Id.* at 1183. A departing lawyer should, of course, consult all case law applicable in the practice jurisdiction.

and avoid the conduct the court found actionable, such as secretly attempting to lure firm clients to the new firm (even when the departing lawyer originated and had principal responsibility for the clients' matters) and lying to clients about their right to remain with the old firm and to partners about the lawyer's plans to leave. Although that case involved civil litigation, other courts have imposed discipline on lawyers for similar conduct because it involved dishonesty, fraud, deceit, or misrepresentation in violation of Rule 8.4(c).[18]

Entitlement to Files, Documents, and Other Property Depends on the Model Rules and Other Law

A lawyer moving to a new firm also may wish to take with her files and other documents such as research memoranda, pleadings, and forms. To the extent that these documents were prepared by the lawyer and are considered the lawyer's property or are in the public domain, she may take copies with her. Otherwise, the lawyer may have to obtain the firm's consent to do so.

The Committee is of the opinion that, absent special circumstances, the lawyer does not violate any Model Rule by taking with her copies of documents that she herself has created for general use in her practice. However, as with the use of client lists, the question of whether a lawyer may take with her continuing legal education materials, practice forms, or computer files she has created turns on principles of property law and trade secret law. For example, the outcome might depend on who prepared the material and the measures employed by the law firm to retain title or otherwise to protect it from external use or from taking by departing lawyers.

Client files and client property must be retained or transferred in accordance with the client's direction.[19] A departing lawyer who is not continu-

ABA Formal Ethics Opinions (Selected)

---

18. *See, e.g.,* In the Matter of Cupples, 979 S.W.2d 932, 935 (Mo. 1998); In re Cupples, 952 S.W.2d 226, 236-37 (Mo. 1997) (in separate disciplinary proceedings involving a lawyer in connection with his departure from two different law firms, the court held that the lawyer's conduct, which included secreting client files as he prepared to withdraw from a firm, removing files without client consent, failing to inform client of change in nature of the representation, and other actions constituted conduct involving dishonesty, fraud, deceit, or misrepresentation in violation of Missouri's counterpart to Model Rule 8.4(c)). See also In re Smith, 853 P.2d 449, 453 (Or. 1992) (Before leaving law firm, lawyer met with new clients in his office, had them sign retainer agreements with him, and took files from the office. In imposing a four (4) month suspension from practice of law, the Court stated that "[a]lthough there is no explicit rule requiring lawyers to be candid and fair with their partners or employers, such an obligation is implicit in the prohibition of DR 1-102(A)(3) against dishonesty, fraud, deceit, or misrepresentation.").

19. *See* Model Rule 1.16(d), *supra,* n.8. Pending client instructions, client property must be held in accordance with Model Rule 1.15.

ing the representation may, nevertheless, retain copies of client documents relating to her representation of former clients, but must reasonably ensure that the confidential client information they contain is protected in accordance with Model Rules 1.6 and 1.9.

Conclusion

Both the lawyer who is terminating her association with a law firm to join another and the responsible members of the firm who remain have ethical obligations to clients for whom the departing lawyer is providing legal services. These ethical obligations include promptly giving notice of the lawyer's impending departure to those current clients on whose matters she actively is working.

The lawyer does not violate any Model Rule in notifying the current clients of her impending departure by in-person or live telephone contact before advising the firm of her intentions to resign, so long as the lawyer also advises the client of the client's right to choose counsel and does not disparage her law firm or engage in conduct that involves dishonesty, fraud, deceit, or misrepresentation. After her departure, she also may send written notice of her new affiliation to any firm clients regardless of whether she has a family or prior professional relationship with them.

Before preparing to leave one firm for another, the departing lawyer should inform herself of applicable law other than the Model Rules, including the law of fiduciaries, property and unfair competition. She also should take care to act lawfully in taking or utilizing the firm's information or other property.

Formal Opinion 09-455   October 8, 2009
Disclosure of Conflicts Information
When Lawyers Move Between Law Firms

When a lawyer moves between law firms, both the moving lawyer and the prospective new firm have a duty to detect and resolve conflicts of interest. Although Rule 1.6(a) generally protects conflicts information (typically the "persons and issues involved" in a matter), disclosure of conflicts information during the process of lawyers moving between firms is ordinarily permissible, subject to limitations. Any disclosure of conflicts information should be no greater than reasonably necessary to accomplish the purpose of detecting and resolving conflicts and must not compromise the attorney-client privilege or otherwise prejudice a client or former client. A lawyer or law firm receiving conflicts information may not reveal such information or use it for purposes other than detecting and resolving conflicts of interest. Disclosure normally should not occur until the moving lawyer and the prospective new firm have engaged in substantive discussions regarding a possible new association.[1]

Many lawyers change law firm associations during their careers. New York's highest court noted more than a decade ago that the "revolving door" is a modern-day law firm fixture.[2] Usually these changes are voluntary, but often they are not. The Model Rules of Professional Conduct recognize lawyer mobility. Comment [4] to Rule 1.9, "Lawyers Moving Between Firms," states that the rule on duties to former clients should not be so broadly cast as to preclude other persons from having reasonable choice of legal counsel or unreasonably hamper lawyers from forming new associations and accepting new clients. The February 2009 amendment of Rule 1.10(a) to permit screening of lawyers moving between firms to prevent imputed disqualification of the new firm is grounded on that premise. The importance of clients being free to choose counsel after a change of association is also identified in Comment [1] to Rule 5.6.

The Need for Conflicts Analysis

When a lawyer moves between law firms, the moving lawyer and the new firm each have an obligation to protect their respective clients and for-

ABA Formal
Ethics Opinions
(Selected)

---

1. This opinion is based on the Model Rules of Professional Conduct as amended by the ABA House of Delegates through August 2009. The laws, court rules, regulations, rules of professional conduct, and opinions promulgated in individual jurisdictions are controlling.
2. *Graubard Mollen Dannet & Horowitz v. Moskovitz*, 653 N.E.2d 1179, 1180 (N.Y. 1995).

mer clients against harm from conflicts of interest. A moving lawyer whose current clients may wish to become clients of the new firm must determine whether the new firm would have disqualifying conflicts of interest in representing those clients.[3] The prospective new firm has a corresponding duty to determine the conflicts in its current representations that could arise if the moving lawyer actually joins the firm. Comment [3] to Rule 1.7 advises lawyers to adopt reasonable procedures, appropriate for the size and type of firm and practice, "to determine in both litigation and non-litigation matters the persons and issues involved" to ascertain whether proposed new matters are permitted under the conflicts rules. Comment [2] to Rule 5.1(a) includes policies and procedures designed to "detect and resolve" conflicts of interest among those measures that law firm managers must establish to give reasonable assurance that all lawyers in the firm conform to the Rules.

The obligation to detect and resolve conflicts of interest derives from the common law as well as the lawyer ethics rules.[4] When lawyers move between firms, early detection and resolution of conflicts of interest is also prudent risk management. "A common and often serious problem for law firms is the conflict of interest involving a newly hired lawyer ... and his or her former clients or adversaries. Accordingly ... it is essential to conduct prior conflict screening as thoroughly as possible before making hiring decisions."[5] Other authorities have deemed it essential in order to facilitate the necessary conflicts screening to include client identification and subject matter in the new firm's conflicts database for all former clients of lawyers joining the law firm.[6]

Tension between Confidentiality and Conflicts Analysis

Despite the need for both a lawyer considering a move and the prospective new firm to detect and resolve conflicts of interest, some commentators have expressed concern that the Model Rules do not specifically permit disclosure of the information required for conflicts analysis.[7] This concern

ABA Formal
Ethics Opinions
(Selected)

---

3. ABA Comm. on Ethics and Prof'l Responsibility, Formal Op. 99-414 (September 8, 1999) (Ethical Obligations When a Lawyer Changes Firms) n.12.

4. *See* RESTATEMENT (THIRD) OF THE LAW GOVERNING LAWYERS § 121, cmt. *g* (2000); and RICHARD E. FLAMM, LAWYER DISQUALIFICATION: CONFLICTS OF INTEREST AND OTHER BASES § 3.9 (2003).

5. ANTHONY E. DAVIS AND PETER R. JARVIS, RISK MANAGEMENT: SURVIVAL TOOLS FOR LAW FIRMS 109 (2d ed. 2007).

6. LAWRENCE J. FOX AND SUSAN R. MARTYN, RED FLAGS: A LAWYER'S HANDBOOK ON LEGAL ETHICS § 6.07 (ALI-ABA 2005).

7. *See, e.g.,* Paul R. Tremblay, *Migrating Lawyers and the Ethics of Conflict Checking,* 19 GEO. J. LEGAL ETHICS 489, 506-08 (2006); and Eli Wald, *Lawyer Mobility and Legal Ethics: Resolving the Tension between Confidentiality Requirements and Contemporary Lawyers' Career Paths,* 31 J. LEGAL PROF. 199, 203-07 (2007).

arises from the definition of information covered by Rule 1.6(a), which is "all information relating to the representation, whatever its source."[8] Thus, the persons and issues involved in a matter generally are protected by Rule 1.6 and ordinarily may not be disclosed unless an exception to the Rule applies or the affected client gives informed consent.[9]

Disclosure of conflicts information does not fit neatly into the stated exceptions to Rule 1.6. The exception in Rule 1.6(a) for disclosures "impliedly authorized in order to carry out the representation" typically is limited to disclosures that serve the interests of the client. Examples cited in Comment [5] to Rule 1.6 include facts that must be admitted in litigation or a disclosure that facilitates a satisfactory conclusion to a matter, disclosures clearly necessary to advance a client's representation. Another example was recognized in ABA Formal Opinion 98-411,[10] which found limited disclosure outside a law firm in a lawyer-to-lawyer consultation impliedly authorized "when the consulting lawyer reasonably believes the disclosure will further the representation by obtaining the consulted lawyer's experience or expertise for the benefit of the consulting lawyer's client." This interpretation is consistent with general agency law: an agent's implied authority is limited to acts "necessary or incidental" to achieving the principal's objectives.[11] There may well be instances where client representations are advanced by lawyers moving between firms, but most such moves appear to take place for the sake of the lawyer rather than advancement of the client's representation. Absent a demonstrable benefit to a client's representation from the disclosure of conflicts information, it is unlikely that the disclosure would be "impliedly authorized" within the generally understood and accepted meaning of that exception.

A second stated exception to Rule 1.6(a) that might arguably allow dis-

ABA Formal
Ethics Opinions
(Selected)

---

8. Rule 1.6 cmt. 3.

9. *See, e.g.*, Comment [4] to Rule 1.6 (use of hypothetical to discuss representation permissible so long as there is no reasonable likelihood that listener could ascertain identity of client or situation involved); ABA Formal Op. 96-399 (Jan. 18, 1996) (Ethical Obligations of Lawyers Whose Employers Receive Funds from the Legal Services Corporation to their Existing and Future Clients When Such Funding is Reduced and When Remaining Funding is Subject to Restrictive Conditions), in FORMAL AND INFORMAL ETHICS OPINIONS 1983-1998 at 384-85 (ABA 2000) (lawyers may be unable to comply with proposed condition of Legal Services Corporation funding to disclose identity of all clients); and ABA Formal Op. 01-421 (February 16, 2001) (Ethical Obligations of a Lawyer Working Under Insurance Company Guidelines and Other Restrictions) (insurance defense lawyer may not disclose billing records relating to insured's representation to third-party auditor designated by insurer without insured's informed consent).

10. ABA Formal Op. 98-411 (August 30, 1998) (Ethical Issues in Lawyer-to-Lawyer Consultation).

11. *See* RESTATEMENT (THIRD) OF AGENCY § 2.02(1) (2006).

closure of conflicts information incident to lawyers moving between firms is Rule 1.6(b)(6), which permits disclosure of information "the lawyer reasonably believes necessary ... to comply with other law." However, Comment [12] to Rule 1.6 seems to limit "other law" to law other than the Rules. Compliance with Rule 1.7 would therefore not seem to fall within the exception. Comment [12] also notes that the disclosure must be "required" by the other law. Because the movement of lawyers between firms is not mandated by some external law, it is unlikely that disclosure of conflicts information to comply with Rule 1.7 qualifies as required by other law outside the Rules. Finally, as explained in Comment [12], when disclosure of information relating to the representation appears to be required by other law, the lawyer must discuss the matter with the client to the extent required by Rule 1.4. Such a discussion at the time conflicts information is provided often would not be practicable.

Obtaining clients' informed consent, as defined in Rule 1.0(e), before a lawyer explores a potential move could resolve the tension between the broad scope of Rule 1.6(a) and the need to disclose conflicts information, but there are serious practical difficulties in doing so. Many contemplated moves are never consummated. In the common situation where a lawyer interviews more than one prospective new firm, multiple consents would be required. Consent of all former clients, as well as all current clients, also would be necessary. Further, seeking prior informed consent likely would involve giving notice to the lawyer's current firm,[12] with unpredictable and possibly adverse consequences.[13] Routinely requiring prior informed consent to disclose conflicts information would give any client or former client the power to prevent a lawyer from seeking a new association with no incentive for a client or former client to give such consent unless the client plans to follow the lawyer to the new firm. Nevertheless, as noted below, there may be unusual situations where the persons and issues involved are so sensitive that a moving lawyer may need to seek informed client consent or take alternative protective measures before disclosing that information.

Permissive Disclosure of Conflicts Information

In most situations involving lawyers moving between firms, however, lawyers should be permitted to disclose the persons and issues involved in a matter, the basic information needed for conflicts analysis. The Model Rules are "rules of reason" to be "interpreted with reference to the purposes

---

12. *See* Robert W. Hillman, Hillman on Lawyer Mobility: The Law and Ethics of Partner Withdrawals and Law Firm Breakups § 2.2.4 (2d ed. 2009 Supp.).

13. For a discussion of when a lawyer changing firms must give notice to clients for whom the lawyer has active matters, *see* ABA Formal Op. 99-414, *supra* note 3.

of legal representation and of the law itself."[14] Interpreting Rule 1.6(a) to prohibit any disclosure of the information needed to detect and resolve conflicts of interest when lawyers move between firms would render impossible compliance with Rules 1.7, 1.9, and 1.10, and prejudice clients by failing to avoid conflicts of interest. Such an interpretation would preclude lawyers moving between firms from conforming with the conflicts rules.

The need to disclose conflicts information has been recognized when lawyers change firms as well as in other contexts. As noted above, a moving lawyer with a current client that may wish to become a client of the new firm "must ensure that her new firm would have no disqualifying conflict of interest.... In order to do so, she may need to disclose to the new firm certain limited information relating to this representation."[15] Providing guidelines for employing temporary lawyers in compliance with the Rules, ABA Formal Opinion 88-356 advises: "The second firm should make appropriate inquiry [of the temporary lawyer] and should not hire the temporary lawyer or use the temporary lawyer on a matter if doing so would disqualify the firm from continuing its representation of a client on a pending matter."[16] ABA Formal Opinion 99-415 gives guidance regarding representations adverse to an organization by its former in-house lawyer, and advises in-house lawyers to maintain logs describing those matters on which they worked because determination by the new firm of whether there was a conflict of interest with the former employer required "an inquiry into the responsibilities of the lawyer" during the former employment.[17] Further, the February 2009 revision of Rule 1.10(a) that permits screening of lawyers moving between firms to avoid imputing the disqualification of the moving lawyer to the new firm becomes relevant only if a former client conflict of the moving lawyer has been recognized by the new firm, presumably on the basis of information obtained from the moving lawyer. These opinions and amended Rule 1.10(a) clearly acknowledge that disclosure of conflicts information is permitted to facilitate compliance with the obligation to deal with conflicts of interest.

The importance of a lawyer's compliance with the Rules has justified limited disclosure of protected information in other circumstances. Rule 1.6(b) was amended in 2002 to clarify that disclosures reasonably necessary to secure legal advice about the lawyer's compliance with the Rules are

ABA Formal
Ethics Opinions
(Selected)

---

14. Scope, Paragraph [14].

15. ABA Formal Op. 99-414 n.12.

16. ABA Formal Op. 88-356 (Dec. 16, 1988) (Temporary Lawyers), in FORMAL AND INFORMAL ETHICS OPINIONS 1983-1998 (ABA 2000) at 41.

17. ABA Formal Op. 99-415 (Sept. 8, 1999) (Representation Adverse to Organization by Former In-House Lawyer).

proper even when not impliedly authorized under the stated exception to 1.6(a) because of the overriding importance of compliance with the Rules.[18]

As discussed above, before a moving lawyer joins a new firm, the Model Rules and the common law require the lawyer and the firm to detect and resolve conflicts of interest to protect their clients and former clients, even if only one party to the move undertakes the actual conflicts analysis. Conflicts analysis cannot be accomplished without sharing conflicts information generally about the persons and issues involved in a matter. Because conflicts information is needed to detect and resolve conflicts of interest when lawyers move between firms, as a general matter and subject to the limitations stated below, disclosure of conflicts information otherwise protected by Rule 1.6 should be considered permissible as necessary to comply with the Rules.

This conclusion is consistent, although not congruent, with a comment to the current ethics rules of one state and at least four bar association opinions. Comment [5A] to Colorado Rule 1.6 (which defines protected information substantially the same as Model Rule 1.6) states that a lawyer moving or contemplating a move from one firm to another may disclose client identity and the basic nature of the representation to insure compliance with the conflicts rules. Boston Bar Association Opinion 2004-1 concluded that without implicit authorization to share limited conflicts information, the requirement of Rule 1.7 to check for conflicts of interest as well as the protection of lawyer mobility and a client's right to choose a lawyer under Rule 5.6 could not be reconciled.[19] Opinions from jurisdictions that did not adopt the Model Rules definition of protected information, but rather retained the 1969 Model Code of Professional Responsibility formulation of confidences and secrets, reached similar results.[20]

---

18. A LEGISLATIVE HISTORY: THE DEVELOPMENT OF THE ABA MODEL RULES OF PROFESSIONAL CONDUCT, 1982-2005 (ABA 2006) at 125. *See also* Comment [9] to Rule 1.6 (even when not impliedly authorized, paragraph (b)(4) permits disclosure to secure legal advice because of importance of compliance with Rules).

19. Boston Bar Ass'n Eth. Comm. Op. 2004-1 (May 20, 2005) ("The 'Do's and Don'ts' of Revealing 'Conflict-checking Information'"), available at http://www.bostonbar.org/sc/ethics/op04_1.pdf. Massachusetts Rule 1.6(a) protects only "confidential information relating to representation of a client."

20. *See* D.C. Bar Ass'n Eth. Op. 312 (April 2002) (Information That May Be Provided To Check Conflict When a Lawyer Seeks to Join a New Firm), available at http://www.dcbar.org/for_lawyers/ethics/legal_ethics/opinions/opinion312.cfm; New York State Bar Ass'n Eth. Op. 720 (August 27, 1999) (Successive Representation; Moving Lawyer; Conflict Check.), available at http://www.nysba.org/AM/Template.cfm?Section=Ethics_Opinions&CONTENTID=18917&TEMPLATE=/CM/ContentDisplay.cfm; and Association of the Bar of the City of New York Eth. Op. 2003-03 (Oct. 2003) (Checking For Conflicts of Interest), available at http://www.abcny.org/Ethics/eth2003-3.html.

Limitations on Disclosure

Permissive disclosure of conflicts information otherwise protected by Rule 1.6(a) incident to the process of lawyers moving between firms is limited in scope. Consistent with Comment [14] to Rule 1.6, any disclosure of conflicts information when lawyers move between firms should be no greater than reasonably necessary to accomplish the purpose of detection and resolution of conflicts of interest. As noted in Comment [3] to Rule 1.7, conflicts information typically includes the persons and issues involved in the relevant matter, and disclosure of that information would be permitted. In some cases, conflicts of interest that would likely frustrate a contemplated move can be discovered even before disclosure of client-specific information is necessary. For example, if it is recognized that moving lawyer's current firm and the prospective new firm are adverse in numerous existing matters or regularly represent commonly antagonistic groups (*e.g.*, landlords and tenants or management and unions), then discussions regarding a potential move probably would proceed no further. In other cases, simply comparing client lists or the general nature of the practices of the moving lawyer and the prospective new firm will often reveal the absence or presence of potential conflicts without the need for additional disclosure; initial disclosures of conflicts information thus can often be limited to names of clients or areas of practice. In any case, if information beyond the persons and issues involved appears necessary for conflicts analysis, alternative measures such as those discussed below should be considered.

Another important limitation is that disclosing conflicts information must not compromise the attorney-client privilege or otherwise prejudice a client or former client.[21] There are matters, albeit rare, in which the identity of the client or the nature of the representation or both are protected by the attorney-client privilege.[22] There are also situations (*e.g.*, clients planning a hostile takeover, contemplating a divorce, or appearing before a grand jury) in which disclosure of non-privileged information to the prospective new firm of the persons and issues involved would likely prejudice the client or former client.

In some situations, resolving whether a lawyer's move to a new firm would result in a conflict of interest requires fact-intensive analysis of information beyond just the persons and issues involved in a representation.

ABA Formal
Ethics Opinions
(Selected)

---

21. *See* ABA Formal Op. 98-411, *supra* footnote 9 and accompanying text (consulting lawyer in lawyer-to-lawyer consultation impliedly authorized to disclose certain information relating to the representation without client consent, but may not waive attorney-client privilege or otherwise prejudice client).

22. *See* EDNA SELAN EPSTEIN, THE ATTORNEY-CLIENT PRIVILEGE AND THE WORK-PRODUCT DOCTRINE 88-93 (5th ed. 2007).

Such an analysis will often be required in determining whether there is a "substantial relationship" between two matters for purposes of Rule 1.9. In such cases, the firm may be able to resolve the question based on information available from sources other than the moving lawyer. If not, the moving lawyer must either seek prior client consent, be screened from the current representation pursuant to Rule 1.10(a)(2), forgo the move, or persuade the prospective firm to undertake an alternative method of detecting and resolving the conflicts of interest issue consistent with the stated exceptions to Rule 1.6.

An alternative suggested by some commentators is retention by the moving lawyer, the prospective new firm, or both, of an independent or intermediary lawyer to receive and analyze conflicts information in confidence. This approach should not compromise any privilege nor frustrate the reasonable expectations of a client. It also conforms to Rule 1.6(b)(4), which expressly permits disclosure of protected information to secure legal advice about a lawyer's compliance with the Rules. The intermediary lawyer then may advise one or both, without disclosing any facts to the other, of the intermediary lawyer's conclusion on the resolution of, or the inability to resolve, any conflicts of interest that may have been detected. Procedures involving use of intermediary lawyers when lawyers move between firms have been described by Professors Tremblay,[23] and Wald,[24] as well as by Professors Hazard and Hodes.[25] If a client has instructed the moving lawyer not to reveal particular information to any other person, including other firm lawyers, that information cannot properly be imparted to the intermediary lawyer.[26]

In every case, a lawyer or law firm receiving conflicts information has a duty not to reveal that information. Use of conflicts information by the receiving lawyer or firm should be limited to the detection and resolution of conflicts of interest, and dissemination of conflicts information should be restricted to those persons assigned to or involved in the conflicts analysis with respect to a particular lawyer.

Timing of Disclosure

Timing is also important. Conflicts information should not be disclosed until reasonably necessary, but the process by which firms decide to offer lateral lawyers positions varies widely among firms and usually differs

---

23. 19 Geo. J. Legal Ethics at 544.

24. 31 J. Legal Prof. at 227.

25. *See* GEOFFREY C. HAZARD, JR. AND W. WILLIAM HODES, THE LAW OF LAWYERING § 14.4, note 2 at 14-40 (3d ed. 2009 Supp.).

26. *See* Comment [5] to Rule 1.6.

within firms according to the age and experience level of the lawyer under consideration. Many firms might not ask conflicts information of younger lawyers until making an offer of employment, which will be contingent on resolution of conflicts. For partner-level lawyers, the process is more complicated. As a consequence, conflicts issues may need to be detected and resolved at a relatively early stage.[27]

In any event, negotiations between the moving lawyer and the prospective new firm should have moved beyond the initial phase and progressed to the stage where a conflicts analysis is reasonably necessary, which typically will not occur until the moving lawyer and the prospective new firm have engaged in substantive discussions regarding a possible new association. In another context, ABA Formal Op. 96-400[28] explored at length the issue of when a lawyer considering potential employment with an adverse firm or party must consult with and seek consent of the involved client. The analysis there concluded that participation in substantive discussions by the moving lawyer and the prospective employer best identified the point at which such consideration needed to occur. Thus, conflicts information normally should not be disclosed when conversations concerning potential employment are initiated, but only after substantive discussions have taken place.

ABA Formal Ethics Opinions (Selected)

---

27. *See, e.g., Roberts & Schaefer Co. v. San-Con*, 898 F. Supp. 356, 363 (S.D.W.Va. 1995) ("Lawyers and law firms must consider and address the effects of mergers and new associations on their clients well in advance of when such events occur.").

28. ABA Formal Op. 96-400 (January 24, 1996) (Job Negotiations with Adverse Firm or Party), in FORMAL AND INFORMAL ETHICS OPINIONS 1983-1998 (ABA 2000) 391 n.9.

Formal Opinion 10-457   August 5, 2010
Lawyer Websites

Websites have become a common means by which lawyers communicate with the public. Lawyers must not include misleading information on websites, must be mindful of the expectations created by the website, and must carefully manage inquiries invited through the website. Websites that invite inquiries may create a prospective client-lawyer relationship under Rule 1.18. Lawyers who respond to website-initiated inquiries about legal services should consider the possibility that Rule 1.18 may apply.[1]

I. Introduction

Many lawyers and law firms have established websites as a means of communicating with the public. A lawyer website can provide to anyone with Internet access a wide array of information about the law, legal institutions, and the value of legal services. Websites also offer lawyers a twenty-four hour marketing tool by calling attention to the particular qualifications of a lawyer or a law firm, explaining the scope of the legal services they provide and describing their clientele, and adding an electronic link to contact an individual lawyer.

The obvious benefit of this information can diminish or disappear if the website visitor misunderstands or is misled by website information and features. A website visitor might rely on general legal information to answer a personal legal question. Another might assume that a website's provision of direct electronic contact to a lawyer implies that the lawyer agrees to preserve the confidentiality of information disclosed by website visitors.

For lawyers, website marketing can give rise to the problem of unanticipated reliance or unexpected inquiries or information from website visitors seeking legal advice. This opinion addresses some of the ethical obligations that lawyers should address in considering the content and features of their websites.[2]

---

1. This opinion is based on the ABA Model Rules of Professional Conduct as amended by the ABA House of Delegates through August 2010. The laws, court rules, regulations, rules of professional conduct, and opinions promulgated in individual jurisdictions are controlling.

2. We do not deal here with website content generated by governmental lawyers or offices or by non-profit law advocacy firms or organizations. *See, e.g., In re Primus,* 436 U.S. 412 (1978) (discussing how solicitation of prospective litigants by nonprofit organizations that engage in litigation as form of political expression and political association constitutes expressive and associational conduct entitled to First Amendment protection, which government may regulate only narrowly).

ABA Formal Ethics Opinions (Selected)

II. Website Content

A. Information about Lawyers, their Law Firm, or their Clients

Lawyer websites may provide biographical information about lawyers, including educational background, experience, area of practice, and contact information (telephone, facsimile and e-mail address). A website also may add information about the law firm, such as its history, experience, and areas of practice, including general descriptions about prior engagements. More specific information about a lawyer or law firm's former or current clients, including clients' identities, matters handled, or results obtained also might be included.

Any of this information constitutes a "communication about the lawyer or the lawyer's services," and is therefore subject to the requirements of Model Rule 7.1[3] as well as the prohibitions against false and misleading statements in Rules 8.4(c) (generally) and 4.1(a) (when representing clients). Together, these rules prohibit false, fraudulent or misleading statements of law or fact. Thus, no website communication may be false or misleading, or may omit facts such that the resulting statement is materially misleading. Rules 5.1 and 5.3 extend this obligation to managerial lawyers in law firms by obligating them to make reasonable efforts to ensure the firm has in place measures giving reasonable assurance that all firm lawyers and nonlawyer assistants will comply with the rules of professional conduct.

As applied to lawyer websites, these rules allow a lawyer to include accurate information that is not misleading about the lawyer and the lawyer's law firm, including contact information and information about the law practice.[4] To avoid misleading readers, this information should be updated on a regular basis.[5] Specific information that identifies current or former clients

ABA Formal
Ethics Opinions
(Selected)

---

3. *See, e.g.,* Arizona State Bar Op. 97-04 (1997), *available at* http://www.myazbar.org/ Ethics/opinionview.cfm?id=480; California Standing Committee on Prof'l Resp. and Conduct Formal Op. 2001-155, 2001 WL 34029609 (2001); Hawaii Sup. Ct. Disc. Bd. Formal Op. 41 (2001), available at http://www.odchawaii.com/FORMAL_WRITTEN_OPINIONS. html; South Carolina Bar Eth. Advisory Committee Op. 04-06, 2004 WL 1520110 *1 (2004); Vermont Advisory Eth. Op. 2000-04, *available at* http://www.vtbar.org/Upload%20 Files/WebPages/Attorney%20Resources/aeopinions/Advisory%20Ethics%20Opinions/ Advertising/advertising. htm. Many state and local ethics opinions are published online can be accessed through the ABA Center for Professional Responsibility website at http:// www.abanet.org/cpr/links.html.

4. *See, e.g.,* North Carolina State Bar Formal Eth. Op. 2009-6 (2009) (firm may provide case summaries on website, including accurate information about verdicts and settlements, as long as it adds specific information about factual and legal circumstances of cases ((complexity, whether liability or damages were contested, whether opposing party was represented by counsel, firm's success in collecting judgment)) in conjunction with appropriate disclaimer to preclude misleading prospective clients).

5. *See, e.g.,* Missouri Bar Inf. Advisory Op. 20060005 (2006) (firm must remove lawyer's biographical information within reasonable time after lawyer leaves firm).

or the scope of their matters also may be disclosed, as long as the clients or former clients give informed consent[6] as required by Rules 1.6 (current clients) and 1.9 (former clients).[7] Website disclosure of client identifying information is not normally impliedly authorized because the disclosure is not being made to carry out the representation of a client, but to promote the lawyer or the law firm.[8]

B. Information about the Law

Lawyers have long offered legal information to the public in a variety of ways, such as by writing books or articles, giving talks to groups, or staffing legal hotlines. Lawyer websites also can assist the public in understanding the law and in identifying when and how to obtain legal services.[9] Legal information might include general information about the law applicable to a lawyer's area(s) of practice, as well as links to other websites, blogs, or forums with related information. Information may be presented in narrative form, in a "FAQ" (frequently asked questions) format, in a "Q & A" (question and answer) format, or in some other manner.[10]

Legal information, like information about a lawyer or the lawyer's services, must meet the requirements of Rules 7.1, 8.4(c), and 4.1(a). Lawyers may offer accurate legal information that does not materially mislead reasonable readers.[11] To avoid misleading readers, lawyers should make sure

---

6. *See, e.g.*, Ohio Advisory Op. 2000-6, 2000 WL 1872572 *5 (2000) (law firm may list client's name on firm website with client's informed consent). *See also* New York Rule of Professional Conduct 7.1(b) (2) (2009) (lawyer may advertise name of regularly represented client, provided that client has given prior written consent).

7. These rules apply to "all information relating to the representation, whatever its source" including publicly available information. Model Rule 1.6 cmt. 3. The consent can be oral or written. Rules 1.6 and 1.9(c) require informed consent, but do not require a written confirmation.

8. *See* ABA Committee on Eth. and Prof'l Responsibility, Formal Op. 09-455 (2009) (Disclosure of Conflicts Information When Lawyers Move Between Law Firms) (absent demonstrable benefit to client's representation, disclosure of client identifying information, including client's name and nature of matter handled, is not impliedly authorized under Rule 1.6(a)).

9. Model Rule 7.2 Comment [1] acknowledges that the "public's need to know about legal services can be fulfilled in part through advertising," a need that may be "particularly acute" in the case of persons who have not made extensive use of, or fear they may not be able to pay for, legal services.

10. *See, e.g.*, Vermont Advisory Eth. Op. 2000-04, *supra* note 3 (lawyer may use "frequently asked questions" format as long as information is current, accurate, and includes clear statement that it does not constitute legal advice and readers should not rely on it to solve individual problem).

11. Rule 7.1 Comment [2] provides that a "truthful statement is also misleading if there is a substantial likelihood that it will lead a reasonable person to formulate a specific conclusion ... for which there is no reasonable factual foundation."

ABA Formal
Ethics Opinions
(Selected)

that legal information is accurate and current,[12] and should include qualifying statements or disclaimers that "may preclude a finding that a statement is likely to create unjustified expectations or otherwise mislead a prospective client."[13] Although no exact line can be drawn between legal information and legal advice, both the context and content of the information offered are helpful in distinguishing between the two.[14]

With respect to context, lawyers who speak to groups generally have been characterized as offering only general legal information. With respect to content, lawyers who answer fact-specific legal questions may be characterized as offering personal legal advice, especially if the lawyer is responding to a question that can reasonably be understood to refer to the questioner's individual circumstances. However, a lawyer who poses and answers a hypothetical question usually will not be characterized as offering legal advice. To avoid misunderstanding, our previous opinions have recommended that lawyers who provide general legal information include statements that characterize the information as general in nature and caution that it should not be understood as a substitute for personal legal advice.[15]

---

12. ABA Law Practice Management Section, *Best Practice Guidelines for Legal Information Web Site Providers* 1 (Feb. 2003), *available at* http://meetings.abanet.org/webupload/commupload/EP024500/relatedresources/best_practice_guidelines.pdf (website providing legal information should provide full and accurate information about identity and contact details of provider on each page of website, as well as dates on which substantive content was last reviewed).

13. Model Rule 7.1 cmt. 3. *See, e.g.,* ABA Law Practice Management Section, *Best Practice Guidelines, supra* note 12 at 2 (website providers should avoid misleading users about jurisdiction to which site's content relates, and if clearly state-specific, the jurisdiction in which the law applies should be identified).

14. *See, e.g.,* Arizona State Bar Op. 97-04, *supra* note 3 (because of inability to screen for conflicts of interest and possibility of disclosing confidential information, lawyers should not answer specific legal questions posed by laypersons in Internet chat rooms unless question presented is of general nature and advice given is not fact-specific); California Standing Committee on Prof'l Resp. and Conduct Formal Op. 2003-164, 2003 WL 23146203 (2003) (legal advice includes making recommendations about specific course of action to follow; public context of radio call-in show that includes warnings about information not being substitute for individualized legal advice makes it unlikely lawyers have agreed to act as caller's lawyer); South Carolina Bar Eth. Advisory Committee Op. 94-27 *2 (1995), 1995 WL 934127 (lawyer may maintain electronic presence for purpose of discussing legal topics, but must obtain sufficient information to make conflicts check before offering legal advice); Utah Eth. Op. 95-01 (1995), 1995 WL 49472 *1 ("how to" booklet on legal subject matter does not constitute practice of law).

15. ABA Inf. Op. 85-1512 (1985) (Establishment of Private Multistate Lawyer Referral Service by Nonprofit Religious Organization), in FORMAL AND INFORMAL ETHICS OPINIONS: FORMAL OPINIONS 1983-1998, at 550, 551 (ABA 2000) (not unethical to prepare articles of general legal information for lay public, but may be prudent to include statement that information furnished is only general and not substitute for personalized legal advice); ABA Inf. Op. 85-1510 (1985) (Establishment of Multistate Private Lawyer

ABA Formal Ethics Opinions (Selected)

Such a warning is especially useful for website visitors who may be inexperienced in using legal services, and may believe that they can rely on general legal information to solve their specific problem.[16] It would be prudent to avoid any misunderstanding by warning visitors that the legal information provided is general and should not be relied on as legal advice, and by explaining that legal advice cannot be given without full consideration of all relevant information relating to the visitor's individual situation.

C. Website Visitor Inquiries

Inquiries from a website visitor about legal advice or representation may raise an issue concerning the application of Rule 1.18 (Duties to Prospective Clients).[17] Rule 1.18 protects the confidentiality of prospective cli-

---

Referral Service for Benefit of Subscribers to Corporation's Services), in FORMAL AND INFORMAL ETHICS OPINIONS: FORMAL OPINIONS 1983-1998, at 544, 545 (corporate counsel may author articles of general legal information for corporations' subscriber newsletter, but "good practice" to include a statement that information is only general in nature and not substitute for personal legal advice).

16. *See, e.g.,* ABA Law Practice Management Section, *Best Practice Guidelines, supra* note 12 at 3 (websites that provide legal information should give users conspicuous notice that information does not constitute legal advice). Some state opinions also warn against providing specific or particularized facts in a lawyer's communication to avoid creating a client-lawyer relationship. *See also* District of Columbia Bar Eth. Op. 316 (2002), *available at* http://www.dcbar.org/for_lawyers/ethics/legal_ethics/opinions/opinion316.cfm (online chat rooms and listserves); Maryland State Bar Ass'n Committee on Eth. Op. 2007-18 (2008) (lawyer conducting domestic relations law seminars for lay public); New Jersey Advisory Committee on Prof'l Eth. Op. 712 (2008) (Attorney-Staffed Legal Hotline For Members of Nonprofit Trade Association), *available at* http://lawlibrary.rutgers.edu/ethics/acpe/acp712_1.html (lawyer staffing telephone hotline); New Jersey Advisory Committee on Prof'l Eth. Op 671, 1993 WL 137685 (1993) (Activities and Obligations of Pro Bono Attorneys), (lawyer-volunteer at abused women shelter); New Mexico Bar Op. 2001-1 (2001) (Application of Rules of Professional Conduct to Lawyer's Use of Listserve-type Message Boards and Communications) (listserves); Wisconsin Prof'l Eth. Committee Op. E-95-5 (1995), *available at* http://www.wisbar.org/AM/Template.cfm?Section=Legal_Research&Template=/CustomSource/Search/Search.cfm&output=xml_no_dtd&proxy stylesheet=wisbar5&client=wisbar5&filter=1&start=0&Site=SBW&q=%22formal+opinion%22+E%2D95%2D5&submit=ethics (lawyervolunteer at organization that provides information about landlord-tenant law). The Model Rules defer to "principles of substantive law external to these Rules [to] determine when a client-lawyer relationship exists." Scope cmt. 17.

17. *See, e.g.,* Arizona State Bar Op. 02-04 (2002), *available at* http://www.myazbar.org/Ethics/opinionview.cfm?id=288 (lawyer does not owe duty of confidentiality to individuals who unilaterally e-mail inquiries to lawyer when e-mail is unsolicited); California Standing Committee on Prof'l Resp. and Conduct Formal Op. 2001-155, *supra* note 3 (lawyer may avoid incurring duty of confidentiality to persons who seek legal services by visiting lawyer's website and disclose confidential information only if site contains clear disclaimer); Iowa Bar Ass'n Eth. Op. 07-02 (2007), *available at* http://www.iowabar.org/ethics.nsf/e61beed77a215f6686256497004ce492/cb0a70672d69d8c1862573380013fb9d?OpenDocument (message that encourages detailed response about case could in some situations be considered bilateral); New Hampshire Bar Ass'n Eth. Committee Op. 20092010/1(2009),

ABA Formal
Ethics Opinions
(Selected)

ent communications. It also recognizes several ways that lawyers may limit subsequent disqualification based on these prospective client disclosures when they decide not to undertake a matter.[18]

Rule 1.18(a) addresses whether the inquirer has become a "prospective client," defined as "a person who discusses with a lawyer the possibility of forming a client-lawyer relationship."

To "discuss," meaning to talk about, generally contemplates a two-way communication, which necessarily must begin with an initial communication.[19] Rule 1.18 implicitly recognizes that this initial communication can come either from a lawyer or a person who wishes to become a prospective client.

Rule 1.18 Comment [2] also recognizes that not all initial communications from persons who wish to be prospective clients necessarily result in a "discussion" within the meaning of the rule: "a person who communicates information unilaterally to a lawyer, without any reasonable expectation that the lawyer is willing to discuss the possibility of forming a client-lawyer relationship, is not a prospective client."

For example, if a lawyer website specifically requests or invites submission of information concerning the possibility of forming a client-lawyer relationship with respect to a matter, a discussion, as that term is used in Rule 1.18, will result when a website visitor submits the requested information.[20] If a website visitor submits information to a site that does not specifically request or invite this, the lawyer's response to that submission will determine whether a discussion under Rule 1.18 has occurred.

A telephone, mail or e-mail exchange between an individual seeking

---

available at http://www.nhbar.org/legal-links/ethics1.asp (when law firm's website invites public to send e-mail to one of firm's lawyers, it is opening itself to potential obligations to prospective clients); Ass'n of the Bar of the City of New York, Formal Op. 2001-1 (2001) (Obligations Of Law Firm Receiving Unsolicited E-Mail Communications From Prospective Client), *available at* http://www.abcny.org/Ethics/eth2001-01.html (where firm website does not adequately warn that information transmitted will not be treated as confidential, information should be held in confidence by lawyer receiving communication and not disclosed to or used for benefit of another client even though lawyer declines to represent potential client); New Jersey Advisory Committee on Prof'l Eth. Op. 695, 2004 WL 833032 (2004) (firm has duty to keep information received from prospective client confidential); San Diego County Bar Ass'n Eth. Op. 2006-1 (2006), *available at* http://www.sdcba.org/index. cfm?Pg=ethicsopinion06-1 (private information received from non-client via unsolicited e-mail is not required to be held as confidential if lawyer has not had opportunity to warn or stop flow of information at or before the communication is delivered).

18. Lawyers do not normally owe confidentiality obligations to persons who are not clients (protected by Rule 1.6), former clients (Rule 1.9), or prospective clients (Rule 1.18).

19. For example, in ABA Committee on Eth. and Prof'l Responsibility, Formal Op. 90-358 (1990) (Protection of Information Imparted by Prospective Client), this Committee considered the obligations of a lawyer who engaged in such a "discussion" in the context of a face-to-face meeting.

20. Rule 1.18 cmt. 1.

ABA Formal Ethics Opinions (Selected)

legal services and a lawyer is analogous.[21] In these contexts, the lawyer takes part in a bilateral discussion about the possibility of forming a client-lawyer relationship and has the opportunity to limit or encourage the flow of information. For example, the lawyer may ask for additional details or may caution against providing any personal or sensitive information until a conflicts check can be completed.

Lawyers have a similar ability on their websites to control features and content so as to invite, encourage, limit, or discourage the flow of information to and from website visitors.[22] A particular website might facilitate a very direct and almost immediate bilateral communication in response to marketing information about a specific lawyer. It might, for example, specifically encourage a website visitor to submit a personal inquiry about a proposed representation on a conveniently-provided website electronic form which, when responded to, begins a "discussion" about a proposed representation and, absent any cautionary language, invites submission of confidential information.[23] Another website might describe the work of the law firm and each of its lawyers, list only contact information such as a telephone number, e-mail or street address, or provide a website e-mail link to a lawyer. Providing such information alone does not create a reasonable expectation that the lawyer is willing to discuss a specific client-lawyer relationship.[24]

---

21. *See, e.g.,* Virginia Legal Eth. Op. 1842 (2008), *available at* http://www.vacle.org/opinions/1842.htm (absent voicemail message that asks for detailed information, providing phone number and voicemail is an invitation only to contact lawyer, not to submit confidential information); Iowa State Bar Ass'n Eth. Op. 07-02 ("Communication from and with Potential Clients), *available at* http://www.iowabar.org/ethics.nsf/e61b-eed77a215f6686 256497004ce492/cb0a70672d69d8c1862573380013fb9d?OpenDocument (telephone voicemail message that simply asks for contact details does not give rise to bilateral communication, but message that encourages caller to leave detailed messages about their case could be considered bilateral).

22. *See, e.g.,* Arizona State Bar Op. 02-04 (2002), *available at* http://www.myazbar.org/Ethics/opinionview.cfm?id=288 (lawyers who maintain websites with e-mail links should include disclaimers to clarify whether e-mail communications from prospective clients will be treated as confidential); Massachusetts Bar Ass'n Op. 07-01 (2007), *available at* http://www.massbar.org/publications/ethics-opinions/20002009/2007/opinion-07-01 (lawyer who receives unsolicited information from prospective client through e-mail link on law firm website without effective disclaimer must hold information confidential because law firm has opportunity to set conditions on flow of information); South Dakota Bar Eth. Op. 2002-2 (2002) (lawyer's website that invites viewers to send e-mail through jump site creates expectation of confidentiality).

23. *See, e.g.,* Iowa State Bar Ass'n Eth. Op. 07-02, *supra* note 21 (web page inviting specific questions constitutes bilateral communication with expectation of confidentiality) and Virginia Legal Eth. Op. 1842 *supra* note 21 (website that specifically invites visitor to submit information in exchange for evaluation invites formation of client-lawyer relationship).

24. E-mails received from unknown persons who send them apart from the lawyer's website may even more easily be viewed as unsolicited. *See, e.g.,* Arizona State Bar Op. 02-04, *supra* note 22 (e-mail to multiple lawyers asking for representation); Iowa State Bar

A lawyer's response to an inquiry submitted by a visitor who uses this contact information may, however, begin a "discussion" within the meaning of Rule 1.18.

In between these two examples, a variety of website content and features might indicate that a lawyer has agreed to discuss a possible client-lawyer relationship. A former client's website communication to a lawyer about a new matter must be analyzed in light of their previous relationship, which may have given rise to a reasonable expectation of confidentiality.[25] But a person who knows that the lawyer already declined a particular representation or is already representing an adverse party can neither reasonably expect confidentiality, nor reasonably believe that the lawyer wishes to discuss a client-lawyer relationship. Similarly, a person who purports to be a prospective client and who communicates with a number of lawyers with the intent to prevent other parties from retaining them in the same matter should have no reasonable expectation of confidentiality or that the lawyer would refrain from an adverse representation.[26]

In other circumstances, it may be difficult to predict when the overall message of a given website communicates a willingness by a lawyer to discuss a particular prospective client-lawyer relationship. Imprecision in a website message and failure to include a clarifying disclaimer may result in a website visitor reasonably viewing the website communication itself as the first step in a discussion.[27] Lawyers are therefore well-advised to con-

Ass'n Eth. Op. 07-02, *supra* note 21 (website that gives contact information does not without more indicate that lawyer requested or consented to sending of confidential information); San Diego County Bar Assn. Op. 2006-1, *available at* http://www.sdcba.org/index.cfm?Pg=ethicsopinion06-1 (inquirer found lawyer's e-mail address on state bar membership records website accessible to the public).

25. *See, e.g.,* Iowa State Bar Ass'n Committee Eth. Op. 07-02, *supra* note 22 (lack of prior relationship with person sending unsolicited e-mail requesting representation was one factor in determining whether communicator's disclosures were unilateral and whether expectation of confidentiality was reasonable); Oregon Eth. Op. 2005-146, 2005 WL 5679570 *1 (2005) (lawyer who sends periodic reminders to former clients risks giving recipients reasonable belief they are still current clients).

26. *See, e.g.,* Virginia Legal Eth. Op. 1794 (2004), *available at* http://www.vacle.org/opinions/1794.htm (person who meets with lawyer for primary purpose of precluding others from obtaining legal representation does not have reasonable expectation of confidentiality); Ass'n of the Bar of the City of New York Committee on Prof'l and Jud. Eth. Formal Op. 2001-1 (2001), *available at* http://www.abcny.org/Ethics/eth2001.html ("taint shoppers," who interview lawyers or law firms for purpose of disqualifying them from future adverse representation, have no good faith expectation of confidentiality).

27. *See e.g.,* Massachusetts Bar Ass'n Op. 07-01, *supra* note 22 (in absence of effective disclaimer, prospective client visiting law firm website that markets background and qualifications of each lawyer in attractive light, stresses lawyer's skill at solving clients' practical problems, and provides e-mail link for immediate communication with that lawyer might reasonably conclude that firm and its individual lawyers have implicitly "agreed to consider" whether to form client-lawyer relationship).

sider that a website-generated inquiry may have come from a prospective client, and should pay special attention to including the appropriate warnings mentioned in the next section.

If a discussion with a prospective client has occurred, Rule 1.18(b) prohibits use or disclosure of information learned during such a discussion absent the prospective client's informed consent.[28] When the discussion reveals a conflict of interest, the lawyer should decline the representation,[29] and cannot disclose the information received without the informed consent of the prospective client.[30] For various reasons, including the need for a conflicts check, the lawyer may have tried to limit the initial discussion and may have clearly expressed those limitations to the prospective client. If this has been done, any information given to the lawyer that exceeds those express limitations generally would not be protected under Rule 1.18(b).

Rule 1.18(c) disqualifies lawyers and their law firms who have received information that "could be significantly harmful" to the prospective client from representing others with adverse interests in the same or substantially related matters.[31] For example, if a prospective client previously had disclosed only an intention to bring a particular lawsuit and has now retained a different lawyer to initiate the same suit, it is difficult to imagine any significant harm that could result from the law firm proceeding with the defense of the same matter.[32] On the other hand, absent an appropriate warning, the prospective client's prior disclosure of more extensive facts about the matter may well be disqualifying.

Rule 1.18(d) creates two exceptions that allow subsequent adverse representation even if the prospective client disclosed information that was significantly harmful: (1) informed consent confirmed in writing from both the affected and the prospective client, or (2) reasonable measures to limit the disqualifying information, combined with timely screening of the disqualified lawyer from the subsequent adverse matter. Rule 1.18(d) (2) specifically would allow the law firm (but not the contacted lawyer) to "undertake or continue" the representation of someone with adverse interests without receiving the informed consent of the prospective client if the lawyer who initially received the information took reasonable precautions to limit the

ABA Formal Ethics Opinions (Selected)

---

28. Rule 1.18(b) allows disclosure or use if permitted by Rule 1.9. Rule 1.9(c) (2) and its Comment [7] in turn link disclosure to Rule 1.6, the general confidentiality rule, which requires client informed consent to disclosure.

29. Rule 1.18 cmt. 4.

30. Rule 1.18 cmt. 3.

31. *See also* RESTATEMENT (THIRD) OF THE LAW GOVERNING LAWYERS § 15 (2) (2000).

32. Rule 1.18 cmt. 5 also allows lawyers to condition an initial conversation on the prospective client's informed consent to subsequent adverse representation in the same matter or subsequent use of any confidential information provided.

prospective client's initial disclosures and was timely screened from further involvement in the matter as required by Rule 1.0(k).

III. Warnings or Cautionary Statements Intended to Limit, Condition, or Disclaim a Lawyer's Obligations to Website Visitors

Warnings or cautionary statements on a lawyer's website can be designed to and may effectively limit, condition, or disclaim a lawyer's obligation to a website reader. Such warnings or statements may be written so as to avoid a misunderstanding by the website visitor that (1) a client-lawyer relationship has been created;[33] (2) the visitor's information will be kept confidential;[34]

---

33. *See, e.g.,* New Mexico Bar Op. 2001-1 (2001), *available at* http://www.nmbar.org/legalresearch/ethicsadvisoryopinions.html (appropriate disclaimers of attorney-client relationship should accompany any response to listserve message board, but any response that would suggest to reasonable person that, despite disclaimer, relationship is being or has been established, would negate disclaimer); North Carolina State Bar Formal Eth. Op. 2000-3, 2000 WL 33300702 *2 (2000) (Responding to Inquiries Posted on a Message Board on the Web) (lawyers who do not want to create client-lawyer relationships on law firm message board should use specific disclaimers on any communications with inquirers, but substantive law will determine whether client-lawyer relationship is created); Ass'n of the Bar of the City of New York Committee on Prof'l and Jud. Eth. Formal Op. 1998-2 (1998), *available at* http://www.abcny.org/Ethics/eth1998-2.htm (disclaimer that "if specific legal advice is sought, we will indicate that this requires establishment of an attorney-client relationship which cannot be carried out through the use of a web page" may not necessarily serve to shield law firm from claim that attorney-client relationship was established by specific on-line communications); Utah State Bar Eth. Advisory Op. Committee Op. 96-12, 1997 WL 45137 *1 (1997) ("if legal advice is sought from an attorney, if the advice sought is pertinent to the attorney's profession, and if the attorney gives the advice for which fees will be charged, an attorney-client relationship is created that cannot be disclaimed by the attorney giving the advice"); Vermont Bar Ass'n Advisory Eth. Op. 2000-04 (2000), *supra* note 3 (despite website caveat and disclaimers, nonlawyer may still rely on information on website or lawyer's responses; disclaimer cannot preclude possibility of establishing client-lawyer relationship in an individual case).

34. The Committee does not opine whether a confidentiality waiver might affect the attorney-client privilege. *See, e.g.,* Barton v. U.S. Dist. Ct. for the Cent. Dist. of Cal., 410 F. 3d 1104, 1111-12 (9th Cir. 2005) (checking "yes" box on law firm website that acknowledged providing information in answer to questionnaire "does not constitute a request for legal advice and I am not forming an attorney-client relationship by submitting this information" did not waive attorney-client privilege because confidentiality was not mentioned in attempted disclaimer and questionnaires were nevertheless submitted in course of seeking attorney-client relationship in potential class action). *Cf.* Schiller v. The City of New York, 245 F.R.D. 112, 117-18 (S.D.N.Y. 2007) (although privilege may protect pre-engagement communications from prospective clients, it does not apply to person who completed questionnaires soliciting information from N.Y. Civil Liberties Union to allow it to "effectively advocate for change"). *See also* David Hricik, *To Whom it May Concern: Using Disclaimers to Avoid Disqualification by Receipt of Unsolicited E-Mail from Prospective Clients,* 16 ABA PROFESSIONAL LAWYER 1, 5 (2005) (agreement that waives all confidentiality tries to do too much and might destroy the ability of prospective client who eventually becomes firm client to claim privilege).

ABA Formal Ethics Opinions (Selected)

(3) legal advice has been given;[35] or (4) the lawyer will be prevented from representing an adverse party.[36]

Limitations, conditions, or disclaimers of lawyer obligations will be effective only if reasonably understandable, properly placed, and not misleading. This requires a clear warning in a readable format whose meaning can be understood by a reasonable person.[37] If the website uses a particular language, any waiver, disclaimer, limitation, or condition must be in the same language. The appropriate information should be conspicuously placed to assure that the reader is likely to see it before proceeding.[38]

Finally, a limitation, condition, waiver, or disclaimer may be undercut if the lawyer acts or communicates contrary to its warning.

---

35. *See* note 15 *supra.*

36. Rule 1.18 cmt. 5.

37. *See, e.g.*, California Bar Committee on Prof'l Resp. Op. 2005-168, 2005 WL 3068090 *4 (2005) (finding disclaimer stating that "confidential relationship" would not be formed was not enough to waive confidentiality, because it confused not forming client-lawyer relationship with agreeing to keep communications confidential).

38. *See, e.g.*, District of Columbia Bar Eth. Op. 302 (2000), *available at* http://www.dcbar.org/for_lawyers/ethics/legal_ethics/opinions/opinion302.cfm (lawyers may want to use "click through" pages that automatically direct the reader to another webpage containing disclaimers to ensure that visitors are not misled and other devices such as confirmatory messages that clarify nature of relationship); Virginia Legal Eth. Op. 1842, *supra* note 21 (approving of prominent "click through" disclaimers that require readers to assent to terms of disclaimer before submitting information). Courts have refused to uphold disclaimers or licensing agreements that appeared on separate pages and did not require a reader's affirmative consent to their terms because they did not provide reasonable notice). *See, e.g.*, Sprecht v. Netscape Communications Corp., 306 F.3d 17, 31-32 (2d Cir. 2002). On the other hand, courts have upheld website restrictions that provided actual knowledge by presenting the information and requiring an affirmative action (a click through or "clickwrap" agreement) before gaining access to the website content. *See, e.g.*, Register.com v. Verio, 356 F.3d 393, 401-02 (2d Cir. 2004).

ABA Formal
Ethics Opinions
(Selected)

Formal Opinion 466 April 24, 2014
Lawyer Reviewing Jurors' Internet Presence

Unless limited by law or court order, a lawyer may review a juror's or potential juror's Internet presence, which may include postings by the juror or potential juror in advance of and during a trial, but a lawyer may not communicate directly or through another with a juror or potential juror.

A lawyer may not, either personally or through another, send an access request to a juror's electronic social media. An access request is a communication to a juror asking the juror for information that the juror has not made public and that would be the type of ex parte communication prohibited by Model Rule 3.5(b).

The fact that a juror or a potential juror may become aware that a lawyer is reviewing his Internet presence when a network setting notifies the juror of such does not constitute a communication from the lawyer in violation of Rule 3.5(b).

In the course of reviewing a juror's or potential juror's Internet presence, if a lawyer discovers evidence of juror or potential juror misconduct that is criminal or fraudulent, the lawyer must take reasonable remedial measures including, if necessary, disclosure to the tribunal.

The Committee has been asked whether a lawyer who represents a client in a matter that will be tried to a jury may review the jurors' or potential jurors'[1] presence on the Internet leading up to and during trial, and, if so, what ethical obligations the lawyer might have regarding information discovered during the review.

Juror Internet Presence

Jurors may and often will have an Internet presence through electronic social media or websites. General public access to such will vary. For example, many blogs, websites, and other electronic media are readily accessible by anyone who chooses to access them through the Internet. We will refer to these publicly accessible Internet media as "websites."

For the purposes of this opinion, Internet-based social media sites that readily allow account-owner restrictions on access will be referred to as "electronic social media" or "ESM." Examples of commonly used ESM at the time of this opinion include Facebook, MySpace, LinkedIn, and Twitter. Reference to a request to obtain access to another's ESM will be denoted as an "access request," and a person who creates and maintains ESM will be denoted as a "subscriber."

Depending on the privacy settings chosen by the ESM subscriber, some information posted on ESM sites might be available to the general public, making it similar to a website, while other information is available only to a fellow

ABA Formal
Ethics Opinions
(Selected)

---

1. Unless there is reason to make a distinction, we will refer throughout this opinion to jurors as including both potential and prospective jurors and jurors who have been empaneled as members of a jury.

subscriber of a shared ESM service, or in some cases only to those whom the subscriber has granted access. Privacy settings allow the ESM subscriber to establish different degrees of protection for different categories of information, each of which can require specific permission to access. In general, a person who wishes to obtain access to these protected pages must send a request to the ESM subscriber asking for permission to do so. Access depends on the willingness of the subscriber to grant permission.[2]

This opinion addresses three levels of lawyer review of juror Internet presence:

1. passive lawyer review of a juror's website or ESM that is available without making an access request where the juror is unaware that a website or ESM has been reviewed;
2. active lawyer review where the lawyer requests access to the juror's ESM; and
3. passive lawyer review where the juror becomes aware through a website or ESM feature of the identity of the viewer;

Trial Management and Jury Instructions

There is a strong public interest in identifying jurors who might be tainted by improper bias or prejudice. There is a related and equally strong public policy in preventing jurors from being approached ex parte by the parties to the case or their agents. Lawyers need to know where the line should be drawn between properly investigating jurors and improperly communicating with them.[3] In today's Internet-saturated world, the line is increasingly blurred.

For this reason, we strongly encourage judges and lawyers to discuss the court's expectations concerning lawyers reviewing juror presence on the Internet. A court order, whether in the form of a local rule, a standing order, or a

---

2. The capabilities of ESM change frequently. The committee notes that this opinion does not address particular ESM capabilities that exist now or will exist in the future. For purposes of this opinion, key elements like the ability of a subscriber to control access to ESM or to identify third parties who review a subscriber's ESM are considered generically.

3. While this Committee does not take a position on whether the standard of care for competent lawyer performance requires using Internet research to locate information about jurors that is relevant to the jury selection process, we are also mindful of the recent addition of Comment [8] to Model Rule 1.1. This comment explains that a lawyer "should keep abreast of changes in the law and its practice, including the benefits and risks associated with relevant technology." See also Johnson v. McCullough, 306 S.W.3d 551 (Mo. 2010) (lawyer must use "reasonable efforts" to find potential juror's litigation history in Case.net, Missouri's automated case management system); N. H. Bar Ass'n, Op. 2012-13/05 (lawyers "have a general duty to be aware of social media as a source of potentially useful information in litigation, to be competent to obtain that information directly or through an agent, and to know how to make effective use of that information in litigation"); Ass'n of the Bar of the City of N. Y. Comm. on Prof'l Ethics, Formal Op. 2012-2 ("Indeed, the standards of competence and diligence may require doing everything reasonably possible to learn about jurors who will sit in judgment on a case.").

case management order in a particular matter, will, in addition to the applicable Rules of Professional Conduct, govern the conduct of counsel.

Equally important, judges should consider advising jurors during the orientation process that their backgrounds will be of interest to the litigants and that the lawyers in the case may investigate their backgrounds, including review of their ESM and websites.[4] If a judge believes it to be necessary, under the circumstances of a particular matter, to limit lawyers' review of juror websites and ESM, including on ESM networks where it is possible or likely that the jurors will be notified that their ESM is being viewed, the judge should formally instruct the lawyers in the case concerning the court's expectations.

Reviewing Juror Internet Presence

If there is no court order governing lawyers reviewing juror Internet presence, we look to the ABA Model Rules of Professional Conduct for relevant strictures and prohibitions. Model Rule 3.5 addresses communications with jurors before, during, and after trial, stating:

A lawyer shall not:

(a) seek to influence a judge, juror, prospective juror or other official by means prohibited by law;
(b) communicate ex parte with such a person during the proceeding unless authorized to do so by law or court order;
(c) communicate with a juror or prospective juror after discharge of the jury if:
  (1) the communication is prohibited by law or court order;
  (2) the juror has made known to the lawyer a desire not to communicate; or
  (3) the communication involves misrepresentation, coercion, duress or harassment . . .

Under Model Rule 3.5(b), a lawyer may not communicate with a potential juror leading up to trial or any juror during trial unless authorized by law or court order. *See, e.g., In re Holman,* 286 S.E.2d 148 (S.C. 1982) (communicating with member of jury selected for trial of lawyer's client was "serious crime" warranting disbarment).

A lawyer may not do through the acts of another what the lawyer is prohibited from doing directly. Model Rule 8.4(a). *See also In re Myers,* 584 S.E.2d 357 (S.C. 2003) (improper for prosecutor to have a lay member of his "jury selection

---

4. Judges also may choose to work with local jury commissioners to ensure that jurors are advised during jury orientation that they may properly be investigated by lawyers in the case to which they are assigned. This investigation may include review of the potential juror's Internet presence.

team" phone venire member's home); *cf.* S.C. Ethics Op. 93-27 (1993) (lawyer "cannot avoid the proscription of the rule by using agents to communicate improperly" with prospective jurors).

Passive review of a juror's website or ESM, that is available without making an access request, and of which the juror is unaware, does not violate Rule 3.5(b). In the world outside of the Internet, a lawyer or another, acting on the lawyer's behalf, would not be engaging in an improper ex parte contact with a prospective juror by driving down the street where the prospective juror lives to observe the environs in order to glean publicly available information that could inform the lawyer's jury-selection decisions. The mere act of observing that which is open to the public would not constitute a communicative act that violates Rule 3.5(b).[5]

It is the view of the Committee that a lawyer may not personally, or through another, send an access request to a juror. An access request is an active review of the juror's electronic social media by the lawyer and is a communication to a juror asking the juror for information that the juror has not made public. This would be the type of ex parte communication prohibited by Model Rule 3.5(b).[6] This would be akin to driving down the juror's street, stopping the car, getting out, and asking the juror for permission to look inside the juror's house because the lawyer cannot see enough when just driving past.

---

5. Or. State Bar Ass'n, Formal Op. 2013-189 ("Lawyer may access publicly available information [about juror, witness, and opposing party] on social networking website"); N.Y. Cnty. Lawyers Ass'n, Formal Op. 743 (2011) (lawyer may search juror's "publicly available" webpages and ESM); Ass'n of the Bar of the City of N.Y. Comm. on Prof'l Ethics, *supra* note 3 (lawyer may use social media websites to research jurors); Ky. Bar Ass'n, Op. E-434 (2012) ("If the site is 'public,' and accessible to all, then there does not appear to be any ethics issue."). *See also* N.Y. State Bar Ass'n, Advisory Op. 843 (2010) ("A lawyer representing a client in pending litigation may access the public pages of another party's social networking website (such as Facebook or MySpace) for the purpose of obtaining possible impeachment material for use in the litigation"); Or. State Bar Ass'n, Formal Op. 2005-164 ("Accessing an adversary's public Web [sic] site is no different from reading a magazine or purchasing a book written by that adversary"); N.H. Bar Ass'n, *supra* note 3 (viewing a Facebook user's page or following on Twitter is not communication if pages are open to all members of that social media site); San Diego Cnty. Bar Legal Ethics Op. 2011-2 (opposing party's public Facebook page may be viewed by lawyer).

6. *See* Or. State Bar Ass'n, *supra* note 5, fn. 2, (a "lawyer may not send a request to a juror to access non-public personal information on a social networking website, nor may a lawyer ask an agent to do so"); N.Y. Cnty. Lawyers Ass'n, *supra* note 5 ("Significant ethical concerns would be raised by sending a 'friend request,' attempting to connect via LinkedIn.com, signing up for an RSS feed for a juror's blog, or 'following' a juror's Twitter account"); Ass'n of the Bar of the City of N.Y. Comm. on Prof'l Ethics, *supra* note 3 (lawyer may not chat, message or send a "friend request" to a juror); Conn. Bar Ass'n, Informal Op. 2011-4 (friend request is a communication); Mo. Bar Ass'n, Informal Op. 2009-0003 (friend request is a communication pursuant to Rule 4.2). *But see* N.H. Bar Ass'n, *supra* note 3 (lawyer may request access to witness's private ESM, but request must "correctly identify the lawyer . . . [and] . . . inform the witness of the lawyer's involvement" in the matter); Phila. Bar Ass'n, Advisory Op. 2009-02 (lawyer may not use deception to secure access to witness's private ESM, but may ask the witness "forthrightly" for access).

ABA Formal
Ethics Opinions
(Selected)

Some ESM networks have a feature that allows the juror to identify fellow members of the same ESM network who have passively viewed the juror's ESM. The details of how this is accomplished will vary from network to network, but the key feature that is relevant to this opinion is that the juror-subscriber is able to determine not only that his ESM is being viewed, but also the identity of the viewer. This capability may be beyond the control of the reviewer because the notice to the subscriber is generated by the ESM network and is based on the identity profile of the subscriber who is a fellow member of the same ESM network.

Two recent ethics opinions have addressed this issue. The Association of the Bar of the City of New York Committee on Professional Ethics, in Formal Opinion 2012-2[7], concluded that a network-generated notice to the juror that the lawyer has reviewed the juror's social media was a communication from the lawyer to a juror, albeit an indirect one generated by the ESM network. Citing the definition of "communication" from Black's Law Dictionary (9th ed.) and other authority, the opinion concluded that the message identifying the ESM viewer was a communication because it entailed "the process of bringing an idea, information or knowledge to another's perception—including the fact that they have been researched." While the ABCNY Committee found that the communication would "constitute a prohibited communication if the attorney was aware that her actions" would send such a notice, the Committee took "no position on whether an inadvertent communication would be a violation of the Rules." The New York County Lawyers' Association Committee on Professional Ethics in Formal Opinion 743 agreed with ABCNY's opinion and went further explaining, "If a juror becomes aware of an attorney's efforts to see the juror's profiles on websites, the contact may well consist of an impermissible communication, as it might tend to influence the juror's conduct with respect to the trial."[8]

This Committee concludes that a lawyer who uses a shared ESM platform to passively view juror ESM under these circumstances does not communicate with the juror. The lawyer is not communicating with the juror; the ESM service is communicating with the juror based on a technical feature of the ESM. This is akin to a neighbor's recognizing a lawyer's car driving down the juror's street and telling the juror that the lawyer had been seen driving down the street.

Discussion by the trial judge of the likely practice of trial lawyers reviewing juror ESM during the jury orientation process will dispel any juror misperception that a lawyer is acting improperly merely by viewing what the juror has revealed to all others on the same network.

While this Committee concludes that ESM-generated notice to a juror that a lawyer has reviewed the juror's information is not communication from the lawyer to the juror, the Committee does make two additional recommendations to lawyers who decide to review juror social media. First, the Committee sug-

ABA Formal
Ethics Opinions
(Selected)

---

7. Ass'n of the Bar of the City of N.Y. Comm. on Prof'l Ethics, *supra*, note 3.
8. N.Y. Cnty. Lawyers' Ass'n, *supra* note 5.

gests that lawyers be aware of these automatic, subscriber-notification features. By accepting the terms of use, the subscriber- notification feature is not secret. As indicated by Rule 1.1, Comment 8, it is important for a lawyer to be current with technology. While many people simply click their agreement to the terms and conditions for use of an ESM network, a lawyer who uses an ESM network in his practice should review the terms and conditions, including privacy features—which change frequently—prior to using such a network. And, as noted above, jurisdictions differ on issues that arise when a lawyer uses social media in his practice.

Second, Rule 4.4(a) prohibits lawyers from actions "that have no substantial purpose other than to embarrass, delay, or burden a third person . . ." Lawyers who review juror social media should ensure that their review is purposeful and not crafted to embarrass, delay, or burden the juror or the proceeding.

Discovery of Juror Misconduct

Increasingly, courts are instructing jurors in very explicit terms about the prohibition against using ESM to communicate about their jury service or the pending case and the prohibition against conducting personal research about the matter, including research on the Internet. These warnings come because jurors have discussed trial issues on ESM, solicited access to witnesses and litigants on ESM, not revealed relevant ESM connections during jury selection, and conducted personal research on the trial issues using the Internet.[9]

In 2009, the Court Administration and Case Management Committee of the Judicial Conference of the United States recommended a model jury instruction that is very specific about juror use of social media, mentioning many of the popular social media by name.[10] The recommended instruction states in part:

> I know that many of you use cell phones, Blackberries, the internet and other tools of technology. You also must not talk to anyone at any time about this case or use these tools to communicate electronically with anyone about the case . . . You may not communicate with anyone about the case on your cell phone, through e- mail, Blackberry, iPhone, text messaging, or on Twitter, through any blog or website, including Facebook, Google+, My Space, LinkedIn, or YouTube. . . . I expect you will inform me as soon as you become aware of another juror's violation of these instructions.

9. For a review of recent cases in which a juror used ESM to discuss trial proceedings and/or used the Internet to conduct private research, read Hon. Amy J. St. Eve et al., *More from the #Jury Box: The Latest on Juries and Social Media*, 12 Duke Law & Technology Review no. 1, 69-78 (2014), *available at* http://scholarship.law.duke.edu/cgi/viewcontent.cgi?article=1247&context=dltr.

10. Judicial Conference Committee on Court Administration and Case Management, *Proposed Model Jury Instructions: The Use of Electronic Technology to Conduct Research on or Communicate about a Case*, USCourts.gov (June 2012), http://www.uscourts.gov/uscourts/News/2012/jury-instructions.pdf.

These same jury instructions were provided by both a federal district court and state criminal court judge during a three-year study on juries and social media. Their research found that "jury instructions are the most effective tool to mitigate the risk of juror misconduct through social media."[11] As a result, the authors recommend jury instruction on social media "early and often" and daily in lengthy trials.[12]

Analyzing the approximately 8% of the jurors who admitted to being "tempted" to communicate about the case using social media, the judges found that the jurors chose not to talk or write about the case because of the specific jury instruction not to do so.

While juror misconduct via social media itself is not the subject of this Opinion, lawyers reviewing juror websites and ESM may become aware of misconduct. Model Rule 3.3 and its legislative history make it clear that a lawyer has an obligation to take remedial measures including, if necessary, informing the tribunal when the lawyer discovers that a juror has engaged in criminal or fraudulent conduct related to the proceeding. But the history is muddled concerning whether a lawyer has an affirmative obligation to act upon learning that a juror has engaged in improper conduct that falls short of being criminal or fraudulent.

Rule 3.3 was amended in 2002, pursuant to the ABA Ethics 2000 Commission's proposal, to expand on a lawyer's previous obligation to protect a tribunal from criminal or fraudulent conduct by the lawyer's client to also include such conduct by any person.[13]

Model Rule 3.3(b) reads:

(b) A lawyer who represents a client in an adjudicative proceeding and who knows that a person intends to engage, is engaging or has engaged in criminal or fraudulent conduct related to the proceeding shall take reasonable remedial measures including, if necessary, disclosure to the tribunal.

Comment [12] to Rule 3.3 provides:

Lawyers have a special obligation to protect a tribunal against criminal or fraudulent conduct that undermines the integrity of the adjudicative process, such as bribing, intimidating or otherwise unlawfully communicating with a witness, juror, court official or other participant in the proceeding, unlawfully destroying or concealing documents or other evidence or failing to disclose information to the tribunal when re-

ABA Formal
Ethics Opinions
(Selected)

---

11. *Id.* at 66.

12. *Id.* at 87.

13. Ethics 2000 Commission, *Model Rule 3.3: Candor Toward the Tribunal*, AMERICAN BAR ASSOCIATION, http://www.americanbar.org/groups/professional_responsibility/policy/ethics_2000_commission/e2k_rule33.html (last visited Apr. 18, 2014).

quired by law to do so. Thus, paragraph (b) requires a lawyer to take reasonable remedial measures, including disclosure if necessary, whenever the lawyer knows that a person, including the lawyer's client, intends to engage, is engaging or has engaged in criminal or fraudulent conduct related to the proceeding.

Part of Ethics 2000's stated intent when it amended Model Rule 3.3 was to incorporate provisions from Canon 7 of the ABA Model Code of Professional Responsibility (Model Code) that had placed an affirmative duty upon a lawyer to notify the court upon learning of juror misconduct:

> This new provision incorporates the substance of current paragraph (a)(2), as well as ABA Model Code of Professional Responsibility DR 7-102(B)(2) ("A lawyer who receives information clearly establishing that a person other than the client has perpetrated a fraud upon a tribunal shall promptly reveal the fraud to the tribunal") and DR 7-108(G) ("A lawyer shall reveal promptly to the court improper conduct by a venireperson or juror, or by another toward a venireperson or juror or a member of the venireperson's or juror's family, of which the lawyer has knowledge"). *Reporter's Explanation of Changes, Model Rule 3.3.*[14]

However, the intent of the Ethics 2000 Commission expressed above to incorporate the substance of DR 7-108(G) in its new subsection (b) of Model Rule 3.3 was never carried out. Under the Model Code's DR 7-108(G), a lawyer knowing of "improper conduct" by a juror or venireperson was required to report the matter to the tribunal. Under Rule 3.3(b), the lawyer's obligation to act arises only when the juror or venireperson engages in conduct that is *fraudulent or criminal*.[15] While improper conduct was not defined in the Model Code, it clearly imposes a broader duty to take remedial action than exists under the Model Rules. The Committee is constrained to provide guidance based upon the language of Rule 3.3(b) rather than any expressions of intent in the legislative history of that rule.

By passively viewing juror Internet presence, a lawyer may become aware of a juror's conduct that is criminal or fraudulent, in which case, Model Rule 3.3(b) requires the lawyer to take remedial measures including, if necessary, reporting the matter to the court. But the lawyer may also become aware of juror conduct that violates court instructions to the jury but does not rise to the level of criminal or fraudulent conduct, and Rule 3.3(b) does not prescribe what the

---

14. Ethics 2000 Commission, *Model Rule 3.3 Reporter's Explanation of Changes*, AMERICAN BAR ASSOCIATION, http://www.americanbar.org/groups/professional_responsibility/policy/ethics_2000_commission/e2k_rule33rem.html (last visited Apr. 18, 2014).

15. Compare MODEL RULES OF PROF'L CONDUCT R. 3.3(b) (2002) to N.Y. RULES OF PROF'L CONDUCT R. 3.5(d) (2013) ("a lawyer shall reveal promptly to the court improper conduct by a member of the venire or a juror....").

lawyer must do in that situation. While considerations of questions of law are outside the scope of the Committee's authority, applicable law might treat such juror activity as conduct that triggers a lawyer's duty to take remedial action including, if necessary, reporting the juror's conduct to the court under current Model Rule 3.3(b).[16]

While any Internet postings about the case by a juror during trial may violate court instructions, the obligation of a lawyer to take action will depend on the lawyer's assessment of those postings in light of court instructions and the elements of the crime of contempt or other applicable criminal statutes. For example, innocuous postings about jury service, such as the quality of the food served at lunch, may be contrary to judicial instructions, but fall short of conduct that would warrant the extreme response of finding a juror in criminal contempt. A lawyer's affirmative duty to act is triggered only when the juror's known conduct is criminal or fraudulent, including conduct that is criminally contemptuous of court instructions. The materiality of juror Internet communications to the integrity of the trial will likely be a consideration in determining whether the juror has acted criminally or fraudulently. The remedial duty flowing from known criminal or fraudulent juror conduct is triggered by knowledge of the conduct and is not preempted by a lawyer's belief that the court will not choose to address the conduct as a crime or fraud.

Conclusion

In sum, a lawyer may passively review a juror's public presence on the Internet, but may not communicate with a juror. Requesting access to a private area on a juror's ESM is communication within this framework.

The fact that a juror or a potential juror may become aware that the lawyer is reviewing his Internet presence when an ESM network setting notifies the juror of such review does not constitute a communication from the lawyer in violation of Rule 3.5(b).

If a lawyer discovers criminal or fraudulent conduct by a juror related to the proceeding, the lawyer must take reasonable remedial measures including, if necessary, disclosure to the tribunal.

ABA Formal
Ethics Opinions
(Selected)

---

16. *See, e.g.*, U.S. v. Juror Number One, 866 F.Supp.2d 442 (E.D. Pa. 2011) (failure to follow jury instructions and emailing other jurors about case results in criminal contempt). The use of criminal contempt remedies for disregarding jury instructions is not confined to improper juror use of ESM. U.S. v. Rowe, 906 F.2d 654 (11th Cir. 1990) (juror held in contempt, fined, and dismissed from jury for violating court order to refrain from discussing the case with other jurors until after jury instructions delivered).

Formal Opinion 471   July 1, 2015
Ethical Obligations of Lawyer to Surrender Papers and Property to which Former Client is Entitled

Upon the termination of a representation, a lawyer is required under Model Rules 1.15 and 1.16(d) to take steps to the extent reasonably practicable to protect a client's interest, and such steps include surrendering to the former client papers and property to which the former client is entitled. A client is not entitled to papers and property that the lawyer generated for the lawyer's own purpose in working on the client's matter. However, when the lawyer's representation of the client in a matter is terminated before the matter is completed, protection of the former client's interest may require that certain materials the lawyer generated for the lawyer's own purpose be provided to the client.

This opinion addresses the ethical duties of a lawyer pursuant to the ABA Model Rules of Professional Conduct, when responding to a former client's request for papers and property in the lawyer's possession that are related to the representation. The opinion does not address a client's property rights or other legal rights to these materials.

A lawyer has represented a local municipality for 10 years pursuant to a contract for legal services. The contract term expired. After publishing a request for proposals, the municipality chose a different lawyer to provide the municipality with future legal services. The municipality requested that the lawyer provide the municipality's new counsel with all files – open and closed. The lawyer has been paid in full for all of the work.[1] The lawyer asks what materials must be provided to the former client.[2]

The scope of a lawyer's ethical duty pursuant to the Rules of Professional Conduct to provide a former client with papers and property to which the client is entitled at the termination of the representation arises with regularity. Many jurisdictions, through case law on property rights, agency law, or ethics opinions under the jurisdiction's Rules of Professional Conduct, have examined the question and determined which papers and property a lawyer must return, reproduce, and/or provide to a client. There may be other obligations defined in a jurisdiction's case law or court rules.[3] Lawyers are cautioned to review the law

---

1. Because the lawyer has been paid in full, this opinion does not address retaining liens.

2. The ABA Model Rules of Professional Conduct do not directly address the length of time a lawyer must preserve client files after the close of the representation. Many jurisdictions provide guidance on this issue through court rule or ethics opinions.

3. *See,* Corrigan v. Teasdale Armstrong Schlafly Davis & Dicus, 824 S.W.2d 92 (Mo. 1992) (client has a conditional right of access to a lawyer's notes, research, and drafts if the client needs the notes, research, and drafts to understand completed documents).

in the jurisdiction in which they practice because lawyers have been disciplined for failing to surrender to the client papers and property to which the client is entitled.[4]

ABA Informal Ethics Opinion 1376 (1977) addressed a lawyer's ethical duty to deliver files to a former client. The opinion interpreted Rule 9-102(B)(4) of the Model Code of Professional Responsibility that read, "A lawyer shall: [P] romptly pay or deliver to the client as requested by the client the . . . properties in the possession if the lawyer which the client is entitled to receive." It concluded: "The attorney clearly must return all of the materials supplied by the client to the attorney. . . . He must also deliver the 'end product' . . . On the other hand, in the Committee's view, the lawyer need not deliver his internal notes and memos which have been generated primarily for his own purpose in working on the client's problem."

That opinion was issued prior to the adoption of the Model Rules of Professional Conduct and prior to advances in technology that have affected virtually all aspects of the practice of law, including how lawyers create, communicate, use, and store materials related to client representations. This opinion clarifies and updates a lawyer's ethical duty to provide a former client with papers and property pursuant to Model Rules of Professional Conduct 1.15 and 1.16, and addresses practical considerations attendant to those obligations.

Model Rule 1.15 provides that a lawyer must safeguard a client's property and promptly deliver it to the client upon the client's request.[5] By its terms, Rule 1.15 applies to a client's and third party's money and to "other property" that comes into a lawyer's possession in connection with a representation.[6] Although not specifically defined in the Rule, "other property" may be fairly understood to include, for example, (a) tangible personal property, (b) items with intrinsic value or that affect valuable rights, such as securities, negotiable instruments, wills, or deeds and (c) any documents provided to a lawyer by a client.[7] Therefore, as

---

4. *See In re* Brussow 286 P.3d 1246 (Utah 2012). In Brussow, the respondent represented a client in post-dissolution matters and was publicly sanctioned for refusing to turn over the file to the client. Brussow argued that the client owed him money for the cost of deposition transcripts which the client's second husband agreed to pay. The Utah Supreme Court noted that Utah's Rule 1.16 "differs from the ABA Model Rule in requiring that papers and property considered to be part of the client's file be returned to the client notwithstanding any other laws or fees or expenses." *Id.* at 1252. Brussow was also admonished for failing to account for fees paid in advance. *See also In re Thai*, 987 A.2d 428 (D.C. 2009). Thai delayed returning a client's file and "actively obstructed the efforts of his former client and the successor attorney to obtain the file." *Id.* at 430. Thai was disciplined for violating Rule 1.16 as well as for violations of Rules 1.1, 1.3, and 1.4 involving the same client matter.

5. ABA MODEL RULE 1.15, Safeguarding Property.

6. ABA MODEL RULE 1.15(a).

7. This obligation exists with respect to all materials whether in paper or electronic form. *See* ABA MODEL RULE 1.0(n) defining writing as "a tangible or electronic record of a communication . . . including audio or video recording, and electronic communications." *See also* N.H. Bar Ass'n Advisory Op. 2005-06/3 (2005).

an initial matter, and in the absence of other law[8] or a valid dispute under Rule 1.15(e), the lawyer must return all property of the municipality that the municipality provided in connection with the representation. *See* ABA Informal Ethics Opinion 1376 (1977). This would necessarily include original documents provided by the client.

When a representation ends, ABA Model Rule 1.16(d) mandates that the lawyer take steps that are "reasonably practicable to protect a client's interests . . ."[9] "Reasonable," when used to describe a lawyer's actions "denotes the conduct of a reasonably prudent and competent lawyer."[10] These steps include, but are not limited to, "surrendering papers and property to which the client is entitled."[11]

The Model Rules do not define the "papers and property to which the client is entitled," that the lawyer must surrender pursuant to Rule 1.16(d). Jurisdictions vary in their interpretation of this obligation. A majority of jurisdictions follow what is referred to as the "entire file" approach.[12] In those jurisdictions, at the termination of a representation, a lawyer must surrender papers and property related to the representation in the lawyer's possession unless the lawyer establishes that a specific exception applies and that certain papers or property may be properly withheld.[13] Commonly recognized exceptions to surrender include: materials that would violate a duty of non-disclosure to another person;[14] materials containing a lawyer's assessment of the client;[15] materials containing information, which, if released, could endanger the health, safety, or welfare of the client or others;[16] and documents reflecting only internal firm communica-

---

8. *See* ABA MODEL RULE 1.15, cmt. [4] for a discussion of third party liens. *See* ABA MODEL RULE 1.16(d) and cmt. [9] and ABA Comm. on Ethics & Prof'l Responsibility, Informal Op. 86-1520 (1986) for a discussion of lawyer retaining liens.

9. ABA MODEL RULE 1.16, Declining or Terminating Representation.

10. ABA MODEL RULE 1.0(h), Terminology.

11. ABA MODEL RULE 1.16(d). This duty applies even when the lawyer believes the client's discharge is unfair. *See* ABA MODEL RULE 1.16, cmt. [9].

12. *See, e.g.,* Iowa Sup. Ct. Attorney Disciplinary Bd. v. Gottschalk, 729 N.W.2d 812 (2007) (failure to return entire file to client violates disciplinary rules); Alaska Bar Ass'n Ethics Comm. Op. 2003-3 (2003); Ariz. Formal Op. 04-01 (2004); Colo. Bar Ass'n. Formal Op. 104 (1999); D.C. Bar Op. 333 (2005); Or. Bar Ass'n Formal Op. 2005-125 (2005); Va. State Bar Op. 1399 (1990).

13. This approach is also advocated by the RESTATEMENT (THIRD) OF THE LAW GOVERNING LAWYERS. *See* RESTATEMENT (THIRD) LAW GOVERNING LAWYERS (2000) §46 ("On request, a lawyer must allow a client or former client to inspect and copy any document possessed by the lawyer relating to the representation, unless substantial grounds exist to refuse.")

14. *See, e.g.,* Colo. Bar Ass'n Formal Op. 104 (1999) ("A lawyer has the right to withhold pleadings or other documents relating to the lawyer's representation of other clients that the lawyer used as a model on which to draft documents for the present client."); *In re* Sage Realty Corp. v. Proskauer, Rose, Goetz & Mendelsohn LLP, 689 N.E.2d 879,883 (N.Y. 1997).

15. *See, e.g., In re* Sage Realty Corp. v. Proskauer, Rose, Goetz & Mendelsohn LLP, 689 N.E.2d 879, 883 (N.Y. 1997).

16. RESTATEMENT (THIRD) LAW GOVERNING LAWYERS (2000) §46, cmt. c.

ABA Formal Ethics Opinions (Selected)

tions and assignments.[17] The entire file approach assumes that the client has an expansive general right to materials related to the representation and retains that right when the representation ends.

Other jurisdictions follow variations of an end-product approach.[18] These variations distinguish between documents that are the "end-product" of a lawyer's services, which must be surrendered and other material that may have led to the creation of that "end-product," which need not be automatically surrendered. Under these variations of the end-product approach, the lawyer must surrender: correspondence by the lawyer for the benefit of the client;[19] investigative reports and other discovery for which the client has paid;[20] and pleadings and other papers filed with a tribunal. The client is also entitled to copies of contracts, wills, corporate records, and other similar documents prepared by the lawyer for the client. These items are generally considered the lawyer's "end product."

Administrative materials related to the representation, such as memoranda concerning potential conflicts of interest,[21] the client's creditworthiness, time and expense records,[22] or personnel matters,[23] are not considered materials to which the client is entitled under the end- product approach. Additionally, the lawyer's personal notes,[24] drafts of legal instruments or documents to be filed with a tribunal,[25] other internal memoranda, and legal research[26] are viewed as generated primarily for the lawyer's own purpose in working on a client's matter, and, therefore, need not be surrendered to the client under the end product approach.

Final documents supersede earlier drafts. Earlier drafts and lawyer notes are part of the process of completing the final draft and, when electronic documents go through a process of continuing changes, it can become difficult or

---

ABA Formal
Ethics Opinions
(Selected)

17. *See, e.g.*, Colo. Bar Ass'n Formal Op. 104 (1999); D.C. Bar Op. 333 (2005).

18. Ala. Ethics Comm. Advisory Op. 1986-02 (1986); Ill. State Bar Ass'n Advisory Op. 94-13 (1995); Kan. Bar Ass'n Op. 92-5 (1992); Miss. Bar Formal Op. 144 (1988); Utah State Bar Ass'n Advisory Op. 06-02 (2006).

19. *See, e.g.*, Neb. Lawyer's Advisory Comm. Advisory Op. 12-09 (2012); Ill. State Bar Ass'n Advisory Op. 94-13 (1995).

20. *See, e.g.*, Corrigan v. Teasdale Armstrong Schlafly Davis & Dicus, 824 S.W.2d 92, 98 (Mo. 1992); Neb. Lawyer's Advisory Comm. Advisory Op. 12-09 (2012).

21. Ohio Bd. Comm'rs on Grievances and Discipline Advisory Op. 2010-2 (2010); Colo. Bar Ass'n Formal Op. 104

22. Saroff v. Cohen, No. E2008-00612-COA-R3-CV, 2009 WL 482498 , 2009 BL 39364 (Tenn. Ct. App. Feb. 25, 2009) (Invoices for legal work performed are a law firm's business records, not prepared for the client's benefit, and need not be turned over upon client request. Proper procedure for securing this information when client is suing firm is to make a discovery request.).

23. Colo. Bar Ass'n Formal Op. 104 (1999); Alaska Bar Ass'n Ethics Comm. Op. 2003-3 (2003); D.C. Bar Op. 333 (2005).

24. Womack Newspapers Inc. v. Town of Kitty Hawk, 639 S.E.2d 96, 104 (N.C. 2007).

25. Miss. Bar Formal Op. 144 (1988); Utah State Bar Ass'n Advisory Op. 06-02 (2006).

26. Ill. State Bar Ass'n Advisory Op. 94-13 (1995); San Diego Cnty. Bar Ass'n Op. 1984-3 (1984).

impossible to determine what constitutes a distinct "draft."[27] Thus, drafts and other documents representing work by a lawyer are often of relatively small value to clients and can be burdensome for a lawyer to preserve, catalogue, and maintain.

In ABA Informal Ethics Opinion 1376 (1977), the Committee addressed, under the Code of Professional Responsibility, what properties a lawyer must provide to a client at the conclusion of the representation in a trademark matter. We advised that the lawyer must provide the client with "end product—the certificates or other evidence of registration of the trademark," searches conducted and paid for, "significant correspondence, applications and materials filed in aid thereof, receipts, documents received from third parties, significant documents filed in the administrative and court proceedings, finished briefs whether filed or not if they pertain to the right of the client to the use or registration of the mark in question." The Committee noted that the lawyer "need not deliver" to the client "internal notes and memos."

The Committee affirms the position taken in Informal Ethics Opinion 1376 as it states the minimum required by the Rules. However, there may be circumstances in individual representations that require the lawyer to provide additional materials related to the representation. For example, when the representation is terminated before the matter is concluded, protection of the client's interest may require the lawyer to provide the client with paper or property generated by the lawyer for the lawyer's own purpose.

As noted above, Model Rule 1.16(d) requires a lawyer to take steps to the extent reasonably practicable to protect a client's interest. Such steps include "surrendering papers and property to which a client is entitled . . ." Comment [9] to Rule 1.16 further clarifies that the lawyer "must take all reasonable steps to mitigate the consequences [of withdrawal] to the client." Although surrendering papers and property which the client is entitled to receive does not necessar-

---

27. This opinion does not address a lawyer's obligations to retain specific material relating to a representation in the first instance (whether in paper or electronic form). However, a lawyer's duty under Rule 1.16(d) to "surrender papers and property to which the client is entitled" at the termination of a representation necessarily requires some consideration of this issue. In general, a lawyer's ethical obligation to retain and safeguard material relating to a representation arises pursuant to a lawyer's duties of competence and diligence and will depend on the facts and circumstances of each representation. *See* ABA MODEL RULE 1.1 and ABA MODEL RULE 1.3. *See also* Ass'n of the Bar of the City of N.Y. Comm. on Prof'l & Judicial Ethics, Formal Op. 2008-1 (2008); S.C. Bar Formal Op. 15 (2013). Further, a lawyer's decision whether to retain specific material related to a representation, in most cases, ultimately rests in the professional judgment of a lawyer consistent with his or her ethical and legal duties to the client. For example, in most instances, a lawyer will not need to retain non-substantive email communication to a client such as an email confirming a meeting or providing driving directions to the lawyer's office. By contrast, the lawyer likely would need to retain an email to the client in which the lawyer communicates and evaluates a settlement offer from an opposing party. Consistent with duties under the Model Rules, lawyers are encouraged to develop good document management policies.

ily give rise to a client's entitlement under the Rules of Professional Conduct to *all* materials in the lawyer's custody or control related to the representation, at a minimum a lawyer's obligation under the Rules reasonably gives rise to an entitlement to those materials that would likely harm the client's interest if not provided.[28] We agree with Colorado Ethics Opinion 104 (1999) that in this context, unless the law of the jurisdiction provides otherwise, "the ethical entitlement is based on the client's right to access the document related to the representation to enable continued protection of the client's interest."[29]

Therefore, on the facts presented, at a minimum, Rule 1.16(d) requires that the lawyer must surrender to the municipality:

- any materials provided to the lawyer by the municipality;
- legal documents filed with a tribunal - or those completed, ready to be filed, but not yet filed;[30]
- executed instruments like contracts;[31]
- orders or other records of a tribunal;
- correspondence issued or received by the lawyer in connection with the representation of the municipality on relevant issues, including email and other electronic correspondence that has been retained according to the firm's document retention policy;
- discovery or evidentiary exhibits, including interrogatories and their answers, deposition transcripts, expert witness reports and witness statements, and exhibits;
- legal opinions issued at the request of the municipality; and
- third party assessments, evaluations, or records paid for by the municipality.

ABA Formal Ethics Opinions (Selected)

28. The Committee recognizes that while Model Rule 1.16(d) specifies "papers and property," many lawyers have moved or are moving to a paperless practice in which few documents are available in tangible form. The use of the term "paper" in Rule 1.16(d) includes all communications noted above, whether tangible or electronic. *See* ABA MODEL RULE 1.0(e) defining writing as a "tangible or electronic record of a communication." While this opinion does not address whether and in what circumstances a lawyer must convert an electronic document into paper for a client or who will bear the cost of this conversion, the Committee agrees with the reasoning in D.C. Bar Op. 357 (2012) which explained, "Lawyers and clients may enter into reasonable agreements addressing how the client's files will be maintained, how copies will be provided to the client if requested, and who will bear what costs associated with providing the files in a particular form; entering into such agreements is prudent and can help avoid misunderstandings."

29. *See also* Corrigan v. Teasdale Armstrong Schlafly Davis & Dicus, 824 S.W.2d 92, 97 (Mo. 1992) ("The purpose of the Rule, however, gives it meaning. The Rule is designed to protect a client's interest. It imposes a duty upon the attorney 'to take steps to protect' a former client's interest. 'Surrendering papers and property to which the client is entitled' is one example of a step an attorney must take to protect that interest. But, this duty 'to surrender papers and property' need not be supported or justified by any property concepts.")

30. ABA Comm. on Ethics & Prof'l Responsibility, Informal Op. 1376 (1977).

31. *Id.*

In contrast, under these facts, it is unlikely that within the meaning of Rule 1.16(d), the client is entitled to papers or other property in the lawyer's possession that the lawyer generated for internal use primarily for the lawyer's own purpose in working on the municipality's matters.[32] This is particularly true for matters that are concluded.

Therefore, under the facts presented, under Rule 1.16(d) the lawyer need not provide, for example, the following to the municipality:

- drafts or mark-ups of documents to be filed with a tribunal;
- drafts of legal instruments;
- internal legal memoranda and research materials;
- internal conflict checks;
- personal notes;
- hourly billing statements;
- firm assignments;
- notes regarding an ethics consultation;
- a general assessment of the municipality or the municipality's matter; and
- documents that might reveal the confidences of other clients.

The Committee notes that when a lawyer has been representing a client on a matter that is not completed and the representation is terminated, the former client may be entitled to the release of some materials the lawyer generated for internal law office use primarily for the lawyer's own purpose in working on a client's matter.[33]

In this fact scenario, if the lawyer has materials that are: (1) internal notes and memos that were generated primarily for the lawyer's own purpose in working on the municipality's matter, (2) for which no final product has emerged, and (3) the materials should be disclosed to avoid harming the municipality's interest, then the lawyer must also provide the municipality with these materials. For example, if in a continuing matter a filing deadline is imminent, and as part of working on the municipality's matter the lawyer has drafted documents to meet this filing deadline, but no final document has emerged, then the most recent draft and relevant supporting research should be provided to the municipality.

Finally, as part of the lawyer's duty pursuant to Rule 1.4 to keep the client "reasonably informed about the status of the matter," a lawyer may already have provided much of this information to a former client during the course of the representation. As Comment [4] to Rule 1.4 explains, "A lawyer's regular communication with clients will minimize the occasions on which a client

---

32. ABA Comm. on Ethics & Prof'l Responsibility, Informal Op. 1376 (1977).

33. A number of jurisdictions approve lawyer generated "summary of facts" or redacted memorandum that essentially provide the "useful" part of the documents to the client while preserving the internal thoughts/impressions of the lawyer as unnecessary for protecting the clients' interests. *See* Ohio Bd. Comm'rs on Grievances and Discipline Advisory Op. 2010-2 (2010).

will need to request information concerning the representation." The Committee encourages lawyers to regularly provide clients with information and copies of documents during the course of the matter and encourages lawyers to advise clients to maintain these documents. The fact that copies of certain materials may have been previously provided to a client is not dispositive of whether the lawyer must also provide such materials at the termination of a representation.[34] This fact may not, however, be dispositive of who—the lawyer or the client—should pay for the time and cost of duplication of such materials upon termination of the representation.[35]

Conclusion

Upon the termination of a representation, a lawyer is required under Model Rules 1.15 and 1.16(d) to take steps to the extent reasonably practicable to protect a client's interest, and such steps include surrendering to the former client papers and property to which the former client is entitled such as materials provided to the lawyer, legal documents filed or executed, and such other papers and properties identified in this opinion. A client is not entitled to papers and property that the lawyer generated for the lawyer's own purpose in working on the client's matter. However, when the lawyer's representation of the client in a matter is terminated before the matter is completed, protection of the former client's interest may require that certain materials the lawyer generated for the lawyer's own purpose be provided to the client.

ABA Formal Ethics Opinions (Selected)

---

34. *See generally* Travis v. Comm. on Prof'l Conduct, 306 S.W.3d 3 (Ark. 2009) (the client has no duty to maintain a file on his or her own behalf).

35. Lawyers are encouraged to explain in their retainer letters who is responsible for the costs of copying and under what circumstances.

Formal Opinion 472   November 30, 2015

Communication with Person Receiving
Limited-Scope Legal Services

Under Model Rule 1.2(c), lawyers are authorized to provide limited-scope legal representation. Although not required by Rule 1.2(c), the Committee recommends that lawyers providing limited-scope representation confirm the scope of the representation in writing provided to the client.

Although Rule 4.2 does not require a lawyer to ask a person if he or she is represented by counsel before communicating with that person about the subject of the representation, a lawyer's knowledge that the person has obtained assistance from another lawyer may be inferred from circumstances. If the lawyer has reason to believe that an unrepresented person on the opposing side has received limited-scope legal services, the Committee recommends that the lawyer begin the communication with that person by asking whether that person is or was represented by counsel for any portion of the matter so that the lawyer knows whether to proceed under ABA Model Rule 4.2 or 4.3. When a lawyer has knowledge that a person is represented on the matter to be discussed, the lawyer must obtain the consent of counsel prior to speaking with the person.

If the person states that he or she is or was represented by counsel in any part of a matter, and does not articulate either that the representation has concluded or that the issue to be discussed is clearly outside the scope of the limited-scope representation, the lawyer requesting information should contact the lawyer providing limited-scope services to identify the issues on which the inquiring lawyer may not communicate directly with the person receiving limited-scope services.

The lawyer must comply with Rule 4.2 and communicate with the person's counsel when the communication concerns an issue, decision, or action for which the person is represented. Under Rule 4.3, however, the lawyer may communicate directly with the person on aspects of the matter for which no representation exists. On aspects of the matter for which representation has been completed and the lawyer providing limited-scope services is not expected to reemerge to represent the client, a lawyer may communicate directly with the other person. Communication with a person who received limited-scope legal services about an issue for which representation has concluded should not include inquiries about protected communications between the person and the lawyer providing limited-scope services.

In this opinion the Committee addresses the obligations of a lawyer under ABA Model Rule of Professional Conduct 4.2, *Communication with Person Represented by Counsel*, commonly called the "no contact" rule, and ABA Model Rule of Professional Conduct 4.3, *Dealing with Unrepresented Person*, when communicating with a person who is receiving or has received limited-scope representation under ABA Model Rule of Professional Conduct 1.2, *Scope of Representation and Allocation of Authority Between Client and Lawyer*.[1] We also provide recommendations for lawyers providing limited-scope representation.

Like all the Model Rules of Professional Conduct, Rules 1.2, 4.2, and 4.3 are intended to be rules of reason and must be construed and applied "with reference to the purposes of legal representation and the law itself."[2] In a limited-scope representation, the Model Rules in general, and Model Rule 4.2 specifically, must be interpreted accordingly because limited-scope representations do not naturally fit into either the traditional full-matter representation contemplated by Model Rule 4.2 or the wholly pro se representation contemplated by Model Rule 4.3.

Rule 1.2, Scope of Representation and Allocation of Authority Between Client and Lawyer

Model Rule 1.2(c) reads: "A lawyer may limit the scope of the representation if the limitation is reasonable under the circumstances and the client gives informed consent."[3] Today lawyers increasingly represent clients on a limited-scope basis.

Limited-scope representation may include assisting a litigant who is appearing before a tribunal pro se, by drafting or reviewing one or more documents to be submitted in the proceeding. "This is a form of 'unbundling' of legal services, whereby a lawyer performs only specific, limited tasks instead of handling all aspects of a matter." *See* ABA Formal Ethics Opinion 07-446 (2007).[4]

Although limited-scope representation is not restricted to low-income clients or small claims matters, the ABA Ethics 2000 Commission explained that the proposed amendments to Model Rule 1.2(c) and its Comments regarding limited-scope representations were in part "intended to provide a framework within which lawyers may expand access to legal services by providing limited

ABA Formal
Ethics Opinions
(Selected)

---

1. This opinion is based on the Model Rules of Professional Conduct as amended by the American Bar Association House of Delegates through February 2013. The laws, court rules, regulations, rules of professional conduct, and opinions promulgated in the individual jurisdiction are controlling.

2. MODEL RULES OF PROF'L CONDUCT, Preamble & Scope [14].

3. MODEL RULES OF PROF'L CONDUCT R. 1.2(c).

4. ABA Formal Op. 07-447 (2007) addressed the scope of representation of a client in a collaborative law setting. In that Opinion, the Committee determined that "[A] lawyer may provide legal assistance to litigants appearing before tribunals 'pro se' and help them prepare written submissions without disclosing or ensuring the disclosure of the nature or extent of such assistance." The Committee rejected the argument that courts are deceived by lawyers who "ghostwrite" legal documents for pro se litigants or that such conduct is "dishonest," noting that the conduct does not mislead the court or any party.

5. A LEGISLATIVE HISTORY: THE DEVELOPMENT OF THE ABA MODEL RULES OF PROFESSIONAL CONDUCT, 1982-2013, at 59 (Art Garwin ed., 2013).

but nonetheless valuable legal services to low- or moderate-income persons who otherwise would be unable to obtain counsel."[5]

Rule 1.2(c) requires a lawyer to secure the informed consent of a client when providing limited-scope services. Informed consent is defined as: "the agreement by a person to a proposed course of conduct after the lawyer has communicated adequate information and explanation about the material risks of and reasonably available alternatives to the proposed course of conduct."[6] The Colorado Bar Association advised in Formal Ethics Opinion 101 that a lawyer providing limited-scope services to a client should "clearly explain the limitations of the representation, including the types of services which are not being provided and the probable effect of limited representation on the client's rights and interests."[7] The D.C. Bar Legal Ethics Committee advised in its Opinion 330 (2005) that the "client's understanding of the scope of the services" is fundamental to a limited-scope representation.[8] Opinion 330 recommended that lawyers reduce such agreements to writing:

> Because the tasks excluded from a limited services agreement will typically fall to the client to perform or not get done at all, it is essential that clients clearly understand the division of responsibilities under a limited representation agreement . . . Particularly in the context of limited-representation agreements, however, a writing clearly explaining what is and is not encompassed within the agreement to provide services will be helpful in ensuring the parties' mutual understanding.[9]

Similarly, the Ethics 2000 Commission recommended adding a formal Comment to Rule 1.2 that a "specification of the scope of representation will normally be a necessary part of the lawyer's written communication of the rate or basis of the lawyer's fee as required by Rule 1.5(b)." However, because the House of Delegates rejected the Commission's parallel proposal to amend Rule 1.5(b) — which would have required written fee agreements that included an explanation of the scope of the representation, the basis or rate of the fee, and the expenses for which the client will be responsible — this proposed Rule 1.2 Comment language was not advanced.[10]

Therefore, although not required by Rule 1.2(c), the Committee nevertheless recommends that when lawyers provide limited-scope representation to a client, they confirm with the client the scope of the representation—including the tasks the lawyer will perform and not perform—in writing that the client can

---

6. Model Rules of Prof'l Conduct R. 1.0(e).
7. Colorado Bar Ass'n Formal Op. 101 (1998, rev. by addendum 2006).
8. D.C. Bar Op. 330 (2005).
9. *Id.*
10. A Legislative History, *supra* note 5, at 61-62.

read, understand, and refer to later. This guidance is in accord with Model Rule 1.5(b) which explains:

> The scope of the representation and the basis or rate of the fee and expenses for which the client will be responsible shall be communicated to the client, preferably in writing, before or within a reasonable time after commencing the representation, except when the lawyer will charge a regularly represented client on the same basis or rate. Any changes in the basis or rate of the fee or expenses shall also be communicated to the client.

The Committee notes that some state rules of professional conduct require a written agreement when a lawyer provides limited-scope services. *See, e.g.,* Maryland Lawyers' Rules of Professional Conduct, Rule 1.2(c)(3); Missouri Rule of Professional Conduct 1.2(c); Montana Rule of Professional Conduct 1.2(c) (2); and New Hampshire Rule of Professional Conduct 1.2(c) and 1.2(g). Other states explain that a written agreement is preferred. *See* Ohio Rule of Professional Conduct 1.2(c) and Tennessee Rule of Professional Conduct 1.2(c). Additionally, some state rules of civil procedure require a limited-scope appearance filing with the court identifying each aspect of the proceeding to which the limited-scope appearance pertains. *See, e.g.,* Illinois Supreme Court Rule 13(c) (6). Therefore, lawyers providing limited-scope representation are advised to review their state rules to determine whether a written agreement is required for their limited-scope representation.[11]

If a lawyer who is providing limited-scope services is contacted by opposing counsel in the matter, the lawyer should identify the issues on which the inquiring lawyer may not communicate directly with the person receiving limited-scope services. A lawyer providing limited-scope legal services to a client generally has no basis to object to communications between the opposing counsel and the client receiving those services on any matter outside the scope of the limited representation.

These issues would best be resolved at the inception of the client-lawyer relationship by the client giving the lawyer providing limited-scope representation informed consent to reveal to opposing counsel what issues should be discussed with counsel and what issues can be discussed with the client directly.

---

11. Because a tribunal may require disclosure of the scope of the services performed by the lawyer, and because a client receiving limited-scope services may desire to disclose to opposing counsel the scope of services performed by the lawyer, the Committee cautions lawyers providing limited-scope services to draft their limited-scope legal service agreement so that the agreement does not reveal information beyond that necessary for the client, opposing counsel, or the tribunal to determine the scope of the representation. For an example of a limited-scope agreement that lists services to be performed, see Reporter's Notes to Maine Rule of Professional Conduct 1.2 Limited Representation Agreement. The agreement lists 20 categories of legal services.

ABA Formal Ethics Opinions (Selected)

Model Rule 4.2, Communication with Person Represented by Counsel: Is there a duty to ask?

The ABA ethics rules have included a "no-contact" rule since the 1908 adoption of the ABA Canons of Professional Ethics.[12] Current Model Rule 4.2 reads:

> In representing a client, a lawyer shall not communicate about the subject of the representation with a person the lawyer knows to be represented by another lawyer in the matter, unless the lawyer has the consent of the other lawyer or is authorized to do so by law or a court order.

Model Rule 4.2 protects clients who have chosen to be represented by a lawyer from having another lawyer interfere with the client-lawyer relationship by, for example, seeking uncounseled disclosure of information and/or uncounseled concessions and admissions related to the representation.[13] A lawyer directly communicating with an individual, however, will only violate Rule 4.2 if the lawyer *knows* that the person is represented by another lawyer in the matter to be discussed.[14] "Knows" is defined by the Model Rules as "actual knowledge of the fact in question. A person's knowledge may be inferred from circumstances."[15]

ABA Model Rule 4.3 reads:

> In dealing on behalf of a client with a person who is not represented by counsel, a lawyer shall not state or imply that the lawyer is disinterested. When the lawyer knows or reasonably should know that the unrepresented person misunderstands the lawyer's role in the matter, the lawyer shall make reasonable efforts to correct the misunderstanding. The lawyer shall not give legal advice to an unrepresented person, other than the advice to secure counsel, if the lawyer knows or reasonably should know that the interests of such a person are or have a reasonable possibility of being in conflict with the interests of the client.

---

12. ABA Canon 9: "Negotiations with Opposite Party. A lawyer should not in any way communicate upon the subject of controversy with a party represented by counsel; much less should he undertake to negotiate or compromise the matter with him, but should deal only with his counsel. It is incumbent upon the lawyer most particularly to avoid everything that may tend to mislead a party not represented by counsel, and he should not undertake to advise him as to the law." Canon 9 is available at: http://www.americanbar.org/content/dam/aba/migrated/cpr/mrpc/Canons_Ethics.authcheckdam.pdf.

13. MODEL RULES OF PROF'L CONDUCT R. 4.2, cmt. [1].

14. *See, e.g.,* Okla. Bar Ass'n v. Harper, 995 P.2d 1143 (Okla. 2000) (lawyer did not violate Rule 4.2 without actual knowledge of the representation. "Ascribing actual knowledge to a lawyer based on the facts is not the same as applying the rule under circumstances where the lawyer should have known.").

15. MODEL RULES OF PROF'L CONDUCT R. 1.0(f).

Lawyers confronted with a person who appears to be managing a matter *pro se* but may be receiving or have received legal assistance, often are left in a quandary. May the lawyer assume that such persons are proceeding without the aid of counsel and, therefore, speak directly to them about the matter under Model Rule 4.3, or should the lawyer first ask whether they are represented in the matter and then proceed accordingly under either Rule 4.2 or 4.3?

Interpreting Model Rule 4.2 in July 1995, ABA Formal Ethics Opinion 95-396, noted:

> It would not, from such a practical point of view, be reasonable to re-
> quire a lawyer *in all circumstances* where the lawyer wishes to speak
> to a third person in the course of his representation of a client first to
> inquire whether the person is represented by counsel: among other
> things, such a routine inquiry would unnecessarily complicate perfectly
> routine fact-finding, and might well unnecessarily obstruct such fact-
> finding by conveying a suggestion that there was a need for counsel in
> circumstances where there was none, thus discouraging witnesses from
> talking.[16] (Emphasis added.)

Thus, while the black letter of Model Rule 4.2 does not include a duty to ask whether a person is represented by counsel, this Committee reiterates the warning of Comment [8] to Rule 4.2 that a lawyer cannot evade the requirement of obtaining the consent of counsel before speaking with a represented person by "closing eyes to the obvious."[17]

In circumstances involving what appears to be an unrepresented person, but in fact may be a person represented by a lawyer under a limited-scope agreement, a lawyer's knowledge that the person has obtained some degree of legal representation may be inferred from the facts.[18] Such circumstances include, for example:

ABA Formal
Ethics Opinions
(Selected)

---

16. ABA Formal Op. 95-396, fn. 39 (1995). Immediately after the release of Formal Opinion 95-396, Rule 4.2, Comment [5] was amended to read: "The prohibition on communications with a represented person only applies, however, in circumstances where the lawyer knows that the person is in fact represented in the matter to be discussed. This means that the lawyer has actual knowledge of the fact of the representation; but such actual knowledge may be inferred from the circumstances. See Terminology. Such an inference may arise in circumstances where there is a substantial reason to believe that the person with whom communication is sought is represented in the matter to be discussed. Thus, the lawyer cannot evade the requirement of obtaining the consent of counsel by closing eyes to the obvious." However, the Ethics 2000 Commission recommended to the ABA House of Delegates that the sentence explaining "inference" be deleted, and the House adopted this recommendation in 2002. According to the "Reporter's Observations" document submitted to the House with the Ethics 2000 Commission resolution, this description of the knowledge requirement was "inconsistent with the definition of 'knows' in Rule 1.0(f), which requires actual knowledge and involves no duty to inquire." *See* A LEGISLATIVE HISTORY, *supra* note 5, at 566, citing ABA House of Delegates Report 401 (Feb. 2002).

17. MODEL RULES OF PROF'L CONDUCT R. 4.2, cmt. [8].

18. MODEL RULES OF PROF'L CONDUCT R. 1.0(f) (defining "knows").

when a lawyer representing a client faces what appears to be a pro se opposing party who has filed a pleading that appears to have been prepared by a lawyer or when a lawyer representing a client in a transaction is negotiating an agreement with what appears to be a pro se person who presents an agreement or a counter-offer that appears to have been prepared by a lawyer.[19]

Therefore, the Committee recommends that, in the circumstances where it appears that a person on the opposing side has received limited-scope legal services, the lawyer begin the communication by asking whether the person is represented by counsel for any portion of the matter so that the lawyer knows whether to proceed under ABA Model Rule 4.2 or 4.3. This may assist a lawyer in avoiding potential disciplinary complaints, motions to disqualify, motions to exclude testimony, and monetary sanctions, all of which could impede a client's matter.[20] It is not a violation of the Model Rules of Professional Conduct for the lawyer to make initial contact with a person to determine whether legal representation, limited or otherwise, exists.

If the person discloses representation under a limited-scope agreement and does not articulate either that the representation has concluded (as would be the case if the person indicates that yes, a lawyer drafted documents, but is not providing any other representation), or that the issue to be discussed is clearly outside the scope of the limited-scope representation, then the lawyer should contact opposing counsel to determine the issues on which the inquiring lawyer may not communicate directly with the client receiving limited-scope services.[21]

When the communication concerns an issue, decision, or action for which the person is represented, the lawyer must comply with Rule 4.2 and communicate with the person's counsel.

The lawyer may communicate directly with the person on aspects of the matter for which there is no representation.[22] For these communications, the lawyer must comply with Rule 4.3. On aspects of the matter for which representation has been completed and the lawyer providing limited-scope services is not expected to reemerge to represent the client, a lawyer may communicate directly with the other person. We note that Rule 1.6 and the confidentiality of

ABA Formal
Ethics Opinions
(Selected)

---

19. *See generally* State Bar of Arizona Op. 05-06 (2005) (filing of documents prepared by lawyer but signed by client receiving limited-scope representation is not misleading because ". . . a court or tribunal can generally determine whether that document was written with a lawyer's help.").

20. *See, e.g.*, Weeks v. Independent School Dist. No. I-89, 230 F.3d 1201 (10th Cir. 2000) (affirming district court's disqualification of lawyer who interviewed members of control group in violation of Rule 4.2).

21. Model Rules of Prof'l Conduct R. 4.2, cmt. [3] ("A lawyer must immediately terminate communication with a person if, after commencing communication, the lawyer learns that the person is one with whom communication is not permitted by this Rule.").

22. Model Rules of Prof'l Conduct R. 4.2, cmt. [4] ("This Rule does not prohibit communication with a represented person . . . concerning matters outside the representation.").

communications between a lawyer and the lawyer's client does not end when the limited representation concludes. Therefore, any communication with a person who received limited- scope legal services about an issue for which representation has concluded should not include inquiries about communications between the person and the lawyer providing limited-scope services.

If at any point in the matter the person—or the lawyer providing the limited-scope representation to that person—notifies the communicating lawyer that the scope of the representation was expanded, the communicating lawyer must act in accordance with Rule 4.2 as to any issues, decisions, or actions implicated by the expansion of the scope of services.

Conclusion

Under Model Rule 1.2(c), lawyers are authorized to provide limited-scope legal representation. Although not required by Rule 1.2(c), the Committee recommends that lawyers providing limited-scope representation confirm the scope of the representation in writing provided to the client.

Although Rule 4.2 does not require a lawyer to ask a person if he or she is represented by counsel before communicating with that person about the subject of the representation, a lawyer's knowledge that the person has obtained assistance from another lawyer may be inferred from circumstances. If the lawyer has reason to believe that an unrepresented person on the opposing side has received limited-scope legal services, the Committee recommends that the lawyer begin the communication with that person by asking whether that person is or was represented by counsel for any portion of the matter so that the lawyer knows whether to proceed under ABA Model Rule 4.2 or 4.3. When a lawyer has knowledge that a person is represented on the matter to be discussed, the lawyer must obtain the consent of counsel prior to speaking with the person.

If the person states that he or she is or was represented by counsel in any part of a matter, and does not articulate either that the representation has concluded or that the issue to be discussed is clearly outside the scope of the limited-scope representation, the lawyer requesting information should contact the lawyer providing limited-scope services to identify the issues on which the inquiring lawyer may not communicate directly with the person receiving limited-scope services.

The lawyer must comply with Rule 4.2 and communicate with the person's counsel when the communication concerns an issue, decision, or action for which the person is represented. Under Rule 4.3, however, the lawyer may communicate directly with the person on aspects of the matter for which no representation exists. On aspects of the matter for which representation has been completed and the lawyer providing limited-scope services is not expected to reemerge to represent the client, a lawyer may communicate directly with the other person. Communication with a person who received limited-scope legal services about an issue for which representation has concluded should not include inquiries about protected communications between the person and the lawyer providing limited-scope services.

Formal Opinion 473   February 17, 2016

Obligations Upon Receiving a Subpoena or
Other Compulsory Process for Client Documents
or Information

*A lawyer receiving a subpoena or other compulsory process for documents or
information relating to the representation of a client has several obligations.
If the client is available, the lawyer must consult the client. If instructed by
the client or if the client is unavailable, the lawyer must assert all reasonable
claims against disclosure and seek to limit the subpoena or other initial demand on any reasonable ground. If ordered to disclose confidential or privileged information and the client is available, a lawyer must consult with the
client about whether to produce the information or appeal. If the client and
the lawyer disagree about how to respond to the initial demand or to an order
requiring disclosure, the lawyer should consider withdrawing from the representation pursuant to Model Rule 1.16. If disclosure is ordered and the client
is unavailable for consultation, the lawyer is not ethically required to appeal.
When disclosing documents and information—whether in response to an
initial demand or to an order, and whether or not the client is available—the
lawyer may reveal information only to the extent reasonably necessary. The
lawyer should seek appropriate protective orders or other protective arrangements so that access to the information is limited to the court or other tribunal
ordering its disclosure and to persons having a need to know.*

I. Introduction

Recently the Committee was asked to revisit Formal Opinion 94-385 (July 5,
1994) regarding subpoena of a lawyer's files because Model Rule 1.6(b)(6) was
adopted in 2002, more than a decade ago (at that time as 1.6(b)(4)). Model Rule
1.6(b)(6) provides: "A lawyer may reveal information relating to the representation of a client to the extent the lawyer reasonably believes necessary to comply
with *other law or court order.*"[1]

---

1. ABA MODEL RULE 1.6(b)(6) (2015) (emphasis added). The phrase "other law" refers, generally, to statutory or regulatory requirements. See, e.g., State Bar of Michigan Advisory Op.
RI-311 (1999) (regulation requiring lawyer to report the names and addresses of clients to the
Legal Services Corporation); State Bar of Michigan Advisory Op. RI-54 (1990) (Internal Revenue Code requirement that cash transactions exceeding $10,000.00 be reported to the Internal
Revenue Service). Although there is overlap in the two phrases, this opinion addresses principally the obligations of a lawyer who receives a subpoena or other initial demand that is or
may be enforced by a court or other tribunal. Throughout this opinion, "subpoena," "demand,"
"compulsory process," and similar terms are used interchangeably to refer to any initial demand by an entity or person or government agency seeking information protected by Model
Rule 1.6(a) that is or may be enforced by compulsory process. "Court" or "tribunal" refers to a
court, an arbitrator in a binding arbitration proceeding or a legislative body, and an administrative agency or other body acting in an adjudicative capacity and includes any other "tribunal"
within the meaning of Model Rule 1.0(m).

When Formal Opinion 94-385 was issued, Model Rule 1.6(b) permitted a lawyer to disclose confidential information *in only two circumstances*: (i) to prevent certain crimes, and (ii) to establish certain claims or defenses on behalf of the lawyer.[2] Relying in part on then Comment [20], Formal Opinion 94-385 advised that the lawyer "must comply with the final orders of a court or other tribunal of competent jurisdiction requiring the lawyer to give information about a client."[3] The Opinion explained that this "does not mean that the lawyer should be a passive bystander to attempts by a governmental agency—or by any other person or entity for that matter—to examine her files or records."[4] Rather,

> [W]here a government agency serves on the lawyer a subpoena or court order directing the lawyer to turn over to the agency the lawyer's files relating to her representation of the client—the lawyer has a professional responsibility to seek to limit the subpoena, or court order, on any legitimate available ground (such as the attorney-client privilege, work product immunity, relevance or burden), so as to protect documents as to which the lawyer's obligation under Rule 1.6 apply. Only if the lawyer's efforts [at limiting the subpoena or order] are unsuccessful, either in the trial court or in the appellate court (in those jurisdictions where an interlocutory appeal on this issue is permitted), and she is specifically ordered by the court to turn over to the governmental agency documents which, in the lawyer's opinion, are privileged, may the lawyer do so.[5]

In the twenty-one years since publication of Formal Opinion 94-385 and the fourteen years since the Ethics 2000 amendments, additional questions have arisen regarding how a lawyer should respond to subpoenas, demands, or other compulsory process for client information and documents. These questions include: If disclosure is to be made, how extensive should it be? What, if any, protective measures should or must the lawyer seek? Are the obligations different when the client is not available for consultation? When the client is available for consultation but responding to the demand is outside the scope of a current representation, how should the lawyer handle retention and fee arrangements? If the client and the lawyer disagree about how to respond—either to the initial demand or after disclosure is ordered—what are the lawyer's obligations? Must the lawyer appeal an adverse decision for a client who is unavailable? Should or may the lawyer provide for these contingencies in retainer letters? This opinion provides guidance on these and related questions. The advice offered here updates and extends the advice offered in Formal Opinion 94-385.

ABA Formal
Ethics Opinions
(Selected)

---

2. *Compare* ABA Model Rule 1.6(b) (1994), with ABA Model Rule 1.6(b) (2015).

3. ABA Comm. on Ethics & Prof'l Responsibility, Formal Op. 94-385 (1994), at 2.

4. *Id.*

5. Id. at 3 (footnotes omitted).

II. Discussion

Rule 1.6(b) permits but does not require a lawyer to disclose information relating to the representation of a client ("[a] lawyer may reveal information") that the lawyer would otherwise be barred from disclosure under Rule 1.6(a).[6] Each of the seven 1.6(b) provisions specifies an exception to the 1.6(a) prohibition, and under each provision disclosure is permitted.[7]

For example, Rule 1.6(b)(6) makes clear that a lawyer cannot argue 1.6(a) bars compliance with a court order. Rule 1.6(a) permits disclosure of information relating to the representation, "if such disclosure is permitted by paragraph (b)," and subparagraph (b)(6) permits the lawyer to disclose information "to comply with other law or court order." A lawyer must obey a court order, subject to any right to move the court to withdraw or modify the order or to appeal the order.[8] But a lawyer facing a court order requiring the disclosure of client confidential information still is faced with complex, critical and fact-intensive questions on how to respond—e.g., what challenges should be considered, what specific information should be disclosed, and what protective measures should be sought. In making these judgments the lawyer must balance obligations inherent in the lawyer's dual role as an advocate for the client and an officer of the court. [9] In doing so, the lawyer should disclose client confidential information only to the extent "the lawyer reasonably believes necessary" to comply with the order.[10] Provision (b)(6) enables—indeed calls upon—the lawyer to make these delicate judgments.

---

6. ABA Model Rule 1.6(a) (2015) provides: "A lawyer shall not reveal information relating to the representation of a client unless the client gives informed consent, the disclosure is impliedly authorized in order to carry out the representation or the disclosure is permitted by paragraph (b)."

7. See, e.g., ABA Model Rule 1.6(b)(1) (2015) (a lawyer *may* reveal confidential information "to prevent reasonably certain death or substantial bodily harm") (emphasis added); ABA Model Rule 1.6(b)(2) (2015) (a lawyer *may* reveal confidential information "to prevent the client from committing a crime or fraud that is reasonably certain to result in substantial injury to the financial interests or property of another and in furtherance of which the client has used or is using the lawyer's services") (emphasis added). ABA Model Rule 1.6(b)(6) is, by its terms, and consistent with (b)(1) through (b)(5), also permissive. See ABA Model Rule 1.6(b)(6) (2015) ("[a] lawyer *may* reveal information . . . to comply with . . . a court order") (emphasis added). See also A Legislative History: The Development of the ABA Model Rules of Professional Conduct, 1982-2013 130 (Art Garwin ed., 2013); Margaret Love, *The Revised ABA Model Rules of Professional Conduct: Summary of the Work of Ethics 2000*, 15 Geo. J. Legal Ethics 441, 451 (2002).

8. See, e.g., ABA Model Rule 3.4(c) (2015) ("A lawyer shall not . . . knowingly disobey an obligation under the rules of a tribunal"); ABA Model Rule 8.4(d) (2015) ("It is professional misconduct for a lawyer to . . . engage in conduct that is prejudicial to the administration of justice"); ABA Model Rule 8.4(a) (2015) ("It is professional misconduct for a lawyer to . . . violate or attempt to violate the Rules of Professional Conduct"). See also Restatement of the Law Governing Lawyers (3d) § 105 (2000) ("In representing a client in a matter before a tribunal, a lawyer must comply with applicable law, including rules of procedure and evidence and specific tribunal rulings.").

9. See Dike v. Dike, 448 P.2d 490, 493 (Wash. 1968) (discussing whether a lawyer should be ordered to disclose confidential information the court said, "[I]t is important to recognize that an attorney has a dual role [in this context] — he is both an advocate for his client and an officer of the court . . . . Neither duty can be meaningfully considered independent from the other.").

10. ABA Model Rule 1.6 cmt. [16] (2015).

A. Notice and Consultation

The lawyer's obligations of notice and consultation upon receiving a demand for client files and information are essentially the same for current and former clients. First, the lawyer must notify—or attempt to notify—the client.[11] For former clients, the lawyer must make reasonable efforts to reach the client by, for example, internet search, phone call, fax, email or other electronic communications, and letter to the client's last known address. The specific efforts required to reach particular clients will depend on the circumstances existing when the lawyer receives the demand. But these efforts must be reasonable within the meaning of Model Rule 1.0(h), and should be documented in the lawyer's files.

The lawyer's obligations to the client will differ depending on whether the client is available for consultation. Where the client is available, the lawyer must consult the client about how to respond to the demand.[12] Model Rule 1.4 should guide this consultation.

---

11. *See, e.g.*, State Bar of Michigan Advisory Op. CI-925 (1983) (lawyer must notify client upon receipt of a subpoena for documents relating to the lawyer's representation of the client) (citations omitted); Alaska Bar Ass'n Op. 96-3 (1996) (upon receiving a demand for confidential information or documents, the lawyer should attempt to contact the client concerning the request). *See also* Linda G. Bauer, *Subpoena Savvy: What to Do When Your Client's File Is Subpoenaed* (Nov. 2002), www.mass.gov/obcbbo/subpoena.htm (". . . [T]he lawyer should first attempt to contact the former client to determine whether the client consents to the disclosure."); D.C. Bar Op. 14 (1976), at 2 ("an attorney should promptly notify his former client when he receives a subpoena asking for documents that came into his possession during the course of the representation of that former client or documents that affect or may affect that former client"); Pennsylvania Legal Ethics & Prof'l Responsibility Comm. Op. 2002-106 (2003) ("a lawyer may comply with an order issued in a private arbitration to reveal confidential client information, but must first raise the confidentiality issue with the arbitration panel and notify any clients whose confidences are implicated. The lawyer should try to limit the scope and impact of the disclosure.").

12. *See* ABA MODEL RULE 1.6 cmt. [15] (2015) (client consultation is required by Rule 1.4 before responding to an order or demand for information relating to a representation by "a court or by another tribunal or governmental entity"). The protection of 1.6 is provided to former clients through Model Rule 1.9(c)(1) and (2), which provide: "A lawyer who has formerly represented a client in a matter or whose present or former firm has formerly represented a client in a matter shall not thereafter: (1) use information relating to the representation to the disadvantage of the former client except as these Rules would permit or require with respect to a client . . . or (2) reveal information relating to the representation except as these Rules would permit or require with respect to a client." *See also* Swidler & Berlin v. U.S., 524 U.S. 399 (1998) (obligations of confidentiality continue even after the death of a client); Jamaica Pub. Serv. Co. v AIU Ins. Co., 684 N.Y.S.2d 459, 462 (N.Y. 1998) (an attorney owes a "continuing duty" to a former client not to reveal confidences learned in the course of a professional relationship). *See also* ABA Comm. on Ethics & Prof'l Responsibility, Formal Op. 10-456 fn8 ("[t]he lawyer's obligation to protect the attorney-client privilege ordinarily applies when the lawyer is called to testify or provide documents regarding a former client no less than a current client"); Rhode Island Supreme Ct. Ethics Advisory Panel Op. 2013-05, at 3 (2013) (obligations under 1.6 continue even after death of client; even then a "lawyer has a professional responsibility to seek to limit [a] subpoena or court order on any legitimate grounds such as attorney-client privilege, work product immunity, burden or relevance, to protect information to which obligations under Rule 1.6 apply") (citing ABA Formal Opinion 94-385).

ABA Formal Ethics Opinions (Selected)

Rule 1.4 directs the lawyer to "promptly inform the client of any decision or circumstance with respect to which the client's informed consent" is required and to "explain [the] matter to the extent reasonably necessary to permit the client to make informed decisions."[13] Rule 1.6(a) allows the lawyer to disclose information relating to the representation with the client's informed consent.[14] "'Informed consent' denotes the agreement by a person to a proposed course of conduct after the lawyer has communicated adequate information and explanation about the material risks of and reasonably available alternatives to the proposed course of conduct."[15]

The content of the consultation will depend on the circumstances. It should include, at a minimum, (i) a description of the protections afforded by Rule 1.6(a) and (b), (ii) whether and to what extent the attorney-client privilege or work product doctrine or other protections or immunities apply, and (iii) any other relevant matter. Other relevant matters include, for example, "to the extent that the disclosure of confidential client information in a civil proceeding may raise potential criminal liability for the client, the consequences should be explained to the client during the consultation process."[16] The lawyer also may need to discuss whether the subpoena or other demand is valid and whether the requested document contains self-incriminatory information that might form the basis of a Fifth Amendment privilege claim against disclosure.

If, after consultation, the client wishes to challenge the demand, the lawyer should, as appropriate and consistent with the client's instructions, challenge the demand on any reasonable ground. If, after making the challenge, the court or other tribunal rules against the motion to withdraw or modify the order or demand for production, "the lawyer must consult with the client about the possibility of appeal to the extent required by Rule 1.4."[17] If the client decides not to appeal and gives informed consent to disclosure, the lawyer must produce the documents and information consistent with the client's instructions and as described in Part IIC of this opinion.

The lawyer has several options and some obligations if the lawyer and client disagree about how to respond to the initial demand or to an adverse ruling, or if the client wishes to retain new counsel. For a current client, where the initial demand or the appeal is within the scope of the retention, for example, the lawyer may seek to withdraw in compliance with Model Rule 1.16.[18] Where the initial demand or the appeal constitutes a new matter for a current client or relates to a former client and the client wishes to seek other counsel, the lawyer

---

13. ABA Model Rule 1.4 (2015).

14. *See* ABA Model Rule 1.6(a) (2015) (prohibiting a lawyer from revealing confidential information unless the client gives "informed consent").

15. ABA Model Rule 1.0(e) (2015).

16. *See* Bauer, *supra* note 11.

17. ABA Model Rule 1.6 cmt. [15] (2015).

18. *See* ABA Model Rule 1.16(b)(1), (4), (7) & 1.16(c) (2015).

should take reasonable steps to protect the client's interest during the client's search for other counsel.[19]

B. Fee Arrangements

When responding to a demand that is outside the scope of a current retention, or when the demand relates to information and documents of a former client, the lawyer may need to discuss fee and retention arrangements during the consultation. In doing so, however, the lawyer must comply with the relevant rules. For example, under Model Rule 1.5(b) "[t]he scope of the representation and the basis or rate of the fee and expenses for which the client will be responsible shall be communicated to the client, preferably in writing, before or within a reasonable time after commencing the representation, except when the lawyer will charge a regularly represented client on the same basis or rate."[20]

Lawyers also may consider providing for these situations in initial retainer letters by including provisions that (i) the client will keep the lawyer informed on how to reach the client, even after the representation has ended, (ii) in the event the lawyer receives a subpoena or other demand for information protected by Model Rule 1.6, the client will promptly respond to the lawyer's request for instructions, and (iii) the client agrees to pay all reasonable fees and costs associated with any production or judicial proceedings in response to a subpoena or other demand. Even if no fee agreement is reached—either in the initial retainer letter or during a consultation following the lawyer's receipt of the demand—the lawyer nevertheless may be required to challenge the initial demand, as discussed below.[21]

C. Where the Client Is Unavailable for Consultation

Where the client is unavailable for consultation after the lawyer has made reasonable efforts to notify the client, the lawyer "*should* assert on behalf of the client all non-frivolous claims that . . . the information sought is protected against disclosure by the attorney-client privilege or other applicable law."[22] The law-

ABA Formal
Ethics Opinions
(Selected)

---

19. *See* ABA MODEL RULE 1.16(d) (2015).

20. ABA MODEL RULE 1.5(b) (2015).

21. *See, e.g.,* D.C. Bar Op. 288 fn4 (1999) (" . . . [even] if no agreement on fees and expenses is reached regarding the efforts to protect the confidential information [demanded by a subpoena], the lawyer must nevertheless take all ethically required steps to protect the privilege even if not compensated for the services by the client."). A later suit in *quantum meruit* for the services rendered may be available to the lawyer but that is an issue of law beyond the jurisdiction of this Committee. Alternatively, a lawyer may seek to withdraw as appropriate under Rule 1.16.

22. ABA MODEL RULE 1.6 cmt. [15] (2015) (emphasis added). *See* RESTATEMENT OF THE LAW, *supra* note 8, § 63 cmt. b ("A lawyer generally is required to raise any reasonably tenable objection to another's attempt to obtain confidential client information . . . from the lawyer if revealing the information would disadvantage the lawyer's client and the client has not consented . . ."); Bd. of Prof'l Responsibility of the Supreme Ct. of Tennessee Formal Op. 2014-F-158 (2014) ("[i]n the absence of informed consent of the client, the lawyer must reveal the information or document if ordered to [do] so by the tribunal, but only after the lawyer has raised all non-frivolous objections

yer has this obligation to assert all reasonable objections and claims when the lawyer receives the initial demand.[23] During the proceeding before the court or other tribunal, the lawyer should explain the lawyer's diligent but unsuccessful efforts to reach the client. If the lawyer is ordered to produce the documents and records, paragraph (b)(6) permits the lawyer to comply with the court order, as discussed below.

D. Complying with the Court Order

As noted, relying in part on then Comment [20], Formal Opinion 94-385 declared that a "lawyer must comply with the *final* orders of a court or other tribunal of competent jurisdiction requiring the lawyer to give information about the client."[24] Other authorities also direct a lawyer to comply with "final" orders of a court or other tribunal.[25] Questions have arisen as to whether the reference

---

that the information sought is protected against disclosure by the attorney-client privilege or other applicable law"); D.C. Bar Op. 288 (1999) (" . . . . A lawyer generally is required to raise any reasonably tenable objection to another's attempt to obtain confidential information . . . , unless disclosure would serve the client's interests . . . ." (citations omitted); D.C. Bar Op. 14 (1976) (". . . [W]hen documents are subpoenaed or an effort is otherwise made to compel their disclosure, it is the lawyer's ethical duty to a former client to assert on the former client's behalf every objection or claim of privilege available to him when to fail to do so might be prejudicial to the client"); Kentucky Bar Ass'n Op. E-315 (1987) (upon receiving a grand jury subpoena for client documents a lawyer "must respond by asserting any privilege (i.e., the attorney-client privilege) . . . .") (citations omitted); New Jersey Advisory Comm. on Prof'l Ethics Op. 145 (1969) (". . . if the client fails to respond to the attorney's letter his silence cannot be construed as consent and it would be improper to turn over copies of the [client's documents absent a court order] . . . .").

23. Appropriate objections and claims may vary with the jurisdiction. In some states, e.g., California, a lawyer may be *required* to raise certain claims or objections. *See, e.g.,* Cal. Evidence Code § 955 (1965) (lawyer who received or made a communication subject to the privilege under this article shall claim the privilege whenever he is present when the communication is sought to be disclosed and is authorized to claim the privilege under subdivision (c) of § 954). In other states, by contrast, a lawyer may be *forbidden* from raising certain objections or claims.

24. ABA Comm. on Ethics & Prof'l Responsibility, Formal Op. 94-385, at 2 (emphasis added). Prior to the adoption of the amendments in 2002, Comment [20] to Model Rule 1.6 also said, a "lawyer must comply with the *final* orders of a court or other tribunal of competent jurisdiction requiring the lawyer to give information about the client." *See* A Legislative History, *supra* note 7, at 129 (emphasis added).

25. *See, e.g.,* Rhode Island Supreme Ct. Ethics Advisory Panel Op. 98-02 (1998) (upon receiving a demand for confidential information a lawyer "has professional responsibility to seek to limit subpoena [sic] or court order on any legitimate ground, such as attorney-client privilege, work product immunity, burden or relevance . . . . The . . . attorney must comply, however, with the *final* orders of a court requiring him/her to produce the documents sought or to give information about the former client" (emphasis added) (citing ABA Formal Opinion 94-385)). *See also* State Bar of Arizona Op. 00-11 (2000) (discussing, *inter alia,* a comment to Arizona RPC 1.6, which says, "'The lawyer must comply with the *final* orders of a court or other tribunal . . . [requiring disclosure]" but noting that "[w]hat constitutes a 'final order' is problematic. Criminal attorneys might well argue that before revealing any such confidential information . . . the lawyer must await a final order by the highest court of appellate review and the mandate is spread relative thereto, if the original order of the lower court is appealed") (emphasis added).

to "final order" in Formal Opinion 94-385 and elsewhere requires a lawyer to appeal an adverse ruling when the client cannot be located or is unavailable for consultation.

Model Rule 1.6(b)(6) makes no reference to a "final" order. The comments adopted in 2002 make no reference to "final" orders. Comment [15] reads simply, "In the event of an adverse ruling, the lawyer must consult with the client about the possibility of appeal to the extent required by Rule 1.4. Unless review is sought, however, paragraph (b)(6) permits the lawyer to comply with the court's order."[26] The text thus suggests that omitting the reference to "final" orders was meant to relieve the lawyer from the added burden of pursuing an appeal or other "final" disposition, unless appropriate arrangements are made with an available client. The obligation of the lawyer with regard to an appeal is particularly relevant if the client or former client is unavailable.[27]

Requiring a lawyer to take an appeal when the client is unavailable places significant and undue burdens on the lawyer. An appeal costs money and takes time away from other clients. Taking an appeal on behalf of an unavailable client forces the lawyer to act without consultation and direction. While such clients need and deserve protection in response to an initial demand—to avoid improper and unjustified access to information and documents that the rules protect even after the client's death[28]—the balance changes once a court or other tribunal has ruled on the lawyer's initial objection. In the absence of instructions from the client to appeal, the ethics rules do not require a lawyer to shoulder further burdens. Accordingly, a lawyer is not ethically required to take an appeal on behalf of a client whom the lawyer cannot locate after due diligence.[29]

Once a lawyer determines disclosure is appropriate—in response to an initial demand or to an order and whether or not the client is available—the lawyer may produce documents and information "only to the extent the lawyer reasonably believes . . . is necessary . . . ."[30] The lawyer should seek appropriate protective orders and similar arrangements "to the fullest extent practicable."[31] "[D]isclosure should be made in a manner that limits access to the information to the tribunal or other persons having a need to know it . . . ."[32]

ABA Formal
Ethics Opinions
(Selected)

---

26. ABA MODEL RULE 1.6 cmt. [15] (2015).

27. *See* the Reporter's comment in A LEGISLATIVE HISTORY, *supra* note 7, at 132.

28. Swidler & Berlin v. U.S., 524 U.S. 399 (1998) (obligations of confidentiality continue even after the death of a client); Jamaica Pub. Serv. Co. v. AIU Ins. Co., 684 N.Y.S.2d 459, 462 (N.Y. 1998) (an attorney owes a "continuing duty" to a former client not to reveal confidences learned in the course of a professional relationship).

29. When challenging the subpoena or other demand in the first instance the lawyer should explain to the court or other tribunal the lawyer's efforts to locate the client and the client's unavailability.

30. ABA MODEL RULE 1.6 cmt. [16] (2015).

31. *Id.*

32. *Id.*

III. Conclusion

A lawyer receiving a subpoena or other compulsory process for information or documents relating to the representation of a client has several obligations. If the client is available, the lawyer must consult the client. If instructed by the client or if the client is unavailable, the lawyer must assert all reasonable claims against disclosure and seek to limit the subpoena or other demand on any reasonable ground.

If ordered to disclose confidential or privileged information and the client is available, a lawyer must consult with the client about whether to produce the information or to appeal. If the client and the lawyer disagree about how to respond to the initial demand or to an order requiring disclosure, the lawyer should consider withdrawing pursuant to Model Rule 1.16. If disclosure is ordered and the client is unavailable for consultation, the lawyer is not ethically required to appeal.

When disclosing documents and information—whether in response to an initial demand or to a court order and whether or not the client is available—the lawyer may reveal information only to the extent reasonably necessary. The lawyer should seek appropriate protective orders or other protective arrangements so that access to the information is limited to the tribunal ordering its disclosure and to persons having a need to know.

Where the client is available, the lawyer is not required to act without a fee but arrangements regarding the scope of the work and fee arrangements must conform to the relevant rules.[33] Where the client is unavailable to make retention and fee arrangements, the lawyer is nevertheless required to challenge the demand in the first instance. Lawyers should consider providing for these situations in retainer agreements.

ABA Formal Ethics Opinions (Selected)

---

33. *See, e.g.*, ABA Model Rule 1.5 (2015).

Formal Opinion 474   April 21, 2016
Referral Fees and Conflict of Interest

Rule 1.5(e) allows lawyers who are not in the same firm to divide a fee under certain circumstances. A lawyer who refers a matter to another lawyer outside of the first lawyer's firm and divides a fee from the matter with the lawyer to whom the matter has been referred, has undertaken representation of the client.

Fee arrangements under Model Rule 1.5(e) are subject to Rule 1.7. Unless a client gives informed consent confirmed in writing, a lawyer may not accept a fee when the lawyer has a conflict of interest that prohibits the lawyer from either performing legal services in connection with or assuming joint responsibility for the matter.

When one lawyer refers a matter to a second lawyer outside of the firm and the first lawyer either performs legal services in connection with or assumes joint responsibility for the matter and accepts a referral fee, the agreement regarding the division of fees, including client consent confirmed in writing, must be completed before or within a reasonable time after the commencement of the representation.

The question presented is under what circumstances lawyers may divide a fee when one lawyer refers a matter to another lawyer outside the firm.[1] Our analysis starts with Model Rule 1.5(e), which reads:

A division of a fee between lawyers who are not in the same firm may be made only if:
(1) the division is in proportion to the services performed by each lawyer or each lawyer assumes joint responsibility for the representation;
(2) the client agrees to the arrangement, including the share each lawyer will receive, and the agreement is confirmed in writing; and
(3) the total fee is reasonable.

Comment [7] to Rule 1.5 explains that lawyers in different firms may divide a legal fee. This practice is often used when the fee is contingent and the division is between a referring lawyer and a trial lawyer.[2]

---

1. This opinion is based on the ABA Model Rules of Professional Conduct as amended by the ABA House of Delegates through February 2016. The laws, court rules, regulations, rules of professional conduct, and opinions promulgated in individual jurisdictions are controlling.

2. MODEL RULES OF PROF'L CONDUCT R. 1.5 cmt. [7] (2016). *See also* MODEL RULES OF PROF'L CONDUCT R. 1.1 (2016), which requires a lawyer to provide competent representation. Comment [6] to Rule 1.1 notes that "before a lawyer retains or contracts with other lawyers outside the lawyer's own firm to provide or assist in the provision of legal services to a client, the lawyer should ordinarily obtain informed consent from the client and must reasonably believe that the other lawyers' services will contribute to the competent and ethical representation of the client. . . . The reasonableness of the decision to retain or contract with other lawyers outside

Model Rule 1.5(e)(1) establishes two different standards for such division of fees: either the division must be in proportion to the services performed or the lawyers must assume joint responsibility for the representation.[3] Thus the Rule permits a lawyer to associate with another lawyer (often a trial lawyer) in a different firm, refer a client to that lawyer, and divide a fee either in proportion to the services performed by each lawyer, or by having each lawyer involved in the representation assume joint responsibility for the matter, provided that the client agrees to the participation of all lawyers involved, including the share each lawyer will receive, the agreement is confirmed in writing, and the total fee is reasonable.[4]

Joint responsibility is not defined by the black letter of Model Rule 1.5(e). However, Comment [7] to Rule 1.5 provides guidance noting that "Joint responsibility for the representation entails financial and ethical responsibility for the representation as if the lawyers were associated in a partnership."[5] Implicit in the terms of the fee division allowed by Rule 1.5(e) is the concept that the referring lawyer who divides a legal fee has undertaken representation of the client.[6]

Because the client is represented by both the referring lawyer and the lawyer to whom the client was referred, a referral fee arrangement under Model

---

the lawyer's own firm will depend upon the circumstances, including the education, experience and reputation of the nonfirm lawyers; the nature of the services assigned to the nonfirm lawyers; and the legal protections, professional conduct rules, and ethical environments of the jurisdictions in which the services will be performed, particularly relating to confidential information."

3. There is wide variation in state adoptions of Model Rule 1.5(e). Some states have eliminated the specific requirement of proportionality or joint responsibility, simply requiring client consent and a reasonable total fee. *See, e.g.,* CALIFORNIA RULES OF PROF'L CONDUCT R. 2-200; CONNECTICUT RULES OF PROF'L CONDUCT R. 1.5(e); DELAWARE RULES OF PROF'L CONDUCT R. 1.5(e); MICHIGAN RULES OF PROF'L CONDUCT R. 1.5(e); OREGON RULES OF PROF'L CONDUCT R. 1.5(d). A limited number of states either prohibit referral fees altogether or have declined to adopt any version of subsection (e). *See, e.g.,* COLORADO RULES OF PROF'L CONDUCT R. 1.5(e) & WYOMING RULES OF PROF'L CONDUCT R. 1.5(f). LOUISIANA RULES OF PROF'L CONDUCT R. 1.5(e) requires the provision of substantive legal services to justify a fee division, which would also appear to preclude fee division solely for a referral. Other states require that a fee division always be accompanied by ongoing joint responsibility, or joint financial responsibility, for the matter. *See, e.g.,* ARIZONA RULES OF PROF'L CONDUCT R. 1.5(e); ILLINOIS RULES OF PROF'L CONDUCT R. 1.5(e); WISCONSIN RULES OF PROF'L CONDUCT R. 20:1.5(e).

4. MODEL RULES OF PROF'L CONDUCT R. 1.5 cmt. [7] (2016).

5. MODEL RULES OF PROF'L CONDUCT R. 1.5 cmt. [7] (2016). Comments do not add obligations to the Rules but provide guidance. *See* MODEL RULES OF PROF'L CONDUCT, PREAMBLE AND SCOPE [14] (2016). The Ethics 2000 Commission is the source of the current language of Comment [7]. *See* A LEGISLATIVE HISTORY: THE DEVELOPMENT OF THE ABA MODEL RULES OF PROFESSIONAL CONDUCT, 1982-2013, at 99 (Art Garwin ed., 2013). The Ethics 2000 Commission relied on ABA Comm. on Ethics & Prof'l Responsibility, Informal Op. 85-1514 for the amendments.

6. *See generally* Connecticut Bar Association Prof'l Ethics Comm., Informal Op. 2013-04 (2013); Maine Bd. of Bar Overseers Op. 145 (1994).

ABA Formal
Ethics Opinions
(Selected)

Rule 1.5(e) subjects both lawyers to the conflict provisions of Rule 1.7.[7] Model Rule 1.7(a) reads:

(a) Except as provided in paragraph (b), a lawyer shall not represent a client if the representation involves a concurrent conflict of interest. A concurrent conflict of interest exists if:

(1) the representation of one client will be directly adverse to another client; or

(2) there is a significant risk that the representation of one or more clients will be materially limited by the lawyer's responsibilities to another client, a former client or a third person or by a personal interest of the lawyer.

Illustration by Hypothetical: Part One

Application of Rule 1.5, and the relationship between Rules 1.5 and 1.7, can be illustrated using a hypothetical. Assume the following situation: for many years, Lawyer has represented The Flower Shoppe Inc., which is jointly owned by Daisy and Rose. Rose was in a car accident while on a personal errand driving a car owned by The Flower Shoppe. Rose, as a co-owner of the Shoppe, had permission to use the Shoppe vehicle to perform the errand. Rose was not at fault but was injured in the accident. Knowing Lawyer does not practice personal injury law, Rose asked Lawyer to refer her to a personal injury trial lawyer. Lawyer will not assist the trial lawyer in preparation of the case. Rose would like Lawyer to receive a referral fee, and Lawyer wants to accept joint responsibility for the matter. When Rose requests the referral, Lawyer reasonably believes that The Flower Shoppe will not be a party to the matter. Before assuming joint responsibility for the matter, Lawyer must determine whether a conflict of interest exists under Rule 1.7(a).

On the facts presented here, Lawyer can proceed with the referral to the trial lawyer because there is no conflict of interest under Rule 1.7(a). The representation of one client is not directly adverse to another client and there is not a significant risk that the referral of Rose will be materially limited by Lawyer's responsibility to The Flower Shoppe. Thus, the requirements of 1.7(a) are satisfied.[8]

ABA Formal Ethics Opinions (Selected)

---

7. The Commission on Evaluation of Professional Standards (commonly referred to as the Kutak Commission) explained, "A fee arrangement [envisioned by this paragraph of Rule 1.5] is subject to the conflict provisions of Rule 1.7 and 1.8." See PROPOSED FINAL DRAFT, MODEL RULES OF PROFESSIONAL CONDUCT 37 (1981). See also Illinois State Bar Ass'n, Advisory Op. 90-26 (1991); Massachusetts Bar Ass'n Op. 80-10 (1980); State Bar of Michigan, Informal Op. RI-116 (1992).

8. We assume that when Lawyer conducted the conflict check, Lawyer determined that Lawyer's representation was also not limited by Lawyer's responsibilities to another client, a former client or a third person, or by a personal interest of Lawyer.

Illustration by Hypothetical: Part Two

Assume again that for many years, Lawyer has represented The Flower Shoppe Inc., which is jointly owned by Daisy and Rose. Rose was in a car accident while on a personal errand driving a car owned by The Flower Shoppe. Rose, as a co-owner of the Shoppe, had permission to use the Shoppe vehicle to perform the errand. Rose was injured. Fault is in dispute. Rose asked Lawyer to refer her to a personal injury trial lawyer. Lawyer will not assist the trial lawyer in the representation. Rose would like Lawyer to receive a referral fee, and Lawyer wants to accept joint responsibility for the matter.

Lawyer recognizes that sometime in the future the other driver in the accident will file a claim against Rose and may file a claim against The Flower Shoppe as owner of the car. If the other driver adds The Flower Shoppe as a party and Lawyer continues to represent The Flower Shoppe, Lawyer believes that there is a significant risk that Lawyer's representation of Rose will be materially limited by Lawyer's responsibilities to The Flower Shoppe and vice versa.[9]

Therefore, in order to receive a referral fee for referring Rose to a trial lawyer, Lawyer must meet the requirements of Model Rule 1.7(b).[10]

Illustration by Hypothetical: Part Three

Assume again that for many years Lawyer has represented The Flower Shoppe Inc., which is jointly owned by Daisy and Rose. Rose was in a car accident while on a personal errand driving a car owned by The Flower Shoppe. Rose, as a co-owner of the Shoppe, had permission to use the Shoppe vehicle to perform the errand. Rose was injured. Fault is in dispute. Rose asked Lawyer to refer her to a personal injury trial lawyer. Lawyer will not assist the trial lawyer in the representation. Rose would like Lawyer to receive a referral fee and Lawyer wants to accept joint responsibility for the matter.

The other driver has filed a claim against Rose and The Flower Shoppe, and Lawyer has determined that Rose's interests in the suit are adverse to The

---

9. MODEL RULES OF PROF'L CONDUCT R. 1.7 cmt. [8] (2016) explains that a conflict of interest exists "if there is a significant risk that a lawyer's ability to consider, recommend or carry out an appropriate course of action for the client will be materially limited as a result of the lawyer's other responsibilities or interests. . . . The mere possibility of subsequent harm does not itself require disclosure and consent. The critical questions are the likelihood that a difference in interests will eventuate and, if it does, whether it will materially interfere with the lawyer's independent professional judgment in considering alternatives or foreclose courses of action that reasonably should be pursued on behalf of the client." In this hypothetical, the facts provide that Lawyer reasonably believes that there is a significant risk that Lawyer's representation of Rose and The Flower Shoppe will be materially limited by Lawyer's responsibilities to the other. Thus Lawyer's reasonable belief establishes the conflict under Rule 1.7(a)(2).

10. Circumstances at the outset also could make accepting a referral fee improper. Changing a few facts in this hypothetical would prohibit Lawyer from referring Rose to the trial lawyer and receiving a referral fee. For example, if at the outset the other driver sued both Rose and The Flower Shoppe Inc., Lawyer represented The Flower Shoppe in the suit, and Rose and The Flower Shoppe asserted claims against each other, then Lawyer would have a conflict that a client could not consent to. See MODEL RULES OF PROF'L CONDUCT R. 1.7(b)(3) (2016).

Flower Shoppe's interests. While Lawyer does not expect to represent The Flower Shoppe in the suit, The Flower Shoppe will continue to be Lawyer's client. Lawyer's representation of Rose, through the referral, is a conflict of interest under Rule 1.7(a)(1).[11]

To receive a referral fee for referring Rose to the trial lawyer, Lawyer must meet the requirements of Model Rule 1.7(b).

Informed Consent to the Conflict

Rule 1.7(b) reads:

Notwithstanding the existence of a concurrent conflict of interest under paragraph (a), a lawyer may represent a client if:

> (1) the lawyer reasonably believes that the lawyer will be able to provide competent and diligent representation to each affected client;
> (2) the representation is not prohibited by law;
> (3) the representation does not involve the assertion of a claim by one client against another client represented by the lawyer in the same litigation or other proceeding before a tribunal; and
> (4) each affected client gives informed consent, confirmed in writing.

Assuming that Lawyer reasonably believes that Lawyer will be able to provide competent and diligent representation to each affected client, that the representation is not prohibited by law, and that at this time the representation does not involve the assertion of a claim by The Flower Shoppe against Rose in the same litigation, then under Rule 1.7(b)(4) Lawyer must still secure the informed consent, confirmed in writing, of each affected client.[12] Under hypotheticals two and three, Lawyer needs the informed consent of both Rose and The Flower Shoppe to refer Rose to the trial lawyer outside the firm and divide the legal fee.

Informed consent is defined by Model Rule 1.0(e) as "the agreement by a person to a proposed course of conduct after the lawyer has communicated adequate information and explanation about the material risks of and reason-

ABA Formal
Ethics Opinions
(Selected)

---

11. MODEL RULES OF PROF'L CONDUCT R. 1.7 cmt. [6] (2016) provides, "Loyalty to a current client prohibits undertaking representation directly adverse to that client without that client's informed consent. Thus, absent consent, a lawyer may not act as an advocate in one matter against a person the lawyer represents in some other matter, *even when the matters are wholly unrelated*. The client as to whom the representation is directly adverse is likely to feel betrayed, and the resulting damage to the client-lawyer relationship is likely to impair the lawyer's ability to represent the client effectively. In addition, the client on whose behalf the adverse representation is undertaken reasonably may fear that the lawyer will pursue that client's case less effectively out of deference to the other client, i.e., that the representation may be materially limited by the lawyer's interest in retaining the current client." (Emphasis added).

12. MODEL RULES OF PROF'L CONDUCT R. 1.0(b) (2016) explains, "'Confirmed in writing,' when used in reference to the informed consent of a person, denotes informed consent that is given in writing by the person or a writing that a lawyer promptly transmits to the person confirming an oral informed consent."

ably available alternatives to the proposed course of conduct."[13] Comment [6] to Model Rule 1.0 explains:

> The lawyer must make reasonable efforts to ensure that the client or other person possesses information reasonably adequate to make an informed decision. Ordinarily, this will require communication that includes a disclosure of the facts and circumstances giving rise to the situation, any explanation reasonably necessary to inform the client or other person of the material advantages and disadvantages of the proposed course of conduct and a discussion of the client's or other person's options and alternatives . . .

Before Rose or The Flower Shoppe can provide informed consent to the conflict of interest, Lawyer must provide both with information about the conflict of interest. For example, if Lawyer is representing The Flower Shoppe in the suit as noted in hypothetical two, and if after Lawyer has referred Rose to the trial lawyer the other driver sues both Rose and The Flower Shoppe Inc. resulting in Rose and The Flower Shoppe Inc. asserting claims against each other, then a conflict under Model Rule 1.7(b)(3) would prohibit representation.[14]

Rule 1.5(e) Fee Disclosures

Rule 1.5(e) requires that a client agree to the fee division and that the agreement be confirmed in writing.[15] The agreement must describe in sufficient detail the division of the fee between the lawyers including the share each lawyer will receive.[16] Rule 1.5(e)(3) mandates that the total fee be reasonable. If a contingent fee is divided between a referring lawyer and another lawyer, the total fee cannot be increased because of the referral.[17]

Rule 1.5(e)(2) uses the future tense in the phrase "including the share each lawyer *will receive*" to describe what the fee division agreement must include, and Comment [7] to Rule 1.5 explains "the client must agree to the arrangement, including the share that each lawyer *is to receive* . . . ." The use of the future tense envisions that the fee division agreement will precede the division of fees. Such an agreement should not be entered into toward the end of such a relationship.

---

13. Model Rules of Prof'l Conduct R. 1.0(e) (2016).

14. This opinion does not address whether Lawyer would be required to withdraw from representing both Rose and The Flower Shoppe in hypothetical two, if such a conflict did arise. *See* Model Rules of Prof'l Conduct R. 1.7 cmt. [29] (2016). Nor does this opinion address under what circumstances Lawyer might also be required to repay a referral fee that was already paid to and received by the Lawyer.

15. Model Rules of Prof'l Conduct R. 1.5(e)(2) (2016).

16. *Id.*

17. *See, e.g.*, Illinois State Bar Ass'n, Advisory Op. 90-18 (1990).

ABA Formal Ethics Opinions (Selected)

Instead, the division of fees must be agreed to either before or within a reasonable time after commencing the representation.[18]

Conclusion

Rule 1.5(e) allows lawyers who are not in the same firm to divide a fee under certain circumstances. A lawyer who refers a matter to another lawyer outside of the first lawyer's firm and divides a fee from the matter with the lawyer to whom the matter has been referred, has undertaken representation of the client.

Unless a client gives informed consent confirmed in writing, a lawyer may not accept a fee when the lawyer has a conflict of interest that prohibits the lawyer from either performing legal services in connection with or assuming joint responsibility for the matter.

When one lawyer refers a matter to a second lawyer outside of the firm and the first lawyer either performs legal services in connection with or assumes joint responsibility for the matter and accepts a referral fee, the agreement regarding the division of fees, including client consent confirmed in writing, must be completed before or within a reasonable time after the commencement of the representation.

ABA Formal
Ethics Opinions
(Selected)

18. At least two courts have questioned the efficacy of fee division agreements signed after settlement. Wagner & Wagner, LLP v. Atkinson, Haskins, Nellis, Brittingham, Gladd & Carwile, P.C., 596 F.3d 84, 92 (2d Cir. 2010) (rejecting referring lawyer's argument that "technical" requirement of joint responsibility letter required by New York Rule DR 2-107 could be satisfied by complying "before fees have been paid"; court explained that fee division provision "clearly anticipates compliance with its requirements early on in the representation. . . . Moreover, the undertaking of joint responsibility is difficult (to say the least) to accomplish, other than as a charade, after a settlement with the defendant has been reached."); Saggese v. Kelley, 837 N.E.2d 699, 706 (Mass. 2005) (while affirming the enforcement of an agreement to divide fees that client agreed to "toward the end of the attorney-client relationship," court holds that after the issuance of the decision, referring lawyer required to disclose fee sharing before the referral is made and secure client's consent in writing). *But see* Cohen v. Brown, 93 Cal. Rptr. 3d 24, 38 (Ct. App. 2009) (California's Rule 2-200 "requires only that the client's consent to a division of fees be given prior to the actual *division* of the fees. It does not require client consent prior to the commencement of work by the associated-in attorney/law firm."). *See also* MODEL RULES OF PROF'L CONDUCT R. 1.1 cmt. [6] (2016) "before a lawyer retains or contracts with other lawyers outside the lawyer's own firm to provide or assist in the provision of legal services to a client, the lawyer should ordinarily obtain informed consent from the client . . . ."

Formal Opinion 475   December 7, 2016
Safeguarding Fees That Are Subject to Division with Other Counsel

A lawyer may divide a fee with another lawyer who is not in the same firm if the arrangement meets the requirements of Model Rule 1.5(e). When one lawyer receives an earned fee that is subject to such an arrangement and both lawyers have an interest in that earned fee, Model Rules 1.15(a) and 1.15(d) require that the receiving lawyer hold the funds in an account separate from the lawyer's own property, appropriately safeguard the funds, promptly notify the other lawyer who holds an interest in the fee of receipt of the funds, promptly deliver to the other lawyer the agreed upon portion of the fee, and, if requested by the other lawyer, provide a full accounting.

Model Rule 1.5(e) provides for the division of fees between lawyers who are not in the same firm.[1] A division of a fee "is a single billing to a client covering the fee of two or more lawyers who are not in the same firm."[2] Rule 1.5(e) provides that such agreements are permissible only if the division is proportionate to the services performed by each lawyer or both lawyers assume joint responsibility for the representation, the client agrees to the arrangement including the share each lawyer will receive, the arrangement is confirmed in writing, and the total fee is reasonable. Model Rule 1.15(a) provides in pertinent part that a lawyer "shall hold property of . . . third persons that is in a lawyer's possession in connection with a representation separate from the lawyer's own property."

When lawyers are dividing a fee pursuant to Rule 1.5(e), a question arises regarding how an earned fee received from a client by one of the lawyers must be handled when both lawyers have an interest in the paid fees. Should the other lawyer who holds an interest in the earned fees be treated as a third person under Rule 1.15? We conclude that for the purposes of a division of fees between lawyers, when one lawyer receives fees on behalf of all lawyers in the matter, the answer is yes.

Model Rule 1.15 provides the answer. It explains in relevant part:

> (a) A lawyer shall hold property of clients or third persons that is in a lawyer's possession in connection with a representation separate from the lawyer's own property. Funds shall be kept in a separate account maintained in the state where the lawyer's office is situated, or elsewhere with the consent of the client or third person. Other property shall be identified as such and appropriately safeguarded. Complete records of such account funds and other property shall be kept by the

ABA Formal Ethics Opinions (Selected)

---

1. This opinion is based on the ABA Model Rules of Professional Conduct as amended by the ABA House of Delegates through August 2016. The laws, court rules, regulations, rules of professional conduct, and opinions promulgated in individual jurisdictions are controlling.

2. Model Rules of Prof'l Conduct R. 1.5, cmt. [7] (2016).

lawyer and shall be preserved for a period of [five years] after termination of the representation.

...

(d) Upon receiving funds or other property in which a client or third person has an interest, a lawyer shall promptly notify the client or third person. Except as stated in this rule or otherwise permitted by law or by agreement with the client, a lawyer shall promptly deliver to the client or third person any funds or other property that the client or third person is entitled to receive and, upon request by the client or third person, shall promptly render a full accounting regarding such property.

Rule 1.15 applies in many situations including fee advances, advances of costs, receipt of settlement funds, holding client funds to which creditors have claims, and fee disputes between the lawyer and the client. Whatever the context, Rule 1.15 requires the safekeeping of any property that comes into the lawyer's possession in connection with the representation of a client[3] in which the client or any "third person" has an interest.

Thus, if two or more lawyers have an agreement that satisfies Rule 1.5 regarding a division of fees, and one lawyer receives a payment that must be divided with the other lawyer pursuant to their agreement, the other lawyer is a "third person" for purposes of Rule 1.15. However, the designation of a person as a "third person" under Rule 1.15 addressing safekeeping property of others is limited to the purposes of Rule 1.15 (i.e., safekeeping the property of others). It is not necessarily indicative of the status of the person beyond the scope of Rule 1.15 (e.g., a lawyer who is co-counsel and a third person under Rule 1.15 for the purposes of safekeeping property is not a third person for the purposes of Rule 1.6).

The receiving lawyer, therefore, must, under Rule 1.15(a), deposit the funds in which co-counsel holds an interest in an account (typically a trust account) separate from the lawyer's own property.[4] Rule 1.15(d) requires the lawyer who receives the earned fees subject to a division agreement to promptly notify the other lawyer who holds an interest in the fee of receipt of the funds, promptly deliver to the other lawyer the agreed upon portion of the fee, and, if requested by the other lawyer, provide a full accounting.

ABA Formal
Ethics Opinions
(Selected)

---

3. Rule 1.15(a) explicitly applies to property in the lawyer's possession in connection with a representation of a client. Rule 1.15(d) does not contain this explicit limitation and some authorities have applied Rule 1.15(d) outside the context of a representation of a client. *See, e.g.,* Att'y Grievance Comm'n v. Johnson, 976 A.2d 245 (Md. 2009) (applying what is now Maryland Rule 1.15(d) to facts involving a lawyer serving as a settlement agent for a title company); State Bar of Arizona Comm. on Rules of Prof'l Conduct, Op. 04-03 (2004) (applying Arizona Rule 1.15(d) to facts involving funds delivered to a seller's former divorce lawyer by escrow agent in connection with a home sale in which the lawyer did not represent the former client).

4. Applicable state implementation of Rule 1.15 may require that the funds be deposited into an IOLTA (Interest on Lawyer Trust Accounts) account.

Finally, if there is any dispute as to the interest of the receiving lawyer and the lawyer with whom the receiving lawyer is dividing a fee, Rule 1.15(e) requires that the receiving lawyer keep the disputed funds separate from the lawyer's own property until the dispute is resolved.

Conclusion

A lawyer may divide a fee with another lawyer who is not in the same firm if the arrangement meets the requirements of Model Rule 1.5(e). When one lawyer receives an earned fee that is subject to such an arrangement and both lawyers have an interest in that earned fee, Model Rules 1.15(a) and 1.15(d) require that the receiving lawyer hold the funds in an account separate from the lawyer's own property, appropriately safeguard the funds, promptly notify the other lawyer who holds an interest in the fee of receipt of the funds, promptly deliver to the other lawyer the agreed upon portion of the fee, and, if requested by the other lawyer, provide a full accounting.

ABA Formal Ethics Opinions (Selected)

Formal Opinion 476   **December 19, 2016**

Confidentiality Issues When Moving to
Withdraw for Nonpayment of Fees in Civil Litigation

In moving to withdraw as counsel in a civil proceeding based on a client's fail-
ure to pay fees, a lawyer must consider the duty of confidentiality under Rule
1.6 and seek to reconcile that duty with the court's need for sufficient informa-
tion upon which to rule on the motion. Similarly, in entertaining such a mo-
tion, a judge should consider the right of the movant's client to confidentiality.
This requires cooperation between lawyers and judges. If required by the court
to support the motion with facts relating to the representation, a lawyer may,
pursuant to Rule 1.6(b)(5), disclose only such confidential information as is
reasonably necessary for the court to make an informed decision on the motion.

Withdrawal from a Civil Matter Based on a Client's Failure to Pay Fees[1]

Model Rule 1.16 addresses a lawyer's duties and responsibilities when withdrawing from the representation of a client. Rule 1.16(a) sets forth the circumstances when a lawyer is required to withdraw, and Rule 1.16(b) describes the
circumstances when a lawyer may be permitted to withdraw from a representation.[2] Among the permissive reasons, Rule 1.16(b)(5) provides that a lawyer may

---

1. This opinion does not address the additional and unique issues raised when a lawyer
seeks to withdraw from representation in a criminal matter. The opinion is based on the ABA
Model Rules of Professional Conduct as amended by the ABA House of Delegates through February 2016. The laws, court rules, regulations, rules of professional conduct, and opinions promulgated in individual jurisdictions are controlling.

2. Rule 1.16, paragraphs (a) and (b) read:
(a) Except as stated in paragraph (c), a lawyer shall not represent a client or, where representation has commenced, shall withdraw from the representation of a client if:
    (1) the representation will result in violation of the Rules of Professional Conduct or
other law;
    (2) the lawyer's physical or mental condition materially impairs the lawyer's ability to
represent the client; or
    (3) the lawyer is discharged.
(b) Except as stated in paragraph (c), a lawyer may withdraw from representing a client if:
    (1) withdrawal can be accomplished without material adverse effect on the interests of
the client;
    (2) the client persists in a course of action involving the lawyer's services that the lawyer
reasonably believes is criminal or fraudulent;
    (3) the client has used the lawyer's services to perpetrate a crime or fraud;
    (4) the client insists upon taking action that the lawyer considers repugnant or with
which the lawyer has a fundamental disagreement;
    (5) the client fails substantially to fulfill an obligation to the lawyer regarding the law-
yer's services and has been given reasonable warning that the lawyer will withdraw unless
the obligation is fulfilled;

ABA Formal
Ethics Opinions
(Selected)

withdraw from representing a client when "the client substantially fails to fulfill an obligation to the lawyer regarding the lawyer's services and has been given reasonable warning that the lawyer will withdraw unless the obligation is ful-filled." Comment [8] to the Rule states: "A lawyer may withdraw if the client re-fuses to abide by the terms of an agreement relating to the representation, such as an agreement concerning fees or court costs . . . ." In addition, Rule 1.16(b)(6) provides that a lawyer may withdraw where "the representation will result in an unreasonable financial burden on the lawyer or has been rendered unreason-ably difficult by the client." As the courts have decided in the cases cited below, if a client fails over time to pay a lawyer's fees, and that failure continues after a lawyer provides a reasonable warning to the client, the lawyer may be permit-ted to withdraw.[3] In effectuating a withdrawal, a lawyer should do so in a man-ner that minimizes any prejudice to the client.[4]

The Duty of Confidentiality in Moving to Withdraw, Generally

A permissive withdrawal under Rule 1.16(b) is subject to the requirements of Rule 1.16(c). Rule 1.16(c) provides that when representing a client in a matter before a tribunal,[5] a lawyer must comply with the applicable law of the tribu-nal in seeking to withdraw.[6] Under the rules of most courts, a motion to with-draw is required when a substitute lawyer does not simultaneously enter an appearance.[7]

In preparing a motion to withdraw a lawyer must consider how the duty of confidentiality under Rule 1.6 may limit the information that can be disclosed

---

(6) the representation will result in an unreasonable financial burden on the lawyer or has been rendered unreasonably difficult by the client; or

(7) other good cause for withdrawal exists.

3. *See* Restatement (Third) of the Law Governing Lawyers § 32(g) cmt. k (2000). *Cf.* Brandon v. Belch, 560 F.3d 536, 538 (6th Cir. 2009).

4. Model Rules of Prof'l Conduct R. 1.16(d) (2016). *See also* Ronald E. Mallen, Legal Malpractice § 33.71 (2016).

5. "Tribunal" is defined in Rule 1.0(m), and "denotes a court, an arbitrator in a binding ar-bitration proceeding or a legislative body, administrative agency or other body acting in an adjudicative capacity. A legislative body, administrative agency or other body acts in an adjudi-cative capacity when a neutral official, after the presentation of evidence or legal argument by a party or parties, will render a binding legal judgment directly affecting a party's interests in a particular matter."

6. ABA Model Rule 1.16(c) states: "A lawyer must comply with applicable law requiring notice to or permission of a tribunal when terminating a representation. When ordered to do so by a tribunal, a lawyer shall continue representation notwithstanding good cause for terminat-ing the representation."

7. *See, e.g.,* Ariz. R. Civ. P. 5.1(b)(2); Cal. R. App. P. 8.36; D.C. Sup. Ct. R. Civ. P. 101(c); Fla. R. Jud. Admin. 2.060; Ill. R. Civ. P. 13; Mass. R. Civ. P. 11(c); N.D. Ct. R. 11.2; Va. R. Civ. P. 1:5. Under ABA Model Rule 3.4(c), it is ethical misconduct for a lawyer to "knowingly disobey an obligation under the rules of a tribunal, except for an open refusal based on an assertion that no valid obligation exists."

ABA Formal Ethics Opinions (Selected)

in the moving papers.[8] Under Rule 1.6(a), the duty of confidentiality applies broadly to "information relating to the representation," unless the client provides "informed consent," disclosure is "impliedly authorized to carry out the representation," or one of the enumerated exceptions in Rule 1.6(b) applies. The exceptions in paragraph (b) permit disclosures only "to the extent the lawyer reasonably deems necessary" to address the purpose of a particular exception. *See* Rule 1.6 Comment [16].[9] For example, in *In re Gonzalez*, 773 A.2d 1026 (D.C. 2001), the respondent was given an informal admonition, not for informing the court that fees were owed by the client, but for also disclosing extraneous and embarrassing client information in connection with the motion. Accordingly, when in doubt, a lawyer should err on the side of non-disclosure.

The more difficult question is when is a lawyer permitted to disclose *any* confidential client information in filing a motion to withdraw, and if so, how much. The tension between a lawyer's obligation to provide the court with sufficient facts to rule on a motion and the lawyer's duty of confidentiality has been characterized in one treatise as "a procedural problem that has no fully

---

8. ABA Model Rule 1.6, titled "Confidentiality of Information," provides as follows:

(a) A lawyer shall not reveal information relating to the representation of a client unless the client gives informed consent, the disclosure is impliedly authorized in order to carry out the representation or the disclosure is permitted by paragraph (b).

(b) A lawyer may reveal information relating to the representation of a client to the extent the lawyer reasonably believes necessary:

(1) to prevent reasonably certain death or substantial bodily harm;

(2) to prevent the client from committing a crime or fraud that is reasonably certain to result in substantial injury to the financial interests or property of another and in furtherance of which the client has used or is using the lawyer's services;

(3) to prevent, mitigate or rectify substantial injury to the financial interests or property of another that is reasonably certain to result or has resulted from the client's commission of a crime or fraud in furtherance of which the client has used the lawyer's services;

(4) to secure legal advice about the lawyer's compliance with these Rules;

(5) to establish a claim or defense on behalf of the lawyer in a controversy between the lawyer and the client, to establish a defense to a criminal charge or civil claim against the lawyer based upon conduct in which the client was involved, or to respond to allegations in any proceeding concerning the lawyer's representation of the client;

(6) to comply with other law or a court order; or

(7) to detect and resolve conflicts of interest arising from the lawyer's change of employment or from changes in the composition or ownership of a firm, but only if the revealed information would not compromise the attorney-client privilege or otherwise prejudice the client.

(c) A lawyer shall make reasonable efforts to prevent the inadvertent or unauthorized disclosure of, or unauthorized access to, information relating to the representation of a client.

9. ABA Model Rule 1.6, Comment [16] states: "Paragraph (b) permits disclosure only to the extent the lawyer reasonably believes disclosure is necessary to accomplish one of the purposes specified…In any case, a disclosure adverse to the client's interest should be no greater than the lawyer reasonably believes necessary to accomplish the purpose. If the disclosure will be made in connection with a judicial proceeding, the disclosure should be made in a manner that limits access to the information to the tribunal or other persons having a need to know it and appropriate protective orders or other arrangements should be sought by the lawyer to the fullest extent practicable."

satisfactory solution."[10] Ultimately, however, lawyers wishing to withdraw must choose some manner in which to phrase their request for relief.[11]

The Duty of Confidentiality in Motions to Withdraw for Unpaid Legal Fees

Neither Rule 1.6(b) nor the Comments expressly refer to motions to withdraw for unpaid fees. The Comments do, however, recognize that some disclosure of confidential client information otherwise protected by Rule 1.6(a) is permitted in fee-collection suits by lawyers, based on the "claim or defense" exception in Rule 1.6(b)(5).[12] Similarly, motions to withdraw based on a client's failure to pay fees are generally grounded in the same basic right of a lawyer to be paid pursuant to the terms of a fee agreement with a client. Nonetheless, courts have differed widely as to whether any specific information regarding a lawyer's reasons for seeking withdrawal is required in a motion to withdraw, and if so, how much.

Comment [16] to Rule 1.6 provides that a lawyer may disclose information under 1.6(b) only "to the extent the lawyer reasonably believes the disclosure is necessary to accomplish one of the purposes specified." In support of the idea that specific information should not be required with respect to a motion to withdraw for nonpayment of legal fees, Comment [3] to Rule 1.16 states:

> The court may request an explanation for the withdrawal, while the lawyer may be bound to keep confidential the facts that would constitute such an explanation. The lawyer's statement that professional considerations require termination of the representation ordinarily should be accepted as sufficient. Lawyers should be mindful of their obligations to both clients and the court under Rule 1.6 and 3.3.

---

10. GEOFFREY C. HAZARD JR., W. WILLIAM HODES & PETER R. JARVIS, THE LAW OF LAWYERING § 21.16 (4th ed. 2015). *See also* Byrd v. Mahaffey, 78 P.3d 671, 676 (Wyo. 2003) ("[A]n artful balance between confidentiality and providing an adequate basis for withdrawal must be maintained by counsel requesting to withdraw.").

11. In ABA Formal Opinion 92-366, the Committee discussed the possibility of a "noisy withdrawal" to avoid assisting client misconduct. That Opinion was issued under a prior version of the Model Rules that did not include exceptions for disclosures to prevent or rectify client crime or fraud in furtherance of which the client used the lawyer's services. Currently, ABA Model Rule 1.6(b)(2) and (b)(3) expressly permit such disclosures.

12. ABA Model Rule 1.6(b)(5) permits disclosures "to establish a claim or defense on behalf of the lawyer in a controversy between the lawyer and a client." Comment [11] states: "A lawyer entitled to a fee for services rendered is permitted by paragraph (b)(5) to prove the services rendered in an action to collect it. This aspect of the rule expresses the principle that the beneficiary of a fiduciary relationship may not exploit it to the detriment of the fiduciary." *See also* the RESTATEMENT (THIRD) OF LAW GOVERNING LAWYERS § 65, stating: "A lawyer may use or disclose confidential information relating to the representation when and to the extent that the lawyer reasonably believes necessary to permit the lawyer to resolve a dispute with a client concerning compensation or reimbursement that the lawyer reasonably claims the client owes the lawyer."

ABA Formal Ethics Opinions (Selected)

See also N.Y. State Bar Ass'n Comm. on Prof'l Ethics, Advisory Op. 1057 (2015), 2015 WL 4592234, at *3 ("the Rules anticipate that the court will usually not demand the disclosure of confidential information if the lawyer advises the court that 'professional considerations' require withdrawal").

Notwithstanding this authority, however, many courts have issued decisions that recite details as to the money owed by the clients, the specific legal services performed and related facts, indicating that the court required more from the lawyer than just a statement that the motion to withdraw was motivated by "professional considerations." While the courts in the following cases did not address a lawyer's duty of confidentiality, the decisions demonstrate that these courts found such details pertinent to their assessment of the motions. *See, e.g., In re Franke*, 55 A.3d 713, 724 (Md. Ct. Spec. App. 2012) (vacating trial court's denial of attorney's motion to withdraw based on client's nonpayment of $120,000 in unpaid fees as an abuse of discretion and as wrongly causing attorney "to provide free legal services"); *Team Obsolete Ltd. v. A.H.R.M.A. LTD.*, 464 F. Supp. 2d 164 (E.D.N.Y. 2006) (granting motion to withdraw based on supporting affidavit filed under seal revealing that the moving law firm had a dispute with their client regarding unpaid legal fees); *King v. NAID Inflatables of Newport, Inc.*, 11 A.3d 64, 67 (R.I. 2010) (the Supreme Court of Rhode Island, with the benefit of an *amicus* brief from the Rhode Island Bar Association, reversed the trial court's denial of a motion to withdraw by a law firm filed before trial, stating that "the hearing justice did not accord adequate weight to the financial burden that would befall [the law firm] if [it] were required to continue to represent a nonpaying client."); *Brandon v. Blech*, 560 F.3d 536, 538-39 (6th Cir. 2009) (reversing trial court's denial of motion to withdraw for a client's nonpayment of fees, stating: "As other circuits recognize, compelling attorneys to continue representing clients who refuse to pay imposes a severe burden" (quoting then from *Rivera-Domenich v. Calvesbert Law Offices PSC*, 402 F.3d 246, 248 (1st Cir. 2005)); *Fid. Nat'l Title Ins. Co. v. Intercounty Nat'l Title Ins. Co.*, 310 F.3d 537, 540 (7th Cir. 2002) (reversing the denial of a motion to withdraw by a law firm that was owed more than $470,000 in fees, stating that it was "difficult to see why [the law firm] should be obliged to provide them free legal services"); *Reed Yates Farms, Inc. v. Yates*, 526 N.E.2d 1115, 1121 (Ill. App. Ct. 1998) (upholding trial court's granting of a motion to withdraw, stating: "If during the course of litigation attorney fees are not paid when due, an attorney may demand payment of accrued fees and withdraw from the case if the fees are not paid in a reasonably time." [internal citation omitted]); *City of Joliet v. Mid-City Nat'l Bank of Chi.*, 998 F. Supp. 2d 689, 694 (N.D. Ill. 2014) (granting motion to withdraw by lawyers who were owed more than $5 million in fees, explaining that "to force unwilling attorneys to labor free of charge in a civil case where parties are not entitled to free representation is not in the interests of justice").

In *Team Obsolete Ltd. v. A.H.R.M.A. LTD.*, 464 F. Supp. 2d 164 (E.D.N.Y. 2006), the moving lawyer provided the reasons for the motion by submitting an affidavit *in camera*. Opposing counsel sought to unseal the affidavit. The court granted the motion to withdraw for nonpayment and denied the motion to unseal, but

ABA Formal Ethics Opinions (Selected)

expressly ruled that the opposing party was entitled to know that the motion was based on an assertion that the client had failed to pay the agreed-upon fees, stating that it "hereby informs" [the opposing parties] "that the basis for [movant's] motion to withdraw is a dispute regarding AHRMA's failure to pay its legal bills." *Id.* at 165.[13]

Thus, when filing a motion to withdraw a lawyer often will not know whether the court will accept the assertion that "professional considerations" warrant withdrawal, or whether the court will require more information. Under the narrow facts of this opinion, when a judge has sought additional information in support of a motion to withdraw for failure to pay fees, Rule 1.6(b)(5) authorizes the lawyer to disclose information regarding the representation of the client that is limited to the extent reasonably necessary to respond to the court's inquiry and in support of that motion to withdraw. We turn now to the issues facing judges who are called upon to rule on motions to withdraw based on unpaid fees.

The Judicial Inquiry with Respect to Such a Motion

In ruling on a motion to withdraw, judges seek to balance their need for information about the facts underlying the motion with the client's right to confidentiality.[14] In Formal Opinion 93-370, this Committee addressed the need for judicial sensitivity to lawyers' duty of confidentiality in the context of pretrial settlement discussions with judges, stating: "The judge should be sensitive to these ethical constraints on counsel and sensitive as well to the superior position of authority the judge enjoys with respect to the lawyer . . . ."[15] This need for judicial sensitivity applies as well when the judge is considering a motion to withdraw.

Trial courts have wide discretion when ruling on motions to withdraw. In addition to considering a lawyer's reasons for seeking to withdraw, trial courts also have a duty to consider such matters as the likely impact of a withdrawal on the parties and on the court's control over its calendar. *See generally Laster v. D.C.*, 460 F. Supp. 2d 111, 113 (D.C. 2006) ("[C]ourts may consider the disruptive impact that the withdrawal will have on the prosecution of the case."); *In re Kiley*, 947 N.E.2d 1, 7 (Mass. 2011) ("[T]he judge did not abuse his discre-

---

13. As also indicated in *Team Obsolete*, the procedural rules in that court require that motions to withdraw be accompanied by facts showing a sufficient basis to grant the motion. Local Civil Rule 1.4 of the U.S. District Court for the Eastern District of New York, states that motions to withdraw "may be granted only upon a showing by affidavit or otherwise of satisfactory reasons for withdrawal . . . ." Team Obsolete Ltd. v. A.H.R.M.A. LTD., 464 F. Supp. 2d 164, 166 (E.D.N.Y. 2006).

14. The Model Code of Judicial Conduct provides only broad based guidance on this matter. Model Code of Judicial Conduct R. 2.5(A) states: "A Judge shall perform judicial and administrative duties, competently and diligently." Comment [4] to Model Code of Judicial Conduct R. 2.5 states that "[i]n disposing of matters promptly and efficiently, a judge must demonstrate due regard for the rights of the parties to be heard and to have issues resolved without unnecessary cost or delay. A judge should monitor and supervise cases in ways that reduce or eliminate dilatory practices, avoidable delays and unnecessary costs."

15. ABA Comm. on Ethics & Prof'l Responsibility, Formal Op. 93-370, at 4 (1993).

tion in refusing to release the Kiley firm from the representation where the case was already three years old, discovery was delayed, and no successor counsel could be found."); *Brandon*, 560 F.3d at 538 (discussing topics of strategically timed or coercive behavior, prejudice); *McDonald v. Shore*, 953 N.Y.S.2d 650, 651 (App. Div. 2012) ("Generally, where the insurer of a defendant in a personal injury action issues a contested disclaimer of coverage in the midst of litigation, it is inappropriate to grant a motion to withdraw by the attorney the insurer has provided for that defendant.") In some jurisdictions the procedural rules provide criteria for the court to consider in ruling on motions to withdraw. *See In re Franke*, 55 A.3d at 722 (quoting Rule 2-132(b) of the Maryland Rules of Civil Procedure, permitting a court to deny a motion to withdraw "if withdrawal of the appearance would cause undue delay, prejudice, or injustice."). *See also Team Obsolete*, 464 F. Supp. 2d at 1662 (Local Civil Rule 1.4.).

In some instances, such as when a motion to withdraw is filed early in a case, a court's decision may be relatively straightforward. In other cases, such as when a matter is complex, extensive discovery has been conducted, and the trial date is approaching, a court's decision may be more difficult. To accommodate the individual facts of any particular case, the scope of information that may be deemed pertinent to a particular withdrawal motion is necessarily one that is left to the trial judge's discretion under applicable law.

As with settlement negotiations, judges should recognize the ethical constraints on lawyers who move to withdraw, and work with the lawyers to obtain the information needed to rule on the motion while cognizant of the lawyer's duties under Rule 1.6. In some instances, judges may conclude that the procedural history and status of the case is sufficient to decide the motion without further inquiry. Or a judge may consider asking the lawyer merely to assure the court that the motion is brought in good faith and without purpose of undue delay. A judge should not require the disclosure of confidential client information without considering whether such information is necessary to reach a sound decision on the motion. When a judge decides that confidential information is required, the judge should consider whether there are ways to reduce or mitigate harm to the client. For example, in *Gonzalez*, the court noted that two means of mitigation are to direct that the disclosures be made under seal and *in camera* [16] and for sensitive

ABA Formal Ethics Opinions (Selected)

---

16. By "*in camera*" we mean a submission only to the court under seal, to be reviewed in chambers, with a copy to the client. While opposing counsel or opposing parties do not receive copies of the *in camera* submission, they are nonetheless generally aware that it has been submitted. Opposing counsel and parties do not have the same unconditional or unrestricted right to all information relating to a motion to withdraw as they would with other motions. *See* MALLEN, *supra* note 4 (noting that "The adverse party's interest in the submission usually is unrelated to the litigation of the merits and not sufficient to warrant disclosure."). While some may suggest that such submissions violate Model Code of Judicial Conduct Rule 2.9, prohibiting judges from engaging in substantive *ex parte* communications, the Committee does not believe that such *in camera* submissions, when made with full knowledge of the opposing party, are an *ex parte* communication and thus, they do not fall within that prohibition. "An *ex parte* communication is one that excludes any party who is legally entitled to be present or notified of the

or unnecessary information to be redacted.[17] Another option available to the court is to issue a protective order. As discussed below, these approaches, while sometimes useful, will not be appropriate in every case, nor are they "silver bullets" that resolve all issues.

Limiting Disclosures to Mitigate Harm to Clients

Comment [16] to Rule 1.6 provides that disclosures under Rule 1.6(b) are permitted only to the extent the lawyer reasonably believes necessary to accomplish the purpose specified. Of course, where practicable, a lawyer should first seek to persuade the client to take suitable action to remove the need for the lawyer's disclosure. When such persuasion is not practicable or successful, and disclosure of some confidential information is required, "If the disclosure will be made in connection with a judicial proceeding, the disclosure should be made in a manner that limits access to the information to the tribunal or other persons having a need to know it *and appropriate protective orders or other arrangements* should be sought by the lawyer to the fullest extent practicable."[18] Thus, Comment [16] anticipates the use of *in camera* submissions for disclosures where any of Rule 1.6(b)'s exceptions may apply. The situation is similar to discovery disputes over claims of privilege, whereby competing claims are often resolved by a court's review *in camera* of the documents at issue and such procedures can help reconcile the competing issues involved in ruling on motions to withdraw as well.

But while *in camera* submissions are a useful tool, a lawyer's disclosure of client information *in camera* is itself a form of "revealing" under Rule 1.6. It is therefore generally not sufficient under Rule 1.6 for a lawyer to proceed in the first instance by providing confidential information *in camera*, without first attempting to file a withdrawal motion with a formulaic reference to "professional considerations" or a similar term as the grounds for the motion, as suggested in Comment [3] to Rule 1.16. At that point the trial court might grant the motion without further inquiry; it might state that a motion will be denied absent further information; it might request further information; or it may order the lawyer to provide further information.

Thus, in order to comply with Rule 1.6, a lawyer who has a good faith basis for withdrawal under Rule 1.16(b)(5) and/or 1.16(b)(6), and who complies with the applicable procedural prerequisites of the court for such motions, could: (1) initially submit a motion providing no confidential client information apart from

ABA Formal Ethics Opinions (Selected)

---

communication and given an opportunity to respond." ANNOTATED MODEL CODE OF JUDICIAL CONDUCT 176 (2d ed. 2011). The prohibition on *ex parte* communications in MCJC Rule 2.9 is directed mainly to surreptitious contacts of which an adversary has no notice or awareness.

17. The *Gonzalez* court implied that the lawyer's disclosure of information relating to the fee claim, if done *in camera* and with certain redactions, would not have violated Rule 1.6, stating: "[W]e agree with the Board [on Professional Responsibility] that Gonzalez could have submitted his documentation in camera, and that he could also have made appropriate redactions of the material most damaging to his client . . . ." *In re Gonzalez*, 773 A.2d 1026, 1032 (D.C. 2001).

18. MODEL RULES OF PROF'L CONDUCT R. 1.6 cmt. 16 (2016) (emphasis added).

a reference to "professional considerations" or the like;[19] (2) upon being informed by the court that further information is necessary, respond, when practicable, by seeking to persuade the court to rule on the motion without requiring the disclosure of confidential client information, asserting all non-frivolous claims of confidentiality and privilege; and if that fails; (3) thereupon under Rule 1.6(b)(5) submit only such information as is reasonably necessary to satisfy the needs of the court and preferably by whatever restricted means of submission, such as *in camera* review under seal, or such other procedures designated to minimize disclosure as the court determines is appropriate. If the court expressly orders the lawyer to make further disclosure, the exception in Rule 1.6(b)(6) for disclosures required to comply with a court order will apply, subject to the lawyer's compliance with the requirements of Comment [15].[20]

We consider here disclosures only in the context of a motion to withdraw in a civil case based on a client's failure to pay a lawyer's fees. Given the competing rights and responsibilities implicated in such motions, these steps should satisfy a lawyer's ethical duties under Rule 1.6. If a motion to withdraw is based on grounds other than a failure to meet financial obligations, other Rules and principles may apply.

As stated in the Scope section of the Model Rules, "The Rules of Professional Conduct are rules of reason."[21] The Scope section also states: "The Rules presuppose a larger legal context shaping the lawyer's role. That context includes court rules, statutes relating to matters of licensure, law defining specific obligations of lawyers and substantive and procedural law in general."[22]

Conclusion

In moving to withdraw as counsel in a civil proceeding based on a client's failure to pay fees, a lawyer must consider the duty of confidentiality under Rule 1.6 and seek to reconcile that duty with the court's need for sufficient information upon which to rule on the motion. Similarly, in entertaining such a motion, a judge should consider the right of the movant's client to confidentiality. This requires cooperation between lawyers and judges. If required by the court to support the motion with facts relating to the representation, a lawyer may, pursuant to Rule 1.6(b)(5), disclose only such confidential information as is reasonably necessary for the court to make an informed decision on the motion.

---

19. Of course a lawyer can recite her compliance with procedural steps, such as prior notice to the client, and can recite the procedural history and status of the case as reflected on the docket and the court's file.

20. *See* ABA Comm. on Ethics & Prof'l Responsibility, Formal Op. 473 (2016), relating to a lawyer's duties when responding to a subpoena or compulsory process to provide privileged information. *See also* Oregon Formal Op. 2011-185 (2011), 2011 WL 11741926, at *2 (Lawyer may reveal information relating to the representation of Client under Oregon RPC 1.6(b)(5), but may only do so to the extent "reasonably necessary" to comply with the court order.) The court's mere statement that the motion will not be granted absent more information is not "a court order" and does not trigger the exception under Rule 1.6(b)(6) until the lawyer has taken steps to prevent or limit disclosure of confidential information.

21. MODEL RULES OF PROF'L CONDUCT, Scope [14] (2016).

22. *Id.* at [15].

ABA Formal Ethics Opinions (Selected)

Formal Opinion 477   May 11, 2017
Securing Communication of Protected
Client Information

A lawyer generally may transmit information relating to the representation of a client over the internet without violating the Model Rules of Professional Conduct where the lawyer has undertaken reasonable efforts to prevent inadvertent or unauthorized access. However, a lawyer may be required to take special security precautions to protect against the inadvertent or unauthorized disclosure of client information when required by an agreement with the client or by law, or when the nature of the information requires a higher degree of security.

I. Introduction

In Formal Opinion 99-413 this Committee addressed a lawyer's confidentiality obligations for e-mail communications with clients. While the basic obligations of confidentiality remain applicable today, the role and risks of technology in the practice of law have evolved since 1999 prompting the need to update Opinion 99-413.

Formal Opinion 99-413 concluded: "Lawyers have a reasonable expectation of privacy in communications made by all forms of e-mail, including unencrypted e-mail sent on the Internet, despite some risk of interception and disclosure. It therefore follows that its use is consistent with the duty under Rule 1.6 to use reasonable means to maintain the confidentiality of information relating to a client's representation."[1]

Unlike 1999 where multiple methods of communication were prevalent, today, many lawyers primarily use electronic means to communicate and exchange documents with clients, other lawyers, and even with other persons who are assisting a lawyer in delivering legal services to clients.[2]

Since 1999, those providing legal services now regularly use a variety of devices to create, transmit and store confidential communications, including desktop, laptop and notebook computers, tablet devices, smartphones, and cloud resource and storage locations. Each device and each storage location offer an opportunity for the inadvertent or unauthorized disclosure of information relating to the representation, and thus implicate a lawyer's ethical duties.[3]

ABA Formal Ethics Opinions (Selected)

---

1. ABA Comm. on Ethics & Prof'l Responsibility, Formal Op. 99-413, at 11 (1999).

2. ABA Comm. on Ethics & Prof'l Responsibility, Formal Op. 08-451 (2008); ABA COMMISSION ON ETHICS 20/20 REPORT TO THE HOUSE OF DELEGATES (2012), http://www.americanbar.org/content/dam/aba/administrative/ethics_2020/20120508_ethics_20_20_final_resolution_and_report_outsourcing_posting.authcheckdam.pdf.

3. *See* JILL D. RHODES & VINCENT I. POLLEY, THE ABA CYBERSECURITY HANDBOOK: A RESOURCE FOR ATTORNEYS, LAW FIRMS, AND BUSINESS PROFESSIONALS 7 (2013) [hereinafter ABA CYBERSECURITY HANDBOOK].

In 2012 the ABA adopted "technology amendments" to the Model Rules, including updating the Comments to Rule 1.1 on lawyer technological competency and adding paragraph (c) and a new Comment to Rule 1.6, addressing a lawyer's obligation to take reasonable measures to prevent inadvertent or unauthorized disclosure of information relating to the representation.

At the same time, the term "cybersecurity" has come into existence to encompass the broad range of issues relating to preserving individual privacy from intrusion by nefarious actors throughout the Internet. Cybersecurity recognizes a post-Opinion 99-413 world where law enforcement discusses hacking and data loss in terms of "when," and not "if."[4] Law firms are targets for two general reasons: (1) they obtain, store and use highly sensitive information about their clients while at times utilizing safeguards to shield that information that may be inferior to those deployed by the client, and (2) the information in their possession is more likely to be of interest to a hacker and likely less voluminous than that held by the client.[5]

The Model Rules do not impose greater or different duties of confidentiality based upon the method by which a lawyer communicates with a client. But how a lawyer should comply with the core duty of confidentiality in an ever-changing technological world requires some reflection.

Against this backdrop we describe the "technology amendments" made to the Model Rules in 2012, identify some of the technology risks lawyers' face, and discuss factors other than the Model Rules of Professional Conduct that lawyers should consider when using electronic means to communicate regarding client matters.

II. Duty of Competence

Since 1983, Model Rule 1.1 has read: "A lawyer shall provide competent representation to a client. Competent representation requires the legal knowledge, skill, thoroughness and preparation reasonably necessary for the representation."[6] The scope of this requirement was clarified in 2012 when the ABA recognized the increasing impact of technology on the practice of law and the duty of lawyers to

ABA Formal
Ethics Opinions
(Selected)

---

4. "Cybersecurity" is defined as "measures taken to protect a computer or computer system (as on the Internet) against unauthorized access or attack." CYBERSECURITY, MERRIAM WEBSTER, http://www.merriam-webster.com/dictionary/cybersecurity (last visited Sept. 10, 2016). In 2012 the ABA created the Cybersecurity Legal Task Force to help lawyers grapple with the legal challenges created by cyberspace. In 2013 the Task Force published The ABA Cybersecurity Handbook: A Resource For Attorneys, Law Firms, and Business Professionals.

5. Bradford A. Bleier, Unit Chief to the Cyber National Security Section in the FBI's Cyber Division, indicated that "[l]aw firms have tremendous concentrations of really critical private information, and breaking into a firm's computer system is a really optimal way to obtain economic and personal security information." Ed Finkel, Cyberspace Under Siege, A.B.A. J., Nov. 1, 2010.

6. A LEGISLATIVE HISTORY: THE DEVELOPMENT OF THE ABA MODEL RULES OF PROFESSIONAL CONDUCT, 1982-2013, at 37-44 (Art Garwin ed., 2013).

develop an understanding of that technology. Thus, Comment [8] to Rule 1.1 was modified to read:

> To maintain the requisite knowledge and skill, a lawyer should keep abreast of changes in the law and its practice, *including the benefits and risks associated with relevant technology*, engage in continuing study and education and comply with all continuing legal education requirements to which the lawyer is subject. (Emphasis added.)[7]

Regarding the change to Rule 1.1's Comment, the ABA Commission on Ethics 20/20 explained:

> Model Rule 1.1 requires a lawyer to provide competent representation, and Comment [6] specifies that, to remain competent, lawyers need to "keep abreast of changes in the law and its practice." The Commission concluded that, in order to keep abreast of changes in law practice in a digital age, lawyers necessarily need to understand basic features of relevant technology and that this aspect of competence should be expressed in the Comment. For example, a lawyer would have difficulty providing competent legal services in today's environment without knowing how to use email or create an electronic document. [8]

III. Duty of Confidentiality

In 2012, amendments to Rule 1.6 modified both the rule and the commentary about what efforts are required to preserve the confidentiality of information relating to the representation. Model Rule 1.6(a) requires that "A lawyer shall not reveal information relating to the representation of a client" unless certain circumstances arise.[9] The 2012 modification added a new duty in paragraph (c) that: "A lawyer shall make reasonable efforts to prevent the inadvertent or un-

ABA Formal
Ethics Opinions
(Selected)

---

7. *Id.* at 43.

8. ABA Commission on Ethics 20/20 Report 105A (Aug. 2012), http://www.americanbar. org/content/dam/aba/administrative/ethics_2020/20120808_revised_resolution_105a_as_ amended.authcheckdam.pdf. The 20/20 Commission also noted that modification of Comment [6] did not change the lawyer's substantive duty of competence: "Comment [6] already encompasses an obligation to remain aware of changes in technology that affect law practice, but the Commission concluded that making this explicit, by addition of the phrase 'including the benefits and risks associated with relevant technology,' would offer greater clarity in this area and emphasize the importance of technology to modern law practice. The proposed amendment, which appears in a Comment, does not impose any new obligations on lawyers. Rather, the amendment is intended to serve as a reminder to lawyers that they should remain aware of technology, including the benefits and risks associated with it, as part of a lawyer's general ethical duty to remain competent."

9. Model Rules of Prof'l Conduct R. 1.6(a) (2016).

authorized disclosure of, or unauthorized access to, information relating to the representation of a client."[10]

Amended Comment [18] explains:

> Paragraph (c) requires a lawyer to act competently to safeguard information relating to the representation of a client against unauthorized access by third parties and against inadvertent or unauthorized disclosure by the lawyer or other persons who are participating in the representation of the client or who are subject to the lawyer's supervision. See Rules 1.1, 5.1 and 5.3. The unauthorized access to, or the inadvertent or unauthorized disclosure of, information relating to the representation of a client does not constitute a violation of paragraph (c) if the lawyer has made reasonable efforts to prevent the access or disclosure.

At the intersection of a lawyer's competence obligation to keep "abreast of knowledge of the benefits and risks associated with relevant technology," and confidentiality obligation to make "reasonable efforts to prevent the inadvertent or unauthorized disclosure of, or unauthorized access to, information relating to the representation of a client," lawyers must exercise reasonable efforts when using technology in communicating about client matters. What constitutes reasonable efforts is not susceptible to a hard and fast rule, but rather is contingent upon a set of factors. In turn, those factors depend on the multitude of possible types of information being communicated (ranging along a spectrum from highly sensitive information to insignificant), the methods of electronic communications employed, and the types of available security measures for each method.[11]

Therefore, in an environment of increasing cyber threats, the Committee concludes that, adopting the language in the ABA Cybersecurity Handbook, the reasonable efforts standard:

ABA Formal
Ethics Opinions
(Selected)

> . . . rejects requirements for specific security measures (such as firewalls, passwords, and the like) and instead adopts a fact-specific approach to business security obligations that requires a "process" to assess risks, identify and implement appropriate security measures responsive to

---

10. *Id.* at (c).

11. The 20/20 Commission's report emphasized that lawyers are not the guarantors of data safety. It wrote:

"[t]o be clear, paragraph (c) does not mean that a lawyer engages in professional misconduct any time a client's confidences are subject to unauthorized access or disclosed inadvertently or without authority. A sentence in Comment [16] makes this point explicitly. The reality is that disclosures can occur even if lawyers take all reasonable precautions. The Commission, however, believes that it is important to state in the black letter of Model Rule 1.6 that lawyers have a duty to take reasonable precautions, even if those precautions will not guarantee the protection of confidential information under all circumstances."

those risks, verify that they are effectively implemented, and ensure that they are continually updated in response to new developments.[12]

Recognizing the necessity of employing a fact-based analysis, Comment [18] to Model Rule 1.6(c) includes nonexclusive factors to guide lawyers in making a "reasonable efforts" determination. Those factors include:

- the sensitivity of the information,
- the likelihood of disclosure if additional safeguards are not employed,
- the cost of employing additional safeguards,
- the difficulty of implementing the safeguards, and
- the extent to which the safeguards adversely affect the lawyer's ability to represent clients (e.g., by making a device or important piece of software excessively difficult to use).[13]

A fact-based analysis means that particularly strong protective measures, like encryption, are warranted in some circumstances. Model Rule 1.4 may require a lawyer to discuss security safeguards with clients. Under certain circumstances, the lawyer may need to obtain informed consent from the client regarding whether to the use enhanced security measures, the costs involved, and the impact of those costs on the expense of the representation where nonstandard and not easily available or affordable security methods may be required or requested by the client. Reasonable efforts, as it pertains to certain highly sensitive information, might require avoiding the use of electronic methods or any technology to communicate with the client altogether, just as it warranted avoiding the use of the telephone, fax and mail in Formal Opinion 99-413.

In contrast, for matters of normal or low sensitivity, standard security methods with low to reasonable costs to implement, may be sufficient to meet the reasonable-efforts standard to protect client information from inadvertent and unauthorized disclosure.

In the technological landscape of Opinion 99-413, and due to the reasonable expectations of privacy available to email communications at the time, unencrypted email posed no greater risk of interception or disclosure than other non-electronic forms of communication. This basic premise remains true today for routine communication with clients, presuming the lawyer has implemented basic and reasonably available methods of common electronic security mea-

ABA Formal
Ethics Opinions
(Selected)

---

12. ABA CYBERSECURITY HANDBOOK, *supra* note 3, at 48-49.

13. MODEL RULES OF PROF'L CONDUCT R. 1.6 cmt. [18] (2013). "The [Ethics 20/20] Commission examined the possibility of offering more detailed guidance about the measures that lawyers should employ. The Commission concluded, however, that technology is changing too rapidly to offer such guidance and that the particular measures lawyers should use will necessarily change as technology evolves and as new risks emerge and new security procedures become available." ABA COMMISSION REPORT 105A, *supra* note 8, at 5.

sures.[14] Thus, the use of unencrypted routine email generally remains an acceptable method of lawyer-client communication.

However, cyber-threats and the proliferation of electronic communications devices have changed the landscape and it is not always reasonable to rely on the use of unencrypted email. For example, electronic communication through certain mobile applications or on message boards or via unsecured networks may lack the basic expectation of privacy afforded to email communications. Therefore, lawyers must, on a case-by-case basis, constantly analyze how they communicate electronically about client matters, applying the Comment [18] factors to determine what effort is reasonable.

While it is beyond the scope of an ethics opinion to specify the reasonable steps that lawyers should take under any given set of facts, we offer the following considerations as guidance:

1. *Understand the Nature of the Threat.*

   Understanding the nature of the threat includes consideration of the sensitivity of a client's information and whether the client's matter is a higher risk for cyber intrusion. Client matters involving proprietary information in highly sensitive industries such as industrial designs, mergers and acquisitions or trade secrets, and industries like healthcare, banking, defense or education, may present a higher risk of data theft.[15] "Reasonable efforts" in higher risk scenarios generally means that greater effort is warranted.

2. *Understand How Client Confidential Information Is Transmitted and Where It Is Stored.*

   A lawyer should understand how their firm's electronic communications are created, where client data resides, and what avenues exist to access that information. Understanding these processes will assist a lawyer in managing the risk of inadvertent or unauthorized disclosure of client-related information. Every access point is a potential entry point for a data loss or disclosure. The lawyer's task is complicated in a world where multiple devices may be used to communicate with or about a client and then store those communications. Each access point, and each device, should be evaluated for security compliance.

3. *Understand and Use Reasonable Electronic Security Measures.*

   Model Rule 1.6(c) requires a lawyer to make reasonable efforts to prevent the inadvertent or unauthorized disclosure of, or unauthorized access to, information relating to the representation of a client. As comment [18] makes clear, what is deemed to be "reasonable" may vary, depending on the facts and circumstances of each case. Electronic dis-

ABA Formal
Ethics Opinions
(Selected)

---

14. See item 3 below.

15. *See, e.g.*, Noah Garner, *The Most Prominent Cyber Threats Faced by High-Target Industries*, TREND-MICRO (Jan. 25, 2016), http://blog.trendmicro.com/the-most-prominent-cyber-threats-faced-by-high-target-industries/.

closure of, or access to, client communications can occur in different forms ranging from a direct intrusion into a law firm's systems to theft or interception of information during the transmission process. Making reasonable efforts to protect against unauthorized disclosure in client communications thus includes analysis of security measures applied to both disclosure and access to a law firm's technology system and transmissions.

A lawyer should understand and use electronic security measures to safeguard client communications and information. A lawyer has a variety of options to safeguard communications including, for example, using secure internet access methods to communicate, access and store client information (such as through secure Wi-Fi, the use of a Virtual Private Network, or another secure internet portal), using unique complex passwords, changed periodically, implementing firewalls and anti-Malware/Anti-Spyware/Antivirus software on all devices upon which client confidential information is transmitted or stored, and applying all necessary security patches and updates to operational and communications software. Each of these measures is routinely accessible and reasonably affordable or free. Lawyers may consider refusing access to firm systems to devices failing to comply with these basic methods. It also may be reasonable to use commonly available methods to remotely disable lost or stolen devices, and to destroy the data contained on those devices, especially if encryption is not also being used.

Other available tools include encryption of data that is physically stored on a device and multi-factor authentication to access firm systems.

In the electronic world, "delete" usually does not mean information is permanently deleted, and "deleted" data may be subject to recovery. Therefore, a lawyer should consider whether certain data should *ever* be stored in an unencrypted environment, or electronically transmitted at all.

4. *Determine How Electronic Communications About Clients Matters Should Be Protected.*

Different communications require different levels of protection. At the beginning of the client-lawyer relationship, the lawyer and client should discuss what levels of security will be necessary for each electronic communication about client matters. Communications to third parties containing protected client information requires analysis to determine what degree of protection is appropriate. In situations where the communication (and any attachments) are sensitive or warrant extra security, additional electronic protection may be required. For example, if client information is of sufficient sensitivity, a lawyer should encrypt the transmission and determine how to do so to sufficiently protect it,[16] and

---

16. *See* Cal. Formal Op. 2010-179 (2010); ABA CYBERSECURITY HANDBOOK, *supra* note 3, at 121. Indeed, certain laws and regulations require encryption in certain situations. *Id.* at 58-59.

ABA Formal
Ethics Opinions
(Selected)

consider the use of password protection for any attachments. Alternatively, lawyers can consider the use of a well vetted and secure third-party cloud based file storage system to exchange documents normally attached to emails.

Thus, routine communications sent electronically are those communications that do not contain information warranting additional security measures beyond basic methods. However, in some circumstances, a client's lack of technological sophistication or the limitations of technology available to the client may require alternative non-electronic forms of communication altogether.

A lawyer also should be cautious in communicating with a client if the client uses computers or other devices subject to the access or control of a third party.[17] If so, the attorney-client privilege and confidentiality of communications and attached documents may be waived, and the lawyer must determine whether it is prudent to warn a client of the dangers associated with such a method of communication.[18]

5. *Label Client Confidential Information.*

Lawyers should follow the better practice of marking privileged and confidential client communications as "privileged and confidential" in order to alert anyone to whom the communication was inadvertently disclosed that the communication is intended to be privileged and con-

---

17. *See, e.g.*, ABA Comm. on Ethics & Prof'l Responsibility, Formal Op. 11-459 (2011) (discussing the duty to protect the confidentiality of e-mail communications with one's client); Scott v. Beth Israel Med. Center, Inc., Civ. A. No. 3:04-CV-139-RJC-DCK, 847 N.Y.S.2d 436 (Sup. Ct. 2007); Mason v. ILS Tech., LLC, 2008 WL 731557, 2008 BL 298576 (W.D.N.C. 2008); Holmes v. Petrovich Dev Co., LLC, 191 Cal. App. 4th 1047 (2011) (employee communications with lawyer over company owned computer not privileged); Bingham v. BayCare Health Sys., 2016 WL 3917513, 2016 BL 233476 (M.D. Fla. July 20, 2016) (collecting cases on privilege waiver for privileged emails sent or received through an employer's email server).

18. some state bar ethics opinions have explored the circumstances under which e-mail communications should be afforded special security protections, *See, e.g.*, Tex. Prof'l Ethics Comm. Op. 648 (2015) that identified six situations in which a lawyer should consider whether to encrypt or use some other type of security precaution:

- communicating highly sensitive or confidential information via email or unencrypted email connections;
- sending an email to or from an account that the email sender or recipient shares with others;
- sending an email to a client when it is possible that a third person (such as a spouse in a divorce case) knows the password to the email account, or to an individual client at that client's work email account, especially if the email relates to a client's employment dispute with his employer . . . ;
- sending an email from a public computer or a borrowed computer or where the lawyer knows that the emails the lawyer sends are being read on a public or borrowed computer or on an unsecure network;
- sending an email if the lawyer knows that the email recipient is accessing the email on devices that are potentially accessible to third persons or are not protected by a password; or
- sending an email if the lawyer is concerned that the NSA or other law enforcement agency may read the lawyer's email communication, with or without a warrant.

ABA Formal Ethics Opinions (Selected)

fidential. This can also consist of something as simple as appending a message or "disclaimer" to client emails, where such a disclaimer is accurate and appropriate for the communication.[19]

Model Rule 4.4(b) obligates a lawyer who "knows or reasonably should know" that he has received an inadvertently sent "document or electronically stored information relating to the representation of the lawyer's client" to promptly notify the sending lawyer. A clear and conspicuous appropriately used disclaimer may affect whether a recipient lawyer's duty under Model Rule 4.4(b) for inadvertently transmitted communications is satisfied.

6. *Train Lawyers and Nonlawyer Assistants in Technology and Information Security.*

Model Rule 5.1 provides that a partner in a law firm, and a lawyer who individually or together with other lawyers possesses comparable managerial authority in a law firm, shall make reasonable efforts to ensure that the firm has in effect measures giving reasonable assurance that all lawyers in the firm conform to the Rules of Professional Conduct. Model Rule 5.1 also provides that lawyers having direct supervisory authority over another lawyer shall make reasonable efforts to ensure that the other lawyer conforms to the Rules of Professional Conduct. In addition, Rule 5.3 requires lawyers who are responsible for managing and supervising nonlawyer assistants to take reasonable steps to reasonably assure that the conduct of such assistants is compatible with the ethical duties of the lawyer. These requirements are as applicable to electronic practices as they are to comparable office procedures.

In the context of electronic communications, lawyers must establish policies and procedures, and periodically train employees, subordinates and others assisting in the delivery of legal services, in the use of reasonably secure methods of electronic communications with clients. Lawyers also must instruct and supervise on reasonable measures for access to and storage of those communications. Once processes are established, supervising lawyers must follow up to ensure these policies are being implemented and partners and lawyers with comparable managerial authority must periodically reassess and update these policies. This is no different than the other obligations for supervision of office practices and procedures to protect client information.

7. *Conduct Due Diligence on Vendors Providing Communication Technology.*

Consistent with Model Rule 1.6(c), Model Rule 5.3 imposes a duty on lawyers with direct supervisory authority over a nonlawyer to make

ABA Formal
Ethics Opinions
(Selected)

---

19. *See* Veteran Med. Prods. v. Bionix Dev. Corp., Case No. 1:05-cv-655, 2008 WL 696546 at *8, 2008 BL 51876 at *8 (W.D. Mich. Mar. 13, 2008) (email disclaimer that read "this email and any files transmitted with are confidential and are intended solely for the use of the individual or entity to whom they are addressed" with nondisclosure constitutes a reasonable effort to maintain the secrecy of its business plan).

"reasonable efforts to ensure that" the nonlawyer's "conduct is compatible with the professional obligations of the lawyer."

In ABA Formal Opinion 08-451, this Committee analyzed Model Rule 5.3 and a lawyer's obligation when outsourcing legal and nonlegal services. That opinion identified several issues a lawyer should consider when selecting the outsource vendor, to meet the lawyer's due diligence and duty of supervision. Those factors also apply in the analysis of vendor selection in the context of electronic communications. Such factors may include:

- reference checks and vendor credentials;
- vendor's security policies and protocols;
- vendor's hiring practices;
- the use of confidentiality agreements;
- vendor's conflicts check system to screen for adversity; and
- the availability and accessibility of a legal forum for legal relief for violations of the vendor agreement.

Any lack of individual competence by a lawyer to evaluate and employ safeguards to protect client confidences may be addressed through association with another lawyer or expert, or by education.[20]

Since the issuance of Formal Opinion 08-451, Comment [3] to Model Rule 5.3 was added to address outsourcing, including "using an Internet-based service to store client information." Comment [3] provides that the "reasonable efforts" required by Model Rule 5.3 to ensure that the nonlawyer's services are provided in a manner that is compatible with the lawyer's professional obligations "will depend upon the circumstances." Comment [3] contains suggested factors that might be taken into account:

- the education, experience, and reputation of the nonlawyer;
- the nature of the services involved;
- the terms of any arrangements concerning the protection of client information; and
- the legal and ethical environments of the jurisdictions in which the services will be performed particularly with regard to confidentiality.

Comment [3] further provides that when retaining or directing a nonlawyer outside of the firm, lawyers should communicate "directions appropriate under the circumstances to give reasonable assurance that the nonlawyer's conduct is compatible with the professional obligations

ABA Formal
Ethics Opinions
(Selected)

---

20. MODEL RULES OF PROF'L CONDUCT R. 1.1 cmts. [2] & [8] (2016).

of the lawyer."[21] If the client has not directed the selection of the outside nonlawyer vendor, the lawyer has the responsibility to monitor how those services are being performed.[22]

Even after a lawyer examines these various considerations and is satisfied that the security employed is sufficient to comply with the duty of confidentiality, the lawyer must periodically reassess these factors to confirm that the lawyer's actions continue to comply with the ethical obligations and have not been rendered inadequate by changes in circumstances or technology.

IV. Duty to Communicate

Communications between a lawyer and client generally are addressed in Rule 1.4. When the lawyer reasonably believes that highly sensitive confidential client information is being transmitted so that extra measures to protect the email transmission are warranted, the lawyer should inform the client about the risks involved.[23] The lawyer and client then should decide whether another mode of transmission, such as high level encryption or personal delivery is warranted. Similarly, a lawyer should consult with the client as to how to appropriately and safely use technology in their communication, in compliance with other laws that might be applicable to the client. Whether a lawyer is using methods and practices to comply with administrative, statutory, or international legal standards is beyond the scope of this opinion.

A client may insist or require that the lawyer undertake certain forms of communication. As explained in Comment [18] to Model Rule 1.6, "A client may require the lawyer to implement special security measures not required by this Rule or may give informed consent to the use of a means of communication that would otherwise be prohibited by this Rule."

V. Conclusion

Rule 1.1 requires a lawyer to provide competent representation to a client. Comment [8] to Rule 1.1 advises lawyers that to maintain the requisite knowledge and skill for competent representation, a lawyer should keep abreast of the ben-

---

21. The ABA's catalog of state bar ethics opinions applying the rules of professional conduct to cloud storage arrangements involving client information can be found at: http://www .americanbar.org/groups/departments_offices/legal_technology_resources/resources/charts _fyis/cloud-ethics-chart.html.

22. By contrast, where a client directs the selection of a particular nonlawyer service provider outside the firm, "the lawyer ordinarily should agree with the client concerning the allocation of responsibility for monitoring as between the client and the lawyer." MODEL RULES OF PROF'L CONDUCT R. 5.3 cmt. [4] (2017). The concept of monitoring recognizes that although it may not be possible to "directly supervise" a client directed nonlawyer outside the firm performing services in connection with a matter, a lawyer must nevertheless remain aware of how the nonlawyer services are being performed. ABA COMMISSION ON ETHICS 20/20 REPORT 105C, at 12 (Aug. 2012), http://www.americanbar.org/content/dam/aba/administrative/ethics _2020/2012_hod_annual_meeting_105c_filed_may_2012.authcheckdam.pdf.

23. MODEL RULES OF PROF'L CONDUCT R. 1.4(a)(1) & (4) (2016).

efits and risks associated with relevant technology. Rule 1.6(c) requires a lawyer to make "reasonable efforts" to prevent the inadvertent or unauthorized disclosure of or access to information relating to the representation.

A lawyer generally may transmit information relating to the representation of a client over the Internet without violating the Model Rules of Professional Conduct where the lawyer has undertaken reasonable efforts to prevent inadvertent or unauthorized access. However, a lawyer may be required to take special security precautions to protect against the inadvertent or unauthorized disclosure of client information when required by an agreement with the client or by law, or when the nature of the information requires a higher degree of security.

ABA Formal
Ethics Opinions
(Selected)

Formal Opinion 477R*   **May 11, 2017**
Revised May 22, 2017

Securing Communication of Protected Client Information

A lawyer generally may transmit information relating to the representation of a client over the internet without violating the Model Rules of Professional Conduct where the lawyer has undertaken reasonable efforts to prevent inadvertent or unauthorized access. However, a lawyer may be required to take special security precautions to protect against the inadvertent or unauthorized disclosure of client information when required by an agreement with the client or by law, or when the nature of the information requires a higher degree of security.

I. Introduction

In Formal Opinion 99-413 this Committee addressed a lawyer's confidentiality obligations for email communications with clients. While the basic obligations of confidentiality remain applicable today, the role and risks of technology in the practice of law have evolved since 1999 prompting the need to update Opinion 99-413.

Formal Opinion 99-413 concluded: "Lawyers have a reasonable expectation of privacy in communications made by all forms of e-mail, including unencrypted e-mail sent on the Internet, despite some risk of interception and disclosure. It therefore follows that its use is consistent with the duty under Rule 1.6 to use reasonable means to maintain the confidentiality of information relating to a client's representation."[1]

Unlike 1999 where multiple methods of communication were prevalent, today, many lawyers primarily use electronic means to communicate and exchange documents with clients, other lawyers, and even with other persons who are assisting a lawyer in delivering legal services to clients.[2]

Since 1999, those providing legal services now regularly use a variety of devices to create, transmit and store confidential communications, including desktop, laptop and notebook computers, tablet devices, smartphones, and cloud

---

1. ABA Comm. on Ethics & Prof'l Responsibility, Formal Op. 99-413, at 11 (1999).
2. ABA Comm. on Ethics & Prof'l Responsibility, Formal Op. 08-451 (2008); ABA COMMIS-SION ON ETHICS 20/20 REPORT TO THE HOUSE OF DELEGATES (2012), http://www.americanbar. org/content/dam/aba/administrative/ethics_2020/20120508_ethics_20_20_final_resolution_ and_report_outsourcing_posting.authcheckdam.pdf.

---

*The opinion below is a revision of, and replaces Formal Opinion 477 as issued by the Committee May 11, 2017. This opinion is based on the ABA Model Rules of Professional Conduct as amended by the ABA House of Delegates through August 2016. The laws, court rules, regulations, rules of professional conduct, and opinions promulgated in individual jurisdictions are controlling.

resource and storage locations. Each device and each storage location offer an opportunity for the inadvertent or unauthorized disclosure of information relating to the representation, and thus implicate a lawyer's ethical duties.[3]

In 2012 the ABA adopted "technology amendments" to the Model Rules, including updating the Comments to Rule 1.1 on lawyer technological competency and adding paragraph (c) and a new Comment to Rule 1.6, addressing a lawyer's obligation to take reasonable measures to prevent inadvertent or unauthorized disclosure of information relating to the representation.

At the same time, the term "cybersecurity" has come into existence to encompass the broad range of issues relating to preserving individual privacy from intrusion by nefarious actors throughout the internet. Cybersecurity recognizes a post-Opinion 99-413 world where law enforcement discusses hacking and data loss in terms of "when," and not "if."[4] Law firms are targets for two general reasons: (1) they obtain, store and use highly sensitive information about their clients while at times utilizing safeguards to shield that information that may be inferior to those deployed by the client, and (2) the information in their possession is more likely to be of interest to a hacker and likely less voluminous than that held by the client.[5]

The Model Rules do not impose greater or different duties of confidentiality based upon the method by which a lawyer communicates with a client. But how a lawyer should comply with the core duty of confidentiality in an ever-changing technological world requires some reflection.

Against this backdrop we describe the "technology amendments" made to the Model Rules in 2012, identify some of the technology risks lawyers face, and discuss factors other than the Model Rules of Professional Conduct that lawyers should consider when using electronic means to communicate regarding client matters.

II. Duty of Competence

Since 1983, Model Rule 1.1 has read: "A lawyer shall provide competent representation to a client. Competent representation requires the legal knowledge, skill, thoroughness and preparation reasonably necessary for the

ABA Formal
Ethics Opinions
(Selected)

---

3. *See* JILL D. RHODES & VINCENT I. POLLEY, THE ABA CYBERSECURITY HANDBOOK: A RESOURCE FOR ATTORNEYS, LAW FIRMS, AND BUSINESS PROFESSIONALS 7 (2013) [hereinafter ABA CYBERSECURITY HANDBOOK].

4. "Cybersecurity" is defined as "measures taken to protect a computer or computer system (as on the internet) against unauthorized access or attack." CYBERSECURITY, MERRIAM WEBSTER, http://www.merriam-webster.com/dictionary/cybersecurity (last visited Sept. 10, 2016). In 2012 the ABA created the Cybersecurity Legal Task Force to help lawyers grapple with the legal challenges created by cyberspace. In 2013 the Task Force published The ABA Cybersecurity Handbook: A Resource For Attorneys, Law Firms, and Business Professionals.

5. Bradford A. Bleier, Unit Chief to the Cyber National Security Section in the FBI's Cyber Division, indicated that "[l]aw firms have tremendous concentrations of really critical private information, and breaking into a firm's computer system is a really optimal way to obtain economic and personal security information." Ed Finkel, Cyberspace Under Siege, A.B.A. J., Nov. 1, 2010.

representation."[6] The scope of this requirement was clarified in 2012 when the ABA recognized the increasing impact of technology on the practice of law and the duty of lawyers to develop an understanding of that technology. Thus, Comment [8] to Rule 1.1 was modified to read:

> To maintain the requisite knowledge and skill, a lawyer should keep abreast of changes in the law and its practice, *including the benefits and risks associated with relevant technology,* engage in continuing study and education and comply with all continuing legal education requirements to which the lawyer is subject. (Emphasis added.)[7]

Regarding the change to Rule 1.1's Comment, the ABA Commission on Ethics 20/20 explained:

> Model Rule 1.1 requires a lawyer to provide competent representation, and Comment [6] [renumbered as Comment [8]] specifies that, to remain competent, lawyers need to "keep abreast of changes in the law and its practice." The Commission concluded that, in order to keep abreast of changes in law practice in a digital age, lawyers necessarily need to understand basic features of relevant technology and that this aspect of competence should be expressed in the Comment. For example, a lawyer would have difficulty providing competent legal services in today's environment without knowing how to use email or create an electronic document. [8]

III. Duty of Confidentiality

In 2012, amendments to Rule 1.6 modified both the rule and the commentary about what efforts are required to preserve the confidentiality of information relating to the representation. Model Rule 1.6(a) requires that "A lawyer shall not reveal information relating to the representation of a client" unless certain

---

6. A LEGISLATIVE HISTORY: THE DEVELOPMENT OF THE ABA MODEL RULES OF PROFESSIONAL CONDUCT, 1982-2013, at 37-44 (Art Garwin ed., 2013).

7. *Id.* at 43.

8. ABA COMMISSION ON ETHICS 20/20 REPORT 105A (Aug. 2012), http://www.americanbar. org/content/dam/aba/administrative/ethics_2020/20120808_revised_resolution_105a_as_ amended.authcheckdam.pdf. The 20/20 Commission also noted that modification of Comment [6] did not change the lawyer's substantive duty of competence: "Comment [6] already encompasses an obligation to remain aware of changes in technology that affect law practice, but the Commission concluded that making this explicit, by addition of the phrase 'including the benefits and risks associated with relevant technology,' would offer greater clarity in this area and emphasize the importance of technology to modern law practice. The proposed amendment, which appears in a Comment, does not impose any new obligations on lawyers. Rather, the amendment is intended to serve as a reminder to lawyers that they should remain aware of technology, including the benefits and risks associated with it, as part of a lawyer's general ethical duty to remain competent."

ABA Formal Ethics Opinions (Selected)

circumstances arise.[9] The 2012 modification added a new duty in paragraph (c) that: "A lawyer shall make reasonable efforts to prevent the inadvertent or unauthorized disclosure of, or unauthorized access to, information relating to the representation of a client."[10]

Amended Comment [18] explains:

> Paragraph (c) requires a lawyer to act competently to safeguard information relating to the representation of a client against unauthorized access by third parties and against inadvertent or unauthorized disclosure by the lawyer or other persons who are participating in the representation of the client or who are subject to the lawyer's supervision. See Rules 1.1, 5.1 and 5.3. The unauthorized access to, or the inadvertent or unauthorized disclosure of, information relating to the representation of a client does not constitute a violation of paragraph (c) if the lawyer has made reasonable efforts to prevent the access or disclosure.

At the intersection of a lawyer's competence obligation to keep "abreast of knowledge of the benefits and risks associated with relevant technology," and confidentiality obligation to make "reasonable efforts to prevent the inadvertent or unauthorized disclosure of, or unauthorized access to, information relating to the representation of a client," lawyers must exercise reasonable efforts when using technology in communicating about client matters. What constitutes reasonable efforts is not susceptible to a hard and fast rule, but rather is contingent upon a set of factors. In turn, those factors depend on the multitude of possible types of information being communicated (ranging along a spectrum from highly sensitive information to insignificant), the methods of electronic communications employed, and the types of available security measures for each method.[11]

Therefore, in an environment of increasing cyber threats, the Committee concludes that, adopting the language in the ABA Cybersecurity Handbook, the reasonable efforts standard:

> . . . rejects requirements for specific security measures (such as firewalls, passwords, and the like) and instead adopts a fact-specific approach to

---

9. MODEL RULES OF PROF'L CONDUCT R. 1.6(a) (2016).

10. *Id.* at (c).

11. The 20/20 Commission's report emphasized that lawyers are not the guarantors of data safety. It wrote:

"[t]o be clear, paragraph (c) does not mean that a lawyer engages in professional misconduct any time a client's confidences are subject to unauthorized access or disclosed inadvertently or without authority. A sentence in Comment [16] makes this point explicitly. The reality is that disclosures can occur even if lawyers take all reasonable precautions. The Commission, however, believes that it is important to state in the black letter of Model Rule 1.6 that lawyers have a duty to take reasonable precautions, even if those precautions will not guarantee the protection of confidential information under all circumstances."

business security obligations that requires a "process" to assess risks, identify and implement appropriate security measures responsive to those risks, verify that they are effectively implemented, and ensure that they are continually updated in response to new developments.[12]

Recognizing the necessity of employing a fact-based analysis, Comment [18] to Model Rule 1.6(c) includes nonexclusive factors to guide lawyers in making a "reasonable efforts" determination. Those factors include:

- the sensitivity of the information,
- the likelihood of disclosure if additional safeguards are not employed,
- the cost of employing additional safeguards,
- the difficulty of implementing the safeguards, and
- the extent to which the safeguards adversely affect the lawyer's ability to represent clients (e.g., by making a device or important piece of software excessively difficult to use).[13]

A fact-based analysis means that particularly strong protective measures, like encryption, are warranted in some circumstances. Model Rule 1.4 may require a lawyer to discuss security safeguards with clients. Under certain circumstances, the lawyer may need to obtain informed consent from the client regarding whether to the use enhanced security measures, the costs involved, and the impact of those costs on the expense of the representation where nonstandard and not easily available or affordable security methods may be required or requested by the client. Reasonable efforts, as it pertains to certain highly sensitive information, might require avoiding the use of electronic methods or any technology to communicate with the client altogether, just as it warranted avoiding the use of the telephone, fax and mail in Formal Opinion 99-413.

In contrast, for matters of normal or low sensitivity, standard security methods with low to reasonable costs to implement, may be sufficient to meet the reasonable-efforts standard to protect client information from inadvertent and unauthorized disclosure.

In the technological landscape of Opinion 99-413, and due to the reasonable expectations of privacy available to email communications at the time, unencrypted email posed no greater risk of interception or disclosure than other non-electronic forms of communication. This basic premise remains true today

---

12. ABA Cybersecurity Handbook, *supra* note 3, at 48-49.
13. Model Rules of Prof'l Conduct R. 1.6 cmt. [18] (2016). "The [Ethics 20/20] Commission examined the possibility of offering more detailed guidance about the measures that lawyers should employ. The Commission concluded, however, that technology is changing too rapidly to offer such guidance and that the particular measures lawyers should use will necessarily change as technology evolves and as new risks emerge and new security procedures become available." ABA Commission Report 105A, *supra* note 8, at 5.

for routine communication with clients, presuming the lawyer has implemented basic and reasonably available methods of common electronic security measures.[14] Thus, the use of unencrypted routine email generally remains an acceptable method of lawyer-client communication.

However, cyber-threats and the proliferation of electronic communications devices have changed the landscape and it is not always reasonable to rely on the use of unencrypted email. For example, electronic communication through certain mobile applications or on message boards or via unsecured networks may lack the basic expectation of privacy afforded to email communications. Therefore, lawyers must, on a case-by-case basis, constantly analyze how they communicate electronically about client matters, applying the Comment [18] factors to determine what effort is reasonable.

While it is beyond the scope of an ethics opinion to specify the reasonable steps that lawyers should take under any given set of facts, we offer the following considerations as guidance:

1. Understand the Nature of the Threat.

   Understanding the nature of the threat includes consideration of the sensitivity of a client's information and whether the client's matter is a higher risk for cyber intrusion. Client matters involving proprietary information in highly sensitive industries such as industrial designs, mergers and acquisitions or trade secrets, and industries like healthcare, banking, defense or education, may present a higher risk of data theft.[15] "Reasonable efforts" in higher risk scenarios generally means that greater effort is warranted.

2. Understand How Client Confidential Information is Transmitted and Where It Is Stored.

   A lawyer should understand how their firm's electronic communications are created, where client data resides, and what avenues exist to access that information. Understanding these processes will assist a lawyer in managing the risk of inadvertent or unauthorized disclosure of client-related information. Every access point is a potential entry point for a data loss or disclosure. The lawyer's task is complicated in a world where multiple devices may be used to communicate with or about a client and then store those communications. Each access point, and each device, should be evaluated for security compliance.

3. Understand and Use Reasonable Electronic Security Measures.

   Model Rule 1.6(c) requires a lawyer to make reasonable efforts to prevent the inadvertent or unauthorized disclosure of, or unauthorized access to, information relating to the representation of a client. As Comment [18]

ABA Formal
Ethics Opinions
(Selected)

---

14. See item 3 below.

15. *See, e.g.,* Noah Garner, *The Most Prominent Cyber Threats Faced by High-Target Industries,* TREND-MICRO (Jan. 25, 2016), http://blog.trendmicro.com/the-most-prominent-cyber-threats-faced-by-high-target-industries/.

makes clear, what is deemed to be "reasonable" may vary, depending on the facts and circumstances of each case. Electronic disclosure of, or access to, client communications can occur in different forms ranging from a direct intrusion into a law firm's systems to theft or interception of information during the transmission process. Making reasonable efforts to protect against unauthorized disclosure in client communications thus includes analysis of security measures applied to both disclosure and access to a law firm's technology system and transmissions.

A lawyer should understand and use electronic security measures to safeguard client communications and information. A lawyer has a variety of options to safeguard communications including, for example, using secure internet access methods to communicate, access and store client information (such as through secure Wi-Fi, the use of a Virtual Private Network, or another secure internet portal), using unique complex passwords, changed periodically, implementing firewalls and anti-Malware/Anti-Spyware/Antivirus software on all devices upon which client confidential information is transmitted or stored, and applying all necessary security patches and updates to operational and communications software. Each of these measures is routinely accessible and reasonably affordable or free. Lawyers may consider refusing access to firm systems to devices failing to comply with these basic methods. It also may be reasonable to use commonly available methods to remotely disable lost or stolen devices, and to destroy the data contained on those devices, especially if encryption is not also being used.

Other available tools include encryption of data that is physically stored on a device and multi-factor authentication to access firm systems.

In the electronic world, "delete" usually does not mean information is permanently deleted, and "deleted" data may be subject to recovery. Therefore, a lawyer should consider whether certain data should *ever* be stored in an unencrypted environment, or electronically transmitted at all.

4. Determine How Electronic Communications About Clients Matters Should Be Protected.

Different communications require different levels of protection. At the beginning of the client-lawyer relationship, the lawyer and client should discuss what levels of security will be necessary for each electronic communication about client matters. Communications to third parties containing protected client information requires analysis to determine what degree of protection is appropriate. In situations where the communication (and any attachments) are sensitive or warrant extra security, additional electronic protection may be required. For example, if client information is of sufficient sensitivity, a lawyer should encrypt the transmission and determine how to do so to sufficiently protect it,[16] and

---

16. *See* Cal. Formal Op. 2010-179 (2010); ABA CYBERSECURITY HANDBOOK, *supra* note 3, at 121. Indeed, certain laws and regulations require encryption in certain situations. *Id.* at 58-59.

consider the use of password protection for any attachments. Alternatively, lawyers can consider the use of a well vetted and secure third-party cloud based file storage system to exchange documents normally attached to emails.

Thus, routine communications sent electronically are those communications that do not contain information warranting additional security measures beyond basic methods. However, in some circumstances, a client's lack of technological sophistication or the limitations of technology available to the client may require alternative non-electronic forms of communication altogether.

A lawyer also should be cautious in communicating with a client if the client uses computers or other devices subject to the access or control of a third party.[17] If so, the attorney-client privilege and confidentiality of communications and attached documents may be waived. Therefore, the lawyer should warn the client about the risk of sending or receiving electronic communications using a computer or other device, or email account, to which a third party has, or may gain, access.[18]

---

17. ABA Comm. on Ethics & Prof'l Responsibility, Formal Op. 11-459, Duty to Protect the Confidentiality of E-mail Communications with One's Client (2011). Formal Op. 11-459 was issued prior to the 2012 amendments to Rule 1.6. These amendments added new Rule 1.6(c), which provides that lawyers "shall" make reasonable efforts to prevent the unauthorized or inadvertent access to client information. See, e.g., Scott v. Beth Israel Med. Center, Inc., Civ. A. No. 3:04-CV-139-RJC-DCK, 847 N.Y.S.2d 436 (Sup. Ct. 2007); Mason v. ILS Tech., LLC, 2008 WL 731557, 2008 BL 298576 (W.D.N.C. 2008); Holmes v. Petrovich Dev Co., LLC, 191 Cal. App. 4th 1047 (2011) (employee communications with lawyer over company owned computer not privileged); Bingham v. BayCare Health Sys., 2016 WL 3917513, 2016 BL 233476 (M.D. Fla. July 20, 2016) (collecting cases on privilege waiver for privileged emails sent or received through an employer's email server).

18. Some state bar ethics opinions have explored the circumstances under which email communications should be afforded special security protections. See, e.g., Tex. Prof'l Ethics Comm. Op. 648 (2015) that identified six situations in which a lawyer should consider whether to encrypt or use some other type of security precaution:

- communicating highly sensitive or confidential information via email or unencrypted email connections;
- sending an email to or from an account that the email sender or recipient shares with others;
- sending an email to a client when it is possible that a third person (such as a spouse in a divorce case) knows the password to the email account, or to an individual client at that client's work email account, especially if the email relates to a client's employment dispute with his employer . . . ;
- sending an email from a public computer or a borrowed computer or where the lawyer knows that the emails the lawyer sends are being read on a public or borrowed computer or on an unsecure network;
- sending an email if the lawyer knows that the email recipient is accessing the email on devices that are potentially accessible to third persons or are not protected by a password; or
- sending an email if the lawyer is concerned that the NSA or other law enforcement agency may read the lawyer's email communication, with or without a warrant.

ABA Formal Ethics Opinions (Selected)

5. Label Client Confidential Information.

Lawyers should follow the better practice of marking privileged and confidential client communications as "privileged and confidential" in order to alert anyone to whom the communication was inadvertently disclosed that the communication is intended to be privileged and confidential. This can also consist of something as simple as appending a message or "disclaimer" to client emails, where such a disclaimer is accurate and appropriate for the communication.[19]

Model Rule 4.4(b) obligates a lawyer who "knows or reasonably should know" that he has received an inadvertently sent "document or electronically stored information relating to the representation of the lawyer's client" to promptly notify the sending lawyer. A clear and conspicuous appropriately used disclaimer may affect whether a recipient lawyer's duty under Model Rule 4.4(b) for inadvertently transmitted communications is satisfied.

6. Train Lawyers and Nonlawyer Assistants in Technology and Information Security.

Model Rule 5.1 provides that a partner in a law firm, and a lawyer who individually or together with other lawyers possesses comparable managerial authority in a law firm, shall make reasonable efforts to ensure that the firm has in effect measures giving reasonable assurance that all lawyers in the firm conform to the Rules of Professional Conduct. Model Rule 5.1 also provides that lawyers having direct supervisory authority over another lawyer shall make reasonable efforts to ensure that the other lawyer conforms to the Rules of Professional Conduct. In addition, Rule 5.3 requires lawyers who are responsible for managing and supervising nonlawyer assistants to take reasonable steps to reasonably assure that the conduct of such assistants is compatible with the ethical duties of the lawyer. These requirements are as applicable to electronic practices as they are to comparable office procedures.

In the context of electronic communications, lawyers must establish policies and procedures, and periodically train employees, subordinates and others assisting in the delivery of legal services, in the use of reasonably secure methods of electronic communications with clients. Lawyers also must instruct and supervise on reasonable measures for access to and storage of those communications. Once processes are established, supervising lawyers must follow up to ensure these policies are being implemented and partners and lawyers with comparable managerial authority must periodically reassess and update these policies. This is

ABA Formal Ethics Opinions (Selected)

---

19. *See* Veteran Med. Prods. v. Bionix Dev. Corp., Case No. 1:05-cv-655, 2008 WL 696546 at *8, 2008 BL 51876 at *8 (W.D. Mich. Mar. 13, 2008) (email disclaimer that read "this email and any files transmitted with are confidential and are intended solely for the use of the individual or entity to whom they are addressed" with nondisclosure constitutes a reasonable effort to maintain the secrecy of its business plan).

no different than the other obligations for supervision of office practices and procedures to protect client information.

7. Conduct Due Diligence on Vendors Providing Communication Technology.

Consistent with Model Rule 1.6(c), Model Rule 5.3 imposes a duty on lawyers with direct supervisory authority over a nonlawyer to make "reasonable efforts to ensure that" the nonlawyer's "conduct is compatible with the professional obligations of the lawyer."

In ABA Formal Opinion 08-451, this Committee analyzed Model Rule 5.3 and a lawyer's obligation when outsourcing legal and nonlegal services. That opinion identified several issues a lawyer should consider when selecting the outsource vendor, to meet the lawyer's due diligence and duty of supervision. Those factors also apply in the analysis of vendor selection in the context of electronic communications. Such factors may include:

- reference checks and vendor credentials;
- vendor's security policies and protocols;
- vendor's hiring practices;
- the use of confidentiality agreements;
- vendor's conflicts check system to screen for adversity; and
- the availability and accessibility of a legal forum for legal relief for violations of the vendor agreement.

Any lack of individual competence by a lawyer to evaluate and employ safeguards to protect client confidences may be addressed through association with another lawyer or expert, or by education.[20]

Since the issuance of Formal Opinion 08-451, Comment [3] to Model Rule 5.3 was added to address outsourcing, including "using an Internet-based service to store client information." Comment [3] provides that the "reasonable efforts" required by Model Rule 5.3 to ensure that the nonlawyer's services are provided in a manner that is compatible with the lawyer's professional obligations "will depend upon the circumstances." Comment [3] contains suggested factors that might be taken into account:

- the education, experience, and reputation of the nonlawyer;
- the nature of the services involved;
- the terms of any arrangements concerning the protection of client information; and
- the legal and ethical environments of the jurisdictions in which the services will be performed particularly with regard to confidentiality.

---

20. MODEL RULES OF PROF'L CONDUCT R. 1.1 cmts. [2] & [8] (2016).

ABA Formal
Ethics Opinions
(Selected)

Comment [3] further provides that when retaining or directing a nonlawyer outside of the firm, lawyers should communicate "directions appropriate under the circumstances to give reasonable assurance that the nonlawyer's conduct is compatible with the professional obligations of the lawyer."[21] If the client has not directed the selection of the outside nonlawyer vendor, the lawyer has the responsibility to monitor how those services are being performed.[22]

Even after a lawyer examines these various considerations and is satisfied that the security employed is sufficient to comply with the duty of confidentiality, the lawyer must periodically reassess these factors to confirm that the lawyer's actions continue to comply with the ethical obligations and have not been rendered inadequate by changes in circumstances or technology.

IV. Duty to Communicate

Communications between a lawyer and client generally are addressed in Rule 1.4. When the lawyer reasonably believes that highly sensitive confidential client information is being transmitted so that extra measures to protect the email transmission are warranted, the lawyer should inform the client about the risks involved.[23] The lawyer and client then should decide whether another mode of transmission, such as high level encryption or personal delivery is warranted. Similarly, a lawyer should consult with the client as to how to appropriately and safely use technology in their communication, in compliance with other laws that might be applicable to the client. Whether a lawyer is using methods and practices to comply with administrative, statutory, or international legal standards is beyond the scope of this opinion.

A client may insist or require that the lawyer undertake certain forms of communication. As explained in Comment [19] to Model Rule 1.6, "A client may require the lawyer to implement special security measures not required by this Rule or may give informed consent to the use of a means of communication that would otherwise be prohibited by this Rule."

---

21. The ABA's catalog of state bar ethics opinions applying the rules of professional conduct to cloud storage arrangements involving client information can be found at: http://www.americanbar.org/groups/departments_offices/legal_technology_resources/resources/charts_fyis/cloud-ethics-chart.html.

22. By contrast, where a client directs the selection of a particular nonlawyer service provider outside the firm, "the lawyer ordinarily should agree with the client concerning the allocation of responsibility for monitoring as between the client and the lawyer." Model Rules of Prof'l Conduct R. 5.3 cmt. [4] (2016). The concept of monitoring recognizes that although it may not be possible to "directly supervise" a client directed nonlawyer outside the firm performing services in connection with a matter, a lawyer must nevertheless remain aware of how the nonlawyer services are being performed. ABA Commission on Ethics 20/20 Report 105C, at 12 (Aug. 2012), http://www.americanbar.org/content/dam/aba/administrative/ethics_2020/2012_hod_annual_meeting_105c_filed_may_2012.authcheckdam.pdf.

23. Model Rules of Prof'l Conduct R. 1.4(a)(1) & (4) (2016).

V. Conclusion

Rule 1.1 requires a lawyer to provide competent representation to a client. Comment [8] to Rule 1.1 advises lawyers that to maintain the requisite knowledge and skill for competent representation, a lawyer should keep abreast of the benefits and risks associated with relevant technology. Rule 1.6(c) requires a lawyer to make "reasonable efforts" to prevent the inadvertent or unauthorized disclosure of or access to information relating to the representation.

A lawyer generally may transmit information relating to the representation of a client over the internet without violating the Model Rules of Professional Conduct where the lawyer has undertaken reasonable efforts to prevent inadvertent or unauthorized access. However, a lawyer may be required to take special security precautions to protect against the inadvertent or unauthorized disclosure of client information when required by an agreement with the client or by law, or when the nature of the information requires a higher degree of security.

ABA Formal Ethics Opinions (Selected)